-2

THE PALACE PAPERS

Inside the House of Windsor—
the Truth and the Turmoil

TINA BROWN

RANDOM HOUSE
LARGE PRINT

Cover design: Amy Musgrave
Front cover photographs: Peter Summers/Getty Images (Queen Elizabeth), Max Mumby/Getty Images (Duchess of Cornwall, Duchess of Cambridge, Duchess of Sussex)
Back cover photographs: Agencja Fotograficzna Caro/Alamy Stock Photo (Prince Charles), Max Mumby/Getty Images (Prince William), Geoff Pugh/Shutterstock (Prince Harry), David Moffitt/Getty Images (Prince Andrew)

Photograph credits appear starting on page 827.

The Library of Congress has established a Cataloging-in-Publication record for this title.

ISBN: 978-0-593-61251-4

www.penguinrandomhouse.com/large-print-format-books

FIRST LARGE PRINT EDITION

Printed in the United States of America

1st Printing

This Large Print edition published in accord with the standards of the N.A.V.H.

For my beloved Harry,
always

CONTENTS

PROLOGUE

KRYPTONITE

THE OPRAH WINFREY INTERVIEW WITH PRINCE Harry and Meghan, Duke and Duchess of Sussex, in March 2021 was one of the most ballyhooed in television history. It was recorded one year after their bolt for the royal exit in the palmy gardens of an undisclosed mansion in Montecito, their California Elba perched high above the Pacific coast. Oprah's outsized glasses magnified her wonder at the couple's nuclear revelations about the House of Windsor.

"Were you silent or were you **silenced**?" the TV oracle demanded in her most commanding tone over the ominous soundtrack in the teaser to the two-hour special. The camera panned to Meghan's narrowed eyes, then cut off before we could learn her response. Forty-nine million people globally tuned in to find out. The Duchess wore smoky, tragedy eye makeup, first deployed by Diana, Princess of Wales, in her notorious interview with Martin Bashir, and her hair was in a low bun for confessional gravitas. There was much parsing amongst Meghan fans of the white lotus detail (resurrection!) on the long black Giorgio Armani dress belted high over her baby bump.

Royal code breakers noted that on Meghan's left wrist was her late mother-in-law's Cartier diamond tennis bracelet, signifying that the mantle of wronged royal woman was now hers. Harry, for his part, was lambasted on Twitter for the sartorial fail of his disconsolately saggy socks and undistinguished J.Crew suit. The main theme of his complaint was that his dad, the Prince of Wales, had misread his statement about seeking financial independence and cut off his money.

A damning charge sheet was presented by the House of Sussex: institutional disregard of Meghan's mental health; the Palace's inaction at her character assassination by the press; family jealousy; and, most serious of all, the explosive charge of racism against an unnamed Royal Family member who had raised "concerns" about how dark-skinned the unborn Archie could be.

It was kryptonite.

Prince William's terse response several days later to press trailing him on an engagement was: "We are very much not a racist family." But how would he know? Meghan Markle is the first person of color to marry a Mountbatten-Windsor, and the diversity percentage amongst Buckingham Palace employees is 8.5 percent.

The social media maelstrom immediately showed a heated transatlantic divide in the audience reaction. Americans who have never forgiven the Windsors for their rejection of Diana mostly cheered the Sussexes for blowing the whistle on the monarchy's whole crumbling theme-park enterprise. Against the backdrop of the Black Lives Matter movement, the racism allegation only confirmed that royal dinosaurs should no longer rule the earth. Even President Biden's press secretary Jen Psaki weighed in, praising Meghan's courage for airing her anxiety and depression.

The British reaction predominantly went the other way—outrage at the display of such arrant disrespect for the monarchy and an angry focus on the many disputable, unchallenged claims by the couple. There was widespread skepticism at Meghan's assertion that she had nowhere to turn with her thoughts of suicide except the Buckingham Palace HR department—a surreal-sounding place that few people had ever heard of (and that sounded ripe for a BBC sitcom written by Ricky Gervais). Wasn't Harry, who had himself spent years in therapy, also one of the founders of Heads Together, a royal initiative with Prince William and Kate to end the stigma around mental illness? Whatever adjustment problems Meghan experienced, they were clearly too painful for Harry to watch. On both sides of the pond, the younger generation was ardently on Team Meghan for saving her sweet, sexy husband from his crusty, clueless relations.

Less discussed were Meghan's puzzling—and to me, fascinating—comments about her lack of preparation for royal life. "I didn't fully understand what the job was," she told Oprah. "What does it mean to be a working royal? What do you do? . . . As

Americans especially, what you do know about the
royals is what you read in fairy tales. . . . I grew up in
L.A., you see celebrities all the time. This is not the
same but it's very easy, especially as an American, to
go, 'These are famous people.' [But] this is a completely different ball game."

Uh, yes. The notion that the countryside-rooted,
duty-obsessed, tradition-bound senior members of
the British Royal Family bear any resemblance at all
to Hollywood celebrities is head-explodingly off-
track. Celebrities flare and burn out. The monarchy
plays the long game. There is no time stamp on the
public's interest in you as long as it's clear that your
interest is the public's. As the Queen's grandmother
Queen Mary once said to a relative, "You are a member of the British royal family. We are never tired
and we all love hospitals."

THE DAZZLE OF ROYALTY that captivated Meghan
is an optical illusion. It was hard for her to grasp that
the organic lemon and elderflower dessert served at
her fairy-tale Windsor Castle wedding was Alice in
Wonderland's "Eat Me" cake. Even as she became a
bigger and bigger star on the global stage, she would
have to simultaneously shrink into the voiceless re-
quirements of service to the Crown.

Meghan's curious failure to prepare for a vocation
that was the royal equivalent of taking the veil was a
surprise to many of her former colleagues on the
USA Network show **Suits**, where she appeared as a

supporting player for seven years. According to a colleague on the show, Meghan as an actress had always been known for "doing her homework," exhaustively grilling anyone who could help her for "notes."

It's baffling she did not do the same for the most important role of her life. The main reason that Diana's Mr. Wonderful, the heart surgeon Hasnat Khan, whom she dated after her separation from Charles, didn't want to marry her is that he knew he couldn't live with being traduced every day on the front pages of the tabloids.

A former member of the royal household told me,

I suppose my sense from the beginning was that you had in Meghan someone who had no context through which to comprehend the institution. And in the Palace, you had an institution that had no context for understanding Meghan. So, you had this huge problem of two worlds colliding, that had no previous experience of each other.

The British monarchy is a more than one-thousand-year-old institution with a ninety-six-year-old CEO and a septuagenarian waiting in the wings. It cannot be expected to be nimble. It builds its social capital with steady, incremental acts of unexciting duty. Every so often the glacier moves, usually after a resounding shock to the system: the abdication of Edward VIII to marry the divorced American Wallis Simpson, when it tightened to repel any more intruders; the death of Diana and the ensuing public hysteria, when it reassessed and quietly became more accessible; and the crisis of "Megxit," when the Duke and Duchess of Sussex made a choice between the Commonwealth and Netflix and followed the money. It will be several years before we know how seriously the monarchy has reckoned with its failures to reflect the diversity of the country it symbolizes—and works for.

But change it will. The backstory of what propelled the British monarchy from the era when Princess Margaret could not marry the man she loved in 1955 because he was divorced, to twenty-six years later, when Prince Charles was made to marry a twenty-year-old virgin with a suitable pedigree, to the momentous milestone of 2018, when a divorced, biracial American received the Queen's blessing to marry her grandson: All are potent reminders that the monarchy's prime goal is to survive.

"I didn't do any research," Meghan admitted to Oprah in the interview.

I did. Over two years, in person, and over Zoom as the COVID-19 pandemic descended, I talked to more than 120 people, many of whom have been intimately involved with the senior royals and their households during the turbulent years since Diana died.

My focus for this book is the ensuing twenty-five years up until today. But as we shall discover, the fascination of monarchy is that its themes—and its problems—repeat themselves over time through its reliably fallible and all-too-mortal protagonists. To understand the House of Windsor as it is today, one must understand the forces, human and historical, that shaped it. I have structured **The Palace Papers** into chapters centered on the key individuals who have molded the monarchy's recent history: Diana, Camilla, Charles, Philip, Margaret, Andrew, and, more recently, William, Harry, Kate, Meghan, and their families. We shall travel back in time, from World War II to the lurid nineties, from modernizing millennial Britain to the "Peak London" of the Olympics, from the angry divisions of Brexit to the shared pain of a world pandemic. We shall meet prime ministers, influential courtiers, powerful spin doctors, lowly hangers-on, lovers, rivals, and even outright enemies. We'll parse the layers of aristocracy as well as the complex relationship between the royals, the media, and the public.

Above all, I hope we will get closer to understanding the woman who matters more than anyone else: the Queen.

The book in your hand is the one I wish Meghan had been able to read before she packed up her house in Toronto and boarded the plane to England to plan her wedding to the younger son of the heir to the British throne. She would have learned that no one is a bigger brand than the Firm.

PART ONE

CHAPTER
1

NEVER AGAIN

———

The Royals Confront
a Post-Diana World

———

IN THE FIRST YEARS OF THE TWENTY-FIRST century, a damp melancholy seemed to hang over the British royals that extended to their friends, servants, and hangers-on. Research for my biography of Princess Diana in 2006, almost ten years after her death, took me to the fading walk-up flats in far-flung London postal codes of former courtiers and retainers. The smell of their stair carpets always filled me with gloom, a waft of downward mobility and pointless, genteel sacrifice. The light always seemed to go out on the third-floor landing because of the time switch. The door would open to a small, heavily book-lined one-bedroom apartment full of tasteful knickknacks, a world of remnants from a life of palace duty. What had any of these courtiers got, really, out of all their loyalty and discretion toward the institution of monarchy? The Queen's "regard," a

Seago watercolor, a few courtly thank-you letters signed in royal cursive.

Nowhere was the creak of irrelevance and decay more apparent than at a memorial service in March 2006 at the Guards' Chapel at Wellington Barracks in Westminster for the Queen's cousin and society photographer Lord Lichfield. I was there because I worked with the suavely charming Lichfield often in the early 1980s when I was editing **Tatler,** and once spent a riotous weekend with him and two other legendary photographers, Helmut Newton and David Bailey, covering the Monaco Grand Prix.

Court Circular stalwarts filled the Guards' Chapel that rainy day, including the Queen's fifty-five-year-old daughter, Princess Anne, who is also known as the Princess Royal, and Camilla Parker Bowles, newly elevated to HRH The Duchess of Cornwall since her marriage to Prince Charles the previous year. The ex–king and queen of Greece trudged past to their pew behind Camilla's once-dashing ex-husband Brigadier Andrew Parker Bowles in his usher's morning suit. Camilla and Andrew continue to move inextricably among all the same circles. In one of those inbred social details that baffle royal outsiders, he had joined the Queen to watch the Grand National in a side room at Windsor Castle after Charles and Camilla's wedding blessing at St. George's Chapel.

"No one rises for the Greeks anymore. Isn't it perfectly awful?" hissed the Queen Mother's former steward William "Backstairs Billy" Tallon. He also acted very surprised that the Queen didn't come her-self: "She was his cousin after all."

"Yes, except she was more a cousin from his point of view than hers," said a man to Billy's right, the royal biographer Hugo Vickers, whose observation seemed to encapsulate the relationship of royals to everyone else. Princess Anne, seated with the Greek party, looked dowdy and gruff, Andrew Parker Bowles like a walking pink gin. A decrepit Lord Snowdon, ex-husband of the Queen's sister, Princess Margaret, displayed a bad-tempered air as he was borne along by his son and lowered into a seat. The Duchess of Cornwall's box-shaped hat capped off a dour air-stewardess suit. This was a crowd that could well afford the best Harley Street dentist, but you could root for truffles in the forests of bad teeth.

What a depressing posse they made as they filed out of the chapel! Even the younger generation looked pale and discontented. Tallon murmured to me about a drug problem every time one of them got up to speak. One longed for the tall, blond glory of Princess Diana to appear in a blaze of paparazzi. A guest said that he saw Brigadier Parker Bowles after-ward on the London tube, strap-hanging in his morning suit. Princess Michael of Kent, the Silesian interloper and former interior designer, was the only one in the royal party who added a frisson of glamour. She married the Queen's cousin HRH Prince Michael of Kent in the late 1970s, and be-came known as "the Führer" by Princess Diana after **The Mirror** revealed her father was a member of the

SS. Striding down the aisle with her hair left long under an elegant black hat with a netted veil and a big curly smile, she had retained her Valkyrie good looks. Perhaps because her husband's only achievements have been to grow a beard that increases his resemblance to Tsar Nicholas II and to sink from seventh to fifty-second in the order of succession, she'd made more of an effort to keep her end up.

It was clear that day that deep dullness had returned to the Royal Family, a dullness for which they, if not the tabloid newspapers, were extremely grateful. The lack of excitement around them was hard-won.

Ever since the death of Diana in 1997, the Queen had made it clear to all those who advised her that **it** could never happen again—the **it** being Diana's explosive celebrity, the problem of the British monarchy being upstaged, outshone, drowned out by one overweening, dangerously popular member of the family other than the Queen or the heir to the throne. The refrain most repeated at the pinnacle of the Palace was "We don't want another Diana." The press, the public, and the younger generation of the Windsor family needed to be schooled to understand that the Crown is not a "platform," nor is the extended Royal Family the monarchy. The sovereign is the monarchy and the direct heirs are the only ones who truly count. They and all others watching the Queen's birthday flyover by the Royal Air Force from the Buckingham Palace balcony are there to serve, support, and promote not themselves, but the Crown. They are high-born scaffolding.

Princess Diana's global fame, so unplanned for when she was first earmarked by the Queen Mother as the perfect English rose to pluck for Prince Charles, hit Buckingham Palace like a meteor. Her heat singed the Queen's tiara. And it made all the royals question their own performance and relevance for the first time.

At first, she'd seemed like a savior. England was in a sullen mood in the late seventies after an era of Labour Party government rife with industrial disputes. The monarchy was increasingly seen as an anachronism, mocked by the Sex Pistols with a snarling 1977 punk anthem "God Save the Queen." During the so-called Winter of Discontent in 1978 to 1979, ambulance drivers, refuse collectors, and gravediggers went on strike. For the Royal Family, the young Lady Diana Spencer was both a tonic and a joyful national distraction. She was lightning in a bottle, but they had no idea what to do when the lightning escaped.

Until Diana, the hierarchy of public attention and adoration was preordained. The Queen drew the most royal crowds besides the Queen Mother (described as "radiant" more than nine million times according to Google at last search). Princess Margaret, still with the aura of her renegade youth, was thought to be glamorous into her sixties. Then came Prince Charles, whose Dumbo ears were offset by his excellent tailoring and debonair polo prowess; his younger sister, the dogged Princess Anne, who could shine up well for a gala and, when out of jodhpurs, display very good legs; Prince Andrew, always the Queen's favorite son, who, thanks to fifteen minutes of fame in the Falklands War as a serving naval officer (and as yet unsoiled by his association with an American pedophile ringmaster), could pass for dashing in a uniform. The Queen's youngest boy, Prince Edward, was perhaps a little **wet**, as her husband Prince Philip—let's not forget **his** perennially virile presence—would put it, but no one asked much of Eddie. (He became useful to the Foreign Office for meeting visiting dignitaries at airports.) And so on, down through the assorted carriages of Kents and Gloucesters who composed that marginal grace-and-favor tribe otherwise known as "minor royals," lodged in free housing belonging to the Crown.

Then, boom! Once Diana hit the world stage, nobody wanted to see **them** anymore. So what if Princess Anne did more than 450 charitable assignments a year? No one was interested. The Prince of Wales discovered for the first time in his life what it felt like to have someone looking over his shoulder at a shimmering vision on the other side of the room. If they opened a hospital on a rainy day in Grimsby, the other royals were unlikely to get their pictures in the paper at all, let alone the front page. It made them all not only cranky, but afraid.

The monarchy had been shaken before by the perils of limelight and self-indulgence. Edward VIII was a rock-star Prince of Wales in the 1920s—progressive seeming, communicative, and empathetic in style—until his obsession with the American divorcée Wallis

Simpson prompted him to abdicate to marry her. This supreme act of selfishness or romantic act of self-sacrifice, whichever way you look at it, thrust his younger brother, Princess Elizabeth's reluctant, agonizingly shy father, "Bertie," onto the throne as George VI.

In the years after the abdication, the Windsors believed that it was mass adulation as much as personal weakness that had turned Edward VIII from the course of his royal duty. Edward's unsuitability for the duties of a sovereign was profound. He was feckless and disloyal, and he harbored Nazi sympathies. Musing on Edward's personal failings, Prime Minister Winston Churchill once encapsulated his character as that of a "morning glory," named after the flower whose ephemeral blaze fades before noon. In exile in France, wandering around the United States and the schlosses and châteaus of Europe, living an extravagantly faux-royal life, and making embarrassing statements, the Duke and Duchess of Windsor proved almost as much of a problem as if they had stayed in the UK. The Duke agitated constantly for a "real job," but it was impossible for the royals and the British government to decide which was more undesirable—that the former king succeed at something and become a rival royal power center, or fail and shame the monarchy. So in limbo Edward and Wallis remained.

In the reign of George V, the monarchy, shorn of its executive power, had been reinvented as the protectorate of national morality and guardian of the

British way of life. The personal had become the institutional. Throughout the dark days of the Second World War, the images of his son George VI's sunny nuclear family came to represent the wholesome purpose of good versus evil. Protecting the interests of the immediate family—and their direct descendants—was the Queen Mother's lifelong (often ferocious) priority.

The King and Queen always believed that it was the excess public attention that had promoted Edward's delusion of outsize significance and the coddling of dangerous emotional needs. They were doubly appalled when in his abdication broadcast Edward revealed his personal feelings about Wallis to the British public. The naturally reserved Queen Elizabeth II was schooled to erect inflexible, lifelong barriers around her private thoughts and feelings. In the seventy years of her reign, she has never given an interview, which has only enhanced her mystique. "A different monarch with a more outgoing or extrovert temperament would lose the special mystery of reticence," Lady Elizabeth Longford observed. Her former royal governess Marion Crawford, known to the family as "Crawfie," wrote how the twenty-year-old Princess Elizabeth detested the crowd calling out "Where's Philip?" when their romance was first rumored. Its intensity frightened her and made her feel a commodity.

Crawfie paid dearly for sharing that insight with the public when she published it in 1950 in what was the first tell-all royal bestseller, **The Little Princesses.**

Her saccharine but up-close account of life in the royal nursery outraged the Queen Mother by offering some hints of the King's famous temper tantrums, his wife's frost toward the Windsors, and the (true) notion that neither the King nor the Queen were greatly concerned with the higher education of their daughters.

Crawfie was long demonized as a treacherous snake, but a 2000 Channel 4 documentary by Hamish Mykura suggests that the articles in **Ladies' Home Journal** on which her book was based originated as a clumsy attempt by the Palace and the British government to boost the image of the Royal Family in America. Far from acting disloyally, the unfortunate Crawfie thought she was doing her mistress's bidding. (A more realistic gloss is that she was manipulated by the unscrupulous top editors of **Ladies' Home Journal,** who reworked and sensationalized her copy without her consent and led her to think her agreement with the Royal Family held more latitude than it did.)

Like many a biography subject before and since, once the Queen Mother read the manuscript, she felt differently. She bitterly resented any glimpse of daylight shed on royal magic. "Our late & completely trusted governess has gone off her head," she wrote to Lady Astor. Crawfie was summarily ejected from Nottingham Cottage, the grace-and-favor house on the grounds of Kensington Palace that she had been gifted for life, and was never spoken to by any of the family again.

Prince Philip, too, came to very much regret it

after allowing BBC cameras to penetrate the inner sanctums for the **Royal Family** documentary shown in June 1969. Though the film was as prim and anodyne as Crawfie's efforts, it sent the message that the media was now invited in. The Crown cannily retained the copyright, and the ninety-minute period piece showing a Philip-manned barbecue at Balmoral Castle at which the family banters in impenetrably clipped upper-class accents had rarely been seen since, until it turned up on YouTube in 2021.

Under a forthright exterior Philip was as personally guarded as his wife. His childhood was so unstable he had to grow layers of emotional fortifications simply to survive. His uncle King Constantine I was forced to abdicate the throne of Greece to his eldest son in 1922 in a military coup. His father, Prince Andrew, was arrested and court-martialed during the 1922 Revolution and banished into exile in Paris. Philip was of no fixed address from the time he was an infant, bouncing around between England, France, and Germany. The Queen Mother found it less than endearing when considering his suitability to marry her daughter that the bloodline of the Danish ruling family of Greece was dominated by its unfortunate German strand. Philip's four elder sisters were all married to highborn German aristocrats who were Nazi sympathizers, which made for some awkward social moments. When Philip was eight, his mother, Princess Alice of Battenberg, the great-granddaughter of Queen Victoria, was diagnosed with paranoid schizophrenia and institutionalized after a series of harrowing psychiatric medical measures that rivaled the barbaric leeching of King George III. He didn't see his mother from the age of ten until he was sixteen, when his favorite sister, Cécile, her husband, and their two young sons were killed in a plane crash, and mother and son were reunited at the funeral in Darmstadt. Eventually, Princess Alice invented her own religious order and wandered around the world dressed as a nun.

Philip's father, the exiled Prince Andrew, spent the rest of his life with his mistress in Monte Carlo, only seeing his son occasionally. After the age of eighteen, when the war intervened, Philip never saw him again. While at Gordonstoun, the spartan boarding school to which he was dispatched in Scotland, Philip literally had no idea where and with which relative he would be spending his school holidays.

Author and broadcaster Gyles Brandreth told me he was always trying to draw the acerbic Philip into reflecting on the difficulties of his rootless and tragedy-stricken childhood, without success:

BRANDRETH: Did His Royal Highness find it, uh, eccentric that his mother always dressed as a nun?

PHILIP: What do you mean? She wasn't eccentric at all! Simply a costume, do you see? Instead of wasting money on frocks and things and having her hair done, she dressed as a nun.

Philip's rootless royal past reinforced a conviction that the monarchy's survival is built on and bounded by a commitment to duty. It made him less than sympathetic about Princess Margaret's inconvenient love affair with the divorced, much-older equerry Group Captain Peter Townsend. Bewitching and oh-so-bored, Margaret was a sexy sideshow who was always catnip to the press. Smoking Balkan Sobranies through a long cigarette holder and carousing at fashionable London nightspots with a circle of society bucks, she was an irresistible foil to the virtuous young monarch. (A new generation fell in love with Margaret anew whenever she appeared in Peter Morgan's Netflix series **The Crown**.) As in later life, the Queen sometimes felt sandwiched between the irritating effulgence of her mother and the romantic histrionics of her more exciting sister.

Margaret's affair pitted the Queen's love for her sister and her desire to make her happy against her trusted counselors' advice and desire to observe constitutional purity. For a long time the monarch was paralyzed, but ultimately handled the peril of the Townsend affair with a precocious flash of steel. The Royal Marriages Act of 1772 decreed that, until Margaret was twenty-five years old, Elizabeth would have to give her consent to the union, which, as head of the strongly opposed Church of England, she could hardly do. A deft establishment ruse was concocted that Margaret always blamed on the Queen's advisers, but that actually had the Queen's full accord. Margaret was told she had to wait two years, until she had passed the age of the need for the sovereign's consent, to marry Townsend. Procrastination worked. They drifted apart. The Princess's repudiation of Townsend after the separation was ultimately a pragmatic decision made by them both. Faced with losing the HRH title, Margaret came to realize what an exit from royalty actually meant—living as Mrs. Townsend in a cottage on a group captain's salary with a man fifteen years older than herself and two beefy stepsons. No more motorcycle outriders or baths drawn by her personal maid or cruises on HMY **Britannia** (where divorced persons were banned); all royal rights and prerogatives, all specialness gone.

Doing the right thing for whatever motive made Margaret a romantic heroine for a while. But the peril of celebrity is that it curdles. After the failure of her marriage to the fashionable photographer Lord Snowdon, the press cast her in the royal soap opera as the spoiled palace diva who drank too much and made offensive comments. She became a recurring double-page spread of the wrong kind with her very public dalliances in the Caribbean island Mustique with Snowdon's younger doppelgänger, Roddy Llewellyn. (The press always painted Roddy as a toy boy rather than what he truly was—a charming gentleman gardener who treated Margaret with the kindness she craved.)

If Margaret acted out all her life, she never disrespected her elder sister's sovereignty. Her rebellions did not subvert the unassailable authority of the

Crown. Simply by renouncing her first love, she showed the British public that she ultimately understood that royal duty must trump personal feelings. She was genuinely outraged when she perceived any demeaning of the Queen, by anyone. The embarrassments to the monarchy of her own love life were mistakes of the heart at a time when social mores outside the strictures of royal life were rapidly changing. However lurid the coverage, she would never have "gone public" with her unhappiness as Diana was to do in later years. The mystery of royalty was preserved by the maxim "Never complain, never explain."

II

The challenge for the royals when Diana came along was that she understood the changing media much better than Margaret, and knew how to make lethal use of it. If there was any residual reticence in the coverage of Margaret's recklessness, it had evaporated by Diana's time, burnt off by the heat of animating market forces.

Diana's media moves always predicted the zeitgeist. Her bombshell interview with the BBC's Martin Bashir in November 1995 was an Oprah confessional without Oprah. It has since emerged that Bashir successfully manipulated Diana's paranoia by showing her brother, Earl Spencer, forged documents that "proved" her closest advisers had betrayed her to the Palace, inflaming her desire to speak out for herself. Bashir lied his way to the biggest TV scoop of the twentieth century.

But Diana was adept at deception herself. With exquisite cunning, she arranged for the camera crew to film her at Kensington Palace on a Sunday when the staff were off. She disguised the equipment as the delivery of a new hi-fi system, applied her own panda-eyed makeup with maximum haunted pallor, and stunned the monarch with a direct challenge to her authority in the interview: "I'd like to be a queen of people's hearts." (Impudent!) . . . "I was the separated wife of the Prince of Wales." (Jab!) . . . "I was a problem, full stop. Never happened before—what do we do with her? . . . She won't go quietly." (Threat!) And the quote that will live forever: "There were three of us in this marriage." (He cheated. On me.)

It's often been alleged that Diana came to see the Bashir interview as a grave mistake. She surely would have done so had she known of the dishonesty in his approach. But she was also subsequently clear that she had said exactly what she wanted to say on camera. Gulu Lalvani, the wealthy, British, Pakistani-born entrepreneur who briefly dated Diana in the last year of her life, told me that the Princess said in July 1997 that "she was pleased about it [the interview]. She didn't have a bad word to say about Martin Bashir. She realized it served her purpose." She was right. Her "purpose" was to frame herself to the British public as a betrayed woman, before the increasingly inevitable divorce from Charles. Opinion polls in the wake of the interview showed support for the Princess at 92 percent. She had the public in the palm of her hand.

After the divorce, Charles's campaign to overhaul perceptions of his deeply unpopular self was top of his agenda. To speed this along, in 1996, the Prince hired the thirty-year-old communications hotshot Mark Bolland, whose relationship with the tabloids had been well-honed during his prior employment at the Press Complaints Commission. Bolland, wily and deft with an urbane patina over meritocratic origins, was a strong ally of Camilla. He was suggested for the post by her former divorce lawyer. William and Harry referred to him as "Blackadder," sensing his assassin's skill at planting and killing stories with only one beneficiary in view, the Prince of Wales. It was clear that anyone who worked for the Prince and did not like Camilla was eliminated fast.

Charles was obsessed with the two central problems of his life that were inextricably intertwined: how to regain the approval of the British public who blamed him for the misery he caused Diana; and how to win acceptance for the love of his life, Camilla. He was desperate to bring his mistress out of the shadows, but the public continued to see her only through Diana's eyes as "the Rottweiler," whose hold over Charles had gaslighted the naïve twenty-year-old bride until she realized the painful truth of where his heart lay.

One might imagine that Charles deserved points for wanting the polar opposite of a trophy wife with whom to settle into middle age. Camilla resisted all improving tucks and Botox. There was honesty in her countryside complexion and crinkly, smiling eyes. Her hair never presented any unsettling surprises. It remained the same old blond seventies blowout with the feathery, Carmen-rollered side wings. Her offense, perhaps, was to overthrow the sexist magazine nostrums of what a mistress ought to look like. The tabloids expended an endless volley of creative insults in her direction: old boiler, old trout, old bag, prune, hatchet face, horseface, fat, gaunt, weather-beaten, witch, vampire, frump (as memorably itemized by Allison Pearson in **The New Yorker** in 1997). The best she could achieve was to have an entrée named after her at Green's Restaurant and Oyster Bar in St. James's: Smoked Haddock Parker Bowles. Camilla took this in stride, but Charles did not. He wanted to make an honest kedgeree of his mistress.

A major part of Bolland's job was supposed to be wooing and spinning the **Daily Mail,** which had become Britain's most powerful tabloid under the leadership of the buccaneering editor David English. English told Bolland, "One of your jobs is to teach the Prince of Wales that we were never against him, we were just for Diana. . . . It was a commercial decision. Diana sells newspapers. Charles doesn't. If he does something that sells newspapers, then we will back him." Charles, lugubrious at the best of times, found this report especially depressing. He felt he was always re-marketing himself to the press, doing

the rounds of the newspaper editors to try to ingrati-
ate himself. He said to Bolland, "When I was young
I did all this, but what's the point? They still believe
all the terrible things Diana says about me."

Bolland was, nonetheless, effective. Working with
Charles's private secretary Stephen Lamport, he
gradually remade Camilla for the public in the con-
text of charity events, creating press moments where
she could be seen in respectful proximity to the
Queen. One carefully managed myth peddled by
Bolland was that the boys had warmed to Camilla.
But they tolerated her at best. In his early thirties,
Harry was still complaining bitterly to friends that
Camilla had converted his old bedroom at Highgrove,
Charles's Gloucestershire estate, into an elaborate
dressing room for herself.

Yet, in the summer of 1997, convincing the public
of the rightness of his life with Camilla wasn't going
fast enough for Charles. On August 5, the Archbishop
of Canterbury had declared at a press conference in
Sydney to mark the 150th anniversary of the Anglican
Church's foundation in Australia that if the divorced
heir to the British throne remarried, it would plunge
the Church of England into a crisis. He also pointed
out that the Prince of Wales had given no indication
he wanted to remarry following his divorce from
Diana, and thus it was a nonissue. That was unwelcome news for Camilla. Two years after her own
divorce from Andrew Parker Bowles and a year
after Charles's divorce from Diana, she still had to
see Charles on the quiet, visiting once a week from

her own house in Wiltshire, forbidden by the Queen from joining him at Balmoral Castle, the family's Scottish retreat in the Highlands, or at Sandringham, their twenty-thousand-acre estate on the Norfolk coast, unless Her Majesty wasn't there. The couple longed to go to the theater together or spend long weekends at Birkhall, the Queen Mother's summer home on the Balmoral estate. The Queen, however, was obdurate. When asked whether she would receive Mrs. Parker Bowles, the Queen replied, "Why?" To her, the Prince of Wales's options were either to accede to the throne and repudiate Camilla, or marry her and go the way of the Duke of Windsor.

Peter Mandelson, spin doctor to Prime Minister Tony Blair, describes in his memoir how three weeks before Diana's death in August 1997, he was summoned by Bolland for a private lunch with the Prince of Wales and Camilla at Highgrove. Charles showed him around his beloved garden in a light drizzle and unburdened himself about the media pressure he was enduring. He denied being in a rush to marry Camilla, and said they "just wanted to lead a more normal life." He asked Mandelson how he was viewed by the public. Mandelson told Charles that he was more admired than he might expect for his championing of so many worthy causes, but that "people had gained the impression you feel sorry for yourself, that you're rather glum and dispirited. This has a dampening effect on how you are regarded.'" The public didn't want a Prince Eeyore.

Candor is a rare commodity for members of

the Royal Family. Charles seemed "momentarily stunned," and there was a sudden look of mistressly concern in Camilla's eyes. But afterward, the Prince thanked Mandelson for his honesty and followed it up with a grateful note. It led Mandelson to reflect on the unique oddity of the royal predicament. "At least for me and other politicians, there was a dividing line to defend," he wrote. "For Charles and the Queen, their lives were quite literally their job. Every move they made, every smile or raised eyebrow, every relationship made or severed, was seen as part of their defining function: simply to be the royal family."

III

For the Queen, the shock of Diana's death at the age of thirty-six on August 31, 1997, was a traumatic comingling of the public and the private. Diana was not simply her son's ex-wife whose life had been cut short in a calamitous car crash. She was also the mother of the future king and the adored icon of the nation.

At the rate of six thousand an hour, people who'd never met the Princess of Wales streamed into London to mourn her death. The diversity of the crowd as much as the size was a revelation: old and young, Black and white, South Asian and East Asian; wearing shorts and saris, pinstripes and hijabs; in wheelchairs and on crutches; carrying young children aloft on their shoulders or pushing them in prams. As the bouquets of flowers piled up outside Kensington Palace and the death of Mother Teresa on September 5 went largely ignored, the troubled and turbulent Princess of Wales was on her way to becoming a celebrity saint—not just in Britain but in every nook of the globe. No British royal in history has had such a magnetic hold on the world's imagination, a fact not lost on Prime Minister Blair when he winningly declared her on her death "the People's Princess."

In the tsunami of the nation's grief, the monarchy's emblematic role that had held good for so long was suddenly not enough. The Queen's usual impeccable sense of how to do the right thing—"simply to be," as Peter Mandelson put it—was beset by the need for a new kind of emotional response that met the moment of the crisis. Her deepest personal desire had been to stay in Balmoral to console her grandchildren, and she resented public hysteria that told her otherwise. "She grasped the enormity of the event, but in her own way," wrote Tony Blair in his memoir, **A Journey.** "She was not going to be pushed around by it. She could be very queenly in that sense. . . . In the strange symbiosis between ruler and ruled, the people were insisting that the Queen acknowledge that she ruled by their consent, and bend to their insistence."

Their will prevailed. After five days of tumult, Her Majesty, with steely reluctance, returned to London for a public walk-about amidst the ululating crowds and flower tributes outside Buckingham Palace. She made a rare live TV broadcast to the nation, expressing an empathy she almost certainly did not feel (it was Downing Street that urged her to refer to herself as a "grandmother"), and she capitulated at last to the crowd's and the tabloids' demand to lower the Union Jack over Buckingham Palace. I am told that Prince Philip regarded it as a great humiliation.

IV

The most awful task of Charles's life was waking up his twelve- and fifteen-year-old sons at 7:15 A.M. at Balmoral to deliver the news of their mother's death. In a documentary by Nick Kent on the twentieth anniversary of Diana's death, Harry expressed a sentiment that seems forgotten in his more recent interviews: "One of the hardest things for a parent to have to do is to tell your children that [the] other parent has died. . . . But you know, he was there for us. He was the one out of two left, and he tried to do his best and to make sure that we were protected and looked after."

Prince William recalled, "The shock is the biggest thing, and I still feel [it]. . . . People go 'Shock can't last that long,' but it does," and "The trauma of that day has lived with me for twenty years, like a weight."

The scramble to arrange Diana's funeral in just a week was fraught. When the Archbishop of Canterbury, George Carey, sent the Dean of Westminster the prayers he proposed to read at the service, he was told that the Spencer family didn't want any mention of the Royal Family. In retaliation, Buckingham Palace insisted they have a separate prayer for the Royal Family, and that the words "People's Princess" be removed.

The disagreements among the family about which of the royal men would walk behind the gun carriage bearing Diana's coffin raged for four days, relayed between the Queen's private secretary Robert Fellowes in London and his deputy Robin Janvrin. The latter was on point at Balmoral Castle. Every so often, Prince Philip's voice would come booming over the speakerphone as he listened in.

A person on the funeral planning committee told me, "The Spencer side had been saying what the role of the children had to be. Philip suddenly blasted, 'Stop telling us what to do with those boys. They have lost their mother!' His voice was full of emotion, a real voice of the grandfather speaking." It was also the voice of a man who had effectively lost his own mother at the age of ten.

Alastair Campbell, Tony Blair's press secretary, recorded in his diary of September 4, 1997, that Prince William, "consumed by a total hatred of the media" because of the fatal hounding of his mother, was refusing to walk behind the gun carriage, and he and Harry were holding firm. Prince Charles, meanwhile, was supposed to be traveling to Westminster Abbey with Charles Spencer, but the Earl hated him so much he was refusing to be in the same car with him. Finally, Philip, ever the family decider, gently cajoled the boys with, "If I walk, will you walk with me?" He reminded them how these images would be seen around the world. Though Harry still talks about the personal agony it caused him, from the Crown's point of view, Philip was right. The unforgettable sight of three generations of royal males solemnly walking behind Diana's coffin made the powerful dynastic statement the monarchy required.

Inside the Abbey the silence was heavy, interspersed only by the sniffle of quiet weeping. Editor Geordie Greig, whose sister was once Diana's flatmate and lady-in-waiting, told me that "the somberness of the occasion was so profound [that] you felt you were in the heart of the body of the world that was grieving."

Nothing could have shocked and outraged Her Majesty and Prince Philip more in their life of public service than the accusatory oration by Diana's brother, Earl Spencer. His address from the pulpit was a hand grenade, aimed at every sitting member of the House of Windsor. In his eulogy for Diana the Hunted, the thirty-three-year-old Earl, whose literary flair has since been proved in numerous immensely readable histories, displayed the same instinct for risk-taking as his royal sister. After promising Diana that "we will not allow [the young princes] to suffer the anguish that used regularly to drive you to tearful despair," he went on to pledge "that we, your blood family, will do all we can to continue the imaginative and loving way in which you were steering these two exceptional young men so that their souls are not simply immersed by duty and tradition, but can sing openly as you planned."

Blood family! Spencer had publicly kicked the frozen-faced Royal Family in the teeth. In another time, the hotheaded Earl would have been summarily executed in the Tower of London. Especially insulting was the salvo implying Diana was bigger than her HRH: "[She] proved . . . she needed no royal title to continue to generate her particular brand of magic." A burst of applause from outside the Abbey where the service was being broadcast washed through the Great West Door and down the nave until for the first time in the history of the great church the whole congregation—except for the Royal Family—was clapping. Diana's astrologer Debbie Frank, sitting beside the sobbing television host Michael Barrymore, recalls thinking it was the sound of thunder. Archbishop Carey was appalled by Earl Spencer's eulogy, which he deemed "vengeful and spiteful." Prince Philip was so angry he had to be talked down afterward by Earl Mountbatten's son-in-law Lord Brabourne. "Very bold" was all the Queen Mother reportedly said between clamped teeth. (Even the Queen found it hard to rise above. Nearly seven years later at the opening of the Diana, Princess of Wales Memorial Fountain in Hyde Park, she tossed a gibe at Earl Spencer: "I hope you feel satisfied.")

Never again.

V

On the Monday after the funeral, hoping to distract the boys, Tiggy Legge-Bourke, their kindly big-sister caregiver appointed by Charles after his separation from Diana, took them to follow the Beaufort Hunt on foot. They were greeted with all the right sensitivity by an old family friend, Captain Ian Farquhar, joint master of the Duke of Beaufort's Hunt. "It's good to see you, sirs," he said to the shattered young princes. "I just want you to know that we are all very, very sorry about your mother. You have our deepest sympathy and we were all incredibly proud of you on Saturday. That's all I am going to say, and now we're going to get on with the day."

"Thank you. Yes, you're right," William gravely replied, as if the Queen's stoic genes had fully asserted themselves in her grandson. "We all need to get on with the day."

Harry, always more fragile, struggled mightily to manage without a mother. In the weeks after her death, to try to cheer him, Charles took his younger son at half term on a five-day tour of South Africa, Swaziland, and Lesotho, then sent him off on a safari to Botswana with a party led by his bluff one-time equerry and former Welsh Guards officer Mark Dyer, whom he later recruited as the boys' mentor. Dyer made the boy's day in Johannesburg by scoring him a backstage visit with the Spice Girls. Writer Anthony Holden, who accompanied the royal press corps to South Africa, recalls in his memoir waiting to see if

Harry appeared at the concert wearing a T-shirt and jeans, as he would have done with his mother, or a suit and tie, which meant the Windsors had prevailed. Harry "duly materialized in a suit and tie," signifying, Holden writes, that "Diana's memory [was] already being expunged."

In his harassed, fogeyish way, Prince Charles made every earnest effort to be an attentive father. He read Rudyard Kipling stories to the boys before they went to sleep. He took them to Stratford-upon-Avon to see Royal Shakespeare Company productions and go backstage to meet the cast. Actor and writer Stephen Fry, who accompanied them to **The Tempest,** told me he was enchanted by how much the boys teased their father, which he thought was "a truly healthy sign." At breakfast at Highgrove, Fry was inspecting the buffet when he lifted a tureen that offered Charles's preferred heap of linseed. Prince William said, "Oh no, don't go near the bird table, Stephen, that's only for Pa."

Despite Earl Spencer's vow that Diana's boys would be "steered by his blood family," William and Harry were raised not as Spencers but as Windsors. No more paparazzi-trailed school breaks at European resorts and private islands in the Caribbean. They holidayed almost exclusively at Balmoral and Sandringham, where Prince Philip regaled them with stories of military history and taught them to shoot. Their friends were the children of their father's circle. It was Diana's more sober-sided sister, don't-rock-the-boat Jane, who became a steady presence in the boys' lives, hosting them on country weekends in Norfolk with their cousins. Thanks to her marriage to Robert Fellowes, who stayed a life-long loyalist to the Queen after he retired as her private secretary, she was almost a Windsor by osmosis.

Mostly it was Tiggy Legge-Bourke, who had joined Harry on the Africa trip, who provided maternal warmth and structure. A jolly hockey-sticks blonde from minor nobility, Tiggy was a Charles loyalist to the core who believed that boys should be distracted by "fresh air, a rifle, and a horse." She caught flak from the press—and Charles—when she allowed the boys to rappel down a fifty-meter dam in Wales without safety lines or helmets. Charles was reportedly unamused to see a picture in the newspapers of Tiggy at the wheel of the car with a cigarette between her lips while Harry was shooting rabbits through the open window. In 2006, Harry invited her to watch his "passing-out" (graduation) parade as an officer at Sandhurst and, in 2019, privately made her Archie's godmother. (One of Bashir's worst calumnies was to tell Diana that Tiggy was having an affair with Charles and had had an abortion. In 2021, Tiggy, now Mrs. Charles Pettifer, was reportedly offered substantial damages from the BBC.)

A draconian agreement with the Press Complaints Commission in the post-Diana moral reshuffle meant that photographers and royal reporters rarely penetrated William and Harry's private terrain during their childhood. Scarred by the public's fury after Diana died pursued by paparazzi, some editors were almost grateful for the clarity of the PCC's Editors' Code of Practice, which spared them from having to make editorial decisions that could have reaped a public backlash. According to Lord Black, who was then director of the PCC, newspapers were constantly offered stories about the princes from other boys at school, and liked having the protection of the code to reject them. The princes' holidays were similarly off-limits unless access was choreographed by the Palace.

It's easy to forget now that the boys' famous fun-filled excursions with Diana to Disney World, movie theaters, and McDonald's became iconic only because the press was always there, snapping, following, and making Diana cry. The contrast contributed to the myth that what the Windsors offered was boring and constrained. But in truth there was more freedom for the young princes inside the royal cocoon than out of it: dirt biking at Balmoral in the privacy of fifty thousand acres of grouse moors and farmland; blasting pheasants out of the Norfolk sky over Christmas and New Year's at Sandringham; foxhunting at a thrilling pace during weekends at Highgrove. In the evenings at Balmoral, the whole Windsor family and houseguests played jolly games of charades.

Princess Diana acknowledged to me in June 1997, when she visited Manhattan for the charity auction of her dresses at Christie's, that she found it hard to compete with what Charles offered the boys at the multiple royal homes. In the July before her death, she took them for what she hoped would be a fun holiday at Harrods owner Mohamed Al Fayed's Saint-Tropez spread, with interludes sailing on his £15 million yacht, the **Jonikal**, but the young princes didn't like it much. The flash and excess of Al Fayed's hospitality—the groaning buffets and the palatial bathrooms—embarrassed William in particular. At sea, he stayed belowdecks much of the time to avoid the long lenses of the paparazzi. The press presence also ruined a trip with Diana to a local funfair. Harry, meanwhile, got into an altercation with Al Fayed's younger son, Omar, who refused to give up the room Harry wanted to sleep in. In the post-Diana years, the boys could disappear from the media noise into the woods and fields of the royal estates. On one occasion William elected to stay at Sandringham popping pheasants with his grandfather rather than go skiing with Charles in Klosters, where the press might pursue them on the slopes.

Windsor-world gradually swallowed up the boys. Earl Spencer soon piped down about his thundering promise from the pulpit about the preeminence of Diana's "blood family." His own private life was consumed by two acrimonious divorces, and he was not a central figure in his nephews' circle of influence. When William turned to him to urge Harry to slow down his rush to the altar with Meghan, the younger brother viewed it as a gross intrusion by William. Diana's memory became an Althorp tourist attraction, where a somewhat eerie, dimly lit ensemble of artifacts such as her frothy fairy-tale wedding dress, childhood photographs, and touchingly ordinary letters from boarding school were displayed to the ticket-buying public to donate to the Diana, Princess of Wales Memorial Fund.

Diana's former circle was pruned from the boys' lives. Though Harry often turned to his mother's scrupulously private school friend, grief counselor Julia Samuel, for support, her other intimates, like the Honourable Rosa Monckton, with whom Diana spent her last girls' vacation in Greece, and Lucia Flecha de Lima, the Brazilian ambassador's wife who was one of her closest confidantes, were cut from their orbit. Rosa was considered a leak risk because she had shared her memories of Diana with the press. Even though she was the chairman of the committee for the Diana Memorial Fountain in Hyde Park, and her disabled daughter, Domenica, was Diana's godchild, her letters to the princes on milestones such as their birthdays went unanswered. Lucia was snubbed for the wedding of William and Kate in 2011, and watched it on TV instead. The **Daily Mail**'s Richard Kay, Diana's favorite royal correspondent, who always had the inside track and talked to her on the phone the last day she was alive, similarly received no access to her sons.

By the turn of the century, the waters at last seemed to be closing over the charred landscape left by the Diana years.

The royals believed that the painful, institution-rattling crisis was something they could weather, and it was. But the media universe that manufactured and amplified the Diana phenomenon was only at the beginning of its twenty-first-century transformation.

If her untimely death was the first global electronic real-time saturation event, it's chilling to imagine how much more intense it would be today. Martin Bashir's interview with Diana, like Meghan and Harry's with Oprah, would be played in endlessly devastating loops on YouTube. The banned pictures and footage of the Princess dying in the mangled car in the Alma tunnel in Paris would be all over what is called, with mostly unconscious irony, social media. The multiple conspiracy theories that got traction over the following months would have been unleashed instantaneously and developed deadly credence among a global horde of believers. If the angry crowd in the Mall had been told on Twitter that the Princess had been bumped off by MI6 at the behest of Prince Philip, might the chant to lower the flag have become a roar for the monarchy's downfall? "Never complain and never explain," the dictum that had worked for so long for the royals, now feels like the distant signal from a shipwrecked liner.

But all this was still to come. For now, the furies of media blame and public censure abated. The Queen privately remained shaken by what her aides called "the revolution." Her Majesty would not forget the time when her perceived aloofness from the British people's grief over Diana's death caused them to turn on her. Or what she had felt obliged to do when Diana's coffin passed the Palace: For the first and only time, except for a head of state—she waited for her. Then bowed her head.

Never again.

CHAPTER
2

SEX AND SENSIBILITY

Why Charles Loves Camilla

THE IMPORTANT THING TO REMEMBER ABOUT Camilla is that she said she never wanted to marry Prince Charles. And now she's his wife. She said she would not be a public figure. And she now does more than two hundred royal engagements a year. And she said (or Clarence House did) that after Charles's coronation as king, she will be known as Princess Consort. But that cautious plan, too, has been discarded, and a Queen Camilla is in Britain's future.

Meanwhile, even though she has every right to be known as the Princess of Wales, Camilla chose to be styled HRH The Duchess of Cornwall. She was shrewd enough to know it would be bad karma to assume a title forever associated with a princess so beloved. She has now, let us remember, been married to Prince Charles longer than Diana.

Camilla has always been sexual and emotional comfort food for the Prince of Wales. The ease of her charm from the moment she first met him at the age of twenty-four in 1972 unwound the tight wrapping of his princely training. The royal mistress gene was in her blood: Her great-grandmother Alice Keppel was for twelve years, until his death, the chief favorite of King Edward VII. Alice, a socially accomplished and witty charmer, was the King's last major fling after a lifetime of juggling an unceasing cast of aristocratic mistresses and continental prostitutes. At the time Alice arrived in his life at the age of twenty-nine to his fifty-seven, Bertie, as he was known, was a wheezing, malodorous figure, addicted to cigars and so obese that he sometimes had to be trussed up to achieve penetration. Alice was a stunning beauty. Her daughter Violet Trefusis, better known later for her tempestuous Sapphic love affair with the writer and garden designer Vita Sackville-West, remembered her possessing a "brilliant, goddess-like quality" and marveled at her mother's "ripe curves," her "alabaster skin, blue eyes, chestnut hair, large breasts, kindness and charm."

Alice's staying power in Bertie's life can be attributed as much to shrewd intelligence as it was to beauty. Consuelo Vanderbilt, Duchess of Marlborough, tells us, "She invariably knew the choicest scandal, the price of stocks, the latest political move; no one could better amuse the [then] Prince during the tedium of the long dinners etiquette decreed." Alice also understood how to play the mistress game with the utmost propriety, especially with regard to Queen Alexandra. She helped Bertie commission pleasing gifts of jeweled animals for his wife's Fabergé collection. A signed photograph of the Queen was ostentatiously displayed on the mantel of her drawing room. Always canny about money, she tapped the King's financial adviser to turn her royal handouts into lucrative investments. In evening hours, her daughter Violet remembered her "resplendent in a perpetual tiara." Two maids laid out her four wardrobe changes a day into one of her many silk Worth gowns, bedecked with long ropes of pearls and sparkling diamond collars.

Edwardian adultery in aristocratic circles was an artful **La Ronde** conducted only after marriage with people of parallel social station, usually involving deft room-swapping at whispering country house weekends. Most of Bertie's mistresses had compliant husbands who were happy, as was the Honourable George Keppel, with the status their wives' royal liaison conferred. One of Bertie's favorite mistresses, Daisy Brooke, Countess of Warwick—also known as "Babbling Brooke"—proved something of a liability, and attempted to sell the King's old letters after he died to the **Daily Express** until the Crown quashed it.

Belowstairs gossip in the Keppel household whispered that the effete, low-testosterone George vacated Alice's bed early in the marriage. By the time she first mesmerized the Prince of Wales in 1898, she'd developed a faithful stream of afternoon callers while her indifferent husband twirled his waxed moustache at his gambling club in Piccadilly. She may have been the toast of high society, but as a former maid of the household put it, Alice Keppel was "a right dirty bird." That suited the libidinous Bertie, who had a large scattering of illegitimate offspring, as well as his six children by the long-suffering Queen Alexandra. There were persistent rumors that Alice Keppel's younger daughter, Sonia, grandmother of Camilla, was in fact the daughter of the King, thus making the Duchess of Cornwall a possible blood relation of Prince Charles.

A century later there are many similarities in the circumstances and dynamic between Alice and Bertie and Camilla and Charles. Like Bertie, Charles has had to wait decades for the throne. Queen Victoria finally left the scene after reigning for sixty-three years, during which she thought her son was so hopeless she rigorously excluded him from affairs of state. Though never overtly rancorous like Bertie's relations with Queen Victoria, Charles's push for a bigger royal role has led in the past to rivalrous tensions between his own household and Buckingham Palace. The Queen has been known to comment to advisers that she finds him "maddening," and only in the last decade, when she has depended on him to help share the burden, has she seen him as more than a recalcitrant child.

By the time Bertie became King Edward VII at fifty-nine, he felt it was all too late. "I don't mind praying to the eternal father," he muttered during a church service marking Queen Victoria's Diamond Jubilee, "but I do mind being the only man in the country afflicted with an eternal mother." Charles, too, has felt frustrated and sometimes despairing about his own thwarted life in the wings. He is now the longest-serving heir apparent in history, the longest-serving Duke of Cornwall, and the longest-serving Duke of Rothesay (as he is known north of the border). He made his disappointments clear in 1992 after the funeral of Diana's father, Earl Spencer, in a conversation with the late earl's twenty-eight-year-old son and heir. "He did not seem to appreciate how I felt at my loss," the young Earl Spencer told his family. "We had just buried my father and he kept telling me how lucky I was to have inherited so young!"

Like Bertie, Charles felt bruised by his childhood and miserable school days, misunderstood by his domineering father, and deprived of an emotional connection with his mother. His strongest tie was with his ultra-traditionalist former nanny, Mabel Anderson—to whom Camilla is said to have a telling resemblance. Like Bertie, he is a natural aesthete, subject to sentimentality and tantrums, and needs to be soothed and amused by a woman who can be both maternal and subtle in her controlling hand. Like Alice, Camilla's winning card has always been her ability to entertain. A place next to her at dinner is prized among guests at Highgrove, who find her sophisticated and earthy, worldly and direct, and marvelously salty fun. One frequent male attendee told me one of her great charms is to make you feel like the most important person in the room. "I've insisted that you sit next to me," she says in her deep, confiding voice. "She has an extraordinary skill of making you feel that you belong," the guest told me. "For a long time, she and I were the only people likely to be smokers at these events and she managed to make that into a kind of joyous secret." Like Alice, Camilla has never challenged the status quo. She's a rooted embed in aristocratic life who needed no coaching in etiquette around the royals. Like Alice, Camilla had, in Major Andrew Parker Bowles, a **mari complaisant**, apparently unfazed by the joke around town that he was "the man who had laid down his wife for his country." Like Edward VII with Alice, Prince Charles cannot live without her.

II

It was his old Cambridge flame Lucia Santa Cruz, daughter of the Chilean ambassador, who introduced Charles to Camilla in the summer of 1971 when he was twenty-two and Camilla had just turned twenty-four. Roy Strong, the director of the National Portrait Gallery, met Charles around this time and describes him as "a pleasant young man, earnest, with a boyish grin and a non-sophisticated sense of humor, prank-ish, thoughtful, kind and shy. He dresses in a very middle-aged way with narrow lapels and tiny shirt collars and narrow ties." As a student at Cambridge, where Charles met Lucia, he turned up on the first day of term wearing an impeccably tailored suit and tie. It was October 1967, the year of the Summer of Love. Not surprisingly for a prince with rarefied social exposure, he was having trouble making any authentic romantic connection.

Lucia and Camilla lived in the same block of flats in Cundy Street, Belgravia, on the Grosvenor Estate, a hub for trust fund daughters and deb's delights. Camilla was the untidy flatmate of Conservative minister Lord Carrington's daughter Virginia on the ground floor. Lucia said the Prince "was coming for a drink or to pick me up, and I said 'Can Camilla come up?'" She knew he was lonely. She told him Camilla was "just the girl" for him who had "enormous sympathy, warmth and natural character." Charles was drawn to her immediately. When Lucia introduced them, she joked, "Now, you two, be very careful. You've got genetic antecedents. Careful, CAREFUL!" A playful introduction that seems much more likely than the oft-quoted raunchy apocrypha of Camilla's supposed nudge-nudging reply: "My great-grandmother was the mistress of your great-great-grandfather—so how about it?"

Camilla had no need to tout her own antecedents. The Shands were a charismatic family whose deep roots in aristocratic life were amplified by their considerable personal charm.

Camilla's father was the dashing war hero Major Bruce Shand, her mother the Honourable Rosalind Cubitt, daughter of the third Baron Ashcombe.

Major Shand, who was joint master of the Southdown Hunt in East Sussex, was admired as much for his Jason Robards good looks as his impressive combat record in the Second World War. He was held for three years by the Germans as a prisoner of war, and was awarded two military crosses for his daring ingenuity and sangfroid under fire. "One of his biggest complaints about being a POW was not mistreatment by the Nazis, but the fact that Spangenberg Castle, a prison for officers, was like being back at boarding school," said the writer James Fox, whose family moved in the same Sussex circles.

Fox remembers the galloping Major Shand as "the opposite of the tabloid image of a Colonel Mustard." He spoke excellent French from his early training in the wine business at Bordeaux and, after the war, became a partner in the posh vintner Block, Grey, and Block in Mayfair. His style of disapproval would be a laconic "look" rather than a roar of reproach. He later took a live-and-let-live attitude to Camilla's complicated life.

Rosalind Shand, Camilla's mother, was a celebrated society beauty named Debutante of the Year in 1939. She was the great-great-great-granddaughter of the nineteenth-century master builder Thomas Cubitt, whose legacy is London's most coveted real estate: the great wedding-cake mansions of Belgravia, the white stucco terraces of Pimlico near the House of Commons, and the east frontage and extended balcony of Buckingham Palace. George VI and his consort Elizabeth attended Rosalind's coming-out ball at the majestic Holland House in Kensington, the last glittering occasion there before it was destroyed in the Blitz. She often smoked a small cigar and was generously bosomed, vivacious, and witty. Camilla recalls her as being "quite fierce" when it came to manners.

Rosalind was unusually public-spirited. Two or three days a week, she would volunteer as a nurse for thalidomide-affected children at Chailey Heritage, a school for the disabled near the Shand family home in Plumpton, East Sussex. She used to invite the kids over to swim in the pool and asked a group of her mentees to both her daughters' weddings.

Camilla, along with her sister, Annabel, who became a successful society decorator, and the youngest sibling, Mark, were known in London society as the "sexy Shands." The real beauty of the trio was Mark. During the 1970s, he was one of the most lusted-after bachelors in London, a muscular blond god who was a serial dater of top models and "It" girls. Like his friend and peer Peter Beard, but less wacky, he was an adventurer from the nineteenth-century Sir Richard Burton school who wandered the world on extravagant connections and an adequate trust fund. His epic 750-mile trek on an elephant from Konarak on the Bay of Bengal to Sonepur on the Ganges was chronicled in a bestselling memoir, **Travels on My Elephant.** Among his group of raffishly exalted friends were the Earl of Westmorland's son Harry Fane, with whom he shared a house in Bali and started an antiques business; the photojournalist

Don McCullin; and the heartthrob cricket hero Imran Khan, who would later become prime minister of Pakistan. Some of Shand's more colorful capers were suggested by the multiple tattoos on his person, "a serpent on my forearm, which I got when I was working in the packing room of Sotheby's, the crab on my shoulder in Texas, and a tiger I found after I woke up with a bunch of Algerian soldiers. On my foot I've got some markings which were made by Dayaks in Borneo while I was fairly intoxicated on anything that was remotely available," he told writer Camilla Long. One female admirer called him "a real-life Indiana Jones." His sudden death at the age of sixty-two in New York in 2014 from a fall outside the Gramercy Park Hotel's Rose Bar after a Sotheby's fundraiser for his elephant foundation was devastating to Camilla. She told friends, "When I heard [Mark's] voice on the phone saying 'Camillsy' . . . I knew immediately he wanted something. But God, I miss him."

The Shand children were raised with the kind of secure affection that breeds absolute self-assurance. Home was a comfortable former rectory, The Laines, where Ashcombe heirlooms merged with an easy profusion of eclectic objects, handwoven Moroccan kilims, and deep sofas that welcomed dog hair. The house had wonderful views of the South Downs. One of its charms was a sequence of tumbling secret gardens planted by Rosalind, whose green thumb was evident in their homegrown vegetables and loose arrangements of fresh flowers. Unusually for her class and era, Rosalind did not employ a nanny. She picked the girls up herself from their day school, Dumbrells in Ditchling, every afternoon and then spirited them off in the summer to the beach at Hove. She let Camilla and Annabel go on riding and camping excursions over the Downs and stay the night out in their sleeping bags. At dinner, Bruce would pour the children a glass of wine and water like the French do, and they were allowed to stay up late, hanging out with Rosalind as she sipped her crème de menthe. Their friends were jealous of the Shands' easygoing, relatable parents.

Through Rosalind, the young Shands had cousins and relatives all over **Burke's Peerage**, a skein of intertwined connections that rotated them through the house parties, hunt balls, shooting weekends, and dinner parties of the grandest houses in England. For sure, it was a less august pedigree than Princess Diana's, whose gold-dust lineage boasted the Earldom of Spencer on Diana's father's side and on her mother's the Barony of Fermoy. There was no stately home like Althorp in the Shand picture. But Diana's family was so fractured and antagonistic, she never forged particularly deep roots in aristocratic country life. Fourteen years older than Diana, Camilla was far more adjusted to royal circles. Generationally as well as socially, she was linked to multiple friends and houses that formed the texture of Prince Charles's world.

Her social self-confidence increased her appeal to the opposite sex. Camilla's allure was her husky baritone voice, candid blue eyes, curvaceous figure, and smiling accessibility. The year they connected, Prince Charles was at the start of his career in Her Majesty's Armed Forces, training as a jet pilot before completing a course at the Britannia Royal Naval College in Dartmouth. Neither the Queen nor Prince Philip opted to come to his passing-out parade in 1971. For the milestone of his cadet ceremony, Lord Louis Mountbatten, former viceroy of India and First Sea Lord, and, more important, Charles's closest confidant and "honorary grandfather" as he fondly called him, flew down by helicopter from his home in Hampshire to ensure there was a family presence at the ceremony.

The guided missile destroyer HMS **Norfolk** in Gibraltar awaited Charles next, his first assignment in a career in the Royal Navy like his father, grandfather, and both great-grandfathers before him. "Poor Charles," the Queen remarked to a dinner guest at this time. "Hopeless at maths and they made him a navigation officer!" For the next five years, despite his royal status, Charles was expected to grind his way up through the ranks from acting sub-lieutenant to sub-lieutenant to lieutenant. (One perk of being royal is that he continues to accrue rank though not on active service. Hopeless or not at maths, he's now Admiral of the Fleet.)

Free from the scrutiny of the press and the censure of his parents, Charles did his best in the navy to be "one of the boys." He didn't love sharing an already tiny cabin with two other officers, but came to embrace the communal spirit of service life enough to briefly grow a George V beard. "I was to be treated like any other Sub Lieutenant," he wrote in his naval diary, "but there were obviously differences and I suspect no one was sure how I would behave or how pompous I would be." One of those "differences" he resented was being kept out of aircraft and anti-submarine helicopters deemed too dangerous for the heir to the throne to try. In 1976, he made it to the command of his own ship, the minesweeper HMS **Bronington**. Unfortunately, in an Inspector Clouseau incident recounted by Anthony Holden, Charles ordered the lowering of the anchor without having noticed on his chart an underwater telecommunications cable linking Britain and Ireland. It was snagged, and the two divers sent down to dislodge it nearly drowned. "I've got to live with the GPO [the General Post Office, then the national telecommunications agency] for the rest of my life. What happens if I break the damn thing?" he reputedly lamented. After twenty-four hours, he was forced into the severe embarrassment of slipping anchor, earning a "stern rebuke" from the brass at the Ministry of Defence. He left the Royal Navy in December 1976 with obvious relief, and used his £7,400 severance pay to found his first charity, the Prince's Trust.

Charles's career in the navy may not have been as illustrious as his father's and Mountbatten's, but it played well in the press. It's hard to overstate what a glamorous figure the Prince of Wales cut in the early and mid-seventies. He was the most eligible bachelor in Britain, manly, dashing, and heir to around 53,000 hectares of the Duchy of Cornwall, which brought him an annual income of £80,000. Impressively shrewd financial management has increased his portfolio of land, buildings, and financial investments to around £22 million a year. The royal press corps photographed him in perpetual motion, parachuting out of helicopters, windsurfing, and galloping around the polo field with a millionaire tan. Shortly before he met Camilla, he had pulled off a derring-do incident when he jumped out of an RAF aircraft, caught his feet in the rigging lines of a parachute, and descended 1,200 feet toward the sea upside down before landing upright off the Dorset coast.

Interest in him was such that a worldwide TV audience of 500 million watched the live broadcast of his 1969 investiture as Prince of Wales at Caernarfon Castle. (One of those who watched was the eight-year-old Diana Spencer, who was spellbound by the romance of the pageantry and the man at the center of it.) There had been twenty English Princes of Wales crowned before him, beginning in 1301 when King Edward I gave the title to his heir apparent, Prince Edward, after the brutal subjugation of Wales was complete. Charles was "shit-scared" according to Lord Snowdon, who designed the setting of the event, but he looked impossibly noble in his hand-woven purple velvet robe and ermine cape with solid gold clasps, his head crowned by the specially made gold coronet encrusted with diamonds and topped by a golden orb that resembled a burnished golf ball. (It actually was a ping-pong ball encased in gold.) Viewed today, the photographs seem not fifty years ago, but five hundred. As the Queen lowers the crown onto his head, the twenty-year-old Prince in profile has a thin Plantagenet nose and wears a prayerful expression. Always dutiful, he had spent the nine weeks before the ceremony cramming with a tutor at Aberystwyth University so he could make his acceptance speech in Welsh. Poet Laureate Sir John Betjeman celebrated the occasion with these words: "You knelt a boy, you rose a man / And thus your lonelier life began."

III

Immediately after he met Camilla, Charles was in hot pursuit. A romance began that lasted until he disappeared off to sea in December 1972 to join the naval frigate HMS **Minerva.** There were intense late-night phone calls, evenings dancing groin to groin at the Mayfair nightclub Annabel's, and suppers à deux after the opera at Covent Garden. Charles loved to entertain her with his impersonations of the characters in Peter Sellers and Spike Milligan's antic BBC Radio comedy **The Goon Show,** and she was polite enough to find them uproariously funny. He drove her in the blue Aston Martin his parents gave him for his twenty-first birthday to spend long private weekends at Broadlands, the Romsey home of Earl Mountbatten. A columnist sighted them double-dating at Annabel's with Princess Anne and her escort Gerald Ward.

Sometimes they managed furtive meetings at her grandmother Sonia Cubitt's house in Hampshire, which was within easy reach of his ship's docking at Portsmouth. Hosting the Prince and Camilla must have been piquant for Sonia, who nurtured childhood memories of her mother, Alice Keppel, entertaining the stout, bearded man she knew only as "Kingy." A butler for Sonia told how one afternoon Camilla had been wandering around all day in jeans done up in front with a safety pin. Mrs. Cubitt demanded to know whether she was going to change into something more appropriate for an impending visit from the Prince of Wales. "I can even see your drawers, Camilla," she apparently bellowed, to which Camilla replied, "Oh, Charles won't mind about that." When the Prince arrived at six P.M., they "vanished into thin air" together. He clearly appreciated her sexual joie de vivre. "Pretend I am a rocking horse," she is said to have urged him, to conquer his early diffidence in bed. Charles showed his appreciation of her grandmother Sonia's welcoming discretion by gifting her a silver trinket box engraved with Prince of Wales feathers.

The earliest photographs of Charles and Camilla together are at polo matches at Smith's Lawn in Windsor Great Park, locked in an intimate sidebar as they lounged in the car park or under a tree looking at each other with a clear-eyed understanding—she in a red T-shirt and jeans and he bronzed and still sweaty in his striped team shirt and jodhpurs. Camilla was pony mad from the age of five and had become a keen equestrian under her father's tutelage. She loved the whole lusty, gutsy sport of foxhunting with the Southdown, the mad chase through the open East Sussex downland, the hearty hunting teas afterward in the homes of tallyho friends. The Prince adored her carelessness and utter absence of sycophancy. And he was charmed by her family, whose relaxed warmth was the polar opposite of his own. The supermodel Marie Helvin, who dated Mark Shand for several years, told me that at country weekends, "Camilla used to come in in big, muddy boots with her hair all blown around and good skin, and she just looked great somehow. She had dirt under her fingernails and it wouldn't bother her. That was appealing if you are an uptight man like Charles." When Camilla rode to hounds, her father's master-of-the-hunt etiquette demands prevailed. She always looked whip-crackingly equestrian in thigh-hugging jodhpurs, crisp white stock, and taut black snood.

The ease with which the Shands could move up and down the stylistic register was sometimes perplexing for arrivistes in their confident world. Mark was known to show up at a seated lunch party at home in a pair of ragged shorts. Marie Helvin remembers feeling mortified when she descended the stairs for Christmas breakfast at the Shand house wearing a white satin Dior negligee and matching peignoir only to find the rest of the family eating eggs and bacon wearing old hunting jackets over crumpled pajamas. Apparently Camilla's and Annabel's young sons never forgot the vision of her entrance.

The Shands' unostentatious house could acquire sudden polish for a grand dinner party. The family's easeful character was underpinned by social rigor. Camilla was from the last generation of British women who were schooled in the necessity—and the skills—of being amusing. In 2017, she reminisced to Geordie Greig about how her mother would drag her and her siblings downstairs, and make them join a dinner with boring neighbors:

> We used to complain and say, "Can't we stay here and watch the television over fish fingers?" and she'd sit us down at the dinner table and the minute there was silence, she used to say, "Talk! I don't care what you talk about, talk about your budgie or your pony, but keep the conversation going. . . ." And so, I've never been able not to talk. It's in the psyche, not to leave a silence.

To Camilla's generation of upper-class girls, academics were irrelevant. From the age of ten through her teenage years, Camilla attended the elite London day school Queen's Gate near the family's South Kensington townhouse. It was a good launchpad for her debutante season. According to the novelist Penelope Fitzgerald, who taught French at Queen's Gate, it was very much a place "where the girls were taught how to write checks, play bridge, and recognize a well-laid table." Camilla left school with one O level, a good address book, and an ability to fence. A Swiss finishing school on the banks of Lake Geneva where the students learned French conversation, wine tasting, flower arranging, and the skills of running a big house completed Camilla's lack of formal education. More gloss was added as she drifted off to France for six months to study French and French literature at the University of London Institute in Paris.

Camilla's debutante year, 1965, was poised on the cusp of two worlds. The old social ritual of "doing the season," when freshly finished "fillies," as her father called them, were presented at court before being launched into a whirlwind of cocktail parties, racing events, and glittering country house balls, had been on the downdraft since the late 1950s. The last presentations at court, always held at Buckingham Palace, took place in 1958. Apparently, Prince Philip had long campaigned to get rid of the ritual on the grounds that it was "bloody daft," a sentiment in sync with the British public's souring of deference toward the ruling class, and the rising tide of satire and social conscience drama. Princess Margaret was no fan either. "We had to stop them," she said. "Every tart in London was being presented." Queen Charlotte's ball, which used to launch the season, survived until 1976 with debutantes curtseying to the cake instead of to the sovereign. (A select few were taught how to do so by Lucie Clayton, doyenne of the eponymous charm school, who was known as "the battle-axe of Bond Street.")

By Camilla's year, counterculture vibes were streaming through the ballroom door. Girls were divided between those rolling their overstuffed joints and teetering around in Mary Quant miniskirts, knee-length boots, and elfin Twiggy haircuts, and their more conservative peers, like Camilla, who stuck to Buck's Fizz, strands of pearls, and parties at the Guards Polo Club.

Hers was a bumper year of stylish aristocratic girls, from the fey Duke of Northumberland's daughter Lady Caroline Percy, to Lady Mary-Gaye Curzon, daughter of Edward Curzon, sixth Earl Howe and later the mother of Prince Harry's pre-Meghan girlfriend, Cressida Bonas. Lady Mary-Gaye was written up in the gossip columns so often she had a blue Curzon cocktail (for her blue blood) named after her at Claridge's. A blond dazzler with amazing legs, she epitomized the risqué spirit of the times by posing with her delicate face smeared in engine oil (in homage to her racing driver grandfather) and a lot of bare skin for the **Birds of Britain** coffee-table book.

In the afternoon, after a bout of shopping, a posse of debs including Camilla used to meet up on the green leather armchairs on the banking floor of Harrods, then head across the road for a lunch of cold roast chicken and peas at the Brief Encounter restaurant.

It seems Camilla has no regrets about her butterfly years. She never wanted a career. For ten minutes, she had a pretend job with the decorator Colefax and Fowler, but was fired for coming in late after a night of dancing. So what? There was an inheritance of £500,000 in the wings that would come to her on the death of her grandmother Sonia Cubitt.

Today some of her contemporaries bitterly resent that girls of their generation were denied a good education and were stuck as boarders in such schools as the debs wasteland of Heathfield in Berkshire, which one alumnus of the period described as "a Jane Eyre establishment gone wrong." Camilla, now a voracious reader and an avid consumer of culture and current affairs, is more inclined to see value in what she learned in a system now vanished. "Thank goodness I was brought up with the grounding of my parents, and taught manners," she told Geordie Greig.

It sounds, especially in this day and age, sort of snobbish but we left school at sixteen, nobody went on to university unless you were a real brainbox. Instead, we went to Paris and Florence and learned about life and culture and how to behave with people, how to talk to people. This was very ingrained in my upbringing and if I hadn't had that, I would have found royal life much more difficult.

Indeed, Camilla was so perfectly trained for life with the heir to the throne, in contrast to the abjectly unprepared Diana, that it feels baffling today that she was ever considered unsuitable. But with neither a grand title nor a record of chastity, and with names like Princess Marie-Astrid of Luxembourg being bandied around as a possible royal bride, the chances of the Prince of Wales proposing to Camilla were slim. The unwritten rule of the season was, as Christopher Wilson once put it, "If good girls don't, Camilla did." She had a yearlong tumble with Kevin Burke, the rich nineteen-year-old son of an aviation magnate who flashed around town in a yellow Jaguar E-Type she called "The Egg," and another whirl with the sleek banking heir Rupert Hambro.

But the recurring theme in her life was Andrew Parker Bowles, scion of a wealthy racehorse-owning family and the most panted-after dinner partner on the social circuit. None of her boyfriends could compete with the sexual panache of Andrew, who was seven years older than Camilla and cut a dashing figure as an officer in the Royal Horse Guards, a prestigious regiment of the Household Cavalry. For Camilla, it was a **coup de foudre** from the moment his younger brother Simon introduced them in 1966. They hooked up in the summer that year at a dance in Scotland, and she was soon overnighting at his Portobello Road flat, which often showed evidence of the last female visitor.

Camilla understood that the achingly archaic requirement of virginity in a royal bride was a deal breaker in her relationship with Charles. It would also prove lethal to his future happiness. Finding an intact woman in her late twenties amongst his contemporaries might have seemed easy from the Queen Mother's point of view, but in the freewheeling sexual mores of seventies London society, it was about as likely as a sighting of the Loch Ness monster. No wonder he wound up marrying the twenty-year-old ingénue Lady Diana Spencer.

It's also doubtful that Camilla would have accepted a proposal from Charles anyway. For seven years, she remained in headlong pursuit of the sexier, more dangerous Parker Bowles. Maddeningly, Andrew's style was to pick her up and drop her at will. (In the early seventies he had a torrid fling with the young Princess Anne. They remain close friends, and he still escorts her to racing events. In March 2020, the eighty-year-old Andrew, in a well-worn fedora, could be seen steering Anne around the Cheltenham Festival, where some of the crowd, including him, contracted COVID-19.) Camilla often regaled Rupert Hambro with furiously funny tales of Andrew's two- (or three-) timing. No one was fooled. Camilla Shand was obsessed with Parker Bowles.

It seems likely her dalliance with Charles was a ploy to make Andrew jealous. The time span of her romance with the Prince tallies with the major's six-month deployment in Northern Ireland and Cyprus, where the rumors of Camilla's new admirer would have surely lit a fire under him to propose.

To ensure Andrew did put a ring on her finger, Major Shand conspired with Andrew's father, Derek

Parker Bowles, to post news of an engagement in **The Times** on March 15, 1973, before he'd actually proposed, citing a wedding date four months hence. It was a risky move that paid off. Prince Charles was crushed to learn of the engagement while still at sea on the HMS **Fox** in the West Indies. "After such a blissful, peaceful and mutually happy relationship fate had decreed it should last a mere six months," he mourned in a letter seen by biographer Jonathan Dimbleby. The Roman Catholic ceremony on July 4, 1973 (Andrew was Catholic; Camilla did not convert), was a full-blown high-society turnout with eight hundred guests—so packed that one hundred of them had to stand—at the Guards' Chapel, Wellington Barracks. The Queen Mother and Princess Anne were in attendance, with Princess Margaret joining for the reception afterward at St. James's Palace. Anne, still smitten with Andrew, was apparently "in pieces" about the wedding and shortly afterward became engaged herself to Captain Mark Phillips, a less virile, intellectually dimmer version of Parker Bowles, gently dissed by Charles as "Fog." The Prince, fortuitously, could not attend, as he was on his way to Nassau to represent the Queen at a ceremony of imperial downsizing. (It couldn't have helped his mood when, at the handover of constitutional documents to the newly independent Bahamas, a canopy crashed down on top of them all.)

At least he was saved from having to witness Camilla looking dazzling in lashings of tulle, and her hair sparkling with diamonds, escorted up the aisle on the arm of her father to the handsome military man awaiting at the altar. When the bride and groom left the chapel, they proudly walked beneath the crossed swords of officers in the Blues and Royals. The Queen Mother signed the registry as principal witness.

IV

Across the distance of time, Andrew Parker Bowles has a whiff of the Jane Austen character George Wickham, the good-looking militia officer in **Pride and Prejudice** who later turns out to be an unreliable libertine—except that Camilla Shand, unlike Austen's Elizabeth Bennet, always knew Andrew's weakness for other women. "His power over [them] was extraordinary," an ex-lover said.

> Women had no hesitation believing what he said. He seemed to compel them into loving him, although he sometimes dropped them so quickly their heads spun. He could be completely ruthless in that sense.

> A woman he never won over was Rosalind Shand. She found him annoyingly preoccupied with his social connections and believed that he was never going to stop his philandering.
> She was correct. Andrew Parker Bowles would be as unfaithful during his nearly twenty-two-year

marriage to Camilla as he was for the seven years that preceded it. "When I was with Andrew," Lady Caroline Percy said, "she would come up to me at parties and ask me what I was doing with her boyfriend. She was always doing this to girls at parties. But I got fed up with it and said to her, 'You can have him back when I've finished with him.'" It's evidence of her innate optimism or how infatuated she was, and remained, that it didn't deter Camilla from becoming his wife.

They were a classic country couple. When Camilla was pregnant with their first child, Tom, in 1974, they lived at Bolehyde Manor, a sprawling seventeenth-century house at Allington near Chippenham in Wiltshire. Their friends were a close-knit group of sociable stately-home-owning earls: Pembroke, Shelburne, and Suffolk. Marie Helvin noted to me how "tight" the Parker Bowleses were as a couple, demonstrative and friendly, often talking animatedly to each other across guests at dinner parties.

Horses were a deep bond. Andrew competed hard at polo and was steeped in the racing world. As an amateur jockey, he had ridden his horse, The Fossa, in the 1969 Grand National steeplechase even though he had a steel plate in his back from a fall two years before at Ascot. For both Andrew and Camilla, a big appeal of Bolehyde Manor was that it fell within the territory of the Beaufort Hunt, one of the oldest, largest, and most prestigious of the foxhunting packs in England. A fellow rider described Camilla as formidable on horseback: "You often hear her screaming as you approach a fence, 'Bloody hell, get out of the fucking way!'"

Underneath all this brio was an uncomfortable truth she preferred not to discuss. Even after the birth of Tom and Laura, Camilla never knew where her husband was or with whom during the week. When he wasn't posted abroad, he was flagrantly playing the field in London in a flat he shared with his brother-in-law Nicolas Paravicini. The Greek playboy and writer Taki Theodoracopulos remembers having a run-in with Andrew in the early 1980s when he went after a girl Taki was with at a nightclub:

> I said, "Better luck next time, Andrew," and he said, "You are a fourth-rate fellow." To which the only answer was "As a sixth-rate fellow, you should know."

Andrew and Paravicini invented a code of milk bottles placed outside the door to signal to the other whether there was a girl in the bedroom. Lord Lichfield, who once shared a bachelor flat with Andrew in the pre-#MeToo days of the 1990s, summed it up to me as "They fucked him and forgave him."

Women—and riding—were the basis of Andrew's unlikely friendship with Lucian Freud. In the early eighties, the contrarian artist turned to Andrew in his position of commanding officer of the Household Cavalry Mounted Regiment with the rank of lieutenant colonel, to find him horses to ride and paint. Freud was obsessed with the thrill of the racetrack and the company of jockeys, punters, and bookies, many of whom he painted. (By Geordie Greig's estimation in **Breakfast with Lucian**, the artist lost £3 million to £4 million on bad bets.)

Parker Bowles and Freud used to gallop around Hyde Park together, traveled to Paris for one of Freud's exhibitions and to Ireland to see Freud's bookmaker. They shared a love of beautiful women as well as good meals. From 2003 to 2004, Freud painted Andrew for his wonderfully ironic homage to James Tissot's famous 1870 portrait of the debonair Royal Horse Guards officer Frederick Burnaby reclining on a sofa in shiny black patent leather boots. Freud's seven-foot-tall portrait of Andrew shows a once-dashing man going to seed, the open jacket revealing the expanding girth beneath, the blotchy face wearing an expression of dissolute indifference. In 2015, **The Brigadier** was sold at Christie's in New York for $34.9 million. Andrew told **Tatler** that he didn't have three or four million dollars to spare at the time and "secondly a seven-foot picture of myself looking rather red-faced and fat wasn't my idea of fun."

Meanwhile, after Camilla married, the Prince of Wales moved on. Throughout the mid-seventies, he engaged in a frantic quest for The One he didn't really want, working his way through the cream of the crop in society blondes. The daughters of earls, dukes, admirals, and ambassadors competed for his favor. There were passing flings with movie starlets and "It" girls and steady return matches with the wives of obliging friends. Most of the romances foundered because of press harassment or the ultimate irritation the girls felt with his princely entitlement. No longer the diffident amateur, Charles understood the pulling power of his rank and soon took it for granted.

"There's no doubt that being Prince Charles's girlfriend makes you feel very special," Sabrina Guinness, who was one of them, told me in 2005. "Suddenly, everyone is very interested in you and you are seen by your own circle as very special and glamorous." Lady Diana Spencer's eldest sister, Sarah, one of Charles's dates for a country ball, didn't appreciate being crammed in the back of his Aston Martin coupe on the drive back to London while a Colombian beauty he had just met was enthroned next to him in the front seat. Others complained they were offered no protection from the press. There was a selfishness in the royal disregard for the invasion of their privacy. Girls were offered zero defense from the voyeurs and the hounding, but were dropped like a hot potato if they wound up too often in the gossip columns.

Deftly, Camilla wove the Prince of Wales into her married life with Andrew. There is a sense that she was playing her own careful double game, keeping alive the sexual charge with Charles as a power play against her husband. It was an insurance policy for her own **amour propre**. Like Alice Keppel with Bertie, she remained the Prince of Wales's best listener, an always empathetic sounding board for his romantic adventures and frustration with the constraints of his lofty métier. In a way, she subsumed the role played in Charles's life by the Queen Mother, the woman who always made him the center of her world, the buttery scone to his mother's steamed broccoli. You can hear the solicitous tones on the notorious leaked "Camillagate" tapes illicitly recorded in 1989 by a ham radio fan from a phone call Charles made to Camilla at her marital home in Wiltshire:

CAMILLA: I'm so proud of you.
CHARLES: Your great achievement is to love me.
CAMILLA: Oh, darling, easier than falling off a chair.

Pure Noël Coward. A visitor to Bolehyde reported seeing the Prince "sitting patiently like a small, cold child in the kitchen waiting for Camilla to see her guests off after a dinner party." There was doubtless piquancy in the fact that when he vented about his parents, she was hearing the inside dope on the Queen and Prince Philip, but as the years rolled by, the Prince of Wales's attention was more than gratifying flattery. His unswerving devotion to Camilla was a deep comfort, their bond an emotional sustenance to protect. Constantly distracted by Andrew, she may have loved Charles more than she really knew.

A few months before the wedding of Charles and

Diana in 1981, I visited the Parker Bowleses at Bolehyde with the photographer Derry Moore for a **Tatler** picture story on the grand houses of Wiltshire. I was fascinated by the couple's dynamic, a kind of electric indifference. Andrew, at forty-one, had restless autocratic good looks and a terse military manner.

"Do you hunt?" he asked me.

"No."

"Do you fish?"

"No."

"Real intellectual, are you?" he said with a slight patrician sneer.

Camilla, softer in manner but practiced in self-protection, kept up a light banter that was determinedly disarming, telling us stories about the ghost of a "very randy monk." Her charm was all about the deep voice and the anything-goes smile. She described her neighbor Mrs. Rupert Loewenstein as a "not tonight, darling" type, a mood one felt rarely applied to herself.

By that time the Prince of Wales and Camilla were again lovers, or known to be. It is likely they never stopped. Corroborating evidence is offered by the late Sir Martin Charteris, who was then the Queen's private secretary and claimed that in 1973, the year Camilla married Andrew, he told the Queen that "Prince Charles was sleeping with Camilla Parker Bowles, the wife of a fellow officer in the Brigade of Guards, and that the Brigade of Guards did not like it." The Queen, said Charteris, said nothing. "Her face didn't change in any way," but courtiers were told never to include Mrs. Parker Bowles on the guest list of any formal event in future.

Like George Keppel, Andrew was amused and flattered that the Prince was still clearly enamored of his wife. When Charles agreed to be Tom Parker Bowles's godfather, it was a sign of status that Andrew seemed to relish. The Prince was usually one of the party when the couple went to stay at Birkhall with the Queen Mother, a longtime family friend of Andrew's. It seems the affair had varying degrees of intensity, dialed up by Camilla when she sensed a rival in view.

V

One woman she kept a beady eye on was Dale Harper, known as "Kanga," a platinum-blond Australian with luscious lips who was the daughter of a wealthy Melbourne publisher and the wife of Charles's sporting friend Lord Tryon. Camilla revealed her rivalrous feelings to me when she alluded to a piece **Tatler** had run about Dale a couple of months before my visit. "All this stuff about Lady Tryon being such a friend of Lady Diana," she said with an arch look. "She's never even **met** Diana Spencer," adding, "frightfully amusing all the stuff about Dale being such a country girl!"

Charles had met the sparky charmer Dale at a sock hop at the Timbertop campus of Geelong Grammar School in Victoria, where he spent six months at the age of seventeen. After moving to London and marrying Lord Tryon, she became a trusted confidante. Dale's directness, warmth, and talent at country entertaining were just the kind of attributes that Charles admired in Camilla. She allegedly strengthened her hold on Charles when Camilla was **hors de combat** with her pregnancies. It did not make Camilla happy that Dale put it around that Charles was said to have declared Dale "the only woman who ever understood me," a compliment he usually reserved for the Queen Mother and her surrogate, Mrs. Parker Bowles.

In the midseventies, both married women were on call for the Prince while their husbands looked the other way. A fellow social Aussie in my acquaintance, Lyndall Hobbs, described Lord Tryon as "extremely posh and cold-faced and kind of a bore," but everyone loved the ebullient Dale. She launched a fashion line of frothy frocks called the Kanga line. Princess Diana wore one of her deeply off-brand multi-patterned polyester dresses to the Live Aid concert at Wembley in 1985 just to make Camilla insane. The Tryons were invited to Balmoral, where Dale rode out with the Queen, who apparently found her brashness amusing. Charles was the godfather, too, of their middle son named, uh, Charles. The Prince often stayed at the Tryons' summer fishing lodge in Iceland, which supplied perfect private time with Dale. He was with her on August 27, 1979, when he heard the news of the murder of his adored great-uncle, Lord Mountbatten, by the IRA at his estate in Ireland, receiving from Dale the solace that was usually Camilla's to provide.

Diana never feared Dale like she did Camilla, rightly so since Dale was no match for Mrs. Parker Bowles. It takes layers of aristocratic grooming to know how to play the royal mistress game to win. You just have to wait for the upstart to make mistakes. Dale became too obviously enthralled with Charles's attention, talking too much about him, letting it be known she was his favorite. He dropped her or, rather, "created distance," as the royals know how to do better than anyone.

Dale kept believing that when the Prince's marriage to Diana went publicly awry, he would return to her welcoming arms. Instead, Charles grew closer to Camilla. Dale began to fall apart. After repeated bouts with ill health, including cancer, she became addicted to painkillers and, in an incident that shocked their circle, unaccountably fell twenty-five feet from the window of Farm Place, a Surrey drug-and-alcohol rehabilitation clinic. The fall paralyzed her below the waist and left her in a wheelchair. Things turned even darker when she insisted she was pushed. Her husband first asked for a divorce and then had her committed. Society pulled away. In July 1997, she showed up at a polo match at Tidworth and frantically pursued Prince Charles in her wheelchair. After the bizarre story leaked out, the Prince made a chilly statement saying they were no longer the friends they once were.

Dale died of septicemia three months after Diana in 1997 at the age of forty-nine, leaving behind mystery and silence. In a raw 2011 interview with the

Daily Mail, her daughter exposed the emotional truth of being the child of parents living in a supposedly civilized sexual "arrangement": "The pain of that time didn't go away for us as a family, just because Mum had passed away and Charles had married Camilla Parker Bowles," Lady Victoria Tryon said. "It might seem a long-forgotten scandal, but for us, the Tryon family, we are still having to live with its effects."

VI

As his parents' pressure to find a suitable wife became impossible to ignore, Charles's relationship with Camilla picked up momentum, even acquiring a slightly desperate edge. Both of them seemed to want to get caught. Many of the Prince's friends believe it was the shattering murder of Mountbatten that destabilized him and reheated the sexual soufflé, but Camilla had her own reasons to raise the stakes. After six years of marriage and two children, Andrew's eye was roving again. In 1979, he was posted to Rhodesia as senior military liaison officer to Lord Soames, who was serving as governor of Southern Rhodesia during its transition to the majority-rule state of Zimbabwe. His job was to work with the returning armies of Mugabe and Nkomo and aid the process of keeping the peace before the elections. It seems he excelled. He won a citation for "exceptional courage" when he faced down a renegade force of four hundred Zimbabwe African National Liberation Army guerrillas, and managed to bring them into the assembly area without casualties on either side.

More relevantly, however, as far as Camilla was concerned, he also found the time to conduct a very public flirtation with the governor's beautiful daughter, Charlotte Soames.

Mrs. Parker Bowles was unafraid of marital intrigue. She flew into Rhodesia, now Zimbabwe, with the Prince of Wales for the handover ceremonies, acting as his official escort for the trip. According to Christopher Wilson's account, the British Foreign Office was outraged at the impropriety. "The hauling down of the British flag was a humiliating enough circumstance without everyone knowing the royal envoy has brought his **popsy** along with him," complained one empurpled FO source. Charles's canoodling with Camilla in his private compartment was noted with dismay by all in the royal party. As was his overt behavior during dinner festivities at Government House on April 16, 1980, where Brigadier Parker Bowles and the Soames family, including Charlotte, were also present. "Christopher Soames unwisely sat Charles next to Camilla, probably at Charles's request," the Queen's former press secretary Michael Shea told me. "They behaved so blatantly it was appalling." Realizing this was going to be the dinner party from hell, Lady Soames, the daughter of Winston Churchill, looked heavenward and commented dryly, "And pray God may the claret be good."

The recklessness of Charles's behavior was no doubt fueled by panic. It was becoming oppressively imperative that he find a wife. He was now thirty-one, one year older than the age he had once ill-advisedly said was the best time to get married. He was intelligent enough to understand the futility of his own predicament, dispatched all over the world to watch the lowering of flags over outposts of the British Empire while the only real point of his existence was to produce an heir so the dynastic irrelevance could continue. In August 1980, he used the Duchy of Cornwall's funds to buy Highgrove House. The 347-acre estate near the market town of Tetbury in Gloucestershire was and is a romantic dream of an eighteenth-century manor. He especially loved the outstretched arms of the magnificent two-hundred-year-old cedar tree on the west side of the house. He snapped up the property for around a million dollars.

The press all assumed this was the act of a man preparing to settle down. His favorite sibling, Princess Anne, lived seven miles down the road at Gatcombe Park. Charles was easing into the life of a cosseted rich bachelor whose horses were saddled in the morning, whose fishing tackle was always ready, whose tweed jacket and corduroys were laid out for him the night before—and whose mistress lived fourteen miles away. Those on the inside knew that this was Highgrove's star attraction: its proximity to Camilla. (In 1985, downsizing after the children left for boarding school, she and Andrew moved to

Middlewick House in Corsham, still keeping close
to Highgrove.)

Charles was clearly heading for emotional chaos.
As the Palace moved with ever more purpose to put
a pin in the name of nineteen-year-old Lady Diana
Spencer, and Prince Philip demanded that he, for
God's sake, stop dithering, the Prince of Wales was
suddenly linked with someone new. He met the attractive haughty blonde Anna "Whiplash" Wallace,
the twenty-five-year-old daughter of a rich Scottish
landowner, foxhunting with the Belvoir while staying at the Duke of Rutland's estate. Hunting? Camilla
didn't like that detail of Anna's biography one bit.
Women who risk the speed and danger of the hunt
are likely to be sexually adventurous. Just at the
time when all her friends knew that Andrew was
enamored with Charlotte Soames, Camilla, now
thirty-three, began to feel threatened by the Prince
of Wales's susceptibility to younger rivals.

She routed Anna Wallace on a hot night in June
1980 during a string of summer balls. By then, rumors had been swirling that Charles had already
proposed to Wallace. She was his date at a significant
Royal Family event, the Queen Mother's eightieth
birthday ball hosted by the Queen at Windsor Castle.
Mrs. Parker Bowles enticed the Prince of Wales onto
the dance floor and kept him there all night. Anna
did not disguise her irritation: "Don't ever, ever ignore me like that again," she hissed. "No one treats
me like that, not even you!" But he was the Prince of
Wales and he did, a week later when she was again

his date at a polo ball at Stowell Park, hosted by the heir to a meat fortune, Lord Vestey. The sexual fireworks continued. The Parker Bowleses were seated at the Prince's table. Camilla and Charles's behavior on the dance floor was overtly demonstrative. "On and on they went, kissing each other, French kissing, dance after dance. . . . [It] was completely beyond the pale," Jane Ward, an old flame of the Prince, recalled. Even Rosalind and Major Shand were discomfited by such a blatant display of intimacy in front of Camilla's husband. They need not have worried. Uttering a line that could have been delivered by George Keppel in 1898, Andrew Parker Bowles opined to a guest, "HRH is very fond of my wife. And she appears to be very fond of him." Anna did not stick around this time to voice her outrage. She commandeered Lady Vestey's BMW and screeched out of the gates of Stowell Park and out of Charles's life.

Camilla had had a scare with Anna Wallace, and adopted a new strategy. She now became as insistent a proponent as the Queen and Prince Philip for the Prince of Wales finding a wife—someone young, pliant, and, with a bit of luck, perpetually pregnant. After all, the supremacy of Alice Keppel as Edward VII's immovable mistress was shored up by the quiet elegance of Queen Alexandra at his side. Her presence headed off the dangerous ambitions of young pretenders.

As the Prince wavered with reluctance and indecision, Camilla vetted the blushing Lady Diana Spencer. Charles noted with unease that at nineteen,

Diana was still a child, "exquisitely pretty, a perfect poppet . . . but she is a child." Better yet, noted Camilla, she didn't hunt, leaving plenty of opportunity for her and Charles to meet.

From the Palace's point of view Diana checked every box. Pedigree? Check. Younger? Check. Virgin? (Diana boasted she always knew she had "to keep myself very tidy" for a future husband.) The Spencer girl had long familial associations with the royals. Diana's grandmother Lady Fermoy was one of the Queen Mother's most beloved ladies-in-waiting. Her father, Earl Spencer, had been an equerry to both King George VI and Queen Elizabeth II. Diana had been close to the Windsors' way of life forever. That meant she would know how things were done and would not complain.

The Queen did have some reservations. "She's never **stuck** to anything," she noted about Diana's thin résumé, but when the news of the royal engagement broke, Princess Margaret spoke for all the family circle when she said to a friend, "We're extremely relieved—but [Camilla] has no intention of giving him up." As if to reinforce the status quo, Andrew Parker Bowles was appointed by the Prince of Wales to be head of security at the wedding.

What a pity that the Queen, so gifted at reading the bloodlines of horses, misread so profoundly the Spencers' suitability to join with royal stock. Yes, in terms of pedigree, they were flawless. Generations of Spencers had served as courtiers and servants to the Crown. But their power and independence were such that they saw themselves as serving the monarch they chose. The Spencers were kingmakers and schemers. The men were bad-tempered and choleric, and the women were said to be, in the parlance of upper-class misogyny, "out of control." As a Spencer relation once said:

The Spencers are difficult. . . . As a family, they like to live among dramas. There's never a moment when they are all speaking to each other. Spencers are not as others. They are not straightforward.

In a keynote speech she gave at European Drug Prevention Week in 1993, Diana spoke of the "skilled survivors" of dysfunctional families. It was generally assumed she was delivering coded messages about her husband's cold and formal upbringing starved of physical affection, but she could just as easily have been speaking of herself. Her parents' divorce was not simply acrimonious; it was steeped in treachery.

At eighteen, her mother, the rich and aristocratic Frances Roche, was one of the youngest brides ever to walk up the aisle at Westminster Abbey when she married the thirty-year-old heir to Althorp, John Spencer. Alas, behind his impeccable manners and affable veneer, Johnnie turned out to be a bullying, patriarchal personality who became abusive after a few drinks. In order to produce an heir, he made Frances go through six pregnancies in nine years, of which only four were carried to term, and he resented her having any independent life.

The five-year-old Diana used to listen behind the door of the drawing room to the sounds of rows so violent that her sister Sarah had to turn up the gramophone to drown them out. One of the bitterest moments of Frances's life was when her husband refused to let her see the baby son who had died shortly after birth. She struggled from the bed and banged frantically on the locked door of the nursery to which he had been snatched away. "My baby was taken from me and I never saw his face. Not in life. Not in death. No one ever mentioned what had happened," she recalled later. It was not for many years that Frances saw the baby's death certificate, with the entry "extensive malformation."

Frances found her marriage intolerable by the time she met Peter Shand Kydd, the heir of a wallpaper fortune, who swept her off her feet. When she and Johnnie separated in 1968, she never expected her husband to win custody of their children. The testimony against her by a genteel viper, her mother, Lady (Ruth) Fermoy, who valued above all her position at court with the Queen Mother, was a decisive factor. Ruth chose to brand Frances as a "bolter" rather than go up against as embedded an establishment figure as Johnnie Spencer. Frances attempted to regain custody in 1971, but lost again.

"Her mother's testimony was a bitter hurt, a deep wound," Barbara Gilmour, the wife of one of Diana's godfathers, told me. "It created a lifelong rift between them that was never healed. I will never understand what motivated Ruth."

The pain inflicted on Frances by Lady Fermoy was the final twist in the primal wound that shaped Diana's life. The children were not told the truth of why Frances was leaving. Diana everlastingly internalized her exit as a cruel abandonment. When Frances returned to Park House to renew her efforts to collect Diana and her younger brother months later, the door was shut in her face. "The house was so huge the children couldn't hear me from inside calling out to them," Frances remembered.

Her move with Peter Shand Kydd to the remote Isle of Seil to escape the mean gossip of Norfolk gentry was a double deprivation for the Spencer children. The gloomy void left by her vibrant mother instilled in Diana a lifelong insecurity and fear of loss. Before she even met Prince Charles, a mutinous rage beneath her ladylike façade played out in explosive scenes whenever she felt slighted.

At fifteen, Diana was aghast when her father remarried the overblown social doyenne Raine Legge, ex-wife of the ninth Earl of Dartmouth. The Spencer children learned the news by reading it in the newspaper. There was a glittering celebration ball at Althorp to which none of them were invited. Significantly, it was the blushing teenage Diana who was deputed by her siblings to execute a fittingly vindictive reprisal. As her father's favorite, she felt the most displaced. She confronted Johnnie at Althorp on her return from school. As she advanced for what her father thought was a warm embrace, she drew back her hand and hit him stingingly across the face. "That's from all of us for hurting us," she hurled at him with scarlet cheeks.

That wasn't all. On the eve of her brother Charles's wedding to the model Victoria Aitken in 1989, Diana became so furious at Raine's dismissive treatment of Frances that she pushed her stepmother down the stairs and watched her tumble in a heap on the landing. "[It] gave me enormous satisfaction," Diana told her speech coach Peter Settelen two years later. "I was so angry. I wanted to throttle that stepmother of mine. . . . She kept saying to me, 'Oh, but Diana, you're so unhappy in your own marriage. You're just jealous of Daddy's and my relationship.' In reply, Diana said, "We've always hated you."

Wow. There was probably never a more dangerous candidate than Diana to unwittingly enter a loveless marriage. Charles's inability to give Camilla up would tap into her most abject terrors of childhood rejection. The violence of her panic later expressed itself in self-harm. The Duke of Marlborough told the influential politico Woodrow Wyatt's daughter, Petronella, that on one occasion Diana cut up all of Prince Charles's ties and stabbed at herself with a pair of scissors.

But none of these unsettling undercurrents could be detected in the big blue eyes of the nineteen-year-old Spencer girl. The British public fell in love with Diana's freshness from the moment they beheld her picture in **The Sun,** shyly holding two toddlers in her arms outside of the Young England Kindergarten and wearing a translucent flowered summer skirt, backlit to reveal, unknowingly, the long slender legs beneath. The photograph became iconic the way Marilyn Monroe's had done decades earlier, except that Diana's was a chaste allure.

Two years later, the usually canny Mrs. Parker Bowles asked herself how in the world she could have got the "perfect poppet" so hopelessly wrong.

CHAPTER
3

THE WILDERNESS YEARS

How Camilla Hung In

T HE MISERIES OF THE WALES MARRIAGE, AND Camilla's role in it, remained deniable until two bombs went off. One was detonated by Diana, the other was the Camillagate tapes, the illicit recording of the six-minute raunchy phone call between Charles and his mistress one ill-starred December evening in 1989 and leaked four years later.

Andrew Morton's tell-all book **Diana: Her True Story**, in essence the Princess's revenge memoir, was published in June 1992. Patrick Jephson, her former private secretary, described the Palace tension in the buildup to the release: "It was like watching a slowly spreading pool of blood seeping from under a locked door."

Morton ripped open the curtain of discreet collusion that had allowed Camilla's years of adultery with Charles to persist, exposing her as his mistress.

His book shamed her as the de facto wrecker of the happily-ever-after myth of Charles's marriage to an adored fairy-tale princess. Camilla had no Palace machine to protect and spin for her as the royals did. She was deluged with hate mail. The Parker Bowleses were forced to change their phone number. The press camped out on their doorstep. "It was entirely normal to be chased at high speed by these people on motorbikes or cars," her son, Tom, has said. "They're bullies, half these people, and they made you very angry."

The day of the first serialization of Morton's publication, the Parker Bowleses appeared together with Tom at the Alfred Dunhill Queen's Cup polo match in Windsor Great Park as guests in the Queen's box. "I'm certainly not going to bury myself away because of what the papers say," Camilla told reporters defiantly. "Absolutely not. Why should I?" The couple needed the show of unity as much for their children as themselves. Andrew, recently promoted from the preposterously named post of Lieutenant Colonel Commanding the Household Cavalry and Silver Stick-in-Waiting to Queen Elizabeth II, to the rank of Brigadier, didn't much relish all the covert merriment about how often his silver stick was made to wait for his wife. He was taunted several days later by the hearty fool Charles Spencer-Churchill at Royal Ascot as "Ernest Simpson," after the cuckolded husband of Wallis.

The Morton revelations were doubly shocking to Tom, seventeen, at Eton and Laura, fourteen, at a country boarding school. They had been less exposed than William and Harry to any disharmony between their parents. Camilla had to contend with the confusion and hurt of sensitive teenagers. Genial familiarity with the Prince of Wales's involvement in their mother's and father's lives was now transformed from a source of pride to painful embarrassment. Laura, especially, felt protective of her father. She refused to give her mother the message when the Prince called to speak to her. Laura reportedly used to pick up an extension when they talked and would shout down the receiver, "Why don't you stop calling Mummy and leave our family alone." The only salvage was saying nothing or labeling it all a lie. Andrew Parker Bowles's stoic response: "It's fiction, fiction. I've nothing to say."

One of Morton's most damaging allegations was that relations between Camilla and the Prince never ceased after he married Diana. Among many clues, Charles sometimes surreptitiously removed himself with (one can't help imagining) one of those huge first-generation mobile phones to talk to Camilla from the Highgrove bathroom.

It was easy for his flattered mistress to keep the flames alive by deploying the same skills she'd used in the early years of her union with Andrew, sharing all the Prince of Wales's interests and remaining his constant listener at whatever time of day he called. Michael Shea told me that Princess Anne said that sometime after the birth of Harry, the three royal siblings were thinking of writing to Charles, protesting his behavior. "The Queen and Prince Philip felt the same," Shea told me. If they did write, it had no effect. "Charles was hypnotized by Camilla sexually," said Shea.

Whatever Diana's suspicions, it's likely Charles did not return to Camilla's bed until just after Prince Harry was born in September 1984, which was two years earlier than he admitted, but later than Diana believed. Most indications are that he followed the traditions of upper-class adultery by pausing while the breeding was done. Once he had fulfilled his royal duty with an heir and a spare, he turned off the light. "Something happened in his head," Diana confided to Lady Colin Campbell of his behavior at that time. ("Oh God, it's a boy . . . and he's even got red hair!" he had exclaimed when he first saw baby Harry. He had wanted and expected a girl.)

As Princess Margaret of Hesse saw it: "One day, he'd had enough. It was as simple as that. One day—a day neither she [Diana] nor anyone else can identify—she pushed him over that invisible line. He didn't realize it at the time, but she'd goaded him past the point of endurance. After that, he retreated into himself." All Charles's life, his needs had been met by others. Diana's own needs were so unappeasable, he had neither the ability nor the inclination to try to answer them. His old friends' view was that the Princess of Wales turned Charles into a nervous wreck. He retreated to his garden at Highgrove while Diana followed him out and berated him about his callous behavior. Was it truly the Prince's feelings for

Camilla, his friends asked, that had turned his wife into what they considered an "unmanageable termagant"? Or had Diana really been unstable all along?

Former staffers say Diana was not always the quietly sobbing victim of Morton's narrative, but a spoiled celebrity princess who cavalierly leased a $130,000 red Mercedes at a time of widespread unemployment, making herself the only Royal in memory to drive a foreign car. Or, spitefully, kept the boys away from her husband when they came home from boarding school, demanding dinner on a tray with them upstairs while Charles sat forlornly waiting for them at the dinner table. The Princess blew hot and cold on the staff with such caprice they had no idea how to please her.

Ronnie Driver, a polo-playing friend of Charles, recalled the scene one weekend when the Prince left to ride out with the Beaufort Hunt—and, by extension, with Camilla, in her tight white breeches and shiny black dominatrix boots. "Diana saw Charles slinking off, after he had promised to spend the day with her and William . . . and she started screaming . . . accusing him of being selfish, a bastard, and a few four-letter words." The Prince's circle argued that the Princess of Wales would have been wise to take up hunting herself. Or gardening. Or embraced, rather than banished, his old friends, but such tactics are easier when you acknowledge that you are in an arranged marriage rather than naïvely thinking you had married for love. Guile goes out the window when pain is so raw.

Camilla was strongly of the view that Diana was emotionally damaged. When Diana's uncle Lord Fermoy shot himself after a struggle with depression in 1984, there was more chatter in the Gloucestershire set about "bad blood." The Queen's cousin Lady Kennard admitted in an officially sanctioned BBC documentary: "The Queen, or anybody else, would never quite understand what Princess Diana was about. She was very damaged—her background and her childhood—and it is very difficult to know."

The cruel joke that went around was that the Princess, like much of the cattle in the British Isles at the time, was suffering from mad cow disease. Concern for how badly Charles's reputation was shredded by Diana's manipulation of the press made Camilla feel she was his only champion. Andrew didn't need her, but Charles did. Saving the suffering Prince had now become her mission. She was finally over Andrew and fully committed to Charles. There is no other explanation for how else Camilla could have tolerated the successive humiliations that rained down on her in the mid-1990s, when it appeared that she was held in scorn by the entire nation. Her steadiness in adversity won points with all his friends. "Camilla has been absolutely constant and unflinching. She has never attempted to defend herself or succumbed to the temptation to set the record straight," her old Sussex neighbor William Shawcross said. "I think it's been one of her great strengths, and for that dignity she has earned a lot of quiet praise. People have said, 'My God, she's put up with a lot,' and she did."

As her own marriage frayed, she and Charles clung to each other more and more.

II

In January 1993, seven months after the publication of Andrew Morton's book, the Camillagate tape robbed the two lovers of any cover at all. For the first time, the heir to the throne had nowhere to hide. The incontrovertibility of the evidence busted every layer of upper-class obfuscation, every vestige of the dignity of disavowal. "Game, set, and match," Diana exclaimed triumphantly to her personal protection officer Ken Wharfe, clutching a copy of the **Mirror** containing the transcript. For Camilla, coming seven months after Morton, it brought mortification times ten. The brutal exposure ended any murmuring mystique around the status of "royal mistress" and reduced it to something that sounded furtive and squalid and earned the mockery of the world:

CAMILLA: You're awfully good at feeling your
   way along.
CHARLES: Oh stop! I want to feel my way
   along you, all over you and up and down
   you and in and out.
CAMILLA: Oh!
CHARLES: Particularly in and out.
CAMILLA: Oh, that's just what I need at the
   moment. . . .

CHARLES: I'll just live inside your trousers or
something. It would be much easier!
CAMILLA: What are you going to turn into, a
pair of knickers?
CHARLES: Or, God forbid a Tampax. Just
my luck . . .

Tampax jokes lit up every comedy show. Cartoons
featured Charles talking dirty to his plants. In Italy,
they called him **Prince Tampacchino.** Camilla Parker
Bowles was now a household name hounded by the
press. She retreated to Middlewick House and pulled
up the drawbridge. She had never felt more isolated.
Meeting Charles was now nearly impossible with so
much surveillance, and she feared calling him in case
their phones were bugged.

Without identifying the reason for her twelve
months of purdah, Camilla told Geordie Greig
twenty-four years later, in 2017:

I couldn't really go anywhere. But the children
came and went as normal—they just got on with
it—and so did great friends. I would pass the
time by reading a lot—I thought, well, if I'm
stuck here I might as well do something positive
like read all the books I want to read, and try
to learn to paint—though that wasn't a huge
success!—and after a while, life sort of went on.

Life sort of did, but it took Camilla several years
to recover her game face. Friends were concerned

about how the pressure impacted the state of her health. "I am genuinely worried about her," one of them told Christopher Wilson. "The spark has gone out of her life and she looks haunted and hunted." Unlike Charles, who had castle gatekeepers and protection officers to shield him, Camilla had only her front door in Wiltshire. "She has no desire to be famous, or popular," Mark Bolland said in 2004.

The period when she was demonized and traduced by newspapers was very upsetting for her, and it upset [Charles] enormously too, because he felt responsible for it.

One source of support was her father, Major Shand. "I remember once when he was staying with me at Middlewick," Camilla recalled in her seventieth birthday year to the **Mail,** "and the press were outside. Every couple of minutes they'd be rattling the door, coming down the chimney, banging on the window. . . . After a while, my father calmly went to the front door and he summoned them all. They came clustering round thinking there was about to be some great statement about me, and he said, 'Gentlemen, in our family, we keep our traps shut, thank you very much,' and walked in again. He closed the door with a smile and that was it. I don't think the press could believe what they'd heard but that was always how we were brought up: never complain and never explain. Don't whinge—just get on with it."

How downcast she really felt can be detected in a telling **Mirror** photograph that appeared in March 1993, which shows her driving up to Middlewick House wearing a drab babushka headscarf and looking despondent: no guards, no protection, a woman hung out to dry. There was cold comfort from those who were named in the lovers' colluding aristocratic circle. The tape laid bare a cynical code of marital morals that was socially discomfiting to peers who often had their own arrangements. Camilla and Charles had mortified not just themselves, but an entire class.

Royal mistresses had been tolerated and even expected in the past, but that was in the age of deference, when privacy could always be maintained. At a London dinner party, the Queen's cousin Princess Alexandra of Kent raised the topic with Woodrow Wyatt. Wyatt noted in his journal of February 16, 1993, that Alexandra "rather nervously asked me . . . did I think the monarchy would survive. They are obviously all very rattled."

Charles himself feared the answer to the question—as well as the fact that the question was even being asked. If you could die of embarrassment, he had. He was deeply aware that he had brought the monarchy into disrepute and that the constant ridicule would undermine the important work he was doing with his many philanthropies. His popularity numbers were in the tank at 4 percent. When he attempted a low-key royal appearance at a hostel center for the mentally ill in east London, he was heckled: "Have you no shame?" The Queen, who had always been restrained about her disapproval of Camilla, was frozen with disgust. Prince Philip ruminated that Charles was "not King material." The British public agreed with Philip: 42 percent of the Queen's subjects now thought Charles should never become king and 81 percent, when asked if he should take over the throne "within the next couple of years," stated "No." This was of real concern to his parents. It would not have been lost on them that five European kings and queens who attended Lord Mountbatten's funeral fifteen years before were all now in exile. Even though Diana had herself just been humiliatingly exposed in another salaciously leaked phone call with her admirer James Gilbey, whose term of endearment for her was "Squidgy," she remained the Royal Family's most popular member. The press unkindly noted that at a memorial service for the Earl of Westmorland in November 1993, Diana looked radiantly beautiful while Camilla looked old enough to be her mother.

Nine months after the Camillagate tape was released, architectural historian and celebrated diarist James Lees-Milne reported in his entry of September 4, 1993, about spending time with the Parker Bowleses and their children as guests of two of Charles's closest friends, the Duke and Duchess of Devonshire, at Chatsworth. Camilla, he wrote, "is not beautiful, and has lost her gaiety and sparkle. Doubtless worn by tribulations undergone. Women spit at her in supermarkets; cameramen snoop at her at the Fair. Walks with bowed head, and has trained her fluffy hair to cover her cheeks." Charles's stalwart circle of aristocratic friends were recipients of even more tortured late-night calls from him than usual. He seemed to have an alarming preoccupation with the suicide in the 1880s of Crown Prince Rudolf, heir to the throne of the Austro-Hungarian Empire, who was found shot to death with his lover in the hunting lodge at Mayerling, a small village southwest of Vienna. "Wouldn't the media have a field day if I took the same way out?" he demanded morosely.

There were rumors he was looking at property in Tuscany, an ominous sign given its reputation as "the paradise of exiles." The Queen Mother was so dismayed by this drift that she invited the Prince to lunch at Clarence House and (without mentioning Tuscany) prodded him to remember his visit to the sad, exiled Duke of Windsor at his house in the Bois de Boulogne in Paris at the end of his life. It was her subtle way of reminding him of what happens when you abandon duty, and of the futility of Edward VIII's life after abdication.

III

There was another debacle ahead: a disastrous appearance by the Prince of Wales on June 29, 1994, in a TV documentary by his friend Jonathan Dimbleby in which he confirmed his adultery. Titled **Charles:**

The Private Man, The Public Role, it preceded Dimbleby's distinguished official biography. This timing was clearly a mistake for both author and subject. It meant that a thoroughly researched, much-praised 620-page tome was subsumed forever in an explosive documentary sound bite.

Charles had cooperated with the charming scion of the BBC broadcasting family to a reckless degree, serving up ten thousand personal letters and diaries and long, introspective interviews. The Queen and Prince Philip were appalled at his naïvety in doing so, and offended by the content. "The Queen reportedly sighed, pursed her lips, and murmured, 'So it's come to this.'" His parents had no time for sob stories about the brutalities Charles endured at Gordonstoun. (One that was especially memorable was how the boys in his dorm beat him over the head with pillows all night because he snored.) His younger brothers, after all, seemed to have attended the school without undue emotional scars. The Queen resented the portrait of her as a remote, unfeeling parent. Philip did not appreciate being depicted as an insensitive tyrant, remembering Charles's childhood very differently: the jolly Balmoral picnics, reading him **The Song of Hiawatha** before he went to sleep (noted by Dimbleby, but ignored by the press), and the summer holidays cruising on the twelve-meter yacht **The Bloodhound** with sister Anne.

For Camilla, the worst harm was that defining sound bite delivered three-quarters through the discussion on a chintz-covered sofa at Highgrove. Dimbleby asked whether Charles, after he married Lady Diana Spencer in 1981, had tried "to be faithful and honorable to [his] wife." "Yes, absolutely," replied the Prince, adding the terminal caveat, "until it became irretrievably broken down, us both having tried." Bingo, adultery. For the tabloid press, there was a feast of headlines. Piers Morgan's **News of the World** rushed out a late edition that blasted the news: "Charles: I've Never Loved Diana."

James Lees-Milne was one of many of the country's squirearchy who watched the interview in incredulity. The universal condemnation of Charles's admission was a precursor of the opprobrium that would descend on Prince Andrew after his disastrous sit-down with the BBC's Emily Maitlis in 2019, to clear his name about his relationship with the American millionaire pedophile Jeffrey Epstein and the seventeen-year-old Virginia Roberts. "I only saw a few minutes of the Prince Charles interview," wrote Lees-Milne in his diary of June 28,

but it was enough to make me deplore the whole exercise. This idealistic middle-aged man struggled to get the words out and writhed with intellectual deficiency, wrinkling his forehead and making grimaces. A great mistake for him to admit marital infidelity. He should have refused to discuss such matters, whatever the pressure.

The Queen's former press secretary Dickie Arbiter concurred. "The programme was a complete whinge, a terrible own goal, that not just affected relations between the Prince and the Princess, but between St. James's Palace [where Charles's office was headquartered] and Buckingham Palace," he said. It was a double whammy that Diana went out the night of the interview to the **Vanity Fair** party at the Serpentine Gallery wearing a slinky black Christina Stambolian cocktail number that was swiftly dubbed her "revenge dress."

As Camilla fought off more ugly press from Charles's confirmation of their adultery, she was also in deep distress over the health of her mother, Rosalind. Like Sonia Cubitt before her, Mrs. Shand was dwindling away with severe osteoporosis. She shrank eight inches and became so bent over she could no longer properly digest food. "It was terrible, because we didn't know anything about it," Camilla said in a BBC documentary in 2021. "Occasionally, when she moved or you touched her, she literally screamed. I remember when a friend of hers came in one day just to give her a hug, her rib broke." She died in July 1994 at the age of seventy-two. In Camilla's role as president of the Osteoporosis Society, her first ever philanthropic leadership position, which she assumed seven years after Rosalind died, she spoke of the "pain and ignominy of the disease. . . . I believe that the quality of her life became so dismal, and her suffering so unbearable, that she just gave up the fight and lost the will to live."

The pain of her mother's death was now compounded by her husband Andrew's desire for a divorce.

Many of the Parker Bowleses' friends believe that, if not for Dimbleby, Andrew and Camilla might never have ended their marriage, for reasons of habit, face, and money—even though Andrew had been deep in an affair since 1986 with the ex-wife of an old army friend. But Charles's admission of infidelity on camera was said to be the last straw for Andrew. One might ask why it took this long for Mr. Silver Stick-in-Waiting to finally draw a line in the sand. Wasn't Morton's book enough? The Tampax colloquy? It seems that in the upper-class adultery code, the only truly dishonorable thing to do is to tell the truth. Within three months, Andrew was summoning a matrimonial lawyer, and, by December, proceedings were issued. With warp speed, the divorce was heard in January 1995 and finalized by March the same year. It was just as well. Diana retaliated against Dimbleby with her lethal November 20, 1995, interview with Martin Bashir on **Panorama**, which directed an even sharper laser on the reasons her marriage to Charles had collapsed.

One last **scandale** attached to Andrew and Camilla as a couple. They were betrayed by one of their Middlewick household staff, Margaret Giles, who lived in a cottage at the end of the drive. Andrew had gone to tell her in person of the impending divorce and warn her of probable press harassment. Her response was to steal a cache of family pictures out of her employers' personal photograph albums and flog them off to **The Sun.** The Parker Bowleses sued, and the paper settled out of court, agreeing to pay £25,000, which went to charity.

Their children, Laura and Tom, were not handling the successive parental embarrassments well. Laura blamed Charles for the breakup of her parents' marriage and feuded about it with Prince William. The **Sunday Express** reported that a family friend said, "William would blame Camilla for all the hurt she had caused his mother, which would send Laura into a rage. . . . Laura was not having any of it. She would take a hard line and fire back at William, 'Your father has ruined my life.'" In April 1995, Camilla's son, Tom, still at Oxford, was arrested for possession of ecstasy tablets and cannabis after being searched leaving a south London nightclub. "I didn't help myself getting into all sorts of trouble, nothing serious, mucking around, just dabbling in stuff and, you know, not being clever with whatever I was caught with," Tom told an Australian TV station in 2015, by which time he was a successful food critic. Tom managed not to be sent down from Oxford, but he was cautioned by the police.

In February 1996, Andrew married his mistress, the very rich and vivacious Rosemary Pitman, at the Chelsea Register Office with their children present. Perhaps he just wanted some peace and to draw a line under the whole undignified marital mess with Camilla that had played out for so many years in the press. The ex–Mrs. Parker Bowles was left fragile and exposed and skating on thin ice, facing the prospect of rattling around in an empty nest in Wiltshire with her two Jack Russells.

IV

For the first time Camilla felt she was losing the upper hand. If the Prince discarded her now, her social standing and long-term security would be seriously reduced. She was already keenly worried about money. In the divorce settlement with Andrew, Middlewick House was swiftly off-loaded. (It was bought by Pink Floyd's drummer, Nick Mason.) The couple split the proceeds, and Camilla's share went toward Ray Mill House, a mid-nineteenth-century stone pile on seventeen acres secluded at the end of a long drive, which she bought for £850,000 in May 1995. She furnished it with cozy charm, displaying family heirlooms and a grand portrait of Alice Keppel that dominated the living room. Its privacy was perfect, as was its location at Chippenham in Wiltshire, near enough to Highgrove, but the outlay left her cash poor. She was said to have soon run up an overdraft with Coutts bank of nearly £130,000. Ray Mill was in a somewhat shabby state, and she could never afford to have it renovated. One of her plans was to bring her widowed father to live in a converted barn on the property as company for them both, but she was denied planning permission and he had to live instead with Annabel. Her only other visible asset was some family land in Lincolnshire divided with her siblings. Her share gave her an income of £15,000 a year.

Adding to her financial difficulties were the losses she had sustained in the midnineties as an investor, or "name," in Lloyd's of London, the world's preeminent insurance market. "Names," as they are called, provide financing to the underwriting syndicates and share in the profits. There was a cachet to being a name, just as there was to banking at Coutts. But when things turned bad, the underwriters have to shell out, as **The Guardian** put it, "right down to the last cufflink." A large number of the names were unenquiring aristos used to cashing their checks without reading the small print. They now found themselves liable for huge claims as Lloyd's racked up losses of £8 billion between 1988 and 1992, mainly due to asbestos and pollution policies from the United States and ferocious storms in northern Europe. Among those stung were Prince Michael of Kent, £1 million; Princess Diana's mother, Frances Shand Kydd, £1.3 million; the Duchess of York's father, Ronald Ferguson, £1 million; and former prime minister Edward Heath, £1.4 million. Camilla lost £400,000, left to her by her grandmother, in two syndicates that failed. To protect her from exposure to Lloyd's, Ray Mill's ownership was placed in a trust.

Some of Camilla's shortage of cash was likely strategic. The thinking would have been that the Prince's unfortunate blabbing to Dimbleby had triggered

Andrew into divorcing Camilla. Now Mrs. Parker Bowles needed a big house to live in to keep her in the necessary style as the Prince of Wales's mistress. He had a duty of care to provide for her. She would clearly run out of cash, and the Prince would have to front for it. "Camilla is a smart poker player," remarked a friend of hers who subscribes to this theory.

Camilla began to accumulate perks from the Prince to improve her post-divorce life. When she hosted a dinner party at Ray Mill, the Highgrove chef was dispatched to cook. Bernie Flannery, the Highgrove butler, shopped for her at Sainsbury's and charged it to the Prince's account. Stabling her horse, Molly, at Highgrove reduced her hunting costs. A consignment of flowers, bushes, and trees from the Prince's estate was sent over in a horse trailer to beautify her property. Two gardeners and two housekeepers were added to her staff. The Prince replaced her battered car with a shiny new Ford Mondeo Estate. When her road flooded, he gifted her a Range Rover. Given how critical the press was of her appearance, a dress allowance was granted from the Wales war chest. It might sound like small potatoes given Charles's personal wealth, but the royals tend to be blithely unaware of other people's financial needs.

Camilla exerted increasing control of Charles's diary. In 1996, one of her oldest friends, Virginia Carrington, joined the Prince's staff to run his personal schedule. Camilla often joined the all-important diary meetings at St. James's Palace. A favorite line in

Bolland's background briefings to the press was, "While the Prince is anxious to improve his public image, the question of Mrs. Parker Bowles is non-negotiable." Members of his team were amused by another oft-repeated line that described Camilla as "the woman who waited." A former colleague of his said that "it was Bolland who invented that fiction. It was quite an aggressive campaign."

One evening in June 1997, while Camilla was driving to have dinner with the Prince at Highgrove, a nerve-racking accident earned her another upgrade. On a narrow country lane near Malmesbury in Wiltshire, Camilla crashed headlong into fifty-three-year-old Carolyn Melville-Smith's Volvo station wagon, ripping off her own front wheel and flipping the Volvo over in a ditch. Mrs. Parker Bowles had "appeared like a missile" in her Ford Mondeo, claimed Miss Melville-Smith, who suffered chest injuries. Although dazed and with a sprained wrist, Camilla managed to call the police and ambulance service and then the Prince at Highgrove on her mobile phone, taking off from the scene to get a better signal on higher ground. This was not great optics since, at the time, Melville-Smith was trapped upside down in the ditched car because her skirt was shut in the door.

Charles immediately dispatched his own police bodyguard to the scene with two of his valets and two other members of staff. When local cops arrived, the distraught Melville-Smith alleged that Camilla had departed the scene of the accident. The implausible first explanation offered was that she had been trained in anti-terrorism techniques to leave the scene immediately. "I think in shock you do funny things. I am sorry for her really. It was not very nice not to come and help me," Melville-Smith commented to the Associated Press. A month later, the Crown Prosecution Service decided that there was insufficient evidence to bring charges. Melville-Smith declined to make an official complaint, perhaps computing that the "Crown" in "Prosecution Service," was the Prince of Wales's mother. "I don't want Camilla to be prosecuted because it won't get me anywhere," she told **The Independent**, with the vaguely threatening coda:

> So long as I am not left out of pocket I am happy to let the matter rest. . . . It would be really bitchy if I did pursue it because Camilla has a hard enough time anyway and she would only get more bad press.

What if the collision had proved fatal? The effect on public sympathies would surely have ended any chance the Prince of Wales had to bring Camilla formally into his life. She needed to be assigned protection. The Prince arranged for a round-the-clock man-and-wife chauffeur team to be housed near her property.

To maintain momentum, a more overt show of the Prince's commitment was needed. Camilla's fifti-eth birthday party on July 18, 1997, was the right occasion, preceded by a flattering Channel 5 TV documentary. Defying an attempt by Robert Fellowes to seek the Queen's veto, the Prince of Wales told his closest aide and maestro of mise-en-scène, Michael Fawcett, to pull out the stops with a festive five-course banquet for Mrs. Parker Bowles at Highgrove. It would be followed in September by Camilla stepping out as a philanthropic woman of substance, chairing a fundraiser with her sister, Annabel, for the National Osteoporosis Society. Billed as an "evening of enchantment," the charity gala would show her humanity by having her speak movingly about her mother's long decline. Fifteen hundred invitations had already been sent out to VIPs and top media people with tickets priced at £100 apiece. The timing was not inauspicious for Charles himself. His ex-wife's halo was slipping. Diana was attracting all the wrong kind of press by cavorting in the south of France on Mohamed Al Fayed's boat.

Contrastingly sedate items were planted by Bolland, stating that the Prince and Camilla planned a September vacation together at Birkhall. (Cue bagpipes.) As the fiftieth birthday party approached, Robert Fellowes and his allies at the Palace were not alone in their misgivings. Major Shand, too, made it clear that he thought it was "entirely wrong," a friend of Camilla's says.

But she would not be denied her moment of triumph, one that was defiantly supported by the Prince of Wales. This birthday night there would be no sneaking into Highgrove by a side entrance.

Corralled by Bolland, the press were allowed rare access. As the woman of the hour's chauffeur-driven car swept into Highgrove's front drive, the cameras caught her smiling joyfully in the back seat, wearing an alluring dark navy silk dress and a whopping diamond-and-pearl necklace that fashion editors like to call a "statement piece." The necklace was the Prince's fiftieth birthday present. It was said to have once belonged to Alice Keppel, and it was retrieved by Charles from a private collection.

Highgrove's garden was ablaze with harpists serenading the eighty guests drinking champagne under an Arabian Nights–themed tent. A pre-Instagram-era splash of cultural appropriation was afforded by the sight of waiters wearing white dishdasha and scarlet turbans. No other royals, nor Charles's sons, attended, but all the couple's grand friends and Camilla's relatives did. The Prince and Mrs. Parker Bowles danced the night away with the relaxed intimacy of husband and wife.

Fade to black.

V

Six weeks later, the world was mad with grief.

It was Bolland who first got through to Camilla in the early hours of August 31, 1997, to tell her that Diana had died. Until that moment, she thought the Princess had been merely injured in the crash. Her first response was as a mother. "Those poor, poor boys," she replied in sorrow. Her next concern was for Charles. Would he fall apart? He must not, for the sake of the boys. She knew him well enough to understand how harshly he would blame himself for the tragedy.

There would be no possibility now of joining him at Birkhall in September. Forget about that glittering "evening of enchantment" fundraiser that was going to relaunch her as a woman of philanthropy. With Diana being canonized by the public, the Other Woman who had caused her so much pain had become radioactive. Camilla went to ground, hiding out at her house in Wiltshire. Charles's office sent two policemen to sit outside in a car in case some nutter unhinged by grief for Diana tried to get in. Even for the mistress who knew better than anyone how to play the long game, the odds had horribly lengthened.

As the world mourned Diana, Camilla had plenty of time to ponder the impact the Princess's death would have on her own future. Charles called her constantly in a state of panic and despair. As usual, his mistress was a soothing balm. He was tormented, I was told, by a toxic combination of sorrow, thwarted hope, and self-pity. Solitary grieving walks in the Balmoral heather could not assuage his sense of guilt. When there was still hope that the Paris doctors might save Diana's life, Charles agonized over the possibility that the mother of his children might be returned to London brain-damaged or paralyzed. Buried tenderness from their early days together added to his pain. She was so young when he married her! "I always thought that Diana would come back to me, needing to be cared for," he brooded in a reverie of magical thinking that erased all the years of anger and accusation.

What hope now was there for the successful completion of what Mark Bolland used to call Operation PB (or Operation Parker Bowles)? Diana was on that reckless holiday with Dodi Fayed in Paris only because she had been spurned by **him,** Charles. The public thought it would have all been different but for his obsession with his "horse-faced" mistress, Camilla. He feared they would never forgive him now. How would this affect his standing as future king? He was forty-eight years old and still toiling for public approbation in the penumbra of his sovereign mother's rectitude. Now this catastrophe. He would be cast into outer darkness. Would he wind up like the Duke of Windsor, driven into exile because of his stubborn love for a married woman who had ruined the now-sainted Diana's happiness? Monkish loneliness would be the only alternative as he tried to raise his motherless sons.

Cloistered at her Wiltshire home, Camilla watched the funeral of the Princess along with 2.5 billion other viewers on television. It was unclear how long she would need to disappear while the press bayed for someone other than itself to blame. Right now, Camilla was Public Enemy Number One, the purest anathema. That could change. If she navigated with care, the demise of Diana might turn out to be something only uttered sotto voce by the Queen Mother: "providential"—for the future of the monarchy, and for her.

Eight months later, the Camilla campaign was back on track. In 1998, Charles mandated for Mrs. Parker Bowles an annual stipend of £120,000 paid quarterly from his private funds with all perks accrued. It was agreed with his advisers that if, to satisfy her debt, the bank foreclosed on Ray Mill House, known by all to be the home of his non-negotiable partner Camilla Parker Bowles, it would cause more damning coverage for the Prince of Wales. That thought perhaps prodded him to take care of her overdraft at Coutts. Thanks to Mark Bolland's efforts, the Prince of Wales was soon recast as a sympathetic single father adored by his two sons. By the end of 1998, Charles had overtaken Tony Blair in the BBC Radio 4 poll as Man of the Year.

CHAPTER
4

MOTHER OF THE NATION

—

The Queen's Twenty-first-Century Headaches

—

THE DAWNING OF THE THIRD MILLENNIUM
was an anxious time for Queen Elizabeth II.
Normally, she would have been in Norfolk surrounded by family and friends for her annual New
Year's Eve celebration at Sandringham House.
Instead, on the night of December 31, 1999, she had
gone to bed at Windsor Castle distinctly disgruntled. She and Prince Philip had been obliged to join
Prime Minister Tony Blair and his wife, Cherie, at
the disastrous New Year's celebration for the grand
opening of the Millennium Dome. The enormous
white fiberglass structure built on forty-eight acres
of derelict land in Greenwich was conceived both to
revive an abandoned part of London and house a
Festival of Britain–type exhibit that would ignite national optimism on the eve of the twenty-first century.

Even though it had been started by Blair's Tory predecessor, John Major, the Dome, designed by the celebrated architect Sir Richard Rogers, had become a signature project of Prime Minister Blair and New Labour's Cool Britannia ethos. It was unwisely touted by Blair as "a triumph of confidence over cynicism, boldness over blandness, excellence over mediocrity" and therefore—perhaps inevitably—became a much-relished object of derision for the British press. Its beleaguered, overrun construction turned into a slug-fest of warring cultural stakeholders, overweening sponsors, and interfaith activists. For Blair haters, of whom there were now many, it was soon regarded as a metaphor not for Cool Britannia, but for New Labour's empty promises and half-baked modernity. When Robert Fellowes attended a windy meeting with civil servants, Downing Street advisers, and other establishment bigwigs about the dangers of Y2K—the fears, wildly overblown in hindsight, that the world's computers would crash as 1999 ticked over into 2000—he was asked what the Queen's plans were for New Year's Eve. "Well, I think probably she'll want to go to church," the hale Fellowes said. The whole table was reduced to silence as everyone realized that the new millennium also signified two thousand years since the incarnation of Christ.

True to form, the Dome's grand opening on New Year's Eve 1999 was one of the most monumental cock-ups in public relations history. There was a bomb scare in the southbound lane of the Blackwall

Tunnel (under the Dome), and the whole event was nearly called off. Media leaders and VIPs were supposed to be ferried to the Dome on the tube, but a bottleneck of ticketing at the Stratford station meant that the top TV and newspaper executives of England were stranded for hours in the bitterly cold weather. In his memoir, Tony Blair confesses hollering at Lord Falconer, his secretary of state for justice (dubbed "Dome Secretary" by the press when he was given oversight of the accursed project), at the Cabinet Office, "Please don't tell me it doesn't matter if they're not here for midnight, Charlie, or I will club you to death on the spot." The much-touted River of Fire stunt on the Thames was a dud, "a damp squib, barely visible," Blair's media guru Alastair Campbell recorded. Mortifyingly, London's celebration was clearly upstaged by Paris, which chose to present the simple beauty of the Eiffel Tower illuminated by twenty thousand strobe lights and a fireworks display that could have taught Blair's team a thing or two.

The Queen and Prince Philip arrived by boat at Greenwich after an already exhausting evening. They had been obliged to inspect a crisis shelter in Southwark followed by a service at Southwark Cathedral before boarding the sightseeing boat **Millennium of Peace** at Bankside Pier to take them to Greenwich. Every member of the Royal Family was deployed that evening to fan out and cover various worthy outposts of the British Isles. Prince Charles was dispatched to Scotland to visit the Royal

Infirmary of Edinburgh, a Salvation Army hostel, and a church service at St. Giles Cathedral in Edinburgh. Prince Andrew was given nautical assignments at the National Maritime Museum in Greenwich and dinner with the trustees. Princess Anne was deployed at an event for homeless people in Westminster. Prince Edward, the Earl of Wessex since his marriage to PR executive Sophie Rhys-Jones, landed the plum gig of touring the Surrey police headquarters and the Guildford Fire Station before lighting the millennium beacon on the top of Guildford Cathedral tower.

It was already past their usual bedtime when the Queen and Prince Philip, accompanied by Princess Anne and her second husband, Commodore Timothy Laurence, disembarked at the Queen Elizabeth II Pier. Inside the Dome, they were greeted with rows and rows of empty seats. Alastair Campbell noted in his diary **Power and Responsibility** that the royal party were clearly "pissed off to be there":

> TB [Blair] worked away at them . . . but Anne was like granite. Cherie [Blair's wife] even curtsied to the Queen, a bit of a first I think, but it didn't seem to do much good. . . . [They] tried to get the Royals going a bit once "Auld Lang Syne" came on, but it was pretty clear they would rather be sitting under their travelling rugs in Balmoral. The Queen did kiss Philip and took his and TB's hands [with obvious freezing reluctance, the press noted] for "Auld

Lang Syne," but they did not look comfortable with the whole thing. TB claimed Philip said to him it was "brilliant," but his body language did not radiate in that direction.

Blair himself says he was obsessed throughout by the conviction that an acrobatic show with performers flying through the air with no harnesses was going to end with one of them landing on the Queen's head.

The royal couple were not fans of Blair at the best of times (though after nine prime ministerial August weekends at Balmoral, the Queen somewhat warmed to him, his wife claims). In the period after Diana's death, when he was new to the job, the Queen found her forty-four-year-old prime minister's much-publicized efforts to mediate her response to popular feeling overly inflated. Robert Lacey reports that in 2001, the Downing Street briefing room heard how the prime minister had been talking to the Queen in audience about "the" Golden Jubilee to receive some gentle correction. "My Golden Jubilee," the Queen said.

Blair had got royal relations off to a chilly start with his government's 1997 decision not to replace the forty-three-year-old royal yacht **Britannia**, with its crew of twenty officers and 220 yachtsmen. It was a political hot potato he had inherited from John Major's government, and Blair felt he had no choice but to go through with it to appease the lefties in his own party. Philip had openly complained about the decision. In December 1997, at the ship's decommissioning ceremony, the Queen shed a rare tear. **Britannia** represented not only memories of grand and glamorous state visits but also some of her happiest times with the family. She and Philip had been closely involved in its conception from scratch—the sole home they had actually designed to suit themselves. It was the only way she could holiday privately. Every summer, the first leg of their annual journey to Balmoral began with a cruise around the coast of the western isles to Aberdeen, anchoring at Caithness to call in on the Queen Mother at the Castle of Mey for a picnic. A guest recalls seeing the draft of a ship's signal from the Queen Mother to **Britannia:** "Dearest Lilibet [the family's name for Elizabeth], Bring lemons, have run out."

Another irritation from New Labour was the termination of all but ninety-two of the hereditary peers from the House of Lords in 1999. Six hundred and fifty-eight of the aristocratic old guard were swept out, ending eight centuries of parliamentary history on the spot. Still ahead—Labour's infuriating foxhunting ban, and an impolitic call from one of Blair's favorite cabinet office ministers, Dr. Mo Mowlam, for the Royal Family to move out of Buckingham Palace into a modern building more reflective of the times. When Prince Philip was asked in the early 2000s if he was a modernizer, he replied (no less impolitic than Mowlam), "No, no, not for the sake of modernising, not for the sake of buggering about with things in some sort of Blairite way."

The Millennium Dome represented everything the Queen most disliked—hype, expense (it was financed with hundreds of millions in National Lottery money), and ersatz patriotic emotion. It increased her unease about how to strike the right tone in her impending Golden Jubilee in 2002. For the first time in her reign since her earliest days, she was feeling unsure. The aftermath of Princess Diana's death—when she had so clearly misjudged the popular mood—damaged her normally implacable confidence. She remained bruised, too, from the "annus horribilis," as she called it, of 1992, when the marriages of three of her four children collapsed, her beloved childhood home Windsor Castle went up in flames, and the British public, disaffected by so much family scandal, was noisily resentful about funding its repairs. "No institution—City, Monarchy, whatever—should expect to be free from the scrutiny of those who give it their loyalty and support," she said humbly in her speech to mark the fortieth anniversary of her accession, on November 24, 1992. Her placatory tone helped revive the nation's esteem, as did the monarchy's volunteering to start paying income tax for the first time and its funding of Windsor's repairs by opening Buckingham Palace to the public.

To compound her uncertainties, all the scandals of the 1990s gave added fuel to a republican movement in Australia, climaxing in a referendum in November 1999—chaired by lawyer and merchant banker Malcolm Turnbull—on the abolition of the monarchy Down Under. (The Queen's Australian title rolls off the tongue as Elizabeth the Second, by the Grace of God Queen of Australia and Her Other Realms and Territories, Head of the Commonwealth.) By 1999, a growing number of Australians found this whole concept a grating anachronism, particularly when they considered that any day soon they could find themselves bowing to His Majesty King Charles III (whom many Aussies regarded as an eccentric drip). All Australian polls indicated the monarchy would lose the referendum, and the Queen was preparing to be philosophical about being given the heave-ho. She actually preferred that to happen in her own reign rather than her son's. A new Australian republic could provoke a domino effect in Canada and the rest of the Commonwealth, which would be a humiliating start to Charles's reign.

To everyone's surprise, Australians voted no to a republic, 55 to 45 percent. Domestic politics had complicated the referendum's process and handed a victory to the Crown. In March 2000, the Queen visited Australia to show that there were no hard feelings. Her speech at the Sydney Opera House struck the right note of humility, a tone she was having to get good at these days. She reminded people that her formal commitment to Australia "will have spanned almost precisely half of this country's life as a federated nation," but that "the future of the monarchy in Australia is an issue for you, the Australian people, and you alone to decide by democratic and constitutional means." Fifteen years later, Turnbull, the republican leader, became prime minister. It is a tribute to the Queen's diplomatic skills that he swore off republicanism for as long as she was monarch. Disarmed by the Queen's graceful handling of the Australian referendum, Turnbull even declared himself an "Elizabethan."

A more rising concern at the Palace was the monarchy's lackluster image in its own country. The Queen feared her looming Golden Jubilee, like the Dome, would be a resounding flop. A planning committee was set up, and, in September, a smart former British Airways communications executive, Simon Walker, came in with a team to help conceive it under the direction of Robin Janvrin, who had succeeded Robert Fellowes as the Queen's private secretary. After twenty-two years of service, Fellowes had at last quit his job on the heels of a stitch-up in **The Mail on Sunday.** The paper accused him of being "one of the prime instruments in the destruction of the monarchy's public esteem," which was hardly fair. He blamed the piece on Bolland, who shared the Prince of Wales's conviction that Fellowes was the major blockade in Buckingham Palace's acceptance of Camilla. The Queen showed her gratitude to her faithful private secretary by ensuring he was given a life peerage as Baron Fellowes of Shotesham in the County of Norfolk in her Birthday Honours List of 1999.

In truth, she needed a new broom. Robin Janvrin was a far more congenial presence than his uptight predecessor, and could be trusted to improve relations with the Prince of Wales's court. The Palace has many flaws, but what it's very good at is planning. Energized by Janvrin, all the Queen's advisers embraced the idea of the jubilee having the atmosphere of a huge national party rather than a solemn celebration. As an ex-royal aide put it, "The Golden Jubilee was the culmination of several years of thinking: What would it take to close the door on the nineties?"

The month of June was chosen for the centerpiece weekend. There was an enthusiastic lobby for Her Majesty to take a ride on the new London Eye, the cantilevered observation wheel on the South Bank of the Thames that Tony Blair opened for the millennium celebrations. Her response: "I am not a tourist."

The suggestion of a major pop concert in Buckingham Palace Garden dubbed "Party at the Palace" went over somewhat better. The Queen's only concern was possible damage to the Buckingham Palace lawns. Asked, with some apprehension, if she would sign off on the inclusion of Ozzy Osbourne, the outré rocker who was formerly the lead singer of the heavy metal band Black Sabbath, she replied, "Oh, that's all right as long as he doesn't bite the head off a bat." The jubilee team were surprised at Her Majesty's familiarity with this nugget of pop culture history. (Osbourne had performed this stunt at a concert in Des Moines in 1982. When it was realized the bat thrown onto the stage by a fan wasn't made of rubber, he was rushed to the hospital for a rabies shot. In 2019, Osbourne marked the thirty-seventh anniversary of the incident with a tweet that read "Today marks the 37th Anniversary since I bit a head off a f*cking bat! Celebrate with this commemorative plush [bat] with detachable head.")

Mostly, the Queen deputed Prince Philip to meet the jubilee group about the plans. It was a well-tested way for her to off-load the things that didn't really interest her, like the minutiae of public occasions, onto her more detail-orientated husband. As usual, he barked his responses with little tolerance for sloppy thinking. Then he would say he had to consult the Queen over the weekend, and it would turn out she agreed with all his suggestions.

One decision that seems to be her own was consenting to sit for a portrait with Lucian Freud to be unveiled shortly before the jubilee. It was brokered by Robert Fellowes, who had sat for Freud himself. Although Freud's preeminence in the British art world made the choice less than daring, some considered it a risk to embrace an artist most celebrated for his fleshy, pendulous nudes. Breaking a lifelong rule of insisting his subjects come to his studio, Freud traveled to the Picture Conservation Studio at Friary Court at St. James's Palace, where from May 2000 to December 2001, the Queen sat for fifteen sessions. They reportedly had "a whale of a time" and talked about horses and racing nonstop.

The resulting portrait was as unforgiving as one might expect from Freud: grim, coarse-featured, and imposing. There's a fixed resolution to the sovereign jaw and a weighty crown plonked on her head. One critic argued that the Queen should have Freud locked up for such an ugly image. The editor of **The British Art Journal** was quoted as saying, "It makes her look like one of the royal corgis who has suffered a stroke," but unlike Winston Churchill, who descended into a thunderous mood in 1954 when he saw Graham Sutherland's unflattering eightieth-birthday portrait, the Queen displayed her usual absence of personal vanity on the unveiling of the Freud portrait. "Very interesting," she remarked gnomically. Perhaps it helped that it was small (six by nine inches). In 2017, recognizing its significance in the artist's oeuvre, she approved the hanging of the portrait in the Queen's Gallery at Buckingham Palace. (Gyles Brandreth notes that, at an art exhibit a few years after she sat for Freud, the Queen adroitly moved out of a photographer's shot that nearly caught her gazing up at the assertive scrotum of a sprawling Freud nude. Her host inquired, "Haven't you been painted by Lucian Freud, ma'am?" She smiled and said, sotto voce, "Yes, but not like that.")

As jubilee planning progressed, Her Majesty was distracted by more worrying matters. Her relationship with the heir to the throne was at a low ebb. They rarely spoke except through intermediaries. The invitation to Charles's fiftieth birthday party at Highgrove two years after Camilla's came not from him, but via his friend and neighbor the Earl of Shelburne. When the Queen learned Camilla would be present, she declined (as did his three siblings). In recent years neither she nor the Queen Mother had relented regarding ever being in the same room as Mrs. Parker Bowles. At the formal fiftieth birthday party hosted for Charles at Buckingham Palace, Camilla did not make the list. The Queen had had many discussions with Robert Fellowes on the issue and concluded that receiving her would imply she was part of the Royal Family, and the resulting media frenzy would get out of hand.

It was nonetheless clear that Mark Bolland was slowly but surely managing Camilla's reemergence: easing her into the Prince of Wales's weekend parties at Sandringham, joining Charles on a weeklong cruise in the Aegean. An "accidental meeting" between Camilla and William took place (and, to William's fury, was leaked) just before his sixteenth birthday in June 1998. Camilla was overnighting at St. James's Palace when William returned for a visit from school and, as usual, went straight to his apartment at the top of York House next door. The Prince of Wales took the plunge and escorted Camilla up for a thirty-minute meeting with his son over a drink, the first of a couple of cautious lunches and teas. The temperature of William's resistance was said to be reduced. It would take longer to break the ice with Prince Harry. A member of the household told me that when the younger boy was eventually prevailed upon to be in the presence of Mrs. Parker Bowles, he unnerved her with long silences and smoldering, resentful stares.

With the Queen still intractable on the Camilla question, Charles agreed with Bolland that his best recourse was to turn up the gas with the media. They decided to use the occasion of Camilla's sister Annabel's fiftieth birthday party at the Ritz Hotel for a defining moment in her coming-out campaign. The press would be tipped off by St. James's Palace to capture the Prince and Mrs. Parker Bowles openly leaving the event together shortly after midnight. Stepladders providing the best view started to appear outside the Ritz two days before. As the couple emerged from the party and Charles steered Camilla to the car, more than two hundred photographers blinded them with flashbulbs. "No secret about their relationship now, none possible at all," a BBC newscaster intoned. "The photograph that people have waited so long for; the picture that people have waited so long to see." There followed a rush of other "couple" sightings— theater visits, an engagement in Scotland to thank charity supporters, and a fundraising dinner where Camilla wore the potent signifier of their intimacy— a brooch with the Prince of Wales feathers.

II

The Queen knew she was being pressured and didn't like it one bit. Her problems with Charles went deeper than Camilla. The Dimbleby book that aired her son's feeling that she was an emotionally remote mother cut deep, probably because she knew there was some truth in it.

Yes, affairs of state had intervened in young motherhood when she acceded the throne in 1952 at the age of twenty-five, but often when she had the chance to be with her baby son, she had chosen not to be. In the happy months she spent as a naval wife in Malta with Prince Philip before she became Queen, she elected to take two trips of six weeks apiece—one over Christmas—leaving the twelve-month-old Charles behind to be taken care of by his nanny and the Queen Mother. At the end of the first Malta sojourn (during which Princess Anne was conceived), instead of rushing straight back to see Charles at Sandringham as one might expect, she lingered in London for a few days, catching up on admin at Clarence House and attending an engagement at Hurst Park Races, where she had a horse running. She missed his second and third Christmases and his third birthday. Charles told biographer Anthony Holden that his earliest memories of childhood were of his first pram, "lying in its vastness, overshadowed by its high sides," as good a metaphor as any for glum royal grandeur. Growing up, he often spent weeks at Holkham Hall, the family seat of the Earl of Leicester, whose daughter became Lady Anne Glenconner. He would come to stay whenever he contracted a childhood disease like chicken pox, because the Queen, having never been to school, had not been exposed to it.

For a young mother in the fifties who was also the sovereign, work-life balance was not an issue that occupied much discussion. Plus, the Queen often used affairs of state to withdraw from topics she preferred to ignore. "Ostriching" was the family's name for her routine avoidance of confrontation, usually by retreating to work through her all-consuming red boxes—the scarlet leather briefcases that convey dispatches and sensitive papers from the government to the monarch every day except Christmas Day and Easter Sunday. One of Prince Charles's former private secretaries commented to **The Telegraph**'s Graham Turner:

> If she'd spent less time reading those idiotic red boxes—to what effect, one asks?— and taken being a wife and mother more seriously, it would have been far better. Yes, she can handle prime ministers very well, but can she handle her eldest son—and which is the more important?

There's a whiff of crusty misogyny to these judgments that are unlikely to have been leveled at a man. Although Her Majesty is required to be politically neutral, the monarch retains the right to be consulted and "advise and warn" her prime ministers, an eventuality for which she likes to be rigorously prepared. Discretion forbids them from sharing it when she does. She cannot be faulted for taking her job seriously.

There is a deep poignance that any working mother can relate to in an anecdote told by Gyles Brandreth in his biography **Philip and Elizabeth:** As a small boy, Charles went to the Queen's study and asked if she would play, and she gently closed the door, saying, "If only I could."

The Queen loved her job and was good at it. She still is. Her keen mind enjoys the minutiae of government. A foreign prime minister who had an audience with the Queen in July 2017 told me that HM possesses a forensic grasp of every detail behind the Grenfell Tower tragedy that had occurred the month before. The catastrophic fire in a twenty-four-story block of North Kensington flats killed seventy-two people, setting off an impassioned national debate about the inequities of public housing. "If she had been a cabinet officer," said the visiting prime minister, "you would have considered her unusually well-briefed."

Absorbed by her duties and temperamentally undemonstrative, the Queen's low-intensity maternal engagement continued all Charles's life. In 1976, a former senior member of the royal household recalled the Prince coming through on the phone to his parents during dinner at Balmoral. Prince Philip took it, and the Queen asked what her son had to say. "He's coming out of the Navy next week," Philip replied.

"Oh," said the Queen, "I thought he wasn't coming out till next spring."

Some of this obliviousness was typical of her class, and doubtless greatest-generational. The war made for some unsentimental parenting, but it's always stunning from a modern perspective to hear how casually neglectful some aristocratic mothers of the Queen's era were raised to be. Lady Pamela Hicks, the redoubtable daughter of Lord Mountbatten and almost the same age as the Queen, recounted blithely how in July 1935, as Mussolini prepared to invade Abyssinia, it was decided that all naval families should leave the Mediterranean. After a quick kiss, her mother, Lady Edwina Mountbatten, deposited six-year-old Pamela and her eleven-year-old sister, Patricia, with the nanny and governess in a small hotel in the mountains located two hours east of Budapest and surrounded by pine forest, then drove off for a motoring holiday in her Hispano-Suiza with her lover, Lieutenant Colonel Harold "Bunny" Phillips. Unfortunately, Lady Mountbatten lost the piece of paper with the hotel's name on it and didn't return for four months. When I asked Lady Pamela how she felt about that at the time, she replied, "Well, when the weather got cold, we were a bit short of clothes as we'd run out of money. Terribly funny really."

Lady Anne Glenconner regales us with another lighthearted horror story in her 2020 memoir **Lady in Waiting.** At the outbreak of war in 1939, when she was seven years old, her mother, Lady Elizabeth Coke, went off to join her father, who was a member of the Scots Guards in Egypt. She didn't return for three years. She left Anne and her five-year-old sister, Carey, in Scotland with their Ogilvy cousins and an abusive governess, Miss Bonner, who tied Anne to the bed all night. In the end, her aunt sacked Miss

Bonner not for her cruelty, but for being a Roman Catholic and taking Anne to Mass. No wonder these ladies were tough or, at any rate, accustomed to not being asked—as Meghan Markle famously expected people to do after she married Prince Harry—if they were "okay."

In contrast, the Queen Mother was an affectionate and attentive parent to the young Elizabeth and Margaret, but an implacable enforcer of royal infallibility. Society photographer Cecil Beaton memorably called her "a marshmallow made on a welding machine."

She was unyielding in her opposition of Margaret's marriage to Group Captain Peter Townsend. On the agonizing night that Margaret repudiated the love of her life, the Queen Mother went off to an evening engagement, says Hugo Vickers, "unaware or unconcerned that her daughter would be having dinner alone on a tray." Even her special relationship with Charles and her long friendship with the Parker Bowleses as a couple did not alter her dedication to form over feeling. Once it was public that Camilla was the Prince of Wales's mistress, she refused to receive her with or without him.

Even so, Charles adored his grandmother, and the obviousness of his devotion sometimes got on the Queen's nerves. A lady-in-waiting recalled that when Charles arrived at a picnic at Balmoral, he would say to the Queen Mother:

"Oh, your Majesty, I'm graciously honoured to

see you!" and she would reply, [and one can almost hear the creamy, flirtatious tone], "Would
it please Your Royal Highness to have a drink?"
Then he would kiss her all the way up her arms!

There was rarely a day when Charles and his
grandmother were at their London residences that
the Prince did not drop in on her either in the morning or for a drink. The Queen felt that the old
mischief-maker exacerbated tensions between Philip
and Charles, and that her high-living example encouraged him in financial excesses.

Extravagance has always been a bête noire for the
Queen. She and Prince Philip themselves were
trained to be wartime thrifty. A former girlfriend of
Charles told me that when she was dating Charles in
1979 and came back to Windsor Castle for tea, the
"Queen was in a fluster because she'd been going
through the Windsor heating bills and claimed she
was being overcharged." She has been known to
walk the halls of Buckingham Palace at night turning off the lights and to request that an untouched
lemon slice be returned to the kitchen to avoid waste.
Cherie Blair noted that when she stayed at Balmoral,
the prime minister's suite was heated with an electric
heater not dissimilar to that of her working-class
grandma in Liverpool.

Prince Philip's study in his private quarters at
Wood Farm, the house on the Sandringham Estate
where he spent much of his retirement years, was as
minimal and uncluttered as the boardroom of a ship.

His was always the leanest operation of the Palace machine, deploying only two private secretaries, an equerry, and a librarian to execute several hundred royal engagements a year. Despite his peremptory manner, he was by far the most popular member of the family to work for—"very unassuming and knows that it is not always as easy to do something as it is to ask for it be done," as one household servant put it. In 2008, he gave his Savile Row tailor (John Kent of Norton & Sons) a fifty-one-year-old pair of trousers to be altered.

The Prince of Wales, unfortunately, chose to emulate his big-spending grandmother, who insisted on living in Edwardian grandeur, maintaining five fully staffed homes. Charles, senior courtiers felt, wanted to "out-granny Granny" in old world elegance. When he traveled to stay at friends' country houses, a truck arrived the day before, bringing his bed, furniture, and even pictures, which his pampering aide Michael Fawcett ensured would be hung in his allotted bedroom in place of the possessions of his host. Unlike the Queen, who always ate what she was served, the Prince stipulated his menu preferences up front, and sometimes arrived at dinner with his protection officer bearing a martini premixed and ready to be handed to the butler and served in his own glass. He employed an overall staff at St. James's Palace and at Highgrove of ninety (including ten gardeners at the country estate). "He has to have eight rooms!" the Queen reportedly exclaimed in dismay when he visited Sandringham with Diana.

Her Maj lamented, too, the way he demanded his senior staff drive three hours from London to Highgrove for meetings and were left hanging around half the day.

The sorry truth was that Charles, in his material character, just wasn't the kind of person the Queen admired. "Charles is absolutely desperate for his mother's approval and knows he'll never really get it," a Highgrove regular said. "He's the wrong sort of person for her—too needy, too vulnerable, too emotional, too complicated, too self-centered, the sort of person she can't bear. Arts, charitable causes that aren't wrapped in a rigid sense of duty—it's all anathema to her."

Her son's unrelenting obsession with Camilla was the greatest vexation of all. The Queen handled it as she handled most emotional problems: by ignoring it. Three successive private secretaries wanted her to insist before and during Charles's marriage to Diana that the Prince of Wales stop seeing Camilla. The Queen instilled enough dynastic fear in her son that, if she'd demanded it, he would have had to accede. Yet she held back, perhaps from some primordial sense that it was unwise to get between a man and his passions. Or the deeper concern that faced with a choice—like his great uncle Edward VIII—he would have chosen the woman he loved.

Philip disliked mess of any kind, and after Diana's death, he just wanted to see Charles clean it up. It was not the mistress he objected to; it was the emotional spillage. Charles's "wet" romanticism versus his own scrupulously pragmatic approach to private life was always a source of conflict, but by 2000 the Queen's new private secretary, Sir Robin Janvrin, could see expunging Camilla was never going to happen, and the Queen needed to repair her relationship with the heir to the throne. Even the Archbishop of Canterbury had lightened up on the long-running affair—an important factor for the Queen. He had met with Camilla in secret at his son's East Peckham home to avoid the press and have some obsequious getting-to-know-you sessions, much to her ungodly amusement.

Janvrin helped oil the wheels to get the Queen to attend an informal sixtieth birthday lunch at Highgrove on Saturday, June 3, 2000, that Charles was hosting for former king Constantine II of Greece. Tino, as Charles called him, an affable buffer who was driven into exile in 1967 in a coup by a vengeful military junta and finally deposed in 1973, is a cousin of Prince Philip and the godfather of Prince William. Possessing an abundance of European royal relatives, he's always been a useful networking tool within the family for the staging of rapprochements. Dashing as a young man when he won Greece's first Olympic gold medal since 1912—for sailing—he lived for the ensuing forty-six years of his exile in a stockbroker mansion in London's Hampstead Garden Suburb with his wife, Princess Anne-Marie of Denmark, until the Greek government finally let him come back as a private citizen in 2013. Princess Diana often dropped her boys off for playdates in the 1990s with their five children. Everyone in the British Royal Family loved Tino, so what better function to insert Camilla into than the occasion of his sixtieth birthday party?

It's an index of the glacial state of the relationship between Charles and his mother that he learned the news that the Queen had agreed to come to the party not from her, but from Tino. Charles was openly astonished. "Are you sure?" he said.

As a rapprochement, however, it was only a partial success. The Queen, fully aware of the semiotics of acceptance, declined to be formally introduced to Mrs. Parker Bowles—acknowledging her, but not going all the way—and let it be known they had to be seated far apart (something of a Kabuki exercise given that she'd known Camilla for decades as the wife of Andrew Parker Bowles). Bolland made hay with the supposed royal perestroika in the press, but a few weeks later, the Queen thwarted any excessive media assumptions. On June 21, 2000, she hosted what was named the "Dance of the Decades" at Windsor Castle, the biggest Royal Family celebration since the anniversary ball for her golden wedding anniversary with Prince Philip. Eight hundred guests were invited for a black-tie supper and dancing to celebrate the Queen Mother's one hundredth, Prince Andrew's fortieth, Princess Margaret's seventieth, and Princess Anne's fiftieth birthdays.

The castle was banked with a thirty-foot display of the Queen Mother's favorite flowers. The Prince of Wales arrived in his open-top Aston Martin wearing full polo kit. (Prince William, who turned eighteen that day, was toasted in absentia as he prepared for an A-level examination at Eton.) The Queen was in great dancing form. Graham Dalby, who played the party with his swing band, the Grahamophones, said:

I've never seen the Queen so animated, she had a really lovely smile on her face and she was wearing a lovely powder blue dress and she was looking absolutely stunning. She was just grabbing people and pulling them onto the dance floor. She nearly grabbed me and I thought "Ah don't grab me I can't dance" and she got the man next to me and he couldn't dance either.

Two of Prince Andrew's guests included his old friend and newspaper proprietor's daughter Ghislaine Maxwell and her plus-one, the American financier Jeffrey Epstein, two relationships that would come to haunt him.

Another unexpected guest was the disgraced Duchess of York, who had been let in from the cold after a three-year exile. Ever since tabloid photographs surfaced in 1992 showing her toes being sucked by her "financial adviser," Texas businessman John Bryan, as she sunbathed topless in the south of France, the former Sarah Ferguson had been banned from Royal Family functions at the insistence of Prince Philip. It was a major diss for Camilla to be excluded, but it seems that welcoming **two** of her sons' disfavored partners at once was a bridge too far for the Queen and, undoubtedly, for the Queen Mother.

Camilla was relegated instead to attend a B-list function with the Prince of Wales the night before: a dull dinner for the launch of the Prince's foundation in Shoreditch, where she wore a diamond serpent necklace that perhaps reflected her mood. During the Windsor Castle event itself, she had to gnash her teeth and wait for Charles in her suite at St. James's Palace as a gathering of multiple crowned heads and all her aristocratic friends feasted on a midnight champagne breakfast of eggs, sausage, bacon, black pudding, and kedgeree in the glamour of the state apartments at the castle and danced to the music of three live bands and a disco. The Queen Mother stipulated she must be seated "only with the young," which was as well since most of her own friends were dead. Ever the night owl, she lasted longer than the ailing Princess Margaret even though she had spent all day at the Ascot races, dispensing smiles under a pink upturned cartwheel hat. The band serenaded her one hundredth birthday with her favorite wartime hit, "A Nightingale Sang in Berkeley Square."

Charles stayed to toast his grandmother, but left early to return to the excluded Camilla. Afterward, he took her on a cruise off the south of France aboard an Iraqi donor's yacht that caused yet more consternation for his parents. Philip, ever the nativist royal, detested his son's unseemly financial cultivation of "foreign toadies," whether for charity or not. The Queen found it especially irritating that so much of Charles's overseas travel was to Arab countries on the hunt for new donors while he showed little interest in the countries of her beloved Commonwealth. The former New Zealand deputy prime minister Don McKinnon, who did a spell as Commonwealth secretary-general, told biographer Tom Bower he received a "ghastly British brush-off" when trying to persuade the future king to focus more of his attention on the Commonwealth. "Why does he prefer to meet dictators and not democratically elected leaders of the Commonwealth?" he complained of Charles's fascination with the royal fraternity of the Gulf.

III

As the situation with Charles slid downhill again, the Queen was hit by more repercussions of her ostriching, due this time to Prince Edward. Andrew may be the Queen's favorite child, but her last-born, Edward, occupies a soft spot in the maternal pantheon. A friend of Edward's, the suave New York–based public relations adviser Peter Brown, told me, "I once said to him when we were at home the two of us, 'Well, Edward, who's the favorite with your mother?' And there was this pause. 'Well, I am the baby,' he said." Edward was the only one of the royal siblings whose photograph was displayed in Prince Philip's office. Philip wanted Edward to inherit his title, Duke of Edinburgh, when the Queen dies, but in July 2021, Charles rather meanly let it be known that he has other plans. Edward is already in charge of the Duke of Edinburgh's Award. To mark his fifty-fifth birthday in 2019, the Queen, who often hands out unexpected gongs for relatives of whom she's feeling fond, gave Edward the additional Scottish title of Earl of Forfar.

Problems from the affable Eddie were the last things anyone expected in the Golden Jubilee year. He had caused little aggravation since 1987, when he bailed out of the Royal Marines after only four months and was brutally ridiculed in the tabloid press. (In fact, he was brave. According to his former prep school headmaster, Edward "had been bullied and teased about 'gayness' until he couldn't take it any more. Physically, he did not have a problem, as he was very tough despite his angelic looks.") The Queen was icily displeased by Edward's decision, which she saw as a dereliction of duty, but Prince Philip was unexpectedly supportive. Having served himself, he never thought Edward should have joined the Royal Marines in the first place. He wanted him to do something perhaps even worse, as far as the arts-loving Edward was concerned: become an accountant.

Edward's marriage in June 1999 to Sophie Rhys-Jones, a young woman with a modest resemblance to Princess Diana, was greeted with a certain amount of relief. "You wouldn't pick her out of a crowd," was the Queen's dry first comment on meeting Sophie, the daughter of a Kent tire salesman, but she quickly grew to like and respect her lack of pretension. All agreed that Sophie's public relations experience, personable demeanor, and strenuous desire to follow royal protocol ("She literally bobbed up and down the entire time," one Balmoral guest told me of Sophie's constant curtseying to the multiple members of the family who preceded her in rank) would be a useful asset as a Windsor spare wheel.

Unfortunately, Edward, now thirty-five, had media aspirations. His attempts to get into the television business had been a low-wattage embarrassment for some time. After a brief delusion that he could be an actor and a job as a production assistant at Andrew Lloyd Webber's Really Useful Group, he had formed Ardent Productions, a TV company funded by himself and a few royal charity donors such as the sultan of Brunei, in 1993. The company undertook documentaries like **Edward on Edward** about his great-uncle, the Duke of Windsor, in which Eddie was so reticent on camera, **The Guardian**'s Andy Beckett noted, that he couldn't bring himself to ask the only living witness to a notorious meeting between the Duke and Hitler what they had actually talked about. Ardent became an industry joke, churning out unwatchable shows on subjects such as the medieval sport of real tennis, and musty meditations on English warships, royal residences, and the Windsor Castle fire. Beckett summed up the experience of viewing a few dozen hours of Ardent's output as entering "a strange kingdom where every man in

Britain still wears a tie, where pieces to camera are done in cricket jumpers, where people clasp their hands behind their backs like guardsmen. . . . Women are called 'girls.' Voiceovers are reverential and royal, or in accents from the old Commonwealth. . . . Commercial breaks are filled with army recruiting advertisements."

In September 2001, Ardent's camera crews showed up at the University of St. Andrews in Scotland, where the nineteen-year-old Prince William had just arrived as a freshman student. Knowing that there was a press ban brokered by Lord Black and the Press Complaints Commission on photographing or filming him at college without permission, William contacted his father to complain. Father and son were both astonished to learn the crew belonged to none other than the misbegotten TV company run by Uncle Eddie.

Mark Bolland let the press know Prince Charles was "incandescent" at this fraternal betrayal and took full advantage of showcasing him as a protective father. It was leaked that Charles had called his brother a "fucking idiot." Edward had already faced accusations of using official royal visits abroad to secure business for Ardent. His productions—like the cheesy E! Entertainment Television deal to produce a show titled **The A to Z of Royalty,** for which he was filming at St. Andrews—were clearly inappropriately milking the royal brand. It all highlighted the Prince of Wales's conviction that working members of the Royal Family should not pursue their own careers, a lofty stance that irritated his brothers who did not have his cushy Duchy of Cornwall income.

Compounding Edward's affront to decorum was an even worse blunder a few months before, by the hitherto inoffensive Sophie. The new Countess of Wessex had been allowed to maintain her career as the director of her public relations firm, RJH. Amazingly, she now fell afoul of a crass sting perpetrated by an infamous trickster known as the Fake Sheikh, aka Mazher Mahmood, an investigative reporter for Rupert Murdoch's **News of the World.** Posing as the emissary of a lucrative new client who owned a Dubai leisure complex, the bearded dishdasha-wearing phony and his similarly attired photographer taped her at the Dorchester Hotel in a series of mortifying indiscretions. She said of Tony Blair, "We call him President Blair over here anyway because he thinks he is"; babbled on about Charles and Camilla being "number one on the unpopular people list"; and dismissed Chancellor of the Exchequer Gordon Brown's latest budget as "a load of pap."

Even worse, her business partner in a separate meeting chatted to the "sheikh" about setting up his boss with "nice" boys for entertainment and answered a question about whether Prince Edward was gay with "I'm a great believer that there's no smoke without fire." It was clear from both conversations that to secure a £500,000 public relations contract, Sophie's company was selling her royal connections with abandon. When she learned she had been duped, she panicked and made it worse. A deal was negotiated to trade the Fake Sheikh transcript with a "candid" Sophie Wessex interview in the **News of the World.** It ran appropriately enough on April Fools' Day with the headline "SOPHIE: My Edward Is NOT Gay," and revived rumors that provided a double gossip whammy. After a week of sensational leaks from the tapes in the **Daily Mail,** the **News of the World** reneged on its agreement and published the full mother lode of the Fake Sheikh transcripts.

For the Queen, this hurricane of scandal was all too reminiscent of the dreaded annus horribilis she thought was behind her. Would it ever be possible to "close the door on the nineties," as the Palace was working so hard to do? In that turbulent decade, it wasn't only Princess Diana who was hounded by the media. Nearly every member of the Royal Family—and anyone who associated with them— was bloodied and gored. The invasiveness and mockery were cruel and unrelenting.

A real-time picture of that epoch's press barbarism-in-action can be found in the diaries of editorial swashbuckler Piers Morgan, more lately the 800-pound gorilla of British morning TV and scourge of Meghan Markle. Piers got the job as editor at the **News of the World** in January 1994 at the startling age of twenty-eight, but quickly moved on to the **Daily Mirror,** where he cranked out reckless scoops on the biggest royal stories of the Diana decade. He was fired in 2004 for showing zero contrition for publishing faked pictures of torture in Iraq.

Morgan was the era's young Lord of Misrule. He reveled in transgression. He sometimes bought scoops from a source called "Benji the Binman," who scoured the trash of celebrities looking for sellable scoops. When **The Sunday Times**—a sister paper in the Murdoch stable—acquired an excerpt of Jonathan Dimbleby's biography of Prince Charles, Morgan dispatched a reporter, Rebekah Wade, in a cleaner's uniform to steal a copy from **The Sunday Times**'s press room as the first edition printed. Morgan then gleefully pirated the best headlines for the **News of the World**'s second edition. Rupert Murdoch just laughed when he learned of the copyright theft.

Reading Morgan's diaries today, it is stunning how intimately the royals and their press secretaries were involved with trying to manage or outwit Morgan, and the rest of the yellow press, on a daily basis. They had such intimacy with their tabloid torturers. The year after Diana's death, Morgan describes how her mother, Frances Shand Kydd, called him in tears, "gutted," when he published a sensationalist piece by Mohamed Al Fayed accusing the royals of murdering her daughter. "Who cares about the boys in all this, Piers?" she sobbed. "**Who?** . . . I spoke to you the day before you did this and you didn't tell me what else you were doing!"

During the so-called War of the Waleses, Charles's camp did as much leaking and briefing as Diana's via the very tabloids they both professed to detest. Charles spun furiously; he was just less good at it. And other self-inflicted royal scandals dropped into the media's lap. The marital woes and commercial missteps of Fergie and Prince Andrew in the nineties were on such indiscreet display that they provided a never-ending lurid subplot in the royal **opera buffa.**

Whatever the high-minded stance toward the vulgarity of publicity, all the households competed furiously—and still do—for positive coverage or, in the case of the minor royals, to get coverage at all. There is an unwritten rule that they will not step on one another's media moment in deference to the royal hierarchy within the family, though in Prince Charles's case, news bombs from outlier family dramas have the habit of exploding whenever he is about to step up to a podium. The humbling truth is that without the popular press—though markedly less so since the launch of social media—the monarchy is not visible except by public appearances, which, in turn, without coverage, are a tree that falls in the forest. As the Queen once commented when advisers tried to pare down her engagements, "I have to be seen to be believed."

The Queen's successive press secretaries in the nineties were amazed by her sangfroid in the face of relentless media carnage. One former press secretary told me:

People have said [to me], "That must be the most ghastly job," and I said, "Well, it has its difficult times, but actually I work for someone who is totally unflappable." It doesn't matter whether things are going badly wrong or wrong.

She will get up in the morning, she will look at her brief, take a call or have a meeting on something really rather gruesome. And then 10 minutes later, go out into a walkabout . . . talking to people in the streets as if she didn't have any other concerns.

Unflappable the Queen may be, but the nineties' scars could not be reopened. The Wessex imbroglio with the Fake Sheikh required fast action. As usual, Her Majesty turned to Philip to help solve an issue that would continue to haunt the Windsors for the next two decades: How are the spare royal children supposed to combine privilege with a profession and not compromise the integrity (and dignity) of the Crown? In a conference with Edward and Sophie at Windsor, Philip was clear. It is **not** possible. You are in or you are out. There is no such thing as a part-time royal.

When decisions are finally made, the ostrich Queen's management style turns lethal, even when she used Philip to drop the boom. We saw the same tough-minded resolve in Princess Margaret's crisis over Group Captain Peter Townsend and in the question of Charles and Diana's divorce. The force of the Queen's fury with the press came through clearly in the statement sent out by Buckingham Palace just days after the Fake Sheikh scandal broke. It was one of the strongest salvos ever fired from the ramparts of that cautious institution. The Queen was said to "deplore the entrapment, subterfuge, innuendo and untruths" to which the Earl and Countess of Wessex had been subjected in recent days. Deploying an artful double play, Her Majesty voiced her strong support for Edward and Sophie pursuing their independent careers—"It is not an easy option and they are breaking new ground, but it is right in this day and age that they should be allowed to do so"—only to have, in the same statement, the couple declare they were doing the reverse.

Sophie apologized profusely for any embarrassment she'd caused the Queen by succumbing to the sheikh's subterfuge. She added that while she was grateful for Her Majesty's support and for being able to continue working, after she "discussed the situation with the Queen," she had decided to "step aside" as chairman of her PR company to "reassess [her] own role." The statement added that both the Earl and the Countess "vigorously deny" exploiting their royal status in pursuit of their business interests. No one was in any doubt that it was curtains for the Wessexes' career plans. Just as notably, it put any ambitions held by other minor royals, present or future, on alert. In July 2001, the Palace unveiled new guidelines designed to prevent conflicts of interest between family members' business activities and their royal duties.

Ardent, a longtime money pit, was wound up. A chastened Prince Edward explained, "It is quite obvious that in this year, the Golden Jubilee, we are required more than ever to support the Queen and to help my family shoulder some of the increasing responsibilities and workload in the future." To compensate for the loss of income, the Queen increased her financial support of the Wessexes to around £250,000 a year.

She now hoped that this tiresome issue for the Palace had been put firmly to bed. And it might have been, in a different era. But modern expectations of freedom make indefinite dependence on your monarch mother, without any recourse to outside income, both infantilizing and dangerously unrealistic. It was an issue that would explode and rock the monarchy again and again.

CHAPTER
5

A QUESTION OF
INDEPENDENCE

———

How Elizabeth and Philip Made It Work

———

THE COMBINATION OF MARRIAGE AND DUTY
was a subject that the Queen absorbed over many
decades of her own complicated marital minuet. It
began in 1953, in the rustling, ermined silence of
her coronation as Queen Elizabeth II at Westminster
Abbey. The thirty-one-year-old Philip Mountbatten,
Duke of Edinburgh, removed his own coronet, knelt
at the feet of the young woman he'd wed six years
before, and swore an oath of allegiance: "I, Philip,
Duke of Edinburgh, do become your liege man of
life and limb and of earthly worship . . . so help
me God."

That Philip kept that oath for the next sixty-eight
years—and the Queen found a way to make him
want to—is a miracle not only of the modern monarchy but also of modern matrimony.

It wasn't easy, God knows, for Philip to assume a

role in which he would always walk two paces behind his wife. The Duke was the unsettling definition
of a full-on alpha male: devastatingly handsome,
vigorously self-assured, impatient with fools—and
not just fools. When he leaned from his considerable
height and bore down on a recalcitrant fact or factotum, it could be a shriveling experience for whoever
had got it wrong.

His biographer Gyles Brandreth told me there was
a fierce exchange over a passage in his manuscript
about Philip's wartime service aboard the HMS
Ramillies (Philip had given the author editorial independence over everything except error):

> PHILIP, IRATE: What do you mean I served
> on HMS **Ramillies**?
> BRANDRETH: You did, sir. I know you
> served. I gave you the logbooks to see.
> PHILIP: I did not.
> BRANDRETH: You did, sir. You served on
> HMS **Ramillies**.
> PHILIP: I did not serve on HMS **Ramillies**.
> You don't live on your house, man, do
> you? I served **In HMS Ramillies! In HMS
> Ramillies!** Just stick to the facts!

"The Queen must have understood from the beginning that this was a very, very strong character
with a ramrod straight backbone, and he wasn't
going to be buggered about," Sir Nicholas Soames, a
friend of Prince Charles, said to me in 2021.

Elizabeth and Philip's was no contrived union like the disastrous marriage of Charles and Diana. It was a love match from the start. The Queen had been crazy about him since 1939, when she was thirteen and Prince Philip of Greece and Denmark, an eighteen-year-old navy officer cadet, squired her around the Royal Naval College at Dartmouth.

In time, he fell in love with her, he told her in a 1946 letter quoted in Philip Eade's biography, "completely and unreservedly." When he proposed to the twenty-year-old Elizabeth at Balmoral, neither her father, the King, nor her mother thought he was a safe bet. Philip may have been related to half the crowned heads of Europe, but his family had been booted into exile, and he was the penniless prince of nowhere.

The shy, observant Princess Elizabeth was undaunted. She saw in Philip the unflinching character who would be what she would call on their fiftieth anniversary "my strength and stay all these years." The two were bonded by a sense of duty and a desire to serve that was framed by World War II. Philip was mentioned in dispatches for exceptional service aboard the British battleship HMS **Valiant,** and had been awarded the Greek Maritime War Cross.

Smothered by deference, Elizabeth trusted Philip's subversive impatience. Surrounded by excruciating formality, she could always depend on him to make her laugh. "The Queen was always passionately in love with him," a member of the royal circle said. "Part of that love was that she knew she would always get an honest answer from him." His gift to her was the shared secret that the formalities were both utterly absurd and absolutely necessary. In return, she provided Philip with an emotional safe place his childhood had lacked.

The marriage succeeded on strategy as much as love. The Queen's challenge was how to harness her husband's prodigious energies in the service of the Crown without making him feel unmanned.

No battle was either more painful—or more public—for Philip than the question of his children's surname. It was of preeminent importance to him that Charles, Anne, and later Andrew and Edward should be christened as Mountbattens, rather than with the created dynastic name of Windsor. The Queen Mother and the Queen's advisers, notably including Winston Churchill, were adamantly against it. They insisted she must stay with the popularized Windsor name. King George V had chosen it—in perpetuity—over the Saxe-Coburg-Gotha surname, which became a liability during the anti-German sentiment of the First World War. To Philip's bitterness, his wife capitulated—though not immediately—to her advisers. "I am the only man in the country not allowed to give his name to his children," he famously exploded. "I'm nothing but a bloody amoeba." There were few models then for how to build a marriage in which the balance of power was so entirely weighted toward a wife, unless you count Queen Victoria and Prince Albert.

Marital conflict over the matter continued, bringing

the Queen "close to tears," said the Conservative politician R. A. "Rab" Butler, who was privy to it. After an audience with Her Majesty, who was then pregnant with Prince Andrew, Prime Minister Harold Macmillan recorded in his diary that the "Queen only wishes (properly enough) to do something to please her husband—with whom she is desperately in love. What upsets me . . . is the prince's almost brutal attitude to the Queen over all this." A compromise was ultimately reached in which any descendants not entitled to the designation of "royal highness" would be called Mountbatten-Windsor.

With her customary quiet savvy, the Queen found sly ways to manage her husband while she got on with weighty matters of state. She put Philip in total charge of all the royal estates and houses, which he oversaw—as the Queen Mother put it sourly—like a "German junker." Within weeks of moving into Buckingham Palace with the Queen in 1953, he (and his private secretary Mike Parker) had inspected every one of its more than six hundred rooms and ordered an immediate upgrade of the internal communications system and a commission of the refurbishment of the private apartments.

Accepting that he was shut out of her red box life, Philip threw himself into a blizzard of charity chairmanships. One of his most serious successes as a patron was his vigorous presidency of the World Wildlife Fund. He was strikingly ahead of the curve in raising money for projects like the preservation of tiger habitats in India, seen today as the cool, no-brainer causes of William and Harry. He created the Duke of Edinburgh's Award scheme, which recognized adolescents and young adults for achievements in volunteering, physical activity, or planning an adventurous expedition—now adopted by more than 140 countries.

Despite the imbalance of power in their private life, they adhered to traditional gender roles. As one of her friends summarized it to me, her "template for womanliness was her mother, and her template for being sovereign was her father: He ran the shooting. She brought the lunch." At formal dinners the Queen would always wait to see whether Philip chose to talk first to the woman on his left or on his right, then turn in the same direction for conversation herself.

She left him to take the lead on most major decisions about the children. The Queen Mother argued strongly, and with prescience, that the thirteen-year-old Prince Charles should be sent to Eton, where he would know many of the boys and could cultivate his interest in the arts and culture. But Philip wanted his son to go to his austere alma mater, Gordonstoun, in Scotland. "He might as well be at school abroad. He would be terribly cut off and lonely up in the far north," the Queen Mother protested. But the Queen deferred to Philip, and Charles was shipped off to Gordonstoun for five years of miserably inventive bullying.

Philip had the habit of treating the heir to the

throne as a project that had to be whacked into shape. In the 2021 posthumous BBC documentary **Prince Philip: The Royal Family Remembers**, it's poignant to see that the Prince of Wales's recollections of his father are so often about disappointing him:

> I used to enjoy playing polo with him. I used to get endless shouting. "Get up! Stop mucking about!" And I remember playing in a football match, he used to give me instructions. . . . "Get up! DO SOMETHING." . . . He tried to teach me to drive a carriage, but that didn't last very long. [inaudible] With him getting more and more annoyed that I wasn't concentrating properly. You certainly wanted to please my father when given instructions.

The Queen wanted to please Philip, too. She encouraged any activity that made her husband feel truly autonomous. He got his private pilot's license in 1959. Like William, who chose to become a search-and-rescue pilot, Philip found it liberating to fly the lonely skies. No bloody reporter or disapproving courtier would pursue him in the clouds.

Those same bloody reporters labeled him as a gaffe machine, but most of his impolitic comments reflected what he actually thought, ranging from the blunt—"Your country is one of the most notorious centers of trading in endangered species in the world," he told his affronted hosts when accepting a conservation award in Thailand in 1999—to the downright offensive—"How do you keep the natives off the booze long enough to pass the test?" he inquired of a Scottish driving instructor in 1995. The Queen's poker face in public was no guide to how she might have chided him in private.

Other more private rebellions of behavior were also untamed.

Philip's rumored (but vigorously denied) infidelities with a string of society beauties and actresses may well have been the only way such a hard-charging red-blooded husband could assert his masculine autonomy amidst the frustrations of fealty. He was lucky to have been born into an age more protective of the monarchy's penumbral spaces. Such is the unilateral respect for the Queen that the press—even in these less reverential times—settled for suggestion over investigation. When my late husband, Sir Harold Evans, became editor of **The Sunday Times** in 1967, the chief executive of Times Newspapers, Sir Denis Hamilton, a man well wired in the British establishment, warned him to be careful of how the paper reported on Prince Philip because his private life was of interest to MI6.

A seductive blond socialite who was a regular in Mustique told me how in 1977, when the Queen and Prince Philip visited Princess Margaret on the island for the first time toward the end of the Silver Jubilee tour of the West Indies, she was on the beach as the cutter from **Britannia** brought the royal party ashore. She was taking photos of the Queen's lily-white skin being devoured by mosquitoes—"I told you I didn't want to come to this bloody island," the socialite heard her say—when Philip, looking especially handsome in a pale blue shirt with buttons down the back, saw her and winked. Later at Lord Glenconner's reception at the Cotton House hotel, Philip's equerry came over and gave her a card with a private number on it. "The Duke says to keep in touch," he said. "I nearly fainted," the socialite remembered, "but, unfortunately, I lost the bloody card. He was so gorgeous I will always be pissed that I didn't take him up on it."

In 1971, when he felt too old for polo, Philip became enthused by competitive carriage driving. Perched on the box seat of an antique "Balmoral dog-cart" retrofitted by the Sandringham mechanics, he whipped on a team of four galloping Cleveland bays. He became such an enthusiast that he was influential in establishing carriage driving as a sport, and competed on the British team at world and European championships. (The last time he was sighted careening through the Sandringham Estate on a coach and with two female aides was at the age of ninety-eight.)

More often than not, his sporting companion for the last twenty-five years of his life was Lady Penelope Romsey, a tall, slender blonde thirty-one years his junior, who once dated the Prince of Wales. Charles was best man when Penelope Eastwood, as she then was, went on to marry one of his closest friends, Norton Romsey, the grandson of Lord Mountbatten. (Lady Romsey was one of the few friends to tell Charles she thought Diana was much too jejune for him as a future wife.) Penny became the Countess Mountbatten in 2017 when her husband inherited the title. As a longtime family friend, Philip is said to have made the suggestion she learn to carriage drive when she was thirty-five, as a distraction from grief after the death of her five-year-old daughter in 1991.

Whatever the evolution of their friendship, Romsey possessed the beauty, poise, and sense of humor to hold Philip's attention for longer than anyone else except his wife. In photographs, it is obvious that he's always laughing when they're together. "Flirtatiousness at his age is quite good for him," said one of the Queen's oldest friends (in 2015), carefully. "It keeps him chirpy." On summer weekends in the last two decades, the two of them could be seen at carriage-driving house parties all over England.

Once in a while there was a gossip flare-up about Romsey. The Queen's response was to invite her to travel in the car with her to church on Sunday, and they were photographed chatting amicably. Her Majesty apparently approved of the Countess's strength of character, especially the way she had handled the crisis in her marriage in 2010 when Norton Romsey took off after thirty years with an attractive fashion designer in the Bahamas. Without breaking stride, Penny assumed the running of the six-thousand-acre Broadlands estate, and her husband's ceremonial duties as High Steward of Romsey until he returned to the marital mansion with his tail tucked between his legs. She banished him to a converted stable block, inviting him back into the house only after he developed health problems.

The Queen seems to have decided that Romsey was necessary for her husband's good humor. A figure in the royal circle said in 2015, "She shrugs her shoulders and says, 'Philip likes to have her around.'" She gamely absorbed her into her personal circle, and Romsey was frequently on the guest list at Windsor Castle and sometimes part of the royal lineup on the balcony of Buckingham Palace for Trooping the Colour. "[The Queen] accepted that he took a lot of amusing," a close figure told Richard Kay in 2015. "I've always felt his need for amusement outside his marriage had something to do with him being such an active and demanding consort, while having to take a back seat to his wife. But his loyalty to her is unquestioning."

Perhaps, as the Duchess of Devonshire said of her sixty-three-year marriage to the serially unfaithful Duke, the Queen simply had reached "the wonderful moment when you realize you are anaesthetized." She comes from a class and generation of women raised to believe you should outlast your husband's distractions or, failing that, accept them. Anything else would be tiresome and hysterical. She knew that if his eye roved, his devotion to her could not be questioned. Philip himself responded with a long, silent stare when a reporter from **The Independent** once dared to raise the issue of extramarital affairs. He finally erupted, "Good God woman. I don't know what sort of company you keep."

A former member of the Queen's staff told me that, in his nineties, Philip asked, "Do you want some marriage advice? Spend enough time apart, and make sure you don't have all the same interests."

II

The Queen shared the greatest passion of her life with someone else. Despite Philip's love of equestrian sports, he didn't share his wife's obsession with the horses themselves. Bloodstock is the subject that brings the Queen most alive, and that was the unchallenged realm of her closest male friend, Henry George Reginald Molyneux Herbert, seventh Earl of Carnarvon.

Porchey, as he was known from an earlier title of Lord Porchester, was the Queen's racing manager from 1969 to the end of his life. No one other than family enjoyed the same kind of intimacy with the Queen. He was one of the few people who had Her Majesty's mobile phone number, and called her almost every day with the hot horse news, often holding up the phone at bloodstock sales where he was bidding on her behalf so she could hear the action. He was her companion at nearly every race, her consigliere on private visits to stud farms in Kentucky, her partner in her obsession with breeding, fettle, and form. Their bond was much deeper than racing manager and monarch. They were partners in the pursuit that gave the dutiful Queen untrammeled pleasure.

Porchey's friendship with the Queen spanned six decades. George VI had asked the teenaged boy to squire his young daughter to race meetings, where they quickly bonded over their love of horses. He joined the young princesses' madrigal singing group at Buckingham Palace after the war.

The Queen Mother might have been content to consider Porchey a second-line suitor for Elizabeth's hand after the ducal eligibles on her list. His family seat was Highclere Castle in Hampshire, the setting for Julian Fellowes's TV hit **Downton Abbey**. He was one of those low-key aristocrats much richer than you would expect. His grandfather, the fifth Earl of Carnarvon, sponsored the archeologist Howard Carter in the search for King Tutankhamun's tomb in Egypt, and died of blood poisoning after a mosquito bite in 1923, just four months after finding the tomb's entrance.

Not long after he assumed the earldom in 1987, Porchey learned from a family butler that a hoard of some three hundred antiquities from his grandfather's tours in Egypt had lain undisturbed in cupboards and unused rooms at Highclere for more than seventy years. It was a good excuse to make the castle pay its way, and the doors to Highclere were opened to the public in 1988. (Its Italianate spires more than pay their way today with **Downton**'s filming and merchandise.)

A glimpse of the Queen and Porchey's unique trust can be seen in an entry in the diary of one of his closest friends, Labour peer Lord Bernard

Donoughue. In an entry dated Tuesday, April 7, 1998, Donoughue records that Carnarvon told him "two touching stories about the Queen":

> First was when she went racing in Normandy on an official visit to France to celebrate the 1944 Normandy landings. Henry took her to a French restaurant in Honfleur. She did not know how to order her meal. Told him she had never ordered a meal from a menu before. Second was when she recently went to a pub for the first time in her life. She liked it but again she didn't know you had to order a drink from the bar. So she stood there and waited, expecting a drink to arrive on a tray. Said she would have loved a gin martini, but had nothing. Her aides should have told her to go to the bar and order—not her fault.

The last sentence speaks volumes. Carnarvon telling the story with obvious affection, but swift to point out that the Queen's behavior was not because she was spoiled or foolish, but because courtiers who should have known better let her down. "Her Majesty is my lifelong best friend," he once said to Donoughue.

The Queen's affinity with Porchey was so deep there were rumors it could have been something more. Once upon a time, London gossips loved to talk about a strong resemblance between Prince Andrew's coarsely handsome mug and Carnarvon's, but I see neither likeness nor likelihood there.

Porchey more resembled a refined Alfred Molina in a fedora, and was authentically furious when romantic rumors first began to fly. He was the Queen's devoted **cavaliere servente,** ready to defend her to the last and, no doubt, a source of strength when Philip's restless frustrations left her feeling exposed.

III

The Queen's happy place has always been Balmoral. On the eve of Philip's funeral, she chose to release a shot of them relaxing together on the hills of the Coyles of Muick taken by Sophie Wessex in 2003. Philip sprawls on the picnic blanket rug with his hat placed jauntily on his right knee, and the smiling Queen is her version of informal in a tartan skirt, blouse and cardigan, and a string of pearls. The air of unassailed contentment says it all.

Balmoral is so sequestered from the world that in pre-COVID times the family could withdraw into its fifties time warp. As the Queen played patience with herself and a guest pored over the enormous jigsaw puzzle permanently laid out on a table, it was easy to imagine you had just stumbled into that 1969 period piece, the BBC documentary **Royal Family.** There's a reason the sovereign could feel so profoundly detached from the mood of the British people during the crowd hysteria over Diana's death. The Highland estate, with its wild encircling hills, is literally its own world. Purchased by Prince Albert

for Queen Victoria in 1848, the castle, with its tur-
rets and spires, is like a little piece of Bavaria dropped
into a Scottish forest. The Queen has sometimes
been sighted wielding a butterfly net trying to catch
the bats that lurk in the upper reaches of the castle.
At night she indulges a love of stargazing. From her
bedroom window, she can make out every curve
and paw belonging to the great Ursa Major. She
once urged her dresser, Angela Kelly, to go stand in
front of the castle shortly before midnight to get the
best view.

The Queen has spent three months at Balmoral
every year since the first summer of her life in 1926.
When Her Majesty's dark green Range Rover sweeps
into the drive, the entire staff of the estate—including
seventeen gardeners, five cooks, and four scullery
maids—forms a chorus line to greet her at the entrance. It's the moment the monarch can exhale and
know she is at last free of irksome royal engagements
to be her true self.

The Queen is a country woman to her well-trod
Wellies. Until the age of eighty-five, she was known
to be an accomplished "picker-up," following the
guns on shooting parties to wring the necks of
wounded birds or knocking them on the head with
a "priest," a sort of miniature police baton with a
weight at the end. Sometimes she dispatched her
gun dogs with a repertoire of whistles to retrieve the
damaged prey. She told Lucian Freud that she was
once knocked down by a wounded cock pheasant
that flew out of a hedge as she was "picking up" at a

friend's estate. Her would-be protection officer saw the blood, thought she had been shot, and threw himself on her to administer mouth-to-mouth resuscitation. "I consider we got to know each other rather well," she told Freud.

Her cousin and lifelong friend, the late Honourable Margaret Rhodes, said how much the young Elizabeth always relished crawling on her stomach through the undergrowth—"with her nose up to the soles of the stalker's boots"—until she was close enough to take aim. The beast would then be disemboweled, strapped on the back of a horse, taken down to the castle larder for skinning, and served the following week for dinner once the meat had been hung long enough to grow tender. (Her Majesty killed her last stag in 1983.)

One of the Queen's top courtiers was very amused by a pivotal scene in Stephen Frears's 2006 Oscar-nominated movie **The Queen,** when the sovereign, played by Helen Mirren, is shown close to tears as she walks alone in the Balmoral heather in the terrible days after Diana's death. Suddenly, a noble stag appears on a hill before her and her expression turns to joy, wonder, an epiphany that appears to give her strength. The courtier laughed. "The Queen would have shot it," he told me.

Dogs are one of her few areas of visible sentiment. On the death of one of Her Majesty's favorite corgis, Lady Pamela Hicks sent her a sympathy note and received a six-page letter back from the Queen. It was especially notable given that when Pamela's father, Earl Mountbatten, was murdered by the IRA, neither she nor her sister, Patricia, received a personal letter of condolence from the Queen. "A dog isn't important, so she can express the really deep feelings she can't get out otherwise," Lady Pamela suggested, but it's more likely the opposite is true. Dogs and horses are her true emotional peers. They have no interest in her rank, love her for herself, and never bore her by asking what Winston Churchill was really like.

IV

The Queen rarely watches television in the afternoon, unless it's a horse race. But on September 11, 2001, she was in her Balmoral sitting room mesmerized by the calamitous images pouring out of New York City. The last time she had beheld anything close to the World Trade Center destruction was during the Blitz and in the photographs that followed the Japanese attack on Pearl Harbor in 1941, an event that at last brought President Roosevelt to Winston Churchill's aid in the war. Would the obliteration of nearly 3,000 lives—67 of them British—draw the UK into a foreign war, as well?

The nightmarish scenes of the terrorist attacks coincided with a phone call bringing the Queen devastating personal news. The seventy-seven-year-old Earl of Carnarvon, Porchey, had suffered a fatal heart attack at Highclere Castle. His wife, the Wyoming heiress Jeannie Wallop, said that Carnarvon, too, had been watching the coverage of the attacks. He became agitated and collapsed, dying in the ambulance.

Once again, as with the death of Diana, the magical remoteness of Balmoral was pierced by inescapable human pain. There would be no more exuberant calls from Porchey on her mobile to brighten dutiful afternoons. Multiples of human loss on the other side of the Atlantic collided with the Queen's own intimate bereavement at home, but her public duty as sovereign allowed her little time for personal mourning.

The terrorist attacks in the United States were a chance to show a more caring and responsive monarchy to Britain's allies. Lessons had been learned from the death of Diana. There could be no hiding from history at Balmoral. Sir Malcolm Ross, comptroller of the Lord Chamberlain's Office, was already on the phone with an inspired suggestion. Educated at Eton and Sandhurst and later retiring with the rank of lieutenant colonel, Ross was behind most of the memorable details of Diana's funeral procession. He might have had the air of an establishment codger, but his organizational flair, sense of pageantry, and meticulousness were nothing short of genius.

The Queen immediately blessed his idea for a new twist on the Changing of the Guard at Buckingham Palace. On September 12, the Coldstream Guards marched down the Mall to selections by American military composer John Philip Sousa. The tribute to the dead in the Palace courtyard opened with "The Star-Spangled Banner," played to thousands of mourning American expatriates who had assembled in front of the Palace. They closed with "God Save the Queen," which shares a melody with America's "My Country, 'Tis of Thee," offering a particularly powerful resonance. The Queen then flew down from Balmoral to offer condolences to the American ambassador William Farish and attend the Service of Remembrance at St. Paul's Cathedral, where Prince Philip read stirringly from St. Paul's Letter to the Romans: **"If God is for us, who can be against us?"** The formal acknowledgment of America's tragedy was both emotionally and diplomatically perfect.

Six days later, I attended a September 11 memorial service myself at St. Thomas Church, a soaring Gothic edifice on Fifth Avenue in New York City. It was raining hard, and I huddled under a very British umbrella with historian Simon Schama as we hurried across Fifth Avenue. The Episcopal church was packed with seven hundred exiled Brits, many of whom had lost loved ones in the attacks. Their pain was palpable. The Queen was not there, but Prime Minister Tony Blair, looking suddenly very young and burdened by office, read a moving passage about the survival of love from Thornton Wilder's **The Bridge of San Luis Rey.** Among the weeping congregation, Bill Clinton, Mayor Rudy Giuliani, and Secretary-General of the United Nations Kofi Annan were visibly moved. Schama commented to me on the ironic comfort of hearing, back to back, "The Star-Spangled Banner" and "God Save the Queen." The American anthem, after all, was written to celebrate a proud separation, but the distance that day between Britain and America felt as narrow as that between Brooklyn and Manhattan.

Usually the eloquence of Blair wins the hour, but, unusually, it was the Queen who expressed the most memorable thought in the closing line of the message she sent from England, "so wise and so true that it somehow made people feel better," Bill Clinton later said. It was read from the pulpit by the somber Ambassador Christopher Meyer:

> These are dark and harrowing times for families and friends of those who are missing or who suffered in the attack—many of you here today. My thoughts and my prayers are with you all now and in the difficult days ahead. But nothing that can be said can begin to take away the anguish and the pain of these moments. Grief is the price we pay for love.

The Queen was providing solace to the relatives of the victims of terror when she offered those uncommonly expressive words, but I tend to think that the final sentence was prompted by a private as well as a public loss, that of Porchey, her comrade and comforter of sixty years.

Grief is the price we pay for love.

CHAPTER
6

SWAN SONGS

———

Margaret and the Queen Mother
Leave the Party

———

W HEN EDWARD VIII'S ABDICATION IN 1936 meant their shy, stammering father was unexpectedly going to become the king, Margaret, then six years old, asked her ten-year-old sister if this foretold she would be queen one day. Lilibet replied, "Yes, someday."

"Poor you," said Margaret.

Whether there was sympathy or suppressed envy in Margaret's response, the dividing paths of the sisters' future lives were early drawn. The dynamics of the relationship between them never really changed. It was **Sense and Sensibility** made regal—the glamorous, mercurial Margaret Rose and the graver, more conventional Elizabeth protecting and reproving her wayward sibling. A Guards officer friend of Margaret observed:

The Queen was always able to handle her sister, and with much greater skill than she handled her children. If Margaret didn't want to do something the Queen would smilingly say: "Oh, all right," as if saying, "You won't be missed." That usually brought her to heel.

Former equerry Major Colin Burgess recalls a Christmas incident at Sandringham when a rogue candle on the table set Margaret's hair ablaze. Elizabeth watched in amazement and commented dryly, "Oh look. Margo's on fire!"

Even after the Queen was increasingly—and, for Margaret, painfully—captured by her duties as monarch, the sisters still spoke on the phone every day. Margaret was the only person on the planet who always knew Elizabeth as a peer, exchanging gossip, complaining about their mother, understanding the world through the same peculiar royal prism. When Margaret traveled abroad, she always unpacked a small, silver-framed photograph of the Queen to hang on her wall or place on her dresser. Jane Stevens, one of Margaret's long-standing ladies-in-waiting, remembers the inevitable search on their tours for gifts for the Princess to take home to her elder sister.

Elizabeth sometimes envied Margaret's talent to amuse, saying, "Oh, it's so much easier when Margaret's there—everybody laughs at what Margaret says." The younger sister could enjoy freedoms that were inevitably out of bounds for the monarch. Elizabeth was, apparently, particularly envious of a trip Margaret took with their mother in 1959 to sightsee in Rome and Paris. "In all the years she has been Queen she has never had a proper foreign holiday or been able to say: 'Oh, it's a lovely day, let's go somewhere and take a picnic,'" the Queen's cousin Margaret Rhodes said.

Whatever their difference in rank, both sisters lived in a world where everything around them was controlled by the thermostat of royalty. Margaret's life, though ostensibly more open to the world than the Queen's, was also, in a way, more rarefied. She did not have a robust engagement with politics and public affairs, as did her sister as head of state. Specialness of position unmoored to any tangible purpose meant that nothing was more exotic to Margaret than the mundane. It was one of her lifelong dreams to ride on a bus. When she asked Lady Anne Glenconner to go shopping with her, she excitedly chose the dullest of High Street stores. She derived childlike enjoyment from cleaning Anne's car when she came to stay with her in Norfolk with Roddy Llewellyn. In Mustique, she was never happier than when collecting and washing shells. After swimming, "like a big sister," she loved untangling Anne's hair.

There are times in **Lady in Waiting**, Glenconner's memoir, when Margaret's dreams of being outside the royal cage come through with heartbreaking poignance. In 1999, Margaret had a traumatic accident in Mustique when she turned on the hot tap instead of the cold in the bath and severely scalded her feet.

While the Princess was convalescing on the island, she felt safe only with Anne sleeping in her room. In the end, Anne moved into the single bed next to her and they watched videos. "She was thrilled and said, 'Oh, Anne, is this like boarding school?'" Her hunger to learn what the real world was like went unassuaged.

Being denied a real education was one of Margaret's greatest regrets. Both of the princesses were taught by governesses, but Elizabeth was given stimulating tutorials by then vice-provost of Eton Sir Henry Marten on history and the British constitution, while Margaret was fobbed off with French and piano. The Queen harbored some guilt about the course of their lives being defined by an accident of primogeniture. George VI, before his elder brother, Edward, abdicated, felt bitterly his discrimination compared to the heir to the throne. He was determined that Margaret should not feel the same disregard simply because of her date of birth, and treated her as a favorite. He famously said that Lilibet was his pride, but four-year-old Margaret was his joy. When the twenty-one-year-old Elizabeth left home to marry Philip, her wistful father wrote, "Your leaving us has left a great blank in our lives," adding, "Our family, us four, the 'Royal Family' must remain together with additions of course at suitable moments!" Elizabeth was so aware of Margaret's discontents as the also-ran that she did everything she could to placate her. Robert Lacey records how a cook from 145 Piccadilly, the family's pre–Buckingham Palace London residence from 1927 to 1937, said Princess Elizabeth would go out of her way to spare Margaret the worst duties of the girls' character-building housework by taking them on herself. Later, the Queen felt keenly the enforced role she had to play in Margaret's reluctant repudiation of her first love, Peter Townsend, and was profoundly sad when Margaret's marriage to Tony Snowdon foundered.

It was nonetheless galling to Margaret that, after their divorce, Snowdon stayed on good terms with the Queen and that her mother positively adored him. The Princess felt her sister and mother weren't offended enough by Tony's infidelities simply because, unlike hers with Roddy, he'd managed to keep them quiet. More media savvy and himself a figure of fascination to the media as a celebrated photographer, Snowdon succeeded in framing Margaret to the public as the guilty party even though he had been sexually faithless since day one. During their honeymoon, his ex-girlfriend gave birth to his child. Divorce from Margaret eighteen years later became urgent because of the pregnancy of his mistress, Lucy Lindsay-Hogg, who then became his second wife. It's only in recent years that the full extent of Snowdon's awful behavior has come to light.

On February 10, 2002, chronicles of Margaret's troubled history deluged the media. She had died in her sleep the morning before at the age of seventy-one at King Edward VII's Hospital in London after cardiac problems following a stroke. At her side were her son, forty-year-old Viscount Linley, David Armstrong-Jones, and her daughter, thirty-seven-year-old Lady Sarah Chatto, the children of her marriage to Snowdon.

After the scalding incident in Mustique, her infirmity had been further exacerbated by the first of her strokes (she'd had two since 1998), and she never regained full mobility. She was bitterly conscious of the loss of her looks and refused to see most of her old friends, especially the men. A summer visitor to Balmoral in 2001, who had to pass her room on the way down to dinner, told me that the Princess was a woeful, isolated figure who rarely appeared, like a mad aunt in the attic.

In her last days, her eyesight deteriorated greatly and she lost virtually all movement on her left side. The once great "goer" had been sadly stilled. For those who remembered her in her glory days—the petite, curvaceous figure, the wide, sensuous mouth, and the sparkling blue cat's eyes that communicated both "come-hither" and "touch-me-if-you-dare," her disintegration was shocking. David Griffin, her chauffeur of twenty-six years, was appalled at how ill she looked when he met her from the Concorde flight following her accident. Her scalded legs were bandaged from foot to knee, and he had to gingerly lift her into a wheelchair. There was public shock the last time she was seen out, wheeled with swollen face and dark glasses into the one hundredth birthday party of the Dowager Duchess of Gloucestershire.

Obituaries for Margaret were mostly irreverent or maudlin tributes to an unfulfilled life. The press knew too much about the only one among her generation of royals to have lived her private life in public view. She and Snowdon had moved in circles heavy with writers and artists, always the most disloyal when it comes to colorful leaks to the press. Boring friends from aristocratic circles are the only prudent choice to preserve royal discretion—or, as the Queen Mother would put it, stay "utterly oyster"—but, to her credit, Margaret, whose passions were music, theater, and ballet, never wanted to be dull. Her lively mind sought out intelligent company, but, at private gatherings, she still couldn't resist pulling rank.

In Mustique at a picnic hosted by the Glenconners, with whom I became friends during my years editing **Tatler,** I once witnessed a choice Margaret moment that spoke as much to the absurd impact royalty has on everyone else as to the Princess's own self-importance. "What, no mustard!" the Princess suddenly exclaimed. "How am I expected to eat sausages without mustard!" The whole party leapt to its feet in consternation. At informal occasions she would suddenly interject into the conversation a reminder of her closeness to the Queen. Penny Mortimer, widow of the late barrister and writer Sir John Mortimer, told me her husband sat next to Margaret at a dinner party at Wadham College hosted by the warden Sir Claus Moser shortly before her sixtieth birthday in 1990, and reports the following exchange:

MARGARET: What do you think of the post-
    age stamps nowadays?
MORTIMER: Well, ma'am, I don't really think
    much about them.
MARGARET: I think they're ghastly. Buildings
    and birds and things. I want to see pictures
    of my sister!

II

The Queen was alone at Windsor Castle when she
learned the news of Margaret's demise. Affairs of
state had meant that she had not seen her ailing sister
for a month. Given how the Queen often deploys
the demands of work to avoid difficult emotional
interactions, she perhaps couldn't bear to see the last
miserable decline of a sister with whom she had
shared so much.

Behind her typical public stoicism, the death of
Margaret, just when HM was supposed to be entering an allegro moment in her reign and only five
months after the passing of her best male friend,
Porchey, was a heavy personal blow for the Queen.
Whatever her lifelong vexations with Margaret, she
was now bereft of her most intimate companion and
beloved sibling who helped fill the void of her
uniquely lonely position as monarch. Lilibet and
her 101-year-old mother were now the dwindling
remnants of "us four," and clearly that would not be

for long. The Queen Mother had recently had a series of falls, and everyone had expected her to go first.

Prince Charles drove straight to Norfolk to comfort his grandmother at Sandringham, where she had lingered with a chest cold since Christmas. "This is a terribly sad day for all my family," he said in a televised address. "She loved life and lived it to the full. . . . We shall all miss her dreadfully." He had a deep fondness for his aunt "Margo" as he called her, even though she took Diana's side during their marital difficulties. With her unpredictability and panache, Margaret had been the Diana of her day and knew what it was like to be the media's chew toy. She had told Charles she was going to continue her association with Diana after they separated, a resolve that went out the window after Diana's Martin Bashir interview, which Margaret considered rank disloyalty to the Queen.

The Queen Mother told Charles that Margo's death had "probably been a merciful release" and, after they prayed together in the chapel, she stayed on in Sandringham to mourn her daughter's loss alone. Their relationship had been complicated. Throughout their lives, Margaret and her mother had dueled and bickered—a "slightly strained relationship," Lady Anne Glenconner called it. "One would do things like open all the windows, only for the other to go around shutting them. Or would suggest an idea, and the other would dismiss it immediately. Perhaps they were too similar," she recalled. Both loved the limelight and competing for attention; they were flirtatious women, although the Queen Mother was more coquettish (in keeping with her times) and Princess Margaret more forward. They outdid each other at charades. Glenconner recalls how one summer weekend at Glen—the Glenconner Scottish country seat— Princess Margaret dressed up as Mae West and sang, "Come Up and See Me Sometime."

Both Margaret and her mother felt remaindered when Elizabeth ascended to the throne at the age of twenty-five. Stuck with each other, their most challenging years together followed the Queen's coronation, when they had to move out of their home at Buckingham Palace into the much smaller Clarence House. The Queen knew how marginalized they felt: "Mummy and Margaret have the biggest grief to bear for their future must seem very blank, while I have a job and a family to think about." Glenconner recalled how a private film, commissioned by the Queen, captured twenty-two-year-old Margaret looking forlorn in the midst of all the laughter and backstage jubilation following the coronation (in which Anne herself played a role as one of the Queen's maids of honor). "Of course I looked sad," Margaret later told Anne. "I had just lost my beloved father and, really, I had just lost my sister, because she was going to be so busy."

The more immersed Elizabeth became as Queen, the more excluded Margaret felt and the less she had to do. Margaret became a late-sleeping party girl to fill the languid days, offending her mother's tireless work ethic. The Queen Mother would never allow Margaret to retreat to bed until after an engagement was fully over, even if she was genuinely unwell. At the height of the Peter Townsend drama, tension between them became so bad that Margaret threw a book at her mother's head.

For her part, the Queen mostly considered the bouts of depression and excessive drinking of Margaret's earlier years a cry for attention. Once when one of Margaret's inner circle called her to say her sister was threatening to throw herself out of the bedroom window, the Queen replied, "Carry on with your house party. Her bedroom is on the ground floor."

Rarely sick herself, the Queen considered stamina to be a moral as well as physical attribute. A Balmoral guest told me that both the Queen and Prince Philip were clearly irritated by what they saw as an element of carelessness in Margaret's accident in Mustique. Later, when Margaret was seriously depressed from the strokes, a suggestion was made to the Queen that a therapist might help. "Perhaps when she's better we could consider that," the Queen replied.

She viewed her sister's wheelchair as an almost theatrical indulgence. On mother-daughter visits to Buckingham Palace, a duel took place: Margaret would make a beeline for the wheelchair readied by a footman and intended for her mother as the two of them exited the elevator. "For God's sake, Margaret— get out! That's meant for Mummy!" remarked the

Queen. The passive-aggressive dynamic between them suggested they both declined to accept the reality of Margaret's condition. When the Queen came to visit Margaret for tea, her sister declined to turn off the radio soap opera **The Archers.** The Queen appealed to Anne Glenconner to arbitrate. "Every time I try to say something she just says, 'Shh,'" said the Queen. Anne had to then accompany her back to Margaret's bedroom and firmly say, "Ma'am, the Queen is here, and she can't stay all that long. Would you like me to help pour the tea?" and then switched off the radio.

There was heartfelt sorrow among Margaret's staff on her death. She was a decent boss, and they had stayed with her for decades. On official trips, she always ensured her dresser and maid had pleasant rooms and that off-duty sightseeing excursions were arranged for them. Chauffeur David Griffin said she was loyal as long as you stayed within the old-school guidelines of due deference. (She rebuked Princess Diana once for calling him "David" rather than "Griffin.") He told me:

> Princess Margaret was kind to everyone. . . . She treated them properly and she wasn't petty. . . . She would always give you a present at Christmas, but, strangely, she would never wrap them. If, for example, you wanted an iron, she would call you into her rooms and she would give it to you in a box without wrapping paper. It was just, "Thank you very much. Have a Happy Christmas."

Sometimes her desire to offer a useful item misfired. She once gave a lady-in-waiting a toilet brush because she noticed that she "didn't have one" when she came to stay. Let's hope it was wrapped.

Surprisingly, perhaps for one so self-involved, she was an undisputed success as a mother, affectionate and fun with her children. Sarah Chatto and David Linley (now Earl of Snowdon, who inherited his father's looks but not his mercurial edge) were devoted to her. At one moment of depressed self-recrimination, the Princess told the Queen, "I may not have achieved very much—but I at least feel my life has not been wasted, because I have produced two happy and well-adjusted children."

The remark had the usual buried Margaret zinger, but it was true. Despite the turbulence of the Snowdon marriage, Sarah and David were much less beset by emotional drama than the children of Prince Philip and the Queen: Sarah became a well-regarded painter, contentedly married to an actor turned artist, Daniel Chatto, and David, a successful designer and maker of high-end furniture, solidly married to the daughter of a rich peer. (They quietly separated in 2020 after twenty-six years of marriage.) On BBC Radio 4's show **Desert Island Discs**, her son selected Mozart's Piano Concerto No. 24 in C minor to remember his mother. He said that she had inspired his love of art by taking him and Sarah to the National Gallery to appreciate just one picture at a time, to whet their appetite for more. David was as miserable at his prep school as Prince Charles was at

Gordonstoun, but unlike the Queen and Prince Philip, who insisted Charles tough it out, Margaret unhesitatingly responded by pulling David out and sending him to another school where he was happier.

During her final illness, David moved back into Kensington Palace with his wife and young son, Charles, to be close to her. Just a couple of days before her death, Margaret came to the third birthday party of Sarah's second son with a helium balloon tied to her wheelchair.

Her last formal portrait, due to be included in a Golden Jubilee book, was released on the eve of her funeral. The Princess had been photographed by Julian Calder, who had used reduced light and candles to avoid hurting her eyes. She was hesitant about sitting for the portrait at first, then suddenly changed her mind, perhaps knowing she had very little time to live. Looking solemn and strained in a heavy black brocade top, the Princess elected to wear the diamond, pearl, and turquoise Imperial Order of the Crown of India insignia prominently pinned on a blue ribbon. It was given to her by her father, George VI, then Emperor of India, only months before Indian independence from the British Empire and the consequent extinction of the order. That she chose to wear this grand symbol of a dead age underlined the extraordinary journey of her life. She had begun as the second daughter of the Empire, yet she died stigmatized as the first immediate member of the Royal Family to be divorced since Henry VIII. In her frequently disenchanted royal way, Margaret embodied Britain's journey from a confident imperial past to a humbler, more demotic present. **The Guardian** mused that Margaret's "life, above all, posed that essential question which Diana, in her own way, was trying to answer: what, exactly, is a princess for?" That is what the turbulent, unresolved quest of hers had been about.

The funeral—inside St. George's Chapel at Windsor Castle on February 15, 2002—was a dignified, muted affair. It was fifty years exactly since the Queen Mother, with a devastated Margaret at her side, watched as the twenty-five-year-old new sovereign took a handful of red earth from a silver bowl and scattered it somberly on George VI's coffin before it was committed to the vault. A half century later, his younger daughter's casket, shrouded by her personal Royal Standard and adorned with flowers, was carried by eight servicemen from the regiment of which she was colonel-in-chief—the Royal Highland Fusiliers. The Princess had chosen the music, and Tchaikovsky's **Swan Lake** sounded as the mourners entered the chapel.

The 450 members of the congregation were restricted to family, friends, and household staff, including a deeply saddened David Griffin. Both Lord Snowdon and Roddy Llewellyn were present. Despite a painful end to her relationship with Roddy, when he couldn't handle the drama anymore, the Princess maintained a strong bond with him and welcomed his new wife, Tatiana Soskin, into her circle. Many of the friends who came were from the world of theater, film, and music, including Dame

Judi Dench, Felicity Kendal, Dame Cleo Laine, Johnny Dankworth, Bryan Forbes, and Nanette Newman. Of her eighty-plus royal patronages, her theater and ballet associations were the ones she treasured the most.

Afterward, the Queen gently held the arm of her distraught niece, Lady Sarah, and helped her down the chapel steps. During the service the Queen had shown little emotion, but the sight of her sister's coffin loaded into the hearse made her eyes glisten with tears. "It was the saddest I have seen the Queen," said one of Margaret's closest friends, Reinaldo Herrera.

Breaking with family tradition, Margaret had asked to be cremated, her ashes to be interred alongside her father in the King George VI Memorial Chapel at St. George's Chapel. Her coffin was driven the eight miles to a stained brick municipal crematorium in Slough where it was the sixth committal of the day. The crematorium's gates had been painted white. Otherwise, there would be no further indications of the last journey of a king's daughter. The final tribute that friends and family heard before the hearse drove away was a Gaelic lament played by a duo of pipers. It was selected by the Princess's daughter, and it was called "The Desperate Struggle of the Bird."

III

It was typical of the Queen Mother's sense of obligation that Princess Margaret's funeral would be the last duty she was determined to fulfill. She had often said that she hoped to live to see Lilibet's Golden Jubilee, but greater than that hope was her fear of disrupting the occasion with her death.

While the Queen and Prince Philip left almost immediately after Margaret's funeral for a two-week Commonwealth tour that took them to Jamaica, New Zealand, and Australia, the Queen Mother returned to Royal Lodge, her home in the grounds of Windsor Great Park, and continued her roster of commitments, hosting a lawn meet for the Eton Beagles and a house party for the Grand Military Race Meeting at Sandown Park. She was ecstatic when her horse First Love won the race. With serene efficiency, she then started to make phone calls and dispense small personal gifts to staff and friends that indicated she was bidding farewell. An array of Easter eggs was lined up to be given to the grandchildren, great-grandchildren, and members of her household. She was cogent throughout.

Her biographer Hugo Vickers believes that the Queen Mother's instincts for "devoir"—duty—were so attuned to the royal calendar that she chose to slip away the one day of the year when the family had no external plans. They were all in residence at Windsor celebrating Easter, except for the Prince of Wales and Princes William and Harry, who were skiing in Klosters.

The Queen was out riding in Windsor Great Park on Easter Saturday when the doctor summoned her to her mother's bedside. Canon John Ovenden, the

Queen Mother's chaplain, prayed aloud and read a Highland lament as the 101-year-old matriarch drifted into unconsciousness. The daughter of a Scottish earl, she lost a brother in the First World War and became an icon of national resilience in the Second World War; she was the last empress in British history. With magical numerology, she died fifty days after Margaret and fifty years into the Queen's reign.

Unlike the death of Margaret, which had been so fraught with regret, the Queen Mother's passing was her last gift to Lilibet. It released her faithful elder daughter to emerge at the age of seventy-five as the preeminent **Regina** in her golden year, uncluttered by legends of the royal past.

"Us four" was now One, which is what Elizabeth II was crowned to be. After the long season of sorrow, her advisers noted a perceptible hint of liberation in the Queen. Her mother's influence on her even in her waning years was always more dominant and burdensome than people knew. Her voice was in Elizabeth's ear every day, planting doubts about decisions. She was adamantly opposed to Buckingham Palace being opened to the public. She was appalled at the notion of the monarchy paying income tax. She thought the Queen should have fought to keep the royal yacht and that she certainly should not have agreed to let ministers and other dignitaries make use of the royal train. And she felt more than a twinge of regret when successive colonial countries declared their independence. "Africa's quite gone to pot since we left it" was one exceptionable, oft-expressed sentiment at Clarence House.

The Queen Mother's insistent push for institutional conservatism ran counter to Prince Philip's press for modernity, and this "in-house" tension served only to heighten the Queen's already cautious nature. "In due course" was the phrase the Queen inevitably first uttered when her advisers floated the possibility of any change to the traditional way of doing things. This response was more likely after she spoke to her mother. "The Queen's picture of her role was derived from her father, and very much reinforced by her mother," a retired courtier said. The Queen Mother "seemed to favor the Monarchy as it was pre-war, and was not embracing the idea of changing things."

Her initial disapproval of Prince Philip as a future husband for Elizabeth was based not only on his itinerant background and lack of a fortune, but also because she saw him as "dangerously progressive." The self-confident sway of "the Hun," as she called Philip, over the infatuated young Queen meant she had a powerful rival for her daughter's ear. Too clever to ever go to outright war with her son-in-law, she found indirect ways to foil him, sometimes out of sheer naughtiness.

As chairman of the Coronation Commission, Philip favored his friend Baron Sterling Henry Nahum, the court and social photographer whose professional name was "Baron," over the Queen Mother's longtime favorite Cecil Beaton for the coveted job of taking the coronation photographs. Out of the blue in May 1953, Beaton learned the job had gone to him. "I had a short opportunity to thank the Queen Mother for what I am sure must have been her help in bringing about this 'coup' for me," he noted. "She laughed knowingly with one finger high in the air." Philip got used to this kind of subtle sabotage and always took care to treat his mother-in-law with impeccable courtesy. But during an interview with Philip, then seventy-nine, at the time of the Queen Mother's one hundredth birthday, Gyles Brandreth tried to nudge him into saying something effusive about his mother-in-law. "Apart from insisting that he had no desire to live so long himself," says Brandreth, Philip "would not be drawn."

In the early days of her daughter's reign, the Queen Mother's difficult adjustment to being a back number was an acknowledged vexation at Buckingham Palace. Standing with Martin Charteris, her then assistant private secretary, in Clarence House—a mere three weeks after her accession to the throne—the Queen saw her mother's car driving up to the front of the house and turned to Charteris and murmured, "Here comes the problem."

There was a battle of wills between them almost immediately over her reluctance to move out of Buckingham Palace. The Queen Mother expected and demanded to set up her own court in the imposing royal mansion Marlborough House in St. James's. Unfortunately, it was already occupied by another royal dowager, the eighty-five-year-old Queen Mary, widow of King George V, with a staff of eighty whom her granddaughter, the new Queen, had no intention of booting out. Suggesting that they share Marlborough House might have made it look, said The Telegraph's Graham Turner, "like a dumping-ground for retired Queens." Besides, it was in such need of repair that an extensive renovation such as the Queen Mother proposed would have been deemed unacceptably expensive by the British tax-payer.

Instead, she grudgingly accepted what she called "a horrid little house," the splendid four-story, nineteenth-century residence Clarence House, which stands beside St. James's Palace. Princess Elizabeth and Prince Philip had lived there content-edly enough before Elizabeth succeeded to the throne and, indeed, having spent a great deal of time and energy renovating it to modern standards, were sorry to leave it. The Prince of Wales and the Duchess of Cornwall live there in grand style today. After Queen Mary died, Elizabeth deftly put Marlborough House out of her mother's reach forever by donating it to the Commonwealth Secretariat to serve as its head-quarters in 1959. The Queen Mother retaliated by spending a fortune on remodeling Clarence House again. Disaffected rumblings from Parliament about the cost occasioned tart rejoinders like, "Perhaps they would like me to retire decently to Kew and run a needlework guild?"

Elizabeth was sensitive to her mother's unhappi-ness, understanding how humiliating it was to see the King's former staff turn away from her to the new regime, leaving her feeling an isolated irrelevance—she, who had been for a decade and all through the dark hours of the war, the pivot of sovereign power. Her marriage to Bertie was a symbiotic partnership in which she wielded incalculable influence, often joining the King and Winston Churchill during the war for weekly lunches at the Palace when the prime minister came to brief.

With her conciliatory nature, the Queen did not protest when her mother asked to receive Foreign Office telegrams after stepping down, meaning she wielded more power than any Queen Consort before her. And she said nothing when her mother continued to sign her name "Elizabeth R" as if the King were still alive. Such was the Queen's dislike of confrontation, she always felt she had to placate her. A courtier recalls her saying in a worried tone, "It's Mummy that matters. We mustn't do anything that hurts Mummy's feelings." Charteris told Gyles Brandreth that "there was an awkwardness about precedence, with the Queen not wanting to go in front of her mother," who was "accustomed to going first." She was acutely aware that her mother was only fifty-one when she was widowed, and that despite the King's ill-health, she had imagined at least another decade of being the power behind the throne.

Bertie had wooed the petite, smiling Lady Elizabeth Bowes-Lyon—then besieged by suitors—for two and a half years, and had proposed to her three times before she finally accepted his hand in marriage. For Bertie, the warmth, lightness, and levity of Lady Elizabeth's family life at the ancient seat of Glamis Castle in Scotland (of **Macbeth** fame) was an enchanting contrast to the stiff restraints of his own royal upbringing. "Everything at Glamis was beautiful, perfect," one of her rejected suitors recalled. "Being there it was like living in a Van Dyck picture. Time and the gossiping, junketing world, stood still. Nothing happened . . . but the magic gripped us all."

At the time, Lady Elizabeth was in love with Bertie's handsome equerry, the Honourable James Stuart, and she had long held higher ambitions for marriage than the painfully shy "spare" to the throne.

It was his older brother, the future King Edward VIII, she had her eye on, but his taste in women ran to worldly sophisticates like the slinky Freda Dudley Ward and, later and more fatefully, the mondaine temptress Wallis Simpson. Edward seems to have been the one person in the British Isles who was impervious to Elizabeth Bowes-Lyon's charm. The rebuff, no doubt, hardened the unyielding ice she would show to the Duke and Duchess of Windsor in exile.

Settling for Bertie was the best decision of her life. Though it was never a marriage of passion on her side, his devotion to her was unconditional. She had the chance to mold an accidental monarch. "He needed to marry a strong and confident wife," said the actress Evelyn Laye, a close friend of Bertie's.

"Thank God for him, and for the country, that he found the right girl. . . . She made him into a great king in a way that no one else could have done. Hers was the strength and resolve that made it possible."

For the fifteen years of George VI's reign, his supportive consort was the joy gene of the House of Windsor, reviving its shaky image after Edward VIII's dispiriting abdication and bringing hope and grace to the British people during the Blitz. Hitler is supposed to have called her "the most dangerous woman in Europe" because of the uplifting effect she had on public morale after refusing to leave London when Nazi bombs fell, even after Buckingham Palace was struck in 1940.

After the King's death, this unfailingly optimistic woman wrote to the poet Edith Sitwell that she was "engulfed by great black clouds of unhappiness and misery." She conceded the stage to a beloved daughter, yes, but one who she knew would be a reticent young queen who could never approach her in natural charisma. Her daughter knew it, too. Countess Patricia Mountbatten, a cherished friend since they were girls, recalls the Queen saying before a Commonwealth tour: "If only Mummy were doing this. . . . She does it so well. I'm not spontaneous like Mummy."

It was Winston Churchill who brought the grieving widow out of the emotional funk that threatened to turn her mourning into a tiresome replay of Queen Victoria's. On his annual prime ministerial visit to Balmoral, he decided to drive over unannounced to Birkhall, the rustic lodge on the Balmoral estate to which the Queen Mother had removed herself now that the castle belonged to her daughter (another status blow). Churchill was keen to have the more old-fashioned Queen Mother as an ally behind the throne to act as a buffer against too much influence from the modernizing Philip.

Whatever Churchill told her, it worked. To her friend Lord Salisbury, she cooed about the old lion's "great delicacy of feeling." Her lady-in-waiting Jean Rankin claimed that "he must have said things which made her realise how important it was for her to carry on, how much people wanted her to do things as she had before." Importantly, he clearly also gave her a frisson of the power-gossip she missed. "I realized suddenly how very much I am now cut off from 'inside' information," she confided to Lord Salisbury.

In no time, she was reinventing herself as the feathery, sparkling, ever-smiling grandmother of the nation handing out prizes, christening ships, inspecting regiments, unveiling monuments, scattering coveted cultural patronages, and perfecting the art of being universally adored.

The problem was that royal widowhood meant a natural performer lost not only her public platform, but autonomy over her whole life. Her twenty-five-year-old daughter now controlled where she lived, what she spent, and what role, if any, she would be allowed to play on the national stage. Her annual stipend, from the government-approved Civil List, of £643,000 a year was a fraction of what she felt she needed. She hosted bibulous racing house parties at Royal Lodge in the grounds of Windsor, fishing house parties at Birkhall, and black-tie dinner parties all year round with serious jewelry required. Clarence House was a luxurious time capsule, employing a staff of sixty, with three footmen serving full-blown teas fit for a cruise ship, and three or four more waiters at lunch. In her bedroom, two cherubs on her four-poster bed had their angel's clothes washed and starched every month. Her fleet of five or six cars with special number plates was garaged at Buckingham Palace.

Her stable of racehorses alone was an eye-watering expense. She once nearly missed the start of the splendid annual ceremony of the Order of the Garter at Windsor Castle because of a particularly gripping race. The **Daily Mail** reported that she was found in a private sitting room adorned in her Garter finery perched on a fire guard watching the racing on television. "She was shouting at the screen: 'Go in, go in, blast you, go in!'" as her horse balked at entering its starting stall.

Her wardrobe was another annual budget buster. Ever since Norman Hartnell masterminded her all-white Paris wardrobe for her first state visit in 1938, he and his successors produced a steady flow of floaty, frothy Fragonard creations. Chiffon, georgette tea dresses, crinolines shimmering with crystal beading and rhinestone embroidery, ball gowns, velvet coats, and garden dresses—all with shoes (she preferred a two-inch heel) and handbags to match—

filled closet after closet at Clarence House. No austere coat lapel remained unadorned with what she called "a little 'Mmmm,'" an eye-socking piece from her groaning jewelry collection. Her millinery, drenched in peach, lilac, and **eau de Nil** ostrich feathers, arrived by the black-and-white-striped box load. One feathered hat she especially loved had little bells on the side that tinkled in the breeze.

The Queen had to plump up her mother's income out of her personal funds and guarantee an overdraft that ran to £4 million per annum. The Queen did once "affectionately suggest that her mother should not buy so much new bloodstock in one particular year," a friend of the Queen Mother sighed, "but nonetheless a huge bill arrived in due course. All the Queen felt she could do was send her mother a note which simply said, 'Oh dear, Mummy!'" When the size of his grandmother's overdraft eventually hit the press, Prince Charles remarked that "if the reported shortfall were only a tenth of the real figure, the media were at least aiming in the right direction." ("Really," the Queen once said, "what with my mother and her racehorses and my mother-in-law with her nunneries.") Her £643,000 annuity was overspent eight times in every year, and was less than half what it cost just to employ the servants at Clarence House.

In the summer of 1952, on a whim while staying with friends in the north of Scotland, she bought herself an ancient condemned castle in Caithness. Commanding a windswept promontory of the

Scottish coast, the castle overlooks Orkney. She returned it to its original name, Castle of Mey, and spent another small fortune restoring it. (Much to the surprise of everyone who thought the castle a mad folly of widowhood, it became one of her happiest summer escape haunts for nearly five decades.) The blue raincoat and wellingtons she always wore when walking the grounds are still awaiting her arrival in the front hall.

To the end of her life, she was in demand to host fundraisers at Clarence House. Guests would gather in the drawing room while she waited in the adjoining salon knocking back a martini. Then the doors would open and she'd send out a scrabble of smelly corgis to kick up some disturbance to announce that her tiny self was on the way. There ensued such familiar sunny routines as, "Oh, Mr. Branson, how **are** your airplanes these days?"

Though her mother's prickly **amour propre** could be a trial, the Queen's bond with her—and gratitude for her work ethic—was profound. They shared the same wry sense of humor, the same love of horses and dogs, the same formidable physical stamina. (It was one of her mother's lifelong rules never to admit to fatigue, cold, or temperature.)

They spoke every morning after breakfast to swap racing tips and Thoroughbred news. In her long history of backing horses, the Queen Mother had 462 winners who all raced in her personal gold and blue colors. Like the Queen, she relished the full gamut of country pursuits, including fly-fishing. On her sojourns at Birkhall, she could be found until her eighties standing in her waders, rod in hand, in the freezing water of the River Dee. Biographer Ann Morrow recounts how once at Balmoral, when "there had been no sign of the Queen Mother by 8:00 P.M., search parties were sent out, and she was found dragging a 20-pound salmon home in the dark." ("This is the salmon's revenge," she later joked when a salmon bone lodged in her throat at dinner in 1982.)

She could usually thaw the Queen's mood by making her laugh. Once, when student protesters threw toilet rolls at her, the Queen Mother picked them up and handed them back saying, "Was this yours?" She was able to tease the Queen as no one else could. "Have you been reigning today, Lilibet?" she would ask in her droll drawl when her daughter returned feeling spent from an engagement. Sometimes the Queen surprised her mother with an act of generosity, like installing, unasked, a stairlift for her at Birkhall. "You now have a form of mechanized assistance to ascend **'les escaliers'** without Your Majesty's feet touching the floor," Prince Charles wrote to his grandmother in his quaint way, never failing to use her royal title even in a private note.

It was in the social atmosphere of their homes that mother and eldest daughter differed most. Clarence House was a whole lot more fun to work in than Buckingham Palace, which was rife with stuffy factotums. When the Queen Mother left the Palace for her new home, some of the more spirited servants wanted to go with her. She may have been an icon of wartime fortitude, but the era that defined her entertaining ethos was the 1920s.

Widowhood meant that, out of the public eye, she could return to living in her own personal Jazz Age. Liberated from the leaden banquets of a royal consort, she became an inspired and often hilarious hostess to the culturati, the racing crowd, and the grand old aristocracy. (One of her returning guests was the surveyor of the King's—and later the Queen's—pictures: Anthony Blunt, who, in an uncomfortable revelation, turned out to be a Soviet spy from the infamous Cambridge espionage ring that also included Guy Burgess, Harold "Kim" Philby, Donald Maclean, and John Cairncross.)

She was famous for her irreverent toasting games and would lift her glass high-high-high for people she liked and low-low-low under the table for people she didn't, a gesture met by gales of laughter and accompanied by copious amounts of alcohol. Like the Queen, who can do swift, wicked renderings of anyone she has just met, the Queen Mother was a sly mimic. Her Blackadder was said to be very good, but even better was a rendering of Ali G, much appreciated by Prince Harry. She would say, "Darling, lunch was marvelous—respec'."

For decades, her parties were choreographed by her pricelessly camp steward William Tallon—my pew mate at Lord Lichfield's memorial—who presided as master of ceremonies in white tie and tails. "Backstairs Billy" joined the Royal Household at the age of fifteen and stayed in service until the Queen

Mother's death. His partner, Reginald Wilcock, was the page of the presence. The grace-and-favor gate-house where they lived was party central for the Palace's downstairs gay subculture. Billie's backstage tyranny was unassailable because he was the Queen Mother's indispensable right hand.

As chronicled in Tom Quinn's entertaining biography, his day began at six A.M., when he would descend to the kitchens to inspect the Queen Mother's breakfast tray with "a very serious look" and then "stalk off like an elegant if rather gloomy heron." Tallon spun the Gershwin records, walked the corgis, curated the guests, and refilled the Queen Mother's glass with her favorite gin and Dubonnet before lunch. If a guest asked for a non-alcoholic drink, he served them wine anyway to ensure everything went with a bang.

At Birkhall, he used to get people down for lunch by ringing a bell and swinging a censer like a Catholic priest. He was her dance partner at Balmoral's annual Ghillies Ball for the staff, and sometimes five minutes before her luncheon guests arrived at Clarence House, he would whirl her around her private sitting room in a waltz. He claimed she could dance him off his feet even into her eighties. She would say, "We really are a sprightly pair of old girls, aren't we, William?"

One of her distinguished male friends told me that after an evening at the ballet, when she was eighty-two years old, he helped lift her from her car into dinner at Wiltons fish restaurant. He did so with an aide on her other side so that her little feet scarcely touched the ground. He hissed to the waiter not to serve her crab claws like everyone else in the group because she had just recovered from the salmon-bone-stuck-in-the-throat incident. But she looked around and said, "Oh! Everyone has crab claws. Why not me?" and ate three.

As the decades sped by and the Queen became an accomplished, seasoned monarch, the Queen Mother meddled less and savored more her crowd-pleaser role. She was seen as one of the only members of the family untainted by scandal and divorce, preserving her royal mystique even during the coarsest tabloid onslaughts of the 1990s. Her high-spirited longevity became a source of national wonder. Lady Elizabeth Longford describes how after the christening of Prince William, which happened to coincide with her eighty-second birthday, the Queen Mother clambered onto an upturned flowerpot so the crowds could see her wave on her birthday morning:

> She was later shown on television greeting the white-coated butchers at Smithfield—a small figure in perpetual motion, laughing, gesticulating, turning this way and that, determined to collect them all into her own particular magic circle.

Now that perpetual motion was forever stilled. And the question for Buckingham Palace planners was how much the British public would want to mourn her. To die at 101 does not ignite the same kind of emotion as at 36, the age Princess Diana broke the world's hearts. There was concern that the national celebration of an ancient royal icon— following so soon after Princess Margaret's death and only three months before the climax of the Golden Jubilee in June—would be a dusty affair with an unimpressive turnout.

The Palace advisers wondered: Should the celebrations be postponed? Knowing how her mother would feel about it, the Queen was adamant that everything would go on as planned. To forestall any sense of false expectations, the Palace press office took the precaution of drafting possible statements in case there was a public shrugging about her loss.

As feared, the press was less than deferential. There was a big uproar from monarchists because BBC newscaster Peter Sissons, who announced the Queen Mother's death, did so wearing an unconventional (and, it was said, disrespectful) burgundy necktie rather than the traditional black for mourning; and on a special BBC Radio program, instead of celebrating the epic days of the old Queen's life, James Cox asked Lady Pamela Hicks if the Queen Mother had "outlived her usefulness." Republican elements, who made up in volume what they lacked in countable support, decried the government's recall of Parliament in recognition of the Queen Mother's passing as "an embarrassing spectacle."

A **Guardian** headline declared "Uncertain Farewell Reveals a Nation Divided." Columnist

Jonathan Freedland wrote that unlike the outpouring for Princess Diana, the crowds outside
Buckingham Palace were thin and the lines to sign
books of condolence brisk to nonexistent. He attributed the shortening of the official period of
mourning from thirteen days to nine to Palace concern that the nation's grief wouldn't stretch that
long. Piers Morgan recorded in his diary:

> My 37th birthday, and I was looking forward to
> a splendid night's entertainment in the fleshpots
> of London when a phone call came through
> mid-afternoon saying the Queen Mother had
> died. I wish I could say my first reaction was to
> bow my head and pay silent tribute to Her
> Majesty for all she'd done for this country in
> her amazing life, before racing to the newsroom
> to start work on Monday's paper. But all I could
> think of was that she had died on a Saturday.

As Tony Blair's team debated whether to try to
insert the prime minister into the proceedings, Sir
Malcolm Ross, was in his element. Operation Tay
Bridge, as the plans for the Queen Mother's funeral were coded, had been carried home in his
briefcase at night for seventeen years. Ross had
every detail planned down to the last choirboy. Sir
Roy Strong, who attended the funeral rehearsal at
Westminster Abbey, wrote in his diary that he was
stunned by how immaculately it was choreographed. Ross even ordered the cobblestones

outside Westminster Abbey to be gone over with a vacuum cleaner.

Before the cortege left Windsor, Canon Ovenden led the Queen and her family in prayer on Sunday at the foot of her mother's coffin. It lay in state for four days in Westminster Hall, placed on a catafalque and draped in her personal standard. After keeping vigil with the Queen Mother's three other grandsons—the Duke of York, the Earl of Wessex, and Viscount Linley—the Prince of Wales returned alone for his own private twenty minutes of silent prayer. With emotion, he told the nation in his tribute that his grandmother had served the United Kingdom with "panache, style, and unswerving dignity" for nearly eighty years:

> Somehow, I never thought it would come. She seemed gloriously unstoppable and, since I was a child, I adored her. . . . Oh, how I shall miss her laugh and wonderful wisdom born of so much experience and an innate sensitivity to life. She was quite simply the most magical grandmother you could possibly have, and I was utterly devoted to her.

Abracadabra! The magical grandmother waved her wand for the last time. Was there ever an occasion when she had not pulled in the crowds? Did anyone really think she would disappoint on the last great performance of her life? Trouncing all the gloomy predictions, an astonishing two hundred thousand members of the British public filed solemnly past the

Queen Mother's coffin as it lay in state before she was finally laid to rest at Windsor, alongside the body of her late husband and the ashes of Princess Margaret. Over a million lined the streets for her final journey from the Abbey to Windsor, numbers comparable to those of the mourners who turned out for George VI and Winston Churchill. The BBC (and others) had to eat crow. The **Daily Mail** trumpeted **The Guardian**'s failed barometer of national feeling with the headline "Paper that got it so badly wrong."

"It was a huge mix of young and old," recorded Strong of the crowd, when he went over to Westminster Hall to pay his respects, "all sorts and conditions, silent, respectful, muttering, often not knowing quite how to react in the presence of something of this kind." In a sign that the passing of her mother meant a more relaxed era could begin, the Queen told Charles that Camilla could be at the funeral as "a friend of the Queen Mother," if not as his partner.

On the chilly spring day of the funeral itself, church, army, and Crown combined in a uniquely British display of majesty, pageantry, and beauty. The service was preceded by 101 chimes from the Abbey's tenor bell, one per minute, for each year of the Queen Mother's life. Among the 2,100-strong congregation in Westminster Abbey were a contingent of twelve chattering crowned heads from Europe (who treated it all as a massive monarchist cocktail party), eight august prime ministers, all the loyal men and women from her far-reaching charity work, plus a murmuring mêlée of dukes and duchesses, earls and countesses, and row upon row of the great and the goodish.

For the order of service, the Queen had chosen lines of popular verse written by the English poet and painter David Harkins (who, perhaps the Queen is unaware, today makes most of his money selling nude paintings of his wife on the internet). Her Majesty had first read it in the printed order of service for the funeral of the Dowager Viscountess De L'Isle and was apparently touched by its sentiments and "slightly upbeat tone."

A Buckingham Palace spokesman said that the verse "reflected her thoughts on how the nation should celebrate the life of the Queen Mother. To move on." Harkins was stunned when he heard that his humble verse had been included in the ceremony. So were literary critics because, as a piece of writing, it's about as good as his nude paintings:

You can shed tears that she is gone
or you can smile because she has lived.

You can close your eyes and pray that she'll come
back
or you can open your eyes and see all she's left.

Thanks to the high-profile occasion of its use, it's become a modern funeral classic.

The Queen was composed throughout the service, but Prince Charles was not. He was close to tears and traveled with his grandmother's coffin to Windsor Castle. He watched the interment in St. George's Chapel before flying off to Scotland to be consoled by Camilla at Birkhall.

In her will, the Queen Mother had left her favorite retreat to her favorite grandson, along with the Castle of Mey, which was placed in a trust. Also following her wishes, Prince Charles moved into Clarence House. In 1994, the Queen Mother put aside two-thirds of her fortune to her great-grandchildren, of which Princes William and Harry share £14 million. (A larger portion of this bequest was sensitively allocated to Harry, whom she knew would never enjoy the level of wealth of his elder brother.) Royal Lodge at Windsor was turned over to Prince Andrew for his use. Prince Charles created a memorial to his grandmother in the Stumpery at Highgrove, an enchanting clearing where tree stumps are sculpted into interesting natural structures and mingled with ferns and foliage. There he erected a small, temple-like shrine displaying a bronze bas relief of the Queen Mother adorned in her pearls and gardening hat.

Before her coffin was carried from the Abbey, the litany of the Queen Mother's numerous titles was read out in language that belonged in Arthurian legend:

Thus it hath pleased Almighty God to take out of this transitory life unto His Divine Mercy the late Most High, Most Mighty and Most

Excellent Princess Elizabeth, Queen Dowager and Queen Mother, Lady of the Most Noble Order of the Garter, Lady of the Most Ancient and Most Noble Order of the Thistle, Lady of the Imperial Order of the Crown of India, Grand Master and Dame Grand Cross of the Royal Victorian Order upon whom had been conferred the Royal Victorian Chain, Dame Grand Cross of the Most Excellent Order of the British Empire, Dame Grand Cross of the Most Venerable Order of the Hospital of St. John, Relict of His Majesty King George the Sixth and Mother of Her Most Excellent Majesty Elizabeth the Second by the Grace of God of the United Kingdom of Great Britain and Northern Ireland and of her other Realms and Territories Queen, Head of the Commonwealth, Defender of the Faith, Sovereign of the Most Noble Order of the Garter, whom may God preserve and bless with long life, health and honor and all worldly happiness.

Outside Westminster Abbey were deep piles of bouquets left by members of the public. One tribute seemed particularly fitting for the small, indomitable Queen who defied Hitler in the war. It was addressed simply to "England."

CHAPTER
7

JUBILEE GIRL

————

The Queen's Encore

————

AFTER THE DOWNER OF MARGARET'S DEATH, the outpouring for the Queen Mother had perfectly prepared the ground for the epic patriotic party to mark the Queen's Golden Jubilee, two years in the planning. Buckingham Palace was ecstatic at the unexpected unleashing of all this public emotion. A former press secretary of the Queen told me that having witnessed the rancor and low opinion polls of the monarchy in the scandal-scarred nineties, the elevation in royalist mood was nothing short of a miracle:

> It was as if, confronted with the void of the Queen Mother's death, people thought, "My goodness, we've got the Queen and she's been on the throne for 50 years and she's been doing this job quietly and getting on with it and never

complaining[.] We've got something marvelous here that other countries don't have." And they were really in the mood for good news that celebrated being British.

When the Queen left the Abbey after the Queen Mother's funeral to return to Buckingham Palace, the onlookers lining the streets waving their Union Jack flags burst into rapturous applause. The Queen was now buoyant. The warmth of her reception manifestly lightened her spirits. She had been through so much in the last three months, but now the burdens were lifting and so was her confidence. Her people loved her still. Free at last from the eclipsing brilliance of her mother, her sister, and the eternal goddess, Diana, she could step out before the nation to rejoice in fifty successful years. With her steadfast liege man Prince Philip at her side on the balcony of Buckingham Palace, the imagery to the massed crowds was of constancy, stability, and virtue rewarded. And the glimpse of her grandsons William (nearly twenty and just completing his first year at St. Andrews) and Harry (seventeen, and about to start his final year at Eton) offered an added dash of excitement for the monarchy's future.

The Queen visited seventy cities and towns in England, Scotland, Wales, and Northern Ireland in fifty counties over thirty-eight days from May to August on a single tour in her jubilee year. The royal train covered 3,500 miles across England, Scotland, and Wales—from as far south as Falmouth in Cornwall and as far north as Wick in Caithness. She received more than 30,000 congratulatory emails, and received and replied to almost 17,500 Golden Jubilee congratulatory letters. There were twenty-eight million hits on the Golden Jubilee website over a six-month period. The supposed lack of interest in street parties reported by the press was all wrong. There were thousands across the United Kingdom, including one in the Antarctic, where twenty scientists of the British Antarctic Survey held a party at a temperature of minus 20 degrees Celsius.

Five hundred miles of cabling were laid in London so that the events of Golden Jubilee Weekend could be broadcast to countries all around the globe. A tepid response from the press? Three thousand, five hundred, and twenty-one members of the media from more than sixty countries were accredited to cover the Golden Jubilee Weekend from London. A million people gathered in the Mall to watch the festivities in early June 2002. The spectacular jubilee parade down the Mall on the afternoon of June 4 attracted 20,000, including a 5,000-strong gospel choir, 2,500 participants from the Notting Hill Carnival, and 4,000 people representing Commonwealth countries. The Palace ensured every multicultural base was covered. The Queen made visits to all four main non-Christian faith communities, visiting a mosque in Scunthorpe, a Hindu temple in north London, a Sikh temple in Leicester, and the Jewish Museum in Manchester. A multi-faith reception at Buckingham Palace was attended by more than seven hundred representatives of different faiths. The leader of the Roman Catholic Church in England and Wales, Cardinal Cormac Murphy-O'Connor, preached at Sandringham for the first time, and the Sunday service during the Golden Jubilee Weekend was an ecumenical service.

The Guardian, most sour of the pre-jubilee bashers in the press, had to accept that something undeniably powerful had happened. "We need to face up to the facts," they conceded:

> The Queen's Golden Jubilee celebrations of 2002 have been in every respect more successful than either the organisers had feared or the critics had hoped. . . . This has undoubtedly been a great weekend for the House of Windsor and for the Queen in particular. It would not be true to say that their popularity has never been greater, but it is undoubtedly true that this is one of the best mornings the monarchy has ever had.

Out of all this glorious affirmation, there was one central event that came to epitomize the success of Queen Elizabeth II's Golden Jubilee: the Party at the Palace, the rock concert in the grounds of Buckingham Palace with a live audience of twelve thousand. One news outlet called it the "best party in a backyard in the nation's history." The tone for the evening was set by Brian May of the iconic band Queen. Planted in lonely splendor on the roof of Buckingham Palace with his long, curly hair flowing in the evening breeze, the rock god delivered an edgy guitar solo of "God Save the Queen." Three and a half hours of music deities followed, from Paul McCartney to Elton John, Eric Clapton, Phil Collins, Aretha Franklin [pre-recorded], Brian Wilson, Ricky Martin, Annie Lennox, Joe Cocker, and more. Ozzy Osbourne, who thought it was a joke when he first heard he had been invited, more than rose to the occasion. As comedian Lenny Henry began to introduce him, Ozzy burst onstage screaming to the crowd, "Rock 'n' roll, rock 'n' roll." He performed the Black Sabbath anthem "Paranoid," to deafening guitars while racing back and forth across the stage chewing gum at the same time. A jubilant Prince Harry and Prince William could be seen clapping above their heads in the royal box.

Party at the Palace was one of the most watched pop concerts in history, attracting around two hundred million viewers internationally. One hundred thousand copies of the CD were sold within the first week of release. It made Queen Elizabeth II the first member of the Royal Family to be awarded a gold disc from the recording industry. It also made her, perhaps for the first time in her reign, cool, launching the rebranding of her image as a pop culture phenomenon who connected the past to a more relevant present, which culminated in her cameo with James Bond at the 2012 Olympics. Sir Roy Strong wrote in his diary:

The Golden Jubilee seemed to round off what had begun with the Queen Mother's funeral, a rediscovery and rebirth of the Island and its patriotism. . . . By that I mean pageantry met pop in an alliance of past and present, which gives the Crown a formula to carry on through this century . . . conservation and innovation hand in hand.

It was clear that the heir to the throne had never looked happier. Smiling benignly at him, for a change, his mother had given him the best augury of all that the monarchy had entered a new era. Sitting in the third row with the rest of the Royal Family was Camilla Parker Bowles. She led the clapping as Phil Collins and Queen drummer Roger Taylor took to the stage to perform the Motown classic "You Can't Hurry Love."

CHAPTER
8

SERVANT PROBLEMS

What the Butler Saw

Bubbling in the wings of the monarchy's champagne pageant was an incipient scandal that threatened to blow up the precious trove of national goodwill restored with so much care.

The danger would be caused by a problem endemic to royal aloofness from real-world necessities—a stinginess toward belowstairs staff. The Palace culture has always been instinctively cheap. Gracious with manners, charming with thank-you notes and little gifts, but mean when it comes to money. A possible explanation is that ever since the French Revolution, the Royal Family felt they might get marched upon by the populace at any moment and need portable property. There are stories of Queen Mary telling the young Elizabeth Bowes-Lyon, "Make sure you keep the jewelry you have. Don't ever sell it. You may need it." The twentieth-century example of the Romanov family's catastrophic end sent a long-lasting shudder through their cousins at Buckingham Palace.

A better explanation, I suspect, is the Royal Family's inability to imagine what it's like to worry about money. The honor of working at any of the royal households for a piddling salary was long considered enough reward to extract an uncomplaining and lifelong loyalty from underlings. True, after ten years at the Palace, a butler or a footman could parlay the royal crest on a reference into a lucrative gig with a sheikh or a rock star, but more often than not, royal employment produced a kind of servile Stockholm syndrome. One of Prince Charles's show-business friends told me that royal servants are like dressers in the theater. "The uniform of deference before their masters combined with foul-mouthed camp in the wings. It usually ends with a warm gin in a bedsitter surrounded by signed photographs." Despite the fact that the Palace was supposed to be on a modernizing streak, one gets a whiff of the feudal atmosphere simply by the staff's titles: "yeoman of the pantries," "head coffee maid," "page of the back passage," also known as "page of the backstairs." (At a dinner hosted by Prince Charles at Buckingham Palace a few years back, a guest remembers that the equerry deputed to show him round shared a memorable insight: "If you want a big dinner, a big occasion like this to work well at the Palace, it is absolutely essential to stay on the right side of the yeoman of the pantry.") Many of them hung around too long, on a slow burn of rising resentment.

The Queen Mother's devoted steward William Tallon was a typical casualty. Outside the chapel at Lord Lichfield's memorial service in 2006, he moaned that when the old matriarch died and he was no longer needed, he was tossed out of his grace-and-favor apartment with only three months' notice. Admittedly, Tallon's alcohol-fueled orgies with frisky members of the staff had been getting out of hand. But there was no denying the heroic fact that for five decades, he had been on duty at Clarence House or Birkhall or Royal Lodge or Castle of Mey from the moment the grand (and not undemanding) Queen Mother rose in the morning to the moment she went to bed at night. Tallon told me he had actually been dying to resign for years, but the Queen Mother couldn't function without him, and how did **he** know she would live to be 101? After his eviction—for that is how he saw it—he decamped to the one-bedroom grace-and-favor apartment of his late partner, Reginald Wilcock, in a dingy, converted south London house in the lowly borough of Kennington. "If I say it quickly people think I say Kensington," he told me with gales of boozy laughter.

Tallon's less-than-graceful treatment by the Palace was not unusual. David Griffin, Princess Margaret's trusted chauffeur of twenty-six years, was left disgruntled when his boss died. After years of "lump[ing] her around in the wheelchair," as he put it, he felt "stitched up" over his redundancy payment and bitter to be told to leave what had been his home. "They didn't give a monkey's about the staff," Griffin concluded.

Royal parsimony and careless oversight at the Palace created a rampant belowstairs freebie culture. It was tacitly accepted that the heaps of extravagant watches, tureens, picture frames, Fabergé eggs, Hermès ties, and gold leaf gewgaws lavished on members of the Royal Family by foreign dignitaries and holders of promotional and philanthropic events would often be passed on to members of staff who could flog them off for pocket money. For instance, Princess Margaret's butler Harold Brown forged a brisk connection with Spink and Son, the fine-art showroom and auction house just off St. James's. In Tallon's Kennington flat, I saw a draping of pearls that he said belonged to the Queen Mother wrapped around a statuette and tables groaning with medals, engraved objects, and discarded bibelots. Whether bestowed or pilfered was anybody's guess.

The Prince of Wales ran a particularly lax household and office. The Queen had long been vexed that Charles was such a hopeless executive. She herself epitomized a crisp leadership style, scrupulously prioritizing the work in her red boxes. From the age of twenty-five, she had been schooled by a series of highly competent private secretaries in how to become an efficient CEO of sovereign affairs. Princess Diana was also an impressive executive. Her emotional tribulations did not prevent her from being an expeditious responder to correspondence. Her cast-iron politeness gave her the lifetime habit of handwriting her thank-you notes as soon as she returned from an event at night and leaving them out for her office to mail in the morning. Prince Charles, however, was unwilling or unable to be run by his private secretaries. He was always late to respond to the contents of his in-tray. He employed a revolving cast of pass-the-buck factotums, and his many initiatives were an octopus of well-meaning but disorganized entities with overlapping missions and individual fundraising targets that jostled for the same donors. Donor fatigue meant he was constantly seeking new sources of money, sometimes from dubious high rollers such as Cem Uzan, a Turkish businessman who was caught up in numerous financial crimes and eventually fled Turkey.

Sir Malcolm Ross had a taste of Charles as an employer when he left his post at Buckingham Palace in 2006 to take over the job of master of the household to the Prince of Wales. According to the author Tom Bower, the Queen told Ross, "You must be quite mad. . . . Work for Charles? Well . . ." Ross later understood what she meant:

> I had three calls from the Queen outside working hours in eighteen years. I had six to eight of them from the Prince of Wales on my first weekend. . . . I was called names I hadn't heard since my early days in the army.

It is not that Charles was lazy. "He never, ever stops working," Camilla complained after she moved in with him at Highgrove. Prince Harry has described how his father returned to his study most evenings after dinner and often fell asleep at his desk, waking up with papers stuck to his forehead. It is just that he always seemed overwhelmed by admin and bedeviled by management problems. "I would never have worked for Prince Charles, not for double the money," the Queen Mother's former equerry Major Colin Burgess said.

The Prince of Wales's court wallowed in intrigue. Contributing to the Byzantine atmosphere was Charles's dogged allegiance to the wildly unpopular maître d' of his private life, Michael Fawcett. This closest of aides supervised every detail of the Prince's various houses, from raking the gravel at Highgrove to supervising the choice of fresh flowers at Clarence House. He won Charles's devotion with his peerless gift for mise-en-scène. For one Highgrove dinner, for example, Fawcett ransacked the vaults of St. James's Palace and found crates of plates, candlesticks, and napery given to the monarch over the centuries dating back to Catherine the Great.

When Charles traveled to a weekend house party, it was Fawcett who oversaw the paraphernalia that preceded his boss like the baggage train of a Tudor traveling court, including the Prince's orthopedic bed, lavatory seat, and Kleenex Velvet lavatory paper, plus two landscapes of the Scottish Highlands. (It always baffled Charles that his mother had zero interest in the beautification of her residences. He couldn't wait to get his hands on the gardens of Buckingham Palace, which he thought looked like a municipal roundabout, and despaired of the table décor every Christmas at Sandringham when the Queen's idea of a festive look was a bare table with no cloth and a poinsettia placed in the middle.)

Fawcett began his royal service in 1981 as a footman to the Queen, moving up to the post of sergeant footman. He then became Charles's assistant valet at Kensington Palace, laying out his bespoke suits and shirts in the morning and packing the polished shoes, handkerchiefs, and ties for overnight engagements between folds of tissue paper. For weekend house parties, he secreted in a plastic shirt bag Charles's childhood teddy bear, which was still patched whenever necessary by the Prince's former nanny, Mabel Anderson, and went everywhere with him. Fawcett was so deeply entrenched in the Prince's tastes—event planner, advance man, social enabler, and babysitter of rich donors for the Prince's foundation work—that Charles felt paralyzed at any suggestion of removing him. "I can manage without just about anyone except for Michael," Charles reportedly said.

"I could never quite work out how a simple valet could rise to this level of authority, because within the royal household his was really quite a minor job," Major Colin Burgess commented. "But he had somehow managed, with the trust and full knowledge and co-operation of the Prince, to build a huge power base which threatened the whole employee structure of St. James's Palace." Fawcett gained notoriety in the press with the revelation that, after the Prince broke his arm at polo in 1990, the devoted

RIGHT: Thick as Thieves: Despite their divided paths, Princess Elizabeth (right) and her younger sister, Princess Margaret Rose (left), chatted on the phone daily.

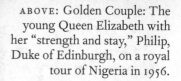

ABOVE: Golden Couple: The young Queen Elizabeth with her "strength and stay," Philip, Duke of Edinburgh, on a royal tour of Nigeria in 1956.

Blue Trinity: The Queen Mother (center) on her eightieth birthday with her two daughters, the Queen (left) and Princess Margaret (right). The Royal Lodge, Windsor, August 4, 1980.

ABOVE: A Special Bond: Prince Charles and the Queen Mother at the Epsom Derby, June 1986.

Prince Philip watches polo with the twenty-two-year-old Penelope Eastwood (soon Lady Romsey), later his close sporting companion. Guards Polo Club, Windsor, June 1, 1975.

LEFT: The Queen—a crisp executive—reviews her daily "red box" government briefings with private secretary Sir Robert Fellowes aboard HMY **Britannia,** May 1991.

The Queen has always been happiest in the country, stalking deer and joining the shoot to pick up pheasants, 1995.

For sixty years, the Queen shared her love of breeding racehorses with her best male friend, "Porchey," seventh Earl of Carnarvon. Epsom Derby, June 8, 1978.

ABOVE: Camilla reaches the "winners' enclosure." Back row: Prince Harry, Prince William, Prince Charles, Camilla, Duchess of Cornwall, Tom and Laura Parker Bowles. Front row: Prince Philip, Queen Elizabeth II, Major Bruce Shand. Windsor Castle, April 9, 2005.

FACING PAGE, RIGHT: The One: Camilla's appeal to Charles was her husky voice and tousled country informality. Middlewick House, Wiltshire, 1992.

FACING PAGE, FAR RIGHT: The Brigadier: Sixty-three-year-old Andrew Parker Bowles OBE captured by his friend Lucian Freud. Painted between 2003 and 2004.

Prince Charles had been in hot pursuit of Camilla Parker Bowles since they met in 1971. Cirencester Park, July 1975.

ABOVE: Laughter and Companionship:
Prince Charles and the Duchess of Cornwall.
Mey Highland Games, Caithness, August 9, 2008.

TOP LEFT: Thirteen-year-old Prince Harry and Charles, South Africa, November 3, 1997.
TOP RIGHT: Diana with the two boys, November 1994.
2ND ROW, RIGHT: Diana with Harry, August 1, 1987.
2ND ROW, LEFT: With twelve-year-old William, her "little wise old man," July 2, 1994.

ABOVE: The nineteen-year-old pin-up Prince William before starting university in Scotland, September 22, 2001. LEFT: A shattered Cornet Harry Wales lands at RAF Brize Norton, March 1, 2008. RIGHT: The brothers embrace at the Invictus Games, September 11, 2014.

TOP RIGHT: Kate Middleton, hounded on her twenty-fifth birthday outside her Chelsea flat, January 9, 2007. 2ND ROW, LEFT: The boys' private secretary Jamie Lowther-Pinkerton and communications secretary Patrick "Paddy" Harverson, October 9, 2012. 2ND ROW, CENTER: Media mogul Rupert Murdoch and Rebekah Brooks—now CEO of Murdoch's News UK—who relentlessly pursued the royals when she ran **News of the World,** July 10, 2011. 2ND ROW, RIGHT: Diana's former butler Paul Burrell leaves the Old Bailey in triumph after his trial for theft collapsed, November 1, 2002.

First Love: Prince Harry with teenage dazzler Chelsy Davy. Cartier International Polo, Windsor, July 30, 2006.

Many thought the Prince would marry the aristocratic Cressida Bonas, but she wanted a different life. Wembley Arena, London, July 3, 2014.

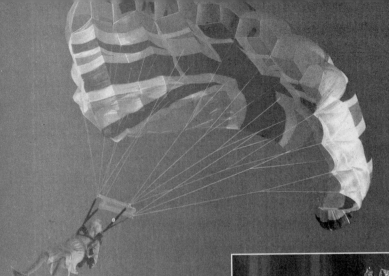

ABOVE: Inspired Madness: The pretend Queen parachutes over the Olympic Stadium after a video of the real Queen stepping into a helicopter with James Bond was played at the opening ceremony of the London Olympics, July 27, 2012.

RIGHT: Gloriana: HM leaves the 2006 State Opening of Parliament. Westminster, November 15, 2006.

Joyful Intimacy: Over their seventy-three-year marriage, Philip always knew how to make the Queen laugh. Braemar Gathering, Aberdeenshire, 2015.

aide would squeeze out the toothpaste on his tooth-brush and hold the urine bottle when a specimen was required.

Fawcett had to resign temporarily in 1998 after being accused of bullying, but was reinstated within a week—and promoted. He received so many free-bies discarded by Charles that he was nicknamed by staff "Fawcett the Fence."

Surrounded by enablers, Charles became oblivi-ous to domestic danger. The Pandora's box burst open with the sensational arrest of Princess Diana's former butler Paul Burrell. The cops were acting on a tip from Princess Margaret's butler Harold Brown, who had been collared after a tip-off to Scotland Yard. It concerned the fishy sale of a two-foot bejeweled silver-and-gold Arabian dhow, specially commissioned from Garrard, the Crown jeweler, as a wedding gift to Charles and Diana by the emir of Bahrain. Brown, described by **The Guardian** as an "archetypal Jeeves" who always dressed in a black coat and pinstripe trousers, had stuffed the dhow into a plastic bag and offloaded it to Spink and Son for £1,200. After he was apprehended and later cleared, Brown started singing about who had sup-plied it to him from Diana's household.

The arrest of Paul Burrell was a news bombshell. Until this moment, the public—and the Royal Family—had bought into the butler's self-promotion as Diana's "rock," her closest confidant, defender, and go-between in the last troubled years of her life at Kensington Palace. Often photographed two steps behind the Princess, he was the obsequious manservant who had supposedly displayed what the Royal household values most: absolute discretion. It was Burrell who rushed to Paris after the car crash and tenderly dressed Diana's body in an evening dress provided by the British ambassador's wife. He was one of the small circle who attended Diana's interment on the private island at Althorp. The Queen bestowed on him the Royal Victorian Medal. He was named a trustee for the Diana Memorial Fund and was given the job of sorting through her possessions.

On January 18, 2001, Scotland Yard officers showed up at Burrell's Cheshire home in a dawn raid and asked a simple question, "Do you have any items from Kensington Palace in this house?"

"No," Burrell replied.

A search of the house exposed him immediately. It was a royal Amazon warehouse stuffed with paintings, photos, drawings, and china belonging to the Princess of Wales. The police discovered two thousand negatives, including a photograph of Charles in the bath with his children, and many others showing the young princes naked. There was a trove of personal notes to and from William at school. In one, the Princess used her favorite nickname for him, writing, "My darling Wombat . . . It was lovely to catch a kiss and a hug from you this morning, even though I would like to run away with you." Even the mahogany desk Burrell was using was inscribed "Her Royal Highness."

Burrell's resolve didn't hold for long. He quickly

collapsed into a chair sobbing. He claimed everything was a gift from Diana, but was speechless when presented with a pencil sketch of Prince William as a baby. As Burrell only blubbered harder, Tom Bower reports, an officer shouted down from the attic, "It's full of boxes, wall to wall!" They were forced open to reveal a huge cache of Diana's underwear, blouses, suits, dresses, and nightgowns. The police loaded two thousand items thought to have been illegally removed from Kensington Palace into a truck. As another car took him to the police station, Burrell reportedly warbled, "I want white lilies on my coffin!"

Some significant items were missing from the Scotland Yard haul: the contents of a large mahogany box that Diana's sister Lady Sarah McCorquodale had alerted the cops to look out for. The stuff was potentially explosive—letters from Prince Philip offering marital advice to Diana, and secret tapes the Princess recorded of sensational revelations by a troubled former valet in Charles's household named George Smith, against Michael Fawcett. (Smith was a disturbed army veteran who suffered from nightmares and flashbacks to the bombing aboard RFA **Sir Galahad,** on which he served in the Falklands War.) After listening to his stories, the Princess, with Burrell at her side, apparently called Charles and urged him to fire Fawcett, saying, "This man is a monster." Charles refused, risking potentially incendiary charges of a cover-up if it came to light.

The possibility that all this dirty laundry could now

be aired sent the Prince of Wales into full panic mode. The more Charles thought about Burrell going public, the queasier he felt. Burrell had been privy to all the tawdry backstage dramas over Charles's subterfuge with Camilla, as well as to the assignations the Princess conducted before and after her divorce.

The butler had been in royal service forever. The son of a Derbyshire truck driver, Burrell had answered an ad in 1976 for the job of household footman at Buckingham Palace after completing a course in hotel management. Within a year, his combination of hard work, boyish charm, and sly sycophancy got him the job as the Queen's personal footman. He accompanied the sovereign and Philip on many royal tours. The Queen used to call him "Little Paul" to distinguish him from another taller footman, Paul Whybrew, known as "Tall Paul," who still serves the Queen. In 1987, Burrell and his wife, Maria, who worked as a housemaid for Prince Philip, agreed to move to the positions of butler and maid and dresser for the Waleses' household at Highgrove. After the marital separation in 1992, they left Highgrove at Diana's request, much to Maria's distress, to work exclusively for the Princess at Kensington Palace.

One of Burrell's more suspect assertions was that he had relayed to the Queen, in a three-hour private conversation in Buckingham Palace, his concern that Diana's sister Sarah was discarding some of Diana's possessions indiscriminately. He explained that he, Burrell, was taking some of the Princess's "papers" into safekeeping. The Queen, he said, had assented to his actions.

Whatever the excuse, Charles wanted the charges against Burrell dropped pronto. His private secretary Stephen Lamport confessed to a colleague that "the Prince of Wales is distraught. The prince will say he gave the things to him and that Burrell's actions were all right." The trouble was that the heir to the throne had no legal say in the issue. He wasn't an executor of his ex-wife's estate. Her mother and sister were the executors.

The Spencer women had long been suspicious of Burrell's maudlin and gaudy loyalty to Diana. They had become increasingly annoyed by the butler launching himself as a celebrity personality, guesting on TV shows, and showboating on the red carpet at the Oscars. He had made a mint out of his infallible devotion. His book **Entertaining with Style** had sold one hundred thousand copies. He was in furious demand as a speaker on cruise ships and wrote a weekly newspaper column on etiquette. "Burrell has chronic red-carpet fever and he will die from it" was the judgment of Diana's former personal protection officer Ken Wharfe.

Other members of the royal households felt similar disenchantment with Burrell. David Griffin told me that he had actually heard the butler on the phone to the press claiming that Diana had called him "my rock," ensuring it became his popular descriptor. Diana's loyal chauffeur Colin Tebbutt, who grieves to this day he was not driving her that last night in Paris, was long enraged at Burrell's claim that he had been the only person outside the family to attend Diana's burial at Althorp. Tebbutt, to whom Frances Shand Kydd was devoted, was also present at the graveside, but was determined to say so only after reading Burrell's claims. Even the butler's long marriage to Maria was a charade. He'd had so many affairs with guardsmen that Diana's chef called him "Barrack-Room Bertha." In 2016, Maria and Burrell finally divorced after thirty-two years, freeing him to marry lawyer Graham Cooper at a ceremony in the Lake District wearing a kilt.

Lady Sarah McCorquodale declared there was no way in hell Burrell would have been authorized to remove Diana's possessions, and explicitly remembered him saying, when offered some of her items, "I can't take anything. I have enough. All of her memories are in my heart." The Spencer women were pressing for his prosecution all the way. Their resolve was no doubt strengthened by the (untrue) rumor that Burrell had been photographed wearing one of Diana's dresses. The always outspoken Frances Shand Kydd proclaimed, "I hope his balls burn."

Sir Robin Janvrin, the Queen's private secretary, was alarmed when he was briefed on the matter by Scotland Yard and the Crown Prosecution Service lawyer. He said he would inform Her Majesty forthwith, but the Queen's response to her private secretary was to go into full ostrich mode. She said not a word. Having discharged his duty to inform,

Janvrin washed his hands of the matter. This was Charles's mess, and Janvrin had matters of state to attend to.

For the next twelve months, the Crown essentially waged a covert war against its own prosecution service. The Prince of Wales's legal team unsuccessfully tried every strategy to get the CPS to drop its case.

But the Burrell prosecution had developed its own unstoppable momentum. With its rich brew of butlers, footmen, crime, and royal embarrassment, it had become irresistible comic relief for the tabloids. Most of them, Palace bashers by instinct, preferred Burrell over Charles. Tabloid reporters had curried favor with the butler for years in the hopes of eliciting some royal dish. The **Daily Mail**'s Richard Kay named Burrell as godfather to one of his children. The **Daily Mirror**'s Piers Morgan believed Burrell was being targeted unfairly. In a diary entry on January 17, 2001, Morgan noted that "what's in [Burrell's] head is worth millions if he ever needed the money why would he need to steal anything?" He also saw the danger a trial represented to the Palace. "A cornered Burrell could be a very dangerous beast." The wounded butler was already making veiled threats. "I wish to emphasize I did not wish to break confidentiality," he said in a statement to the police. An exasperated Mark Bolland, trying to spin some positive press in the midst of all this, found himself reluctantly pulled in to broker a secret détente between the butler and the heir to the throne. Fortuitously, Charles fell off his horse playing polo and went to the hospital instead.

II

In August 2002, Charles was so frustrated with being frustrated that he replaced Stephen Lamport with a new, more formidable private secretary—Sir Michael Peat, fifty-two, an impeccably dressed, dome-headed, former KPMG accountant who was, by turns, iron-fisted and oleaginous. At Buckingham Palace, Peat had already been entrusted with such wide-ranging power that some referred to him as "The Bidet": "You know what it's called but you don't know what it's for." The Eton-and-Oxford-educated appa-ratchik had done wonders for Buckingham Palace's fiscal health in his role as the Queen's Keeper of the Privy Purse and Treasurer, and Receiver General of the Duchy of Lancaster. He enacted multiple bean-counting economies at the Palace and halved spending in the space of five years. It won him few friends. He weeded minor royals off the Civil List, bounced out retainers who were past their sell-by date—it was Peat whom David Griffin blamed for his own unceremonious treatment—and closed down the subsidized staff bar. On hearing every journey cost £35,000, he chopped the royal train. At the same time, he was deft at royal PR. It was Peat who persuaded the Queen to pay income tax on her private wealth. A statistic he wielded to good effect was that the Queen cost each of her subjects only fifty-eight pence a year.

Peat aced "the Camilla test" when the Prince sat him beside her at dinner. "Michael was charm itself," said a friend. "He is the only senior member of the Queen's household to properly acknowledge Mrs. Parker Bowles, and that means a lot to her and the Prince."

Her Majesty was undoubtedly happy to bequeath her most skilled courtier and hatchet man to her scattershot son. She knew Peat was equipped to clean up the Prince's household and negotiate a truce in the rivalrous backstabbing between the factions at St. James's and Buckingham Palace. Hopefully, he would also find a way to dispatch Mark Bolland, whom the Queen still distrusted. (Peat achieved this in four months. In December 2002, following an acrimonious phone call, Charles and Bolland mutually agreed that it was time for his skilled spinmeister to depart.)

One thing Peat could not achieve, however, was closing down the prosecution of Paul Burrell. In fact, he may have made things worse, alienating the police by patronizing them at their first meeting. He directed the senior officer on the case, Detective Chief Inspector Maxine de Brunner, to sit on a low chair so that he could look down on her and thereafter, in classic mansplaining malfeasance, directed all his questions to the male junior officer who accompanied her. Both officers were dismayed by the clear indication that Peat, like Charles and his legal team, seemed to forget Burrell was being charged for stealing property that belonged to Diana, not the Prince of Wales, and resented the implication they were supposed, nonetheless, to halt the prosecution.

Inexorably, the trial went ahead. By the time the devastated butler stood in the dock at the Old Bailey on October 14, 2002, his nerves were shredded and he was ashen in appearance. He was accused of stealing 310 items belonging to the late Princess of Wales's estate worth a total of £4.5 million. Other items were left out of the charges because they belonged to either the Prince of Wales or Prince William, neither of whom agreed to testify.

Bold-faced socialites had, in the days before, lined up to vouch for Burrell as Diana's rock. Two of the grandes dames who were likely to testify on his behalf were Lady Annabel Goldsmith, widow of billionaire Sir James Goldsmith, and Diana's close friend Lucia Flecha de Lima. Those summoned on behalf of the prosecution included Frances Shand Kydd, Lady Sarah McCorquodale, and Colin Tebbutt, who was to be called as a character witness. He never got the chance. Tebbutt still has the record of his unheard testimony in boxes at his house in Chichester.

At 8:30 A.M. on day eleven of the trial, something remarkable happened—which can only be described as an episode of magical realism in twenty-first-century Britain. The trial of Paul Burrell was halted by an intervention from the Queen herself. Crown Prosecutor William Boyce was reading his papers in a room adjacent to the court when he was suddenly joined by Commander John Yates of Scotland Yard. Yates told Boyce that he had just had a conversation with Sir Michael Peat, who said, "Her Majesty has had a recollection."

On the previous Friday, the Queen had by chance been driving past the Old Bailey with Prince Charles and Prince Philip on their way to a memorial service at St. Paul's Cathedral for the twenty-eight British victims of the terrorist bombings in Bali. Noticing a crowd outside the courts, Her Majesty asked Charles about it. He told her that Paul Burrell was on trial for theft, and the Queen apparently had no idea. When all was explained to the best-informed monarch in the world, she recalled a meeting five years earlier, soon after Diana's death, when Burrell had sought an audience with her to explain that he was caring for some of Diana's "papers."

The nation's jaw dropped when this revelation became public. Set aside the fact that the Queen reads the newspapers religiously every day and that screaming headlines about Burrell had been adorning them for months. Set aside also the fact that she had been briefed by Sir Robin Janvrin the previous year, and that this incidental car ride was the first time that the three senior royals had discussed the intimately embarrassing prospects of a Burrell trial, and set aside, too, that the sheer size of the butler's trophy haul hardly correlated to taking care of a few discreet boxes of Diana's "papers."

None of this mattered. The issue of dishonorable intent was at the heart of the prosecution case against Burrell. Now the court would be told the Queen had known all about it in advance. **The Guardian** summarized that the Queen was the "star non-witness in Regina v Burrell. If she knew, then it wasn't theft.

Ergo, Mr Burrell couldn't have stolen anything at all." As usual, when it came to her family, the Queen had avoided the problem for as long as she could and then executed a lethal coup de grâce.

The Spencer family was outraged. Frances Shand Kydd believed the Queen had sat back until this late hour and then allowed them to be humiliated in court. The only word from the House of Windsor had been spoken behind Palace doors, further straining the combustible relationship between the two families.

Crown Prosecutor William Boyce was known to be one of the least emotive members of the British bar. His courtroom speeches had once been compared to "being hit on the head with a dead fish," but the news Commander Yates delivered astonished him so much he went visibly pale and removed his wig. It would now be his task to deliver the official version of his mortification to a gobsmacked court:

> Because the Queen's personal property was not involved and because of concerns to avoid any suggestion that Buckingham Palace was trying to interfere with the investigation of this case, the Queen was not briefed on the way in which the case against Mr Burrell was being prepared.
>
> Therefore Her Majesty had no means of knowing until after the trial had started of the relevance to the prosecution of the fact that Mr Burrell had mentioned to her that he had taken items for safe keeping.

Following further clarification with the Queen, steps were taken to bring the information to the attention of the police.

One Whitehall observer said, "Only a golden bullet could have stopped the trial. And they invented it." The trial was over. As Burrell walked out of the courthouse, he crowed to reporters, "The Queen came through for me." It boggles the mind that after halting the trial the Palace failed to lock Burrell down into legally binding silence. The triumphant butler still had in his quiver all the information he was going to use on the stand with no constraints on selling it to the papers. He promptly hired the celebrity agent Dave Warwick, who conducted a frenzied bidding war for Burrell's story. It sold to the **Mirror** in a deal worth up to £300,000, a major coup for Piers Morgan, who stole it out from under the nose of the **Daily Mail**.

No PR offensive could rectify the reputational damage to the Prince of Wales. An avalanche of sleaze poured forth. Publicist Max Clifford somehow obtained Burrell's entire salacious statement and proof of evidence, including explicit details of Diana's relationships with her many lovers, including Hasnat Khan, who had been smuggled into Kensington Palace to see her under a blanket in the trunk of a car. Burrell described canceling Diana's official plans so the two could stay in bed together. He also offered damning revelations about Charles, including how he would sneer at Diana's outfits and call her an "air stewardess." The **News of the World** splashed all the details, leading with the revelation that Diana had seduced Khan wearing only sapphire-and-diamond earrings and her fur coat. Burrell then twisted the knife even further, describing to the **Mirror** how cold the Spencers were. "The Spencers found Diana unacceptable in life. . . . Isn't it ironic how she suddenly became acceptable in death?" he said. "I, for one, would never have paraded her life before a museum and charged £10.50 a time."

On a roll, Burrell flew to America to tell his secrets to the major networks. Even George Smith, the rehabbed valet, went public with his story in **The Mail on Sunday,** and Michael Fawcett won an injunction on October 31, 2003, to keep his name out of it. Eleven days later, **The Guardian** succeeded in getting the injunction lifted. The worst had happened. The royals had lost all control.

Burrell's book **A Royal Duty** was published with a ten-day **Mirror** serialization. It began with a melodramatic letter Diana wrote that stated she feared she would be killed in a car crash, creating explosive headlines all over the world.

The Prince of Wales was once again mired in the kind of lurid revelations and rumors that he had tried to combat for so long. In a BBC Radio 4 poll, listeners were asked which Brit they most wanted to deport. Charles came in fourth. At a dinner party, he reportedly smashed a plate on the floor in anger. The Palace's handling of the Burrell case, Mark Bolland said in a subsequent interview with **The Guardian,** was "a complete fuck-up that should never have happened." Sharpening his words against Prince Charles in particular, Bolland remarked that the Prince of Wales "should have done more to stop it. But he's not a terribly strong person. . . . He lacks a lot of confidence." (To add insult to injury, in 2003 Bolland took to writing a regular column for **News of the World,** a weekly thorn in Prince Charles's side. It was unsettling, to say the least, to have his former trusted aide spinning not for but against him.)

In November 2002, the Prince made a last attempt to clean things up by commissioning Sir Michael Peat to oversee an inquiry into the misconduct in his own household and determine whether the trial of Burrell was improperly terminated. Unsurprisingly, the report came up clear, but the 112-page document made embarrassing reading for Charles, chronicling a litany of sloppy record keeping, lax administration, and bureaucratic foul-ups under his management as well as the practice of staff flouting rules for accepting gifts from royal suppliers. Nineteen of 180 official gifts to the Prince had gone missing.

Fawcett was found to have broken regulations by accepting thousands of pounds' worth of freebies from suppliers. He resigned but, in true Clarence House form, was immediately rehired to complete freelance work for the Prince under the guise of a new Fawcett event planning agency. The report ducked the issue of whether George Smith's allegations against Fawcett were true, but underscored that the valet was a troubled fantasist. The unfortunate valet died in

2005, at the age of forty-four, after a descent into depression and alcoholism.

Charles loyalist Tiggy Legge-Bourke said she believed Fawcett's bullying tactics had hampered Peat's inquiry. She and six others had complained to Prince Charles about Fawcett at the time, but had refused to cooperate fully with the Peat inquiry for fear of retaliation by Fawcett. "None came forward because no one could guarantee Michael would go," she told **The Mail on Sunday** in 2005. "He resigned, then . . . he was back. Everybody was concerned that if you spoke out against him, he could get rid of you."

Sure enough, Fawcett received, along with his £500,000 payoff and the right to remain in his grace-and-favor home, £100,000 a year's worth of guaranteed work with the Prince of Wales. According to **The Mail on Sunday,** he received at least £120,000 a year for organizing Charles's social diary (paid through his company Premier Mode Events); £50,000 as a fundraiser for the Prince's Foundation; £40,000 as an "internal decoration consultant"; £25,000 to "administer the Prince's watercolours"; £20,000 for buying gifts on behalf of the Prince; and an honorary role as the "creative director" of Charles's businesses at Highgrove. By June 2003, he was choreographing Prince William's twenty-first birthday party at Windsor Castle and, in 2006, had the even greater honor of organizing the Queen's eightieth birthday party at Kew Palace.

As reported in **The New York Times:**

Sir Michael Peat said he anticipated charges that his report was a whitewash, but he argued that it disclosed "serious failures" in royal practices and would result in significant reforms: "I am not going to make any excuses. . . . Things have not been well handled in this office. The Prince of Wales has said that he wants everything to be sorted out—he wants his office run to the highest possible standards."

When the report was released, the Prince of Wales was on a tour of Bulgaria, a comfortable distance from the British press—and from any judgment by his mother. And with that, most of the ignominy of the Burrell affair was swept under the Aubusson rugs of St. James's Palace. An official of the Royal Warrant Holders Association said, "Michael Peat did his best to sort out the vipers' nest but failed."

Burrell went on to build a lucrative career as royal commentator and reality show contestant in the United States with a "royal" range of furniture, crockery, and silverware. He lost his popularity in the UK only after **The Sun** published the transcript of an undercover tape in 2008, at the time of Diana's inquest. In response to the paper challenging him about the prosecution's shredding of his credibility on the witness stand, the butler magisterially replied, "Quite frankly, Britain can fuck off."

Charles, ineluctably, remained in Fawcett's thrall. In 2018, Fawcett was named chief executive of the Prince's Foundation, Charles's charity umbrella.

Sleaze followed the troublesome aide yet again. In 2021, questions were raised about Fawcett having put in the fix for a Saudi billionaire to receive an honorary CBE in return for donations totaling £1.5 million, a cash-for-access scandal that Charles maintains he knew nothing about but which drew his charity into an embarrassing investigation by the Metropolitan Police. After Fawcett temporarily stepped down—yet again—in September 2021, Camilla is said to have been determined that this time he wasn't coming back. "She will be merciless in her pursuit of Michael out the door," a source told **The Times.** Fawcett finally bit the dust as the Prince of Wales's alter ego in November 2021. For how long is anybody's guess.

CHAPTER
9

CAMILLA'S LINE
IN THE SAND

___

A New Duchess in the
Winners' Enclosure

___

Mrs. Parker Bowles was restive. By the spring of 2004, she had been divorced from Andrew for nine years, and the sainted sylph Diana had been dead and buried for six. Camilla and Charles were now ensconced much of the time at Clarence House, where Camilla had her own suite of rooms. Charles had renovated the nineteenth-century John Nash–designed jewel with punctilious historic perfection.

When the Prince traveled, Camilla made festive escapes from royal dullness to Ray Mill House, her rambling Wiltshire bolt-hole less than half an hour from Highgrove. She had refused to give it up, for here at least she could loll around, eat peas straight from the garden, enjoy a cigarette without furtively smoking up the chimney as she did when Charles was around, and have raucous dinners in the kitchen with her now-adult kids.

Life had greatly improved since the wilderness years, but she also felt marooned. Despite all the finagling and finessing of Mark Bolland, who had now been gone for over a year, all the patient maneuvering into royal acceptance that seemed to be gathering steam after the death of the Queen Mother and the Golden Jubilee, all her sweet-talking of a succession of private secretaries to the Queen and the Prince of Wales, all the careful overtures to the still guarded Prince William and an outright sullen Prince Harry, there was always some fresh debacle not of her making that drove her underground again.

Being the unofficial consort of the Prince of Wales was a heavy lift. Upbeat encouragement had always been her mistress role. In the thirty-three years they had known each other, she had never said a public word about their relationship. She acknowledged the nuances of royal etiquette even after so long together as a couple—she always referred to her paramour as "the Prince," not "Charles" when they hosted dinners at Highgrove and "Sir" when she addressed him in public. She was the horse whisperer of his emotional needs, and knew how to dispense tough love with charm. A son of one of the Queen's friends told me, "Camilla stops the pompous thing with Charles. She won't let him get away with telling his man to get his gin and tonic. She says, 'Oh don't be so ridiculous. Let me pour the gin and tonic.'"

If Camilla had a family motto, it would be "Thou Shalt Not Whine." That was not always easy when it came to supporting her royal partner. One of her challenges was to sustain Charles through his Diana PTSD. "I remember in the early days of working for Charles, we would have these three-way dinners with Camilla," Mark Bolland told me in 2005 when I spoke to him for **The Diana Chronicles:**

> Charles would go on and on about Diana and how she spun the press. I would say, "We have to move on, sir," and he said, "To understand me, Mark, you have to hear this." And Camilla would say to me afterwards, "He needs to do this, Mark."

On occasion, Bolland had tried to suggest some gracious way for the Prince to acknowledge Diana's legacy, but Charles always punted him to Camilla. "I'm not the block here," she said. "Forget about trying to make him do it. He still has too much pain and anger. It's too great."

Over time, Charles's self-pitying paranoia about never being appreciated enough was a serious bore to all. He moaned endlessly about being undervalued by his mother, the nation, and the press. He complained his life was unbearable when his office was the wrong temperature. In 2004, he reportedly said, "Nobody knows what utter hell it is to be Prince of Wales." It was not endearing coming from a multi-millionaire monarch-in-waiting with a brace of stately homes on tap. The aftermath of Labour Party spin doctor Peter Mandelson's visit to Highgrove in 1997, when he told Charles that British ministers sometimes found him "rather glum and dispirited," was pure panic. The Prince was so unused to hearing the truth that he asked Camilla afterward in a tortured tone, "Is that true? Is that true?" Camilla crisply replied, "I don't think any of us can cope with you asking that question over and over again for the next month."

The Prince was not wrong that his many accomplishments were rarely acknowledged. Despite the excruciating public spectacle certain parts of his life had become, he had succeeded in transforming the nine hundred acres surrounding Highgrove into an early model of sustainable farming, ignoring those who ridiculed him as an heirhead who wasted his time talking to plants. Decades before organic was cool, he had the vision to convert Home Farm completely to that eco-philosophy. The use of pesticides was banned, and visitors were greeted with the words: "Warning: You are now entering a GMO-free zone." A source of princely pride was the preservation of the gene pool of rare breeds, such as Tamworth pigs and Irish Moiled cattle. And he was entrepreneurial with his farming innovations. In 1990, the Highgrove House estate began producing a surprisingly successful line of organic products, which the Prince called Duchy Originals. (At his seventieth birthday party in 2018, the Queen toasted her son for being "in every respect a duchy original.") Since 2009, thanks to a licensing and distribution agreement with the grocery chain Waitrose, which came to the rescue after the 2008 economic crisis, Duchy Originals (now rebranded as Waitrose Duchy Organic) has raised over £30 million for the Prince of Wales's Charitable Fund. In his own idiosyncratic way, Charles proved to have a flair for sustainable business.

The Prince made other efforts to combine enterprise with his environmental passions. In the late eighties, he donated Duchy of Cornwall land in Dorset to build the experimental village Poundbury. The plan reflected his retro-architectural vision of what British rural life should be—low-rise streetscapes built to human scale in an integrated community of shops, businesses, and residences, a third of them affordable housing. Yawns ensued, and ridicule abounded of Poundbury as a feudal Disneyland, a "Toy Town," and a "retro-kitsch fantasia." But over the years, it blossomed into a buoyant three-thousand-strong community. In 2005, the Prince gave a tour to **60 Minutes,** pointing out the convenience store and noting that he is "very proud of it [as] everybody said [it] wouldn't work," and the pub, which "again, nobody wanted to touch." In his usual doleful vein, he added, "I only hope that, when I'm dead and gone, [the British people] might appreciate it a little bit more." In 2012, Poundbury touted its first full-scale anaerobic digester, which turns food waste and maize from surrounding farms into local, renewable, sustainable energy. It generated about as much excited press coverage as one might expect.

Charles was correct in feeling that the prescience of his much-mocked "hobby horses" was validated again and again. After all, he was only twenty-one

when he made his first landmark speech at the
"Countryside in 1970" conference about the "horri-
fying effects of pollution in all its cancerous forms."

In 2018, when he was served an iced coffee at an
Athens café during a visit to Greece, he made headlines for declining a plastic straw while pointing out
that plastic is bad for the environment. Reporters
made no mention of the fact that Charles had first
spoken out about the threat of plastic to the environment way back in 1970 and was largely ignored.

Charles was bold on other topics. In 1993, eight
years before 9/11, he gave an impassioned address
to the Oxford Centre for Islamic Studies about
the need for a greater understanding of Islam by the
West, expressing outrage about the decimation of
the Marsh Arabs of southern Iraq. Reading the
speeches today, one can tell that they are clearly
mostly his own work, full of characteristic Eeyore
asides and self-deprecating statements. It's hard to
imagine either of his sons embracing such a miscel-
lany of offbeat causes.

Nowhere did Charles feel less appreciated than in
the work of his charities for youth advancement. The
Prince's Trust developed significant heft over time.
Perhaps because Charles himself felt so aimless in his
post-naval years, he made the trust's philanthropic
focus kids whom everyone else had written off: the
homeless and those with arrest records or drug hab-
its, or who lived on the dole and never saw themselves
leaving it. At the time the charity was launched,
there was little interest in seventeen-year-olds who

failed at school. Charles felt a genuine affinity for them and wanted to help.

The actor Idris Elba, who grew up on a council estate in Hackney, has thanked the trust for giving him the audition—and £1,500—he needed to launch his career. In a recent tally, the Prince's Trust has helped more than eighty-six thousand young people start a small business.

Why wasn't Charles more celebrated for his strenuous progressivism, and for his demonstrably humane labors? Ironically, he cared about many of the things the liberal bible **The Guardian** espoused, and to which the Murdoch press was instinctively hostile. But as the heir to the throne, he was hardly going to become a poster boy for liberal causes, especially given his cranky dislike of anything that smacked of lefty cultural dogma. As Prime Minister Tony Blair put it: "He was a curious mixture of the traditional and the radical (at one level he was quite New Labour; at another, definitely not), and of the princely and the insecure."

His lack of appropriate royal caution was sometimes admirable, and principled. While Blair was trying to court improved relations with China, Charles pointedly hosted an evening reception at St. James's Palace for the Dalai Lama, in order to express his keen support of Tibet. He harbored deep reservations about the war in Iraq and its effect on Anglo-Islamic relations, but, in that instance, his opposition was probably based on the wrong reasoning: his cozy, fundraising relationships with the Gulf kingdoms.

What caused him the greatest despair was the
never-ending industry of Diana books, documentaries, and tabloid takeouts that kept his negative
image alive. It was understandably frustrating, but
he also invited avoidable ridicule. Consumed by what
he thought were the burdens of his office, he was
frequently clueless about how distorted his worldview was. After a visit to India in October 2003, he
offered as an inspiring example of livability "the
shanty town slum in Bombay" where a population
of close to a million lived with only one fetid bathroom for every fifteen hundred residents on teeming
acreage half the size of the Highgrove estate. His
hopelessly retro style of delivery made it an insur-
mountable challenge to connect with modern
audiences. As Ken Wharfe told me in 2006:

> The trouble with Prince Charles is he's not like
> the rest of us, is he? The other day he was on the
> news in a suit, cloth cap, and polished green
> Wellies on the Duchy of Cornwall estate talk-
> ing about the marvels of organic farming. He
> said in that voice [of his], "What drives me
> mad of course is the way supermarkets today
> dispatch carrots. When I was a child I remem-
> ber wibbly-wobbly carrots."

A window into his loopy perspective was revealed
in an unfair dismissal tribunal involving Elaine Day,
a former personal assistant at Clarence House. In
March 2002, she happened to see what Charles

wrote about her in one of his intemperate annotations of an office memo. "What is wrong with people nowadays?" Charles scrawled in the margins about Day. (She'd had the temerity to suggest that assistants should have the opportunity to train for senior roles in the household.) The memo continued:

Why do they all seem to think they are qualified to do things far above their capabilities? This is all to do with the learning culture in schools. It is a consequence of a child-centred education system which tells people they can become pop stars, high court judges or brilliant TV presenters or infinitely more competent heads of state without ever putting in the necessary work or having the natural ability. It is a result of social utopianism which believes humanity can be genetically engineered to contradict the lessons of history.

Given that the author of this statement holds the rank of Admiral of the Fleet in the Royal Navy, Field Marshal in the British Army, and Marshal of the Royal Air Force without ever having served a day in combat and felt qualified to opine on architectural design and the intellectual product of every ministry in Whitehall without even an undergraduate degree from the Royal Institute of British Architects or an apprenticeship in the civil service, it's not surprising his comments were poorly received by the British media. The memo concluded: "What on earth am I

to say to Elaine? She is so PC it frightens me rigid."
Day lost her case, but inevitably won the PR war.

For a future king who was supposed to be neutral
on matters of public policy, Charles generated unnecessary grief for himself when he used his bully
pulpit to sabotage reputations. In 1984, while at a
gala marking the 150th anniversary of the Royal
Institute of British Architects, he called architectural
plans for an extension to the National Gallery in
Trafalgar Square "a monstrous carbuncle on the face
of a much-loved and elegant friend." The design by
Ahrends, Burton and Koralek was in all fairness
deemed authentically hideous by many less willing
to be candid than Charles. Patrick Jenkin, then Tory
secretary of state for the environment, who was present while Charles delivered these notorious remarks,
muttered that Charles's speech "saved [him] from
making a difficult decision." The "carbuncle" design
was rejected, and forever seen as the index of how
ruthless the Prince could be when his sensibilities
were offended.

Desperate for influence, stature, and attention as
he waited (and waited) for his mother to move on,
Charles poured forth a blizzard of opinionated
suggestions and complaints to Tony Blair and his
ministers. The Guardian got hold of a juicy batch
from 2004 and 2005 with a Freedom of Information
suit. Charles's letters became known as the "black
spider" memos because of the Prince's sprawling
comments, handwritten in black fountain pen.
Topics ranged from his dislike of the Human

Rights Act 1998 and the "degree to which our lives are becoming ruled by a truly absurd degree of politically correct interference," to governmental neglect of rural England and the lack of resources for the armed forces in Iraq—particularly the "poor performance" of the Lynx helicopter.

Blair and his ministers received letter bombs pushing for a cull of Britain's badgers and a protest about the illegal fishing of the Patagonian toothfish. In one letter of April 2002, which his advisers apparently begged him not to send (and would surely have got him "canceled" today), he associated himself with the views of a Cumbrian farmer who asserted, "If we, as a group, were black or gay, we would not be victimised or picked on."

Just as often, though, the tone was more that of an inflamed curmudgeon who fires off "strongly worded" remonstrations from his armchair in the shires to the **Telegraph** letters page. In February 2005, when raising concerns about the future of hospital sites in a note to John Reid, MP, secretary of state for health, the Prince had at least enough self-awareness to acknowledge that he was at "the risk of being a complete bore."

What is interesting and paradoxical about Charles is that there were also times when he was more in touch with subterranean British feeling than either the media or politicians, times when he was not wrong in essence, even if irritating—and profoundly fogeyish—in expression. Many of his blasts to politicians picked up accurately on the growing resentment felt in rural regions toward urban multiculturalism and Whitehall condescension, a widening divide that contributed to the Brexit vote in 2016.

The Blair government's pledge to ban foxhunting in England and Wales was one of the most inflammatory of such issues. It came to epitomize to country dwellers the liberal elite's insular misunderstanding of rural values. Charles strenuously lobbied Blair to drop what he considered an assault on tradition, explaining that hunting is "environmentally friendly" and "relies entirely on man's ancient and, indeed, romantic relationship with dogs and horses." Hunting was not, he endeavored to explain, what so many townies imagined: an activity dominated by toffs who rejoiced in tearing a terrified animal limb from limb (although there were, to be sure, plenty of them enamored with the chase). Hunt supporters insisted that the sport forged bonds between the village community, the landowner, and the farmer. Men and women saddled up in the same spot for generations amongst their neighbors, who all saw the culling of foxes as an environmental necessity. I glimpsed this myself when the **Daily Mail** sent me to Gloucestershire in 1983 to write a slasher piece about snobs on horseback. I didn't find any. "Mostly the people hunting were relaxed, courteous country people, not all aristos by any means," I wrote, surveying the motley turn-out of farmers, publicans, local doctors, and country squires.

The men were gallant, raising their hats at the slightest provocation, the women dignified and strong. Their hunting-speak wafted back to me as they paused to pat their steeds. "I've just come back from the Quorn. Frightful country." "So difficult. It was nose to brush all the way."

This pro-hunting view, of course, was entirely at odds with the urban sensibilities of the reformers, making the foxhunting ban the most elemental sort of culture war.

For Blair, the hunting topic was too radioactive with the Labour Party's class warfare and animal rights activism to drop the ban. He had thrown it as a bone to appease his troublesome left wing and, as the controversy raged on, he came to have more important decisions to defend, such as the Iraq War. For some reason, many pro-hunting campaigners blamed the ban on Cherie Blair, who had always been identifiably more left of center than her husband. In September 2004, several hundred pro-hunt campaigners blocked the roads against guests trying to get to her fiftieth birthday party at Chequers, one of them wearing nothing but a Tony Blair mask and a strategically placed placard. "To be honest, I was never that interested in the hunting ban despite what they all thought," she told me in 2020. "I'm perfectly happy if they kill a whole herd of foxes if you ask me. I don't even like animals."

In his memoir, Blair revealed that the Hunting

Act that finally passed in 2004 was "one of the domestic legislative measures I most regret" and confessed he was "ignorant about the sport" when he made the "rash undertaking" to agree to a ban. Blair claims he became more desperate to avoid a ban as he learned more about the sport. "Prince Charles truly knew the farming community and felt we didn't understand it, in which there was an element of truth," he wrote.

II

Ironically, it was this issue—a subject on which Charles and Camilla (and the entire Royal Family, including William and Harry, who hunted with the Beaufort) were at one in their private opposition— that was the cause of a rare blow-up between the otherwise harmonious couple.

Camilla was passionate about joining her father (who had been joint master of the Southdown foxhounds), her sister, and their friends at the Countryside Alliance's Liberty and Livelihood March through central London in September 2002. Charles told her it was out of the question because it would be "seen as a direct and unacceptable attack on Tony Blair's government." Camilla strongly resisted. "He has had to put his foot down," a friend told **The Times.**

She finally gave in, but defiantly put a pro– Countryside Alliance sticker on her car. Her resentment only increased when the march turned out to be an epic expression of rural rage with four hundred thousand people busing in from the shires to protest the ban, something she would dearly loved to have been a part of. It was the Dance of the Decades all over again, in gumboots.

The ambivalence of Camilla's position was becoming untenable to her. For a while, she had thought that there was an upside to not being Charles's wife. She had always hated flying, speaking in public, dressing up, and getting press attention. She had never had a calendar filled with things she didn't want to do, which essentially defines the royal way of life.

Camilla was naturally good at the things she was required to be good at—the small talk, the charming of dignitaries and donors, the understanding of the royal milieu and its modes—but she had started to resent the curtailment of freedoms without the dignity of being Charles's official consort. For a woman used to running her own domestic show for decades while her military husband served overseas or in London, she found it disheartening, I am told, to be a permanent guest in Charles's multiple grand houses with lugubrious eavesdropping servants always loitering around.

There wasn't even the fun of being a chatelaine who could decorate the way she wanted, as Charles and Michael Fawcett were the fastidious taste barons who supervised every aesthetic detail. She found Highgrove irritatingly perfect. "It's too small

and too Charles," she told her friends. "I can't touch
a thing." When interior designer Dudley Poplak,
who decorated Kensington Palace and Highgrove
for Charles and Diana in airy color schemes, strolled
round Highgrove after their separation, he noted
how Charles's taste had returned to his childhood.
"You can see this is an old man's room now," he
said, surveying the new dark red window hangings
and tapestry-covered sofa. "The Prince is withdrawing into the womb. It's just like one of those rooms
at Sandringham." Two of his other homes, Birkhall
and Castle of Mey, still felt like shrines to the Queen
Mother. Camilla especially hated the heavy, moth-
eaten tartan curtains at Birkhall that Charles refused
to change because they were his grandmother's favorite.

The Prince's routine was relentless. He never ate
lunch, and breakfasted on the same bird seed and
peeled fruit every morning. Punctuality had never
been Camilla's strong suit, but Charles expected her
to be ready for engagements at his own regimented
pace. When she asked where they were going, he
would snap, "Haven't you read the brief?" (After she
joined the Firm, the military tempo and flying, often
in helicopters, which she hated, were not an option
she could refuse.)

Anecdotes about how she was faring leaked to the
press, and she began to feel she couldn't trust people.
She resented policemen and security personnel who
were not her chosen friends, gossiping about her unkempt appearance out of the public eye. "Camilla is

nervy and lacks stamina; she has never worked in her life and is terrified of being on public display," Mark Bolland wrote in **The Times** in April 2005.

One of her friends at that time told me that she had even started to feel some empathy with Diana's manifold discontents.

When the Queen sent Sir Michael Peat over to clean up the chaos of Charles's household in 2002, his brief from the top, despite the good omens of acceptance at the jubilee, was to push back on Camilla's ascendance. "His instructions were to sever Charles's relationship with Mrs. Parker Bowles because it was a mess and was detracting from his work," the well-wired Penny Junor reports.

This is certainly how the people in St James's Palace who worked with Peat during those first months viewed the situation. . . . For a man who would one day lead the Church of England, this was an awkward situation at best. She had to go.

As reported by **The Independent**, Peat prevented Camilla from going with Prince Charles on an official trip to India and scaled back her public appearances with him. He kept her out of Charles's crucial diary meetings. A piece in **Hello!** magazine claimed that Camilla and her family had started to refer to Peat as "The Enemy"—the term that Diana used about the Prince's previous private secretary. In May 2004, Clarence House had to deny reports that

Camilla was "being frozen out of royal life by unnamed courtiers." The intervention came after
reports that "only if Camilla were sidelined could
the Prince of Wales regain popularity after the Paul
Burrell affair and implausible claims that Diana,
Princess of Wales, was murdered."

Peat, however, was nothing if not pragmatic. After
observing the strength of Charles and Camilla's relationship, he realized that trying to obstruct it was a
futile exercise. He began to advocate the reverse to
the Palace and his boss: Charles should marry her
and be done with it. A "trusted royal courtier," who
sounds very much like Peat, would tell **The Times**
only nine months later:

> The Prince will become the Supreme Governor
> of the Established Church and Defender of the
> Faith when he becomes King. We would want
> to avoid the succession being overshadowed by
> any controversy over whether the new King
> should marry his long-time love.

Peat was backed up in his marriage zeal by Charles's
new communications secretary, Paddy Harverson,
who was also put in charge of representing the young
princes. Harverson was an inspired choice for the
role, the definition of a breath of fresh air—six foot
five, confident, modern, easygoing, but a robust defender of a client in trouble. He put the days of faxed
press releases to rest by launching a Clarence House
Twitter account, holding press briefings, and going

on television as the charming, ask-me-anything spokesman for all things the old-guard Buckingham Palace team had never deemed proper to do. He defined the communications role simply as promote and protect.

Harverson had a strong press background as a former **Financial Times** journalist, and three years' experience as communications director at Manchester United Football Club. Peat asked him to meet for a vacancy that had come up at Clarence House. There was a view that more employees were needed from the private sector. Harverson thought the job was an unlikely fit, but he liked Peat (who ingratiatingly described himself as a football fan). As he thought about the challenge of becoming the image maker of Prince Charles and the boys, he realized that his work at Manchester United was a useful qualification. The Palace, much like England's premier football club, was a global institution at the heart of English life with young celebrity players: Prince William, twenty-one, finishing university, and Prince Harry, nineteen, who had just left Eton. The protections provided by the Press Complaints Commission's Code of Practice were soon to fall away. He was keen to show the boys they had someone on their side.

Catching sight of William at a Westminster Abbey service marking the fiftieth anniversary of the Queen's coronation, Sir Roy Strong noted in his diary that "Prince William could become the new David Beckham, a real pin-up, fresh and sweet-natured and shy." No one would be better at representing the new

David Beckham than Harverson, who had represented the real one. He quickly passed the Camilla
test over tea. "I thought she was fantastic," he said.
Unfrightened by all the stuffiness and drama of the
past, he saw that her dynamic with Charles could be
an asset to how the media portrayed the Prince: "It
was most noticeable on overseas tours, he looked
lonely. Yet you would see them privately and they
were fantastic together—funny—and she was so
good for him, you could tell."

With Peat urging Charles to make Camilla official, the Prince, in his usual tormented fashion,
dithered about what it would do to his popularity.
In May 2004, the liberated Mark Bolland gave a
mischievous interview to **The Times** in which he
said that Charles had missed the boat to marry
Camilla: "I think there was a window within the
year or so after the Queen Mother died . . . when all
the indications of opinion were in the right place. I
don't think it is like that now. He is more cloaked in
controversy." He said that Charles, despite his longing to be with Camilla, had long been wary about
being pushed into marriage:

> Every now and then newspapers would run a
> poll about whether they should get married and
> a couple of editors said we should start a cam-
> paign. . . . He would always say, "Just please do
> everything you can to stop them doing that. I
> don't want to be pushed into a corner. I will
> know if the time is right."

The gossip columns started to imply that Charles's interest in Camilla was waning. There were lots of winking references to the oft-quoted Jimmy Goldsmith aphorism that "when you marry your mistress, you create a job vacancy."

Happily for Camilla, the former Archbishop of Canterbury and royal sycophant George Carey weighed in a month later with a more soothing news-break. "He is the heir to the throne and he loves her," Carey told **The Times.**

The natural thing is that they should get married. . . . The Christian faith is all about for-giveness. We all make mistakes. Failure is part of the human condition and there is no doubt that there has been a strong loving relationship, prob-ably since they were very young, that has endured over the years.

Other clerics started to join a chorus of approval. Behind the scenes, Michael Peat was in overdrive, squaring the finer points of church and constitution.

III

Ultimately, it was not august canonical opinions, but an infuriating social incident in November 2004 that pushed Charles across the matrimonial finish line. The twenty-nine-year-old son of one of Charles's closest friends, a Norfolk landowner and horse breeder named Hugh van Cutsem, and his socially ambitious Dutch wife, Emilie, was getting married to the Duke of Westminster's daughter at Chester Cathedral. Edward van Cutsem, the groom, had been a page boy at Charles and Diana's wedding. He was the Prince of Wales's godson, and it was all set to be the society wedding of the year. A guest list of 650 included the Queen and Prince Philip, Charles and Camilla, and William and Harry. The two princes were close friends with all the van Cutsem boys and would be serving as ushers.

Charles and Camilla were apprised of the seating plans the weekend before the wedding. The arrangements revealed Mrs. Parker Bowles to be relegated to the social margins of the event.

She had been expecting to sit directly behind Charles, who, protocol demanded, would join the Queen and Prince Philip at the front, but no, that "Dutch cow" (as Camilla reportedly called Emilie van Cutsem) had stuck Camilla on the other side of the cathedral with the bride's friends at the back and told her that she could not enter or leave by the main door.

"The trouble is Charles wasn't really focusing on all the details of the wedding," a courtier told a reporter at the **Daily Mail**. "I think it was William who alerted him to what was going on. And it sent Camilla over the edge. The Prince has been muttering that this would never have happened if Michael [Fawcett] was still here."

What made the snub especially explosive was

that there was already bad blood between Camilla and the van Cutsems. Camilla was outraged when they informed Charles that they believed her son, Tom, a known drug user, was a bad influence over William and Harry. The van Cutsems believed that Bolland was retaliating by spinning against their own sons and brought lawyers into the row until an uneasy truce was declared. (Not enough of a truce, however, to restore Hugh to the guest list of the Prince's shooting parties or either of the van Cutsems to be a recipient of the annual Clarence House Christmas card.)

Claiming a strict allegiance to royal protocol, Emilie van Cutsem resisted Charles's demands to upgrade Camilla's seat in the cathedral at their son's wedding. Hugh was a stuffed shirt whom Princess Diana always considered "heavy furniture" when she drew him as a dinner partner. Dislike of Emilie, the haughty daughter of an Amsterdam banker, was one of the few judgments that Camilla and Diana shared. A point in her disfavor was that she was one of six female confidantes to whom Charles gave a special brooch when he married Diana, suggesting a closeness neither wife nor mistress liked.

Camilla refused to be understanding this time. She would not be humiliated in front of all of Charles's snotty circle and, more important, the Royal Family. The Prince had to choose between attending the wedding without her or snubbing his closest friends and his godson. **Basta!** It was Camilla's line in the sand.

Fortunately, there is always an exit if you are the Prince of Wales.

On the day of the wedding, duty suddenly called. He found himself obliged to visit the barracks at Warminster in Wiltshire to meet with the families of soldiers from the Black Watch serving in Iraq. Three members of the regiment had been killed in a suicide attack near Fallujah.

Meanwhile, Camilla was "otherwise engaged." The absence of the groom's royal godfather at the wedding was a devastating social setback for Hugh and Emilie van Cutsem, but one that they had to bear with a stiff upper rictus. Game, set, and match to Mrs. Parker Bowles. The Prince of Wales had made an unprecedented show of support for the woman he loved.

That was satisfying, but not sufficient for Camilla. At this point, she felt there would always be some reason why the moment wasn't right to make her partnership with the Prince of Wales official. Her feelings were supported by the mildest of men with the strongest of principles: her father, Major Shand. Now aged eighty-seven, he had become increasingly concerned that his beloved daughter was being put in a shoddy position. "Although he loved the Prince dearly, he thought him weak, and was worried about how vulnerable he had made Camilla by allowing her to live in limbo," royal biographer Penny Junor says. The Major decided to make a rare intervention. "He took the Prince aside and said, 'I want to meet my maker knowing my daughter's all right.'" He was speaking for the entire extended family. Charles, who had a deep respect and affection for the old war hero, felt chastened enough to pay attention. The humiliation of the van Cutsem affair could not be repeated. "It's nonsense, it's insulting," Charles acknowledged. "And I'm not going to put Camilla through it anymore." What would happen, for instance, if William married first? Mrs. Parker Bowles banished again to the back of the church?

Charles proposed to Camilla at last over New Year's at Birkhall on bended knee. They had each spent Christmas with their families and Charles had briefed his mother, his sons, and the rest of his family at Sandringham on what he planned to do. A Populus poll in 2004 had shown more members of the British public supported the notion of a Charles-Camilla marriage than opposed it, and even more said they didn't care (which was more helpful to Charles than it might seem, for it disarmed those who would raise fears of popular opposition to his remarrying). The Queen, softened up by the prelate and public approval, the constitutional politicking of Sir Michael Peat, and her freedom from the Queen Mother's objections, agreed that cleaning up the Camilla business—"regulariz[ing]" her role, in royal parlance—was the only course that now made sense for the working efficiency of the Firm. "It's been very messy, hasn't it?" one of the Queen's oldest friends said to Gyles Brandreth. "The Queen likes things to be tidy and, despite what's been said, she isn't in the least bit vindictive. Since Camilla isn't going to go away, she may as well be welcomed. That seems to be the view." The Duke of Edinburgh, apparently, was of the opinion that if "they're going to do it, they might as well get on with it." William and Harry would never fully embrace Camilla or understand her appeal, but as everyone else understood, she was "non-negotiable" in their father's life. If their relations were strained, they were, by this time, cordial.

The Queen signed off on Charles choosing Camilla's engagement ring from one of the Queen Mother's collection. It was an art deco heirloom featuring a five-karat emerald-cut diamond in the center, with three diamond baguettes on each side, more valuable than the engagement ring given to Diana. Camilla always loved heritage bling, and Charles loved giving it to her. Shortly before the marital separation in 1992, Diana was particularly aggrieved when she found that an expensive diamond necklace had been marked by Charles to give to Camilla for Christmas while she had been allocated a collection of paste. "I don't want his bloody fake jewels!" she cried in front of Highgrove staff. "I thought cheating husbands took great care to keep their wives sweet with the real things, saving the tawdry stuff for their tarts!" His grandmother would have turned in her grave at Windsor Castle if she had known who was destined to wear her emerald-cut diamond bequest.

For Camilla, the ring on her finger was the ring of fire through which she had passed over thirty tumultuous years. She was inextricably bound to Charles like a Russian vine, entwined in love, protection, and the rough passages of the past. Why had she stuck it out? Some of her friends believe that by temperament and love of independence, she would have preferred the Alice Keppel role, but only in the discreet era that Alice Keppel lived. Mrs. Keppel never had to endure trashings by the British tabloids, the humiliation of the Camillagate tapes, the demonization after the death of the Princess of Wales, and the financial insecurity of divorce. Nor was there the remotest chance that Mrs. Keppel could end up as Queen. Camilla had been patient but never passive in her slow advance. She was about to become the second most important woman in England after the Queen. The "Dutch cow" would have to curtsey to her now!

There were more wins. She was able to ensure the Prince established a "substantial" trust fund for her children and that Charles prevailed against legal advice by waiving a prenuptial agreement, even though he felt he had been "taken to the cleaners" last time around. Given how he never stopped resenting the £17 million settlement he was obliged to pay Diana, the absence of a prenup in the Prince's second marriage was an especially impressive score for Camilla. She had seen enough of royal parsimony to ensure she protected her future.

They chose Valentine's Day 2005 as the date to release the engagement news and Camilla's new title of HRH The Duchess of Cornwall bestowed by the Queen. Clarence House announced that when the Prince succeeded the throne, it was "intended" (a well-chosen weasel word) that his wife would be known by the galleon-like title of Princess Consort. The Queen gave her royal consent to the union after consulting Prime Minister Tony Blair. He expressed his approval and delight with a message of congratulations from the whole cabinet. Clarence House settled down to planning a wedding as different as possible from the unhappy associations of the first celebrated Wales union at St. Paul's Cathedral. A civil ceremony at Windsor Castle on Friday, April 8, 2005, avoided religious controversy. A service of prayer and dedication led by the Archbishop of Canterbury at St. George's Chapel brought ecclesiastical stature. The couple decided to eschew engagement pictures and the hazard of a prenuptial interview, with its horrible hark back to "whatever 'in love' means" when Charles was told he and Diana looked "very much in love." There would be no glamorous honeymoon on the royal yacht (it was gone anyway). Instead, the newly married couple chose a few quiet days tramping around in the biting cold at Birkhall. It would all be very low-key, very elegant, very age appropriate.

Except it wasn't. How could it be when the royal groom was the male version of Calamity Jane? First, in perhaps what American shrinks would see as a gesture of acting out that revealed the true turmoil of his feelings, there was a tabloid furor in January 2005 over leaked pictures of Prince Harry wearing a Nazi uniform from General Rommel's Second World

War Afrika Korps at a costume party. An incensed Charles, who was a nervous wreck before the "Big Announcement," demanded Harry make proper apologies to Jonathan Sacks, chief rabbi of the United Hebrew Congregations of the Commonwealth. Prince Charles also blasted William, who'd reportedly dressed in a skin-tight black leotard with leopard-skin paws and a tail, for allowing his younger brother to make such a witless choice. The House of Commons Public Accounts Committee launched an inquiry into the standards and responsibilities of Clarence House advisers. The always tone-deaf Duchess of York extended the headlines a further cycle by publicly offering Harry her full support.

Next, royal reporter Robert Jobson of the **Evening Standard** caught wind of the wedding scoop and bounced Clarence House into announcing the plans early, on February 10. At first, it seemed all right. Charles and Camilla were due that evening to go to a charity function at Windsor Castle that offered a friendly flashbulb moment outside. Camilla looked radiant in her pink Jean Muir dress. She showed off her ring and told the press she was "just coming down to earth!" The Queen illuminated the Round Tower of the castle as a festive gesture.

The problem: The usually punctilious team led by Michael Peat had made an unfortunate mistake.

The small print in the Marriage Act 1994 allowed marriages to be solemnized in certain "approved premises." That said, if Windsor Castle was given a license to host the civil marriage of Charles and

Camilla, it also meant that any old yobbo could apply to marry at the Queen's home as well. The venue for Charles and Camilla to exchange vows had to be switched from the castle to the Guildhall. The Queen, as supreme governor of the Church of England, felt that her position did not permit her to attend a civil marriage ceremony, particularly one involving the heir to the throne. Nor was she given to showing up at High Street registry offices, inching past the Windsor branch of McDonald's en route. She would now attend only the blessing in St. George's Chapel. The question of the legality of the civil ceremony immediately cropped up. Sir Michael Peat had to ask the help of Tony Blair, who deployed the Lord Chancellor Lord Falconer. The latter put the matter sagely to rest by saying that the Human Rights Act 1998 (the one that Charles had sounded off against in the "black spider" memo) trumped, in effect, the Marriage Act, and affirmed that the marriage was lawful.

All of this offered an irresistible cock-up narrative for the press. The red tops, as British tabloids are sometimes known due to their red mastheads, were already in an angry mood that the **Evening Standard** had scooped them all with the engagement news. The headlines were brutal. "A Bloody Farce!" "Queen Snubs Charles's Wedding!" "Humiliated!" "The Town Hall Bride!" "Wedding Fiasco Deepens Hostility to Charles!"

In March 2005, Charles took the boys skiing over Easter break at the Swiss resort at Klosters.

Reluctantly, he agreed to a press opportunity in the snow that would give William and Harry a chance to express their enthusiasm for the wedding. The boys behaved with media-savvy geniality. Charles asked his sons, "Do I put my arms round you? What do we do?" William suavely said, "Keep smiling." Asked if he looked forward to being a witness, the Beckham pin-up gamely answered, "As long as I don't lose the rings—that's the one responsibility!"

Charles, however, was furious when the BBC's veteran royal correspondent Nicholas Witchell shouted what would seem to be a benignly predictable question about how the Prince was "feeling" with eight days to go before his wedding. "Felt" is always an unwise word to use around a senior member of the Royal Family, as it opens up questions of emotion they have been trained not to discuss. Forgetting the hot mic, Charles voiced his true opinion of Witchell to the world. "Bloody people," he muttered under his breath. "I can't bear that man. He's so awful. He really is." The sentiment surprised everyone since the inconsequential Witchell's only claim to fame until that moment was sitting on a lesbian demonstrator during a protest invasion of the BBC's **Six O'Clock News** studio in 1988. It took several days of negative Charles commentary—that he was "bad-tempered," "petulant," etc.—for that gaffe to go away.

At the end of March, the Bishop of Salisbury, who chaired the Church of England's liturgical committee, got in on the act. He was on the high church

Anglo-Catholic wing of the communion, and seemed to speak for those not happy with the Archbishop of Canterbury's willingness to sanction the remarriage of the future supreme governor and defender of the faith. In a statement, the dyspeptic, ecclesiastical showboat insisted that Charles and Camilla should apologize to Camilla's ex-husband for their part in breaking up the marriage before they were allowed to receive a church blessing. Clarence House didn't even dignify this suggestion with a comment, though it afforded much mirth to those who knew the colorful sexual history of the supposedly wronged Brigadier Andrew Parker Bowles.

Charles was distraught at how the wedding was being received. He made frantic phone calls to his friends. Some of them thought he and Camilla should have just gone off to Scotland like Princess Anne when she married her solid second husband, Commander Timothy Laurence, a former equerry of the Queen, at Crathie Kirk near Balmoral. Nicholas Soames, one of Charles's closest friends, disagreed. "It might have been all right for Princess Anne . . . to do it in a businesslike way and then go back for a cheese sandwich at Gatcombe or whatever they did, but Camilla is a **different gel**," he told **The Spectator**. "She wanted her friends there, for heaven's sake." Charles blamed Peat for the protocol debacles, and Peat in turn blamed his deputy, Kevin Knott, for bollixing up the venue. The twenty-year Palace veteran Knott obligingly resigned. The Queen, always such a stickler for detail herself, was exasperated at yet more indignities blowing up around Charles. Even Camilla wondered aloud to her staff, "Will the nastiness ever end?"

The life of Mrs. Parker Bowles was already beginning to change. She now had an armed protection officer at her side and could never again nip out to a store without one. Being "royal" in comportment would always be an effort for Camilla. A friend remembers seeing her with Charles in Qatar when they were all staying at the Four Seasons. "One time, I was getting into the elevator and Camilla got in wearing only a bathrobe, and I said 'You are a brave woman'—imagine if people had taken a picture of her!" One characteristic she shared with the royals is that she never allowed her stress to show. At a memorial service for Princess Alexandra of Kent's husband, Sir Angus Ogilvy, she was seated with the royal party. Gyles Brandreth noted that she looked "really good":

She has lost weight and gained confidence. Her smile is sustained and unforced. Her only sign of insecurity is her habit of holding on to her hat. Given the years she has had to spend hovering in the shadows, she is entering into the limelight with considerable assurance.

While Charles went on a tour of Australia, New Zealand, Fiji, and Sri Lanka, where he visited tsunami victims, Camilla spent her time with her sister in fittings for her two wedding outfits—one for the

Guildhall and one for the blessing—at the studio of the designer duo Antonia Robinson and Anna Valentine. She visited the hairdresser, though there was no threat of her changing her style, and practiced yoga to reduce angst. Charles's tour of Australia was rewarded with a poll saying 59 percent of Aussies thought he should stand aside and give the throne to William.

Six days before the wedding, the pope died. And not just any pope. John Paul II, who would be canonized in 2014, was the most consequential pontiff of the modern era. He helped end communist rule in his native Poland and eventually all of Europe. His funeral convened the single most august gathering of heads of state outside the United Nations. Millions of mourners gathered in Rome. Dr. Rowan Williams was the first serving Archbishop of Canterbury to attend the funeral of a pope since the Church of England split with Rome in 1534. Seventy presidents and prime ministers, four kings, five queens, and more than fourteen leaders of other religions were on the guest list.

The Queen insisted that Charles represent her on the appointed funeral day, which happened to be the date on which he was supposed to be getting married. "Can anything else possibly go wrong?" whooped the **Daily Mail,** in response to this cosmic eruption into the lives of Charles and Camilla.

The wedding was postponed for twenty-four hours. Religious and political propriety demanded it. On top of the herculean task and expense of reworking every single detail of the arrangements, the televised blessing was now scheduled to clash with the Grand National steeplechase, considered the "crown jewels" of the BBC's sports coverage. The solution was to move the start of the race from 3:40 P.M. to 4:10 P.M., allowing viewers to see both.

The otherwise stalwart Camilla went into meltdown. It must have felt as if Diana and the Queen Mother had joined forces from beyond the grave to rain down thunderbolts on her special day. She developed a chronic case of sinusitis and spent the week at Ray Mill with a group of girlfriends ministering to her shredded nerves. Her old friend Lucia Santa Cruz, who had first introduced her to Charles, arrived from Chile and brought Camilla homemade chicken soup. "She was really ill, stressed," Lucia said, and terrified she wouldn't make it. On the day of the wedding, Penny Junor reports, it took four people to coax Camilla out of bed at Clarence House: "She literally couldn't get out of bed." Camilla's dresser, Jacqui Meakin, was there along with Camilla's sister, Annabel, and daughter, Laura, and a housemaid. Finally, it was Annabel who settled the matter: "Okay, that's all right. I'm going to do it for you. I'm going to get into your clothes." Only then did Camilla get out of bed. Competition was always the best way to galvanize the woman who would, soon, never again be Mrs. Parker Bowles.

Once Camilla's game face was on, she had never looked better. Radiating hesitant joy, she stepped into the Queen's Rolls-Royce Phantom VI to join

Charles for the journey to the Guildhall. It was a killing comparison to know that the world was thinking about that other bride, the enchanting twenty-year-old "lamb to the slaughter," who had gone before up the steps of St. Paul's Cathedral in a riot of princess-doll taffeta, followed by that crumply, over-the-top train. But Camilla had her own muted dazzle that day. Aged fifty-seven, unvarnished, unblushing, un-svelte, she was someone that Diana had never been: the woman whom the Prince of Wales had wanted all along.

The fashion press agreed that Robinson Valentine pulled off a double win with its outfits: a delicate cream chiffon dress under an oyster silk basket-weave coat paired with a wide-brimmed, white-feathered Philip Treacy hat for the civil ceremony; a porcelain-blue chiffon dress and matching coat, embroidered with five varieties of gold thread that glowed in the light of St. George's Chapel for the blessing. Hat maestro Treacy excelled himself a second time with a headdress of gold-leafed feathers, reminiscent of waving cornfields at harvest and a chic rural accent for a bride who loved the country.

The crowds lining Windsor's narrow, winding streets were respectable enough—20,000 to Diana's 600,000 in 1981—and at least they weren't hostile. Twenty-eight guests, including Princess Anne, Prince William, and Prince Harry witnessed Charles and his new Duchess's vows in the modest Ascot Room of the Guildhall with its single brass chandelier and fresh flowers picked from the garden at Highgrove

and Ray Mill. Charles looked immaculate in a morning suit and dove-gray waistcoat. Bride and groom
exchanged wedding rings made of special Welsh
gold. When a cut of it was requested from the family's remaining reserve from the Clogau mine, the
Queen remarked, "There is very little of it left—
there won't be enough for a third wedding." Her gift
to Charles was a broodmare for which she would pay
the expenses.

At St. George's Chapel, eight hundred guests
waited eagerly for the newlyweds to arrive. Energy
was high, bordering on euphoria. This was the
Camilla-Charles home team, the myriad friends and
supporters who had provided safe houses to tryst in.
They had listened patiently to Charles's moans, kept
Camilla's secrets, defended them in the press, and
acted as advocates with the Queen. It was Party in
the Pews, without Ozzy Osbourne, featuring old favorites such as the Duchess of Devonshire, country
stalwarts the Palmer-Tomkinsons, the former king
and queen of Greece, Nicholas Soames, Stephen
Fry, and a brace of old flames, such as Lady Amanda
Ellingworth, and the Duke of Wellington's daughter,
Lady Jane Wellesley. Andrew Parker Bowles appeared
mysteriously gratified. "He was behaving like the
mother of the bride," one of the congregation told me.
Two guests whose absence raised eyebrows were
Hugh and Emilie van Cutsem. Still in mourning for
the pope, it was said.

Fresh off a plane from Rome himself, the
Archbishop of Canterbury, Dr. Rowan Williams,

officiated the blessing. Masterfully, he led the couple in a prayer considered to be the strongest act of penitence in the Church of England. It was written by Thomas Cranmer, Archbishop of Canterbury, to King Henry VIII, who had plenty to be sorry about himself:

> **We acknowledge and bewail our
> manifold sins and wickedness,
> which we, from time to time, most
> grievously have committed,
> by thought, word, and deed, against thy
> divine Majesty,
> provoking most justly thy wrath
> and indignation against us.
> We do earnestly repent,
> and are heartily sorry for these
> misdoings.**

Asked if they would support the Prince in his marriage vows and his loyalty for the rest of his life, the congregation bellowed in unison, "WE WILL!"

The Queen sat through all this with her customary wedding face (to wit, no expression at all), but one of the guests told me there was a marked difference in her demeanor at the after-party, where she exuded genuine affection for both Camilla and her son. Were the long years of exclusion an expression of form rather than feeling? The Prince's supportive and uncomplicated second wife has qualities the Queen always admires—constancy, discretion, stoicism under fire. Nothing kept Her Majesty from her first love, however. When Charles and Camilla emerged to cheers into the sunshine outside the chapel, the Queen disappeared into a side room to watch the Grand National. She emerged into the buzzing reception taking place in the State Apartments at Windsor Castle to make an unusually inspired toast that led the headlines the next day:

> I have two important announcements to make. I know you will want to know who was the winner of the Grand National. It was Hedgehunter. [Deadpan pause.] Secondly, having cleared Becher's Brook and The Chair and all kinds of other terrible obstacles, they have come through and I'm very proud and wish them well. My son is home and dry with the woman he loves. They are now on the home straight; the happy couple are now in the winners' enclosure.

Then she disappeared into the side room again to watch a replay of the race.

Camilla and Charles worked the room with an air of bewildered jubilation. Paddy Harverson remembers it as one of the most joyful weddings he has ever attended, releasing years of pent-up tension within the Royal Family and their entire circle of mutual friends. Stephen Fry remembers:

> There was a moment when there was a mass of people and I was talking to David Frost and I

turned round and, suddenly, there was the Queen next to me. And she said, "Is nobody going to get me any cake?" And I thought, "Wow." There we were at Windsor Castle, and there indeed the cake had been. People were handing it out, and lots of people were eating it, and she wasn't. I said, "You stay, ma'am. I'll go and get you some." So I barged through feeling like I was the most important messenger in a Shakespeare play, you know, saying, "Out of the way, the Queen demands some cake!"

As Her Majesty and Prince Philip headed for the exit, they passed Michael Fawcett. The Queen turned to Philip and said loudly, "Oh look, there's Fawcett. He's got so fat." Coming shortly after the exquisite charm of her toast to Charles and Camilla, it was a moment when the tartness of the offstage Queen revealed itself.

William and Harry rushed outside to hang "Just Married" signs onto the back of their father's Bentley before the bride and groom left for Birkhall. "It was transparent that William was happy for them," a photographer who was up close told Penny Junor, "and Harry, but more so William. You could see that what mattered to him was the happiness of his father and how good Camilla was for him."

What Diana's younger son was thinking only he can tell us, and doubtless will.

PART TWO

CHAPTER
1 0

THE PRINCES NEXT DOOR

———

William's and Harry's
Competing Realities

———

UNTIL HE LOST HIS HAIR, PRINCE WILLIAM was probably the biggest heartthrob to be heir to the throne since the pre-obese Henry VIII.

William had more than a whiff of Diana's shimmer. He had her easy, accessible smile; the faun-like hint of shyness that suggested a need (perhaps even an insistence) to be defended. He had the Spencer coloring in all the right accents: the gentle flush and the auburn lights, in contrast to Harry's tufty carrot-top. And, by the age of sixteen, William possessed the Spencerian height—six foot one—which made him princely even in sneakers.

"You couldn't help but smile when he came into a room because he was always full of fun," Prince Charles's former press secretary Sandy Henney said of William. "It was not like when the Prince [of Wales] walked in and you thought, 'Oh God, where's it coming from today,' good mood, bad mood or whatever?"

From an early age, William was remarkably self-possessed. He was camera-ready at nine months old, accompanying Charles and Diana on their first Australian tour in 1983. He spoke his first words in public the following year, filmed in a striped shirt paired with blue dungarees, kicking a ball in the walled garden of Kensington Palace.

"He's really interested in cameras," Prince Charles told **The Times** in June 1984.

An ITN cameraman obliged by letting Prince William look inside [the camera's] eye-piece, while directing the lens at the rest of the pressmen.

"There are people in there, oooh," Prince Charles said as his son's eyes spread wide at this new toy.

Shifting his attention to a long microphone, Prince William asked, "What's that?"

"It's a big sausage that picks up everything you say—and you are starting early," his father told him.

William was beguiling the British public before he even turned five. In June 1987, he attended his first Trooping the Colour, the military parade that marks the official birthday of the monarch. He traveled in an open carriage with the Queen Mother and Princess Diana, and fixedly watched the rest of the parade from a window overlooking Horse Guards Parade. His media skills were honed by observing Diana's frequent encounters with the press, both friendly and hostile, whether "on the record," "off the record," or "on background." He was curious about (and a little wary of) the boisterous beasts he called "tographers." When he said to his mother on his way to preschool, "Poppa says I have to be very careful of them," Diana replied, "No, they're just doing their job. Be polite and smile and they'll leave you alone."

Off camera, William wasn't so easy. As a toddler, he had been a cause of concern to the Queen when he showed signs of being a brat. She complained to her husband that their grandson was "out of control" and needed a stricter nanny. She was not amused that he loved to say, "When I am king, I'm going to make a new rule that . . ."

Diana herself admitted—after she and Charles returned from an eighteen-day tour of Canada without William in June 1983—that her Wombat was turning into "a holy terror—dashing about bumping into tables and lamps, breaking everything in sight." By the time he was four, he had the unattractive habit of yapping at his nanny, Barbara Barnes, "No one tells **me** what to do! When I am king I will have you punished." Highgrove guards found it less than hilarious when William squirted them relentlessly with a water pistol. Diana fondly called him "my mini-tornado." At Mrs. Mynors' Nursery School, William was considered an entitled little monster and was known as "Basher Wills."

In those days, it was Prince Harry who was the muffled, sensitive son babied by Diana. "Harry is quieter and just watches," she told an interviewer. He often stayed home from school sick, perhaps as a way to have his mother all to himself. "You take care of the heir; I'll take care of the spare," Diana used to say to Darren McGrady, the chef at Kensington Palace, who sometimes was recruited to keep an eye on the boys.

The Waleses' nursery was a kind of kingdom within the kingdom. Indeed, Diana's former private secretary Patrick Jephson, who joined when both boys were under seven years old, called it "almost a court in its own right":

> There were bedrooms, playrooms, a kitchen and a dining room snug under the eaves of Kensington Palace. There were full-time and part-time nannies, policemen, a shared driver. . . . Every Friday morning almost the whole apparatus would transport itself a hundred miles to the west, to spend the weekend at Highgrove in Gloucestershire. There a duplicate set of rooms awaited, together with all the attractions and diversions of life on a small, picture-postcard country estate.

Diana, to her credit, did not want William and Harry to be raised as clueless little Lord Fauntleroys in Start-Rite button shoes. Nor did she like the way the staff at Balmoral spoiled them. At Highgrove, she let them hang out with the Burrell children, which Prince Charles thought was ill-advised. He told Diana the boys were princes and should be raised as such. "They may be princes, but they are my children as well," Diana retorted. "And they need to have a normal life or they will end up as hopelessly out of touch as you are."

When she joined friends for lunch at San Lorenzo, her favorite restaurant in Knightsbridge, she let the boys gambol happily around the restaurant, in and out between the tables.

Around the ages of four and six, the two brothers seemed to absorb their appointed destinies. It's as if nurture kicked in over nature and they traded personality traits. Duty and responsibility were drilled into the heir to the throne—subduing his boisterousness— while Harry became the skinny, exuberant imp of misrule.

For their preparatory years, both boys boarded in the cozy country setting of Ludgrove in Berkshire. Keith Critchlow, one of several academic tutors Charles hired to work with the boys, called William "an extraordinarily natural character" with "an impeccable sense of truth and correctness." William's knightly aura was further enhanced by the Harry Potter scar on his forehead, a token he received from a golfing accident when he was eight. "It glows sometimes," he told a young cancer patient while lending his support for a new children and teenagers cancer center at the Royal Marsden hospital in 2009.

There remained moments where he showed his

sense of entitlement. A former staffer of Diana's told me that the eight-year-old William, on a plane ride back from his first formal trip to Wales, reached over with his fork and speared a hard-boiled egg from the staffer's plate. It was as if the boy had said, "I'm going to be king. You're not and I'm going to have what I like off your plate. . . . What are you going to do about that?" When Diana scolded him, the staffer said, William went into a "right strop"—little short of a temper tantrum—which the staffer attributed to the strains of a St. David's Day walkabout in Cardiff.

While the boy wizard increasingly accepted his manifest destiny, the younger Prince began to sense that he had the freedom to have some fun. "You'll be king one day. I won't. So I can do what I want," a four-year-old Harry teased William, with shades of the young Margaret's "poor you" to the older, graver Lilibet. He zoomed at high speed around the guards' stations and servants' quarters, a blur of springy orange hair. Ken Wharfe, who also protected the boys, nearly had a heart attack when he allowed six-year-old Harry to play with his police radio. Only when he heard the crackle of Harry's whereabouts as "Tower Records, Over" did he realize that the third in line to the throne was halfway down Kensington High Street, a half mile beyond Palace grounds. On another occasion, Harry, after rolling around earlier in the paddock and getting liberally coated with sheep dung, attacked his father from behind just as Charles was boarding a helicopter for an official trip.

The Prince's back was now striped with green and black stains. "Look at me!" the father wailed. "I am absolutely **covered** in sheep shit!" Charles then had to be dried off with a hairdryer.

Diana indulged her younger son. "One of her mottos to me was, you know, 'You can be as naughty as you want, just don't get caught,'" Harry said in Nick Kent's 2017 documentary about his mother.

He knew he could always count on William for an alibi when they got into mischief. When his favorite moorhen at Highgrove was shot, Prince Charles had a strong suspicion those "bloody boys" were responsible and demanded to know the culprit. Press secretary Sandy Henney was deputized to call Eton housemaster Andrew Gailey and get one of the boys to fess up. She later relayed the episode to William's biographer Penny Junor:

Some hours later, I'm driving home and Andrew [Gailey] rings and he's giggling before he starts. He says, "I got them into the office and I said, 'William and Harry. I've had Sandy on the phone and your father's very upset because someone has shot the moorhen.' They're looking at each other and saying, 'Shot the moorhen? Shot the moorhen?' Then William turns to Andrew and says, 'Which moorhen is that, Dr. Gailey?' And Harry says, 'The one you told me not to shoot!' I [then] said, 'Tell Harry he's got twenty-four hours,' and bless his heart he rang his dad and said, 'I'm so sorry Papa, it was me,

I shouldn't have done it.'" Those boys are so close to each other—the loyalty between them and the mischievousness and sense of honesty, not wishing to tell a lie.

They were a tight fraternal alliance in the stifling royal bubble. Together, they'd bomb down the ski slopes in Klosters, throw each other into the swimming pool at Highgrove, and beat each other at the card game Racing Demon. Their routine treats were the stuff of other children's fantasies. During the Christmas season, they went with their mother to see Santa Claus at Harrods. The store opened before the public arrived, giving the boys Santa all to themselves. William, already adept at pulling rank, told the elves, "I am not telling you what I want for Christmas. I'm only talking to Father Christmas." In the store's famous Toy Kingdom, they rampaged through the fourth floor on two mini motorbikes.

William was fiercely protective of Harry. At Ludgrove, he was able to cushion his younger brother's arrival with his two-year head start and his guiding hand. Harry was held back a year from Eton because of bad grades in his exams, which was just as well. Arriving as a new boy in September 1997, a month after his mother died, would have been an impossible stress.

Meanwhile, the sophistication that Eton cultivates had added to William's poise. A combination of extreme wealth and extreme academic selectivity at the school produces the confidence of a breed that assumes itself to be Best in Class. A short walk across the bridge from Windsor Castle, Eton has spawned twenty prime ministers, from Sir Robert Walpole, the first to hold that title, up (or down) to Boris Johnson. Boris himself followed another Old Etonian, David Cameron, with the middle-class Theresa May—condescended to by both—in between.

Sending both boys to Eton was one of the few things on which Charles and Diana agreed, even though it was plain that Harry would not meet the academic standards. "If he doesn't go there," Diana told author Ingrid Seward, "everyone will think he's stupid." It's sometimes forgotten that the People's Princess was much more a princess than she was of "the people." Generations of Spencer men, including her father and brother, had attended Eton. Her tastes and social expectations remained essentially aristocratic. Charles, meanwhile, had no desire to inflict on the boys his own experience of Gordonstoun's "Colditz with Kilts."

Etonians are organized into group houses, each of which has its own distinct character and is overseen by an omnipotent housemaster who supplies men-torship and discipline, supported by a maternal surrogate known as the Dame. Manor House, where William was berthed, fell under the steward-ship of Gailey, an Anglo-Irish scholar and a man of warmth and twinkling humor who kept a sensitive eye on William's progress. Each boy has a room to himself that he can decorate and furnish. The seventeen-year-old William's sported a poster of a spaced-out Rastafarian flying through the clouds with a spliff in his mouth, coupled with the slogan "Don't drink and drive, have a smoke and fly." A sly student offered the picture showcasing William's decked-out digs to the **Mirror.** Excited for a moment by the opportunity to suggest that William was a stoner, Piers Morgan ultimately passed because of the juvenile privacy injunctions of the PCC's Code of Practice.

William's schoolmates, used to a healthy number of high-profile parents, were not overawed by the presence of the heir to the throne in their midst. Along with the sons of Britain's titled aristocracy there were boys on scholarship, heirs of foreign oligarchs and Gulf kingdoms, and the offspring of meritocratic achievers who sought the ultimate educational status symbol of Eton. The former **Daily Mail** editor Paul Dacre, the surly Baron of Middle England, unashamedly sent his son to Eton. Also in William's year was the future Oscar-winning actor Eddie Redmayne.

In keeping with William's instinct for self-protection, his social circle was carefully unadventurous, drawn from those who would be sure to stay discreet. The boys he hung out with rejoiced in recurring aristocratic brand names from the Wales and Windsor past: William van Cutsem, son of the you-can't-shake-'em-off Emilie and Hugh; Thomas van Straubenzee, scion of the Spennithorne landed gentry, and James Meade, son of the forever-hot

Olympic gold medalist equestrian and famous ex-boyfriend of Princess Anne, Richard Meade.

But royal or commoner, William would have been a star at any school. At Eton he was captain of the swimming team and, in addition to playing rugby and football, and rowing for his house, he joined the Combined Cadet Force and won the Sword of Honour. He was later elected to the acme of Eton's elite popularity contest: the senior-year prefect club known as Pop, whose members are allowed to wear their own self-designed waistcoats under their uniform tails. The eighteen-year-old William chose an eye-catching Union Jack emblazoned across his chest, which sent the ironic message of l'état c'est moi. Academically, he kept his end up enough to avoid giving comfort to critics of special privilege. Achieving twelve GCSEs and three A levels with solidly middling grades, he was a Nobel laureate compared to his mother—and perhaps even his father. "My boy's got a good brain," Diana noted with pride, "considering how hopeless both his parents were."

It was tough for Harry at Eton. He struggled academically and was at the bottom of the class. Despite William's attempts to settle him in, he acted out to conceal his academic unease and, no doubt, his yearnings for his mother. The historian Juliet Nicolson attended a Mother's Day event at Eton in 1999 and recalled how poignantly vulnerable Harry looked and how small. "The grown-ups were around the top of the chapel and below were the boys," she told me. "The only redhead in the entire group was just two or three rows below me and it was Harry. It was the second Mother's Day after Diana had died. And I remember it felt like the entire chapel was willing love towards this little head."

Where Harry excelled was on the playing fields. He was a top performer at polo, cricket, and rugby, and was elected house captain of games. His calling was confirmed when he joined Eton's Combined Cadet Force and was chosen to be parade commander, putting the other cadets through their military paces.

More entertaining, more endearing, more relatable, Harry was always the more beloved of the brothers. Encomiums of William's gifts sometimes miss the fact that from the age of seven, Harry was a better horseman, skier, and shot than his elder brother. William sometimes found that discomfiting. Ken Wharfe noticed how the heir belittled Harry on an excursion to the Lippitts Hill shooting range in 1991. "He really doesn't understand things," William scoffed. "Oh shut up, William," Diana said. "We'll see who's been concentrating in a minute."

"Her instinct was proved to be right," Wharfe observed.

Both boys were good but Harry was the star. He hit the center of the target time after time and was given his near-perfect target as a present afterwards that he cherished. I am certain his success that day made him even more determined to follow a career in the military.

The Queen, sensitized by the struggles with her younger sister, always had a particular soft spot for Harry. The whole family from his earliest age could sense the fragility behind his roistering personality. "The affection that HM has for Harry is not a figment of the media's imagination," a former adviser told me. "It is real. She's incredibly fond of him and so is his father, who was always deeply anxious about how he was doing. He often worried about things in the loveliest way. Is he eating properly through the day? Has he got enough to do? Is he happy enough?" Diana had tried to make her sons fully aware of what lay ahead for them. "The Princess believed that the preparation of William, and to a lesser extent, Harry, for their public roles was her primary duty," Wharfe observed, but preparing them for their unequal status was a more nuanced issue harder to address.

Diana never questioned William's rightful destiny to be king. Even at her most bitter ebb with the Royal Family, she was always a monarchist. The Queen was the one person of whom Diana remained in awe. Despite her bomb-throwing instincts toward Charles that splattered the monarchy, she wanted to update the institution and bring it closer to the public. She was, nonetheless, determined that her boys would have the freedom to live in ways her husband had not been permitted. Until they boarded at Ludgrove, she always dropped them off and collected them herself from their north London preschool. She let them go on playdates with their classmates. She tried to leaven her sons' royal

privilege by showing them how the other 99.9 percent lived. She stressed that "everyone is not rich,
has four holidays a year, speaks standard English or
drives a Range Rover." She took the boys on numerous informal charity visits to meet the people she
was trying to help. William's introduction to the
homeless population came when he was eleven years
old, at a center attached to Westminster Cathedral
called the Passage—a rough, intimidating, and over-
crowded place. Sister Bridie Dowd, who ran the
shelter, says William was very shy and stayed close to
his mother. Used to living in a world where every
person he met professed to be more than pleased to
see him, he was shocked when an ornery Scottish
drunk made a pungent comment about a royal showing up. It was a useful exercise. Harry later joined
Wharfe on a visit to the night center, where they
played chess with overnighters.

Poverty tourism? Maybe, but at least Diana tried.
"I want them to have an understanding of people's
emotions, people's insecurities, people's distress, and
people's hopes and dreams," she said. The exposure
to grim addiction shelters and harrowing AIDS
wards made a deep impression on the boys, even if
they were driven home by a chauffeur. "Sleeping
rough, sofa surfing, not having basic comforts a lot
of us take for granted. That really struck me at a
young age, bearing in mind the gulf for me, growing
up in a palace," William said in 2015. The experience
impressed both boys enough for William to pick
up the patronage of one of Diana's favorite causes,

Centrepoint, a charity that supports homeless young adults, and for Harry to carry the torch for her AIDS work with the founding of Sentebale (which means "forget me not") in Lesotho, supporting orphans living with HIV. It was William's idea in 1997 to auction off Diana's famous outfits at Christie's to raise funds for AIDS charities.

The two twenty-first-century princes grew up within a tantalizing, sometimes unbearable, simulacrum of normality. As adolescents, they became adept at faking ordinariness, slouching around in their cool and contemporary off-duty outfits and speaking in the pseudo-Essex accents that were in fashion. The camouflage couldn't disguise, let alone change, the fact that their mother was the most famous woman in the world, their royal protection officers were billeted on the same hall, and when their grandmother was at home, the Royal Standard flew from the Round Tower of Windsor Castle.

At fourteen, William's Eton peers went through their religious confirmation together at College Chapel, but his took place separately, at St. George's Chapel, attended by his mother, Prince Charles, and the Queen. The boys would always be plagued by the bifurcated perspective of two competing realities—profound "specialness" on the one hand and, on the other, strenuous efforts to seem just like everyone else. "I always wanted to be normal. As opposed to being Prince Harry, just being Harry. It was a puzzling life," he would say to Oprah in 2021 on her mental health series **The Me You Can't See.**

Writer Anthony Holden was struck by their bubble world after a lunch with Diana and her sons, when a friend of their mother's gave each boy a £50 note. Diana cooed, "Ooh, look, boys, pink grannies!"

At the age of eighteen, in his last year at Eton, three years after his mother's death, William tried extra hard to project average blokery. He allowed an ITN crew to film him playing football and gamely losing a tackle, tapping at a school computer, splashing in water polo practice, cramming in the library, and trying his hand at cooking a purposely average paella. It was a shrewd communications strategy. He was advised to play down his interest in polo and get pumped about soccer—the national obsession of his countrymen. No need to highlight the fact that the window of William's room was fitted with bulletproof glass or that his course was charted by a star chamber of Palace graybeards, communications professionals, Prince Charles, the Queen, and Prince Philip—with a bishop or two at the ready for pastoral gravitas.

The smallest decision about William's life was scrutinized by the Palace and the press. At Eton, he became accustomed to the point of nonchalance to members of the European media—unconstrained by British press rules about juveniles—sitting on the riverbank with their cameras, watching him row, and waiting for him to fall in.

Spontaneity would never be an option for the heir to the throne. The only person who really understood and shared his unchosen privilege—the golden handcuffs—was his increasingly rebellious younger brother. Fifty years after Princess Margaret claimed that her dream of freedom was to ride a London bus, William and Harry would find their own cage scarcely larger. "Normality" cannot be summoned at will like a genie, or executive-produced by a Palace factotum.

II

From their earliest childhood, the young princes were collateral damage in a cold war between their parents, one that could turn hot in front of them in alarming ways. The two-year age gap between them was critical in forging their distinctive worldviews and, equally so, in shaping their perceptions of their mother. Prince Harry idolized Diana more and understood her less. He would always be her baby, a scamp who was "thick" at his lessons and "naughty, just like me." His emotions, like hers, were always simmering near the surface.

William understood Diana more, but idealized her less. He was privy to her volatile love life. He knew the tabloids made her life hell, but he also knew she colluded with them. By his early teens, he was his mother's most trusted confidant. She used to describe him as "my little wise old man." "He was so sensible that he put the rest of us to shame," Simone Simmons, Diana's psychic pal, recalls. "He was never an ordinary teenager and always sounded much older than his years. . . . That was due in no small part to the way [Diana] was so forthright with him." It was a pity she didn't listen more to his advice. "Mummy, [Bashir] is not a good person," is one warning from William that suggests antennae better than her own.

Like many women whose relationships with their husbands have become dysfunctional, Diana used her elder son as both a stand-in and a buffer, toting him along for meetings with journalists. Piers Morgan describes in his diary a startlingly revealing background lunch with Diana and the thirteen-year-old William at Kensington Palace in 1996 at which, he says, the Princess allowed him to ask "literally anything." William insisted on a glass of wine even when Diana said no, and he seemed thoroughly up to date on all the tabloid rumors about her lovers. "He is clearly in the loop on most of her bizarre world and, in particular, the various men who come into it from time to time," the astonished Morgan noted.

Diana's most recent romantic adventure was with the sturdy hunk Will Carling, captain of the England rugby team, whom she had met in 1995 working out at the Chelsea Harbour Club gym. William idolized Carling and met him several times with Diana. When Carling visited Kensington Palace for a romantic rendezvous, he gave both the boys a rugby shirt. It is unclear when William came to realize that his hero was a sporting visitor in more ways than one. Carling's wife, the television personality

Julia Carling, conclusively enlightened him—and everyone else—when she divorced her husband, making it clear the Princess was at least one of the reasons. "This has happened to [Diana] before," Julia told a reporter. "You hope she won't do these things again, but obviously she does."

Diana was livid about Mrs. Carling's comments. "She's milking it for all she's worth, that woman," she told Morgan over lunch. "Honestly, I haven't seen Will [Carling] since June '95." William interjected, "I keep a photo of Julia Carling on my dartboard at Eton."

The exchange reveals much about the dynamic between mother and son. For Diana to include the future heir to the throne at a meeting with one of the Royal Family's most reckless press tormenters and freely refer to a casual affair was, on its face, amazing. (Try imagining William's wife, the Duchess of Cambridge, and a teenage Prince George doing the same today.) It suggests that her boundaries were dissolving and, with them, her judgment. At thirteen years old, William knew how to slyly dare his mother to deny him his request for wine in front of a journalist. William already understood that his status gave him the upper hand even with her. Not only was he used to hearing about her lovers, as Morgan notes, but he'd also found a way to deal with it at school. Tacking Julia Carling's image onto a dartboard was a gesture of loyalty to his mother that also announced he knew exactly what the other boys were whispering about.

William learned early to veil his emotions. He was more sensitive than his bravado suggested. He always hated going back to Ludgrove at the beginning of term. He would cry copiously, following his father around the flower beds and potting sheds at Highgrove as Charles tried to reassure him with stories of how he used to dread going back himself. Charles told a member of the staff that William's life was made more difficult by who he was.

He might have added that it was also very difficult at home. Was it a coincidence that in the lead-up to the publication of Andrew Morton's veil-rending book, when you could cut the tension between their parents with a knife, the ten-year-old William was so miserable at Ludgrove that Diana had to rush down with Harry to console him? At the start of the following year, the Camillagate tapes were released, and it's excruciating to imagine what kind of Tampax-related ridicule of his father William endured. For a time afterward, he regressed in his studies. The school saw the reemergence of "Basher Wills." He was involved in a bullying incident against a fellow student because the boy impugned his feuding parents.

In this situation at least, William and Harry were just like many boys in their school. Their parents adored them and hated each other. On weekends home, William would try to make stilted conversation at the Highgrove dinner table through his parents' stony silences. Diana cried bitter tears in front of the boys. After one hostile exchange at this time, William followed her upstairs and pushed tissues under the door of her bathroom, saying, "I hate to see you sad." Harry, for his part, once beat on his father's legs with his fists, shouting, "I hate you, I hate you, you make Mummy cry!"

Nonetheless, the boys' own experience of Charles was kind and paternal. When he landed by helicopter at Highgrove on a Friday afternoon, he would spin them around in the air as his two Jack Russell terriers, Tigger and Roo, yapped at his feet. The boys relished their expeditions shooting, stalking, or watching him play polo. Their love of country life was a real bond with Charles. Neither of them felt squeamish about the rabbits Tigger caught or the magpie traps where they found wounded birds. Harry especially liked to hold his father's hand as he showed him the garden. "Harry loves animals and plants," Charles observed. "I tell him all about them and that they have feelings, too." Such tender scenes were alien to Diana's experience of Charles. The mother they adored saw her husband as Public Enemy Number One—heartless, cold, and treacherous.

The war between Charles and Diana tore the household apart. The boys could see their father's anger and hurt when Diana spirited them away from him upstairs on their exeat weekends, but it was such guilty fun to snuggle with her on the sofa watching videos of Mr. Bean. Christmases at Sandringham were especially bleak, with their mother's embarrassing nonattendance at the Queen's evening gatherings. Diana took to ordering dinner on a tray and crying in her room.

Most unsettling for the boys was that for years they had no idea what ailed their mother. All they knew came from hints and whispers, the slamming of doors and the muffling of tears, and the sounds of vomiting in Diana's bathroom until she emerged looking flushed and sedated. ("It gives you a feeling of comfort. It's like having a pair of arms around you," she once said of her bulimia.) They were not yet aware of the unshakable offstage presence of Mrs. Parker Bowles, who haunted Diana's psyche. The boys did not know that after they returned to school on Sunday evening and Diana was on her way to London, their father, after an early dinner, would dismiss the staff, circle Sunday night television shows in the **Radio Times**—shows he had no intention of watching—and borrow the chef's car to drive incognito to his mistress's house.

The hostile, weeping mother they saw when their father was around was almost unrecognizable from the lighthearted playmate who radiated their days. "I remember going to see Diana in Kensington Palace when things weren't particularly easy in her married life," her friend Harry Herbert said.

Suddenly, these two boys came thundering round the corner in their dressing-gowns, this was before bed, and just watching her face light up, going from sad chat to suddenly, boof! You know, I'll never forget that moment, and them, you know, crawling all over her and things flying everywhere. And through all the difficulty of other stuff at that time, you could see the most important thing in her life were her boys.

She took them to theme parks, shooting ranges, movies. On holiday escapes to the Mediterranean and the Caribbean, they buried her up to her neck in sand and fired water balloons at the intruding press. When William started to get seriously interested in girls, she arranged to have a trio of supermodels— Naomi Campbell, Cindy Crawford, and Christy Turlington, no less—wait for him at the top of the stairs when he got home from school. "I think I pretty much fell down the stairs on the way up," William later recalled in the 2017 documentary. Harry cherishes the memories of driving with her in "her old-school BMW" through the country lanes with the roof down, "listening to Enya, I think it was, God, a blast from the past. All of that was part of her being a mum."

On sports day at Harry's preschool, she kicked off her shoes and ran barefoot in the mothers' race. "She would come and watch us play football and smuggle sweets into our socks. And I mean like literally walking back from a football match and having sort of five packets of Starburst," Harry said.

Nowhere were they a more carefree trio than on the rugged, windswept Isle of Seil, near Oban in Scotland. This was where Diana often took them to stay with her mother, who lived there alone, very simply, ever since her second marriage to Peter Shand

Kydd had fallen apart. Despite Diana's feeling of abandonment when Frances left Earl Spencer, mother and daughter retained a complicated bond. They feuded and fought, but they also laughed and confided. In his memoir, Anthony Holden recalls Diana showing up for lunch with Frances at a time when all the tabloids were saying they weren't on speaking terms. The two imposing women were very much alike: tall, spirited blondes with a renegade spirit. (To mark what would have been Frances's eighty-fifth birthday in January 2021, the current Earl Spencer posted on Instagram a photo of the painting of the beautiful, finely boned young Frances that's now hanging in the library of Althorp. The likeness to Diana stunned royal fans. With their huge blue eyes and blond bobs, they look almost identical.)

At the remote cottage on Seil, Frances—or Supergran, as the boys called her—loved packing them all off into her ancient car to take them to the Sea Life Sanctuary. With no spying royal servants around, Diana felt so relaxed that she did the dishes and ironed the boys' clothes.

But there was a destructive side to Diana's mothering, too. Rampant insecurity dictated that Diana always needed to be first in her boys' hearts. They got used to people they loved suddenly disappearing or falling out of favor. On William's first day of preschool, Nanny Barnes—Baba, as he called her—simply vanished. He had been used to toddling into her bed in the morning for a snuggle before going to wake up his mother. After telling

Barnes that it would be "better" if she departed, Diana banned her from any last hugs with her charges or even sending them a postcard. Diana was a "very jealous mother," said deputy nanny Olga Powell, who later replaced Barnes. Twenty-four years later, the chivalrous William showed the depth of his feeling when he not only invited Barnes to his wedding to Kate Middleton but also gave her a prime seat in Westminster Abbey.

Diana's pattern of cutting out people they cared about continued throughout their childhood. The boys' favorite cousins, Fergie's two girls, Beatrice and Eugenie, were banished when Diana fatwa'd her sister-in-law for revealing she had developed verrucae after borrowing Diana's shoes. Because of Diana's resentment of the boys' affection, babysitter Tiggy Legge-Bourke, their beloved "big sister," found herself excised from William's confirmation ceremony in March 1997.

Further fanning Diana's jealousy, William invited Tiggy instead of either of his parents to Eton's Fourth of June annual family picnic later that same year. Diana was so bitter she had her private secretary Michael Gibbins call Piers Morgan to unload on her son's guest for "smoking and guzzling" in front of the cameras. Morgan could hear her dictating to Gibbins in the background. The ensuing press coverage provided yet another mortifying spectacle for a teenage boy who wanted above all to be seen as normal. William was so furious he "had a go at [her]," Richard Kay learned.

Supergran, too, was cut from William's confirmation over some trivial slight. She was reduced to posting a notice of celebration in the Oban cathedral newsletter. Asked why she was not at the confirmation, Diana's mother replied bitterly, "I am not the person to ask. You should ask the offices of William's parents."

"One of the great thrills about being royal is you can make people cease to exist," Patrick Jephson said to me. "It's really, really easy. And there's always somebody to do it for you."

CHAPTER
11

THE LOST BOYS

How the Princes Survived
Their Childhood

FOR WILLIAM AND HARRY, THE MISERY OF their parents' discord was amplified by a dishonest, partisan, cutthroat press. Their father was routinely depicted as either a stiff or a monster. What was the truth? Why was he cruel to their mother? Who should they love best? The Prince's camp believed it was impossible to win against what they saw as Diana's performative parenting. There was no point in trying to top all the images of Diana with the boys that were instant iconic testaments to a mother's love—and to a father's inadequacy. Charles's efforts to protect filial privacy and his genuine off-camera fatherly affection would never amount to a newspaper splash syndicated round the world. "I'm not very good at being a performing monkey," he would say grumpily, admitting to a lethal handicap in the media age.

The War of the Waleses, as it was now dubbed, raged with mounting fierceness. As often happens, the underlings were worse than the protagonists themselves: The two camps of royal advisers were as much to blame for the animosity as the couple, each side constantly spinning stories that would damn the other.

On December 9, 1992, Prime Minister John Major announced in Parliament the news of Charles and Diana's separation. The two princes listened sadly as their parents warned them in advance in the headmaster's sitting room at Ludgrove. "I hope you will both be happier now," said William, with heartbreaking maturity, after both boys had shed their tears.

The media they had been coached to smile at had turned into the rapacious enemy. After the marital separation, it was as if all boundaries fell, all respect evaporated. The pursuit of "Greta Garbo Di," as the tabloids called her, became the paparazzi's lucrative blood sport. The ultimate prize was to make her cry. In **Dicing with Di,** published the year before Diana died, the co-authors, paparazzi Mark Saunders and Glenn Harvey, openly mocked their quarry's distress. Saunders tells how Diana appealed for her sons' privacy: "Your lenses are very daunting, very daunting . . . the children find them so daunting." To which Saunders writes, "[Daunting.] Diana had learnt a new word that day."

Outings with their mother became unbearably fraught. One summer afternoon in 1993, Diana took the boys to a matinee showing of **Jurassic Park** at the Odeon Leicester Square. An ugly scrum of paparazzi waited to pounce as they came out. Harvey writes that a "flash of black shot across [his] view":

> It was Diana, but this was a Diana I had never seen before. It was her face, but it was now red and twisted. She was racing towards us through the crowds. Her eyes were fixed on us and then she let out a scream like a wild animal.

She confronted the photographers, yelling repeatedly, "You make my life hell."

Images such as this would haunt William and Harry in the years ahead. "One of the feelings that always comes up is the helplessness," Harry has since said. "Being too young, being a guy but too young to be able to help a woman. In this case your mother. And that happened every single day." Haunting too were the revelations that kept buffeting their belief in what their parents told them. Their fraternal bond was strengthened by a deep well of mistrust in everyone but each other. All the training they'd endured to present a perfect world of royal propriety was undermined by the squalid truth of their parents' secrets.

They were heartsick at their father's admission to Jonathan Dimbleby that he had been forced into marriage to Diana by Prince Philip, and that he had been unfaithful to Diana with Camilla. On the morning of October 17, 1994, they were summoned to the headmaster's study for a meeting with Diana, who had rushed to Ludgrove once again to perform damage control. They wanted answers. According to Andrew Morton, William, then twelve, asked her, "Is it true, Mother? Is it true that Daddy never loved you?"

Almost simultaneously, they were mortified by the fallout from the publication of **Princess in Love**, a sensational tell-all authored by **Daily Express** journalist Anna Pasternak. Closely based on sixty-four of Diana's love letters to her former lover James Hewitt, the book gave the boys the palpitating account of their mother's furtive affair from 1986 to 1991.

Hewitt had been their adored riding instructor. The redheaded army captain was like a dimmer, buffer version of Prince Charles, with the diction of a man who seemed to have swallowed a mothball. "Uncle James" was a weekend regular at Highgrove—with his dog Jester—when their father was away. He'd been an immediate hit with the boys, enthralling Harry with stories of life in the military. Ken Wharfe was less enthralled. He thought Hewitt was "a real prat." When Diana's lady-in-waiting offered him a cold sausage, he ate it and said, "May I say, my lady, that that was possibly the finest sausage I have ever tasted?") Hewitt took the boys on a guided tour of Combermere Barracks and, in an inspired gift, commissioned two miniature flak jackets, two pairs of army-green trousers, and two berets. He taught them how to march, how to salute, and how to carry a rifle. Best of all, he allowed them to climb into a tank. He sometimes drove them to Devon with Diana for merry sleepovers with Hewitt's mum.

Now it turned out he was her lover. Ludgrove made every attempt to shield the boys from the deluge of dirty laundry. Even though the boys were encouraged to read the papers for a weekly news quiz, certain copies in the common room often tactfully disappeared. It did not fool William, who used to slip into his protection officer's room to watch how his parents' problems were covered on TV news.

The **Princess in Love** publication had an unfortunate result for Harry. It amplified rumors that the redheaded Captain Hewitt was his real father, even though the dates of Harry's conception conclusively don't match up with the Diana-Hewitt affair. (My own skepticism about Harry's paternity was banished by a trip to Althorp, where ancestral portraits on the walls prove that Harry had no need of Hewitt's incursive genes to provide his ruddy coloring. One especially vivid nineteenth-century Spencer forebear was known as the Red Earl because of his vast auburn beard.) Before his first term at Eton in the fall of 1998, Charles sat Harry down and told him categorically that he, not Hewitt, was his father. Harry listened carefully and said nothing. It did not stop the rumors, nor the teasing at Eton. As late as 2002, the **News of the World** was said to be in the market for a clip of Harry's hair to enable a DNA match test with a strand of Hewitt's. Harry had to endure question traps from the press about "following your father into the army." "Navy, actually," he would reply with a hard stare.

Martin Bashir's **Panorama** interview with Diana inflicted more wounds. William, then only two months into his first semester at Eton, chose to view the broadcast alone in Dr. Gailey's study. After a year of turmoil on the home front, he was already in a fragile state. The Queen told a Palace source that she was worried he might have a nervous breakdown. His housemaster was concerned, too. According to Ingrid Seward, when Dr. Gailey heard that the interview was going to air, he called Diana and urged her to prepare William in person for what was coming. "Is that really necessary?" she pleaded, perhaps dreading how her "wise old man" would react. Much had changed since she had rushed to Ludgrove to comfort her emotionally bruised eldest son after the Dimbleby interview. Her intrigues were consuming her, and she preferred not to consider their consequences. Only when Gailey called again and pushed her did she agree.

On the eve of the Bashir interview Diana lay in wait for William outside Eton's fifteenth-century Gothic chapel as students filed out from Sunday service in their black tailcoats and white ties. The last to emerge, he had his head down, a Diana-like stance he had lately begun to adopt more and more. When she called out to him he responded with a sullen stare.

Diana was followed on this mission, of course. Paparazzo Mark Saunders saw it all. He climbed on the roof of a Ford Escort to get a better picture when, after an apparently pleading conversation, Diana took William behind a hedge to talk to him in private. "After a few more moments, he walked away from Diana, making no attempt to kiss her or say goodbye," Saunders recalled. "I watched in amazement as she got into the car and drove off, leaving a sad William watching from the doorway."

William told a classmate that as soon as he saw his mother's face appear on the screen for the interview, he was overcome with a feeling of dread. It's pitiable to think of him sitting there alone, watching his mother offer up to viewers a vignette as intensely private as how he consoled her about Hewitt's book. (She said he produced a box of chocolates with the words, "Mummy, I think you've been hurt. These are to make you smile again.") Harry, still at Ludgrove, declined to watch the broadcast, but later was angry with Bashir for his invasive questions, not with his mother's decision to answer them.

By the time Dr. Gailey returned to his study at Eton to collect William, he found him, Robert Lacey records, "slumped on the sofa, his eyes red with tears." He pulled himself together to rush back to his room. But, when, an hour later, Diana telephoned on the house phone, William refused to take the call.

On his return home his mother felt the full force of his hurt. He was furious that she had denigrated his father, furious that she had mentioned Hewitt. He felt humiliated that it had all been aired on television, which, he knew, would inevitably lead to torment from his friends. The next day, he brought her flowers, but Diana was convinced he would never forgive her. She kept asking Simone Simmons, "What have I done to my children?"

II

If your beautiful thirty-six-year-old mother dies in a car crash and is mourned—canonized, even—by the whole world, an unblemished picture is frozen that erases everything else. William, fifteen, and Harry, twelve, believed—and still believe—that their mother was martyred by the paparazzi.

That Diana was hounded is undeniable. But in her last spiral in Paris, there were many fatal factors. Pumped by Diana's celebrity, her feckless lover Dodi Fayed, unused to being in the eye of the celebrity storm, was overexcited by the thrill of the chase. It was Diana's choice—not the Palace's—to dispense with round-the-clock Scotland Yard protection. In the 2008 inquest into Diana's death, former police commissioner Lord Condon testified that in December 1993, when Diana declined further police protection, and over the next two years, there were ongoing meetings with the Princess and her private office to try to convince her to reconsider. But Diana was adamant, he said, that she did not want protection. She believed that officers spied on her and hampered her love life.

Trevor Rees-Jones, the bodyguard who worked for Dodi's father and traveled with them in the car, could not ensure that the most famous woman in the world was wearing a seatbelt. He was far down the totem pole from Henri Paul, her driver that night, who for nearly eleven years had run interference for the Fayeds. No royal protection officer would have allowed the Princess of Wales to get into a car with a driver like Paul, who had never qualified for a private limousine license, and who turned out to be drunk. Rees-Jones did not have the power to countermand Dodi's insistence that Paul drive, or to prevent Paul from making reckless taunts to the paparazzi, "Don't try to follow us! You won't catch us!" as Paul floored the accelerator and sped off to Dodi's apartment on the Rue Arsène Houssaye and entered the Alma tunnel.

Diana's royal protection officers and chauffeurs often acted as informal go-betweens with photographers to negotiate safer coverage of their famous charge. "It's very tragic to say this," Mark Saunders told me, speculating, "but had Ken Wharfe or Colin Tebbutt been with Diana on the night she died, it wouldn't have happened. They would have spoken to the press, and they would have given the brief outline of what was going to happen, which would have prevented the chasing."

In the hearts and minds of the two young princes. the hunting down of their mother by the paparazzi took on the proportions of myth, especially with Harry. William was so angry about the cascade of sordid revelations from the media during the year after she died that he nearly refused to go to the first anniversary remembrance service at Crathie Kirk because the press would be there too.

Almost as hard to process was the posthumous idolatry of Diana the Saint. Harry acknowledged the dissonance in an interview for Nick Kent's documentary.

"It was very, very strange after her death—the outpouring of love and emotion from so many people that had never even met her," he reflected.

And there was William and I walking around Kensington Palace Gardens here, and the sea of flowers all the way from the Palace gates, all the way back to Kensington High Street. And I was thinking to myself: How is it that so many people that never met this woman, my mother, can be crying and showing more emotion— than I actually am feeling?

A year after her death, the two boys issued an unexpected joint statement to say they had been "comforted enormously by the public sympathy and support they had been given." But they insisted that the time had come to stop grieving. "They believe their mother would now want people to move on," said their father's press secretary Sandy Henney. "Because she would have known that constant reminders of her death can create nothing but pain to those she left behind. They therefore hope, very much, that their mother and her memory will now finally be allowed to rest in peace."

It was a vain plea. Her sons were never fully allowed to move on: A constant drumbeat of scandals, conspiracy theories, books, movies, and legal actions made sure they could never look away. The Burrell betrayal was particularly cruel. William, twenty-one, and Harry, nineteen, were so stunned that the supposedly devoted butler had sold their mother out, they issued another joint statement:

> We cannot believe that Paul, who was entrusted with so much, could abuse his position in such a cold and overt betrayal. It was not only deeply painful for the two of us but also for everyone else affected and it would mortify our mother if she were alive today.

The anniversaries were excruciating. On Diana's tenth, in 2007, William asked his private secretary Jamie Lowther-Pinkerton—without success—to do everything he could do to stop a Channel 4 documentary showing graphic pictures of the Paris crash site. Lowther-Pinkerton wrote to Channel 4:

> These photographs, regardless of the fact that they do not actually show the princess's features, are redolent with the atmosphere and tragedy of the closing moments of her life.
>
> As such, they will cause the princes acute distress if they are shown to a public audience, not just for themselves, but also on their mother's behalf, in the sense of intruding upon the privacy and dignity of her last minutes.
>
> [As they said in their statement last year, after

the first publication of the pictures in an Italian magazine], "... We feel that, as her sons, we would be failing in our duty to her now if we did not protect her—as she once did us."

Did Diana protect them? It's not a debate that William and Harry want to have.

The story is more complicated. Time and again, as we have seen, Diana chose to invade her own privacy, often for the capricious reason of making the men in her life jealous. The most unforgettable "stolen" snap from Diana's last fateful holiday was the famous "kiss" picture of her in a clinch with bare-chested Dodi off the coast of Corsica. It was she who tipped off Italian lensman Mario Brenna—to send a taunting message to the current love of her life, Hasnat Khan.

Nicholas Coleridge, former president of Condé Nast International, tells a story in his memoir of inviting Diana to a boardroom lunch at Condé Nast HQ in 1996. The day before, a picture of the Princess sunbathing topless had appeared in the **Mirror,** causing a furor about invasion of privacy. Coleridge expected the Princess to cancel, but she confirmed her attendance with the request there would be no publicity. Halfway through a beguiling confidential lunch, she said:

"Nicholas, can I ask you something? Please be truthful. Did you see the photograph of me in the **Daily Mirror**? The topless one."

"Um, your Royal Highness, yes, we get all the newspapers in my office. I think I did glance at it . . . not that it was very clear."

"William rang me from Eton. Poor boy, he's only fourteen. He was upset. He said some of the other boys were teasing him, saying my tits are too small." She held on to my elbow. "Nicholas, please be frank, I want to know your real view. Are my breasts too small, do you think?"

I became breathless, I needed oxygen. I went as red as a guardsman's tunic. I stuttered, "Er, Your Royal Highness, in as much as I can see under your suit, they seem, um . . . perfect to me. I wouldn't worry."

"Thank you, Nicholas. I knew you'd tell me the truth. Thank you, I feel better now."

At the end of the lunch, Coleridge walked her to her car outside Vogue House, where she was besieged by paparazzi taking a thousand snaps.

Afterwards, Coleridge rang a newspaper friend, to see if he could find out who'd leaked her visit. He rang back in five minutes. Coleridge writes that his source told him, " 'I just spoke to our picture desk. Diana rang herself from her car, on her way to lunch. She often tips them off about where she'll be.' "

This is classic, authentic Diana—tricky, seductive, playing a double game. Cordless phone mogul Gulu Lalvani told me that in the four months of their relationship in June 1997 they always dined discreetly at his house or at Kensington Palace. One evening she suggested they instead dine at Harry's Bar and have a dance or two afterward at Annabel's. Even though no one had known about the plan in advance, the paparazzi were waiting at the door as they left the nightclub. Lalvani told me, "Whether Harry's Bar called them or she tipped them off, I don't know." (I think we do. . . .) He realizes now that she was using him to inflame the true object of her affections, Hasnat Khan. The pictures of Gulu and Diana that appeared the next day were the whole point.

More unsettling still is the truth behind the apparent treachery of Hewitt in cooperating with Pasternak's tell-all book. Like everything with Diana, it turned out to be more fraught. Diana claimed to be outraged when **Princess in Love** spilled the beans of their affair. "He's sold me out!" she screeched to Simone Simmons. "Men aren't supposed to do that to women. I hope his cock shrivels up!" Hewitt paid dearly and so did the author. The tabloids branded him forevermore as the "love rat," and Pasternak was excoriated for peddling mawkish fantasy. (Hewitt's attorney Mark Stephens felt obliged to advise him that the Treason Act of 1351 stipulates that having sex with the wife of the heir apparent was a capital offense. "I saw his Adam's apple wobble," Stephens told me. "He flushed from here to right over the head and down his neck.") Piers Morgan dressed a **Mirror** reporter in full armor, hired a white horse, and charged Hewitt's home to confront him on allegations of treason.

In 2019, however, Pasternak made a startling disclosure in the **Daily Mail** that Diana had encouraged, indeed urged, Hewitt to cooperate with the writing of the book **Princess in Love**. "He told me that Diana was worried that Andrew Morton's second book, due out that autumn, with which she had not cooperated, was going to expose their affair in unflattering terms," Pasternak wrote. "She was worried and wanted control. She was adamant that if their affair was presented in a book as a true love story, the world would not condemn the couple but would understand why they came together as they did." In 2021 Pasternak told me that she and Hewitt "met halfway between Devon and London in a field, and he said, 'Diana wants the story told but with two conditions. One, it has to come out before Morton's second book, and two, it has to be a love story.'" To oblige her, Pasternak says she crashed it out in five weeks.

Once **Princess in Love** was published, Diana threw both Hewitt and Pasternak under the bus. Besotted to the end, her cashiered toy soldier never revealed whether or not he had done her bidding. He made no comment about Pasternak's revelation.

It's hard to understand how a mother as devoted as Diana would choose, in 1995, a year after Hewitt's book, to drag up her affair with him again in her explosive interview with Martin Bashir. She knew how devastated her boys had been by their father's on-camera confession of infidelity with Camilla in the Dimbleby documentary, and how truly mortified they felt when **Princess in Love** came out. I am told Diana chose to speak about Hewitt because he was the only one of her ex-lovers who wasn't married. She could hardly tell the truth about her affair with the elegant art dealer Oliver Hoare, whose wife became so tired of Diana sitting outside their house in her car making nocturnal phone calls and hanging up that Mrs. Hoare reported them to the police as nuisance calls. All told, as the press feasted on these incidents, Diana had—with a large assist from Charles—put her beloved boys through a good deal of gut-wrenching emotional hell.

When Lord Dyson, one of England's most senior retired judges, issued his 2021 report unmasking the full extent of the BBC cover-up of Bashir's trickery in securing his interview with Diana, it, at least, gave the two princes some rationale for why she did something so destructive to their happiness. William chose to make a grave address on camera that could not quite hide the fury of a still-haunted son. "It is my view that the deceitful way the interview was obtained substantially influenced what my mother said," he told the world. "The interview was a major contribution to making my parents' relationship worse and has since hurt countless others. It brings indescribable sadness to know that the BBC's failures contributed significantly to her fear, paranoia and isolation that I remember from those final years with her."

The words "indescribable sadness" can only hint at her sons' private ordeal, but they also occlude the full picture. I don't subscribe to the now pervasive narrative that Diana was a vulnerable victim of media manipulation, a mere marionette tossed about by malign forces beyond her control. While strongly sympathetic to her sons' pain, I find it offensive to present the canny, resourceful Diana as a woman of no agency, as either a foolish, duped child or the hapless casualty of malevolent muckrakers.

When **Vogue**'s Anna Wintour and I, as editor of **The New Yorker,** had lunch with Diana in Manhattan in July of 1997—six weeks before her death—I was bowled over by the confident, skillful way she wooed us. Diana was always more beautiful in person than in photographs—the huge, limpid blue eyes, the skin like a freshwater pearl, the supermodel height that was even more imposing in three-inch-high Manolos. She told us her story of loneliness and hurt at Charles's hands with an irresistible soulful intimacy that sucked us in, then switched to a startlingly sophisticated vision of how she planned to leverage her celebrity for the causes she cared about. I was struck that day by the clarity of her vision of what would now be considered a "broad media content deal"—a film every two years, each one the centerpiece of a discrete humanitarian campaign. First, she said, she would raise awareness of an issue, then produce a documentary in partnership with one of the television channels, and ultimately leave a structure in place to maintain her involvement with the cause. The issue she wanted to start with was illiteracy. "Thick as a plank," she may have ruefully called herself, but Diana was always ahead of the curve.

Her plan sounds very like what Meghan and Harry are attempting with their entertainment deals today, but with one central difference: It was better thought-out.

There is no doubt that the deplorable Martin Bashir successfully exploited Diana's lonely mistrust of all around her. But the Princess was fully complicit—and satisfied, as Gulu Lalvani told me, with everything she said on **Panorama:** "I'm glad I did it, I know the family didn't like it, but I'm glad," she said to him. She even co-opted lines such as "There were three of us in this marriage," from her writer friend Clive James.

"She was walking a tightrope with her relationships with the press," Saunders told me. "It wasn't the press that had an affair with James Hewitt. It wasn't the press that had an affair with Oliver Hoare and sat outside his house in the middle of the night. . . . She was a normal person with feelings and emotions. But she was also the most famous woman in the world and she was doing things that made the other side want to photograph her."

All Diana's crazier decisions made sense to her at the time. In her wounded fury she lost all sense of the impact of her actions. Weeks after the interview, as the conflagration consumed everyone she loved and hated, the dogged Mark Saunders describes an eerie incident as the Princess sped ahead of him down the highway out of London. His prey knew Saunders's car well, and he could see her looking at him in the rearview mirror:

She indicated left and pulled across to the middle lane, slowing down considerably and forcing me to pass and then, in a moment of insanity . . . she suddenly increased her speed and lurched back into the fast lane, coming up directly behind me. We were traveling at 90 MPH when I felt Diana's bumper touch the rear of my car. If I had slowed down or put on the brakes at that point, the world would no longer have had a Princess of Wales.

Writing these words in 1995, Saunders could have no idea what they foreshadowed. In that last tragic chase into the Alma tunnel, was Diana urging Henri Paul to give the pursuing paparazzi the ride of their lives?

It would be unreasonable to ask that William and Harry forgive the paparazzi who trained their cameras on their beloved mother's dying moments in the Paris tunnel, the hungry clicking of their shutters the last sound she would ever hear. Or to forget how often in their presence one or another of that ruffian gang had made her cry. Or to admit that, even though her own sons were among the "countless others" the Bashir broadcast hurt, she had shrewd, pragmatic reasons for undertaking the interview. The camera was Diana's fatal attraction and her most potent weapon—the source of so much power at the price of so much pain. She was always gambling with those odds.

Today, her sons express their lasting contempt for the press in different ways: William with a grim, steely obsession with control; Harry with tortured, vocal, frequently ill-judged condemnation—and finally a burn-it-all-down gesture that his mother, who—despite her yearning to be free held tight to her diadem—might have well understood. But neither of them has yet been heard to reflect on how much Diana loved to dance with danger.

CHAPTER
12

ENTER KATE

William Meets an Extraordinary, Ordinary Girl

IN 2011, THE QUESTION MARK OVER KATE Middleton was whether a girl of such unexalted origins could successfully evolve into a future queen. Now the only question is how the House of Windsor could survive without her.

If there is one cardinal qualification for marrying into the monarchy, it is not beauty, not pedigree, and certainly not outstanding brains. It's resilience. Most of royal life is crushingly dull. It's like being a battery hen in the Waldorf Astoria. Prince Charles always used to despair that he knew exactly what he would be doing a year in advance. Over the course of seventy years, the Queen has only four times missed her annual January visit to the Sandringham chapter of the Women's Institute at West Newton Village Hall in Norfolk. (On her 2019 visit, she caused great excitement captaining one of the two

Women's Institute teams playing a live version of **Pointless,** one of her favorite TV shows.)

Without resilience, it's impossible to retain individual identity against the inexorable Palace machine. Prince Philip had to fight the "men in grey suits" who tried to marginalize his influence on the Queen. He kept sane by carving out a hyperactive commitment to causes and interests of his own. His success as a consort was all the more remarkable given his red-blooded masculinity and the fragility of his own dispersed family who offered so little support.

The longevity of Camilla Parker Bowles's relationship with the Prince of Wales is sustained by her dauntless self-assurance. Her aplomb never wavered, her pillow talk never leaked. She was insulated from court intrigue by the loyalty and discretion of the Shand clan. She has a robust core formed by the consistency of parental love in her early life, on which, she knew, she could always fall back.

Diana never had that support from her dysfunctional family, and we see how vulnerable it made her. She was always casting around for new messiahs. She never trusted people who could genuinely help her.

Prince William knew all this well. Some might even say harrowingly well. The drama and heartbreak of the past was an imprint on his soul—not just his mother's shocking death, but all that followed and preceded it: the ugliness of his parents' divorce, the river of sleaze fed by leaky servants and hangers-on, the reckless spinning of the media by both parents (not to mention the jealousies and pettiness of the Palace anthill). It's why he later would urge his younger brother to wait before **he** rushed to marry.

William made his own bride, Kate Middleton, wait, and wait, and wait before his cautious nature had assessed she was truly a woman of strength who could carry the royal burden. In doing so, he proved the benefit of a future king marrying a girl who was solidly middle class.

Like Diana, Kate is unexpectedly tall, but unlike Diana, Kate's charm is less about dazzle and more about sheen—the glossy lights in that swingy, conker-colored hair, the subtle polish of impeccable grooming, the luster of her smiling green-hazel eyes. There's a Mona Lisa quality to Kate. No one can quite figure out what she's really thinking, or why, after seeing the royal experience up close, she so terribly wanted a life of such limited freedom and non-negotiable good behavior. She exudes honest intelligence without being threateningly bookish, a desire to support with a strong sense of self, an ability to win the room without upstaging her husband. It is as if she were designed to be the blessed obverse of Diana.

In many ways, Kate belongs in a novel by Anthony Trollope, that great Victorian chronicler of social mobility. As a story, the Middleton family's steady striving and incremental social advancement is too dogged and upstanding for Dickens, with his eye for mega-frauds, chiselers, and shysters. Dickens's heroines were, for the most part, sweet airheads, victims, or what was once called "tarts with a heart." George Eliot's women, by contrast, were too complicated and reflective, though Eliot might have seen the Middleton family as the tempting epitome of tenacious ascent, ripe for a guilty secret. Where Dickens imagines the aristocratic class as stultified and zombie-like, Trollope has a far keener sense of the old oligarchy as vulnerable, open, and desperately in need of an update. That reboot is achieved, as often as not, by the entry into their circles of a bracing breath of middle-class air from a female character, like Isabel Boncassen in **The Duke's Children,** irresistible not because she is rich or even beautiful—though she is that—but because she embodies healthy energy, fresh blood:

> Her hair was dark brown and plentiful; but it added but little to her charms, which depended on other matters. . . . It was . . . the vitality of her countenance,—the way in which she could speak with every feature, the command which she had of pathos, of humour, of sympathy, of satire, the assurance which she gave by every glance of her eye, every elevation of her brow, every curl of her lip, that she was alive to all that was going on.

It's the Kate Middleton template to a T—in any social situation, she exhibits an easy human engagement that projects the bourgeois virtues of sympathy and comforting common sense. Like Kate, the quintessential Trollope heroine has heart and seeks happiness, but within a moral compass. She's a woman who leaves a glow behind her when she works a room.

The Middletons of The Manor, Berkshire, are the bedrock of Kate's aspirational resolve. You only have to look at their real estate trajectory over the past thirty years to see the resolute rise in their social status. They moved from a four-bedroom semi-detached Victorian in the Southend village of Bradfield, forty-eight miles west of London, to the comfortably rambling five-bedroom, three-reception-room Oak Acre in the Berkshire village of Bucklebury, to the crème de la crème site of The Manor on Pease Hill up the road, built on eighteen acres of land prized out of monks in Henry VIII's dissolution of the monasteries. There is handy separate accommodation space for royal police protection officers when required.

Bucklebury has the kind of leafy country charm of BritBox TV detective mysteries, with an ancient village church, pub, and quaint creeper-covered cottages. Until the age of thirteen, Kate lived in the first of the three Middleton homes, the small semi-detached in Bradfield. A real estate agent in 2011 noted that we would have to "go back as far as Boudica's mud hut to find a more modest house that was once home to a future Queen." Her parents' move to The Manor in 2012 coincided with the Cambridges' residency of their current twenty-room, four-story apartment at Kensington Palace.

Kate's father, the mild-mannered Michael Middleton, is a former British Airways flight dispatcher who hails from steadfast West Yorkshire stock. His forebears slogged upward inch by respectable inch from nineteenth-century cabinetmaking to the top levels of the legal profession in Leeds. The Middletons' position in civic society was sealed by a marriage into the Lupton wool and textile manufacturing fortune in the 1920s that sixty years later left enough of a trust fund to send Kate and her two siblings to expensive private schools. Michael Middleton is a man of open countenance; handsome, silver-haired demeanor; genial good judgment; and watertight discretion. "One always feels he can't wait to get back to mow his lawn," one social acquaintance said to me. When he speaks of his three children, Kate, Pippa, and James, he does so as if there's no difference between them. "My daughter murdered me at tennis this weekend," leaving which daughter unsaid.

Kate's mother, Carole, is acknowledged by all as the dynamo in the family. She is the daughter of a sales assistant and a builder-decorator who met Michael when he worked as a member of the ground staff at British European Airways and she was an air stewardess. She married up, and was a hard worker who used to perfect her delivery of passenger announcements by playing them back on tape. Her origins are scrappy working-class, a family of strivers who moved to west London from the mining community of Durham and made a living as carpenters.

Carole was raised in a council flat in Southall, a suburban London district now known as Little Punjab. She inherited her drive from her socially ambitious mother, Dorothy "Dot" Goldsmith, aka "The Duchess," who, according to a snarky relative, "wanted to be the top brick in the chimney" and pushed Carole around in "the biggest Silver Cross pram you've ever seen." Her younger brother, Gary Goldsmith, made a pile in the IT recruitment business, married four times, and enjoyed the high life in a holiday villa in Ibiza he named Maison de Bang Bang. "I'm a Thatcher child," he has said. "I'm Captain Ambitious. I belong to a generation in which class does not exist."

There was always a natural, rangy style to Carole Middleton. She never looks mumsy in a wedding hat. She's a slim, vivacious brunette with elegant legs that are sometimes encased in jeans tucked into knee-length riding boots. Her brother describes her wedding to the affable Michael as everything their mother, "The Duchess," could have dreamed of: "natural, informal and classy [not] pretentious or ostentatious—very unlike the weddings I was used to, which were big booze-ups in a Heathrow hotel with round tables and dodgy speeches."

A comfortable marriage didn't mute Carole's drive. She became a kitchen-table entrepreneur when she was pregnant with James, her youngest, stuffing children's party bags and selling them by mail order in a business she christened Party Pieces. She is one of those managerial mothers who have figured out how to be both warmly maternal and successful with a career. A strategy of marketing Party Pieces with flyers through a children's book club was so successful that Michael quit his job and joined her effort to scale a business now reportedly valued at over £30 million. She was famous for the toughness of her negotiating skills. "Butter wouldn't melt in her mouth most of the time," one of her suppliers has said, "but she was a ferocious negotiator—and if the haggling wasn't going her way, then the decibel level rose."

Carole was a self-made millionaire by the time she was in her thirties, hardly typical for a young mother in the home counties in the 1980s. Her company operated first out of a hut in the garden and later out of a sprawling collection of brick sheds and barns on an estate near the Middleton home. The children were always incorporated into her working life. She never missed a school function or seemed overly stressed by concerns about work-life balance. Kate still rhapsodizes about the "the amazing white rabbit marshmallow cake" Carole made for her when she was seven. The Middleton parents showed up at all the school sports events, bearing an expensive picnic and cheering for their daughters' teams. As a child, Kate sometimes modeled for the catalog, and later set up a "First Birthday" effort while Pippa cranked out the blog and James started a cake-making vertical. The ability to drift in and out of the family business gave the kids cover as they pursued their own minimal careers.

II

Once the Middleton girls had been dispatched to glossy up-market, co-ed schools like the small country prep St. Andrew's in Pangbourne and then as boarders at Marlborough College in Wiltshire, a collision between Kate and Prince William at sporting events or school dances would not have been noteworthy. Many of the elite girls' schools socialized with Eton. Kate did get a glimpse of the nine-year-old Prince when he came from Ludgrove for a hockey match against St. Andrew's School, and she attended a tea afterward. The breathless press later tried to reproduce a Diana-like narrative of the ten-year-old Kate pining for her prince forever after, but Kate brushed that off at the engagement interview. Her heart had yearned for the Levi's guy on a poster on her dorm wall, she insisted briskly, not William.

Marlborough was the making of Kate. Perched over acres of rolling downs on the outskirts of a particularly beautiful market town in Wiltshire, its eighteenth-century redbrick architecture and Hogwarts-like chapel exudes moneyed substance. As one of the first major independent schools to go co-ed in 1968, Marlborough encourages a healthy equipoise between the sexes that doesn't just turn out alpha young women but alpha consorts as well. Prime Minister David Cameron's fashion executive wife, Samantha, was a Marlburian, as was accomplished author Frances Osborne, ex-wife of the former chancellor of the exchequer George Osborne,

and the economist Diana Fox Carney, who married
former governor of the Bank of England Mark
Carney. A recent Marlburian says that given that
British independent boys' schools were for so long
an elitist male club, being inside on equal terms
breeds confidence, a sense of ease around boys, and
the ability to be comfortable in a partnership of
peers.

Marlborough's vigorous atmosphere buoyed Kate
after two tearful semesters at Downe House, a mean-
girl academy in Berkshire. When Kate asked her
wedding guests to contribute to BeatBullying, the
country's leading anti-bullying charity, it was widely
assumed that her Downe House tribulations in the
nineties were the cause. And there is truth, for once,
to a seemingly glib assumption of this kind. Downe
House was a vat of boiling estrogen. Eating disorders
were so common girls had to smoke in the lavato-
ries to conceal the smell of sick. One alum, with the
unlikely name of Taffeta Gray, recalled in the **Daily
Mail** some of the seniors rugby-tackling her when
she came out of the shower, pinning her down,
taking her towel, and spraying her groin with blue
hairspray. Then they threw her out into the corridor
naked. "Girls can be very cruel," a former student
told **The Sunday Times.** "You have to remember it
is in the middle of nowhere, up on a hill. There's
nowhere to run, no way to let off steam or get away.
Bitchiness breeds in that environment, especially as
some will do whatever it takes."

Kate was shy, stringy, and taller than her peers.

She was a day student in a predominantly boarding environment and started at thirteen, two years later than many of her classmates. At her prep school, she was a hockey star, but she was required to play lacrosse at Downe House. "You pick up a lacrosse stick and think you're good at games," the former head teacher Susan Cameron told **The Mail on Sunday** chillingly, "then someone says to you, 'That's not how you pick up a lacrosse stick,' and you feel rather squashed."

The mean girls in the popular group looked down on the girl from Boudica's mud hut. "She was regarded as a nonentity," recalled a classmate. "All the social-climbing girls—and there were lots of them at Downe—thought she was not worth bothering with." Another alum recalled Kate sitting on the stairs of her house crying her eyes out. Head teacher Cameron, who sounds like a corporate version of Roald Dahl's Miss Trunchbull, defended the school in words that made Kate sound like a wet blanket. The girls, she said, "were encouraged to play to their strengths. It could be difficult if you were a shrinking violet type." It was so bad Kate developed stress eczema. Carole and Michael Middleton whipped her out of there fast in the middle of the year.

Kate got her game back at co-ed Marlborough. She doesn't have the bitch gene you need to be a player at a single-sex school. She became joint captain of the tennis team and a star at hockey, and she shone at swimming and netball. She was outstanding at high jump. She won a Duke of Edinburgh's

Award for community work and an expedition that was a four-day hike in the pouring rain. What could be better training for vacations at Balmoral? When she received her award at Buckingham Palace, she was unaware she was shaking hands with her children's future great-grandfather.

Her looks had blossomed by the age of sixteen, as a sleek Kate butterfly emerged from the chrysalis of whey-faced "Middlebum" (as she was first known). She lost her braces and returned from a hockey trip to Argentina after her GCSEs a raging beauty, rating top of the "Fit List" by Marlborough men who had given her a low rating when she first arrived. Academically, she was unflashily bright, winning two A's and a B in her A-level exams. In her senior year, she was chosen to be head of house and was voted "Person Most Likely to Be Loved by Everybody" in the 2000 yearbook. On Marlborough Prize Day, she bobbed up and down receiving so many honors for outstanding conduct that she reportedly could not return to her seat, and had to remain blushing on-stage throughout.

She now ran with the Marlborough chapter of the "Glosse Posse," well-born Gloucestershire girls who still are members of her most intimate circle, and was asked to parties at stately homes. Two of her closest girlfriends, Emilia d'Erlanger, now a godmother to Prince George, and Alice St. John Webster, moved in William's circles. The education that the Middletons paid so much money for was laying the ground for her social quantum leap. In 1999, when Kate was seventeen, Emilia d'Erlanger asked her to a house party also attended by William, without any recorded spark. It's as if they were circling each other and logging up points of future attraction.

Kate had a couple of crushes on boys and a romance with the handsome captain of the rugby team, but she retained a princessly reserve noted by her peers. She rarely got drunk. Hers "was quite an old-fashioned approach—especially at Marlborough where half of the pupils were already having sex," one of her schoolmates, Gemma Williamson, has said, sounding rather old-fashioned herself. "Although she had a couple of very innocent 'snogs,' she just wasn't willing to experiment like other girls. I got the distinct impression that Catherine wanted to save herself for someone special." Or as the Tory men's club mag **The Spectator** haw-hawed in a piece handicapping her chances as a royal bride, Kate still had "her V-plates intact and thus [satisfied] the age-old requisite for future queen consorts."

Her younger sister, Pippa, arrived on a sports scholarship in Kate's second year and was known as "Panface" for her flat features. They were billeted in the same house and, like William and Harry, shared many of the same friends. Pippa was considered a spicier personality than Kate, though it was the shiny good looks of both of them that made the Middleton sisters, as one alum put it to me, "a Marlborough thing." Sharper than Kate academically, and also an athletic star, Pippa exhibited some of the drive and vivacity of her mother. "My focus is on winning and making sure that my hair—fashioned into a slick Sporty Spice 'up do'—is just right. Did I mention the boys watching?" she wrote saucily in a column also in **The Spectator.** Only a year apart, there was a tiny whiff of rivalry between the beautiful sisters reminiscent of the American Bouviers, Jackie Kennedy and Lee Radziwill. Though Kate was an outstanding member of the hockey team at Marlborough, it was Pippa who was team captain and was tipped to play for England. "Kate was always quite jealous of Pippa," a family friend said. "I sensed that she feared being eclipsed by her, because Pippa has more natural effervescence, is socially much more at ease, and was always popular with everyone, especially [her brother] James's friends."

Pippa's social ascent seems more calculated than Kate's. Later, at Edinburgh University, she shared an apartment with two boys whose fathers were dukes. "As soon as Pippa arrived at Edinburgh, she was assiduous about joining the right social circle," an alum has said. "She was very charming about it, but quite ruthless in cultivating the 'right' friends." In 2017, she married forty-one-year-old James Matthews, a rich hedge fund manager and heir to the Scottish feudal title of Laird of Glen Affric. His parents, David and Jane Matthews, own the Eden Rock hotel, a celebrity hangout on the Caribbean island of St. Barts. Jane comes from Rhodesian money with a "rock chic" style and social flair that gives Carole Middleton yet more competitive stress when she sets out the carefully folded napkins and scented candles at Bucklebury dinners. Pippa further evened up the ledger by swiftly producing two picturesque children. Hand it to Carole Middleton, her girls have done well.

It is unlikely Kate would be where she is today without her mother's canny help in negotiating a royal romance. Carole Middleton is usually characterized as a cross between Jane Austen's Mrs. Bennet and the sitcom social climber Hyacinth Bucket, who answers the phone "The Bouquet residence." Neither model is right. Carole has considerable strategic flair. Whenever Kate was bloodied in the ring, she retreated to Bucklebury, where Coach Carole would dress her wounds, advise her on moves, and urge her to keep her eyes on the prize.

Carole's fingerprints are all over Kate's first move on the royal chessboard. When the news was announced in 2000 that Prince William would be spending his university years at the small Scottish university of St. Andrews, Kate suddenly bailed out of Edinburgh University fifty miles away and reapplied at St. Andrews. Andrew Neil, former rector at St. Andrews, told me it is not uncommon for students to apply for both universities and decide at the last minute, often depending on where friends are going. "It's easy for them all to stay in touch regardless," says Neil. "Every weekend scores of poshos (the rich kids) leave St. Andrews for Edinburgh to party with friends (and sometimes vice versa)." But Kate's two best friends, Emilia and Alice, had applied to Edinburgh, too. The trio had already found lodgings to share. Kate had worked hard at Marlborough for her A-level exams and achieved the high grades that qualified her for her first choice, Edinburgh, which Pippa and James later attended.

The two Scottish universities couldn't be more different. In American terms, it was like choosing between a large, broad-based Ivy League university and a bijou liberal arts college. Edinburgh has a humming city and festival life, and a stellar reputation in art history, versus the romantic seclusion of the medieval St. Andrews campus, surrounded by cobblestones marking where Protestant martyrs were burned at the stake. It was not Kate's style to blow off something she had worked so hard to achieve, then blithely take a gap year and reapply to somewhere the exact opposite in ambience. Carole was the chancer in the family, not Kate.

"If you got a place at Edinburgh, you would hang on to it, unless Oxford or Cambridge cropped up," a distinguished Scottish editor told me. "You would only sacrifice that place for St. Andrews for one of the following reasons: (a) There was a course at St. Andrews which offered exactly what you wanted and wasn't available at Edinburgh or (b) You heard that the heir to the throne was going to St. Andrews, and you thought . . ."

Kate spent half her gap year attending the Italian

and art history courses favored by gilded girls at the British Institute of Florence. She stayed in an apartment for three months in the center of town with her cousin Lucy Middleton, demurely taking in the masterpieces like Lucy Honeychurch in E. M. Forster's **A Room with A View** and hanging out with other "poshos," as Andrew Neil would call them, at cappuccino bars. Over dinner one night when the Middleton parents visited, a friend recorded Carole marveling to the waiters about her daughter's appearance. Her natural bloom, that luxurious mane of burnished brown hair! "Look at my English rose. Isn't she so beautiful?"

Now on course, Kate had a Zelig-like ability to keep appearing on the edges of William's life. Even the ten-week Outward Bound–like program she joined after Florence, Raleigh International, supporting sustainable international development in Chile, was the very one that William had just completed. It was an earnest, character-building expedition, very hard to get into without creds like the Duke of Edinburgh's Award and the ability to personally raise £3,000 to be admitted. The challenge demanded three weeks of wilderness trekking, three weeks in an inflatable boat surveying marine life, and a spell helping to build a new fire station for an impoverished community. Kate was rated "one of the fitter and stronger members of the group" who retained "a certain aura." Others say she always looked good and displayed a notable lack of drama.

III

Closer and closer. William had aced Raleigh International, too. He was pushed to do it by Mark Dyer, Charles's erstwhile equerry, who had taken over the job of mentoring his sons in their post-school years. Known as Marko to his friends, Dyer is a copper-haired, six-foot-tall straight-shooting former Welsh Guards officer who once dated Tiggy Legge-Bourke, and today is godfather to Harry's son, Archie. Dyer's Palace brief for gap year guidance seems to have been to follow the Prince Philip credo of pounding the boys with fresh air, exercise, and community service: hectic, macho jungle-training in Belize, a stint on a marine project in Mauritius, a spell in Kenya working on a game reserve, a month cleaning out cow stalls and milking on a dairy farm, and a ten-week expedition with Raleigh International in Chile.

According to plan, it all went wrong. William's Raleigh International group in Chile had to sea-kayak through raging storms. The party was marooned on a beach for five nights in a freezing downpour. One of the at-risk youth participants became agitated, and the only person who could reportedly calm him down was William. The Prince found a way to soothe and connect with the young man that would have made his mother proud. On the last leg of the trip, he mucked in at a primary school in a rough local community, filling the British newspapers for two days with magical shots of Diana's beautiful boy sharing her gift for connecting with disadvantaged children. William's combination of bashful good looks, hardy endurance, and tender relatability has never been so appealing, before or since.

To keep a low profile, he arrived at St. Andrews in September 2001 after the freshmen's meet-and-greet week. It was a somber international moment, twelve days after the 9/11 attacks. There was anxiety about possible further attacks on American allies, compounded by a St. Andrews campus anthrax scare in August. Prince Charles drove William up, trailed by private detectives. (William had two personal protection officers.) They got in some goodwill engagements first in Glasgow and in Edinburgh, where they signed a condolence book at the U.S. consulate. William wrote in it the boyish message "With deepest sympathy, love from William." They squeezed in lunch with his 101-year-old "Gan-Gan," the Queen Mother, at her Highland home. Her parting words were "Any good parties, invite me down."

The young Prince, like Kate, had preferred Edinburgh as a first choice, but royal protection officers deemed the setting too exposed to ensure his safety. Brian Lang, the principal and vice-chancellor of St. Andrews, had multiple conversations with the Palace about the best way to protect him. Prince Charles had visited himself and checked out the proposed hall of residence, St. Salvator's, bouncing on a student bed. ("Hmmn, this will do.") A robust deal was negotiated with the Press Complaints Commission that while William was at St. Andrews, the press would continue to leave him alone until after he graduated. The original deal that the PCC struck with newspaper editors for Eton was extended to cover William until he finished full-time education. (Mostly it was followed, except for the debacle of his uncle Prince Edward's production company showing up.) Lord Black, the former director of the PCC, told me he would never forget a town hall meeting he conducted with St. Andrews students soon before William arrived:

> Andrew [Neil] said that students were worried they would find themselves in the papers if they hung out with or were seen around William. So I went up there. We approached the church where the meeting was taking place and I said, "What's that queue of people?" and it became rapidly clear that it was a line trying to get into a 500-seat church when I was expecting about 50. I was bombarded with questions about whether indiscreet behavior anywhere near William would end up on the front page. It made you realize what that was like for William to have this issue loom so large with people who befriended him.

True friends of William had to get used to being stalked and—it was later revealed—phone-hacked by the press. The Prince was lucky to just miss the launch of Twitter and Facebook in 2006, and all the subsequent torments of social media that doubtless await his son Prince George when he attends university in the future.

The last thing William desired at St. Andrews was the coddled loneliness of his father's experience at Cambridge. He made it known he didn't want to be referred to as His Royal Highness or be addressed as "Sir" and was listed at Sallies—as St. Salvator's Hall of Residence is known—under the name of William Wales of Tetbury (the town in Gloucestershire near Highgrove House). Kate found herself there, too, on the floor below. More kismet? William was also down to study art history. It's hard to imagine that, for reasons of discretion, the students placed near William were not carefully vetted by protection officers, and that the Prince had not checked out their names. William was so paranoid about whom he could trust that he sometimes fed new people in his circle tidbits that were untrue and waited to see if they leaked. "But people who try to take advantage of me and get a piece of me—I spot it quickly and soon go off them," he told the BBC's Jennie Bond in 2001. His welfare was closely monitored by the medieval historian David Corner, the university secretary and registrar who checked in on him with pastoral meetings every three or four weeks.

Given such caution, it was unlikely William's dating patterns would diverge from the long roll call of his former aristocratic conquests, mostly drawn from polo types or landowners' daughters. (The Times listed some of them as Natalie "Nats" Hicks-Löbbecke; Rose, the daughter of Captain Ian Farquhar, master of the Beaufort Hunt; Davina Duckworth-Chad, whose brother, James, was an equerry to the Queen; Lady Katherine Howard, daughter of the Earl of Suffolk; Emma Parker Bowles, Camilla's niece; and Alexandra Knatchbull, the great-granddaughter of Lord Mountbatten.) His social circle was replete with the same old stuffy titles from the Highgrove set whose parents had bored Diana, and the trend threatened to continue in his first year at St. Andrews. He had a romance with Carly Massy-Birch, the vivacious daughter of Devon farmers, and he continued to dally with a beautiful twenty-one-year-old proto-Kate named Arabella Musgrave, whose father managed the Cirencester Park Polo Club. Feelings for her drew him back repeatedly to London.

Other students found him retiring and low-key. The "shy" stance perfected at Eton was self-protection. William was perfectly aware he was a campus rock star. If he showed up at his favorite St. Andrews pub for a pint, the bar immediately filled with a questing hubbub of expectant girls. Royal correspondent Robert Jobson says that "William the bashful" was "a persona he invented—a very effective cover for a boy who was growing in confidence daily." In an interview for his twenty-first birthday, William said he kept his head down a lot in an unsuccessful attempt not to be photographed. "Usually I was photographed with my eyes looking through a big blond fringe. It was very silly . . . but I'm someone who doesn't particularly like being the center of attention."

How for Kate to penetrate? It was easy at least to make sure their paths crossed on their dorm stairs. Marlborough's training in the way to build male friendships without entanglement was critical in Kate's ability to earn William's wary confidence. Unlike the flock of female students—especially Americans—who flagrantly hit on William, she built his trust by seeming uninterested. (It helped her mystique in the first semester that she had a good-looking fourth-year law student named Rupert Finch in her thrall.) After her morning run, she sometimes joined William and his friends for breakfast in the hall. (His clique, known as "the Sallies boys," always sat next to the head table flanked by oil paintings of philosophers from the Scottish Enlightenment.) Or they swam together at the Old Course Hotel in St. Andrews. During their art history classes, they often sat unobtrusively together. She shared her notes when he didn't attend lectures.

Home for Christmas after his first semester in 2001, William horrified his father—and Mark Bolland—with the news he wasn't going back. He was bored by St. Andrews for all the reasons his police protection liked it. It was a small seaside town with very little action that gets dark by four P.M. in winter.

The timing of his news could not have been worse. The Palace had strategic reasons for wanting the heir to the throne to study north of the border. In 1998, Scotland voted for devolution, and after the passing of the Scotland Act, important powers from Westminster were transferred to a newly established

Scottish parliamentary body. There was a feeling at the Palace, and among conservatives generally, that the break might herald something worse—the gradual sliding away of Scotland from the clutches of the Union. The Queen, a master throughout her reign at the art of gracious retreats while somehow preserving the aura of sovereignty, made a stirring speech to the new Scottish parliament in 1999, praising the "grit, determination, humor, and forthrightness of the Scots." Leaving St. Andrews would be a public relations disaster for William, and he would be trashed in the press as a spoiled quitter, like poor Prince Edward had been when he threw in the towel with the Royal Marines.

At this critical juncture, Kate Middleton showed a gentle mastery of soft power reminiscent of how the Queen Mother handled George VI. In a series of earnest conversations, she urged William to drop art history, a subject in which he had little or no interest (and only chose as an easy-sounding option). Why not switch to the gripping subject of geography, Kate soothed. After all, she reminded him, he had done so awfully well at it in A levels at Eton. Andrew Neil says he told university administrators opposed to this change of course, "Do you have any idea of the reputational damage that will be done to the university if [William] drops out? I don't care if he wants to study Welsh basket weaving, I don't give a monkey's. He can study whatever he wants."

Crisis averted, William asked Kate, in an obvious but unspoken declaration of trust, to join his flat share (with Fergus Boyd and another student, Olivia Bleasdale) in off-campus accommodation for their second year at 13A Hope Street, a maisonette in the center of town.

IV

Sexual attraction caught fire at the university's annual "Don't Walk" charity fashion show at the St. Andrews Bay Hotel in March 2002. Principal and Vice-Chancellor Lang, who was standing at the back, remembers it to me as the kind of cozy campus occasion when everyone was laughing about a male student modeling underwear with a sock stuffed down his shorts. The funds raised were going to the victims of the 9/11 attack, and the room was packed. In a **Bridgerton**-esque scene, William had bought one of the most expensive front-row tables for himself and his young buck friends to get a ringside look at the girls parading past. Everyone noticed that he was transfixed by a smoking-hot brunette who waltzed down the catwalk in a diaphanous black-and-gold silk dress with the shortest of short skirts that showed off her figure and supermodel-long legs.

Kate Middleton? His terribly nice future housemate? She of the weighty heart-to-heart about the merits of geography? For William it was a double-take as indelible as Vronsky's first sight of Anna Karenina at the Moscow railway station. At the after-party, William attempted to kiss the toast of the show, but she was still involved with Rupert Finch and pushed him away. One of their friends who observed their connection told Katie Nicholl, "He actually told her she was a knockout that night, which caused her to blush. There was definitely chemistry between them, and Kate had really made an impression on William. She played it very cool." Yet she had also made the decision to sashay past William wearing what was designed as a see-through skirt hoisted up as a dress with her underwear showing through. Reported later as the moment William made his first move, it feels more like the moment when Kate Middleton first made hers.

At their flat-share at 13A Hope Street, Kate got a close-up preview of William's compartmentalized world. Beyond the seclusion of their bubble in November 2002, the Paul Burrell trial was collapsing, and wounding secrets were spilling out about his mother's lovers. In the early days of their friendship in April, the funeral of the Queen Mother required the young Prince to travel to London to walk with other members of the Royal Family behind his great-grandmother's funeral cortege to Westminster Abbey. Collective memories of the flushed, sad boy following Diana's coffin with his small brother through the silent city streets were inescapable. Did William share any of this muffled pain with Kate as they became close? The thread of history inevitably connects the moment to another royal ceremonial funeral, Lord Mountbatten's, when eighteen-year-old Lady Diana Spencer observed with brimming, sympathetic eyes Prince Charles's profound grief at the murder of his great-uncle. "You looked so sad when you walked up the aisle at Mountbatten's funeral," Diana told him later, striking a chord of connection in their first meaningful conversation.

William and Kate became a secret couple, protected by their friends. No PDA. Arrive and depart at separate times. The seclusion of St. Andrews makes it a perfect place to be left alone. As a mecca of golf, town residents were used to seeing local celebrities like Sean Connery buying a newspaper or Michael Douglas having a drink in the pub. Kate loved to cook and host dinners. William made use of a cottage on the Balmoral estate where they would repair at weekends to roam around the moors. William got his girlfriend ready to impress his relatives by teaching her how to shoot.

What is striking is how bourgeois they became so fast. In their third year, they moved farther out with two other male friends of William's, Alasdair Coutts-Wood and Oli Baker, to Balgove House, a four-bedroom cottage on the Strathtyrum estate that resembled a mini Highgrove with two acres of grassland hidden behind a six-foot stone wall owned by a friend of the Royal Family. It was their home for their last two years at St. Andrews. The secret William was much less **un homme ordinaire**. He installed a polished mahogany table that seated seventeen and a well-stocked wine fridge. At an age when most young couples want to hang loose, these two were

full-bore into grocery shopping at Tesco and hosting
black-tie dinners. Harry often came to stay on weekends with an open invitation from Kate that made
him feel it was a home away from home.

The lack of drama provided William with an emotional safe space. There are echoes of the haven
Princess Elizabeth gave to Philip after his years of
orphaned wandering around Europe. Kate never
made jealous scenes. Rivals had a habit of being
nuked by her obliviousness. At William's twenty-first
birthday party at Windsor Castle, when he sat her
on a faraway table and himself next to Jecca Craig,
the striking daughter of conservationists in Kenya,
she showed no pique at his rapt attention to someone else.

Not that she wasn't quietly vigilant. "Kate saw
everybody off," a member of her circle told me. "I
mean, anyone that had had anything in the immediate past, or appeared in parties where he would
sort of cast an eye and cruise across the room and
say, 'Hi,' she absolutely picked them off one by one
in the crosshairs." (She ultimately dispatched Jecca
by visiting the Lewa Wildlife Conservancy in Kenya
with William and wrapping her into a mutual
friendship.)

Whenever their romance hit a speed bump, she
would retreat to Bucklebury for strategy sessions
with Carole. The tightness of the Middleton clan
was one of the strongest weapons in Kate's armory.
Kate is as close to her brother, James, as she is to
Pippa and has always been supportive in his

struggles with depression. Despite his own status as a minor celebrity, like all the Middletons, James has honored the family omertà on anything to do with his now-royal sister.

After a year of dating Kate, William adopted the whole family. "Not only did he fall for her but **them**," one of their acquaintances said to me. "A warm nest with a complete nuclear family and seemingly wonderfully uncomplicated. The dad played the dad, the mum the county's tiger mum, but also he saw the daughters and James getting along—and wanting to get along—with their parents. What a contrast." The prince who could take his pick of palaces and estates to spend weekends wanted nothing so much as tennis, TV, and Carole's creature comforts at the Middleton manse. He was such a regular houseguest he had his quad bike transferred from Highgrove to Bucklebury, and joined them on their well-planned vacations to luxury resorts. The En Masse Middletons, as their togetherness was dubbed by the press, regularly descended on Mustique. Carole, said another islander, is the kind of "fun woman who after a drink or two will pull you into a corner of Basil's Bar for a good gossip while Kate circulates for thirty minutes then melts away with William early." Michael Middleton became like a surrogate father. "If your own father is always hosting dinner parties for fifty on Catherine the Great china or whatever," an older acquaintance of William's said to me, "it's not very relaxing. Whereas the Middletons were like a pipe and slippers, with the wireless on, which is slightly the sort of William and Kate world." The Prince even liked the tattooed, bullet-headed Gary Goldsmith, whom he called "Uncle G." In 2006, he and Kate went to stay with Gary in Ibiza and sailed to Formentera on a yacht he rented.

The couple was so discreet and well protected by their friends that they weren't busted by the press until March 2004. Only when Kate was spied in Klosters riding up the mountain on a T-bar beside an affectionate William was it clear that this radiant brunette occupied a position of settled intimacy.

V

The exposure of their relationship was unhelpful to Kate's quiet campaign. It nettled William into wanting to prove his independence and heading off on a sailing trip in Greece with his childhood friend Guy Pelly—whose Rabelaisian presence usually meant trouble—and a racy all-girl crew. Two formidable possible rivals appeared on the scene later that summer: a vivacious American heiress, Anna Sloan, who hosted William solo on her father's estate in Nashville in August, and the extravagantly named Isabella Anstruther-Gough-Calthorpe, one of the stunning blond actress daughters of the much-married beauty Lady Mary-Gaye Curzon. William was fascinated by her, but Isabella was too beautiful and well-connected to find the hassle of being his girlfriend interesting. She later married a more amusing version of a royal heir: billionaire entrepreneur Richard Branson's son, Sam, at his father's private safari lodge near Kruger National Park.

The stakes were much higher for Kate now that the relationship with William was public. She had to balance widespread humiliation if William dumped her with the need to never push too hard. Her family came under scrutiny with barely veiled sneers about her mother's lower-middle-class origins. A steady drip of blind quotes appeared from unnamed friends or peripheral Palace factotums suggesting "doors to manual" (an airline term before landing) was whispered when the former flight attendant Carole socialized in upper-class circles. Eyes supposedly rolled when Mrs. Middleton said "Pardon?" instead of the brisk bark of the toff-approved "What?" "At first Carole rather enjoyed the attention," a family friend said. "She seemed to find the whole thing quite dizzying, but the constant nit-picking in the press did get to her."

Some of it was probably invented by self-aggrandizing royal commentators but as late as November 2018, after Carole gave a rare interview to mark the thirtieth anniversary of Party Pieces, a writer in the conservative **Telegraph** had this to say about Carole Middleton:

But the voice is what everyone wants to know about. Is it stewardessy (in her early 20s she worked for British Airways)? Elocutioned? Lynda Snell? None of the above. The best description is probably modern posh—not affected, not mockney.

Stewardessy. Gary Goldsmith was wrong when he said that as a "Thatcher child" he belonged to "a generation in which class does not exist." Margaret Thatcher herself was bedeviled by England's class obsession. To Tory grandees, the longest-serving British prime minister of the twentieth century and the first woman to hold that office would always be metaphorically stuck over her father's grocery shop in Grantham, "**trying too hard.**"

The fourth year at St. Andrews was a dangerous passage for the Middleton-Wales liaison. In the sleepy isolation of Balgove House, the atmosphere was edgy. William was behaving like a pampered princeling. How could the second in line to the throne be anything other than a man just a little bit spoiled by a sycophancy he didn't even recognize? The shadow of obstinate privilege sometimes crossed his pleasing, open face. Michael Choong, a rugby-playing friend who visited the couple, told Andrew Morton that William "could be flip and curt with her. . . . He expected Kate to run after him and the longer they knew each other the more he seemed to keep her on a tight leash." Carole counseled, "Give him space." On weekends, Kate left the campus for Bucklebury and toiled away at her dissertation on Lewis Carroll, which combined two subjects that grew in fascination for her: early childhood and photography. William applied himself to a ten-thousand-word study on the coral reefs of Rodrigues, an island 344 miles off the coast of Mauritius.

Each time William felt restive with Kate, he quickly discovered that it wasn't as easy as it looked to replace her with the girls he thought he wanted, or to find anyone he could trust as he trusted her. There were plenty who liked to date him for the frisson of a night with a prince, but the trade-off was the media disruption of their lives, risking the social embarrassment of being one of many. There are women who, forty years later, are still identified by the grubby moniker "a former girlfriend of Prince Charles," whatever their later achievements. Dodging the press quickly got tedious. The romance with Carly Massy-Birch had floundered in part because she grew tired of being smuggled to rendezvous by his bodyguard.

Any young woman involved with William confronted constant issues of unequal status. The prince who wanted to be "just like everyone else" would always inhabit his two realities. Because of strict spouses-only protocol rules, Kate was not invited to Charles and Camilla's wedding in April 2005, though she had by now met them many times. On graduation day, William managed a 2:1 in geography to Kate's 2:1 in art history. The Queen and Prince Philip, Charles and Camilla, all attended the ceremony and the festive garden party that followed, where the Queen, in an especially jolly mood, was escorted around by Principal and Vice-Chancellor Lang. The Middleton family, who were there to cheer for Kate, was advised not to approach the royals. William's live-in girlfriend was not introduced to his grandmother. It took another three years for Kate to be greeted by the Queen at the wedding of Princess Anne's son, Peter Phillips, to Canadian management consultant Autumn Kelly in May 2008.

Until the moment an engagement was announced, a female friend of William's was both prey for the media and a nonperson to the Palace. This became ferociously apparent as soon as the couple left the St. Andrews cocoon.

William was immediately swallowed up by his role as a monarch in training. He acquired an impressive new guide for his next act in Jamie Lowther-Pinkerton, forty-four, who was appointed the princes' first shared private secretary. A former Special Air Service (SAS) officer so well regarded he had been mentioned as a potential commanding officer, Lowther-Pinkerton, a graduate of Eton and Sandhurst, had useful royal experience from his days as a young Irish Guards officer posted to serve as an equerry to the Queen Mother. That job mostly meant opening the bar behind the bookcase at 12:30 P.M. before the old grande dame's lunch parties at Clarence House, where he was treated like a surrogate grandson. How he moved effortlessly from that to leading a two-year SAS operation against Colombian drug cartels is an index of his ability to combine courtliness with ingenuity. No one could be a better choice to both understand the peculiar demands of the royal world and design how the boys could most purposefully serve their country in their post-school and university years. Immediately, William's life course was mapped out.

On June 29, 2005, the twenty-three-year-old heir to the throne was dispatched to represent the Queen on his first solo overseas royal tour in New Zealand. Lowther-Pinkerton designated him to forty-four weeks of army officer training at the Royal Military Academy Sandhurst, one year serving in the Household Cavalry Blues and Royals regiment, and a two-year tasting menu of the Royal Navy and the Royal Air Force.

Kate's role, meanwhile, was to be the Goodbye Girl, available when William needed her. The enigmatic question is whether the future Duchess of Cambridge was preternaturally self-directed from the start or whether she became so invested in the veneer of suitability, she made herself inevitable. The crucible was the press, and how she would survive it.

CHAPTER
13

QUEEN IN WAITING

Kate Closes the Deal

KATE WAS RELENTLESSLY PURSUED IN London. She was hounded when she left her Chelsea apartment in ways reminiscent of the harassment of the young Lady Di. At the benign end, she was photographed putting out the trash at her apartment—"Bin There, Done That. William's Girl Mucks In" (**Evening Standard**)—and led the evening news waiting for a bus. At the ugly end, it was nineties paparazzi excess all over again. As she walked through Paddington Station or an airport, barbaric photographers yelled "Bitch!" "Whore! "Slag, look this way!" to try to get a rise out of her, just as they had with Diana. When the house next door to her parents' flat was being renovated, she discovered scaffolding on which workers were being paid to pass information to a particular paparazzo about her comings and goings. During the same week the

Diana inquest opened in October 2007, there was a horribly ironic echo of the past when photographers gave chase to the car as Kate left a nightclub with William.

Belle Robinson, founder of the mid-market fashion line Jigsaw, for whom Kate worked as a part-time accessory buyer from 2006 to 2007, told the **Evening Standard** that despite what many people believe, Kate received no official Palace help to fend off the photographers and TV crews who waited for her to emerge from work. "Only if she were a fiancée would she get support. She said she can turn to William's press guy if there's a political problem with the press, but only if it's serious."

It is not entirely true that Kate received no help. Behind the scenes, Paddy Harverson would often run interference unofficially. In keeping with her character, Kate's requests for his intervention were rare and always began with the words "I don't want to make a fuss, but . . ." William reportedly arranged for a panic button to the local police station to be installed in her apartment to protect her from the constant threats of intrusion. At Jigsaw, Robinson would say to Kate, "Listen, do you want to go out the back way?" to which Kate would say, "To be honest, they're going to hound us until they've got the picture. So why don't I just go, get the picture done, and then they'll leave us alone." Robinson was impressed with how she handled it all. "I think she's been quite good at neither courting the press nor sticking two fingers in the air at them. I don't think

I would have been so polite." Robinson's own girls, she said, would "never want to be a royal girlfriend."

Kate's submerged identity in the media was now reduced to her wardrobe, the inevitable outcome of having to smile but not speak. What she wore had an impact. The "Kate Effect" could send a £40 monochrome-print Topshop shift or a pair of Penelope Chilvers tassel boots flying out of the stores. Rarely dressing in anything that the British public couldn't afford, she presented as the perfectly pitched girlfriend from the Manor next door in fresh, swingy High Street dresses, cropped blazers, and short skirts. The only suggestion of parental money in the background was a seemingly inexhaustible collection of Longchamp bags. Untroubled, it seems, by the modern anxiety about "not having a voice," she became a mute icon of appropriate style. This disappointed her friends. "When we first came down from St Andrews, it was exciting for us all to be in London together," an old university chum told **The Observer**. "But as it turned out we didn't end up seeing much of Kate. She spent a lot of time with William's friends and sort of stopped coming to our girls' suppers. I don't even think she dropped us deliberately."

The tabloids teased her for her apparent lack of serious employment, and even the Queen, who saw there was more than a chance that Kate might be here to stay, reportedly thought she should get a "real job" or an attachment to high-profile charity work. William was dedicated to a grueling training schedule, but Kate seemed only to be drifting around, dabbling in her parents' company so she could be available when William came home to party. The Queen's discomfort increased after the economic collapse in 2008 when Her Majesty was not at all enamored of images of her grandson and his girlfriend leaving Boujis, the Kensington hot spot for the louche and the loaded. "Army boys up for the weekend, a smattering of Eurotrash types" was how **The Observer** described the ambience of the place, where the Dom Pérignon was marked up to £360 a bottle.

Palace sources briefed that the Queen "was acutely aware that Prince William's public image could suffer if his girlfriend were not recognized as a working professional in her own right." There had been conversations, said the sources, with "a few trusted friends" about how to tackle what was being called "the Kate problem." On the few occasions the Queen had met Kate, Her Majesty apparently thought she was a nice enough girl but had no idea what she actually did (probably an accurate rendition of the Queen's mildly withering turn of phrase). Concerned about his girlfriend's lady-of-leisure rap, it was William who urged her to find employment. When Kate canvassed working at Jigsaw, she "genuinely wanted a job," Robinson recalled. But she told her prospective boss that "she needed an element of flexibility to continue the relationship with a very high-profile man and a life that she can't dictate."

Such undisguised clarity of romantic mission is rare for a contemporary young woman of twenty-four.

Pippa had multiple love affairs, fizzy jobs, and adventures before she married. But Kate's world was William—and only William.

Rarely did she overplay her hand. Almost two months before her twenty-fifth birthday, rumors of a Palace engagement announcement were burning up the media. Woolworths Supermarkets commissioned a series of William and Kate engagement souvenirs. In a thrillingly public show of commitment, William invited Kate and her parents, along with the Queen, Prince Charles, and Camilla, to a significant milestone event in his life: his graduation, or "passing-out," parade at Sandhurst on December 15, 2006. Kate dazzled in a scarlet coat over a black camisole with an unusually statement-y Philip Treacy hat adorned by what looked like enormous heart-shaped broadcast antennae. The Middletons were seated in the front row. Carole, who had given up smoking, made the rare gaffe of chewing nicotine gum throughout, and was hazed for it in the coverage.

William, set to become 2nd Lieutenant Wales, marched out with 223 other newly commissioned officers to be inspected by his commander-in-chief grandmother. Her Majesty said something as she passed that made him break his military stare into a flicker of a smile. At six foot three, the heir to the throne looked spectacularly dashing in his crisp dark blue uniform, white gloves, and red sash. He was carrying a rifle and bayonet that established that his thirty-strong platoon, part of Blenheim Company, had won the honor of carrying the Queen's banner during the parade. "You must be courageous yet selfless, leaders yet carers, confident yet considerate," the Queen told all the graduates in her speech. "And you must be all these things in some of the most challenging environments around the world."

ITV's lip-readers caught Kate saying afterward, "I love the uniform. It's so so sexy."

Before graduation, William had issued his girlfriend the coveted invitation to join him at the Queen's annual Christmas house party at Sandringham. Kate, reflecting the confident mood of her Philip Treacy hat, maintained her resolve that she would not go to such a significant Royal Family gathering unless she had a ring on her finger. She declined. William met her decision with silence.

Kate retreated to Scotland to stay with her parents, who had rented a house in Perthshire for the holidays. After Christmas at Sandringham, William was expected to come up to spend the New Year's holiday with Kate. It's not hard to imagine the social preparations that her mother made to welcome the heir to the throne to the Middleton New Year's feast, nor the twitterings at north-of-the-border dinner parties that the twenty-four-year-old Prince would soon be reeling in their midst and linking arms for "Auld Lang Syne."

He didn't show up.

In Kate's absence at Sandringham, William had taken the opportunity for a heart-to-heart with his father and the Queen. In an ironic re-scripting of the scene between Charles and Prince Philip in 1981—when Philip told him that his dithering over Diana was damaging her reputation—Charles thought it unfair to expose Kate to so much press harassment unless engagement was imminent. (On each occasion, the obvious solution—to provide the girlfriend with more protection—seemed less important than avoiding the appearance of Palace endorsement.) The Queen favored waiting rather than jumping. If her grandson took what the Prince of Wales in his single days used to call "**la grande plonge**," it would be the most significant Windsor union since Charles and Diana. It is an understatement to say the Queen was skittish about any marriage that might fail. So badly had she wanted William to be sure he had the right woman that she had reversed every traditional rule of royal romantic engagement, lending them cottages to tryst in, allowing them to live together before marriage at St. Andrews, and even permitting them to stay together at Clarence House.

For Kate, the humiliation of William's New Year's no-show was intense, and only got worse. On her twenty-fifth birthday on January 9, 2007, the press was so convinced the engagement would be announced that very day that they mobbed her outside her Chelsea apartment. Her usual composed smile was replaced with a testy glare. William phoned to apologize. In an unprecedented public statement, he complained that she was being harassed and said he wanted "more than anything" for her to be left alone. He encouraged her to retain Gerrard Tyrrell of Harbottle and Lewis to complain to the Press Complaints Commission. Even Tory leader David Cameron expressed his "concern about the number of people on Kate Middleton's doorstep."

II

For a girl so dignified and reserved, all this was hell. She didn't want a lawyer. She wanted a ring! "She openly admitted that she expected a formal announcement to be made by Clarence House," a Kate source revealed. In March, Kate and William holidayed uneasily together on the ski slopes in Zermatt, but in pictures taken of them at the races at Cheltenham on their return, they looked bored with each other and boring, in matching hunting-green tweed. It did not need to be pointed out to William (though the press did) that he was fast losing his cool factor as well as his hair and turning into his dad. A William-circle source let the mortifying nugget drop that while the Prince was extremely fond of Kate, he never thought of her as "the one." He was "too young to settle down and wanted to throw himself into his career as an army officer."

"All the fun has gone," William allegedly complained. "I don't want to be nailed down." It is hard not to feel for him. Everything else in his life had been nailed down from birth.

Second Lieutenant Wales's move to Bovington

Camp in Dorset to begin armored reconnaissance
training with his regiment, the Blues and Royals (aka
the Booze and Royals), was the perfect moment to
show what he meant. He was photographed with his
arm around an attractive blond student, who later
described him as a "perfect gentleman," but also one
who had his other hand cupping the breast of a
Brazilian brunette. A rumor circulated that he was
having a fling with a different "well-connected young
woman." **The Sun** quoted a Kate friend saying that
as "far as Kate is concerned, William simply hasn't
been paying her enough attention. She is stuck
in London while he is living in an officer's mess in
Dorset. Kate feels hugely frustrated that their relationship just seems to be going backwards at a rate
of knots."

The death of a Sandhurst colleague and close
friend, 2nd Lieutenant Joanna Yorke Dyer, with
whom he had trained in the Blenheim Platoon, unsettled William further. Joanna, twenty-four, joined
the Intelligence Corps and was serving in Iraq. She
was one of four soldiers killed when their armored
vehicle drove over a powerful roadside bomb. It was
a tragic reminder of the sacrifices William's fellow
cadets were making even as he was cocooned from
such combat. There was no chance he would be allowed to deploy on the front line himself, for fear of
making fellow soldiers a target. If he couldn't serve
his country, and was destined to be in continual
training, he was a man without a mission.

In an awful "let's get it over with" phone call in

April to Kate while she was at the Jigsaw office, he dropped the breakup bomb. She had to excuse herself from a meeting and pace around the parking lot for an hour-long heart-to-heart that left her in pieces. Kate did what she always did when she was devastated. She fled to Bucklebury. Jigsaw gave her compassionate leave. With her daughter's morale at its nadir, Carole Middleton took charge. She whisked Kate off on a trip to a friend's art show in Dublin. A job was created compiling and editing catalogs for Party Pieces. Interested in photography? Kate could get busy taking pictures of decorative cupcakes for the website.

A comeback strategy was devised whose outlines, as summarized by Stefanie Marsh in **The Times**, were to:

Recuperate on holiday with your ex's other former girlfriends. He will admire your lack of jealousy and feel paranoid about what it is you could be talking about. Revise your views on press intrusion. Get yourself photographed doing all of the above as often as possible.

Her sister, Pippa, was a useful co-conspirator. Fresh from graduating from Edinburgh, she was deployed to hit the town with Kate exuding vibes of "Girls Just Wanna Have Fun." Gone was the hunting-green tweed. To William's discomfort, he saw pictures of Kate leaving their old nocturnal haunts late at night in thigh-high skirts. There was even a hint of retaliatory feminist edge when she signed up with an all-women dragon boat crew named the Sisterhood for a twenty-one-mile paddle across the English Channel to raise money for children's charities. (It was a little less edgy when you drilled down. Her fellow rowers included a model, a fashion buyer, a real estate consultant, and a hedge funder.) The riverbanks were soon bristling with paparazzi trying to catch her toned, tight T-shirt look as she trained as the team's helmsman.

By June, it started to dawn on William that his ex was as much of a catch as he was. Beautiful, self-assured, and embossed now with a royal sheen, Kate could have become the wife of a duke or a billionaire in a Highgrove minute. Prince Harry, romantically adrift himself in an erratic relationship with Zimbabwean beauty Chelsy Davy, was a major Kate ally. He referred to her as "the big sister he never had." William, sure enough, was soon begging to have her back. She held out, savoring his contrition, before finally accepting an invitation to the end-of-training Bovington Camp "Freakin' Naughty" party, where she rocked the room dressed as a sexy nurse. The heir to the throne was said to have followed her around all night like a "lost puppy," wearing the abjectly lame getup of hot pants and a policeman's helmet. Soon Kate's Audi was spotted purring back and forth from Clarence House. And there were the En Masse Middletons sitting in the royal box at the anniversary Concert for Diana on July 1, 2007, arranged by William and Harry at Wembley Stadium.

Prince Harry was making out most of the night with Chelsy. But Kate, seated a few rows behind William, maintained social distance to keep the spotlight on the Diana legacy—and the press guessing.

III

The "liberated Kate" narrative was a media hit. Too big a hit, it seems, because the Palace became wary, if not paranoid. It was impossible not to scent a rising, runaway celebrity like—Heaven forfend—the Princess being memorialized on the Wembley Stadium stage. Alarm bells rang louder at the Palace when Kate appeared on the cover of **Hello!** magazine for a story on the dragon boat crew. It coincided, unfortunately, with the publication of a landmark report by Parliament's Culture, Media and Sport Select Committee, fueled by Gerrard Tyrrell's complaint to the Press Complaints Commission about the swarm of photographers outside Kate's apartment on her twenty-fifth birthday. Titled "Self-Regulation of the Press," the report judged that "clear and persistent harassment" was evident. The victory prompted a wave of snarky commentary about Kate's double standards.

In August, the Palace called time on the whole dragon boat escapade. After weeks of training, and just a fortnight before the crew challenged the all-male Brotherhood in the race from Dover to Cap Gris-Nez, Kate was commanded to throw in the towel. Team leader Emma Sayle, a diplomat's daughter, reportedly pleaded with Kate in an emotional phone call, "Remember, this is not just for charity, it is for yourself. Please don't drop out. For the first time in your life you are actually doing something for yourself." It was, Andrew Morton writes, "in vain." The official justification was security fears that might jeopardize the safety of Kate's crewmates. But it was widely suggested that royal aides feared the race was turning into an out-of-control media event. One of the Sisterhood rowers told Richard Kay, "There is no doubt she was leant on. She was our helmsman, very strong and very sporty. It's a huge loss. . . . Now we've got two and a half weeks to find someone, which with the training is probably impossible. . . . Kate's really miffed."

Was she? An edict from the Palace meant Kate unofficially belonged to William again. So what if her edgy new image was eroded by her capitulation to Palace protocol, and she was back to being a gilded appendage to a prince? Kate had crossed a royal Rubicon. The Palace, henceforth, would script her life. There were—let us be honest—compensations. Instead of exhorting a raw-kneed rowing crew across the chilly English Channel, she was paddling on a kayak with the heir to the throne in the balmy waters of the Indian Ocean. William had booked a $750-a-night bungalow at a luxury resort in the Seychelles. In the privacy of their idyll, he gave her the promise of commitment she'd craved. In return, she would wait another three years till he finished his military training and she must be seen to have a "real" job. (For once, discretion was not a help. Working for Party Pieces under the radar meant everyone assumed she was still unemployed. Carole swiftly righted that problem by posting Kate's picture on the website as an employee.)

In October 2010 on a return trip to Kenya, William and Kate stole away to a secluded cabin in the foothills and made their love official. He slipped his mother's sapphire-and-diamond engagement ring on Kate's finger—"my way of keeping [my mother] sort of close to it all," he told the press in their engagement interview. "We had a little private time away together with some friends and I just decided that it was the right time really." The thing people remember about that interview, apart from what Kate wore—a cobalt-blue satin Issa wrap dress that matched her ring—was the couple's easy, familiar joy.

Kate had won by observing every old-fashioned rule of courtship: patience, resilience, and giving her man the space he needed, a playbook that had brought the wholesome middle-class girl from Bucklebury to the brink of the British throne. For William, it was an admission of what he had always known. The rawness, rage, and confusion he had suffered since his mother's death were soothed by something old-fashioned and rare in his fiancée: her constancy. Kate had the healing gene he craved.

In 2020, one of the Duchess's school friends insisted in an interview that William's royal status was immaterial to Kate's willingness to mold her life around his. "She married William despite his position, not because of it," said the friend. "All Catherine ever wanted was a husband, a house in the country, loads of kids, a dog and a kitchen with an Aga."

Perhaps. But Love and Strategy would be a good name for a Kate Middleton perfume. A Trollopian longing for social validation and an irrepressible desire to marry up cannot be overestimated even if it bubbled serenely below the surface. Those girls who thought her infra dig at Downe House? The sneering at her mother's parvenu locutions? The "Waity Katie" jabs in the tabloid columns? If Carole Middleton had come a long way from her working-class roots, the aspiration strain lived on in her eldest daughter. Kate did not wait for eight years for any rich, connected man. She waited for **the** man, the future King William V, by the Grace of God of the United Kingdom of Great Britain and Northern Ireland and of Her Other Realms and Territories King, Head of the Commonwealth, Defender of the Faith—**Your Majesty** to the rest of us.

At her small bachelorette karaoke party hosted by her sister and some old school friends, Kate grabbed the mic and with unusual spontaneity sang her heart out to "Fight for This Love" by Cheryl Cole:

**Quittin's out of the question
When it gets tough gotta fight some more (ohh)
We gotta fight, fight, fight, fight, fight for this
love**

IV

On April 29, 2011, I was a royal commentator for the wedding of William and Catherine, as we must now call her, for ABC News along with the network's Queen Bees of the era, Diane Sawyer and Barbara Walters, reporting from Buckingham Palace, and Robin Roberts, whom I joined on a narrow balcony of the Queen Elizabeth II Centre overlooking Westminster Abbey. The sense that we were part of a big-budget operation the scale of a foreign war weighed heavily on our botoxed brows. The news crew, coming off an exhausting cycle of Arab Spring revolutions and a Japanese earthquake, now faced a cascade of absurd information from royal briefing books the size of the **Almanach de Gotha.** Punctilious details of minor members of the Windsor family and obscure foreign dignitaries rained down on baffled American researchers with as much intensity as had the news of teetering despots and fleeing Tunisian strongmen. If you want to see true news grit in action, it's Cynthia McFadden in a trench coat conjuring bearable news bites out of royalist banality on a freezing April morning, or Barbara Walters's all-night cram on previous royal wedding cakes, just so she could knowledgeably throw out a retrospective passing nugget about Fergie and Andrew's 240-pound confection laced with brandy and rum. William and Kate's eight-tiered traditional fruitcake was so huge, a Palace door had to be removed to get it through. "I hear that you've been dismantling my house," the Queen said to pastry chef Fiona Cairns.

On a conference call the night before the ceremony, the then-head of ABC News, Ben Sherwood, corralled all those anchoring the wedding for a pep talk. "OK," he boomed over the speakerphone, "I hear 'traditional.' I hear 'big.' I hear 'royal' from you guys. But there is one thing I am not hearing here: LOVE. Guys, this is a LOVE STORY! OK?" A humbled silence as Mesdames Walters, Sawyer, Roberts, and Brown digested this insight. Perhaps Middle America might not appreciate the smart-ass observation I was cultivating about the unfortunate fate of previous queens called Catherine: Aragon—divorced; Howard—beheaded. Everyone off-camera agreed that the only wedding events we really wished we could attend were the bride and groom's private disco rave at Buckingham Palace masterminded by Pippa—and Prince Harry's bacon-butty breakfast after-party.

All weddings are made by the unscripted moments. William spent the nervous wedding-night eve at Clarence House buoyed up by the joshing solidarity of his younger brother. After dining with Prince Charles, the two princes made a spontaneous appearance together to greet the crowds camped out in the streets outside the Abbey. Working the lines, Diana's adult boys looked heart-stoppingly tall, dashing, and charming. "I sometimes still think of them as the fifteen- and thirteen-year-olds that they were . . . terrible naughty teenagers, and here they are young men about to launch into a new chapter of William's life. How exciting," said former royal press secretary Colleen Harris on camera.

In honor of William's marriage, the Queen conferred on the heir to the throne the title of HRH Duke of Cambridge, Earl of Strathearn, and Baron Carrickfergus. Much to RAF disappointment (given his flight lieutenant service at the time), William wore the blazing scarlet-and-gold coat of the Irish Guards on his wedding day. Like so many seemingly personal decisions in his life, it was not a choice but an order from his commander in chief, the Queen. "You don't always get what you want, put it that way," he joked. In under three weeks, Her Majesty would make her groundbreaking first trip to the Republic of Ireland. The groom's Irish Guards uniform was a first soft-power flourish of royal statesmanship.

Overnight, Kate Middleton became a royal duchess. Her dress, designed by Sarah Burton of Alexander McQueen, was a flawless expression of new regal confidence. There was TV ecstasy from our narrow broadcasting podium at the swoony reveal of her ivory-and-white satin gazar gown, with lace appliqué on the bodice and skirt handmade by the Royal School of Needlework at Hampton Court Palace, with its nearly nine-foot train. The tight bodice and peaked shoulders gave her the medieval look of a latter-day Queen Guinevere. There was no haute, high-fashion updo for the bride's hair. She wanted to keep her long, glossy tresses loose so William would "recognize" her, she said. Her soft, silk tulle veil was held in place by the Cartier "Halo" tiara, lent to her by the Queen and originally purchased by George VI for the Queen Mother. Perfection, yes, but in a last win of the sister contest, it was Pippa who broke the internet in a dangerously tight ivory satin maid-of-honor sheath dress that hugged her much-touted derriere.

Just as every millennial posted Pippa's epic ass on Facebook, every mother in the land wanted to look like Carole Middleton. Her bespoke Catherine Walker duck-egg blue coat-and-dress ensemble stood out for its modern but appropriate flair. The matching tilted hat was rakish, but not ridiculous like many of the perilously bobbing feathered fascinators, the Duchess of Cornwall's cruise ship–sized Lady Bracknell headgear, and what seemed to be a vast pink felt octopus—or was it antlers?—towering on Princess Beatrice's head. Michael Middleton looked matinee-idol handsome in his morning suit and gray satin waistcoat. If Carole was the catalyst, he was the rock on which this day was built.

For the night before, the Middletons had booked all sixty-nine rooms for their family and friends at the Goring Hotel opposite Buckingham Palace. This was tiresome for the Queen's arrangements because the so-called Boring Goring, always used for Palace staff parties and overflow guests, was where peripheral royal relatives known as the Hons and the Vons and various foreign dignitaries were usually billeted. The Queen had to cram in seeing as many as she could, as well as schlepp over to the Mandarin Oriental in Hyde Park to face-check other royal unavoidables: the Spains, the Denmarks, the Belgiums, and the Norways. Dodgier dignitaries were siphoned off for a champagne-and-sausage-stick reception at Lancaster House. (Flying corps friends of William's got a Kate and Wills mug and a Kate and Wills pillow.)

One of the reasons the wedding was such a logistical work of art was that the Palace team was helmed by Jamie Lowther-Pinkerton, who was experienced in much more daunting operational challenges in the SAS. The private secretary's ten-year-old son, Billy, was one of the two white-breeched, buckle-shoed page boys who stood right next to the lemon-yellow vision of the Queen on the Buckingham Palace balcony. In appreciation for burnishing the monarchy to such a high gloss for the globally tele-vised event, the Queen made Lowther-Pinkerton a lieutenant of the Royal Victorian Order. An even greater honor was given by William and Kate, who named him one of the godfathers of their firstborn, Prince George.

If you ask Palace folk today to name their most outstanding memory of the occasion, they speak of how mysteriously devoid of drama it all was. In 2007, Sarah Goodall, who worked as Prince Charles's deputy private secretary for twelve years, reflected in an interview how a royal engagement (if it happened) would one day change Kate:

There will be massive expectations on Kate's shoulders. When Princess Diana became en-gaged, one courtier turned to her and said, "In

four years, you'll be a complete and utter bitch."
I'm not saying that of Kate, but her life will
undergo the most extraordinary change.

And yet, Kate Middleton was the world's most
unflappable bride—no tearful scenes, no last-minute
panics, no tantrums in meetings to whittle down the
guests to the 1,900 who could be seated in the Abbey.
She had a dedicated team of two to coordinate
what she wanted. "They worked like dogs but had
lots of laughs and broke out the Pinot Noir with
Kate at the end of the day," one of the team commented. I am told the bride's only anxiety on the
wedding day itself was that her stomach rumbling
might be picked up by a hot mic.
The Archbishop of Canterbury, Dr. Rowan
Williams, who officiated the marriage, told me the
sense of calm extended to the bride and groom's religious preparation for the ceremony:

They knew what they were about, they'd thought
about it all, they knew each other well, and of
course, they'd had that experience that can be
quite important for couples of standing back
from the relationship and then re-engaging.
And sometimes that really strengthens relationships, I think. To ask, "Is this really what I want?
Is this the person I'm really going with?"

The Queen was thrilled, he said, that the couple
had chosen to marry in Westminster Abbey, scene of

her own wedding and coronation, rather than St. Paul's Cathedral with the unhappy association of Charles and Diana.

Generations of royal in-laws have complained about being airbrushed out of the picture once the union is announced, but William, who now called Michael Middleton "Dad," made it clear that **his** in-laws were not going to suffer the same fate. Kate's parents reinforced their independence by insisting on sharing with the Queen and Prince Charles the cost of the wedding. (The Middletons' slice was said to total around £250,000.) Palace aides told **The Telegraph** that the Middletons and the Royal Family will play an "equal part" in the couple's lives. Quite so. Except that the Middletons found that none of their guests made the cut for the post-wedding reception at Buckingham Palace, an embarrassment Carole deftly overcame by hosting a flurry of B-list sidebar events.

One relative Carole made sure she took good care of was her brother, Gary. Two years before the wedding he had been caught in a sting by undercover reporters, cutting up lines of cocaine at Maison de Bang Bang. Carole effected brisk damage control—with Gary, not the press. "The minute that story broke, Carole was on the phone apologising to me on behalf of the family, specifically Kate, about me being suddenly thrust into the limelight," Gary has said, unaware that he was being "handled" by his savvy sister. An alienated Gary could have turned into a runaway nightmare for the Middletons, like

Meghan's father, Tom Markle, whose feelings of being dumped spewed out in the lead-up to his daughter's wedding to Harry. Instead, the Middleton clan closed ranks around Uncle Gary, and he not only made the cut for the Westminster Abbey list but was given a prime seat. The Duchess of Cornwall, clearly well-briefed on the possible tripwires, "made a beeline for me," he recalls. "I'm sorry for the bad press," Gary told her. "Don't think twice about it. I get the same myself," replied Camilla, with complicit (and expert) charm.

Carole Middleton was firmly in the center of the newly commissioned Middleton Family coat of arms. A crest had to be specially whipped up to Michael's specifications by the Garter Principal King of Arms and Senior Herald to signify Kate's new royal status. Three acorns and oak sprigs represented each of the Middleton offspring, but the gold chevron cut through the center represented Carole Goldsmith, matriarch of middle-class ascent.

William's bond with his best man, Harry, was touchingly clear to the enchanted British public during the wedding. Never had the two of them seemed more united in private understanding. The pain of the past, the burden of duty, the scrutiny of the press—they had shared it all. The motto on the badge of the black Irish Guards forage cap that William wore on the way to Westminster Abbey spoke as much to their unique fraternal bond as to the military honor code: "Quis Separabit?" or "Who shall separate us?"

The ring that would seal William and Kate's marriage vows was safely waiting in a hiding place in Harry's jacket. His military uniform of the Blues and Royals was so tight-fitting that his tailor came up with the idea of a special gold embroidered cuff with a secret compartment for the precious Welsh gold ring he would pass to his brother.

For the Queen, the wedding day brought a special satisfaction. This new twenty-nine-year-old granddaughter-in-law, the future Queen Consort, was, unlike the child-bride Diana, road tested in resilience as well as royal life. Kate's stoic middle-class origins had proved an incalculable asset. Aristocrats and princes or princesses of the blood had shown themselves to be a hazard for modern royal matrimony. There is too much indulgence in the breeding and centuries of too much time on their hands, a recipe for discontent. Philip was probably the last royal-born consort willing to do what it took. "That was really excellent, wasn't it?" Her Majesty said to her husband after the ceremony in her cool, professional way.

A tear gathered in Carole Middleton's eye when she saw the transcendent vision of her daughter at the Great West Door of Westminster Abbey on her proud father's arm. Kate, like Camilla, had made it into the "winners' enclosure." Sir Hubert Parry's coronation anthem "I Was Glad" soared as father and daughter progressed between an avenue of twenty-foot-high English field maple and hornbeam trees. With every step Kate advanced up the aisle, she also retreated into the remote, airless world of the British Crown. Would the prize be worth it?

Waiting for her at the altar, William bit his lip in a manner reminiscent of his mother. "You look beautiful, babe," he told her when he beheld up close her dear, familiar face.

CHAPTER
14

THE GREAT ESCAPE

———

Harry the Hero Finds His Way

———

FROM THE CRACKLE OF AN URGENT EXCHANGE
on the military radio, Prince Harry deciphered the
news he had been dreading. Ten weeks into his four-
month tour in Afghanistan, his carefully concealed
presence on the front line had been busted by the
press. Harry's heart sank.

It was February 2008, and he was on duty near
the former Taliban stronghold of Musa Qala in the
northern Helmand Province with a seven-strong
Spartan vehicle team. The operation was part of a
push to seize control of a village and carve a route
to the Kajaki Dam, where nearly two years earlier
a British soldier had been killed and six critically
injured when they stumbled upon a Soviet minefield.

Within minutes of learning that the secret of his
Afghan deployment was out, Harry felt a tap on

his shoulder. It was his commanding officer. "Lieutenant Wales, pack up your bag. You're off."

The words were plain, and shattering. In less than an hour, Harry had to abandon his men, grab all his things, and run up the ramp of the Chinook helicopter that was making a dangerous daytime landing to retrieve him. On board were six heavily armed SAS soldiers and his Metropolitan Police backup protection team, who had stayed back at Camp Bastion while Harry was on the front line. An Apache attack helicopter flew overhead, rightly described as a "£46 million flying fortress," equipped with state-of-the-art laser-guided missiles to protect the juicy royal target from Taliban fire. From there it was back to Camp Bastion in the Helmand Province desert and Harry's return to RAF Brize Norton airbase in Oxfordshire.

The heart-crushing curtailment of his Afghanistan deployment was not Harry's first disappointment. Ten months before, he had been all set to head to Iraq with the Blues and Royals as the leader of a unit of twelve soldiers and four Scimitar armored reconnaissance vehicles stationed in Basra. Britain had been at war with Iraq since 2003, when, bedazzled by the notion of playing Winston Churchill in reverse to George W. Bush's Franklin Roosevelt, Prime Minister Tony Blair committed British troops to join America's effort "to remove Saddam Hussein from power and disarm Iraq of its weapons of mass destruction." It was a deeply unpopular war, which, perhaps, made it all the more important that a precious royal was seen sharing the risk of potential loss of life or limb with ordinary Britons.

No sooner had the Ministry of Defence—in its infinite unwisdom—announced Harry's deployment in Iraq than the "tabloid press GPS" worked out where he'd be stationed. And inevitably, a radical cleric, Muqtada al-Sadr, issued credible threats to Harry's life based on that information. British troops were already experiencing increased insurgent attacks. The third in line to the throne would be regarded as a "bullet magnet" who could endanger everybody else around him. In the third week of April 2007, army chiefs feared that a fatal roadside bomb attack on two British soldiers was a dry run for an attempt on Harry's life. In May, the MOD abruptly canceled his deployment to Iraq.

The twenty-two-year-old Prince was gutted. Everything he had trained for had gone up in smoke. He had made it clear how keenly he felt the importance of active service. "I hope I would not drag my sorry arse through Sandhurst. . . . I would not have joined if they had said I could not be in the front line," he told the press on his twenty-first birthday.

As a decorated officer himself, Jamie Lowther-Pinkerton was also deeply frustrated. He had worked for months to make the Iraq deployment happen. The private secretary felt it was essential for the young Prince to get his "knees brown" in operational experience. There had been endless delicate negotiations with Sir Richard Dannatt, chief of the general staff of the British Army, to get Harry to Basra. Now that Iraq was out of the question, there was a strong fear Harry would quit the army altogether. William had to help talk him off the ledge. He told Harry that if he bailed now he would undo all he had achieved as a young officer, and would come off as petulant. Had another opportunity to deploy—this time to Afghanistan—not been created, said Lowther-Pinkerton, "We'd have had a really shattered, disgruntled, sapped—morale-wise—individual on our hands who can kick up and be dangerous if he wants to be."

There was plenty of evidence of that already. Temperamentally, Harry was a human IED. At Eton, he regularly got into fights that turned physical, ending up on crutches after kicking in a window during a dispute with another student over a girl. A former head teacher told writer Chris Hutchins, "We used to say that Harry was like a firecracker, and when other people saw him coming, they used to pass a by-now-familiar warning: 'Don't light the blue touch paper.'" (The British instructions for how to ignite fireworks.)

Harry would have been much happier in the nineteenth century as a pistol-waving, roistering aristocrat of the **Flashman** school (except that Brigadier General Sir Harry Paget Flashman, the hero of George MacDonald Fraser's novels, is a swaggering, cowardly reprobate, which the real Harry is decidedly not). The Spencer annals are full of the intemperance and recklessness of his red-haired ancestors. After a heated argument, Sir William Spencer, in the early 1500s, killed a stag in a rage. The hot-tempered Charles Spencer, third Earl of Sunderland, declared during a debate in the House of Commons that he "hoped to piss upon the House of Lords." The Red Earl appalled Queen Victoria when he was sent to be Lord Lieutenant of Ireland and ended up converting to the cause of Irish independence. Their exploits are all chronicled in a colorful family history by the current Earl Spencer, whose reckless eulogy of Diana was every bit in the tradition of his forefathers.

While William became more and more of a Windsor as the years went by, the Spencer blood coursed hard in Harry's veins. He seems to have embraced it. On the tenth anniversary of Diana's death, at the memorial service held at the Guards' Chapel, Wellington Barracks, William sat (as he no doubt had to) with the Queen and Prince Philip. But Harry chose to sit with all the Spencers. He acknowledged his affinity with Diana's side of the family in his 2021 interview with Oprah: "Family members have said: 'Just play the game and your life will be easier.' But I've got a hell of a lot of my mum in me. I feel as though I am outside the system, but I'm still stuck there."

It's fair to say that joining the army in 2006 saved Harry from going off the rails. While William was away at St. Andrews, and his father was frequently traveling, Harry drank too much and smoked weed with his mates in the basement of Highgrove, where he and William had a teenage den they called Club H. When the brothers were home they were regulars at the nearby Rattlebone Inn, a sixteenth-century pub just a few miles from Highgrove. Its lethal specialty was the snake bite, a cocktail of beer and cider that didn't help Harry's sobriety. A couple of nosy reporters were drinking at the bar in 2001 when a still underage Harry took part in a "lock-in," an illegal but not uncommon British tradition where drinkers spend the night locked in the pub to continue the party. An over-served Harry proceeded to get into a fight with a French employee whom the pre-woke Prince called a "f—ing frog." Things unraveled from there, and Harry was kicked out. The **News of the World** featured the boorish incident in a multipage splash. Harry's late teens and early twenties were a litany of front-page debacles, from punching a photographer in October 2004 when clearly the worse for wear from booze at three A.M. outside a Piccadilly nightclub to wearing that infamous Nazi armband at a costume party in 2005 two weeks before the sixtieth anniversary of the liberation of Auschwitz.

Chris Uncle, the photographer involved in the 2004 paparazzi scuffle, told the **Evening Standard** that Harry had suddenly "burst out of the car" and "lunged" toward him while Uncle was still taking pictures. "He lashed out and then deliberately pushed my camera into my face," Uncle said. Royal protection officers dragged Harry away, and Paddy Harverson artfully spun it as excessive press harassment of an upstanding young man. To add to the princely pandemonium, it happened just as a sacked

Eton art teacher named Sarah Forsyth told an employment tribunal that she had helped Harry with a project required to pass one of the A levels he needed to get into Sandhurst. An exam board cleared him of cheating, but you can hear the pain in Harry's disconsolate gripe: "Maybe it's just part of who I am. I have to deal with it. There's lots of things people get accused of. Unfortunately mine are made public."

Sandhurst gave him a hiding place from all that— "the best escape I've ever had," he called his military career. Never was a temperament as well matched as Harry's with the life of a soldier. It was clear he was a natural, even at Eton, where he was chosen to be parade commander in the school's Combined Cadet Force.

In his zesty twenty-first birthday interview, he said he chose the army over the navy, where his father and grandfather had served, because "I do enjoy running down a ditch full of mud, firing bullets. It's the way I am. I love it." "The navy is so technical now," a retired officer said to me. "Most of the warships are sort of closed down permanently. When you're at sea you're in a sort of dark operations room, not the sort of good old Jack-Hawkins-on-the-bridge type stuff people imagine."

Being a soldier was critical to Harry's self-image. He said he could "easily see" himself spending "thirty-five or forty years" in the army.

Military life was his passport to anonymity. Both Clarence House and Sandhurst made it clear that Officer Cadet Wales would be treated just like everyone else; the same grueling forty-four-week boot camp, the same predawn wake-up calls, the same chores of polishing his boots and making his bed. Like every other cadet, he had to arrive with his own ironing board. His warrant officer famously said at the time, "Prince Harry will call me sir. And I will call him sir. But he will be the one who means it."

Harry preferred a war zone any day to the supposed safety of London, where he had a different target on his back. During missions off base in Afghanistan, his helmet and goggles hid his famous face. The "bro" bonds he forged with soldiers from modest homes were real, not PR confections. At Forward Operating Base Delhi, a godforsaken desert outpost five hundred meters from the Taliban's front line, he shared a room with a constantly changing contingent of Royal Artillery soldiers. "This is what it is all about," Harry told reporters. "Being here with the guys rather than being in a room with a bunch of officers. . . . It's good fun to be with just a normal bunch of guys, listening to their problems, listening to what they think. . . . The guys I am sharing a room [with make] it all worthwhile."

It was balm to Harry after Eton that the army valued innate skills that did not depend on academics. He was an excellent shot for a reason. "He's got extraordinary natural hand-eye coordination and, as a consequence of that, he rolls with things," Major General Buster Howes, former military attaché at the British embassy in Washington, told me. Howes recalled how Harry, on a visit to the U.S. Air Force Academy in Colorado in 2013, was handed an American football and threw two beautiful spiral passes, just as he later whacked two baseballs thrown to him by a Boston Red Sox pitcher.

The army was the one place where the dynamic between Harry and William favored the younger brother. Harry became a commissioned officer at Sandhurst just months after William graduated from St. Andrews. It pleased Harry no end that his older brother would have to salute him. They bonded, says biographer Christopher Andersen, over hearing drill sergeants scream at them, "You 'orrible little prince!" as they scrambled under barbed wire and marched until their feet bled. It was gratifying for the more experienced Harry to be a military mentor to the brother who usually guided him.

If the army was a vocation for Harry from earliest childhood, for William the grueling training was essentially résumé building to burnish his credentials as a future monarch. "I feel it is important for me to understand the military and to be able to look soldiers in the eye with at least a tiny bit of knowledge of what they have gone through," William told a reporter in 2005. And yet, like Prince Charles in the navy, he still found it galling to train endlessly with no hope of real action.

William's decision to join the RAF Search and Rescue Force in 2010 was a stroke of genius. It gave him his operational kicks without putting anyone in danger but himself. Based out of Anglesey for three years, he flew out into the North Atlantic, rescuing yachtsmen, swooping down to pick up stranded climbers on the mountains of Snowdonia, and airlifting bodies from car crashes on the highway. In 2015, he moved on to the East Anglian Air Ambulance, flying a team of doctors and medics to scenes of human distress—accidents, suicides, fires. It gave the young heir a greater insight into the challenges and workings of the National Health Service than any member of the Royal Family before him.

The two brothers did their helicopter flying training at the same time in 2009 at RAF Shawbury and shared a tiny cottage off base together. "The first time and the last time, I can assure you of that," joked Harry in a joint interview. Harry did so well that the military promoted him to training to fly an Apache—considered the most lethal and challenging of aircrafts, weighing nearly twelve thousand pounds. He won the award for best co-pilot gunner in his class. "He is a seriously brilliant pilot and co-pilot gunner," Lowther-Pinkerton said. After Harry trained, he "just suddenly realized, 'I'm brilliant at this. I can't take exams, I can't do this, can't do that,'" one of his military circle said. "But the people that know, they say he's always been exceptional. He went out to Afghanistan, and by all accounts he was absolutely superb. His commanding officer came back and said, 'He was really, really, really twenty-four karat out there.'"

A Palace source made the observation to me that the kind of helicopters each of them flew pretty much summed up their distinctive temperaments, one boy superbly martial, the other bravely empathetic:

Harry flew an Apache armored attack helicopter, which should do about 200 knots at 10 feet above the ground, doing 39 functions at once, firing guns in every direction. Whereas William would fly this big beast of a search and rescue aircraft, with extra fuel tanks, working out the fuel notes, working out a straight line towards it, and hammering his way through the storm, picking somebody out of the ocean and coming back. It's a classic description of the two blokes.

If Harry had dropped out of the army after the Iraq disappointment, Lowther-Pinkerton believes it would have been a disaster not just for the Prince personally, but for the monarchy, blowing up his potential to be a critical asset for the Crown. Evidently, his grandmother thought so too. For the Queen, military service was anything but an ornamental necessity. She is the last head of state to have served in the military during the Second World War and the last, as Robert Hardman put it, to "know the fear, the spirit, even the songs of that generation." She joined, as soon as she turned nineteen, the Auxiliary Territorial Service—the equivalent in the United States of the Women's Army Corps—the first female royal to take a course with regular people with no special rank or privilege at the decree of the King. It equipped her to drive a range of vehicles, including an ambulance, and to deconstruct and rebuild an engine. She adored getting dirt under her fingernails and grease on her hands. It became something of a family joke that over dinner she would earnestly discuss pistons and cylinder heads. If there was any kind of mechanical problem with her Land Rover at Balmoral, she would leap out herself and go under the hood. (In 2003, she shocked the Crown Prince of Saudi Arabia when she drove him round the Balmoral estate herself. The Prince, who never gave women the right to drive during his long reign, had to ask her to slow down. One has to think she was sending him a message.)

On VE Day in May 1945, she and Princess Margaret slipped away with a group of young Guards officers and joined the jubilant throngs, linking arms with the revelers surging round the Palace. The experience of the war was fundamental to shaping the Queen's notion of duty. The uniform of the armed forces has always had a deep emotional resonance for her. Until she ceded the responsibility to Prince Charles in 2017, she regarded the wreath laying at the Cenotaph on Remembrance Day every November as one of her most sacred, and unmissable, royal duties.

A Downing Street insider told me that he believes it was the persistence of the Queen in her sessions with the new Labour prime minister Gordon Brown that resulted in Harry's second chance to deploy—this time to Afghanistan—despite the strong resistance of the military. The Queen was apparently concerned that Harry was showing all the signs of the unhappy drift that bedevils the younger sibling of the heir. She had seen it in Princess Margaret's recalcitrant youth, and in the aimlessness of Prince Andrew. She knew how important it was to Harry to serve his country. "Her Majesty was aware of the limitations of Harry being the 'spare' and the bad things that can happen when you've got a sense of worthlessness," the insider said. "The Queen went out of her way to find an elegant solution. . . . Gordon Brown would never talk about those sessions to anybody, but there was clearly lead being put in his pencil." It was the Queen, as his commander in chief, but more likely in the role of his proud grandmother, who got to tell Prince Harry that he was to finally fulfill his dream of serving in a war zone. With more troops in Afghanistan now than in Iraq and with British soldiers serving at half a dozen locations, army chiefs believed they could protect him—if the media kept quiet.

That would have seemed an outlandish proposition. How to muzzle a voracious and competitive media wolf pack? The only way was to try to co-opt them.

This is where the enterprising double-teaming of private secretary Lowther-Pinkerton and communications maestro Harverson worked to perfection. The Netflix series **The Crown** has spawned an outdated view of Palace advisers as crusty reactionaries. People tend to imagine that the Queen's first private secretary, Tommy Lascelles, unforgettably played by Pip Torrens as a lugubrious mustachioed blood-hound who existed only to thwart a progressive idea, is still running the royal show. In fact, a band of so-phisticated strategists compose the modern Palace's think tank. Things work well or badly for the royals depending on who is employed in the critical private secretary and communications roles at any one time.

In June 2007, Lowther-Pinkerton and Harverson decided to go straight for the beast's belly. They set up meetings with Murdoch's tabloid **The Sun**, and sat down with the limpet-like royal scoop-monger Duncan Larcombe and hoary defense editor Tom Newton Dunn. As recounted in Larcombe's book, **Prince Harry: The Inside Story**, Harverson opened the meeting with "We want to know if you think it will ever be possible for Harry to go to war."

"Have you considered trying to get a media blackout on any future deployment?" Newton Dunn asked.

"Would that really work?" asked Lowther-Pinkerton.

Larcombe replied, "Well, it seems to me that this is the only way Harry would ever be able to serve in the front line. If his deployment is publicized be-fore the event, he will not be able to go. So perhaps this is the only option available."

Bingo. The strategy of co-option landed, and the Palace had even made it appear that the tabloid tor-menters in chief had come up with it. Though neither Larcombe nor Newton Dunn thought the Palace could ever pull off the media going dark on a royal celebrity of Harry's profile and popularity, Lowther-Pinkerton, Harverson, and General Dannatt went into overdrive, meeting with other editors and news producers to sell the idea.

Critical to the success of the scheme was Miguel Head, then chief press officer for the Ministry of Defence, who negotiated agreements with the press that came with a reward. If newspapers could be persuaded to keep mum about Harry's deployment, Head pledged faithfully, the Prince would do interviews before, during, and after his tour, on the condition the conversations would be held until he returned from the front line. With the print media on board, Head next convinced the broadcast media to honor the news blackout. They balked, especially the BBC. It took five months for General Dannatt to persuade them to use as a model the kidnap template, when police have the right to request that media organizations don't report an abduction while negotiations are under way, in case it endangers the hostage. In return, the police accept responsibility to update the media regularly and do a "reveal" on camera once the situation is resolved.

In an interview with **The Journalist's Resource**, Head explained how he shamed the usually rapacious press to stand down on one of the biggest royal stories:

The competitive nature of media had the inverse effect of none of them wanting to be the bad person. Prince Harry is so popular, and back then he was still very young. It had been only 10 years since Diana, Princess of Wales, had died. There was still a very strong sense in the country of the public, in effect, bringing the two young princes into their arms and saying, "We will look after them. And you, press, you had better keep your hands off them. Don't you dare do to them what you did to their mother."

In the end, hundreds of news organizations, including U.S. broadcasters, were brought into what Miguel Head called "the circle of trust." Remarkably, this was a gentlemen's agreement, not a legal one—which is why Head thought the embargo would last for forty-eight hours, tops. Royal watchers who were used to relentless Prince Harry updates were not tipped off by photos disseminated of him riding around in the desert on a rusty motorbike in a mysteriously uncredited location. William took part in the subterfuge by signing up for army duties over Christmas 2007 to help along the fiction that both brothers had elected to spend the day on base with their units. Thankfully, Prince Charles provided a useful news distraction, yelling at a photographer when exercising his horse, "Get out of the way, you annoying little prat!"

While the rest of the royals were eating Christmas pudding, and Princess Anne was picking up dead birds at Prince Philip's Boxing Day shoot, Harry was eating curried goat meat with Gurkha soldiers in the desert of Afghanistan. In many ways, the fates had conspired to pluck him from a war in Iraq that people hated and insert him, instead, into a battle theater—Afghanistan—that was, at that time, less controversial. There is a folk memory of Afghanistan in Britain's fighting forces, and Harry seemed to fit right into a place of which both Kipling and Churchill had written so eloquently.

No one could say that his deployment was a sinecure. For most of it, he lived without running water or heat during the freezing nights. Working as a forward air controller, he scoured the feed of live footage to a laptop terminal, known as "Taliban TV" or "Kill TV." His job was to call in air cover for NATO troops under fire from the Taliban, using his call name Widow Six Seven. Pilots tuned in would hear the message "Cleared Hot" (permission to fire) relayed in Etonian cadences they had no idea belonged to the grandson of the Queen.

It took ten weeks for the anonymity deal with the press to fall apart, which, all things considered, was a credit to the usually carnivorous media, and a testament to Harry's popularity. His cover was almost blown after a month, when a little-known Australian women's magazine called **New Idea** somehow found out about his deployment and, unaware of the blackout agreement, published a small item on its website about the Prince on the front line. (The editor later published an apology and resigned—which did not stop the hate mail and death threats she received for outing the Prince.) Happily for Harry, **New Idea** was on no one's media radar, and the blackout held for a further seven weeks. Miguel Head was right. There was little appetite in the British media to be the delinquent press outlet that blew open a brave warrior-prince's service to his country, but U.S. gossip buccaneer Matt Drudge of the **Drudge Report** had no such concerns. He ran it as his own scoop, trumpeting, "They're calling him 'Harry the Hero!'" The post ended with the ominous signature Drudge sign-off, "Developing . . ."—which he had patented during the Monica Lewinsky scandal.

It was over. When the RAF TriStar troop transporter plane bearing Prince Harry landed at RAF Brize Norton, he was the embodiment of wretchedness. He was wearing his dirty camo uniform and body armor with sand from Afghanistan still in his boots. "He was very upset," Miguel Head recalls. "He was really down. I wouldn't describe him as angry—he's far more mature than that, and he understood why it had happened. He was just very sad about it." He'd had two and a half months of normal life—and only normal because it was war.

His flight home had been traumatic. On board were two seriously wounded British soldiers who were in induced comas with tubes coming out of their arms. One of the men was Ben McBean, a twenty-one-year-old Royal Marine who had lost his right leg and left arm after stepping on a Taliban-planted IED. Tucked into the hand of the other soldier was a test tube of the shrapnel that had been removed from his neck.

Harry never forgot Ben McBean. Five years later, the Prince turned out to cheer him on as he competed—with his prosthetic leg—in a grueling thirty-one-mile run on behalf of an armed forces charity. McBean said afterward he was stunned to see Harry there. The bravery of the injured veterans on the plane had left a forever mark on the Prince's psyche. Their silent suffering later inspired him to found the Invictus Games, which enable wounded veterans to reclaim their sense of worth in competitive sports.

At Brize Norton, Harry's father and brother were there to meet him when he landed. Miguel Head, who was also present, said:

> It was the first time I realized, that I saw with my own eyes, the closeness of the relationship between the two brothers. Think about the mixed emotions Prince William would have had, because he wasn't allowed . . . he never got to go. So he would have known how Prince Harry felt, and he was very protective of him.

On Harry's deployment, William had written him a letter telling him how proud their mother would be.

The media agreement that Miguel Head had negotiated now was an unbearable prospect for the exhausted Prince. He was expected to sit down in front of television lights and do an on-camera interview for the press pool. For once, the British media stood on moral high ground. The leak had come from America, not from the red-tops. Harry thanked them for keeping mum.

"It's a shame," he said with admirable poise. " 'Angry' would be the wrong word to use. I'm slightly disappointed. I thought I could see it through to the end and come back with our guys." Still shaken from the sight of the seriously injured soldiers on the flight, he admitted experiencing shock and a "bit of a choke" in his throat. "Those are the heroes. Those were guys who had been blown up by a mine that they had no idea about, serving their country, doing a normal patrol."

William, watching from the back of the room, sensed how fragile his brother was beneath his media façade. He suddenly stood up and drew his hand across his neck in a gesture that said "Cut."

"It was simply a brother realizing that at that point nothing was more important than his [brother's] welfare, and none of the other agreements mattered at that point," Miguel Head recalled.

And it says something about the closeness of the two brothers and their authenticity, as well. They will not fake who they are simply to play a game or to go along with other people's expectations. And they are perfectly courteous and loyal and they will abide by agreements up to a point. But there will come a point where they say, "Well, actually our humanity is more important."

The BBC producer who had been promised a full-length interview was apoplectic and yelled at Head about the broken agreement. Later the brothers were so appreciative of the way Miguel handled it, they asked Paddy Harverson to hire him as their first joint press secretary, which he duly did.

Harry, Charles, and William quickly exited the scene of the interview. William carried Harry's two duffel bags to a waiting station wagon, and they drove away. Like any family welcoming a beloved soldier safely home from war.

CHAPTER
15

SNOOPERS

How the Press Stalked the Royals

ONE PERSON WHO WAS DELIGHTED that Harry's deployment was cut short was his twenty-two-year-old girlfriend Chelsy Davy, the wild-child daughter of Charles Davy, one of Zimbabwe's largest private landowners. Their relationship had been on-again, off-again for four years, but his absence reheated her affection. Freewheeling outdoorsy-ness and a hard-partying sense of fun defined Chelsy's appeal to Harry as much as her long legs and curtain of platinum hair. He loved her madly for over seven years.

Like Harry, Chelsy had edge. There was allure in the precarious backdrop of her Zimbabwean childhood under the reign of the alligator-faced despot Robert Mugabe. She bombed around Cape Town in a two-seater silver Mercedes. Her parents' wealth gave her an aura of the hedonistic Happy Valley set in Kenya in the 1920s and '30s. Her mother was a famous beauty, Miss Rhodesia 1973, with a face well-known from being plastered in ads on Coca-Cola trucks.

Chelsy grew up running barefoot and hunting snakes on the vast Davy farm. In an interview in **The Times** in 2016, she said that at her preschool "there were monkeys everywhere, stealing your crayons."

By the time Chelsy hit her teens, Zimbabwe was unraveling. She harangued her parents to let her go to school in England. The family settled on the exclusive Cheltenham Ladies' College in Gloucestershire. As a young teenager, she arrived at the uptight upper-class school fresh from the bush, like "Crocodile Dundee with all my snakes." She went on to Stowe, the less prissy, mostly boys boarding school in Buckinghamshire, which her parents hoped would better suit her sensibility.

Back home, her father's pragmatic business ties to allies of Mugabe raised increasingly awkward questions about why his HHK Safaris hunting operation—which catered to American and European high-rollers—continued to thrive in the regime's land grab. With so many white farmers being evicted from their family-run properties, there was a stench about why Charles Davy ultimately surrendered only 140,000 acres. Harry's romance with Chelsy was considered a propaganda coup by Mugabe, less cherished, no doubt, after the Queen stripped the dictator of his honorary knighthood in 2008 in response to British Foreign Office revulsion over his human rights abuses. Charles Davy's big-game hunting business and the postcolonial disintegration of Zimbabwe would have ultimately been explosive elements in Chelsy's story if she had married into the House of Windsor. To avoid diplomatic difficulties, Harry was reportedly counseled by the Palace never to visit Chelsy at home in Zimbabwe, but to rendez-vous instead in countries nearby.

Harry's passion for Chelsy was always inextricably bound up with his longing to flee from the con-straints of royal life. "I wish I could spend more time in Africa," Harry told **Town & Country** in 2017, going on to characterize the diverse peoples of fifty-four countries as a moral and demographic monolith much as his ancestors might have done in less en-lightened times. "I have this intense sense of complete relaxation and normality here. To not get recognized, to lose myself in the bush with what I would call the most down-to-earth people on the planet, people [dedicated to conservation] with no ulterior mo-tives, no agendas, who would sacrifice everything for the betterment of nature." For a time, he said, he longed to be a park ranger.

He first experienced this seduction just weeks after his mother's death, when Charles swept his devas-tated thirteen-year-old son along for some special bonding on that official trip to South Africa, Swaziland, and Lesotho. It was Harry's three days in the bush in Botswana, viewing wildlife from an open-topped Land Rover—while his father bur-nished his own image on his royal road show—that

ABOVE AND RIGHT: A mesmerized Prince William saw his fellow student Kate Middleton in a whole new light modeling at a St. Andrews charity fashion show, March 26, 2002.

LEFT: Bursting with Pride: Carole and Michael Middleton at their Bucklebury home the day Kate and William announced their engagement, November 16, 2010.

ABOVE: Tens of millions watched as William and Kate, now Duke and Duchess of Cambridge, tied the knot at Westminster Abbey under the fatherly gaze of Michael Middleton, April 29, 2011.

LEFT: Relatable Kate, graduating from St. Andrews, June 23, 2005.

FACING PAGE, FAR RIGHT: Golden Girl: Kate rocks the red carpet at the London premiere of the James Bond film **No Time To Die**, September 28, 2021. RIGHT: The Cambridge family celebrates the Queen's official birthday on the Buckingham Palace balcony, June 8, 2019. Left to right: HRH Prince George, HRH Prince Louis, and HRH Princess Charlotte.

Magic Moment: The wedding of the Duke and Duchess of Sussex was a transformative day for Britain and for the House of Windsor. St. George's Chapel, Windsor, May 19, 2018.

2ND ROW, LEFT: Thomas Markle and teenage Meghan, the apple of her father's eye. CENTER TOP: Meghan and Harry's first public date, at the Invictus Games in Canada, September 25, 2017. CENTER ABOVE: Sussex baby Archie Harrison Mountbatten-Windsor in Cape Town, September 25, 2019. 2ND ROW, RIGHT: Prince Charles escorts Meghan's mother, Doria Ragland, out of St. George's Chapel, May 19, 2018.

FACING PAGE: Star Power: The Sussexes radiate happiness as they complete one of their final Royal engagements. Endeavour Fund Awards, Mansion House, London, March 5, 2020.

Annus Horribilis II: A looming Megxit and the scandal of Andrew's involvement with Jeffrey Epstein and the seventeen-year-old Virginia Roberts Giuffre (pictured below right with Prince Andrew and Ghislaine Maxwell) made 2019 one to forget for the Queen. Harry and Meghan's photograph was conspicuously absent in her annual Christmas broadcast at Windsor Castle, December 2019. TOP: The Sussexes caused explosions when they went public with their exit plans in January 2020.

TOP: Mourning Prince Philip: A COVID-era goodbye isolated the Queen in her grief at St. George's Chapel. 2ND ROW, LEFT: The Duke of Edinburgh's coffin—topped by his naval cap and sword—was carried by Royal Marines. CENTER: Lady Romsey—now Countess Mountbatten of Burma—was one of the few invited to attend. 2ND ROW, RIGHT: Anne, Princess Royal, the one most like her father in temperament.

ABOVE: An estranged Harry and William escorted the coffin of their beloved grandfather. Windsor, April 17, 2021.

Pride Before the Fall: Prince Andrew joined his supportive
mother on the Buckingham Palace balcony on June 8, 2019.
On January 13, 2022, HM stripped him of his military honors
and patronages amidst the escalating scandal surrounding Virginia Giuffre's allegations.
RIGHT: Giuffre tells her traumatic story in a BBC interview, December 2, 2019.

Vivat Regina: Her Majesty Queen Elizabeth II traveling to her fifty-fifth
State Opening of Parliament, November 6, 2007. When the longest reign
in British history ends, will the monarchy have the same gravitas and
resonance at home and around the world?

made the deepest impression on Harry at an exquisitely vulnerable time. Accompanied by the tireless
Tiggy Legge-Bourke and a schoolmate, he stayed in
a canvas tent with a reed roof, and was entranced by
the elephants, lions, and giraffes in the wild. Prince
Charles joined him for a boat ride in the Zulu heart-
land, where they floated past flamingos, pelicans,
hippos, and crocodiles. For Harry, it was a mystical
release from the horror and pandemonium of losing
his mother. Ever since that first initiation, he's remained enthralled with Africa, returning again and
again to share his passion for the continent with
someone he loves. When he fell hard for Meghan
Markle after just two dates, he spirited her off to
Botswana to sleep under the stars. He even included
a conflict-free Botswana diamond in her engagement ring.

II

Harry's gap year in 2003—between the end of Eton
and the start of Sandhurst—deepened his sense that
Africa was a place where he flourished. And mentor
Mark Dyer shared Harry's passion for all things
Africa. He'd worked for Save the Children in
Ethiopia and Sudan. Dyer had become almost a
second father to Harry and, with his mop of ginger
hair, could easily have been mistaken for such.
Tasked with designing Harry's gap year, he drew on
a connection with Prince Seeiso, the Crown Prince

of Lesotho, a tiny mountain kingdom landlocked by South Africa that was devastated by the AIDS epidemic.

It was agreed that Harry would spend eight weeks traveling with Seeiso and working at the Mants'ase Children's Home, an orphanage in Lesotho, where numerous children had lost parents to AIDS. The Crown Prince, nearly two decades older than Harry, had some initial trepidation about the responsibility for his nineteen-year-old charge. That was soon dispelled as they bonded over each having lost his mother and the peculiar pressures of being a second royal son. He saw that Harry had a remarkable natural rapport with children, and was a Pied Piper to one little boy who followed him everywhere as he did repairs and painted walls. Harry became so fond of the child—named Mutsu—that he gave him his own special pair of blue Wellies, kept in touch via letters and visits, and, fourteen years later, invited him to his wedding to Meghan at Windsor Castle. Seeiso was Harry's cofounder of Sentebale, his charity to benefit children with HIV, the first patronage that was not thrust upon him by his father or grandmother.

One evening over dinner in Lesotho, Harry disappeared to the back of the outbuilding where he was living, presumably to smoke a cigarette. "I went out to get a glass of water," said a person who was present, "and he was back there. He had just slipped off and was doing the washing up with the ladies. And I thought, he's going to be all right, this boy."

Paddy Harverson flew in to ensure that this leg of Harry's gap year went better than the first, which the Prince spent in Australia on a ranch at Tooloombilla Station, a 39,500-acre cattle estate in central Queensland. Harry was hounded by the media throughout. Instead of doing the prescribed jackaroo tasks of herding cattle and mending fences, the miserable Harry was imprisoned indoors as the press pursued him on the ground and from the air. A swarm of paparazzi was camped just outside the ranch, and helicopter and crop-dusting planes equipped with video cameras buzzed overhead. A livid Mark Dyer told reporters, "I've got a young man in there in pieces. He can't do his job as a jackaroo, he can't go out, he can't even muster cattle in the yards near the road without having his photo taken." To compound the absurdity, the press dubbed him "spoiled and lazy." "Harry is a thoroughly horrible young man who rarely lifted a finger unless it's to feel up a cheap tart in a nightclub or shoot some harmless critter," snorted a **Daily Express** dinosaur.

This was only a small foretaste of future hell. Harry's Lesotho weeks were a rare oasis (and the logistical challenges the kingdom posed to paparazzi were one more reason to love Africa). Now that Harry had left the confines of Eton and the PCC code, the press considered the unpredictable younger brother fair game, especially when they first caught wind of Chelsy Davy, who had captivated Harry on a sidebar excursion from Lesotho to Cape Town. The media bloodhounds sniffed out the couple when they tried to have a romantic getaway before Harry entered Sandhurst, tracking them to the sequestered tropical island of Bazaruto, off the coast of Mozambique. Charles Davy had footed the bill for the private plane that took the infatuated teenagers to their littoral love shack with a heavenly three-mile exclusion zone. That didn't deter Murdoch's **News of the World** from sending reporter Sarah Arnold and a photographer to pose as a honeymoon couple with straw hats concealing their pasty tabloid mugs until the government dispatched eight militia members to demand that the unmasked duo beat it off the island within fifteen minutes.

Even more incendiary to the protective Harry was the way that photographers stalked his girlfriend when they were apart, trailing her as she tried to go about her studies at the University of Cape Town, and upping the harassment further when she moved to Leeds University in England to complete a postgrad degree in law. Chelsy was almost constantly swarmed by Fleet Street's tabloids and their invisible army of lawless outriders. Murdoch's News Group Newspapers, the **News of the World** and **The Sun,** were the worst—followed closely by Viscount Rothermere's **Daily Mail** and **The Mail on Sunday.** The Mirror Group's ostensibly left-leaning **Daily Mirror, Sunday Mirror,** and **People** weren't far behind. In London, the paparazzi were always waiting in packs as Chelsy and Harry emerged after a night of downing Crack Babies, a (tastelessly named) cocktail of passion fruit, vodka, and champagne, at Boujis nightclub. The coverage created a distorted image of Chelsy as nothing but a boozed-up party girl. In reality, she was studying hard at university and later worked long hours in leverage finance at Allen and Overy, a top London law firm. "If you go out once, they take a picture, but they don't take a picture of you going to work every morning. They use one of you falling out of a nightclub at 4 A.M.," she said years later to **The Times.**

The relentless coverage created tension between Harry and Chelsy. When she was back in South Africa, she didn't relish reading the "Dirty Harry" headline in **The Sun** when he had a notably pleasant time with a lap dancer at a strip club in Slough to celebrate the end of his officer training at Sandhurst. Nor was she thrilled by the photo of Harry leaving a party with an old flame, TV presenter Natalie Pinkham, who was overheard by the hacks hiding outside asking the Prince to give her a kiss.

The tabloids expended exhorbitant amounts of time and money on what they saw as the sexy royal romance of the moment. In 2008, **The Sun** sent its royal correspondent and a photographer to lie in wait at the Namibia border just to catch a shot of Harry and Chelsy floating down the Okavango waterway in northern Botswana on a houseboat they rented for some secret R & R.

Chelsy became increasingly vexed with the price she paid for dating Harry. "It was so full-on: crazy and scary and uncomfortable. I found it very difficult when it was bad. I couldn't cope. I was young, I was trying to be a normal kid and it was horrible," she told **The Times** in 2016. The conventional (and sexist) tabloid tropes that her goal was to "land" the Prince were way off the mark. Unlike Kate Middleton, who openly rearranged her life and job around William's schedule, Chelsy clearly intended to forge her own professional identity. She found the royal rigmarole and press invasions an almighty pain in the arse.

What baffled and incensed her—and Harry, too—was how the press always seemed to know where to find them. In April 2006, Chelsy took the precaution of buying a plane ticket with cash at the airport so there would be no electronic trail of her flight from Cape Town to London to join Harry at his graduation ball at Sandhurst. It was a futile attempt at evasion. **The Sun** published a piece credited to the royal correspondent Duncan Larcombe that ended, "In the evening [Prince Harry] will celebrate his achievement at the lavish Passing Out ball, due to take place in the academy's grounds. Harry's girlfriend Chelsy Davy, 20, has flown in from Cape Town to be at the ball. She was given an armed escort for the first time yesterday as she landed at Heathrow—then texted Harry to say she was OK."

How did they know? The answer is the Dark Arts, as the tabloids' shadowy news-gathering techniques were privately referred to, which were practiced in a variety of inventive ways.

Paddy Harverson remembers the pivotal day in 2005 when he was sitting in Jamie Lowther-

Pinkerton's office at the back of St. James's Palace and mentioned that his voicemail had been acting up. "Jamie said he had been noticing the same thing," Harverson told me. "At the same time, the **News of the World** had been printing things that we couldn't understand how they were getting. They were trivial, but spot-on."

By November 2005, Prince William was becoming suspicious, too. He'd noticed that the contents of a particular voicemail, left for him by close friend and ITN correspondent Tom Bradby, had also shown up in the **News of the World.** The message was about how William was going to give Bradby some videotapes so that he could splice them into a spoof news package. Bradby was also going to lend the Prince some broadcasting equipment.

Later, Bradby told the **Daily Express:**

The story—a stupid, uninteresting story—was in the **News of the World.** I like William, I have a good relationship with him, and we've had quite a lot of dealings with each other privately over the years. He knew there was no way I would have told anyone. So he said, "Look, I know it wasn't you, but that was weird." I said, "Yes it was weird—who did you tell?" And he'd told no one apart from his secretary, who would never have dreamed of saying anything. So even though William didn't think for a minute I was responsible, it was embarrassing because only the three of us knew, and suddenly it's in the paper.

Now there were two sources—William and Harverson—raising complaints about the same problem. As Harverson recalls, "We started to twig something was going on." He consulted the go-to media lawyer Gerrard Tyrell, whose client, soccer star David Beckham, had been hacked by Glenn Mulcaire, an ex–soccer pro turned private investigator. Mulcaire had been hired on an exclusive contract by the **News of the World.** One of tabloid journalism's subterranean characters, Mulcaire spoke with a mixture of spy slang and business jargon. He started out with exposés of felons and fraudsters, but as the paper found celebrity journalism more lucrative, Mulcaire's "public interest" investigations gave way to snooping on pop, soccer, and movie stars for a £100,000-a-year retainer. In 2004, he delivered to the **News of the World** a huge exclusive mined from phone hacking about Beckham's alleged extramarital affair with his assistant Rebecca Loos.

Sure enough, Tyrell confirmed to the Palace advisers that the mysterious voicemail glitches were likely evidence of being breached. "There was a clear case to bring in the police to look at it," Harverson told me. "The sneaky-beakies followed the trail, and it didn't take them long at all to trace the calls to the **News of the World** offices." When Scotland Yard examined Mulcaire's handwritten records, they found he had targeted more than six thousand people in all. And he wasn't the only hacker, said Harverson. "The intel people who looked into it saw all these other numbers belonging to **News of the World** journos."

The story was growing to be bigger—much bigger—than one just about the royal brothers and their circle. It would come to rock Britain politically, resulting in the biggest media scandal in the country's modern history.

III

In May 2021, when Prince Harry declared to an American podcast host that his life was "a mix between **The Truman Show** and living in a zoo," listeners may have thought he meant it metaphorically. But it was nothing less than the truth. He had been living his own version of that Jim Carrey movie about a man who has no idea that his whole life is a TV reality show, with near 360-degree surveillance, 365 days a year. The surreal show about Harry's family had begun before he was born. He was just the latest unwitting character to stumble onto the invisible set.

Private investigators had started to market their services to Fleet Street on a big scale as far back as 1985, specifically to squeeze every last droplet of news out of Harry's mother. Princess Diana always believed that it was the Palace and her ex-husband's allies who were spying on her, but it is now clear it was the tabloids who were tracking her calls.

When the **News of the World** suspected her, in 1995, of carrying on an affair with England rugby star Will Carling, they hired Metropolitan Police

officer turned surveillance expert Steve Clarke to
check it out by using a powerful radio scanner, according to an ex-colleague. The device—known in
the trade as a "black box"—enabled Clarke to intercept live calls and possibly home in on the locations
of callers. As soon as the snooper keyed in Diana's
or Carling's mobile number, the electronics inside
locked on to their signal. Immediately, he was able
to listen live as she arranged to meet Carling at
the Chelsea Harbour Club. **News of the World** staff
photographer Nick Bowman was put on a "watch"
at the club. And lo! The tabloid got the "snatched"
pictures of Diana and Carling the editor craved.
Fleet Street's gross absence of ethics was on display
when Bowman was rewarded for his diabolical intrusion with the 1996 **UK Press Gazette** British Press
Award for Photographer of the Year.

The **Sunday Mirror,** looking for a piece of the
Diana action, found a nefarious way to bust open
her affair with Hasnat Khan. The paper paid a private investigator to steal the itemized billing data
from his landline, as evidence that they were calling
each other. By January 1996, the **Mirror** zoned in on
a particular mobile number that they were convinced
was Diana's. To prove it, they tasked a PI with putting in a "blag" call.

Blagging, derived from the French verb **blaguer,**
meaning to joke or to prank, is obtaining information by deception. In America, freelance detectives
refer to scripted scams as "spoofing" or "punking."
In a bid for respectability, blaggers sometimes refer

to themselves as "social engineers" or "creative researchers."

The number of different names used for lying for money is an indication of how widespread and lucrative defrauding people for data has become. In simple terms, private investigators steal the identities of officials, and use their phony authority to con admin staff into revealing private information. Most frequently, the scammers pretend to be telephone engineers fixing broken cables "in the field" to dupe network providers into handing over itemized billing data. Impersonating local doctors to trick hospital staff into giving out medical details over the phone is another favorite ruse.

Diana was creepily entrapped by a blagger named Christine Hart, a thirty-one-year-old hustler who'd cut her teeth battering the phones in a string of London's seamier PI agencies. To verify Diana's phone number, Hart phoned Diana pretending to be a receptionist at the Chelsea Harbour Club wanting to know if a piece of jewelry handed in was hers. "I called the number and a very classy, softly-spoken woman picked up," she admitted to **Byline Investigates** in 2019.

It sounded like it was in a bedroom; it was really, really quiet. I said, "You remember we met that time . . ." and she said, "no," she didn't. I kept calling her "Diana" and told her someone has handed in a gold diamante watch, and we believe it might be yours. I said it was a bit like a

Chanel design, but not actually Chanel and she said "no," that wouldn't be hers. She then joked that if it was real, she might claim it.

Hart—who now says she is "disgusted" by what she did—successfully kept Diana talking for seven minutes on tape, thus proving beyond doubt that they had her correct cell number. By analyzing the itemized phone call data they already had, the **Sunday Mirror** was able to run a front-page exclusive on Diana and Hasnat's frequent contact and their intimate date nights at a restaurant outside London.

How, you might ask, did tabloid journalism—never exactly elevated—sink so very, very low?

The degrading of ethics was a race to the bottom, driven by ever-receding profitability. London's Fleet Street was always a dodgier journalistic address than New York's Newspaper Row. British newspaper journalism—more rough-and-tumble than its U.S. cousins and less burdened by highfalutin principles—has always viewed itself as a jobbing craft, not a solemn calling. A typical "hack," a label a British journalist wears with perverse pride, learns his trade on the job, not in a journalism school. (The word would come to acquire an ironic connotation, too, as events were to show.) A high premium is placed on practical skills: spunky headline writing, swift storytelling, and gut-punching column writing, produced by newsrooms that are, to this day, unabashedly sexist and hard-drinking.

The "voice" of British journalism is high-low and irreverent. American journalism, by contrast, takes itself much more seriously, especially post-Watergate. Even bloodied and gored by the fake news era, it views itself as a profession, even a priesthood, at the upper end of the scale, contravened only by the scavenger exposés of supermarket checkout titles like the **National Enquirer.** No president of the United States—except Donald Trump—would grant access to the editor of the **National Enquirer.** A British prime minister, by contrast, will sit down readily with tabloids that in America would be considered beyond the pale. How else do you reach the working class—or at least appear to be courting it?

Digital disruption in the late nineties and the aughts from Google and Facebook sent British newspapers into a competitive death match. The natural coarseness of tabloid culture turned openly brutal and plunged further down-market. The top editors were drawn increasingly from the showbiz columns, not the newsroom. As the role of the traditional media gatekeepers eroded, a Wild West mentality took over, with the need for faster and faster scoops trumping all else.

The accelerating decline of print and its advertising meant that newsrooms operated on slashed budgets. Management became obsessed with traffic and eyeballs on their money-losing online editions, inevitably stoked by rapid, sensational hits. The demoralized reporters lapsed into what **The Guardian**'s Nick Davies terms "churnalism," recycling thinly researched stories posted by others. In his 2008 book **Flat Earth News,** Davies cited researchers from Cardiff University who discovered that "the average Fleet Street journalist is filling three times as much space as he or she was in 1985." The old-fashioned way of finding things out by foot-slog and working the phones didn't cut it anymore.

This was bad news for such hoary hands at the **News of the World** as royal editor Clive Goodman, a legend in the midnineties for breaking such iconic Diana stories as "My Secret Nights as an Angel," about how the Princess visited terminal cancer patients at night at the Royal Brompton Hospital. (In fact, this was a brilliant decoy feed from Diana herself, to cover nocturnal visits with her lover Dr. Hasnat Khan.) Goodman was known as "the Eternal Flame" because he was always in the office. But his supremacy at the paper would soon wane.

Diana was Fleet Street's golden goose. When she died, the tabloids turned their attention to her teenage sons, but reporters' wings were clipped by the post-Diana censure of the press. The PCC's inhibitions did little to cramp the methods of one newspaper executive: the ruthlessly ambitious **News of the World** editor Rebekah Brooks, née Wade, one of the great divas of London tabloid journalism. She was last glimpsed in this narrative in 1994, dressed as a cleaning lady stealing the first edition of **The Sunday Times** off the presses in order to get a scoop on Prince Charles for the **News of the World.**

With her tumbling mane of curly red hair and

vulpine networking skills, Brooks was lethally successful penetrating the political and media corridors
of power "She can turn people over and have dinner
with them the next day," said former **Sun** editor
David Yelland. Like her paymaster Murdoch, she was
a political chameleon who wooed, in swift succession,
a string of ideologically disparate prime ministers, including Blair, Brown, Cameron, and Johnson. On
weekends she socialized with the "Chipping Norton
set," fellow power mongers who had country houses
in Oxfordshire. They included the Camerons, as well
as Murdoch's daughter Elisabeth, then married to PR
supremo Matthew Freud. She was on such intimate
terms with Gordon Brown's wife, Sarah, that she was
invited to join Sarah's all-girls "slumber party" at
Chequers in 2008, along with Murdoch's then-wife
Wendi Deng and Elisabeth Murdoch.

Brooks had stormed her way up to the top from
the lowly post of a **News of the World** secretary to
become, at age thirty-one in 2000, its youngest-ever
editor. Three years later she moved to Murdoch's
most profitable daily newspaper, **The Sun,** as its first
female editor, leaving the **News of the World** to her
deputy (and on-again, off-again lover) Andy Coulson.

Working together, Brooks and Coulson were a dangerous duo: Brooks, the flamboyant social operator;
Coulson, the fake respectable suit in dark-rimmed
glasses, who used silence to intimidate anyone with
an awkward question.

Brooks won new readers at the **News of the
World** by exploiting primal populist rage, with a

wildly irresponsible campaign to name and shame pedophiles, which led to vigilante mobs terrorizing suspected sex offenders. There were several cases of mistaken identity, including one in which a pediatrician had her house vandalized by inflamed readers who thought her occupation meant she was a pedophile. The paper also did a slap-up job of ruining the lives of cabinet ministers, soccer players, pop stars, and members of the Royal Family.

Brooks perfected an emerging practice in newspapers. The targets of impending **News of the World** exposés were offered pre-publication deals to soften the blow by removing the most damaging revelations in exchange for plumped-up confessions and frothy interviews. Her critics dubbed it "the blackmail model." She wasted no time in using the morally extortionate device on Prince Harry, who at the time was studying for his GCSEs at Eton.

The source of the Harry gossip is a secret to this day. But on the back of a tip that the sixteen-year-old Prince was going off the rails, drinking and taking drugs, Brooks's **News of the World** launched one of the paper's most vicious and exacting operations to date. In a bid to "prove" Harry was using cocaine, they targeted him with a "triple whammy" maneuver. The biggest howitzers were brought to bear: Rebekah Brooks herself, her top undercover reporter Mazher Mahmood—aka the Fake Sheikh who had tormented Sophie Wessex and would later ensnare Sarah Ferguson—and the hacker Glenn Mulcaire. Later, in a bid to defend herself in court in the phone-hacking trials, Brooks would claim that she had only ever used PIs to track down sex offenders in the public interest. The boast proved to be untrue, when the High Court heard that she had also tasked PI Steve Whittamore to investigate her suspicions that her then-fiancé was cheating on her with a woman he met at a pub.

In the early hours of a Friday in August 2001, Harry was snapped "worse for wear," outside a nightclub in Marbella, Spain. Mahmood sweet-talked staff at the nightclub and tried to elicit information on Harry's visit. Despite his best attempts to ascertain whether the waiters and barmen had witnessed Harry score or snort, he drew a blank.

Mulcaire, for his part, monitored the phone records of Harry and his friends. He tracked close confidant Guy Pelly, as well as Harry's drinking buddies at the Rattlebone Inn, to find out whether the boys had been calling drug dealers. Again, there was zero evidence that it was true.

Finally, Brooks herself jumped in to "make it work." Armed with the flimsiest of "dossiers," she managed to bluff Palace aides into thinking the paper had more evidence than it did—an old Fleet Street trick. She had cultivated close relations with Mark Bolland in Charles's office. A PR deal was struck: If Prince Harry admitted that he'd smoked pot, the **News of the World** promised to leave out what it said were the more serious allegations about hard drugs. This was a home run for Brooks, as the hard-drugs material was untrue and a bluff.

As **News of the World** news editor Greg Miskiw put it, "Mazher got nothing. Mulcaire got nothing. But that didn't stop 'Blagga Becka.' She still managed to trick the Palace into a full-on confession, and a story was published."

The full trumped-up "Drugs Shame" sensation was spread over seven pages inside the **News of the World**. The cannabis line—an unrelated confession by Harry to his father that he had partaken—had been fed to Brooks by Bolland as part of the deal. In return, the **News of the World** manipulated the timeline of events, presenting a father-son visit to one of Charles's youth patronages, Phoenix House's Featherstone Lodge rehabilitation center in the early summer of 2001, as a Prince Harry wake-up tour, when in fact the drug allegations were made two months later. The edited timeline was an image-shaping solution concocted by Bolland to make Charles look like a caring **paterfamilias** of a contrite Harry. (Bolland later said he felt "embarrassed" by the paper's "misleading" and "triumphalist" claims.)

An unforeseeable consequence of the story was that serial hackers Mulcaire and freelance PI Gavin Burrows infiltrated Harry and his circle—and it would be many years before they released their grip. Burrows says: "It was all about itemized phone bills and then tapping Harry's friends. This carried on, on and off, for several years." During the investigation, Burrows claims, he put a tap on Tiggy Legge-Bourke. From his tapped recordings, Burrows picked up that Harry was going to be the godfather of Tiggy's child, and then he helped a photographer find out where Harry and William were spending Christmas.

The shocking "Drugs Shame" scandal was a wretched passage for the teenage Harry. Even though his elder brother was just as often a carouser at the Rattlebone Inn, Harry had been pilloried as the problem child. His friends, including the loyal Pelly, had been dragged through the mud. And he had been made to pretend penitence at a drug clinic to sustain a fake narrative, and incidentally prettify his father's PR. He was receiving a bitter lesson in what it meant to be third in line to the throne, and the corrosive scrutiny would only intensify as he approached adulthood.

IV

Chelsy Davy had everything royal reporters wanted—sizzle, youth, and proximity to Harry. Consequently, in the early aughts she was illegally hacked, tapped, and blagged more than any other member of the Prince's circle. Between 2004 and 2010, her voicemails were routinely intercepted. More than a dozen private investigators on two continents were illegally tasked by staff reporters and editors to obtain her phone bills, medical records, travel itineraries, flight details, hotel receipts, bank accounts, and credit card statements. Hundreds of thousands of pounds were paid, some of it to and from shady offshore accounts operated by fly-by-night pop-up companies. At least one PI claims he even tapped Chelsy's landline and the phones of those she talked to—a highly illegal activity that would normally require law enforcement to obtain a warrant from the home secretary.

As I wrote this book, my Virgil through the hacking world was Graham Johnson, a features reporter at the **News of the World** between 1995 and 1997, who moved to the post of investigations editor at the **Sunday Mirror** between 1997 and 2005. In 2013, he was the only newsman who voluntarily told police that he had hacked a phone for one week in 2001. He was sentenced to two months in prison, suspended for one year, and since then has redeemed himself as one of the United Kingdom's most dogged investigative reporters into organized crime, including hacking. He is now the editor of **Byline Investigates,** a valued upstart UK news site.

Johnson told me this: PI Burrows, who also happened to be a self-confessed former drug dealer, says he organized telecoms interception by arranging to break into British Telecom junction boxes outside the homes of Harry's and Chelsy's friends, and selling what he learned to the Murdoch press. On Chelsy, he says he also did "bin spins" (searching her trash), and accessed her itemized bills.

Burrows operated internationally. He claimed to Johnson that he used an Africa-based subcontractor to "pull" her credit card bills and "do" a landline in Cape Town that Chelsy used to call Harry. Burrows extracted numerous stories via these methods, including a short but significant article about Chelsy's being invited to visit Prince Charles at Highgrove. The vast majority of his hits turned out to be one-fact stories that were run as stand-alone "shorts" in diary columns. Alternatively, several eye-catching threads—stark, bald revelations that prompted questions about provenance—were woven, often incongruously, into bigger features, to disguise their shady origins.

In 2006, the South Africa surveillance of Chelsy became more sophisticated. Her movements were monitored by obtaining airline manifests, usually carried out by bribing check-in staff or travel agents.

Though Harry was the main focus, William and Kate were also in the crosshairs throughout the aughts. "It wasn't long before the Middleton family were on the list too," recalls Burrows. "The only reason Harry got done more than William was that William was quite boring." Nevertheless, Burrows purportedly blagged the student house Prince William shared with Kate at St. Andrews, and put a landline tap on the Middleton family home in Berkshire.

Private investigator Steve Whittamore, Johnson learned, carried out fourteen inquiries on the Middleton family. Most were unlawful blags to obtain "friends and family" numbers, registered with British Telecom. By that time, around fifty criminal breaches of the UK's Data Protection Act had taken place on this specific job.

One of the ten numbers on the most-dialed list was Kate's mobile. The reporter rang it, and it went straight to voicemail. Later, the number was passed to a journalist pal. But when he called, an upper-class-sounding young woman picked up. "Is that Kate Middleton?" he asked. "No. It's not Kate. It's Catherine," said the canny future queen.

In 2013, when the truth could no longer be suppressed and hacking transcripts came out in court, the public learned just how blatant the targeting of William and Kate had been. Evidence showed that during a few months in 2005–2006, Kate was hacked 155 times, and Prince William's voicemails were listened to 35 times. The **News of the World** had hacked voicemails left by William on Kate's phone—including one after he'd "nearly got shot" while in military training. Another hacked phone message led to a 2006 exclusive revealing William's private nickname for Kate as "Babykins." (Hold the front page!) The **News of the World** was later ordered to take the stories down.

Call it karma kicking in, but in 2005 the hackers and their taskmasters started to make noticeable mistakes. The editorial overlords were cracking the whip. Eternal Flame Clive Goodman was under pressure from careerist weasel Andy Coulson, who had ascended to Rebekah Brooks's old seat as **News of the World** editor. Coulson thought Goodman's Rolodex was that of a doddering fogey. He was writing about royals who were no longer of interest and failing to bring in exclusives, a cardinal sin for a "big, top operator" at what used to be known colloquially as the "News of the Screws." Stories about Charles,

Diana mysteries, Prince Andrew, Sarah Ferguson—they were all old hat. "The readers wanted youthful William, Harry, Kate Middleton, Harry's girlfriends," **News of the World's** Greg Miskiw asserted.

Goodman was not able to satisfy the editor's demands. His days were numbered. So were Greg Mulcaire's. He made too much money. His wages had gone up to £120,000 per year, boosted by generous payments from Goodman for "royal specials," but still mainly to blag and intercept voicemails six days a week. To defend their respective positions, Goodman and Mulcaire started taking bigger risks. The goal was to bag a few succulent exclusives, prove their worth, and claw back some goodwill from the higher-ups.

Goodman tasked Mulcaire with intercepting the voicemails of four royal aides: Paddy Harverson; Michael Fawcett; Prince Harry's personal secretary Helen Asprey; and Jamie Lowther-Pinkerton. Hacked messages were transcribed and passed on to the news desk. The tidbits provided a steady stream of "shorts" for Goodman's biting weekly column, **The Carvery**. According to Miskiw, Goodman, to show Coulson he was still in the game, began to deploy Mulcaire's hacking on an industrial scale, badgering him several times a day with orders.

Mulcaire, no fool, started to panic about getting caught. He was anxious, too, about being replaced by cheaper, outsourced PIs, who got on better with the current regime. Both worries wrecked his head in equal measure. He was intercepting the messages of the four royal aides too fast, using special "ghost" numbers that "direct-dialed" straight into their mailboxes. Routinely—and in fits of paranoia—he changed the four-digit PINs of the aides' phones, a safety measure he had developed in a bid to stop Goodman and other reporters from doing the hacking themselves and cutting him out. The downside was that the more Mulcaire messed with the voicemail system, the more likely there would be noticeable and alarming glitches.

Goodman, for his part, was running Mulcaire's hacking tips not only too quickly, but in too much detail, without taking enough care to disguise their provenance. "The problem was this," Mulcaire said to Graham Johnson. "I was picking up messages from Harverson and others, which hadn't even been listened to. I advised Clive to use the info cautiously and wait until [it] filtered around the Palace, so that the source would be spread about." Unfortunately, said Mulcaire, Goodman "was so desperate, so under pressure, that he was crashing these things into the paper immediately. That's why it came on top. That's why we got caught."

V

I am told that when Prince Harry and Chelsy Davy learned they had been hacked for years, a certain amount of relief was mixed in with their righteous anger. At last, an explanation for the creepy peepers who sat next to Chelsy on flights to London, the paparazzi who mysteriously turned up at their secret rendezvous, the odd bod "couples" who checked in to her hotel, and the fake tourists who eavesdropped from behind sun loungers. Knowing how the private information of their whereabouts was detected eased the couple's rampant paranoia about whom they could trust.

What they didn't know was that Goodman and Mulcaire, jailed for four and six months, respectively, in January 2007, were only the tip of the iceberg. The two **News of the World** hackers had been thrown under the bus, while endemic data theft at the paper went on with impunity. The police had "sent their message" without damaging their sacrosanct relationship with the press's highest fliers, and the paper had supposedly got rid of its bad apples. Hours after Goodman and Mulcaire were jailed, Coulson resigned from the **News of the World,** but he was soon picked up for a prestige post at Downing Street as David Cameron's director of communications, an appointment for which Cameron would later get much aggravation.

The bad-apple myth would have succeeded but for Nick Davies, the maverick **Guardian** journalist who started digging almost as soon as Goodman and Mulcaire were arrested. Davies, backed by his editor Alan Rusbridger, was certain that "a few royal aides" were not the only victims. The rest of the British press, intimidated by Murdoch, turned a blind eye for two years. Davies alone pursued the clues of the

Murdoch papers' hacking operation through a maze of sources, documents, and hearsay, until he discovered that secret settlements reaching up to a million pounds were being paid out to multiple celebrities for having their phone lines breached.

Eureka! Davies's first piece, published on July 8, 2009, exposed the massive level of the phone hacking of cabinet ministers, members of Parliament, actors, sports stars, and others. It ran in partnership with a follow-up exposé by **The New York Times**, encouraged by Rusbridger, that bolstered protection for **The Guardian** against Murdoch retaliation. The transatlantic news bomb reignited the scandal after four years of dormancy.

The problem with targeting so many of the rich and famous is that they're rich and famous. High-profile victims with means and tenacity tend not to back down. Generally, those in the public eye fear the tabloids' power to make or break careers. But with social media ascendant from 2006 onward, the influence of tabloids was dimming. And when stars choose to speak out, settling in secret is not an option. The names of celebrity victims that came tumbling out—actors Hugh Grant, Sienna Miller, and Jude Law; novelist J. K. Rowling; and footballer Paul Gascoigne—meant a rocketing scandal meter. The High Court hearings became a disclosure machine. Murdoch's News Group Newspapers was forced to hand over at least 35,000 invoices from private investigators, and thousands of cash payment requests. Former **News of the World** staff writer Dan

Evans, who pled guilty in 2013, said the hacking was so common that even "the office cat" knew about it.

Nick Davies cranked out more than a hundred **Guardian** stories about crime in the tabloid empire and its intersection with policy and press failure. Sleep-deprived and racked with nerves as the Murdoch press mobilized against him to discredit his reporting, Davies felt as if he was fighting not just for this particular truth but for the restoration of the depleted morale of investigative journalists everywhere.

As even more **News of the World** staff were implicated, the story slipped from the innermost walls of courtrooms and consciences and into the open. Davies's revelation that the phone of a murdered thirteen-year-old schoolgirl had been hacked after she disappeared—disrupting the investigation into her death and prolonging her parents' hope that she might still be alive—provoked a cascade of public outrage, tipping Britain's mood definitively against the editorial perpetrators.

As with Watergate, the accelerating scandal of the phone-hacking phenomenon was the cover-up. The concealment of evidence at Murdoch's publications went on for years. Executives tried to make sure the taint didn't engulf other journalists. But they were most preoccupied by stopping the spread vertically up the pyramid to Murdoch's younger son, James, who ran his father's operations in Europe and Asia; to Les Hinton, executive chairman of Murdoch's News International; and to Rebekah Brooks, the boss's favorite. Most important, they sought to ensure that it didn't seep into what the newsroom called "deep carpet land," the hushed corporate interior of the office of Rupert Murdoch himself.

The scandal—now beyond any efforts to contain or spin it—did breach that sanctum in the end. On July 19, 2011, it dragged Rupert Murdoch and son James before an excoriating parliamentary hearing on what Murdoch called "the most humble day of my life."

The world's most powerful press baron finally had to acknowledge that a cover-up of astronomical scale had taken place. When he argued that he had been deceived himself, few believed him. His stamp was everywhere on **News of the World** corporate culture. Power and profit, Murdoch's watchwords, drove every decision. His employees didn't have to be told what he wanted. Everyone knew. Sir Harold Evans, my late husband, likened the phenomenon of instinctive compliance that Murdoch generated in his subordinates to the Third Reich syndrome of "Working Towards the Führer." (Harold fought Murdoch on the issue of editorial independence, and was fired by him as editor of **The Times** in 1982.)

Murdoch's pieties before Parliament notwithstanding, what he really thought about his "humbling" was caught on a leaked secret tape in July 2013 and broadcast by **Channel 4 News**. He could be heard dismissively claiming that investigators were "totally incompetent" and acted over "next to nothing," and excusing his papers' actions as "part of the culture of Fleet Street."

The parliamentary select committee report published in 2012 concluded that James Murdoch had showed "wilful ignorance" of the extent of phone-hacking. It found him guilty of "an astonishing lack of curiosity" over the issue, and concluded that both father and son "should ultimately be prepared to take responsibility" for wrongdoing at the **News of the World** and News International. Most damningly, it said that Rupert Murdoch was "not a fit person to exercise the stewardship of a major international company."

When Paddy Harverson and Jamie Lowther-Pinkerton first had their suspicions about glitchy voicemails back in 2005, neither Palace adviser had any idea that they had initiated a process that would lead to such seismic national consequences. There were approximately twenty-five arrests for phone-hacking crimes, leading to eight convictions, plus the resignations of James Murdoch, Les Hinton (a fifty-year apparatchik of Murdoch), and Scotland Yard commissioner Sir Paul Stephenson, who had been tarnished by his close relationship to personnel at the **News of the World.** The once-untouchable Rebekah Brooks was arrested for perversion of justice in March 2012, after police discovered a trash bag containing her laptop, documents, and a phone dumped in an underground parking garage near her house. She and Andy Coulson were put on trial at the Old Bailey in 2013.

Coulson was sentenced to eighteen months of jail time, demoted from Downing Street to Belmarsh prison in the span of four years. Brooks was dramatically cleared of all charges, thanks to the deft lawyering of Angus McBride, who was later appointed as general counsel to Murdoch's News UK empire in 2016. The jury accepted a defense received with widespread eye-rolling by her peers: that this famously hands-on, sharp-elbowed editor had no knowledge that it was illegal to intercept voicemail. It is proof of Murdoch's persistent admiration of Brooks that in 2015 he appointed her as News UK's CEO—the most senior position in his London company—a joint fuck-you to those looking for any genuine penitence.

Even more stunning, perhaps, was how Murdoch responded at the height of the public outcry. In July 2011, advertisers bailed in such volume that he closed the 168-year-old **News of the World** with its 2.6 million in circulation. Overnight, two hundred journalists, good and bad, were sacked. The scandal had hurt him where it counted most, in his wallet, costing him not just an estimated £38 million a year in revenue, but ultimately between £1 billion and £3 billion in payoffs to hacking victims. By 2021, the settlements had made such a hole in profits at **The Sun** that Murdoch had to write down the value of his former cash machine to exactly zero. (Over at the rival Mirror Group Newspapers, hacking charges at time of writing have cost an estimated £100 million.) In 2011, Prime Minister David Cameron ordered a sweeping public inquiry into press malfeasance chaired by Lord Justice Leveson. The resulting two-thousand-page report, published a year later, was a thunderous censure of press recklessness in prioritizing "sensational stories, almost irrespective of the harm the stories may cause and the rights of those who would be affected."

Leveson found that the existing Press Complaints Commission was not sufficient, and recommended a new, independent body with the power to levy substantial fines. Active editors would not be allowed on its board, and it would have the power to levy substantial fines. The British press viewed this proposed oversight as an existential threat. They fought back mightily and, instead, a new, more toothless self-regulating body called the Independent Press Standards Organisation was established in 2014. The victims of hacking felt they had been betrayed, and Hugh Grant emerged as one of the most tenacious pursuers of victim justice and press reform. He has donated generous sums to Hacked Off, a rebel alliance of press abuse victims, academics, and politicians that has continued to keep the issue alive. But four years later, an apparently cowed Theresa May went back on Cameron's pledge to hold a second Leveson inquiry to examine criminality by the press.

Ironically, Leveson exempted the internet from his proposed regulations, saying—which can now only elicit a hollow laugh—that "people will not assume that what they read on the internet is trustworthy or that it carries any particular assurance or accuracy."

Within just a few years, as social media erased the line between truth and lies, it was clear that the worthy judge could not have been more wrong.

The Leveson report and the closure of the scurrilous **News of the World** was doubtless a source of bitter satisfaction to Prince Harry and the rest of the Royal Family. But it did not save his relationship with Chelsy Davy. Worn out by six years of hounding, she realized that a forever-life at Harry's side was not a prospect she could contemplate. In January 2009, the vibrant soulmate whom Harry's friends assumed he'd marry changed her relationship status on Facebook to "Single." They drifted back together on and off for the next two years, but the intensity was gone. In November 2021, Gavin Burrows came out from the shadows and gave a remorseful interview to Amol Rajan for his BBC documentary **The Princes and the Press**. "I was basically part of a group of people who robbed him [Harry] of his normal teenage years," the private investigator said.

It was an understatement. Overall, the media had mortified him on front pages for every adolescent misstep. It had cut short his deployment in Afghanistan. It had destroyed his relationship with Chelsy. His burning anger toward the press—in every shape and form—became unforgiving and irreversible.

CHAPTER
16

GLORIANA

The Windsors' Winning Streak

IF THERE WAS A GOLDEN ERA OF THE TWENTY-FIRST-century monarchy, it was the eight-year stretch after the wedding of William and Kate in 2011 until 2019. The Firm was basking in a bubble bath of national goodwill. The Duchess of Cambridge ensured the succession by producing two irresistibly photogenic children in Prince George and Princess Charlotte. Harry became the nation's hero as an Apache helicopter pilot in his second deployment in Afghanistan. Charles was a cheery new man since his marriage to Camilla ("He looks gleeful as he goes up the stairs to his own quarters at Clarence House where Camilla is going to give him a warm welcome," as one of his friends noted to me), and the Queen was enjoying her own serene heyday by Keeping Calm and Carrying On.

The machine of monarchy and its family

representatives were finally in sync. When yet another jubilee came inexorably around—the Diamond
Jubilee in June 2012 celebrating the Queen's sixty
years on the British throne—there was none of the
Palace apprehension that accompanied the last one.
A **Guardian**/ICM poll on jubilee eve showed the
monarch's personal popularity at a height that "our
despised politicians would die for." A month later
Her Maj was propelled into an uncharted realm—as
pop culture heroine—when she made a cameo appearance as her deadpan self in film director Danny
Boyle's James Bond video spoof that opened the
2012 Olympics.

Thanks to the steady hand of one of the Queen's
most formidably competent private secretaries, Sir
Christopher Geidt, Buckingham Palace was a tight
ship sailing smoothly through the usually treacherous waters of the competing royal households. Geidt
was another former army intelligence officer. "Suave
and charming, very proper, clipped and British with
a regimental tie, but also with a touch of the spook
about him," as one Palace colleague described him.

The Queen loves strong, silent types. Used to
being the only woman in gatherings of power and
sporting prowess, she has never been a great girl's
girl, and has not, to date, had a female private secretary. "She enjoys the company of alpha men," one of
her former aides told me. She especially liked Geidt's
surgical ability to cut to the chase. He was determined to rebuild inter-household trust after the
sour rivalries of the Bolland days, and ran a

weekly three-line whip with the private secretaries from Buckingham Palace, Clarence House, and Kensington Palace, previously locked in internecine squabbles. Geidt made sure that Prince Charles was kept in the loop to assuage his increasingly restive ambitions. With his deputy, Edward Young, he oversaw the Queen's astonishing—and flawless—state visit to the Republic of Ireland in May 2011.

It's hard to overstate the historical and diplomatic importance of a state visit to a place where rancor toward the Crown had been so deeply felt for so long. The Queen was both anxious and excited about the prospect, and more than aware of all the political groundwork that preceded the potent symbolism of her presence on Irish soil. The last time a British monarch, George V, visited Ireland in 1911, he still ruled over it, and neither Elizabeth II nor her father, George VI, had ever set foot in the breakaway republic. The so-called Troubles claimed more than 3,500 lives, including thirteen Irish demonstrators who were brutally gunned down by British troops in 1972 on what became known as Bloody Sunday. The response was a firebombing of the British embassy in Dublin. Three mock coffins were draped in black and placed on the embassy steps, and two Union Jacks and an effigy of a British soldier were set ablaze.

The Troubles were personally harrowing for the Queen. In August 1979, the IRA murdered the man they considered one of the ultimate representations of the British establishment, Lord Mountbatten, the Queen's second cousin and a former chief of the defense staff. The elder statesman was killed along with his fourteen-year-old grandson and two other members of a holiday house party. They had been enjoying an outing aboard Mountbatten's fishing boat in Donegal Bay, near the family's Irish summer home at Classiebawn Castle, when terrorists detonated a fifty-pound bomb they had planted the night before. "The boat was there one minute and the next minute it was like a lot of matchsticks floating on the water," a witness recalled.

Even after the 1998 Good Friday Agreement, crafted with the combined diplomatic muscle of Tony Blair and Bill Clinton, feelings were still too raw for the Queen to travel to Ireland. A window was opened with the release of the long-awaited 2010 Saville report, which found that the Bloody Sunday victims were unarmed, innocent, and shot by British soldiers without warning. The day the report was published, the new Tory prime minister, David Cameron, stood up in the House of Commons and issued a formal apology calling the killings "unjustified and unjustifiable."

The political table was now set for the Queen to personally deliver the pageantry of détente. On the windy spring morning of May 17, 2011, the royal plane touched down at Casement Aerodrome outside Dublin. Her Majesty stepped out, resplendently local in an emerald coat and hat that paid homage to the cherished hue of the host country. Even the choice of airport had conciliatory overtones. Roger Casement, for whom the airport is named, was one of the leaders of the 1916 uprising that set off the Irish War of Independence against the British. The Queen headed straight to the Irish president's residence, where she signed the registry with the squiggle of state, the regal flourish of "Elizabeth R."

The British government shipped a shamrock-green Bentley across the Irish Sea to use during her visit. The streets of Dublin were cordoned off by an estimated eight thousand police officers. There was a frisson of what might be coming when a pipe bomb was found in a tote bag on a bus at the start of the visit. Temperatures were further raised by the impending visit to Ireland of President and First Lady Barack and Michelle Obama a week after the Queen. Palace planners had some concerns that the American firepower might upstage Britain's historic moment, but the Obamas had to cut short their trip when a cloud of black ash started spewing from an Icelandic volcano, threatening to ground Air Force One. (The buttoned-up Palace advance team, I am told, could not resist feeling some quiet schadenfreude when the presidential Cadillac, known as "the Beast" for its impenetrable features, got stuck on a ramp and failed to make it out of the U.S. embassy in Dublin.)

Over the next three momentous days, the monarch proceeded to make every traditional goodwill gesture short of kissing the Blarney Stone—watching the pouring of a perfect pint of Guinness at the Guinness Storehouse Gravity Bar, marveling at the ancient Book of Kells manuscript at Trinity College, touring the Rock of Cashel in County

Tipperary, and smiling through a thunderous performance of Irish step dancers. Her Majesty joined the cast onstage and received a cacophonous five-minute standing O, with cheers and whistles from the two-thousand-strong audience. In a gesture suffused with textbook symbolism, she bowed her head as she laid a wreath at the Garden of Remembrance, which honors all who died fighting for Irish freedom. During the ceremony, the Irish Army band played "God Save the Queen," a surreal improbability only a few decades before, when saving the Queen would have been the very last thing on Irish minds. "For a lot of people we assumed it would be a tricky, wary, mutually suspicious event," broadcaster and author Andrew Marr recalled to me, but by the last day of her visit Irish enthusiasm was so high that security was relaxed to allow joyful thousands to throng the streets of the city of Cork. The Queen insisted on breaking her own protocol to greet them on foot. "They mobbed her like Beyoncé," one of her aides told me. At the English Market, she chatted with Irish fishmonger and wag Pat O'Connell, who amused her so much that she later invited him to Buckingham Palace.

Labour peer Lord Donoughue told me his Irish friends were most struck by the Queen's visit to Croke Park, Dublin's Gaelic football stadium, where, in 1920, the British Army opened fire, killing fourteen spectators and one player, Tipperary captain Michael Hogan, who was shot in the back. Croke was such a notorious symbol of English repression that for the Queen to go there, Donoughue said, "was brave and on the political edge. It showed an acute historical sense."

Irish president Mary McAleese accompanied the Queen as they walked out onto the pitch with Gaelic Athletic Association president Christy Cooney. As they looked up at the stand, Cooney said, "This is named after Michael Hogan, ma'am, killed not far from where you are standing."

"I thought for one second," McAleese told me, "she might break into tears. And she said gently, 'I know, I know.'"

McAleese had insisted that representatives of the Ulster loyalist paramilitaries and republicans be asked to attend. The English security authorities were petrified, but the Queen walked courageously past them, shaking their hands.

The tour wasn't all duty. The Queen made a quick side trip to the Irish National Stud in County Kildare, a horse farm that had bred many of her finest race-horses, and where she had always longed to go in person. Ireland's prime minister (or taoiseach), Enda Kenny, thrilled her with the gift of a book that gave a full account of all the Irish-bred bloodstock that raced in royal colors. The Queen told him she stayed up reading it into the small hours, and we can be certain this is true. Philip, who had looked longingly at the pints of stout there'd been no time to drink at the Guinness Storehouse, now had to trail her around as she did his least favorite thing, horse-talk happily with breeders, jockeys, and trainers.

When a fearsome-looking stallion reared up, the only dignitary who did not flinch was the Queen. The traveling press was hoping for a Philip gaffe, but he did not oblige.

The Queen saved her most stirring gesture of statecraft for the state dinner at Dublin Castle, where, wearing a dress adorned with two thousand hand-sewn shamrocks and a harp brooch, she opened her speech in Gaelic to heartfelt applause and a mouthed "wow" from President McAleese. It was McAleese who had suggested to Edward Young that the Queen tee off in Gaelic as a sensitive acknowledgment of the painful suppression of the native language by the British. HM's delicately worded address had powerful resonance. She conveyed national regret for the long years of violence, but stopped short of apologizing: "So much of this visit reminds us of the complexity of our history, its many layers and traditions, but also the importance of forbearance and conciliation. Of being able to bow to the past, but not be bound by it."

Emotion was high as the 172 dignitaries, politicians, and cultural icons rose for the toast. British prime minister David Cameron was at the Queen's table. "It was incredibly moving to witness our monarch speak of forgiveness," he writes in his memoir. "Every carefully chosen word healed another wound of history. It was a lesson in reconciliation from the best."

Sitting on Cameron's left was the Nobel Prize–winning Irish poet Seamus Heaney, whose other dinner partner was Philip, much to Heaney's unease. The poet had once penned the words "Be advised my passport's green. No glass of ours was ever raised to toast the Queen." Philip, ever the great deflector, spent the dinner telling him "inappropriate" stories. "Bejaysus, that man's a card," Heaney said to Cameron and toasted the Queen as rousingly as everyone else.

"It was the biggest **political** success of her reign," Andrew Marr observed of a monarch who is stead-fastly apolitical. President McAleese told Marr that the Queen and the Duke of Edinburgh had been "prepared to go further" and shake hands with the leader of Sinn Féin, Gerry Adams, but Sinn Féin didn't want to do it. There was hope till the last mo-ment to bring them around, but their seats at the state dinner in Dublin remained empty.

The Queen played a role of even more quiet sig-nificance than has been fully appreciated. The lesser-told story of the normalization of Anglo-Irish relations is the steady contribution of three female leaders: the two Irish presidents Mary Robinson and Mary McAleese, and the Queen. After long coordi-nation between their respective governments, the first public outreach between the countries took the form of a 1993 invitation for tea from the Queen to Robinson, the first woman to lead Ireland. This was a full five years before the Good Friday accords.

Enda Kenny is convinced that "the influence of [these] women leaders [in the peace process] brought about an impact that had not happened under their male counterparts." He treasures the memory of seeing the Queen off at Cork Airport. When they walked out on the red carpet to her plane, she turned to him and said, "Of all the royal visits that I've done in sixty years, this is the one that I really wanted to do."

When David Cameron congratulated her, she downplayed the achievement of her historic trip with a smile. "All I did was decide it was time for a visit," she said.

II

The only directive the Queen gave to the Palace team about her Diamond Jubilee was that it should not cost much. With the Tories' unpopular austerity budget in the wake of the 2008 financial crisis and the countervailing grumblings about billions being thrown at the 2012 London Olympics, the Queen didn't want any populist sniping about jubilee extravagance. The Palace team was instructed to do the whole celebration on a budget of £1 million, tops. Anything beyond that had to be sponsored.

Kate Middleton, now Duchess of Cambridge, was duly marketed to the world as an avid bargain hunter. At her royal speaking debut in March at a children's hospice in East Anglia, the Duchess emphasized the theme of thrift by wearing the blue Reiss dress her mother had worn to Ascot in 2010. There were strategically placed sightings of the Cambridges returning from a ski holiday on easyJet, and of Harry slumming aboard Wizz Air on a flight to Romania. Even on the cheap, the Queen managed to rack up eighty-three public jubilee appearances across the United Kingdom.

The rest of the family were dispatched on a Commonwealth charm offensive. Charles and Camilla hauled ass to Australia, New Zealand, and Papua New Guinea. William and Kate, fending off pregnancy questions, were dispatched to Singapore, Malaysia, Tuvalu, and the Solomon Islands. Prince Andrew, with his usual perfect pitch, took a private jet to visit a Mumbai slum. Family slogger Princess Anne flew commercial to press the flesh in Mozambique and Zambia. Prince Edward and Sophie were unloaded on the Caribbean Islands.

Prince Harry, acing his first solo tour representing Grandma, charmed his way through Jamaica, the Bahamas, and Belize, and provided gold-plated photos racing playfully against Usain Bolt, the fastest runner in the world. Now that William was off the market, the twenty-seven-year-old Harry had assumed the mantle of disheveled royal sex symbol. He was pictured dancing adorably en route to his waiting car at four A.M. after a night at the Bunga Bunga bar in Battersea, and updating royal chivalry by galloping across a polo field in Brazil to aid an American defense contractor who'd been thrown from his mount. "Prince Harry was the first one off his horse, doing the right thing, turning me over to make sure I regained consciousness," said the flattened player. "I remember waking up with these piercing blue eyes looking at me." Britain's hottest pop songstress, Cheryl Cole, told **Marie Claire,** "I had a dream last night that I married [Prince Harry] and was a real-life princess."

The climax of the Diamond Jubilee was a water pageant on the Thames, in which one thousand boats of every size and description, like the little rescue ships of Dunkirk, took to the river in a merry armada. Leading the floating parade was the red-and-gold-draped replica of an eighteenth-century royal galley decked with ten thousand flowers (named, in honor of Winston Churchill, the **Spirit of Chartwell**) and bearing the monarch and her consort, along with Charles and Camilla, William and Kate, and Harry. In boat number two right behind were the rest of the senior royals, former Tory prime minister John Major, and London mayor Boris Johnson, who likened the oarsmen powering the Queen's boat down the river to "oiled and manacled MPs."

The appallingly unseasonable weather subjected the Queen and Prince Philip, at the ages of eighty-six and ninety, respectively, to the ordeal of standing on deck for four hours without a bathroom break on one of the coldest and wettest days of the year. In front of them were two cushy red velvet "thrones" they chose to eschew, because smiling through maximum discomfort is their most priceless skill. (Plus, as one of the Palace team noted, red velvet thrones might have been "a bit too David and Victoria Beckham.")

The unrelenting rain was anyway a necessary part

of the national pageantry of the day. It rained for the Queen's coronation in 1953. It rained for the Silver Jubilee in 1977, which I watched sheltering from the weather in a Brighton pub steamy with drying coats. It's the essence of what the Queen is made for: rain. What is a traditional English summer occasion unless it's pissing down outside? The morose picnics in a squelching car park at Wimbledon; the wet carton of strawberries at Glyndebourne opera house; the sodden scuttle through the church door at Cotswold weddings; the attempt to retain something resembling a hat as the skies open at the Henley Royal Regatta? As historian Simon Schama texted me from London, "the kind of weather that brings back memories of hanging around on college lawns with bits of cucumber bobbing on diluted Pimm's, while fending off chilblains chatting up girls whose faces are turning bluer than their eye shadow." When the royal party arrived at Tower Bridge, the Duchess of Cornwall made a beeline for the hot tea and told David Cameron "she had thought she would expire out there."

The ordeal of standing for so long in a saturated navy uniform took its toll on Prince Philip. He was felled the next day by a bladder infection that meant he was rushed to London's King Edward VII's Hospital. The silver lining was that it enabled him to miss the pop concert on Monday night at Buckingham Palace with Grace Jones gyrating in a hula hoop and a past-his-sell-by-date Tom Jones belting out "Delilah." The Queen solved the problem by wearing earplugs throughout.

Prince Philip's non-appearance gave Charles the chance to escort his mother onstage at the end of the concert. He whipped up a shout-out to the **hors de combat** Philip and kissed his mother's hand after the stirring rendition of "God Save the Queen." His tribute that began "Your Majesty, [pause] Mummy!" got him benign press and some laughs.

The jubilee consolidated an improved standing not only for the heir to the throne but also for his wife. It was a great photo op for Camilla, wearing her ivory mother-of-the-bride Anna Valentine coat-dress to stand on the royal barge next to the Queen, who shimmered in all-white boucle and crystals. It didn't matter that Camilla was completely upstaged by a gorgeous Kate in fire-engine-red Alexander McQueen. Two days later, Camilla had prime real estate again, seated next to the Queen—Philip's usual spot—in the 1902 State Landau that delivered them to Buckingham Palace for the final day of jubilee celebrations.

Ever since the Cambridges' wedding, it had been hard for Camilla to get much love from the cameras. The younger generation was now eclipsing the jaded stories of the old guard, especially after the jubilant announcement in December 2012 that Kate was pregnant. There was a new Everywoman story line when Kate, still in her first trimester, was taken to the hospital for hyperemesis gravidarum (acute morning sickness), leading to acres of empathetic women's page coverage.

Prince George Alexander Louis was born in July

2013 in the private Lindo Wing of St. Mary's Hospital, where his father had been born thirty-one years before. The birth set off celebrations across the Commonwealth for the next male heir, who would be third in line to the throne. Given that three of the greatest and longest-reigning British monarchs have been women—Elizabeth I, Queen Victoria, and Elizabeth II—perhaps it felt the right moment to review the fact that the next three would be kings unless fate intervened. "As a member of the Royal Family, females tend to be treated as honorary men," Princess Anne once said, and there are plenty in Palace circles who believe she is the best king we will never have. In April 2013, Parliament brought gender equality to the line of royal succession. The new act updated seventeenth-century male primogeniture laws to give daughters their proper place in the line for the throne, based on birth order.

Even feeling at her worst, Kate proved she could ace public appearances. Three days before she was hospitalized for morning sickness, she played field hockey in high-heeled boots at her alma mater St. Andrew's. Two years later, when she was pregnant with Charlotte, she undertook a grueling two-day PR mission with William to New York. British consul general Danny Lopez marveled at how buttoned up the Palace prep team were compared to the often chaotic advance work of Westminster's parliamentary secretaries. He noted the professionalism and seamless performances Kate and William pulled off at their meet-and-greets and praised their flawlessly mastered briefs. "They knew what it was to be **on**," he told me.

When he put together a lunch of young achievers at the consul general's residence for Kate, she came up with talking points that were, for example, about "line seventeen from the brief." When Prince Harry had come alone a year earlier, a member of the consulate team noted he had been just as committed but less secure. (Or perhaps he was more attuned to the things that really mattered to people.) He worried about not performing perfectly on a school visit where he would be required to hit a baseball. When he was assured that it would be a piece of cake, Harry replied: "My forgetting one line of your brief at an event is not going to be noticed. Me messing up with a baseball bat will be front page all over the world." As usual, Harry hit all three balls pitched to him and was predictably adored.

The success of the royal rebrand lifted the whole Firm. Camilla was winning points by showing up, smiling, and looking as if she loved her job, which was Paddy Harverson's definition of how to win the public. The trick was to mix old-chestnut appearances like the Chelsea Flower Show with the odd irreverent surprise. The Duchess suddenly popped up on the set of the "zeitgeisty" Danish cop show **The Killing**, where, **The Guardian** reported, she was "given a Faroe Isle cardigan from the show's star, Sofie Gråbøl, who is so proverbially badass that her name rhymes with trouble."

Shots with the Queen and Kate helped embed

Camilla in the royal narrative. The trio traveled together in the car—each in a different shade of blue—on a girly official visit to Fortnum and Mason in Piccadilly, where the message from the monarch was clear: three generations of queens, present and future, solidly united in their enthusiasm for Happy Hound Treats dog biscuits.

More significantly, the Queen allowed Camilla permanent loan of much of the Queen Mother's jewelry collection. The old showboat had left a priceless collection of art deco tiaras, diamonds, and five-strand necklaces, much of it bequeathed to her by the social-climbing hostess Mrs. Ronald Greville. ("A rich old toad," as Hugo Vickers put it, "who preferred to give to the rich rather than the poor.") Charles was never happier than when he could turn Camilla into his grandmother. The bling-loving Duchess made the Greville tiara—also known as the Boucheron honeycomb tiara because of its complex interlocking settings filled with brilliant-cut diamonds—into her signature piece for white-tie dinners. Charles also loved seeing Camilla in Alice Keppel's jewelry. With the help of fine jeweler Wartski, he embarked on a quest to buy up the dispersed pieces, and reputedly paid £100,000 for a diamond tiara he repurposed for Camilla as a necklace and earrings.

In April 2012, Camilla scored a major reputational boost. The Queen bestowed on her the Dame Grand Cross (GCVO), the highest female rank in the Royal Victorian Order. This is the most serious inner-circle gong, connoting services to the sovereign. The Queen gives it at important anniversaries or if she's in a very good mood with the person concerned—or simply wants to keep them on her side. The honor is a telling indication of who's up and who's down in the royal Kremlinology. Neither Sarah Ferguson nor Princess Michael of Kent ever got a GCVO, which is not surprising given how the Queen felt about their antics. Sophie Wessex was over the moon when the Queen made her a GCVO in 2010, a recognition of how diligently her daughter-in-law had slaved to be a stalwart B player in the royal ensemble, uncomplainingly taking on the dullest duties in the diary. Kate was awarded hers on her eighth wedding anniversary in 2019, an acknowledgment by the Queen of how dependent the Firm now was on her loyal glamour. The young Duchess showed it off on its blue satin full-body sash at the state banquet for President Trump. Loyal staff members and private secretaries earn lesser Victorian orders. It was a grievance to Mark Bolland that he never got any of them.

The exclusive hardware from the Queen was an endorsement that gave Camilla a new fillip of confidence. She wore her Dame Grand Cross—the ultimate accessory—when she and Charles went to the Netherlands in April 2013 to witness seventy-five-year-old Queen Beatrix hand over the crown to her forty-six-year-old son. (No such luck for the Prince of Wales, who had to smile wanly as his eighty-six-year-old mother rededicated herself to her British subjects at the Diamond Jubilee.) Camilla wore the coveted cross again, plus the Greville tiara and long white gloves, when, for the first time, she attended the state opening of Parliament a month later. She and Charles sat next to the Queen and the Duke of Edinburgh on the dais of the House of Lords in a regal double date. Dressed in as much white sparkle as the monarch, the former Camilla Parker Bowles had never looked more like the future Queen Consort.

Tabloids, which always back off when HRH appears before a name, began to refer to Camilla as "the Dazzling Duchess." They noted that she was advising Kate on where to go for glossy highlights and the best bee-venom facials. Camilla trimmed down and, always more of a horsewoman than a clothes-horse, now nailed an elegant, age-appropriate style, often in tasteful, monochromatic Bruce Oldfield gowns. The mercurial **Guardian** posed the question "Outcast to national treasure. How did Camilla do that?" and chronicled her journey from "the most hated woman in England" to "an icon of preternatural sixty-something loveliness."

A blessing, as far as Charles was concerned, was that his second wife found the absurdities they often faced on royal tours a source of amusement rather than stress. One of her dinner partners told me how she regaled him with anecdotes about the Saudi trip with Charles in 2013, when she was driven off through the desert for an hour and a half to a huge tent where three thousand unveiled Arab women in Chanel two-pieces were having an enormous tea party in the middle of nowhere. She found it hysterically funny. Camilla and Charles "are always laughing together," one of their aides told me. "If you see them together, they are a glove that fits. She brings out the best in him and he brightens whenever he sees her."

The Duchess's steady ascendance at Charles's side hit only one minor speed bump. There was a frightening incident on the way to a **Royal Variety Performance** at the London Palladium in December 2010. A security snafu allowed Charles's Rolls-Royce to blunder into an ugly protest over the Cameron government's trebling of university tuition fees. A furious mob surrounded the royal couple, who were trapped inside, clutching hands and dressed in formal evening wear, as their chauffeur tried to inch down Regent Street. "Bottles and bins were being thrown," reported the **Evening Standard**. "People were also ripping up barriers from the building sites along the street." As Charles exhibited perfect poker-faced élan, Camilla dived on the floor of the car. Later she stoically laughed off her ordeal, but her caught-on-camera horrified expression was splashed across front pages. The last thing she needed just as she eased into the public's acceptance was images looking like a latter-day Marie Antoinette pelted with paint bombs. It was a reminder of how terrifying unpopularity could be—as it had felt to the royals when the crowd turned on the Queen after Diana's death—and also that the tireless round of goodwill tours were necessary not only for the monarchy's enhancement, but for its survival.

III

The London Olympics in July 2012 provided the capstone of the royal winning streak. The soft power of the Crown was once again in full evidence during the aggressive romancing of the International Olympic Committee by the London Organising Committee, chaired by four-time Olympic medalist Sebastian Coe, the former superstar middle-distance runner.

The thirteen-strong IOC team was invited to a reception at Buckingham Palace at which the Queen made sure that the welcome dinner was a wow—the Royal Standard flying, the Queen's Guards at attention, the Grand Entrance illuminated Olympic torch–style, and a string quartet from the Coldstream Guards serenading the decision makers. Her Majesty visited the site of the stadium as early as 2009, and Coe writes in his memoir of how he walked the Queen down what would eventually be the finishing straight of the running track. "So where am I now?" she asked. "Well, ma'am, if you put in a surge over the next twenty metres, you would be the new 100m Olympic champion," Coe said. When Prince Philip visited Olympic Park, he peppered the group with questions about the architectural nuts and bolts of its construction. He told Coe he didn't really like watching sports. Competing was what he enjoyed, which also applied to his daughter, Princess Anne.

The Games gave the doughty Anne a moment in the PR sun. She was the first member of the Royal

Family to have competed in the Olympic Games herself, when she rode the Queen's horse Goodwill in the equestrian three-day event in Montreal in 1976. She had been appointed a member of the IOC, and was given the honor of accepting the Olympic flame in Athens and bringing it back to Britain for its eight-thousand-mile relay tour of the country.

"Princess Anne has all the traits of the élite competitor," Sebastian Coe writes in his memoir.

> When you're in a sport that demands buckets of bravery, where the only thing that matters is the next training session, whether cross-country or show jumping, with an eye always on the welfare of your horse, you don't have much time to worry about niceties. To know that the press is there solely in the hope that you will fall into the water must be hard to accept. Within that context, her "This-is-who-I-am-and-what-I-stand-for" attitude becomes totally understandable.

After one long-winded interjection by a committee member, Anne forgot to turn her microphone off and her unmistakable brusque voice echoed round the room: "I think this person is probably the most stupid person in world sport."

"She never flinched," Sebastian Coe said in a documentary for Anne's seventieth birthday. "It's as though it never happened and we just moved on. But it is probably one of my favorite moments."

Her daughter, Zara Tindall, cherishes memories of her mother coming back from royal evening engagements in her ball gown and full makeup, putting on her Wellies and going out to feed the chickens and get eggs.

It was positive karma all round that Zara, thirty-one, was following in Anne's footsteps at the London Olympics by competing in the same equestrian three-day event. Great Britain won a silver, and there was a feel-good explosion when Anne presented the team, including her daughter, with their medals.

The bid team had been put together by Tony Blair and sustained by infrastructure provided by Gordon Brown. It now fell to the Cameron government not to bollix it up. "I wanted to wring every conceivable advantage out of this huge opportunity," Cameron wrote in his memoir. Boris Johnson whipped up enthusiasm by declaring that "the Geiger counter of Olympo-mania is going to go 'zoink' off the scale."

London was ready for it. Turbocharged with a population explosion and an influx of European immigrants, the city had become a thrumming liberal nation-state. Britain hadn't gone bust like people thought it might—as Greece had done, and Italy was threatening to do. The financial crisis of 2008 was in the rearview mirror. The city had faced down the terror of the Islamist bombings on July 7, 2005, known as 7/7, that killed fifty-two people on London's public transport system during morning rush hour.

For the first time since the height of Empire,

Britain's capital felt truly global, the culturally effervescent magnet of Europe with the financial buzz of New York City. **The King's Speech,** the film starring Colin Firth that humanized the Royal Family with its moving depiction of George VI's personal struggles with his stammer, won the 2011 Oscar for Best Picture. The Harry Potter blockbuster movie franchise had achieved global domination, a boost for a magical idea of Britishness. Two British music phenoms, Adele and Coldplay, rode the charts.

Rules for work and entry meant it was easier for Europeans, most of whom had a smattering of English, to get a job as a barista at a Café Nero in London than grinding it out in downtown Plovdiv. French lycées opened all over town. The ultra-right-wing UK Independence Party's complaint that England was overrun by Bulgarians who were perfectly equipped to earn a good living at home provoked the stand-up comedian Stewart Lee to demand, "How am I supposed to get cheap tea and coffee unless there is a massively overqualified East European philosophy professor prepared to make it for me for significantly less than the living wage?" There was even the threat that the surge of workaholic American bankers might undermine the ingrained British habit of drinking at lunch time.

Over the previous ten years, the long-running joke about the awfulness of British food had been displaced by the heresy that London had turned into a more vital restaurant city than Paris. The thrill was no longer in the grand dining rooms of the West End hotels, which had become a sterile extension of the luxury goods industry, but had shifted east (and north, south, and west) to shabby storefronts and the back rooms of dying pubs, where a new generation of chefs was reengineering British cuisine. Marco Pierre White, the original hard-drinking, foul-mouthed Visigoth of the 1990s, had retired, but his example was visible in every tattooed media-ready young chef who made his kitchen a stage for fresh and foraged ingredients and adventurous techniques.

Whether they were aware of it or not, the chefs were frontrunners for a new kind of urban development, one brilliantly suited to London's epic, ungainly sprawl. As Brooklyn was demonstrating in New York, neglected neighborhoods could be revitalized by the strategic introduction of two businesses: restaurants and art galleries. These in turn ignited a boom in property values, as they seeded a ready-made bohemian utopia that, at least in their early stages, few people viewed cynically. The idea of gentrification (if not the word) wasn't anathema. Hoxton, Whitechapel, Shoreditch—names that once sounded like they belonged at the scuzzy end of a Monopoly board—were suddenly where young professionals desired to live and tourists wanted to stay. The fastidiously preserved capitals of old Europe could not compete.

Even political life felt optimistic after the irate demonstrations over the Iraq War during Tony Blair's premiership. Boris Johnson won a second term as mayor of London with a persona of shambolic optimism, riding around on a "Boris bike" touting the bicycle-for-hire scheme that he had actually appropriated from Ken Livingstone, his dour Labour predecessor.

At the time, no one in either political or civilian life was particularly fixated on leaving the European Union, except a splenetic wing of the Conservative Party that had been dreaming about it since the Thatcher era. David Cameron was elected prime minister in 2010 by rebranding the Tories as more forgiving and socially liberal, even hip. With his fun, fashionable wife, Samantha (SamCam, as she was known), he was the youngest premier to hold that office in two hundred years. People (at first) liked the fact that Cameron's Tory-ness was tempered by the obligation to share power in a coalition with the Liberal Democrats led by Nick Clegg, who was married to an attractive Spanish international trade lawyer. It was as if Britain's politics were becoming European, too, with slightly forgettable people with mostly good intentions who worked out solutions and didn't stand for very much. No wonder that another subtitled Danish TV political drama series, **Borgen,** with its themes of accountability, ambition, and compromise, was a break-out TV hit with the chattering classes. "I remember there was a feeling of somehow things being eerily okay," said columnist and social historian Andy Beckett. He dubbed the vibrant era "Peak London."

The dark undertow to all this was that the more cynical workings of the Cameron premiership were nothing like the mild-mannered striving of **Borgen'**s

Danish elite. Chancellor of the Exchequer George Osborne's economic austerity program after the Great Recession hacked £30 billion out of welfare payments, housing subsidies, and social services to reduce the deficit. Nick Clegg turned out to be a powerless cipher, and was crushed at the next election for selling out his liberal principles. By 2011, youth unemployment was at 20 percent. It was easy in Peak London to forget the north-south divide and the growing grumbles of predominantly white citizens in forgotten towns like Sunderland, Sheffield, and Northampton. "They were thinking 'You smug sods,' but we smug sods didn't notice that," Andrew Marr told me. If London was awash with fancy foreign restaurants, Middle England was growing bitter while bingeing on traditional comfort food. **The Great British Bake Off** show, launched in 2010 on the BBC, became a ratings phenomenon as contestants vied to make peerless pies, cakes, and puddings. The culture clash masked a major political disconnect.

In London itself, sullen poverty coexisted with all the self-confident affluence. In the dog days of August, while the Royal Family was at Balmoral, and the political elite were offline at their villas in Tuscany, the combustible mood of the neglected inner cities was laid bare in a chain of violent protests. Sparked by the police shooting of a Black man in Tottenham, a deprived, multiethnic area of north London, the mayhem of arson and looting spread to almost every urban area of Britain, including

Liverpool, Manchester, Nottingham, and Leicester. The short, intense, and ominous eruptions had none of the righteous jubilation of what was simultaneously happening in the Arab Spring.

"Now we can see that actually the shock from the financial crisis and from these other things were running under the surface," Andy Beckett said. The most interesting aspect of this summer of madness was that after all Cameron's draconian crackdowns and the media's jeremiads about exploding inequity, what followed in the wake of the 2011 riots was—nothing. By the time the ruling classes had returned from their sunny vacations, youthful fury in England had dissipated like a tropical storm. Boris Johnson didn't cover himself with glory. He was on holiday in Canada at the time, and didn't hurry back. When he did, it was to rush around being, by turns, emollient and punitive—like an Eton housemaster. In 2014, the city bought three German water cannons in case there was a repetition of crowd unrest. It was somehow definitive of the Johnsonian tragicomedy theatrics that they turned out to be unusable and had to be sold for scrap at a net loss of £300,000.

One person who didn't try to gloss over the riots was Prince Charles. Perhaps because he had been shaken by the mob fury he had encountered in the car eight months earlier, he left Balmoral to activate programs from his Trust. While each of Westminster's political party leaders showed up on the streets of Hackney, Lambeth, and Croydon to "show concern" in TV stand-ups, without the cameras they did not come back. Charles did. David Lammy, the Labour MP for Tottenham, the hardest-hit area, told **The Independent:**

> Prince Charles also phoned. He came; he has been back five times and he doesn't just come back to look at it, he's brought all his charities. . . . He hasn't done it with a fanfare, he hasn't put out press releases, he's just done it because he cares.

There was a lesson in this. Charles was more than just a faddish dilettante. He tried to show Britain that he was a worthy—and humane—monarch-in-waiting.

IV

Danny Boyle, the director of the London Olympics opening ceremony, never thought in a million years the Queen would say yes. Boyle, a brilliantly subversive talent whose 2009 hit **Slumdog Millionaire** won eight Oscars, including Best Picture, was determined that London's opening ceremony would be the polar opposite of the overpoweringly martial display of Chinese nationalism at the 2008 Summer Olympics in Beijing. He wanted a pop-up pageant of British history that was emotional and human, with rough edges that could tolerate any surprise, one that would tell the hidden, not the obvious, stories of the country's greatness—from suffragettes and Caribbean immigrants who arrived aboard the **Empire Windrush** in 1948 to fill post-war labor shortages, to the unsung nurses of the National Health Service, embodied by the eight hundred medical volunteers who danced onto the stage in one of the high points of a madcap evening. Boyle's message was that in postcolonial Britain, culture and creativity rule the waves. In the eighty-thousand-seat Olympic stadium in east London, a green and pleasant land grazed by real farm animals gave way to the ominous rising chimney stacks of the Industrial Revolution belching fumes as Isambard Kingdom Brunel, the ingenious British civil engineer who built the Great Western Railway, strode out in the form of actor Kenneth Branagh to declaim Caliban's speech in **The Tempest**: "Be not afeard; the isle is full of noises."

Shakespeare, Captain Hook, and thirty Mary Poppinses descended from the sky through raindrops holding black umbrellas and carpet bags. A huge inflatable Lord Voldemort towered over the stadium, waving a magic wand, and Sir Paul McCartney led a sing-along of "Hey Jude." Boyle turned his back on the jingoism of two world wars and the fight against fascism in favor of joyful cultural celebration and a silent tribute to the wars' fallen dead.

"Could they put in more Churchill?" was one of the refrains of the puzzled Cameron administration traditionalists in the planning meetings. Another was, "Where are the kings and queens?"

There was only one. Whether real or a body

double, Boyle knew that the opening act of the Olympics demanded the iconic presence of the reigning monarch—seen as never before. At first, he wanted the Queen to arrive on the tube, but security would be too big a problem. One of his team suggested filming Her Maj in the flesh at the Palace, and then having her drop into the stadium played by a body double. Boyle being Boyle, he upped the ante by adding to his wish list that the Queen be joined by another Britain-defining cultural icon, James Bond. As Bond, Daniel Craig's role would be to show up at the Palace in a helicopter to rescue the Queen from a security threat that jeopardized her safe arrival at an undisclosed event. "Her Majesty," aka stuntman Gary Connery, would leap from the aircraft dressed in the same peach, crystal, and lace cocktail dress the Queen was planning to wear, and land eight hundred feet below, just outside the Olympic stadium.

Boyle was so stunned when his request to the Palace came back with an immediate yes, he thought it was April Fools' Day. Stephen Daldry, artistic director of the Olympics, told me the main reason the Queen agreed is that she thought it would be a great joke to amuse her grandchildren. Her only real concern was keeping it a secret until the moment when she walked out in person after the "leap" to take her place with Philip in the royal box.

The Queen's dresser, Angela Kelly, often recruited to be a conduit for more personal decisions, was the one who asked the Queen if she would like a speaking part. Without hesitation Her Majesty replied, "Of course I must say something. After all, he is coming to rescue me." The Queen was delighted with the line they came up with: "Good evening, Mr. Bond." Daniel Craig felt that he was in a surreal dream throughout.

Boyle filmed the sequence in the Queen's private sitting room, where she usually meets the prime minister. The crew set up there and then was ushered into another, less formal room. Boyle described the scene:

> It was messy; there were papers and tea trays everywhere. . . . I told her certain specific things about pausing that were important. I didn't have to tell her a second time. . . . It was easy for us because the Queen has the instincts of a performer—she is, after all, "on the stage" all the time—and therefore knows that she has to change with the times. The Queen knew that the Diamond Jubilee celebrations earlier that year would be quite formal, so here was a chance to be the opposite. It was a great instinct.

The stunt could have gone wrong in multiple ways. Sebastian Coe, who was in on the secret, acknowledges how nervous he was:

> If we had judged this wrongly, we knew it would be the only thing anyone would talk about until the athletics got going in the second week, and not in a good way. And, given that Her Majesty's

reputation stood at an all-time high following the extraordinary pageant of the Diamond Jubilee weekend, it was a risk.

The Queen, says Daldry, was the only one unperturbed.

Coe was seated for the opening of the Games next to the Prince of Wales, with Prince Harry and Prince William directly behind:

> None of them knew about the Queen's involvement, nor that the film even existed. So when the sequence began, with the corgis racing up what were obviously very familiar stairs, Prince Charles looked at me and began laughing rather nervously, wondering where on earth this was going. And when the film cut to the shot of the royal back, he had exactly the same reaction as everyone else which was to assume it was the lady who does the impersonations. But the moment she turned around, and everyone realised, "My God! It really is the Queen!" he began roaring with laughter. As for his sons, they were beside themselves. As she started her descent two voices shouted out in unison behind me, "Go, Granny!" For me that was the nicest thing.

Daldry marveled at the perfect sangfroid of the Queen's performance as she walked into the stadium, apparently oblivious of the stunt-Queen's death-defying swan dive. "What was so wonderful was her expression when she came out," he told me. "Not acknowledging what just happened, but knowing she was instrumental . . . perfection . . . in terms of 'I'm taking this entirely seriously, but I know I've just made one of the craziest jokes you could possibly imagine . . . not only in the history of the Olympics, but in the history of the country." The joy in the stadium, in the whole country, was "palpable."

The ethos of Peak London triumphed at the Olympics. Team GB reflected the melting pot of multiculturalism, as exemplified by three athletes who won gold medals in less than an hour on the second Saturday of the Games. Running champ Mo Farah moved from Somalia to London when he was eight years old; track and field champion Jessica Ennis was the daughter of a Jamaican immigrant; and long jumper Greg Rutherford was a pale-faced ginger from the Middle England bastion of Milton Keynes.

It was canny casting by the Palace to have Prince Harry and Kate close the Games to shine a spotlight on the next-gen royals. (William had to report to search-and-rescue duty in Wales.)

But it was the Queen's display of her brilliantly sly sense of humor at the opening ceremony that may be the most remembered moment of the 2012 Olympics. It consolidated a remarkable evolution of public perception that began with Stephen Frears's movie **The Queen.** In the film, which told the story of the only time the Queen got it wrong—after

Diana's death—Helen Mirren had shown her as fallible and conflicted. Boyle did something else. He made the eighty-six-year-old monarch cool. A new generation took the Diamond Queen into their hearts.

CHAPTER
17

THE DUKE OF HAZARD

———

Andrew's Money Pit

———

PRINCE ANDREW WAS OUTRAGED. IT WAS MAY 2011, and Scotland Yard had informed him that his two daughters, Princesses Eugenie and Beatrice, fifth and sixth in line to the throne, respectively, were to be stripped of their twenty-four-hour police protection after rising tensions about the £500,000 annual whammy to the taxpayer.

Andrew had fought ferociously to keep his girls' security detail. His rationale was that with HRH before their names they should be treated accordingly, but he found himself on brittle ground. Princess Anne's daughter, the soon-to-be-married Zara Phillips, had no police protection despite her high profile as an Olympic equestrian. (Nor did she have an HRH: her mother's choice, so that her children could lead a more normal life.) A Scotland Yard cost review looking to prune the £50 million annual security bill for the Royal Family found no clear reason why the government should pay £250,000 a year apiece for two full-time bodyguards to protect twenty-one-year-old Eugenie in her first year at Newcastle University, or for her twenty-three-year-old sister Beatrice, studying in London.

The Queen made it clear that her two granddaughters, of whom she was personally very fond, should expect to get jobs when they left college rather than be supported as working members of the Royal Family. Andrew lobbied hard to reverse the decision. He wanted Beatrice and Eugenie to be designated as working royals. At a dinner in June after the annual Hillsborough Castle garden party in Northern Ireland, he solicited a private drink with Tory MP Hugo Swire to ask him to "have a word" with Prime Minister Cameron about the decision. "He is desperately concerned," Swire's diarist wife, Sasha, wrote. "[His] argument is that they move around in the age of Twitter and Facebook and instant messaging, and that an antagonistic force could be mobilized against them in a matter of minutes."

Unfortunately, those same platforms often showed the sociable young princesses tottering out of expensive London nightclubs in the early hours with protection officers in tow. A purring official SUV waited outside restaurants to ferry them back home, not so much to forestall a kidnapping but as a glorified Uber service.

A year later, Andrew had further reason to feel snubbed. Shortly before he boarded the number two barge—an insult in itself—at the Diamond Jubilee river pageant, he learned that he and his daughters had been cut from the iconic royal photo finish on the Buckingham Palace balcony. Nor were they on the list for the lunch for seven hundred dignitaries at Westminster Hall just beforehand. (It couldn't have been fun for Andrew to hear from staff that he hadn't made the cut and know the decision would have been run by his mother.) Another guest on the follow-up barge heard him whingeing noisily about it with Sophie Wessex, whose invite was also lost in the mail.

Buckingham Palace balcony shots were first initiated by Queen Victoria in 1851, when she waved to the public during celebrations for the opening of the Great Exhibition. Over time these appearances evolved, as the preservation of indelible Royal Family moments in the national photo album. After the Trooping the Colour to celebrate the Queen's official birthday each year in June—done to minimize the risk of bad weather, a practice dating back to George II—the extended Royal Family could be seen with their necks craned, gazing skyward to watch the festive flyby of the Royal Air Force. From the jubilant waves of the young Princesses Elizabeth and Margaret with the King and Queen and Winston Churchill on VE Day, to the newly wedded Charles and Diana and then William and Kate exchanging their first kisses before roaring crowds, getting your face into the balcony shot—or even a straining brim of an ostrich-feathered hat at the back—is the ultimate affirmation of royal belonging.

Not this year. For decades, the Way Ahead Group—the inner cabal of senior royals who meet regularly to discuss big-picture issues facing the monarchy—had discussed slimming down the number of second- and third-generation royals freeloading on the monarchy. Prince Charles had even sent a memo to his private secretary looking for ways to do it twenty years earlier. In George VI's day, it was only "us four" who appeared on the balcony, but as minor members of the family gained their own profiles and procreated, it had become an increasingly unkempt crowd scene.

It wasn't a financial issue alone. Charles was firmly of the opinion that minor royals going rogue provided the media with embarrassing stories that dimmed the monarchy's halo. Always apprehensive about the direction of public mood, and alert to economy since budget slasher Michael Peat joined his household in 2002, Charles was now more eager than ever to reduce numbers.

So was Christopher Geidt, who was always quietly looking ahead to ensure a seamless transition to the next reign. What more appropriate time to start erasing minor royals from the public gaze than the year when everything was being done on the cheap? So in the 2012 Jubilee photo, the Queen, in a mint-green Angela Kelly ensemble, had her usual place of honor in the center of the balcony. But you could count the rest of the royals on one hand: Charles, Camilla, William, Kate, and a pre-Meghan Harry. (Prince Philip was still in the hospital.) That's it. Like newspaper graphics depicting the space for missing members of Saddam Hussein's inner circle, everyone else was erased from the photo op. "I hear there were people literally restraining members of the family trying to get onto the balcony," a former aide told me. One who didn't care the least bit was Princess Anne. "Anne just storms on," said the aide. "Publicity isn't important to her. Sometimes you have to remind her that the charities she visits actually want the press there."

The image of a curated Royal Family struck the right note at a time of austerity. The cost of sustaining them was an issue that reared up regularly in the House of Commons at difficult political moments—such as when the Labour government decommissioned **Britannia** in 1997, a move the Queen regarded as akin to amputation.

National treasure though the Queen Mother was, in her last days her profligacy was tolerated with less goodwill than in more subservient times. She liked to present herself as charmingly skint: "Golly, I could really use £100,000, couldn't you?" she asked a lunch guest, the writer A. N. Wilson, after a morning spent with her bank manager. But when she died in 2002, she left an estate of around £50 million to the present queen. A cantankerous national debate ensued about whether it was time to end the royal privilege of not paying death duties on sovereign-to-sovereign inheritance. The privilege relieved the Queen of paying £20 million in taxes on her mother's bequest, which might have forced her to sell either Balmoral or Sandringham to pay them.

By the time the Cameron government took over in 2010, few people realized that the royal finances were in a parlous state. Historian Andrew Roberts attributes this to the long-term impact of a deal struck by King George III in 1760. In return for giving up rights to the extensive and lucrative Crown Estate, which includes huge swathes of property in the golden mile of Regent Street, Regent's Park, and St. James's, the monarchy was accorded an annual sum by Parliament known as the Civil List. It turned out to be a rotten exchange. In 2001, for instance, while the Crown Estate made a plump post-tax profit of £147 million, the Queen's Civil List came to a stick-figured £6.6 million. The monarchy, opined Roberts, had been "disastrously diddled since 1760." (The Windsors' personal wealth is another matter. In 2019, the Queen's net worth alone was estimated at £390 million.)

Three treasurers oversee the royals' money—the prime minister, the chancellor of the exchequer, and the keeper of the privy purse, who is appointed by the Queen. The chancellor is deputed to oversee royal raises in consultation with the monarch. The Civil List was set as an annual amount in 1952 for the rest of the Queen's reign, but high inflation arrived in the 1960s, and so at the start of the 1970s it was decided to move to setting ten-year budgets. That worked until the 1990s, when the amount set in 1991 proved to be too much. Inflation had fallen sharply. So in 2001 the Palace decided just to spend the surplus they'd built up in the decade before. By 2010 the money had run out—and at an awkward moment. The Cameron government's budget cuts made any raises for the royals a political minefield.

Chancellor George Osborne decided to work up an elegant if characteristically vague idea proposed by Prince Charles. In 2012, Osborne replaced the Civil List with something called the Sovereign Grant, which was based on how the Crown Estate was performing and therefore loosely linked to the economy. That is, as a commercial property company, it would probably be doing well when the economy was doing well and badly when the economy was weak, a concept much easier to sell to the property-obsessed British public. The change was well received by the press and Parliament. It was widely framed as the family sharing in the tough times, though in practice Osborne was using tough times to create a lasting reform that would set their finances right for decades. A Peter Brookes cartoon in **The Times** showed the Queen and the Duke of Edinburgh coming out of Westminster underground station in their state robes saying, "Bloody Osborne," which was exactly the right kind of PR for the Cameron government—and the Crown. A win all round.

The Sovereign Grant funds are spent on the Royal Family's official duties, entertaining and upkeep of royal palaces (but not Balmoral and Sandringham, the Queen's personal homes). It covers such critical needs as staff salaries or, say, repairs, such as those needed in 2007 when Prince Albert's mausoleum was falling down at Frogmore. Though the ten-year refurbishment of Buckingham Palace now under way will cost taxpayers £369 million, the Queen's frugal instincts are known to all. A 2021 **Sunday Times** review of Her Maj's economies noted that "old newspapers are shredded for use as horses' bedding. String from parcels is saved to be tied again. Frayed sheets and dusters are darned and reused. At Balmoral any damage to the walls is patched up by wallpaper bought more than a century ago by Queen Victoria."

Prince Charles and his sons are financed by the income of the Duchy of Cornwall. Philip received a separate annual stipend of around £359,000 that never changed. The Queen personally supplements the stipends of Andrew, Anne, and Edward, as well as those of her now-elderly cousins the Dukes of Gloucester and Kent, and Kent's younger brother Prince Michael and Michael's controversial wife, Marie-Christine. The cousins occupy spacious grace-and-favor apartments at Kensington Palace that they hang on to by their fingernails. KP has housed so many elderly royals in its time, it was once dubbed the Aunt Heap.

The Queen has always been ready to help members of the family, such as her cousin Margaret Rhodes, at straitened moments. "The Queen was just so lovely about helping Mummy when my father was so ill," Rhodes's daughter Victoria Pryor told **The Telegraph**. "Suddenly she said: 'Gosh, Margaret, could you bear to live in suburbia?'"—meaning take possession of a grace-and-favor house on the grounds of Windsor Castle. Margaret gratefully accepted.

The Queen discusses the family allocations of the Sovereign Grant with her keeper of the privy purse. The way she doles it out is remarkably personal. Members of the family wait in trepidation to hear if they are going to get a raise. The Queen meets annually with the chancellor of the exchequer alone, at a small table in her second-floor receiving room with the corgis running around, and produces a piece of paper on which she has written her list. Often, she will make irreverent asides about how people have performed. "The Duke of Kent will get five hundred and fifty thousand and Wren House to use. . . . The Wessexes should get another two hundred—Sophie really is trying. . . . X is **hopeless** with money and hardly does **anything.** . . . I think fifty will do," etc. The chancellor scribbles away and takes the list back to the Treasury, which handles royal finances, and the funds are transferred to Buckingham Palace.

In 2002, the House of Commons Public Accounts Committee raised a stink about the five-bedroom, four-reception-room KP apartment allocated for the past thirty years to the impecunious Prince and Princess Michael of Kent. They performed minimal royal duties, yet paid a rent of only £69 per week. That's less, the **Daily Mirror** pointed out, than a lot of people pay for lousy public housing in a council house. And a hundred times less than they would pay for such a property on the open market. The Queen had to step up and personally fork over the commercial rate of £120,000 annually to cover the cost, until 2009, at which point it was decided the problem was theirs.

The younger Kents' money woes have long been a thorn in the monarch's side. The Queen could, in theory, cut them off, but she is rather attached to the affable seventy-eight-year-old Prince Michael, if less so to Marie-Christine, his towering Wagnerian wife, with her pretentious pronouncements and Brunhild braids.

Always strapped for cash, Prince Michael manages a dubious consultancy business that trades on his dynastic connections in Russia. In 2012 it was reported that he received at least £320,000 over six years from the exiled Russian tycoon Boris Berezovsky to pay his staff. Another business chum was the journalist-snatching despot President Lukashenko of Belarus.

In 2020, the Prince was caught on a Zoom call greedily swallowing the bait of a £200,000 cash-for-access fee in a sting by two **Sunday Times** reporters. The enterprising muckrakers pretended to represent a South Korean company called House of Haedong, seeking Prince Michael's help to break into Putinista circles. The Marquess of Reading, Michael's partner, old school friend, and upper-class bonehead, was recorded assuring the fictional House of Haedong reps that "we're talking relatively discreetly here. Because we wouldn't want the world to know that [Michael] is seeing Putin purely for business reasons, if you follow me." The business wiz added that one of the reasons the Prince enjoyed such privileged access was because of his royal status. "He is just generally regarded as Her Majesty's unofficial ambassador to Russia."

Clearly the Michaels were a low-boil money-grubbing embarrassment, and should be the first to be disappeared in any royal load shedding. But their antics milking the royal brand paled when compared to the sordid depredations of Prince Andrew.

The Duke of York was a coroneted sleaze machine.

II

As the UK's special representative for international trade and investment, a role that allowed him to swan around the world at government expense playing golf, Andrew was the despair of the British Foreign Office. He insisted on flying private, and traveled with an entourage of servants, including a valet who lugged a preposterous six-foot-long ironing board through the lobby of five-star hotels. He described his travel expenses as a "little tiny spot in the ocean by comparison to many people." But that didn't stop the criticism—or the Prince's profligacy. **The Daily Telegraph** reported that in 2010 the Duke of York had spent £465,000 on flights and £154,000 on food and hotels on his trade missions.

International diplomacy rarely offers encounters with angels. The Queen herself has sat down with despots like President Mugabe of Zimbabwe, and if the president of Italy is the licentious charlatan Silvio Berlusconi, the prime minister of the UK has to dunk biscotti with him. In countries that have a royal family like Saudi Arabia, or an authoritarian government like Turkey, the ability of the Foreign Office to deploy a member of the royal family who is not the Queen or her direct heir can be useful to grease the wheels. But Prince Andrew's adhesive contacts with reprehensible foreign riffraff went far beyond what was explicable or acceptable.

A string of international lowlifes, who had nothing to do with British diplomacy and everything to do with unsavory personal deals that he was pursuing on the side, filled the Duke of York's otherwise sparse calendar. In 2011, just three months before Tunisia's regime collapsed in the Arab Spring, he was the proud host at a Buckingham Palace luncheon for Tunisian strongman Zine El Abidine Ben Ali's billionaire son-in-law Mohamed Sakhr El Materi, later sentenced to sixteen years in prison for corruption and property fraud. When Stephen Day, the UK's former ambassador to Tunisia, learned about the lunch, he sent an aghast memo to Downing Street: "Materi was, as we all know, the worst of all the crooks in the presidential family," wrote Day, adding, "Thank goodness there was time for the press to be told it was not done on official advice." In an email published in **The Telegraph**, Andrew's press secretary Ed Perkins scrambled for backup support. "[I] am deploying the line that [Materi] was vice-chairman of the chamber of commerce. Will the UK Trade and Investment Office stand behind [Andrew]? We need some government backing here," he flailed.

One of Andrew's most insalubrious lunch partners was Saif Gaddafi, son of Libyan tyrant Muammar

Gaddafi. Saif, who holds a doctorate from the London School of Economics (and whose thesis is not universally believed to have been written by him), was soon to be a fugitive, wanted for war crimes by the International Criminal Court. Tarek Kaituni, a convicted Libyan gun smuggler, was Andrew's guest at Princess Beatrice's twenty-first birthday party in 2009 at a private villa near Marbella, presenting her with a $30,000 diamond necklace at the same time that he was pushing to get hired as a consultant to a British company with dealings in Libya. Apparently oblivious to the perils and unseemliness of such connections, Andrew invited him back—this time as a guest at the Windsor Castle wedding and black-tie reception of Princess Eugenie in 2018.

A favorite destination of Andrew's was Kazakhstan, best known as the fake birthplace of Borat. Andrew accepted goose-hunting invitations in 2008 with then-president Nursultan Nazarbayev, who was "re-elected" for twenty-nine years, and preemptively passed a law granting himself legal immunity from any criminal charges.

In a questionable transaction typical of Prince Andrew's business affairs, his white-elephant house Sunninghill Park was sold in 2007 to Nazarbayev's baby-faced billionaire son-in-law Timur Kulibayev, for £3 million more than its £12 million asking price, even though there were no other bids on the property. This was doubly puzzling to the press, because the only enhancements to the house since the Yorks' occupation was a new zoning designation under the direct flight path for incoming aircraft at Heathrow Airport. There were so many questions from the press that the Palace felt compelled to protest: "The sale of Sunninghill Park was a straight commercial transaction between the Trust which owned the house and the Trust which bought it. There were no side deals and absolutely no arrangement from the Duke of York to benefit otherwise or to commit to any other commercial arrangement. Any suggestion otherwise is completely false."

Leaked emails from 2011 in the **Daily Mail** gave credence to a report—strongly denied by Buckingham Palace—that Andrew acted as a middleman in helping a Greek sewage company and a Swiss finance house pursue a £385 million contract in Kazakhstan. Andrew was allegedly going to be offered nearly £4 million to convince a Kazakh oligarch to support the bids. Unfortunately for Andrew, the deal fell apart when Kazakh police opened fire on a group of striking oil workers and his partners got spooked. He later tried to get Kazakh associates hooked up with Coutts, the Queen's bankers, but that deal didn't fly. A source at Coutts explained: "Kazakh oligarchs are the sort of people we generally don't touch with a bargepole."

Many who encountered Andrew on trade missions felt the same way about him. Simon Wilson, who hosted him regularly as Britain's deputy head of mission in Bahrain from 2001 to 2005, recalled that much of what the Prince said was "absolute twaddle," and that he was derided by the British diplomatic community in the Gulf as HBH: His Buffoon Highness.

It was the same on his own turf. At a lunch with London Assembly chair Darren Johnson and London mayor Boris Johnson, Andrew made a muddled pitch for such city improvements as fewer traffic lights so that there would be fewer red lights, and a larger Queen Elizabeth II Conference Centre. ("If it's too small it's your mum's fault," Boris allegedly said.) After Andrew was escorted from the lunch, Boris turned to Darren Johnson and commented, "I'm the last person to be a republican but fuck. If I ever have to spend another lunch like that, I soon will be."

Former foreign minister and Labour MP Chris Bryant told me that "it was common parlance that the last thing the FO wanted was Andrew on a trip, because he didn't know the difference between private and public. He'd offend half the people at the dinner table, go off on secret missions and return laden with gifts, and on top of that he was a nightmare because he insisted on more support, more acreage in hotels than any other member of the royal family. When he went to Davos he had a bigger chalet than everyone else, and everyone went, 'Why?' His sense of entitlement was off kilter." In March 2011, Bryant broke parliamentary rules prohibiting attacks on members of the royal family in the House of Commons. "Isn't it increasingly difficult to explain the behavior of the special ambassador for trade, who is not only a very close friend of Saif Gaddafi, but is also a close friend of the convicted Libyan gun smuggler Tarek Kaituni?" he demanded, startlingly, from the floor of the House. "Isn't it time we dispensed with the services of the Duke of York?"

The Speaker instructed Bryant to sit down, but the MP's explosive comment made headline news. A senior Tory told **The Guardian** in 2011: "There appears to be no discernible mental activity upstairs as far as the duke is concerned. I feel sorry for him. He has no friends and so is surrounded by these vile people."

Unfortunately, it was true. Andrew's life had been hurtling downhill since he left the Royal Navy in 2001. He peaked at age twenty-two when, on September 17, 1982, he strode down the gangplank from the battleship HMS **Invincible** in Portsmouth Harbour with a red rose between his teeth, after acquitting himself with honor as a Sea King helicopter pilot in the Falklands War. The Queen and Prince Philip and Princess Anne were there to greet him. Jubilant crowds swarmed the Royal Naval dockyard waving Union Jacks. The Queen was so excited she whipped out her camera and snapped away like a tourist. Her son presented her with the rose, a dashing gesture that fueled ecstatic write-ups in the red-tops. "Nobody called him 'Randy Andy,' a prince whose only claim to fame was his preference for blue-eyed blondes," one tabloid noted. "Now it's Andrew the Warrior Prince, a hero home from the wars."

Like his nephew Prince Harry nearly twenty years later, Andrew had found his métier in the armed services. Or at least his experiences there kept him out of trouble. At the Royal Naval College in Dartmouth as a sub-lieutenant at age twenty-one, he was given the Best Pilot award, bestowed on the school's behalf by his father. Nine months after serving as best man at the wedding of Charles and Diana, Andrew, to the envy of his older brother, found himself sailing off for five months aboard an actual battleship for an actual war.

Few people had heard of the Falkland Islands, a tiny fleck of British Empire off the coast of Argentina, with almost as many sheep on it as people. That is, until April 1982, when Argentina's president, General Leopoldo Galtieri, decided to help himself to the islands. Sending British troops to defend the Falklands provided an opportunity for Tory prime minister Margaret Thatcher to earn her Iron Lady legend, and the British tabloids to go into jingoist ecstasy with headlines in **The Sun** like "Stick It Up Your Junta."

The possibility of Prince Andrew being killed in action made the British government apprehensive and added to the young Prince's aura. The cabinet requested he be moved to desk duty during the conflict, but Andrew was determined to see action. His father, grandfather, and great-grandfather had all served in the navy, and the Queen backed him all the way, releasing a statement that read, "Prince Andrew is a serving officer and there is no question in [my] mind that he should go." Andrew's service did Her Majesty proud. It included flying his helicopter as a decoy target to divert deadly Exocet missiles away from British ships, as well as search and air rescue, and anti-submarine and anti-surface warfare. He witnessed from the air the terrifying sight of the Argentinian attack on the SS **Atlantic Conveyor,** which was hit by two air-launched Exocet missiles, killing twelve sailors. The Prince piloted the helicopter that rescued the surviving British crewmen who'd been thrown into the sea.

Andrew had another brief reputational surge during the Windsor Castle fire ten years later. The thirty-two-year-old prince was the only royal home on November 20, 1992, when a spotlight set a curtain on fire in the Queen's Private Chapel, igniting a blaze that spread to 115 rooms and caused the roof of the magnificent fourteenth-century St. George's Hall to collapse. When Andrew saw the smoke he organized a bucket brigade with some of the resourceful spirit he'd shown in the Falklands. The human chain of the Windsor household salvaged much of the castle's priceless contents, amassed during nine hundred years of royal history: Sèvres porcelain, eighteenth-century furniture, paintings by Van Dyck, Rubens, and Gainsborough from the Royal Collection. Andrew was interviewed outside the eerie scene of flame-lit castle windows as the hero of the hour. It was the first time he had looked really on his game since he returned from war.

There is no doubting the Queen's especially soft spot for Andrew. "Whenever she hears that Andrew is in Buckingham Palace, she'll send him a handwritten note, and he always goes to see her," a former Palace aide told Geoffrey Levy and Richard Kay of the **Daily Mail.** "If he's in jeans, he'll change into a suit. And he always greets 'Mummy' in the same way—bowing from the neck, kissing her hand, and then kissing her on both cheeks. It's a little ritual that she adores. Believe me, he can do no wrong."

He had always received much more of her attention than his siblings. Born in the Queen's second batch, ten years after Princess Anne and four years before Prince Edward, Andrew had a mother who was well settled by then into her sovereign duties. She sometimes allowed herself the time to pick him up from his prep school, Heatherdown, and drive him home herself, or let him play quietly in her study while she received official visitors. He was the first to be christened with the surname Prince Philip fought for, Mountbatten-Windsor.

An ex-girlfriend of Charles told me that when she was staying at Windsor Castle one weekend, she heard the Queen on the phone to one of Andrew's teachers at Gordonstoun, talking worriedly about his academic performance like any mother. Philip liked to say that his second son was a "natural boss." Andrew's temperament—hearty, robust, disruptive (at Heatherdown he loved mixing up everyone's shoes in the dorm)—was more compatible with Philip than Charles. He was less vulnerable to his father's casual Teutonic insensitivities, and undaunted by the rigors of Gordonstoun. The Scottish boarding school took females by the time Andrew got there, reducing the culture of hazing. He didn't make head boy like Charles, perhaps because his classmates didn't like him much. They found him big-headed, arrogant, and deluded about his own intelligence. His penchant for off-color jokes, at which he laughed inordinately, earned him the nickname "the Sniggerer."

One senses that there was always a hollowness in Andrew's personality. That's why he laughed louder and boasted so much and tried to seem important. By the time he went to Gordonstoun, he knew that for all the palaces he lived in and the servants who Sir'd him, he was the second son whose childhood parity with Charles was a mirage. Only the monarch's firstborn wakes up every morning knowing that to advance to the ultimate prize, all he has to do is stay alive. Only the firstborn son is invested as Prince of Wales. Only the firstborn son becomes the Duke of Cornwall, which includes being handed a vast private estate that generates around $30 million in annual income—all of which went to Charles. The winner-take-all calculus has been baked into every generation of the British monarchy. While there are ships, schools, peninsulas, and even a nursery rhyme named for the Duke of York, the title throws off neither an income nor even a stately home. The only certainty for the second son is that, as the years go by, his importance will decline as he slides inexorably down in the line of succession.

The dissonance for Andrew between early promise

and actual destiny was heightened by the media excitement round his early years. As a child, he had been seen very little by the public. The Queen and Prince Philip felt Charles had been overly tormented by the press in his young days, and by the time Andrew was school age there was a constant fear of an IRA bomb. Security forces once had to surround his prep school when there was credible intelligence of an imminent execution plot. As a result, Andrew experienced more coddling than Charles.

By his teens, Andrew was one of the Royal Family's burgeoning assets—debonair, lighthearted, and manly, with a toothy, Kennedyesque smile. When he accompanied his parents at the age of sixteen to the 1976 Montreal Olympics, a Canadian newspaper described him as "six feet of sex appeal." Even Prince Charles admitted his younger brother had "Robert Redford looks." Returning to Canada the following year, he found girls gathered at the Toronto airport to greet him screaming, "We want Andy!" Back in the UK, as Andrew flipped the switch on the Regent Street Christmas lights on live television, girls in the crowd below swooned and even fainted in the frenzy over the young prince. **People** magazine regularly ranked him among the world's best-looking men.

The press were as fixated on Andrew's girlfriends as they had been on Charles's. Andrew preferred minor models and starlets to the **Burke's Peerage** types his elder brother bowled his way through. His first true love was the sprightly twenty-four-year-old-brunette

Koo Stark, an American actress whose oeuvre had featured scenes of lesbian shower sex, masturbation, and sexual molestation by nuns. She met him on a blind date a few months before his twenty-first birthday party at Windsor Castle—"the world's quietest disco," as party guest Sir Elton John put it, "because the Queen was present." They were mutually smitten on sight. "He walked into my life and that was it: He was my life," Stark said in a 2015 interview.

Koo was waiting for Andrew in his rooms at Buckingham Palace when he returned in triumph from the Falklands, and she joined him for a romantic week at Balmoral. The Queen found the actress bright and congenial. She later entertained Koo and Andrew for tea at Windsor Castle, and Her Maj's only comment was, "Oh, I do wish they would call you Kathleen [her real name] and Andrew," remembered Koo. Alas, while the couple was holidaying in Mustique in 1982, topless photos of Koo playing the seventeen-year-old heroine of the modestly erotic coming-of-age movie **The Awakening of Emily** were discovered by the news media. The curtain-twitching tabloid custodians of Middle England love nothing more than to act as the arbiters of who is appropriate as a royal romantic partner. "Overnight, my career and my reputation were irrevocably damaged," Koo said. She could never rub off the porn-star stain. The press made Koo's life hell. Photographers on motorbikes rode into restaurants to try to get a shot of her with Andrew. She was told she was on an IRA hit list. For two years, she moved homes each time her address was published.

Ultimately the pressure was too much for both of them. "I was desperately fond of Koo," Andrew later told a friend, "but marriage would have been an awful mistake. I was terribly immature in those days."

Some people who know Andrew believe that it was ending things with Koo that was the awful mistake. They were genuinely in love. Koo was a smart, creative woman with a credible parallel career in photography. She turned her own camera on the paparazzi when they started to pursue her, and became a protégée of the legendary fashion lensman Norman Parkinson, publishing photo books of her own. For thirty-three years she declined to sell Andrew out, reportedly turning down an offer of a million dollars to spill her secrets. Such was her discretion that she says, for a time, the Palace advised family newcomers seeking advice on how to handle the savage press scrutiny to follow the Koo Stark Rule and simply say nothing. Andrew is the godfather of her daughter. In 2015, she even defended him against "assassinations of character" in the Jeffrey Epstein scandal. She would have probably made an appealing and accomplished Duchess of York, but this was 1983, not 2018, when a divorced American actress married the Queen's grandson at Windsor Castle. Koo's life descended into a sad tale of bankruptcy, a ruinous legal suit against the father of her child, and a bout with breast cancer. Finally, in 2021, to pay her legal bills, she at last seemed to be at work on a tell-all book deal.

III

Sarah Margaret Ferguson, Fergie as she was known, blew into the twenty-five-year-old Prince Andrew's life with her boisterous laugh and exploding mane of Titian-red hair in June 1985. They were introduced by Princess Diana, who wangled Fergie a seat next to Andrew at lunch at the Queen's Ascot weekend house party at Windsor Castle. She and Diana were fourth cousins, and their mothers had gone to school together. Fergie's father, Major Ronald Ferguson, was the Prince of Wales's polo manager, a well-known figure on the fringes of aristocratic society. Andrew and Fergie had once met as children playing on a polo field. "Where else do people meet?" Sarah's mother once remarked.

At the time of the Ascot lunch, Fergie had just been dumped after three years by a rich divorced man twenty-five years older than she. The introduction to Andrew was a godsend. By the end of the lunch, the Prince was coaxing Fergie to eat chocolate profiteroles—and the romance took off from there. The press, beginning to tire of Diana's fashionable supremacy, embraced the breezy, horse-riding country "gel" Fergie as "a breath of fresh air." The Queen was relieved that at least **this** future daughter-in-law could talk with authentic enthusiasm about horses and dogs and the joys of the English countryside.

"Diana may take a better picture," commented **The Washington Post,** "but Fergie is more fun." A new magnet for the media was useful for Diana. She knew her raucous soon-to-be sister-in-law would never offer any real competition. "Fergie lightens the load," she told her ballet dancer friend Wayne Sleep. The press loved it when the two of them tried to gate-crash Andrew's stag party dressed as police-women. On July 23, 1986, there was great national joy when the two twenty-six-year-olds, Sarah and Andrew, were married at Westminster Abbey as the Duke and Duchess of York—with a global audience of five hundred million.

In a sense, the new royal couple were matched not only in their exuberant temperaments but also in their unexpressed anxieties. Like Andrew, Fergie was emotionally stunted by her upbringing. Her noisy, irreverent personality disguised the fact she always felt uncool, overweight, and financially insecure. Her mother, Susan, like Diana's mother, Frances, left home for a **coup de foudre**—in Susan's case with a charismatic Argentinian polo player named Hector Barrantes. She had reasons to leave. The Galloping Major, as the press called Ronald Ferguson, was a priapic old goat who finally got his comeuppance when the press caught him at an erotic massage parlor in 1988, and he was fired from his royal sinecure.

He had raised Fergie and her sister with the help of an unfeeling housekeeper at the family home of the unfortunately named Dummer Down Farm in Hampshire. "Her mother leaving Fergie had a massive effect on her," one of Fergie's closest wingwomen, Kate Waddington, told me in 2006. "It really dictated how she is: her insecurity. Even today if she phones you and you don't phone back she's in a terrible state about what she's done wrong." (In another strange affinity with Diana, Susan Barrantes died in a car crash in September 1998. She was decapitated in a head-on collision on an Argentine provincial highway.) Fergie relays in her memoir an unwittingly tragic scene when her mother briefly returned to Dummer to tell her she was going to Argentina for good. Ever the people pleaser, Fergie told her mother she really liked Hector and hoped she would be happy. "Oh good, so you don't mind then," Susan replied, with that denial of emotion so quintessential to the upper classes.

The York marriage eventually collapsed not because of infidelity, but because of the gloominess of life with Andrew. Or rather, life without him. The Duke of York was home only forty days a year for the first five years of their marriage. Prince Philip refused to let Fergie join her husband in Portsmouth on the grounds that she would be too much of a distraction. Andrew, afraid to take his father on, didn't put up a fight. For all his courage as a warrior, he was a pusillanimous son.

Fergie waited around for her fairy-tale prince in the six doleful rooms of Andrew's former bachelor pad in the East Wing of Buckingham Palace—"damask curtains, pleated lampshades, bland carpeting, brownish wallpaper . . . and sad electric fireplaces," as she described it in her memoir. Her child-man husband's bed was blanketed with fifty stuffed teddy bears, many dressed as sailors, that maids had to place in the exact spot Andrew had ordained. After their marriage, his rambunctious spirit, so manifest in their courtship days, disappeared. He was a couch potato who wanted only to watch TV and golf. His decreasing relevance to the Crown drained his vitality and self-esteem. Former US ambassador to the UK Walter Annenberg's wife, Lee, was appalled when Andrew made a private visit in 1993 to Sunnylands, their magnificent Palm Springs estate in California, and the Duke holed up in his bedroom for two days apparently watching porn.

Fergie performed her royal round with notable gusto, but she was essentially living alone in a huge fusty hotel, where any social spontaneity was curtailed by the need to give a whole day's notice to security and a menu summit with the master of the household. She longed to do something ordinary, like make herself a cheese sandwich. "My solution was simple—for a time I just stopped going out. I would sit and eat my lukewarm supper for one." In 1989, she succumbed to a very public two-year transatlantic affair with a hunky Texan oilman, Steve Wyatt, which Andrew seemed to scarcely notice.

The biggest problem in the Yorks' union was—and always would be—money. Fergie was a crashing spendthrift married to a natural cheapskate who also happened to have much less cash than she had expected. Although far from broke, Andrew was not a rich man (before he sought out unsavory deals to compensate), and he was entirely dependent on the Queen's bounty. Now fourth in line to the throne—the demotions having kicked in with the births of William and Harry—he received £250,000 annually from the Civil List for his official activities, and a Royal Naval pension of about £20,000 a year, plus an unspecified allowance that followed the vagaries of the Queen's goodwill. He had no other capital and no further assets other than a life insurance policy worth £600,000.

"The ridiculous thing was that even when she was with Andrew she paid for all the house decorations herself," Kate Waddington said. "She was always informed, 'There is no money.' Andrew would arrive on a skiing holiday and he'd have no stuff and she'd have to buy it." In an attempt to rake in some funds, Fergie, who was a qualified helicopter pilot, wrote a series of not-bad-at-all children's books about the adventures of a jaunty blue helicopter named Budgie, which she promoted furiously. They were a credible business success, with an animated **Budgie the Little Helicopter** TV series in the United States, but the money was never enough.

She spent with abandon—on expensive vacations, restaurants, jewelry, wardrobe, and grandiose gifts. Dresses "on approval" from couture designers were rarely sent back. Fergie was nothing if not bighearted to her friends, and was always issuing invitations she couldn't pay for. By the time the Yorks separated in March 1992, Fergie was £4 million in debt to Coutts bank. It was clear that, embarrassed though he was by his wife's infidelities, Prince Andrew was reluctant to divorce her. He never really has. The ex-royal maid

Charlotte Briggs claimed Andrew still held a torch for Fergie after he returned to live with his mother at Buckingham Palace after the divorce. Briggs told **The Sun,** "Although [Fergie] did not live there, her make-up was still laid out on the dressing table. . . . Even her wedding dress was still hung up in the wardrobe. It was creepy." Four months before their separation, Woodrow Wyatt recorded in his diary that Angus Ogilvie, husband of the Queen's cousin Princess Alexandra, told him at a dinner party, "Prince Andrew, poor fellow, is still in love with Fergie." When his father told him she had to go, he simply took the path of least resistance.

It was the **Daily Mirror** that did Fergie in. The pictures of her Texan "business manager," John Bryan, sucking and fondling her toes in the south of France in August 1992 irreversibly branded her as a royal deplorable.

"I joined Fergie's staff immediately on the Monday after the pix appeared," Waddington said. "She was shell-shocked, a broken woman." There was little consideration in the press—or the family—of the fact that Andrew and she were separated at the time, or that the pictures were taken by an Italian paparazzo who had brazenly invaded the Duchess's privacy.

Unluckily for Fergie, she was staying at Balmoral with her two daughters when the story hit. An adamant Queen told her to pack her bags and leave immediately. "The redhead is in trouble," Diana paged the **Daily Mail**'s Richard Kay. Prince Philip never spoke to Fergie again. If she walked into a room, he walked out of it. His rage, though theatrical, was genuine. Her pariah status was especially distressing to her on occasions like Kate and William's wedding. Banned from attending the royal event of the decade, she fled to Thailand. "The jungle embraced me," she told Oprah in a 2011 interview. Unprotected by the Palace, she bravely endured years of cruel tabloid misogyny, routinely mocked in the gossip columns as the "Duchess of Pork." "I remember one headline when a newspaper had run a poll and claimed that 82 percent of people would rather sleep with a goat than Fergie," she recalled in an interview in 2021.

Fergie mishandled the terms of her divorce with the same unerring naïvety with which she mishandled everything else. Diana, who knew she would soon face divorce herself, regarded her sister-in-law's negotiations as the road map of how to mess it up. Mistake one was hiring an establishment lawyer, rather than an outsider to royal circles, a mistake Diana avoided when she hired Anthony Julius, who cared nothing for their approval. Mistake two was essentially the same as mistake one. Fergie desperately wanted to claw back a relationship with the senior royals, failing to understand the Windsors' long-practiced art of pulling up the drawbridge irrevocably.

"When I met with Her Majesty, she asked, 'What do you require, Sarah?'" she told one interviewer.

"'Your friendship, ma'am,'" Sarah said she replied, "which I think amazed her because everyone said I would demand a big settlement. But I wanted to be able to say, 'Her Majesty is my friend'—not fight her nor have lawyers saying, 'Look, she is greedy.'"

Her Majesty graciously accepted Fergie's offer of friendship and allowed Andrew's lawyers to make a stingy deal. After ten years of marriage and two children, Fergie wound up with a £350,000 settlement, and for her daughters a £1.4 million trust fund and £500,000 toward a house. Her debts remained unsettled, and she chose to stay on with the girls in a suite of rooms at the Sunninghill house until it was sold in 2007. She became a Flying Dutchman Duchess, pursuing a series of publishing and merchandising deals and TV talk shows in the United States—all of which inevitably cratered.

It's not as if she didn't work hard. A contract with Wedgwood china required her to visit—in twelve months—forty to fifty mid-market American malls, where royalty-struck shoppers turned out to hear her talk up the table settings. And she gamely turned her years of being fat-shamed into a business opportunity. A job as spokesperson for Weight Watchers in the United States at $2 million a year was her most lucrative venture and eventually paid off her debts. In 2006, she sank £700,000 she had saved into Hartmoor, a lifestyle brand with fancy offices on Madison Avenue. It was supposed to be an umbrella company for her publishing, media, and public speaking efforts, but in 2008 Weight Watchers dumped her, and Hartmoor folded from mismanagement and overspending. She was the Real Housewife of the House of Windsor.

In May 2010, she made one of her most person-ally damaging mistakes when she fell for the sting by the **News of the World**'s undercover reporter Mazher Mahmood, who was posing as a businessman seek-ing to buy access to Prince Andrew. This was the very same Fake Sheikh in the bogus burnoose who'd gulled Sophie Wessex ten years earlier. He got Fergie on tape promising to grant access to her ex-husband for £500,000. She told the "businessman" to wire the money to her HSBC bank account, assuring him: "That opens up everything you would ever wish for. I can open any door you want, and I will for you. Look after me and he'll look after you. . . . You'll get it back tenfold."

One former business associate of Fergie's told me that it became impossible to close a deal for Fergie because of the incompetence of the people she sur-rounded herself with. She blew countless bona fide opportunities because of chaotic follow-up or a headstrong lack of it. Like her husband, she had ap-palling character judgment. Her advisory circle was as full of flakes and fools as his was of iffy oligarchs.

But Fergie was also in a position that would continue, in varying degrees, to haunt all the minor royals. They are like creatures in a Middle Eastern harem, captives of luxury everyone resents, but with-out the wherewithal or expertise to pursue successful lives beyond. If they try to do so, they are branded as vulgar and embarrassing and accused of exploiting their royal status. And yet, what else do they have to sell? Weight Watchers wasn't interested in just any jolly zaftig redhead. They were interested—and invested—in the ex-wife of the Queen's second son, a royal duchess who had lived in palaces.

Fergie's parsimonious settlement may have felt like a win for the royals—especially when Charles had to borrow money from the Queen to shell out £17 million three months later for Diana's divorce bonanza—but it was also shortsighted. Just as their failure to pay off the gabby butler Paul Burrell and lock down his secrets offered open season for every tabloid with a checkbook, so, too, were Fergie's ever-rising debts a dangerous vulnerability for the Crown.

Whenever she went on an American TV talk show, they asked her one obligatory question about Weight Watchers, and then, to her chagrin, pivoted to pressing for juice about her life as a royal. The sound bites would bounce eastward across the Atlantic, generating more scorn, sleaze, and tarnishing of the House of Windsor's mystique. And they didn't even get rid of her. In 2008, Fergie moved back in with Andrew at the Queen Mother's former home, Royal Lodge, the thirty-room eighteenth-century jewel-box house on ninety-eight acres in the grounds of Windsor Castle, for which he pays a peppercorn rent. Where Andrew got the £7.5 million to renovate it remains a mystery. They reside there to this day, living in uncoupled coupling as each other's supposed best friends, devoted parents of the two princesses, and proud grandparents. "I stand by him and always will.

The way we are is our fairy tale," Fergie told the **Daily Mail** in 2018.

An American media executive who came to see her at Royal Lodge about a project in 2015 paints a different picture one only hopes was an aberration. "We were having lunch," the media executive told me, "and Andrew came in and sat down and said to me, 'What are you doing with this fat cow?' I was so stunned at his level of sadism. I thought, 'What an asshole.' She has to sing for her supper. She's afraid of him." Whatever the undertow of their curious arrangement, the deal seems to be that he bails her out when she's in trouble, and she backs him up when he's assailed by scandal. It is the symbiosis of sheer survival.

As William and Harry became the heartthrobs of the aughts, Andrew descended into the royal round of rent-a-uniform gigs and booming-voiced business dinners, where he usually embarrassed himself or his host.

Andrew, unfortunately, exhibited classic symptoms of what is scientifically recognized as the Dunning-Kruger effect, the cognitive bias in which people come to believe that they are smarter and more capable than they really are. The combination of minimal self-awareness and dim intellectual wattage leads sufferers of this condition to overestimate their own capabilities. Years of enjoying unearned obeisance to his royal position allowed Andrew to bang on with a combination of overweening self-confidence and unchallenged ignorance. It made him an easy mark for con artists and crooks.

His position as Britain's trade ambassador could not possibly last—and it didn't. In February 2011, Andrew's unsavory private life suddenly blew up, threatening to eclipse William and Kate's wedding just when all was sunny in the royal enclosure.

In February 2011, the **New York Post** published a picture taken the previous December of Andrew strolling in Central Park with the American financier and sex offender Jeffrey Epstein. Andrew appeared to have resumed the friendship with this squalid individual five months after Epstein was released from a Florida jail for procuring a child for prostitution and soliciting a prostitute. These revelations were compounded by news in **The Telegraph** that in 2009, when Fergie had been skirting dangerously close to bankruptcy, Epstein, at Andrew's request, had given money to one of her personal assistants to satisfy a paltry debt of £15,000. When the flak hit, Fergie contorted herself with apologies. "I abhor pedophilia and any sexual abuse of children," she told the **Evening Standard** on March 7, 2011. "I am just so contrite I cannot say. Whenever I can, I will repay the money and will have nothing ever to do with Jeffrey Epstein ever again."

Ironically, Epstein tried to sue her for libel for referring to him as a pedophile.

Enough was enough. It was one thing for Andrew to broker nefarious deals for Kazakh strongmen and party at their homes with big-breasted beauty queens, another to blatantly consort with a convicted

American sex offender and his seraglio of underage girls. In July, the Foreign Office and Christopher Geidt had a quiet word. After which the Duke of York, now drowning in sordid allegations, resigned as Britain's international trade ambassador.

CHAPTER
18

AN INCONVENIENT FRIEND

—

The Lure of Jeffrey Epstein

—

I HAD A FEW RUN-INS MYSELF WITH ANDREW'S shadowy nemesis Jeffrey Epstein in July 2010.

I was sitting at my desk in Manhattan at **The Daily Beast,** the digital news site I founded in 2008, when I received a call from Richard Sarnoff, the executive vice president of Random House. He told me that his cousin Conchita Sarnoff, the Cuban-born sex-trafficking activist, had been working on a book with material that was too great a libel risk to publish. Knowing that I was the instigator of the annual Women in the World summit, which featured courageous female activists taking on such oppressions as child marriage and sex trafficking, he thought I would understand that Conchita was sitting on an important story, and that I would publish it, even though Random House was wary. When I pressed him harder, he mentioned the name of Jeffrey

Epstein. My ears pricked up at that because I'd met him. As a journalistic attendee of the Clinton Global Initiative (CGI), which threw together power people with nonprofit do-gooders at a New York Marriott during the week of the annual UN General Assembly, I'd encountered Epstein at the opening night cocktail party on more than one occasion. I had a dim recollection of a cold-eyed fifty-something guy who was intensely focused on working the room.

Epstein was part of the original group that came up with the idea for CGI. He was so close to Bill Clinton that the former president often flew on Epstein's private plane, making humanitarian pit stops in places such as Haiti and Rwanda. Whether you're a former president or a former CEO, it seems one of the hazards of flying private is that some strange craving enters the soul that makes it unbearable to ever fly commercial again. Epstein used his customized Boeing 727 to perfection. The New York financier—said to be worth at least $500 million from a little-understood investing career—had a rolling manifest (I would later learn from Conchita) of global boldfaces from Harvard super lawyer Alan Dershowitz to former commerce secretary Bill Richardson, to former Israeli prime minister Ehud Barak and token royal Prince Andrew, all of whom loved to fly Air Jeff. He had houses to take them to as well, a gated spread in Palm Beach, his own Caribbean island—Little St. James in the Virgin Islands—a sprawling ranch in Santa Fe, and a $56 million, forty-room Manhattan mansion that commanded nearly the whole block of 71st Street between Fifth and Madison avenues.

The appeal to many of his big-shot frequent fliers was that Epstein wasn't as boring as many hyper-rich businessmen who had planes and homes at their disposal. Epstein purported to be an intellectual with a strong bent for science. He dropped out of Cooper Union, never graduated from NYU's Courant Institute of Mathematical Sciences, and was fired as a mathematics teacher at the prestigious Upper East Side private school Dalton. After ingratiating himself with a parent there who hired him at Bear Stearns (and later fired him, for insider trading), he cultivated strong links with Harvard and MIT through generous donations. The dinners he convened at his 21,000-square-foot mansion combined money players like Apollo Global Management's Leon Black and the billionaire hedge funder Glenn Dubin with big-brained academics like cognitive psychologist Steven Pinker and (we learned in a 2019 **New York Times** news bombshell) Microsoft founder turned philanthropist Bill Gates.

Even if it wasn't the strange vibes of numerous teenage girls coming in and out of Epstein's Manhattan house, one would have thought the "tell" for these guests would be the grotesquely vulgar and very weird décor. Its awfulness wasn't just evidence of the untutored taste of a self-made social climber from Coney Island. There was, **New York** magazine's **The Cut** reported, a life-size female doll hanging from a chandelier, a row of individually framed artificial eyeballs in the hallway, a portrait of Bill Clinton wearing Monica Lewinsky's blue dress, and a huge chessboard at the bottom of the stairs with customized figurines modeled after suggestively attired members of his staff that one guest said was "hair-raising in its commitment to creeping people the fuck out." How was Epstein paying for all of this? He promoted an aura of the mysterious master of many universes, but he was, in fact, a money manager who had only one visible client—the Ohio retail billionaire Les Wexner, owner of Victoria's Secret and the Limited.

The story Conchita Sarnoff wanted to tell for **The Daily Beast**, however, was not about Epstein the dubious financier. It was about Epstein the pedophile. I can proudly say that her reports in the **Beast** were the first to reveal the extent of his depredations.

Conchita's obsession with the case began during her investigations into sex trafficking in Mexico. The country's foreign minister taunted her in an interview, she recalled: " 'You know, you Americans are a bunch of hypocrites. You buy our drugs, you buy our weapons, and now you're stealing our children. The largest number of pedophiles are in the United States.' . . . He then ranted on about gringos, and Americans, and I thought, 'What?' " This set her on her odyssey to find out who they were.

Her investigations took her to the jail cell of a Mexican trafficker in the Palm Beach stockade. Until that moment, Conchita had thought Mexican trafficking victims were provided for drug cartels and other criminal elements, but the trafficker told her that the underage girls he guarded were taken to Palm Beach to service rich older men. His statement suddenly chimed with small, buried items she had read in the Palm Beach press. They noted the arrest— and release after a twelve-month sentence—of a man who Conchita, a glamorous and social woman who moved in high-life circles, knew from around town in New York. A man who had once pursued her for a date: Jeffrey Epstein.

Curiosity took her to the Palm Beach police station, where what she read in the files on the case set her hair on fire. The department had identified seventeen local girls who had contact with Epstein before the age of consent; the youngest was fourteen, and many were younger than sixteen. He referred to one of them, Nadia Marcinkova, as his "Yugoslavian sex slave" because he had imported her from the Balkans at age fourteen. Two or three times a day, whenever Epstein was in Palm Beach, a teenage girl would be brought to his mansion on El Brillo Way. ("The younger the better," he was known to say.) A fund set up to compensate Epstein victims eventually paid out $121 million to 150 of them.

Details eventually emerged that for Epstein's birthday one year, according to allegations in a civil suit, he was presented with three twelve-year-old girls from France who were molested and then flown back to Europe the next day. If Epstein had committed all the crimes against minors listed in these witness statements, thought Conchita, he ought to be serving twenty years in a federal penitentiary, not thirteen months in a private wing of the Palm Beach County Stockade, plus a measly eighteen months under "house arrest," during which time he traveled frequently to his home in New York and his private Caribbean island.

All of these details and more about his lifestyle appeared in the six exposés we published in **The Daily Beast** between July 2010 and March 2011. One of the last included a masked video of the first Jane Doe who had been molested by Epstein at the age of fourteen when she thought she was going to his house to give him a massage. Her mother had reported him to the police, triggering the first investigation that sent him to jail.

The stories Conchita wrote were, above all, accounts of the rank perversion of justice by influence and money. She revealed how the squad of Epstein's all-star lawyers discredited the young victims, many of whom had checkered pasts and came from rough backgrounds, and how the case against Epstein was minimized by the Palm Beach County State Attorney's Office, then bargained down by the U.S. Department of Justice to reduce the charges of multiple perfidies against children to a slap-on-the-wrist charge of two counts of soliciting prostitution.

Conchita interviewed Epstein for many hours at his Palm Beach house until he started to sense that the woman he had once hit on was not planning to write a puff piece. As the first of her stories went through heavy vetting by **Beast** editor Lee Aitken and lawyer Stuart Karle, I received a call from Epstein, now apparently a long-lost friend, telling me that Conchita Sarnoff was nuts and to cease and desist. He offered her through an intermediary, she says, $5 million not to publish the story.

A few days later I had an eerie experience. Returning to my glass-walled office at the **Beast,** I found Jeffrey Epstein sitting there. How he got through front desk security without my assistant being notified or found my office I will never know, but it perhaps speaks to his celebrated gifts for conning his way into anywhere.

He was snake-eyed and terse. There was a morose, menacing air to him that I found sinister. "Just stop," he said heavily as I stood staring at him from the doorway. "Just stop. There will be consequences if you don't." I thanked him for his suggestion and told him to talk to our lawyers. "You heard me," he said. "Stop." And he left.

After the pieces ran, I awaited the legal bomb with trepidation, but it never came. Instead, Epstein let fly a blizzard of press releases about all his philan-thropic activities. Perhaps he gambled that **The Daily Beast** would not generate extensive pickup from other news outlets. He was right about that. The pieces generated chatter in New York circles, but this was pre-#MeToo, before issues of the sexual abuse of women by powerful men triggered much reaction beyond women's empowerment conferences. Epstein was not a household name. There was more interest in what Bill Clinton was doing on that plane.

I was nonetheless surprised to get a call in

December 2010 from the New York publicist and doyenne of celebrity movie screenings, Peggy Siegel, asking me to a "really fabulous" dinner for Prince Andrew at the home of Jeffrey Epstein. The other guests, she enthused, would be Woody Allen (whose estranged adult daughter has accused him of sexually molesting her when she was seven years old), the talk show host Charlie Rose (later "canceled" because of allegations of sexual harassment), and the TV journalists Katie Couric and George Stephanopoulos. By this time I had published five pieces about Jeffrey Epstein's sexual abuse of underage girls, and I exploded with disgust.

"What is this, Peggy," I screeched, "the fucking predator's ball?"

"It's all been overblown," Peggy said. "Jeffrey really is okay. He's been very generous to me. I'm just helping him with his party."

It's been an abiding source of relief to me since then that I abandoned my usual editorial willingness to go to anything I think will yield a good story, and said no to a dinner that became one of Manhattan society's most notorious nights of shame.

II

What did Prince Andrew see in Jeffrey Epstein? The Prince wasn't the first or the last prominent sucker to be taken in. Epstein always knew the right psychic buttons to press. He exploited Andrew's sense of grievance about being relegated increasingly to the royal margins. The wife of a financier who sat next to Andrew at an Epstein dinner told me how the Prince suddenly declared, "I don't know why people don't pay us royals more respect."

Epstein made Andrew feel he had joined the big time—the deals, the girls, the plane, the sexy Manhattan world, where he wasn't seen as a full-grown man still dependent on his mama's privy purse strings or on the harsh pecking order of the Palace. Privately, Epstein told people that Andrew was an idiot, but—to him—a useful one. A senior royal is always a potent magnet abroad. Diplomats in British consulates from New York to Singapore assure me that an invitation to meet the Queen's second son, even one tainted with the swirl of rumors, could still command A-list acceptances from businesspeople otherwise hard to snare. I am told Epstein confided to a friend that he used to fly the Duke of York to obscure foreign markets where governments were obliged to receive him, and Epstein went along for the ride as HRH's investment adviser. With Andrew as front man, Epstein could negotiate deals with these (often) shady players and give Andrew some cream off the cake.

A key figure in the Andrew-Epstein relationship was the woman who introduced them, Ghislaine Maxwell, daughter of the press baron Robert Maxwell, who disappeared mysteriously in November 1991 over the side of his yacht in the Atlantic Ocean off the coast of the Canary Islands. Though little known in the

United States until he bought the debt-laden New York **Daily News** in 1991, Maxwell was a mountainous figure in London with his mellifluous, bellowing voice, huge car-wash-brush eyebrows, and shock of inky dyed black hair. His media empire extended from publishing scientific books with his Pergamon Press to the powerful Mirror Group Newspapers, the Macmillan publishing house, and trophies such as the Oxford United Football Club. The glittering parties he hosted with his French-born wife, Betty, at Headington Hill Hall, their vast showcase mansion, were the Oxfordshire version of Gatsby's festivities at East Egg. Ghislaine, for her part, was an improbably glamorous figure at her Oxford College, Balliol, that was better known for earnest wonks than for headline-making temptresses.

After Maxwell's unsolved death, it was revealed that he was a swindler and crook. He had stolen gargantuan sums of money from the Mirror Group's pension fund, stiffing his own employees. Ghislaine fled to New York to escape the scandal and start a new life with a $100,000-a-year trust fund that wouldn't even cover a few Armani outfits. It's often said that she met Epstein soon after she arrived, and Epstein "took her in," for which she was always "grateful." Given his opportunism, that's neither likely nor true. A former business partner of Epstein's, Steven Hoffenberg, who served eighteen years in jail for running one of the largest pre-Madoff Ponzi schemes in U.S. history, affirmed to me that Ghislaine had already met Epstein in 1980s London through her father. Robert Maxwell, he said, got to know Jeffrey after he left Bear Stearns, and the pair "entered into a deep business relationship."

Ghislaine fell madly in love with Epstein, but the affair was brief. As a mature, strong-willed woman with a pixie haircut, she was nothing like the pliable preadolescent waifs Epstein liked to dominate. Their relationship quickly turned transactional: Epstein made the money, and Ghislaine made the introductions. Unable to hold his sexual attention, she found a way to keep him at her side by recruiting "nubiles" (as she called them) to service his insatiable needs.

Ghislaine was omnipresent in the strata that gathered to celebrate perfume launches, art gallery openings, and air-kissing black-tie charity galas. Sometimes she attended book parties I hosted at my house. She was always a flyby guest who came alone, hovered coquettishly around powerful men, and left. I never really "got" Ghislaine, though we had many mutual friends. There was something about her hard, shiny edge and strained vivacity that suggested an unease at war with her self-confidence.

The truth behind her façade was that for Ghislaine, the plummeting from grace she experienced when her press baron father became a posthumous pariah— seen by all their former adulating social circle as a world-class racketeer—was incalculably traumatic.

In addition, her birth coincided with the car crash of her fifteen-year-old brother, who lingered in a coma for the next seven years. This meant her grief-stricken parents paid her no attention in her early life. Her father later overcompensated by turning his extroverted youngest daughter into the apple of his eye. The primary focus of Ghislaine's life was pleasing and performing for him. Eleanor Berry, daughter of then **Daily Telegraph** owner Lord Hartwell, tells an unsettling story of ten-year-old Ghislaine inviting her to come upstairs and see her bedroom at Headington Hill Hall. Berry noticed an odd-shaped hairbrush, a strap, a slipper, and other implements laid out on the child's dressing room table. Ghislaine said, rather proudly, "This is what Daddy uses to beat me with. But he always allows me to choose which one I want."

When considering the sadistic offering of power to the powerless, her father asking her, in essence, to procure herself for him, one can better understand how Ghislaine fell under the spell of a man like Epstein.

Prince Andrew was Ghislaine's biggest social catch to present to Epstein. He was easy to entertain and satiate. The thirty-nine-year-old prince was as interested in available women as he was in new streams of income. A now divorced horndog eternally on the hunt, with a guffawing, boob-ogling pickup style, Andrew had multiple relationships with different women in the decade after his divorce from Sarah Ferguson.

In January 2001, the Queen was less than gruntled when leaked snaps appeared of Andrew sunbathing on a yacht in Thailand with a gaggle of topless women. The reports of him trawling the red-light districts for action overshadowed his first months on the job as the British government's trade envoy. "One minute you're having your bum pinched and the next minute he is reminding you he is Your Royal Highness," a target of his interest reportedly complained.

The privacy of Epstein's Manhattan mansion and Caribbean island were a valuable perquisite to a prince always trying to avoid Palace censure and the scorn of the press. On visits to New York, when he was expected to stay at the comfortable, centrally located British consulate, Andrew preferred to bed down at Epstein's address only five short blocks away. The Prince stayed with Epstein so often he was given his own grandly decorated guest suite on the third floor. The sardonic Epstein christened it "the Britannica Suite." He even got Andrew out of his suits and ties and made him buy his first pair of sweatpants.

Andrew, Epstein, and Ghislaine became a peripatetic social trio—the Three Musketeers of Lust. In February 2000 they attended an event at Donald Trump's Mar-a-Lago resort in Florida. May 2000 flight records from the Lolita Express—as Epstein's plane was dubbed because of its cargo of young women—show that the Prince flew with Epstein and Maxwell to Palm Beach. Epstein's former handyman, Juan Alessi, alleges that Prince Andrew attended naked swimming pool parties at Epstein's El Brillo Way house, and was treated to massages by attractive girls. In sworn legal papers filed in 2011, Alessi described the house as being "full of pictures of naked young women, and said that the Prince stayed in a blue guest room which contained soap in the shape of male and female genitalia." He also claimed to have set up massage tables on which the royal guest was treated on a daily basis, but never saw him engage in anything untoward.

The quid pro quo to this licentiousness-on-tap was that Epstein got the cachet of attending and being photographed at Royal Ascot with Andrew and Ghislaine, and receiving an embossed invitation with Ghislaine— as the Duke of York's special guests—to the Queen's Dance of the Decades at Windsor Castle in June 2000. In December 2000, Andrew invited the couple for a weekend of pheasant shooting at the royal inner sanctum of Sandringham, a remarkable social ascent for Epstein, the son of a groundskeeper for public parks. Andrew insists that Epstein was there only as Ghislaine's plus-one—but three months after the Sandringham weekend, there they were again, partying together, this time in London.

It is the events of that night, March 10, 2001, that Prince Andrew is still answering tormenting questions about two decades later.

III

Thirty-eight-year-old Virginia Roberts Giuffre, now a married mother of three living comfortably in a suburb of Perth, Australia, on the substantial sum of money she received from winning the 2015

defamation suit she filed against Ghislaine for calling her a liar, is the disregarded girl who turned
into an avenger. A steady-eyed blonde with a composed demeanor, she is credible, appealing, and
direct, and she tells a story that, once heard, cannot
be forgotten.

When Giuffre first caught Ghislaine Maxwell's
eye in the summer of 2000, she was a lithe sixteen-
year-old working at Donald Trump's Mar-a-Lago
resort in Palm Beach as a locker-room attendant. It
was her first stable job after four years of being horribly exploited by predatory middle-aged men. She
had already been molested by a family member and
dispatched by her parents to a lockdown facility. At
the age of thirteen, she ran away and was picked up
at a bus stop in Miami by sixty-three-year-old Ron
Eppinger, who pimped out girls he imported from
Europe and kept Giuffre for himself. According to
her attorney, Brad Edwards, when Eppinger realized
the feds were on to him he stashed her in a barn
in the Ocala woods in northern Florida where he
brutally abused her, then offloaded her to a friend of
the owner of the garish Hot Chocolates club in Fort
Lauderdale, who showed her off as his "girlfriend."
When the FBI eventually caught up with the Eppinger
crew, Virginia was returned to the care of her father,
who worked as a maintenance man at Mar-a-Lago.
He got her a summer job there as a towel girl.

Virginia was leafing through a book about massage therapy on a bench outside the Mar-a Lago spa
when she was approached by a beautiful woman

with a cut-glass English accent. The book had given the perfect opening to Ghislaine for a conversation about a billionaire who lived nearby who was looking for a traveling masseuse.

The deal turned out to entail more than a back-rub. The depraved complicity between Epstein and Ghislaine was immediately clear to Virginia. She alleges that, while laughing, they made her strip down to her pathetic teenage-girl Hello Kitty underwear, then deftly assaulted her with the ball of a white plastic instrument. Ghislaine, she says, demonstrated how Epstein liked to have his nipples pinched, then told her to straddle him "until he finished." He apparently approved of Virginia's performance. "She's a keeper," he told Ghislaine after they showered.

Virginia said in an unpublished manuscript—"The Billionaire's Playboy Club," submitted as evidence in her lawsuit against Maxwell—that when she got home she was distraught, wondering why every path she took seemed to end in sexual abuse. But she was poor, and Epstein paid her more money than she had seen in her entire life.

For the next two years she became his on-call human sex toy, summoned at will and trained by Ghislaine. Ensconced nearby in an apartment Epstein rented for her, Virginia serviced him up to four times a day with erotic massages and oral sex, flying on his Boeing 727—often with a posse of other very young girls—between his homes in the Virgin Islands, New Mexico, and New York.

Ghislaine would often undress and join in. "Their

whole entire lives revolved around sex," Virginia has said. Epstein began to loan her out to his powerful friends. When a friend of Ghislaine's asked her what she thought of the girls she recruited, "she said, 'they're nothing, these girls. They are trash.'"

It's as if the more time Ghislaine spent around Epstein, the more she absorbed his darkness, and justified her actions by reverting to the amorality of her father. Robert Maxwell had also believed he was above the law. His "whiff of chicanery," as biographer John Preston calls it, could just as easily have described Epstein, with his arrogant, smirking, Houdini-like gift of escaping retribution.

A journalist friend of mine told me he once saw Ghislaine in action. He was with a group of friends that included her and the actor Liev Schreiber at Elio's restaurant in the aughts when a posse of beautiful seventeen- or eighteen-year-old models arrived and hung out at the bar. Ghislaine left the table and went over to introduce herself. "What's she doing?" my friend asked. "She's recruiting for Jeffrey," a guest at the table replied.

IV

For those inclined to rationalize Ghislaine's conduct by saying she was, herself, a victim of Epstein, the evidence is unsupportive. It was Ghislaine who industrialized Epstein's hitherto amateurish sexual operation and got the girls to ramp up the turnover by recruiting their own young friends.

One of the famous people to whom Virginia alleged she was trafficked was Prince Andrew. In a December 2014 affidavit sworn under oath, she said she had sex three times with Andrew—the first time in London in March 2001 when she was seventeen. (The flight records of Epstein's aircraft confirm that she flew with him and Ghislaine to London at that time.) On the morning of March 10, in Ghislaine's Belgravia townhouse, Virginia testified, Ghislaine told her, "You are going to meet a prince today," and in the evening, Prince Andrew arrived, and the four of them went to Tramp, the members-only Mayfair club marketed as "London's favorite place to misbehave." Andrew allegedly bought Virginia a drink, and they hit the dance floor in the VIP section. She recalled the Prince was a terrible dancer with overactive sweat glands. She said the four of them went back to Ghislaine's house, where the latter told her, "I want you to do for Andrew what you do for Epstein." Virginia says she obliged, calling it, in her unpublished memoir "the longest ten minutes of her life." She noted the Prince thanked her before he left and that Epstein paid her $15,000. She asserts that she and Andrew had sex again twice: at Epstein's home in New York City a month later, and then, with a group of other young women joining them, on Epstein's Caribbean island of Little St. James.

Her story might never have gained credence but

for the damning photograph that appears to corroborate her account. It was first published by **The Mail on Sunday** in March 2011, when Sharon Churcher persuaded Virginia to tell her story, and features Andrew and the then seventeen-year-old Virginia standing hip to hip on what appears to be the upstairs landing of a London townhouse. Andrew looks like a horny dad about to hit on the teenage babysitter. Virginia wears skintight, hip-hugging pants and a pink tank top, her arm clasped behind Prince Andrew and his arm clasped around her. Ghislaine looms behind them, beaming like a proud madam. Virginia said that Epstein took the picture on her disposable Kodak camera. The article that accompanied the damning picture detailed Virginia's abuse by Epstein, with Andrew's friend Ghislaine identified as his accomplice.

The Queen reportedly sent for her son when the article appeared and demanded that he explain himself. "The Duke assured his mother that he had no sexual relationship with Virginia Roberts or any of Jeffrey Epstein's girls," a Palace source told Edward Klein of **Vanity Fair**. "The Duke talked to the lawyers on the phone, and, with the approval of the Duke and his office, the lawyers drew up a legal document that was meant as a shot across the bow of the press in Britain." (Andrew later insisted that the picture had to be doctored because his real hands have fat fingers.)

The impending nuptials of William and Kate in April had to be safeguarded from any scandal in the

House of York. No doubt with a sigh, the Queen deployed a symbolic Exocet. She made it plain to the press that her second son had her full protection. She summoned Andrew to Windsor Castle and pinned on him the insignia of a Knight Grand Cross of the Royal Victorian Order. Yes, her highest gong. Prince Andrew GCVO was now entitled to wear the red-white-and-blue sash and the noble order's star-shaped insignia that connoted the monarch's deep appreciation of his personal service. The theater worked. The British press went strangely silent about Andrew's tawdry sub-rosa life and turned its attention to the national joy of the Cambridge wedding. In the reports that covered Andrew's exit as British trade ambassador in July 2011, none of them dwelt on the implications of the photograph with Virginia Roberts Giuffre.

Andrew duly hurled himself into a reputation rebrand with the aid of a canny new private secretary, Amanda Thirsk, a Cambridge-educated former banker. She had helped close the deal on the sale of Sunninghill Park to the Kazakh oligarch, and quickly became his closest aide. The strategy was to identify Andrew as the cheerleader for British entrepreneurs. In 2014, they launched Pitch@Palace, a platform for the most promising candidates from tens of thousands of entrepreneurs, selected to make their pitches to a live audience of venture capitalists and other would-be supporters at St. James's or Buckingham Palace.

For once it looked as if Andrew had a success on

his hands. The Pitch@Palace competition went global, with offshoot events in Africa, Australia, the United Arab Emirates, and China. There was applause for such outcomes as an HIV self-test kit; Stasher, a platform to let travelers find a place to stash their bags without checking into a hotel; and Magic Pony Technology, an AI start-up that Twitter scooped up for $150 million. **The Sunday Times** even dispatched their best-regarded business reporter, John Arlidge, to write a cover story on Andrew.

And yet, his shiftlessness could not remain hidden. After declaring to Arlidge, "I am an ideas factory!" the only idea Andrew could take credit for was allowing visitors to use their cell phones inside the Palace. Though Arlidge's team had spent two days negotiating where Andrew would pose for a cover photo, the Duke peremptorily refused to walk three paces to the appointed spot and do so.

The roasting Arlidge gave him made for painful reading for the Palace communications department. "Andrew said it was all the journalist's fault and blamed his staff. He would never admit he effed it up," one of them told me.

Ghislaine Maxwell, too, attempted a makeover of her reputation. She moved on from Epstein and dated Ted Waitt, the billionaire co-founder of Gateway computers, who purchased a triple-decker yacht and installed a submarine for her to pilot. In 2012 she founded a nonprofit named the TerraMar Project, little more than a website with no financial disbursements, to advocate for the sustainable management of the world's oceans. It gave her enough cred to glom on to the TED Talks circuit. The woman who in eight years would be behind bars as a notorious sex offender and procurer of underage girls was now ubiquitous at halo events like the Clinton Global Initiative and the Time 100 gala. She was even seen in 2013, and again in 2014, at the United Nations, giving a virtuous address that cast her as a guardian of our oceans. "She stopped talking about sex and started talking about dolphins," as one of her former friends put it.

But despite her hubris and her high profile, Ghislaine was apparently looking over her shoulder, aware that her past with Epstein would catch up with her. At one of these high-minded convenings, the then–West Coast editor of **The Daily Beast,** Gabé Doppelt, found herself seated next to Ghislaine at dinner. With a journalist's sharp curiosity, Doppelt asked her what it was like to "be [Ghislaine] right now."

"There was bread and butter on the table," Doppelt told me, "and Ghislaine picked up a pat of butter, rolled it into a ball, and proceeded to squash it flat with her fist.

"**Like that,**" she replied, with agonized ferocity.

CHAPTER
19

NUMBER SIX ON THE
CALL SHEET

Meghan Markle's World

EGHAN MARKLE HAD HAD IT WITH
Hollywood—big time. She'd just turned twenty-nine. It had been seven years since she'd graduated from the prestigious Northwestern University in Chicago with a double major in theater and international studies, and instead of being hailed as the next Angelina Jolie, she was stuck in the professional equivalent of Nowhere-stan.

Meghan knew she was destined to be a star from her earliest dazzle, when she played the secretary in a production of **Annie** at Immaculate Heart High School in the Los Angeles neighborhood of Los Feliz. She was raised on the well-tended fringes of the entertainment business. Her father, Tom Markle, worked as a successful lighting and photography director on the Fox comedy **Married . . . with Children** and the long-running ABC soap opera **General**

Hospital. When Meghan would hang around waiting for him in her Catholic school uniform on the set of **Married . . . with Children**, he would shoo her off to craft services during the racy scenes.

Her father's world was "below the line" show business, a milieu of technicians, production managers, and hair and makeup artists who are coddled by their unions but at a considerable remove from the romance of the Hollywood Walk of Fame. If Kate Middleton's story could have sprung from the pages of Trollope, Meghan's was in the back of bound copies of **Variety**. Tom Markle told Fox News that his daughter was first captivated by the red carpet's elusive glamour at the age of twelve, when he was nominated for an Emmy Award for his work on **General Hospital** and he took her as his date to the awards ceremony. "Meghan turned to me and said, 'Daddy, I want to be famous just like you one day.'" On weekends at his house, they watched Busby Berkeley movies together, and her biggest dream was to be a dancer like Eleanor Powell in the tap-dancing thirties.

As early as age eleven, she showed prodigious feminist resolve when she wrote a letter to Procter & Gamble protesting the sexist overtones of a TV ad. It depicted a sink full of dirty dishes with a voice-over intoning "Women are fighting greasy pots and pans with Ivory Clear." Meghan's initiative landed the earnest freckle-faced tween a spot on Nickelodeon's **Nick News**, deadpanning to host Linda Ellerbee that she didn't think "it's right for kids to grow up thinking these things—that just Mom does everything." P&G caved to this precocious telling-off and the next version of the ad announced that "**people** are fighting greasy pots and pans with Ivory Clear." It was an early lesson for Meghan in how to weaponize media successfully.

Tom was so proud of his daughter's progressive drive that he asked if **General Hospital**'s executive producer Wendy Riche would be her mentor on Take Our Daughters to Work Day. He wanted her to see a powerful woman in action. "He said, 'She's so bright and so committed in so many areas of life. I want her to be near the success you have and feel it and know she can achieve it,'" Riche told me. She found the twelve-year-old Meghan bright, positive, warm, alert, and already "aware of issues, a conscious young girl. I thought that was a wonderful thing Tommy did for her, and [what it said about] what he saw in her and wanted for her."

There's a video floating around on YouTube of the eighteen-year-old Meghan in 1999 taken by her best friend, Ninaki Priddy. It shows her cruising along Rodeo Drive in a car with a "Classy Girl" license plate frame talking about the dance audition she had just done for a Shakira video. "It's six hundred dollars for two days. I was really nervous that I was just gonna fall out of my top, I was shaking around so much." Calling out the names of the fancy designer stores they pass in the car, she's any middle-class high schooler window-shopping in the glamorous part of town. At college, she had her pick of the sought-after basketball hunks. She was always clear about who she wanted, her father told me. "Her first year at college, she pointed at one guy and said, 'That boy's going to be my boyfriend.' And he became her boyfriend. . . . She's very, very effective with men."

When she was fourteen, Tom Markle snagged her a tiny part as a young "candy striper" volunteer on **General Hospital.** Seven years later, he secured her first speaking part on the show playing a nurse, a cute background blur who chirrups, "I have his chart right here, Dr. Lambert." She found it disappointing that in the years since, there had been an irksome failure on the part of casting directors to see her as anything more than pass-through eye-candy.

Throughout her childhood, Meghan had struggled with feelings of alienation as the daughter of a white father and an African American mother, Doria Ragland, who divorced when Meghan was six. In seventh grade, Meghan left a census box requesting ethnicity blank. A teacher told her that, as she had to choose one, she should tick Caucasian because that's how she looked—a betrayal, Meghan felt, of the mother she adored. When she told her father what had happened, an irate Tom Markle counseled her: "If that happens again, you draw your own box."

In the early years of her career, her ambiguous ethnicity presented a problem for casting directors. Despite a "closet filled with fashionable frocks to make me look as racially varied as an Eighties Benetton poster," she wrote in an essay for **Elle,** "I wasn't black enough for the black roles and I wasn't white enough for the white ones, leaving me somewhere in the middle as the ethnic chameleon who couldn't book a job."

Growing up in L.A. in the 1980s and '90s, Meghan lived in a predominantly white neighborhood and became used to the distressing frequency with which her mother, a "sweet-eyed" yoga teacher much enamored of California's mindfulness philosophies, was mistaken for her nanny. Even her estranged half sister, Samantha Markle, says in a self-published memoir that she was taken aback by the instinctive racism exhibited by a friend at Taft High School when she first introduced the friend to Doria:

"She's black!"

"So?" I replied. I thought the question was rude and very awkward but I didn't know that Nicole came from a very homogenous family. I thought that racism ended when the 70s ended.

Alas, it did not. Meghan was nine when the vicious 1991 police beating of Rodney King took place. The acquittal, a year later, of the officers responsible triggered looting and arson on the streets of L.A. Meghan and her classmates were sent home. When she saw ash all over the lawns she passed, she thought at first that it was snow.

In high school, she grappled with how to fit in with the cliques of

black girls and white girls, the Filipino and the Latina girls. Being biracial, I fell somewhere in between. So every day during lunch, I busied myself with meetings—French club, student body, whatever one could possibly do between noon and 1pm—I was there. Not so that I was more involved, but so that I wouldn't have to eat alone.

As a teenager, she heard Doria called the N-word when she pulled out of a parking space too slowly for an impatient driver and saw her mother's eyes fill with tears. Not "reading" Black herself, she took on her mother's pain as a helpless witness.

II

Meghan was no breakout ingenue. Four years after her **General Hospital** debut, she was still hoofing it as one of twenty-six "briefcase girls" wearing a shimmery sateen minidress and gold stilettos on the NBC game show **Deal or No Deal.** The girls—all beauties, but none as vividly gorgeous as number twenty-four, Meghan Markle, with her blazing smile—were required to descend a neon-lit staircase en masse at the opening of the show to a raucous soundtrack of pelvic-thrusting electronic guitar music, and chorus "Hi, Howie!" at the rollicking game show barker Howie Mandel. The girl who opens the winning silver briefcase holding anywhere between one cent and a million dollars gets the most airtime. Throughout the 2006 and 2007 seasons in which she appeared, this was rarely Meghan's luck. "I would end up standing up there forever in these terribly uncomfortable and inexpensive five-inch heels just waiting for someone to pick my number so I could go and sit down," she has said. The show recorded up to seven episodes in a single day.

Backstage, the other briefcase girls noted that Meghan was never schmoozing. She was always working, reading scripts, calling her agent, or practicing her lines for her next audition. At night, she would go home and write a doleful anonymous blog about her rejections under the title **The Working Actress**. "I've had to freeze my [acting] union membership, borrow money, work jobs that I hated, endure being treated like s**t on a set, kiss actors with smelly breath and cry for hours on end because I just didn't think I could take it any more," lamented one entry. To make extra money, she freelanced as a calligrapher writing out wedding invitations and Dolce & Gabbana holiday correspondence.

From 2002 to 2011, Meghan's show clips are a parody of a young actress trapped in the male gaze. A 2006 episode of the CBS crime procedural **CSI: NY** features her wearing a sexy maid's outfit and delivering the line, "I may have slept with Grant Jordan, but I didn't kill him." In a 2008 episode of the Fox sitcom **'Til Death**, she's a car salesperson in a tight blue bustier over a T-shirt stroking a red open-topped Corvette. Her opening gambit, "You fellas interested in checking this baby out?," earns the reply, "We're here for donuts so you can save your seductively minty breath." In the morose 2010 melodrama **Remember Me,** panned for its "thunderously overwritten screenplay," she plays a bartender with one line and an attitude. In **Horrible Bosses,** shot the same year, she has a thirty-second cameo in a baseball hat on the receiving end of Jason Sudeikis's assessment, "You're way too cute to be just a FedEx girl."

To make matters even more galling, Meghan did not feel that her producer boyfriend, Trevor Engelson, was helping her get good parts. (He certainly didn't in **Remember Me,** which he produced.) Engelson was a shaggy, genial, high-energy producer and talent manager with a baritone Long Island voice. He had hustled his way to the middle of Hollywood's B-list and had his own management company. Nearly five years older than Meghan and included in **The Hollywood Reporter**'s "Next Gen 2009," a list of up-and-comers ages thirty-five and under, he was used to being the one she needed for connections in the industry. They lived together in Hancock Park, with beer pong and barbecues in the backyard on weekends. They had been together since she was twenty-three, and had a tender dynamic. When he went away on trips, Meghan always packed little love notes in his suitcases, and he was an enthusiastic champion of her on his social media accounts.

Though Engelson was more successful, Meghan exhibited greater ambition. She nagged him to be more aggressive. Friends remember how she urged him to make a more professional impression when they socialized with industry players who were potentially powerful. It irritated Meghan, too, that he seemed to have some exquisite integrity hang-up about pushing on her behalf for better roles—even though he knew plenty of people who could help her. She has described her twenties as "brutal— a constant battle with myself, judging my weight, my style, my desire to be as cool/as hip/as smart/as 'whatever' as everyone else."

In the summer of 2010, when her agent got her a read for the new USA Network drama **A Legal Mind** (as **Suits** was initially titled), Meghan was beside herself. Rachel Zane was a dream role. Set in the gleaming glass offices of a fictional Manhattan law firm, the script by former banker Aaron Korsh was— for a change—snappy and sophisticated. The Rachel Zane character was a self-confident paralegal who exuded Upper East Side class and had enough edge to make her a credible sparring partner of a cocky, boyish new associate attorney with a photographic memory.

A key requisite to play Rachel, the producers told me, was to be believable as a legal professional but also suggest an underlying softness. There had to be an instant sex appeal that made sparks fly in the two characters' meet-cute office orientation scene. A combination of all these qualities in an actress had proved stubbornly difficult to find. Casting director Bonnie Zane (they borrowed her surname when "Rachel Lane" threw up legal problems) went through 150 auditions before she sent her top choices up to the **Suits** decision makers: Aaron Korsh and executive producers David Bartis and Gene Klein. Bonnie Zane had minimal knowledge of Meghan before this cattle call. "She was just an actor for hire," she told me. "No reputation . . . I didn't know Meghan because her résumé was Hot Girl [in an Ashton Kutcher movie]." Happily, this was one audition where Meghan's indeterminate ethnicity was an asset. Director Kevin Bray is biracial himself and was actively pushing for diversity on the show, while middlebrow USA Network was trying to upgrade from being what James Wolcott in **Vanity Fair** called "a spa resort for tired eyes."

By the time of the **Suits** casting in 2010, issues surrounding mixed-race identity were beginning to bloom in the national consciousness. **The New York Times** noted in January 2011 that the latest crop of college students included the largest group of mixed-race people ever to come of age in the United States, a generation at the forefront of a demographic shift driven by immigration and intermarriage. Suddenly, after a long history of sparse roles for people of color, a fluid racial identity offered Hollywood cachet. "They wanted someone more street smart and urbane" for the Rachel part, Kevin Bray told me. "We didn't want the trope of the bouncin' and behavin' Breck hair ad, slow-motion girls coming in. . . . As soon as she walked in, Meghan blew that trope up." The zeitgeist had turned in Meghan's direction at last.

III

One morning in January 2020, I sat in the Terrace Room of the Sunset Tower Hotel in West Hollywood and watched Meghan's auditions for Rachel on casting director Bonnie Zane's iPad. Bonnie is soft-spoken and empathetic, with the long, untidy hair of someone consumed by oblivious passion for her craft and a soulful attachment to all "her" actors. For Meghan's first audition, Bonnie had read the part of the bumptious male attorney character, Mike Ross, who was attempting to hit on Rachel as she took him on a tour of the office. The clip shows Meghan in a youthful spaghetti-strap dress, less polished and more California than she is today. She is natural and freckly with too-shiny lip gloss, but she plays her Rachel lines with unpretentious poise. "I loved her," Bonnie says simply.

Meghan made the initial cut and got a callback. After Meghan read for the **Suits** creatives, director Kevin Bray knew immediately: "We need to bring this young lady back." Meghan thought she blew it. ("They always think they blew it," seen-it-all producer David Bartis said to me.) She called her agent, Nick Collins, at Gersh to bemoan how she had felt distracted and kept forgetting her lines. "I wanted it, and I lost my shot at it," she later described herself thinking.

But this was simple thespian insecurity. Meghan had made the cut again and was invited to test in front of network executives.

Scripted television shows are a complicatedly collaborative business with layers of deciders. Even when there is consensus on a show among the creative executives, network chiefs insist that other finalists must be brought to them in case they disagree. This is the moment when the second-level deciders are as stressed as the talent. So Meghan had to wow not only the showrunner and producers and director but ultimately the corporate uber-bosses at NBCUniversal: Jeff Wachtel, USA Network's chief of original programming at the time, and, over him, in New York, then NBCUniversal Cable Entertainment chairwoman Bonnie Hammer, one of the most powerful executives in television. She would watch the audition tapes, maybe in a moving car on her phone, and make the last call on Meghan's career.

On August 19, 2010, Meghan had her hair blown out at her local Drybar; dressed in jeans, heels, and a skimpy plum-colored top; and drove to the Tribeca West building on Olympic Boulevard in West L.A. for the next round. Told at the last minute that her character's outfit should be conservative—"think hair pulled back and business attire"—she grabbed a $45 black dress off a rack at H&M. All the contenders for Rachel read the same script pages for clear comparison. It was the scene where she asks, like the hopefuls auditioning to play her, to **just be given a chance.** "I'm smart. I know I'd be a good lawyer, but I can't take tests. I don't know what happens to me. I bombed the LSATs. Even if I could get into a law school, there's no way I'd ever pass the bar."

"Even [an established player] has to go into a cold room with bad lighting and bad carpeting at the corporate offices in Burbank and stand in front of twelve people and act," Aaron Korsh told me. The audition process can rattle some actors so much that their agents try to negotiate showing only an artist's taped performances to the deciders. Adding to the tryout tension, the final round of candidates all have hope-inflating option deals pre-negotiated to ensure that, if chosen, they are immediately available. After the pilot is shot, everyone involved, whether veteran or ingénue, has to spend months waiting to find out if the network will pick it up. Will they be employed, sometimes in a contract that spans multiple years and might mean relocating to a different city, or will they be abruptly out of work and back to square one?

Meghan was used to a world of wait-and-see. Unlike the steady generational ascendance of the Middleton family in England, her family had a history of rootless lateral movement. Her mother's paternal ancestors were Georgia slaves whose descendants lit out for California. Her grandparents, Alvin and Jeanette, settled in Cleveland, Ohio, until, in 1956, Alvin drove the family cross-country to Los Angeles to be nearer the Ragland relations and open an antiques shop. In a 2012 public service announcement about racism, Meghan talked about how, as they traversed the United States, her grandparents stopped at a Kentucky Fried Chicken and were sent to the back door for "coloreds" and had to eat their food in the parking lot.

Until she got a college degree as an adult, their daughter Doria drifted between jobs as a makeup artist, yoga teacher, travel agent, and owner of a small gift shop called Distant Treasures.

Meghan's father, big Tom Markle, with his sandy hair and sturdy neck, was one of three brothers of Alsatian stock in small-town Pennsylvania. All three of them did well. One of Tom's brothers became a diplomat and the other a bishop. As soon as Tom was old enough, he took off for the Poconos to work in theater and learn his trade as a lighting director. At eighteen, he moved west to Chicago, where he secured a job at a local news station. He married a local secretary at nineteen; fathered two children, Samantha and Tom Jr.; and ten years later hit the road without them to forge a career in Hollywood. He met the enchantingly petite Doria Ragland, twelve years his junior, when she was a temp makeup artist on **General Hospital.** She was as hippie-dippie and New Age as he was burly and work driven. In a Mother's Day blog post in 2014, Meghan extolled Doria's tasty, healthy cooking and recalled her mother "carefully tossing fresh herbs into the salad, and knowing when the shrimp in the gumbo was juuuuust right." She also celebrated her mother's **joie de vivre:**

Dreadlocks. Nose ring . . . Lover of potato chips & lemon tarts. And if the DJ cues Al Green's soul classic "Call Me," just forget it. She will swivel her hips into the sweetest little dance you've ever seen, swaying her head and snapping her fingers to the beat like she's been dancing since the womb.

Meghan's half sister, Samantha, remembers Doria drifting around the lawn in a bathrobe dreamily smoking.

Tom and Doria were married by a Hollywood guru of the simple life, Brother Bhaktananda, at Sunset Boulevard's Self-Realization Fellowship, shrine of the Hindu guru Yogananda, a stone's throw from the Church of Scientology. Doria wore a little white dress with a Peter Pan collar and a spray of baby's breath in her hair. Meghan was born nearly two years later, in 1981, and was the gurgling apple of her parents' eye.

What broke up Tom Markle's second marriage was residual tension from his first. His two teenage children, Samantha and Tom Jr., were living with him and Doria in Santa Monica before the blended family moved to the bigger house in the prosperous middle-class enclave of Woodland Hills. Samantha, seventeen years older than her baby half sister and eight years younger than her stepmother, seethed with adolescent resentment. She had dreams of being an actress and kept hassling her father to get her parts. Tom Jr. was a high school stoner who slept on a waterbed and hung around with irritating friends smoking weed and fighting with Samantha. When gorgeous, golden Meghan was born, Tom was so besotted with her that Samantha felt even more dis-placed and unattractive, like a "pear on stilts," as she described her appearance. She became curdled with jealousy, the bad fairy at the christening of the serenely sleeping future princess. Over the years, her resentment only grew when her father forked over money from their tight budget to send Meghan to a series of private schools. It was a bitter blow when her radiant half sister's career took off shortly after Samantha learned she had developed multiple sclerosis. She was eventually confined to a wheelchair.

Tom, no doubt relieved to be out of the contentious atmosphere, was rarely home. He had earned himself an enviable reputation and was much in demand, now earning around $200,000 a year. "I always felt safe with him creatively," Wendy Riche told me. "I trusted him. He was professional. Kind. Totally dependable and trustworthy and had a big, big heart." He was beloved by the crew too. The price of bringing in a good salary, however, was a relentless production schedule. He worked grueling hours, going over the lighting script with the director during the daytime, then returning to work from midnight to seven in the morning to light the set before shooting started. (He still seems to live on an eccentric schedule. When I spoke to him at his retirement redoubt on a hilltop in Rosarito, Mexico, he asked me to call him at three A.M.)

"It was a weird life," former **General Hospital** director Shelley Curtis Litvack said to me. "Tommy didn't have a lot of friends. He would never stay for the **General Hospital** parties. He was very private." He rented a small apartment near the studio so he could grab a nap when he had an hour to spare. The perennial Hollywood insecurity of being without a paycheck never left him. His whole world was on set. He may have been beloved for his equable temperament at work, but at home, unless playing with his "beautiful bean" Meghan, he was too drained to be any fun for his young wife. Doria couldn't take it anymore. She scooped up two-year-old Meghan and left him to go live with her mother until she found her own place in the Mid-Wilshire neighborhood of Los Angeles. They were divorced four years later.

Meghan the adorable, the little fashionista who was soon attending tap and ballet classes and who was nicknamed "Flower" by her mother, turned out to be the smartest one in the family about money. Both her parents and her half sister went bankrupt. Her mother's gift shop business cratered in 2002 when Meghan was a junior in college. Her father filed for bankruptcy twice, the last time in 2016 when his property was valued at under $4,000 and his credit card debt at $33,000. Markle told me most of his savings went to contributing to Meghan's Northwestern education and helping out his other two children. He underwrote a florist business for Tom Jr., paid Meghan and Samantha's union dues when they couldn't, and funded expensive stem cell treatment for Samantha's MS. Whatever the truth of where the money went, he lives humbly if comfortably today in his Rosarito aerie.

When Meghan received the final callback for Rachel Zane, she had no idea that this would be her sliding-doors moment that would replace years of demeaning bit parts and scraping-by wages with a multiyear contract playing a non-moronic role in a buzzy show. She sat outside the faceless production office with another nervous would-be Rachel, Cuban American actress Arlene Tur, waiting to be summoned. Meghan felt intimidated when she encountered a statuesque Afro-Latina goddess in the waiting room. This was forty-one-year-old Gina Torres, who won a starring role as senior law partner Jessica Pearson. (She was a compelling presence on **Suits**, striding around in a couture wardrobe and growling with a quiet power, "I will see you in court!")

It was nerve-racking for Meghan that Tur, who was her same physical type, boasted better credits. There was another contender, Kim Shaw, a girl-next-door blonde who was still in the running from a previous round. Shaw's last TV offering, an MTV comedy titled **I Just Want My Pants Back**, might not, on the face of it, sound promising, but it was produced by **Suits** combo David Bartis and Gene Klein, who thought she was terrific.

The finalists were required to audition with rising Canadian leading man Patrick Adams, already cast as the hotshot newcomer attorney Mike Ross. This was the so-called chemistry read to give producers a sense of how they played against each other. The casting of Adams was good news for Meghan. She had done a pilot with him several years before for a show that wasn't picked up. Their on-camera vibes had been good. Chemistry on-screen doesn't necessarily mean sexual attraction. As Bray defined it to me, chemistry is "an organic fluidity about the way they are communicating, where you suspend belief and feel they are really talking to each other in this cold, antiseptic room with seventeen people watching."

The rapport between Meghan and Patrick was immediately clear. The scene has her miming the tour round the law firm, opening and shutting imaginary doors, and deftly blowing him off when he, as Rachel/Meghan puts it, "ogl[es]" her. She has gained in crisp allure since the first audition. There's a firmness about her performance, a forthright intelligence confident enough to project clear-eyed self-esteem. Bray remembers: "Everyone to a man in the room said, 'Where did **she** come from?' It was like group hypnosis." Meghan projected such an uptown aura you would never know that she had arrived at the audition in a rattling secondhand Ford Explorer that required her to climb in through the trunk, as her dwindling bank account would not allow her to get the broken door locks fixed.

The choice was a no-brainer. "She just intrigued us," one of the show's producers told me.

There was an organic attractiveness to her that didn't play to any type. She wasn't a type. She was an interesting human that you just wanted to know more about. So it was a combination of curiosity and kind of a twinkle and ambition that you just somehow knew or believed she would succeed.

Meghan got the call from her agent on August 24, 2010: Rachel was hers. She had been cast in the pilot that would shoot in Manhattan in the fall. Who cared at that moment if the pilot was not picked up? It was validation after eight scrappy years. In 2015, she described in a blog post everything that flowed from this pivotal career moment:

> I had no idea that this late August morning would change my life. That I would get the part. That I would live in a little apartment in Manhattan to shoot the pilot. That over a lunch of lentil salad and muhammara on Beverly Drive, I would get a call saying we were picked up. That I would film the series in Canada. That I would grow up, and still be silly, or that I would find friends in my castmates. First, I was a girl at an audition. Then, I was a girl who got the part. Now I'm a woman who's starting the fifth season of that show. I remember that day like it was yesterday. My cheeks still hurt from how hard I smiled.

There was one milestone omitted from Meghan's reverie. In between shooting the pilot in New York and the seismic news that the show had been green-lit for the next TV season, Trevor Engelson proposed to her on a romantic vacation in Belize. **Suits** required a five-year commitment to live for nine months at a stretch in a different city for shooting (not New York as it turned out, but, for budget reasons, Toronto). She signed on without hesitation. The first season debuted in June 2011 to strong reviews and pleasing attention. Shortly after it wrapped, Meghan married Trevor in a barefoot wedding in Ocho Rios, Jamaica.

The wedding earned a brief write-up in **The Hollywood Reporter.** The bride wore a simple white notch dress with a sparkling silver waistband. "She was 'marrying up,' " her half brother, Tom Markle, Jr., who wasn't there, allegedly said. A planeload of entertainment industry friends came down for four days of partying on the white beach. Both her parents were present—a guest noted how "chill and gracious" Doria was and that Tom Markle bought two seats on the plane for comfort. Meghan and Trevor were lifted aloft in the traditional chair dance, and there was a wheelbarrow race for which Meghan wore a yellow bikini. It was low-key, unpretentious, and informal.

The only jarring note, one wedding guest remembers, is that in the itinerary Meghan sent out was a note requesting "No social media, please."

"We were all laughing because she had been on **Suits** for a few months at that point and we were like, is she kidding me?" the guest told me. "She was already like, 'I'm a really big actress.' " Afterward, the bride returned to Toronto and the groom to L.A. The new Mr. and Mrs. Trevor Engelson settled into a married life that would primarily be conducted on Skype.

Her **Working Actress** blog, that anonymous ballad

of thwarted ambition, had to find a new author. Meghan was now earning around $50,000 an episode. Meghan's next online literary offering would be a stylishly designed lifestyle effort she called The Tig after her favorite full-bodied red wine, Tignanello. (Moments of revelation about life's meaning were termed "Tig moments.") It featured an arty black-and-white "candid" of its creator at the top and roamed between recipes for coconut chai smoothies and suggestions for bath products made by women survivors of domestic abuse. The Tig was an exfoliated, liberal-leaning world of undiscovered travel destinations, soft chats with "influencers" synonymous with Meghan's upward trajectory, and women's empowerment causes where even victims looked their best.

The airbrushing of Meghan's life had officially begun. One who swiftly found he didn't fit the new picture was her husband, whose career was not on the upswing. For nearly two years, Trevor rearranged his life to spend sojourns working from Toronto, but Meghan rarely reciprocated. Trevor started to dread she was going to dump him. A friend tells me she remembers running into him at a wedding where he confided mournfully, "She's not coming back anymore. We are not really talking that much. This is getting ridiculous. She's in another country and we're barely seeing each other. . . . [I have] this awful feeling she's just going to become huge and leave me."

One weekend when he came to see her in Toronto,

she told him she was out of love and it was over. "He
was hurt beyond anything," a woman in his circle
told me. "He was in a lot of pain." He told her, "I am
doing what most men do in this situation. Going
out with a different woman every night." She added,
"He's a decent guy. . . . It was very quick and he
wasn't expecting it. He felt used." Shortly after
Meghan delivered the coup de grâce, a package arrived for Trevor by registered mail in Los Angeles. It
contained his wife's diamond engagement ring and
her gold wedding band.

IV

Toronto, the capital of Ontario, is one of the most
multiethnic and international cities in the world. In
the mid-2000s, it was also a model of immigrant
absorption.

Had **Suits** been shot in New York as the producers
and stars so ardently wanted, Meghan might have
been swallowed up by a city unimpressed by minor
cable stars. In L.A., the entertainment world is
sprawling yet insular. Thousands of Meghans churn
through unremarked. Toronto's charm is that it's
both cosmopolitan and provincial. There's a perme-
able elite that's easy to navigate. Toronto resembles
London in that the political, journalistic, and theatrical worlds all sit at the same table, but it's profoundly
different from London in its equable absence of
snark.

The success of such homegrown music phenom-
ena as the rapper Drake and his R&B protégé the
Weeknd, the adventurous creativity of the annual
Toronto Film Festival, and the explosion of every
denomination and flavor of restaurant catering to
the cascade of immigrants added a cultural swagger
not previously associated with Canada's bland persona. So did tax breaks that drew an influx of overseas
film and TV productions, like **Suits**, using Toronto's
gleaming skyline to stand in for any and every city in
North America. When Soho House, the London-
based membership club for status cultivators, opened
an outpost in 2012 in a three-story Georgian building known as the Bishop's Block, Toronto could
officially claim a cool factor.

For an aspiring cosmopolite like Meghan, who
had always felt othered by her mixed race, the city's
ambience provided a heady cultural and social
accelerant. Within a couple of years, she was hob-
nobbing with the son of former prime minister
Brian Mulroney, TV host Ben Mulroney, and his
style-queen wife, Jessica; the heartthrob crooner
Michael Bublé; and an assortment of celebrity chefs
and film and fashion floaters. As soon as Trevor was
ushered out of the picture, she started dating, first
linked to a hockey hunk named Michael Del Zotto
and, for the two years before she met Harry, the
golden-boy chef Cory Vitiello, who was named as
one of Canada's most beautiful people and whose
restaurant, the Harbord Room, was a hangout for **le
tout Toronto.**

The launch of Instagram in 2010 was a critical tool in Meghan's aspirational arsenal. For those with a fashionable eye and a convincing knack for seeming authentic, Instagram was the new fast track to becoming sort-of famous. To goose ratings, the **Suits** promotion team advised the show's cast to stoke their social media accounts. No one did so more assiduously than Meghan. She rented a cozy three-bedroom house in a hipster district of Toronto and decorated it in the Instagram-ready style of a boutique hotel, right down to the Diptyque candles and shelves of color-coordinated books. Shout-outs to Noam Chomksy's furrow-browed tome **Who Rules the World?** and to **Drift,** a Rachel Maddow treatise on the unmooring of American military power, hinted to her followers that the books were not just adornment. Her two photogenic rescue mutts, Bogart and Guy, one of them procured at the urging of Ellen DeGeneres from a Hollywood dog shelter favored by those in search of furry Instagram enhancers, made frequent cameos. She became known for hosting—and cooking—intimate, groovy dinners that showed off her foodie skills and oeno cred. Her idea of the perfect day, she told **Glamour** magazine, was quintessential California girl in exile:

> Going for a trail run in the ravine with my rescue mutt, Bogart, then going to the farmers' market to get some seasonal produce to grill up with a whole fish and bottle of rosé with friends in my backyard. I grill on a Big Green

Egg (which was my birthday gift to myself last year and this awesome ceramic grill), and I'm obsessed.

The **Suits** gang was a tight-knit unit, especially for the first two years before they knew the show was an assured success. Gina Torres and Sarah Rafferty both became Meghan's close friends. She called them her "sister-wives." Not knowing anyone in Toronto, the cast bonded, with Patrick Adams, a Toronto native, as their glue. They would all drive up north to his house on Lake Huron for three-day weekends with their coolers to play Apples to Apples and charades and drink Scotch. "When I came back to [direct] shows, we would celebrate and party together," Kevin Bray told me. "It was a family."

Like any family, however, there was rivalry. Meghan was desperate to make Rachel Zane more than a support player in the **Suits** lineup. It was vexing that she was not listed higher on the call sheet, that all-important document in the world of film and TV production that's sent out at night by the assistant director to the cast and crew as the strategy map for the next day's shooting. The call sheet is more than a memo to actors stipulating what time and where each should show up. It's also a status register, which makes the whole concept fraught. There can be actors who are listed higher but earn less than an actor further down. The call sheet, one TV producer explained to me, is mostly about the importance of the character in the greater world of the show and how impressive an actor's bargaining leverage is at the time when contracts are signed.

The dream of every rising player is to be listed on the call sheet at number one, with all the perks that go with it—car and driver, your own trailer on location, the first consult on disruptive schedule changes, and generous expenses that include a sheaf of airline tickets for weekends. For the seven years she performed on **Suits**, Meghan Markle was number six on the call sheet.

One of the most influential voices with the show's producers was the veteran TV character actor Rick Hoffman. Meghan quickly sensed his clout and made him her advocate with the executive producers. She asked him to lobby them to get her a car and driver, a bold request because a chauffeured car is a much-desired perk allocated to players listed at number one and two. It was a "safety issue," she argued, because she was working so late and starting so early. Concerned for her well-being, he got it for her.

Meghan was beloved by the show's producers because she never said no to promotion. "Anytime we asked anything extra to be done, whether it was a fundraiser, whether it was supporting the show, going to a Television Critics Association event, basically glad-handing with any of the sales folks and clients . . . Meghan always raised her hand and said, 'Sure, I'll do it,'" I was told by one of the show's executives. "She never complained. She never asked for an extra penny. . . . Meghan would always say, 'I'm there.'" In return, Meghan was able to make

Suits executives powerful sounding boards. She sought advice from producers about how to increase her part "without looking like it's a land grab . . . and expand her role from just a young paralegal to eventually get to the place where she could be part of a true ensemble."

Meghan achieved that up to a point, moving Rachel Zane away from scenes where the script demanded she enter wearing a towel to ones where she became what **The New York Times** in 2018 described as the "show's moral conscience," developing a much-discussed dynamic with her powerful father, played by Wendell Pierce. While Meghan worked to change Rachel, Rachel also changed Meghan. Jolie Andreatta's polished wardrobe choices of tight pencil skirts that fit within an exhale, tastefully unbuttoned fitted white shirts, and sky-high nude heels were wrapped into Meghan's psyche as much as her person. Promotional junket videos show her more confident and sleek with every performance. On **The Tig,** she wrote increasingly about fashion that made her feel "like a lady," "discerning palates," "fancy friends, and role models that make the earth shake." Plugs for cosmetics, travel destinations, restaurants, and self-care products made **The Tig** a dragnet for luxury freebies. She won a reputation amongst the marketers of luxury brands of being warmly interested in receiving bags of designer swag. A publicist for one of them, I am told, was cc'd in a message to a member of Meghan's team soon after she became the Duchess of Sussex. "Make sure [the publicist] knows that she can still send me anything. She's always been one of the good ones." In 2015, to celebrate **Suits** being picked up for a third season, Meghan treated herself to a $5,000 Cartier watch like Rachel's.

Jessica Mulroney—a buzzed-up Toronto taste-maker as well as Ben's wife—was Meghan's thirty-something role model in style and new BFF. Meghan has always been astute in flattering fashionable and famous women and absorbing their networks. There's a long list of strategic besties—Misha Nonoo, the internationally connected British-Bahraini fashion designer; Serena Williams, whom she love-bombed at a 2010 Super Bowl party in Miami; actress Priyanka Chopra, co-opted at a 2016 **Elle** Women in Television dinner; and, soon to come, her ultimate ace-in-the-hole, Oprah Winfrey. Childhood friends like Ninaki Priddy, her closest confidante throughout her school days, hit the bricks like Trevor Engelson.

Physically, Jessica Mulroney could have been Meghan's sister and was just as tireless. She had turned her private life into a permanent destination wedding, posting a ceaseless flow of images about her glossy existence. As a fashion stylist cum marketer, Jessica marked everything in her world with a hashtag. Her own three-day nuptials were covered on Canadian television news, her parenting became a partnership with Pampers, and her trips to the gym a promotional opportunity for Adidas. It could not have escaped Meghan's notice that a crucial factor in Jessica's commercial leverage was her famous husband. "The Brandtastic Life of Ben and Jessica" was the title of a **Toronto Life** magazine puff piece on the Mulroneys. Meghan posted gushing tributes to Jessica's fabulosity and vice versa, with images of their long hair intermingling as they traveled, partied, and savored foodie favorites in matching ripped jeans.

She absorbed Jessica's tactics like a sea sponge. But what sealed her upward trajectory in Toronto was her alliance with the Canadian-born global membership director of Soho House, Markus Anderson, a stubble-chinned social animal who started his career as a waiter in the original London club and rose through the ranks to become the chain's global arbiter of who was—and wasn't—worthy of the exalted status of "influencer." As Meghan's plus-one and travel companion, he was a walking version of Raya, the infamous dating and social connector app. Without Markus's networking skills and Soho House connections, it's unlikely Meghan would have penetrated gilded London circles.

Soho House was Meghan's glide path into a newly porous and aggressively mobile world of shortcut social climbing. Its members had jobs that older clubs neither understood nor welcomed: brand consultants, global marketing gurus, technology evangelists, creative directors, impact investors, media advisers, and movie "gonnabes" (a Soho House term of art). These and other fashion-forward status foragers were "curated" (not "invited," a word that suggests old-fashioned social familiarity) by a membership board drawn from sectors deemed cool by the management. During the Toronto Film Festival, the club was a required pit stop for every movie star in town. Its blended affluence from different sectors gave Meghan entry into the rootless tribe that goes to Art Basel Miami Beach every winter and Mykonos every July, and shares an equal appreciation of bok choy and branding. For three years, usually with Markus Anderson in tow, the club's outposts in far-flung places dictated the direction of most of Meghan's foreign travel. Its social and attitudinal aesthetic defined her relentlessly ambitious world.

V

The rest of the **Suits** team were unaware of Meghan's strenuous efforts to move upward. "You didn't hear about it and she didn't put it up front, but she's playing three-dimensional chess with you," Kevin Bray told me. "Moves that seem like natural moves are moves that are yielding, you know, successful circumstances for just being at the right place at the right time."

The show was mostly filmed in a bleak concrete hangar on a former military base on the outskirts of Toronto where Meghan had to mooch around waiting to be called on set. The hours were brutal. She often was still on set at four A.M. She spent the downtime furiously updating **The Tig**, which she was convinced, not without reason, could emulate the success of Goop, Gwyneth Paltrow's canny second-act creation of a pampering and wellness e-commerce site, with its $550 healing quartz necklaces and $66 yoni eggs for enhanced orgasms. Much mocked by the highbrow press (and attacked for its casual charlatanism), Goop developed an adoring following of millennials that attracted big investment and ultimately became a $250 million business. "Meghan was always talking about Goop," one of the **Suits** team told me.

Viewed today, **The Tig** is impressive for its distinctive minimal elegance and sisterly point of view. It was better than most digital offerings from fashion magazines and was recognized with Best of the Web nods from **Elle** magazine and **InStyle**. What it lacked was Paltrow's sly positioning that she was in on the joke of monetizing eyeballs. The wink-wink sensationalism of Goop's "This Smells Like My Vagina" candle would never have found itself onto Meghan's earnestly tasteful **Tig**. Nonetheless, she soon had a notable following and was humblebragging about being the "little engine that could." Toronto's leading gossip maven Lainey Lui says that by the end of her Toronto sojourn, Meghan was more interesting as the author of **The Tig** than she was as an actress on **Suits**. **The Tig**, Meghan hoped, could be the vehicle that would take her from being an actress forever on the hunt for parts to the lucrative status of a global brand.

But Meghan's Plan B was taking too long. There was a growing dissonance between the cosmopolitan glamour of her Soho House world and the reality of professional opportunity. The movie roles she managed to snag between seasons were a creative sinkhole, indicative of the crapshoot that awaited her after **Suits.** She played an L.A. party girl in the unreviewed low-budget rom-com **Random Encounters;** a lovelorn journalist in the Hallmark TV movie **When Sparks Fly,** which earned a 12 percent audience rating on Rotten Tomatoes; and the girlfriend of a reluctant criminal in **Anti-Social,** a crime drama in which the car heists were deemed to have "all the energy of a dead battery."

Suits, as Meghan saw it, was handicapped by USA Network's mainstream-vanilla positioning in the cable firmament. While the show was popular (during the second season it became the most-watched cable show in the United States among viewers in the 18–49 age bracket), it wasn't even picked up in Canada for the first two years she was there. If **Suits** had been aired on HBO, it might have commanded more cultural cachet. If it had aired on NBC like **Friends,** she could have been the next Jennifer Aniston. She constantly badgered the show's public relations team and independent PR agents to get her on big-time talk shows, but all she could land were small-fry digital entertainment bookings. "Our business is full of people like Meghan," one publicist who encountered her at this time told me. "In it to win it, absolutely focused on fame, celebrity, relevance. You can pick them out in a lineup." But most of her invitations came from Toronto gigs like a

Jimmy Choo shoe store opening at a mall or as the celebrity presence at an Equinox health club gala.

In 2013, she made a career fishing trip to London to see Jonathan Shalit, chairman of the InterTalent Rights Group agency and a big deal in the British entertainment industry. **Suits** had developed something of a cult following in the UK and he was charmed, he told me, by her warmth and poise. He thought he could secure her TV shows and stage work—"**Celebrity MasterChef** would have loved her," he said—but with only a few months off in her shooting schedule, the potential at the time for more projects was slim. "The message we had for her is: London is a great place to work. People love you, come here."

Encouraged, she asked British publicist Neil Ransome, who mostly repped reality stars, to place stories about her in the British press. **Sunday People**'s entertainment editor and gossip columnist Katie Hind described how Ransome called several times before she agreed to meet Meghan on a cold November night in 2013 for a drink on the rooftop of the Karma Sanctum Soho Hotel. Hind did so only with the additional promise that the cocktails would flow on Ransome's marketing tab. Meghan meeting Hind is evidence of a certain desperate flailing. If you are looking to become an upmarket London scene maker, the last place you would start is the **Sunday People**. Meghan offered up her usual girly bonding routine, telling Hind that the footballer Ashley Cole kept looking for a date with her on social media. Hind made Cole's pursuit the subject of an item she wrote about their encounter. The following week, she noted that her interviewee was pictured at a red-carpet event on the arm of an eligible male model—"an old PR ruse designed to set tongues wagging."

Unable to break out beyond a few random articles in women's magazines and some perky panel spots at cable festivals, Meghan cast about for endorsement deals and appearances at women's empowerment fests. She reshaped her résumé to shine up her feminist credentials. Her father's contribution to her Northwestern tuition was eliminated from her list of "scholarships, financial aid programs, and work study [earnings]" by the time she addressed a gathering at the University of the South Pacific in 2018.

She networked the hell out of New York Fashion Week, but hunting for endorsements was like her pre-**Suits** audition days all over again. Her best score was a brand ambassadorship with Reitmans, a midmarket Canadian women's clothing store, which launched an "aspirational girl-next-door" collection inspired by her Rachel Zane character. (Reitmans got lucky when the second collection in 2016 coincided with growing rumors about Meghan's relationship with Prince Harry, and the collection flew off the racks.) She signed on with a minor London speaking and appearance agency, Kruger Cowne, which helped her secure $10,000 red-carpet engagements. More promising was the agency's representation of the One Young World Summit, a well-reviewed convening of emerging global youth leaders that was nudging into the UN space. Her new agent, Gina Nelthorpe-Cowne, mentioned it to her at their first meeting when Meghan opened the door wearing a bathrobe in a hotel suite she was sharing with then-boyfriend Cory Vitiello. Her eyes lit up. She asked Cowne to get her into that, pronto.

VI

Meghan always knew how to surf the zeitgeist. **The Tig** vehicle, the avid brand building, the use of the self-esteem bandwagon to write sensitive women's magazine essays. It is easy to understand her impatience with the shabby clawing after shiny bits and pieces. Writing in **The Working Actress,** she had evoked still-familiar pressures:

> I work long hours. I travel for press. My mind memorizes. My mind spins. My days blur. My nights are restless. My hair is primped, my face is painted, my name is recognized, my star meter is rising, my life is changing.

By 2014, she was famished for prestige, frantic for validation. Stars like Angelina Jolie, Cate Blanchett, and Nicole Kidman were UN goodwill ambassadors, traveling the world in their halos and talking about hunger and refugees. **That should be her!** It seemed not to count that at the age of eleven she had bent

Procter & Gamble to her feminist will, that she had majored in international relations at Northwestern, or that she had worked at the U.S. embassy in Argentina her senior year (the internship procured by her diplomat Markle uncle). All around her were actors and models blabbing bromides on network talk shows and magazine covers about things they knew nothing about and their right to have a "voice."

The challenge was to break into the celebrity and humanitarian nexus that would spring her from the cable ghetto. It did not matter that her first foray—a One Young World panel at their fired-up 2014 summit in Dublin about "the role media plays in the gender gap"—featured a less than stellar lineup of a YouTube makeup star, an Anheuser-Busch executive, and corporate suit from GE. At least it was a start. And Meghan was fresher and more cogent than the others on the panel. In a question about gender portrayal on the big screen versus television, she made the point that in TV the audience assumed almost claustrophobic intimacy because you were right there with them eating pizza in their living room, whereas if you were on the big screen like Angelina Jolie (never far from her mind) you were "larger than life." One senses the longing.

Girl-crush pieces on fashionable women on **The Tig** were replaced by magazine essays about her raised social conscience:

While most become star struck by A-list actors, you'll only see me in awe of leaders effecting change. Politician and diplomat Madeleine Albright, UN Secretary General Ban Ki-moon. These are my heroes. These are my celebrities.

Meghan always did her homework. To penetrate the United Nations, she pitched herself to learn more about its mission by shadowing Elizabeth Nyamayaro, senior adviser to South African powerhouse Phumzile Mlambo-Ngcuka, former under-secretary-general and executive director of UN Women. She had come to the right place. Nyamayaro, a stunning forty-year-old Zimbabwean overachiever, was considered something of a piece of work herself, mowing down the stuffier old guard at the UN in the launch of a flashy, celebrity-heavy campaign called HeForShe whose mission was to co-opt men to advocate for women. It launched with a bang at the 2014 UN General Assembly in New York with an address by UN goodwill ambassador Emma Watson (hosted by Nyamayaro) that netted over four million views on YouTube.

Meghan was determined to be next, and Nyamayaro was receptive. Meghan eagerly took off with UN Women representatives to Rwanda to visit the Gihembe refugee camp and spend time in Kigali with female parliamentarians. It was a **Tig** moment! In an essay in **Elle,** she describes receiving a message from her managers saying that a high-end jewelry company wanted to fly her in for the red carpet at the BAFTA Awards, the British equivalent of the Oscars, something she admits she had always longed to do:

"My brain, heart, and spirit couldn't shift gears that quickly, from the purpose-driven work I had been doing all week in Rwanda to the polished glamour of an awards show. 'No,' my heart said. And it wasn't a soft whisper; it was a lion's roar."

The roar was soon heard at the UN Women's 2015 summit, which marked the twentieth anniversary of the Fourth World Conference on Women in Beijing, where Hillary Clinton had first uttered the words "Women's rights are human rights." Behind that podium at UN headquarters in New York, wearing a serious black dress on International Women's Day, was exactly where UN Women's advocate for political participation and leadership Meghan Markle wanted to be. She knocked off her speech with dazzling aplomb. "Women need a seat at the table," she declared in clarion tones. "They need an invitation to be seated there and, in some cases, where this isn't available, well then you know what, then they need to create their own table." Tom Markle had first taught her that when he told her to draw her own box. Her guest that day was her mother, who saw that Flower was in glorious bloom. Also in the audience was Hillary Clinton, to whom, as First Lady, the eleven-year-old Meghan had lobbed a letter about the infamous P&G ad. Meghan told the story in her speech. In all, it was a tour de force one might think would kick her up to the main stage at the World Economic Forum at Davos the next year.

And yet . . . the traction outside the audience that day was minimal. If you googled "UN speech

Meghan Markle" at the time, Emma Watson's name came up. The write-ups once again were in penny-ante places. She did an enthusiastic interview about her trip to Rwanda with Larry King, but by then he had lost his CNN show. It was on a digital channel and he seemed half-asleep. Meghan was always so close, but never quite there: basic cable, not premium cable, inside the magazines but not on the cover. A UN advocate but not a UN ambassador, a local celebrity in Toronto but an unknown in New York.

As she filmed the fifth and sixth seasons of **Suits**, she was well aware of the clock running down. She was about to turn thirty-five and still had not gotten the call from Anna Wintour to join the red carpet at the Met Gala. Halfway through season six, Patrick Adams started thinking about leaving the show after the next season. His character, Mike Ross, was coming out of prison, and he sensed impending story line irrelevance. Gina Torres planned to peel off, too. Aaron Korsh was enthusiastic about reinventing Rachel Zane's narrative for a new iteration, but few shows maintain their traction past a sixth season. Finding another hit show was perilous terrain. There was no guarantee lightning would strike twice. (In 2019, Torres was given her own **Suits** spin-off, **Pearson,** in which the powerhouse law partner enters the dirty world of Chicago politics. It cratered after one season.)

Besides, Meghan's vision for herself now was as a global celebrity brand synonymous with enlightened causes. As she correctly admitted in **Elle**, "Were it not for my show and website, I would never have been asked to be a global ambassador for World Vision [a charity that took her back to Rwanda] or an advocate for UN Women." There was a further snag she preferred not to mention: that despite the show and the website, very few people had ever heard of her.

Meghan's love life was equally trapped in a cul-de-sac. In 2016, Cory Vitiello, with whom she and her dogs had recently moved in, called it a day. A broadcaster told me she saw Meghan one evening in tears at the Harbord Room, where she used to wait for Vitiello to finish his shift. Always a magnet for beautiful women, he decided he wasn't ready for marriage even if she was.

Meghan's sights once again turned to London. It was the height of the 2016 summer season. Princess Diana used to love this time of year, with the influx of what she called the "July Americans" in town. Meghan's reps scored her a stylish invitation to wear Ralph Lauren's clothes in a celebrity box at Wimbledon, where Serena Williams was playing. Markus Anderson ginned up a discount room for Meghan at her favorite Soho House, the Dean Street Townhouse. She hit the London scene in June with glamour guns blazing.

One stop was a charity dinner hosted by Phones 4u billionaire John Caudwell at his Mayfair mansion. As was her wont, Meghan struck up bonding banter about boyfriends with a footballer's former wife Lizzie Cundy, host of an obscure reality show titled **So Would You Dump Me Now?** Cundy noted that Meghan knew nobody there and later blabbed to the **Daily Mail.** "We were talking girly chat about my life, her life. She said she'd love to have a celebrity boyfriend. She loved Britain and felt very at home there. She loved London life and wanted to stay and work there and have a boyfriend." Cundy suggested the still-on-the-market Ashley Cole.

Meghan pushed ever onward to a strategic drink at the Scarsdale Tavern in Kensington with former tabloid editor Piers Morgan. After a successful run in L.A. and a less successful attempt to fill Larry King's shoes on CNN, Piers had returned to London, hungry for the rude, punchy ebullience of his red-top days of the nineties. His vehicle was **Good Morning Britain,** which he took from a pallid 500,000 viewers to a raucous 1.2 million, while developing a massive Twitter following. He often tweeted about **Suits,** of which he happened to be a fan, and struck up a social media friendship with Meghan. "I'm in London for a week of meetings and Wimbledon," she DM'd him. "Would love to say Hi!"

It was a cor blimey moment for all the men propping up the bar when she walked into the Kensington pub. "She looked every inch the Hollywood superstar," wrote Piers in a 2017 column in the **Daily Mail,** "very slim, very leggy, very elegant, and impossibly glamorous. She was even wearing the obligatory big black shades beloved of LA thespians."

He was impressed with her undisguised ambition. "My mantra is, 'Don't give it five minutes if you're not going to give it five years,'" she told him, and flashed power-woman chestnuts like her Procter & Gamble story and earnest observations about the lost art of calligraphy. "There's still something incredibly romantic and special about a guy writing to a girl and putting pen to paper rather than emailing it, whether his writing is chicken scratch or looks like a doctor's note."

Charm offensive accomplished, she left for a dinner at the uber-posh 5 Hertford Street Club with the Nigerian-born photographer Misan Harriman, who would become the first Black person in the 104-year history of British **Vogue** to shoot the cover of its September issue. But it was thanks to Violet von Westenholz, who had issued Meghan the Wimbledon invitation on behalf of Ralph Lauren, that the cards fell into place. As the daughter of Baron Frederick Patrick Piers von Westenholz, one of Prince Charles's best friends, Violet knew everybody. She was a childhood friend of William and Harry, and her sister Victoria had been romantically linked with Harry. When Meghan once again floated the bait that she was looking for a boyfriend, Violet suggested an idea that was too good to be true. How to make it happen? Markus, of course. No one knew better than he about choreographing high-end social collisions.

Gina Nelthorpe-Cowne had lunch with Meghan at London's Delaunay restaurant on July 1, 2016, and thought her client had never looked more beautiful. Meghan, unable to contain her excitement, shared the secret of whom she was going to meet that night for drinks at Soho House.

"There's no way he's going to be able to resist her," Cowne thought.

CHAPTER
20

FLASHMAN'S FLAMEOUT

———

Harry Confronts His Demons

———

T HE DASHING THIRTY-ONE-YEAR-OLD PRINCE who walked through the door and beheld the seductive vision of a starlet named Meghan was at a complicated juncture of his life. Ostensibly, he was on a roll. He had never been more popular with the British public. While William was losing his hair and being swallowed by the bourgeois maw of domesticity with Kate, Harry was the sexy royal wild card with the Brad Pitt stubble. He had charmed the world standing in for his brother at the closing ceremony of the London Olympics, proved himself impressively brave with his second tour in Afghanistan as an Apache helicopter pilot, and launched the Invictus Games, his wildly successful initiative for wounded and injured veterans.

Just two months earlier, he had opened the second Invictus in Orlando with Michelle Obama, his improbable buddy and Meghan's idol. When the Obamas offered up some smack talk over which country would bring home more gold medals, Harry pulled out the big gun—the Queen—to respond. Grandmother and grandson, sitting side by side on a floral sofa, taped a video in which the Queen, her comic timing impeccable, responds to the Obamas' challenge, with a dry "Oh really?" Message: Harry could even make the Queen have fun.

He had enough goodwill in the bank that the front-page embarrassment of being surreptitiously snapped in August 2012, just a month after the Olympics, playing strip billiards in a high-priced hotel suite in Las Vegas stark naked with a posse of party girls did not tarnish his national appeal. ("Harry Grabs the Crown Jewels!" the **Sun** headline crowed.) While the tabloids roasted him (with a wink) for his loutish lapse of decorum, the British public adored him for it. It was "a classic example of me probably being too much army and not enough prince," was his brilliantly quotable apology for the behavior, no doubt fed to him by the adroit Paddy Harverson. **Good lad, Harry!** was the verdict in most British pubs. He was a bloke like them on a bender, not some stodgy Goody Two-shoes like his princely brother. Everyone, including the Queen, forgave Diana's naughty boy. Bookings to Vegas shot up after the free publicity.

But if his public life was peak Harry, privately he was falling off a cliff. Ever since he left the army in 2015, he had been acting belligerent, carousing all night. Coming out of uniform is often a traumatic experience for those who thrive inside military structure. For Captain Harry Wales, the army had been his hiding place and refuge for ten years. He felt respected, protected, and encircled by a tight band of trusted fellow officers. "He was so much happier there," a close acquaintance of Harry's told me.

> He used to go away for a long period of time. Being in a regimented life with structure and one aim, to kill the enemy. So all your pent-up fury can go down the barrel of a gun. He loved the chaps, was physically brave, and needed the structure. So it was very tough to be brought back and put on a suit and tie and told to do his duties. . . . They pulled him out too early.

It's a commonly held sentiment that Harry should never have left the army, period, but that position is unrealistic. To rise in the ranks requires constant intellectual growth and reassessments at staff college. Instead of the operational assignments at which Harry excelled, military advancement meant desk jobs in the Ministry of Defence, a dismal prospect for a Flashman prince who rarely cracked a book.

With William on a clear path to kingship and his grandmother approaching ninety years of age, Palace advisers deemed there would be plenty for Harry to do, representing the Queen on foreign tours and partnering with his brother on work for the Royal Foundation that they had formed together in 2009 to house the charities of which they were president or patron.

Yet Harry was lost without the army's sense of purpose. Civilian life forced him to contend with the reality of his declining position in the line of succession. He only had to observe his Uncle Andrew's flailing for relevance and income to see the mirror of his own impending fate. The cruelty of primogeniture was more personal in Harry's case. The bond between Charles and Andrew, separated by a twelve-year age gap, had never been tight. With only two years between William and Harry, the inevitability of Harry being pushed aside gave rise to a sorrowful tension that was more like that between Elizabeth and Margaret in their younger years. As "the boys," they had been indivisible, and the public had loved their double act. Their mother even dressed them alike when they were young. But their identical treatment had set up unrealistic expectations. The boys were not, and could never be, equal.

Just as Harry was missing the fraternal ties with his army chums, he also mourned his us-against-the-world bond with William. Though they were still "incredibly close, living next door to each other [at KP], sharing the same office, and hanging out an awful lot," according to a former aide, their relationship hadn't been the same since William married Kate. In May 2015, the Cambridges produced a second child, Princess Charlotte, and Kate made no secret about wanting more. Harry felt displaced by their bougie family unit, and couldn't understand his brother's obsession with his Middleton in-laws, whose Bucklebury world bored Harry to tears.

The Palace communications team would get them to do things together, the three of them. And then, after a while, they stopped, because it was so awkward for Harry. "Much though he loved Kate, he would just find himself looking like a third wheel," a friend of his told me.

In the family tussle between the claims of a brother and loyalty to a wife, it was clear who would win. The Cambridges had become a tight unit, and William a full-on Windsor country bumpkin. On weekends when he wasn't chez Middleton, he was tramping the grounds of Anmer Hall, the redbrick Georgian mansion on the Sandringham Estate that the Queen gave the couple as a wedding present, wearing a flat cap and tweed jacket like his "turnip toff" Norfolk farmer friends. All he needed were George VI's plus fours.

For his part, William felt that Harry's unabated Jack the Lad behavior was getting tiresome. He was less amused than the British public by either the strip billiards debacle in Las Vegas or Harry's ceaseless boozy nightclub forays with his rowdy friends. His younger brother's recklessness exasperated him. Harry was always complaining about the invasion of the press, but at the Vegas hotel he was so wasted on Grey Goose he had got naked with a group of women he had picked up in a hotel bar—unvetted by his protection officers—one of whom was bound to (and did) sell a cell phone picture to the celebrity scandal site TMZ. What was he fucking thinking? The Palace went into overdrive (unsuccessfully) to prevent publication in Britain. Harry was snapped standing outside the hotel nervously checking his mobile about an hour after the picture surfaced on TMZ.

The brothers' jokey persona in joint appearances at this time concealed resentments greater than is widely known. Kate's joining their foundation changed the working dynamic. Friction between the brothers escalated over their professional assignments. William knew he had to be respectful of hierarchy when it came to his father's ownership of the environmental platform, but he was less willing to accede to his younger brother. "The problem was their interests were very close," a Palace source told me. They would agree on territories that they would operate in, and then William would feel that his brother was breaching the agreement.

From Harry's point of view, William was simply "hogging the best briefs," a friend of both of them told me. The younger prince seemed not to have gotten the memo that the future king would always get the juiciest patronages. The friend continued:

Harry felt very frustrated and shortchanged as William definitely moved in, as Harry saw it, on Africa and the environment. Harry hung on to veterans, which he's very good on, but equally he felt that with his work in Lesotho, he should somehow combine elephants and

rhinos and HIV and poverty. Harry still has
Sentebale, but that's a tiny little bit of
Africa. . . . He very much wanted the (African
conservation charity) Tusk Trust (unreason-
ably, since William had been royal patron since
2005), but he got bulldozed off pitch by
William, who also felt strongly. . . . So Harry
was a very, very angry man. I think those were
absolutely Olympic rows.

Unhelpful to Harry's argument was the fact that
floating around online were pictures of him triumphantly posing with a water buffalo he slaughtered
on a big-game hunting trip in Argentina in 2004
with Chelsy Davy, which, though perfectly above-
board, was not a good look for a conservationist. A
member of the brothers' circle told me, "Harry had
done stuff in sub-Saharan Africa that William was
always just really nervous about."

There were other tensions, said the source. William
exhibited more than a tinge of competitive envy.
Harry's Invictus Games had taken off like a bucking
bronco. Harry had been nervous that not enough
spectators would come for the first event, held at the
80,000-seat Queen Elizabeth Olympic Park in 2014.
In fact, more than 65,000 people showed up. Invictus
was perhaps the most immediately impactful new
royal initiative since Prince Philip launched his Duke
of Edinburgh's Awards in 1956.

In his last year in the army, Harry had spent much
of his time visiting recovery centers, NHS hospitals,

and armed forces charities around the country, bolstering his expertise on wounded veterans. "Having been a soldier, having traveled back, God forbid, with body bags all around him on that aircraft, Harry could stand up on a stage in front of fifteen thousand people and speak with absolute authority about what that means. He knew because he lived it," Jamie Lowther-Pinkerton told me. Invictus elevated Harry's star power around the world in a way none of his previous efforts on behalf of his grandmother had.

William's causes, however, somehow felt more shaped from the top, less reflective of personal passion, less well-defined, and therefore less engaging to the public. It became increasingly clear that for all the elder brother's soundness and self-possession, the younger one had a more natural touch with the public. Like his mother, Harry had an easy ability for what the royals call "the chat," while his brother sometimes stiffened behind the podium. "If William makes a speech, everything from 'Good evening' onwards has to be typed out and handed to him," a charity board member told me. "When he came to our dining club one evening, as soon as he got up to speak, he froze." That never happened to Harry, who, like Prince Philip, always knew how to break through an awkward silence with a joke.

Major General Buster Howes cited Harry's spontaneous playfulness on their visit to the U.S. Air Force Academy in Colorado. After Harry's two expert football passes, "he looked at me and smiled and said, 'Watch this.' And the next ball, he threw right into the middle of the expensive cameras. Which was him being mischievous."

Harry was also making a point. He was not constrained by any need to engage with the press, which he hated so much that any encounter made the blood drain from his face. Harry looked at Howes once and said, "Do you want to swap?"

II

If Harry was discontented with his royal duties, he was even more unhappy about the state of his love life. An auspicious two-year affair with Cressida Bonas, the delicate blond daughter of Lady Mary-Gaye Curzon, fell apart in 2014. According to a guest I spoke to, Prince Charles expressed his regret at a Buckingham Palace function sometime after the young couple split. "I don't know what to do about Harry. We so miss Cressida," he told her ruefully.

By contrast, all of Harry's old carousing mates—Tom "Skippy" Inskip, Charlie van Straubenzee, Guy Pelly, and Charlie Gilkes—were engaged or prancing up the aisle with heiresses and "It" girls at destination weddings. Kate was always suggesting new girlfriends to him at the must-have-Harry-over roast chicken dinners she cooked at the Cambridge apartment in Kensington Palace. Harry was a devoted uncle and always brought gifts for Prince George and baby Charlotte. He started to feel like the royal version of Bridget Jones. He blurted out slightly pathetic-sounding comments in interviews about wishing he could settle down. "I would love to have kids right now," he said dolefully. "But there is a process one has to go through. Hopefully I'm doing all right by myself. It would be great to have someone next to me to share the pressure but the time will come and whatever happens, happens."

"Harry will tell anyone who will listen that he is fed up with being single," a member of his set told a journalist. "But girls are wary about dating him."

They should have been, after seeing Cressida Bonas's turbulent experience. There was general agreement that Ms. Bonas had all the makings of a perfect partner for Harry, who was madly in love with her. She was of his world but not obsessed with it, a beauty but not a preening one, with a burgeoning career as an actress on stage and TV after leaving the University of Leeds. (In 2016 she starred as Daisy Buchanan in a production of **The Great Gatsby** at the reputable Leicester Square Theatre.) She was athletic too, winning a sports scholarship to Prior Park College in Bath before attending the co-ed boarding school Stowe like his old flame Chelsy Davy. One of her closest friends was the Yorks' daughter Princess Eugenie, who is said to have introduced her to Harry at a music festival in Hampshire. She drank rum straight up, **Tatler** approvingly reported and, when embarrassed, was heard to exclaim "Cringe de la cringe!"

Cressida was encircled by a discreet but entertaining extended aristocratic family. Her ever-vivacious mother, Lady Mary-Gaye, was the matriarch of a Mitfordesque tribe, most of whom were already known to Harry. There were four more gorgeous-looking half siblings with triple-barreled names from Mary-Gaye's four marriages. As a guest at Sandringham for shooting weekends, Cressida blended easily with Harry's friends. She passed the Africa test on a successful vacation together in the Okavango Delta.

Cressie, as she is known, was amused and forgiving at first when Harry came to stay with her family in the country after the Las Vegas incident with "his tail between his legs, looking like a puppy who had peed on the carpet," as another guest put it. But as their relationship progressed, she found his frat-boy antics beneath him: "Cressida is the kindest, most loving little thing. But she's bossy," a family friend told me. "And I remember her saying to him, 'I just want you to stop being so laddish.' Because he was always one of the boys with their stupid jokes. And Cressida's far too intelligent for that. She said, 'I just want the whole world to be as proud of you as I am.'"

Harry's habitual mood, however, was increasingly truculent. When he wasn't venting about William, he was pouring out resentments about Charles. Father and son mostly communicated through their private secretaries. Harry was especially disgruntled about how his father handled the choice of a present for his thirtieth birthday. Charles, apparently, sent a message through his office asking "What would you like for your thirtieth? Would you like another dinner jacket?" Harry, said my source, sent back the message, "Ok."

> So the man from Savile Row came to measure him and when it arrived . . . one arm was shorter than the other and one leg shorter than the other, so it was picked up and returned in a box which seemed kind of analogous to their whole relationship.

I.e., no communication, and when there was, it went wrong.

Harry also felt perennially aggravated by the power wielded by Camilla, who made him feel like a visitor at Highgrove. He was sensitive about being as excluded by his father's relationship with her as he was from the bond between William and Kate. Their interdependence exacerbated the void left by his mother, whose affection could never be replaced. "I can feel the hugs that she used to give us," he reflected in Nick Kent's documentary, when Harry was thirty-three. "I miss that, I miss that feeling. I miss that part of a family. I miss having that mother to be able to give you those hugs and give you that compassion that I think everybody needs."

More challenging for all was Harry's ever-boiling paranoia about the press. Cressida understood the historical reasons why he hated journalists but believed that he should, like William, come to terms with his royal fame. If the couple emerged from Kensington Palace and Harry saw five press people waiting, he would get white-knuckled. As a close friend said:

> Cressie was a normal twenty-five-year-old who wanted to go out to dinner and touch knees under the table. Harry would walk four paces ahead of her, instead of holding her hand. When they went to the theater, he left at the interval to get out without a hassle. She was either being dragged through the streets being yelled at or ignored while he threw a hissy fit.

It was not as if he showered her in jewelry, either. Harry upheld the Windsor tradition of being tight with a buck. Invited as a couple to Guy Pelly's Tennessee wedding to the Holiday Inn heiress Lizzy Wilson, Harry casually told Cressida, "My office has got my ticket, you get yours," which Lady Curzon's daughter reportedly found not only cheap but disrespectful, especially when she learned he would be off for half the weekend at Pelly's bachelor booze-up. While Cressida kept reading about herself as the glamorous aristocratic girl in a romantic love affair with a prince, the bizarre reality of date nights was glumly eating takeout and watching Netflix at Nottingham Cottage, Harry's tiny and none-too-tidy two-bedroom grace-and-favor bachelor pad on the grounds of Kensington Palace. "Nott Cott," as the house is known in the family, was once inhabited by the Queen's governess Crawfie, until the Queen Mother booted her out. The ceilings are so low that when William lived there with Kate, he had to stoop to avoid hitting his head.

A family friend told me she knew the relationship wouldn't last when there was a blow-up on Valentine's Day. En route to the restaurant, they were driving down Kensington High Street when Harry got word that there was a photographer lying in wait. He slammed on the brakes, did a spin turn in the middle of the street, and gunned it back to Nott Cott for a Valentine's night of pizza. It was like Sean Penn in the old Madonna days.

At Christmas, more unnecessary drama. The couple was staying in the country with Cressida's half sister Isabella and others in the family, and decided to go for New Year's Day lunch to a small local pub in Kidlington, outside Oxford. There were very few guests and they secured a table at the back. A person privy to the incident said:

> Suddenly as they were leaving, this quite elderly, sweet-looking gentleman came out and said, "Oh, sir, so sorry, I know it's Christmastime, but could I just take a photograph to give to my wife who isn't well?" And so Cressida opened her mouth and said, "Oh, of course." And Harry said, "Get out of my way" and went bright red in the face and stormed off in a huff.

Cringe de la cringe.

Their friends expected an engagement announcement at any time, but incidents such as this gave Cressida serious qualms about sharing her life with Harry. It was daunting enough to join the Royal Family with all the restrictions that were sure to hurt her career. Images of Kate and William conquering crowds in New Zealand with the eight-month-old Prince George in tow reportedly spooked Cressida. She found it unimaginable to drag a future baby of her own off on a hectic royal tour, especially with Harry's explosive temperament. Without his army mates to cut him down to size, his sense of entitlement was out of control. His outbursts were ever more frequent and childlike. He took up boxing because, as he later said, he was always "on the verge of punching somebody."

Cressida began to have serious worries about his mental health. It is not widely known that it was she who first persuaded Harry to see a therapist. "She got him to accept he had problems, and see a psychoanalyst," a family friend told me. To find the right therapist, he turned for suggestions to both his mother's old friend Julia Samuel, who worked as a bereavement counselor in the NHS pediatrics department of St. Mary's Hospital, Paddington, and to the advice of British Secret Intelligence Service MI6, whose team of therapists, it was thought, would be an excellent resource. A person close to Harry at the time told me, "There was a need for someone who would be incredibly discreet and who understood what it's like to have a public version of your life and a private version of your life. Therapists at MI6, that's what they do."

"You need to feel it in yourself," Harry told **The Telegraph**'s Bryony Gordon. "You need to find the right person to talk to as well and that's been one of my biggest frustrations over the past few years— how hard it is to find the right person, the right remedy, because there's so much stuff out there."

Harry has said that he eventually found a therapist who helped him start to excavate the trauma of his mother's death. He has since said he now counts himself very lucky that it was "only two years . . . of total chaos" before he learned how to talk about it. "I just couldn't put my finger on it. I just didn't know what was wrong with me." But he said: "It's all about timing." When Cressida suggested he get help, Harry finally agreed.

His meltdown had been a long time in the making. Therapy unlocked the years of buried grief about his mother's death. He at last understood his own evasion of sorrow in tactics that ranged from champagne hooliganism to "sticking my head in the sand, refusing to ever think about my mum, because why would that help?" In the Kent documentary, he said he had only cried twice in the twenty years since she died. He had been expected to hide his anguish while the whole world expressed theirs. "Every time I put a suit on and tie on . . . having to do the role, and go, 'Right, game face,' look in the mirror and say, 'Let's go,'" he said in 2021 on the Apple broadcast **The Me You Can't See**. "Before I even left the house I was pouring with sweat."

Once unburdened, he wanted to share the relief. He had learned that support poured forth once he talked about the concealed torment. No one was more thankful than William that Harry had finally sought professional help. For years, his elder brother had keenly felt Harry's unmoored distress. He knew Harry was having panic attacks. Whatever their territorial tensions, he desperately wanted to help him as he always had when they were growing up. "My brother, you know, bless him," Harry said in his 2017 interview with **The Telegraph**'s Bryony Gordon about mental health, "he was a huge support to me. He kept saying this is not right, this is not normal, you need to talk to [someone] about stuff, it's OK."

William, it should not be overlooked, had suffered grievously himself. His sanctuary was family life. Harry might mock his bourgeois existence with Kate, but the Duke of Cambridge told Alastair Campbell in an interview at this time that he could not do his job without his domestic cocoon. "I have never felt depressed in the way I understand it, but I have felt incredibly sad," he told Campbell. On the days when he feels most weighed down by the trauma of the past, he continued, "I have never shied away from talking about it and addressing how I feel. I have gone straight to people around me and said, 'Listen, I need to talk about this today.'"

In his work as an air ambulance pilot, he said, he found that arriving at the scene of a child's death in a car crash "penetrated [his] armor" because he immediately felt it from the parents' point of view.

"Anything to do with parent and child, and loss, it is very difficult, it has a big effect on me, it takes me straight back to my emotions back when my mother died." He talked with unusual emotion in the 2021 podcast **William: Time to Walk,** about the devastating impact of a rescue call to a car crash with a seriously injured child, Bobby Hughes, nearly the same age as Prince George. It "was as if something had changed inside me," he said. "It was like someone had put a key in a lock and opened it without me giving permission to do that. . . . You just feel everyone's pain, everyone's suffering. And that's not me. I've never felt that before." He has stayed in touch with Bobby and his family ever since.

Shared fraternal grief expressed itself in renewed purpose. Harry's acceptance that he needed help brought the brothers closer for a short time. In May 2016, they launched Heads Together, a high-profile initiative from their foundation suggested by Kate, who saw the thread of combating mental illness in much of the charitable work they undertook. The campaign, whose goal was ending the stigma attached to mental illness, was well-timed, four months after Prime Minister David Cameron's £1 billion pledge for a mental health care "revolution" in England.

Ultimately, the intense focus on Harry's problems to the exclusion of her own was too much for Cressida. To Harry's chagrin, she moved on, later rekindling a romance with another aristocratic Harry, the "towering blonde god," as **Tatler** called him,

Harry Wentworth-Stanley, son of the Marchioness of Milford Haven. She married him in 2020, adding to the store of family multi-hyphenates.

"When [Prince Harry and Cressida] broke up," a friend of theirs told me, "he wrote her a sweet letter saying I admire you, I wish you well and above all thank you for helping me to address my demons and seek help."

"He became very bleak in his outlook," a Palace source told me. "He was convinced he was going to be single for the rest of his life."

The night of July 1, 2016, Harry was in an especially sober mood after returning from a trip to France for the commemoration of the one hundredth anniversary of the Battle of the Somme, the deadliest battle of the First World War, in which a million men were wounded or killed.

It had been a classic day of royal ceremony and national meaning, with the Firm out en masse. Prince Charles and Camilla, Prime Minister David Cameron, Prince Harry, and the Duke and Duchess of Cambridge—she looking impeccably royal in a cream-and-black lace dress—attended a service of commemoration at the Thiepval Memorial in France, close to the battlefields of the Somme, and a military vigil the evening before. "It was in many ways the saddest day in the long story of our nation," Prince William said at his address at Thiepval. "Tonight we think of them. . . . We acknowledge the failures of European governments, including our own, to prevent the catastrophe of world war." Prince Harry, with

a veteran's gravitas, read the poem "Before Action"—
"By all the days that I have lived, make me a soldier,
Lord"—by Lieutenant W. N. Hodgson, published
two days before he fell in the carnage of the Somme.
It was a sacrament of royal duty at its most meaningful. "Not forgetting," maintaining an unbreakable
thread between the nation's history and its present, is
perhaps above all what monarchy is for.

But the trip's solemnity lifted from Harry's shoulders when he walked through the door at Soho
House and was "beautifully surprised" by the sight
of his future wife. "I thought, 'Okay, well I'm really
gonna have to up my game,'" he later said. It was as
if both felt a lack that the other swiftly answered.

CHAPTER
21

SMITTEN

———

The Stars Align for Harry and Meghan

———

THEY BECAME A SECRET SOCIETY OF TWO. BACK-TO-back dates, the third of which was under the night skies of Botswana, Harry's go-to hot-and-heavy glamping retreat. Meghan was soon posting a Love Hearts candy, inscribed "Kiss Me," on Instagram, and the message "Lovehearts in #London." Little did the press know, when they photographed Pippa Middleton and **Vogue** editor-in-chief Anna Wintour in a box at Wimbledon on July 4, 2016, that the unknown actress filed under "incidental people" in the shot was the future bride of the Queen's grandson.

Harry was in orbit. He had always dated heiresses, airheads, or aristocratic girls from within a narrow circle. Meghan was of a breed he had not encountered. As one former Palace adviser put it to me: "Very impressive. Very strong, very motivated, brought up to think she can change the world. It's a very American type; we don't have them here." Harry was fired up not only by Meghan's beauty and poise, but also by the way she was in control of her own life. Compared to her, he was a man-boy whose whole existence had been mapped out for him by others.

But other people's plans weren't working for Harry anymore. They were always predicated on him being a secondary figure. He was boxed in by the overweening dictate of **First, do no harm** to the pinched hierarchy of the monarchy. He was no longer the foolish carouser of his twenties. (Well, sometimes he was. Andrew Morton reports that a few weeks before meeting Meghan, Harry was "dirty dancing" with a pair of brunettes and downing shots at Jak's Bar in west London.) He was not without resources: When he turned thirty, he inherited $13 million from the estate of his mother. And the success of the Invictus Games showed he could be an independent force—or change maker, as Meghan called it—in the larger world beyond the Palace design.

The problem was that no one in that hidebound organization could appreciate this force, or knew how to make use of it. He had spent years in a tumult of inchoate emotion and pointless duty. The contrast of Meghan's crystal-clear focus to his own confusion was thrilling. This amazing woman flew around the world as an actress, a humanitarian, an adventurous traveler at her own instigation—and all on her own dime! She had given a speech at the United Nations **as herself**! She posted about feminist causes on Instagram at the same time as looking fabulous in a bikini in Positano. "It was as if Harry was in a trance," a friend said.

The infatuation was mutual. Meghan had a weakness for tall, buff, overgrown boys with closely cropped golden beards. Harry was the same physical type as Cory Vitiello, but with the additional conferred allure of royalty. Three years younger than Meghan, he was both virile and vulnerable, and he was the solution to every problem she had. With Harry at her side, her star meter wouldn't just rise, it would rocket. From penny-ante panelist to keynote interview. From front-of-book Q and A's to the cover of **Vanity Fair**. From what's-next-after-**Suits** to a global supernova. The morning after their first date, she spoke about Harry to a girlfriend as if he were a hot submission from her agent. "Do I sound crazy when I say this could have legs?"

She took off on a **Suits** promotion junket that sent her to Boston and New York, where a mysterious bouquet of peonies, her favorite flowers, arrived at her hotel. "I am feeling so incredibly joyful right now," she wrote on **The Tig.** "So grateful and content that all I could wish for is more of the same. More surprises, more adventure." A week later, she was experiencing Authentic Africa in a $2,000 deluxe tent at the Meno a Kwena safari camp with Harry in Botswana. By the time the couple returned, the intensity of their feeling for each other was more than a love affair. It was a pact: Us against the World.

Prince Charles was charmed by Meghan in their

first encounters. Over lunch at Highgrove, Meghan, the foodie and **The Tig** tastemaker, listened eagerly to the Prince of Wales extolling his homegrown Charlotte potatoes and Hapil strawberries. Since everyone else in the family rolled their eyes at his obsessions with organic eating, it wasn't hard for Charles to be delighted by a beautiful woman who seemed fascinated by everything he had to say.

The Queen met Meghan after attending church at Windsor, in an informal "drop by" at Royal Lodge, orchestrated, doubtless, by Harry's favorite cousin, Andrew and Fergie's daughter Princess Eugenie, for whom the Queen has a soft spot. Her Maj made the conversation easy and reserved judgment. She was just happy Harry was happy.

But William knew Harry all too well and feared he was heading for trouble. Every time his brother fell in love, it was an eruption of Vesuvius. "You do realize this is the fourth girl you've taken to Botswana," he couldn't help remarking after Harry's starry-eyed account of the trip. William didn't immediately divulge his anxieties about Meghan. Harry introduced her to him in November over relaxed tea in the kitchen of the Cambridges' Kensington Palace apartment. (Kate, to Meghan's disappointment, was off in Norfolk with the kids.) Meghan had prepared herself for a grilling, but William was far too well-mannered for that. "I was looking forward to meeting the girl who has put that silly grin on my brother's face," he told her disarmingly. She felt as welcomed by his effortless charm as she was by the Queen's.

But William was nervous about the speed at which all this was going down. His view was that if the union became permanent, Meghan would be giving up everything she knew: her career, which was a huge part of her identity, and her life in North America. She knew almost nobody in London and had little understanding of British culture. A person close to the Duke of Cambridge told me that William thought she should have more time to build up a life in the UK and make friends who didn't always have to be brought in confidence to the Palace. It had been hard enough for Kate, but Meghan was a glamorous actress who would be the first woman of color to join the Royal Family, factors that would add enormously to the pressure. Unspoken to Harry, the person said, was the older brother's fear that Harry's mental fragility was such that he wouldn't be strong enough to handle all of that on her behalf, as well as his own issues. Her daily life would be lived under scorching scrutiny and harassment that she thought she understood, but Palace veterans knew was nothing remotely like the kind of benign exposure a TV actress had to endure.

To his brother's concerns, Harry's riposte can be summarized as, I am told, "Well, actually the best way that I can protect her is to marry her as quickly as possible, because as soon as I marry her she will then get police protection." Plus, she was a month shy of thirty-five. Her biological clock was ticking.

By September 2016—two months after they first met—Harry was dashing constantly to Toronto, where he stayed at Meghan's house free from hassles, thanks to protective neighbors. It was a magic bubble made possible by the generally low-key Canadians, who tend to leave celebrities alone and provided the couple with privacy in their walks through Toronto's Trinity Bellwoods Park, wearing matching beaded blue bracelets. Whenever Meghan could get to London, they holed up at Nott Cott, seeing only each other. They fell in love, Harry later said, "so incredibly quickly," it was proof the "stars were aligned."

He was so besotted that by December, instead of flying straight back to London from Barbados after representing the Queen on the tour of the Caribbean, he made a 2,400-mile Barbados-to-Toronto detour to see Meghan between filming. Back in London, they were sighted together buying a Christmas tree in Battersea Park. The tree seller described the pair as "totally happy, cute, couple-y—but not overly mushy and gross." To William, it all looked suspiciously like signals of nesting.

It was the **Sunday Express** that first revealed their relationship to the world. The couple had four months of delicious privacy before the paper's royal editor Camilla Tominey broke the news in October 2016 under the headline "Harry's Secret Romance with TV Star." The press reaction was seismic, not least because Tominey scooped all the competitors, resulting in a porcine scramble for every Meghan morsel their Canadian and L.A. stringers could provide. Meghan was swarmed when she left her house for the set of **Suits.** The cable actress who had slogged so long for name recognition now played the part of a besieged celebrity, wearing a long dark coat, beanie hat, and dark glasses.

In the first round of coverage, she was portrayed as Grace Kelly redux, an actress, humanitarian, and gender equality campaigner, making it hard not to believe that the initial leak came from Meghan's side (though a servant tip from the House of York has been fingered). The second round, however, struck a different tone, forcing Meghan to experience the full-on baretoothed barracuda swarm of hacks on the royal beat.

Used to publicist-fed entertainment coverage and magazine puff pieces in return for access, American celebrities often find themselves dazed by the sheer demonic creativity of the British popular press. If you are not the target, the tabloids' tearing through other people's reputations is a guilty pleasure of the English breakfast table, like the tartness of orange marmalade. At their best, they provide pungent demolitions of the pretensions of the rich and pompous. At their worst, they reflect the basest instincts of jeering reactionary trolls.

No one knew better than Harry what the British press was capable of. He had seen it all—from the primordial trauma of his mother's last hours, to the brutal invasions of his previous girlfriends' privacy, and the monstering of every woman in the Royal Family except the Queen. Kate had been tormented about class and social climbing and her mother's Party Pieces business—"Mail Order Bride," one columnist sneered. The jibes didn't end after the wedding, either. She was routinely depicted as a placid nonentity. Booker Prize–winning novelist Hilary Mantel wrote her off (spitefully) in a lecture for the **London Review of Books** as a "shop-window mannequin" who was "as painfully thin as anyone could wish, without quirks, without oddities, without the risk of the emergence of character. She appears precision-made, machine-made."

With Sarah Ferguson, the "Duchess of Pork," the tabloid sharks were merciless about her weight. Camilla Parker Bowles was reviled as ugly and old with such frequency, she took to signing her letters to Charles "your devoted old bag."

"I wouldn't want to put my worst enemy through it," she told an interviewer on her seventieth birthday, recalling the cascade of abuse.

Even the marginal royal trouper Sophie Wessex was trashed so badly over succumbing to the Fake Sheikh's shtick, a former member of the Palace press team told me, "she came into our office on a daily basis, almost in tears because there'd been another bit of shit written about her. And she said, 'My family read this! My friends read this!'"

II

It was perhaps inevitable that the same malevolent scribes who had heaped scorn on the class and looks of the other royal women would go after Meghan on race, practically throwing their backs out as they stooped to new lows. Yet Harry seemed to lay little or no groundwork for the presentation of his biracial girlfriend to the media. His bloody-minded refusal to have any truck with the press, even when it was in his own obvious interests—and hers—made him deny royal correspondents any elegantly pre-planned disclosure of his new relationship. The random tip-off to Camilla Tominey and the **Sunday Express** meant Harry had no control over the other papers, which were now intent on payback.

The **Daily Mail** was the worst offender. Still reigning at the **Mail** after two dozen years, Paul Dacre, the saturnine editorial minotaur who had a matchless flair for defenestrating whichever public figure crossed his Middle England moralist code, ran a team particularly skilled at monstering by association. As in "So and so, a second cousin twice removed of cannibal pedophile Dennis Nilsen and former executive assistant to the brother-in-law of convicted rapist Harvey Weinstein's head of production, now sits at the right hand of the Prime Minister." Dacre's staff referred to his morning editorial meetings as the "Vagina Monologues," because of his habit of calling everybody a "cunt."

When Harry's star was on the rise in 2016, Dacre, in a moment of boredom with the royals, had personally decided that Prince William was having it too easy, and created a new story line that the heir to the throne was a lazy poshie not doing enough to support the Queen. It got traction and dogged William for two years.

The **Mail**'s November 2, 2016, piece about Meghan was a textbook example of monstering by association. Headlined "Harry's Girl Is (Almost) Straight Outta Compton," it was so odiously (and casually) racist it became Exhibit A in Harry and Meghan's righteous war with the press.

"Plagued by crime and riddled with street gangs," read the report, "the troubled Los Angeles neighborhood that Doria Ragland, 60, calls home couldn't be more different to London's leafy Kensington."

Harry's literally palatial homes couldn't be more different from the tatty one-storey homes that dominate much of Crenshaw. And while there have been a total of 21 crimes in the immediate area around Highgrove over the past 12 months, 47 have taken place in Crenshaw in the last week alone—including murder and robbery. . . . Local gangs include Crenshaw Mafia Gangster, which has been plaguing the area since 1981, and Bloods affiliates Center Park Blood. . . . Nevertheless—and in spite of the gangs—parts of Crenshaw are considered to be improving, among them the aptly named Windsor Hills.

Apt indeed, because Windsor Hills was the neighborhood where Doria Ragland's pleasant Spanish colonial bungalow was actually located. City guidebooks describe the affluent Black bastion, with its manicured lawns, superior restaurants, and walking trails, as one of L.A.'s "hidden gems," attracting politicians, basketball stars, and movie actors as residents. Even Crenshaw itself is nothing like the mayhem the **Mail** described, according to a source of mine in the LAPD, who seemed bemused by its portrayal as a gang-infested locus of brazen homicide.

The Sun, meanwhile, went to town with the headline "Fancy a Quick Puck?" alleging Meghan's marriage had broken up because of a fling with the Canadian ice hockey player Michael Del Zotto. They were more revoltingly inventive still with a front-page boxed-out item headlined "Harry's Girl on Pornhub," based on some random guffawing yobbo uploading **Suits** scenes to the porn site without Meghan's knowledge or permission.

"Meghan felt sick to her stomach when she saw that," a friend told biographers Omid Scobie and Carolyn Durand. "She wanted to shout. . . . She was upset and angry." What's more, towering over the Pornhub item about Meghan was a full-length picture of the Duchess of Cambridge at an event wearing a shimmering white gown under the banner "Kate That Got the Cream." The tabloids were already planting the irresistible scenario of a brewing cat fight between virtuous (white) Kate and the racially confounding Meghan.

Harry went ballistic. He stormed in to see the Kensington Palace communications team he shared with Prince William and demanded they blast out a statement of condemnation. His brother was not unsympathetic. He was in a choleric mood with the press himself, having recently ordered up an angry formal reproof when a "pap" broke all civilized protocols and hid in the trunk of a car to snap Prince George playing in the park. But William also reportedly questioned the wisdom of his brother formally confirming his romance with Meghan. He was wary of Harry's fight-or-flight media strategy.

As the future king, William had learned to swallow his own disgust with certain stories because he—and the monarchy—also needed the reliable amplification of the press. He trusted the Paddy Harverson model of carefully controlled access and rare effective intervention. His most thunderous rebuke occurred after a paparazzo for a French magazine stole a shot of Kate sunbathing topless on vacation in Provence in 2012. William secured an injunction against the magazine and pursued the case for five years, until his wife was awarded the victory of £91,000 in damages. The message was noted. When William chose to lash out, it was rare and lethal.

As regards to Meghan, it was unprecedented for the Palace to issue a statement about a girlfriend after a courtship of only four months. Most royal girlfriends without a ring on their finger were left to twist in the wind. The sharp reprimand that William administered to the press in 2007, after Kate Middleton was besieged outside her flat by news crews expecting a wedding announcement, came after a steady relationship of five years.

Meghan's arrival, however, required an amped-up

press strategy. Because she was a divorcee, an American, a woman of mixed race, and an actress, there were too many angles that could generate media mischief. The new Kensington Palace communications chief, Jason Knauf, thirty-two, was a former director of corporate affairs at the Royal Bank of Scotland, and represented the more sophisticated image managers who had entered the Palace in recent years. He advised Harry in the crafting of a robust statement in defense of Meghan.

Released on November 8, 2016, it opened with a windup about Harry's luck in enjoying such a privileged life and his discomfort with the public's interest in it, then condemned in the strongest terms "the smear on the front page of a national newspaper; the racial undertones of comment pieces; and the outright sexism and racism of social media trolls and web article comments."

After outlining all the many ways Meghan had been harassed, Harry ended with classic Spencer saber-rattling:

> He knows commentators will say this is "the price she has to pay" and that "this is all part of the game." He strongly disagrees. This is not a game—it is her life and his. He has asked for this statement to be issued in the hopes that those in the press who have been driving this story can pause and reflect before any further damage is done.

Several weeks later, William issued his own supportive statement, reportedly to quiet rumors of his dissent.

Unsurprisingly, Harry's salvo was a news sensation. Unfortunately, it detonated on Prince Charles during his three-country tour of the Persian Gulf with Camilla (which began with a sword dance in Oman). Palace protocol usually insists on refraining from announcements that might rain on a senior royal's parade, but there was no holding Harry back. After months of Clarence House planning, Charles had briefly fantasized that his statesmanlike exchanges with Gulf leaders would elicit more than pro forma interest from the media. Yet "No comment"—about Harry and Meghan—was the most quoted utterance anyone reported about the Prince in Bahrain.

Letting fly was exhilarating for Harry. He had defended Meghan in a way that he never could have defended his mother. And he was experiencing something new—accolades from the intelligent media. "As I read it, I felt prickles under my skin," a **New Statesman** columnist wrote. "I had never expected to see something as socially momentous as this happen within the British monarchy in my lifetime." A woke House of Windsor was a marvel to behold! For the more prosaic royal correspondents, schooled in the semiotics of Palace statements, the takeaway was that, after a mere five-month courtship, it was time to mount a wedding-watch.

For Meghan, the statement was her quantum leap. It revolutionized her status, from minor celebrity to **cause célèbre.** She was now a global avatar of diversity and style and, on social media, something more potent still: a victim—in actual, ugly fact for sure, yet also imbued with the aura of a woman who could assert she'd been wronged. She absorbed her new identity ravenously. On the moral high ground after clearly heinous press treatment, Meghan was close to invincible.

Seven months before her wedding to Harry, Meghan achieved her heart's desire and burst bare-shouldered onto the cover of **Vanity Fair.** After preparing the interviewer a lunch of "organic greens, a crusty bread to be dipped in olive oil, and pasta tossed with chilies bought from 'a little place called Terroni,'" she broke the royal taboo of discussing her relationship with Harry pre-engagement, as if "forever" was now a fait accompli.

"We're a couple. We're in love. . . . I hope what people will understand is that this is our time. This is for us. It's part of what makes it so special, that it's just ours." Scattering tantalizing narrative bread crumbs for Oprah's delectation in the future, she told the writer, "I'm sure there will be a time when we will have to come forward and present ourselves and have stories to tell."

On November 17, 2017, the couple announced their engagement in the Sunken Garden at Kensington Palace, created in memory of Harry's mother for the twentieth anniversary of her death at one of her favorite spots to sequester in the Palace grounds. Diana was present again in the two diamonds from her personal collection that Harry used for the ring, along with the gem he had acquired in Botswana. On a freezing morning, Meghan's tiny waist was cinched by the belt of a winter white coat with a shawl neckline that crashed the internet and spawned a million knock-offs. "When did I know she was the one? Very first time we met," the Prince said as Meghan gazed up at him with adoration. There was more than sentiment behind the choice of the Sunken Garden for the announcement. It separated the couple by several meters from the press, who had to get their shots from the other side of an intervening ornamental pond.

III

Now that Meghan was a feminist heroine, tensions with the more senior royal beauty, the Duchess of Cambridge, offered an irresistible storyline to the tabloids, who always love to stoke rivalry between women. The two beauties got on impeccably, or well enough, at their first meeting in January 2017.

Meghan later said she found Kate to be cool of temperament, but that's likely because Meghan is a "gusher," who hugged even the guards outside Kensington Palace. Kate is not a woman given to spontaneous rapport. She'd avoided recruiting new girlfriends to her inner circle/slumber party list since Marlborough and St. Andrews. Many members of her core, premarital sisterhood had settled down with children in Norfolk, providing a discreet ring of steel around her—and even they are excluded from the innermost sanctum of her emotional concerns. The only women with whom she is unguarded are her mother and her sister. Preoccupied with two young children and public duty, Kate had no serious reason to see the latest and most glamorous of Harry's string of girlfriends as a potential threat.

And yet, just as in the days when Princess Diana's new updo upstaged the Queen at the opening of Parliament, the increasing media comparisons of Meghan to Kate—invariably casting Kate as dull and dutiful—began to inject tension. From the moment England's most popular weekly magazine, **Hello!**, arrived with a thud at Kensington Palace one week in November 2016, it was clear that the narrative was changing. On the cover, Meghan was bannered as "The Beauty Who Has Won the Prince's Heart," portrayed in an image of daring strapless seduction. The secondary image delivered up the Duchess of Cambridge wearing that same white shimmery evening gown used full length by the **Daily Mail** above the Pornhub story but reduced, this time, to a small top right-hand box.

Kate had worked long and hard for her status as style icon, despite the inhibitions imposed by Palace killjoys. She had ascended alongside the millennial rejection of elitist haute couture and spent the best part of a decade wearing a tastefully inexpensive wardrobe, subsuming her personal views and signaling solidarity with working women. It took her five years after her marriage to pose for an unusually sedate cover of British **Vogue** wearing the kind of conservative brown suede Burberry coat and large vintage hat seen in the crowds of the Cheltenham Horse Show. She put on pantyhose both literally and figuratively, smiling gamely and uncomplainingly for the press. Inside pages of Meghan's **Vanity Fair** cover story showed her not only without pantyhose, but barefoot in a strapless tulle Carolina Herrera bustier gown. It was the same story for the daytime engagement shot. Kate had worn a simple £125 cream silk Whistles blouse, recycling it ten years later to delighted fans in a morale-boosting video during the pandemic. Meghan's choice, nestling against Harry, was a black Ralph & Russo full-skirted, sheer-topped couture ball gown that lit up the fashion press. No one seemed to mind that it reportedly cost $75,000.

It was inevitable that Meghan would be seen as Kate's moral and aesthetic counterweight, but of more concern to the Cambridge camp were Meghan's clearly superior presentation skills. She was a trained and experienced actress, while Kate had always been a reticent public speaker. In February 2018, three months before the wedding, William, Kate, Harry, and Meghan, the "Fab Four"—as they were now unoriginally dubbed—made their first official appearance together to announce that Meghan would become a fourth patron of the Royal Foundation. "I've just been [in the UK] for three months," Meghan acknowledged, before fluently hogging the air time. With blithe proprietorship, she deployed an issue that was not even on the foundation's docket—women's empowerment, then at its fervid height with the acceleration of the #MeToo movement.

"Women don't need to find a voice. They have a voice. They need to feel empowered to use it," Meghan quotably exhorted as Harry looked on with awe and his brother and Kate stood by with expressionless irritation. When it was Kate's moment to speak, she was strikingly less articulate, as well as brief. Few knew that it was she—after years of providing emotional support to her younger brother, James, as he struggled with clinical depression—who had been the prime mover of the foundation's mental health campaign. It was crafted after careful consultation with mental health professionals, policy experts, and Palace advisers. Now here was Meghan championing a fashionable cause anointed by Hollywood and sure to make headlines. It was an awkward dynamic. It was later decided the Fab Four would not play onstage together as a band again.

Meghan had promised in the interview to "hit the ground running," an expression that filled the Palace, an institution of cautious consensus, with dread. The Firm's staff had already seen what that meant. It was swiftly becoming clear that Meghan either didn't know—or didn't want to know—that monarchy is hierarchical. Even before the engagement, she seemed to think that everyone in the shared office of William, Kate, and Harry was now hers to call on.

The British work ethic is a frustration for any alpha American hell-bent on "hitting the ground running." Transatlantic business executives often marvel at the volume of sleepy "out of office" email bounce-backs from the UK. After I'd edited **Vanity Fair** for a year as a transplant in New York in the eighties, my diary records that I dreaded "the rain in the voice" of certain contributors in England that signified I was about to hear why something "just isn't possible."

There is undoubtedly still a quota of drippy debs hanging around the Palace employ who clock in at ten and amble home at five. A former government official told me that transplants from the frenzied pace of the political world or the civil service use a spell in a Palace job as a way to knock off early. One who rotated out observed to me: "In Palace culture, a two-hour visit to a community center is regarded as a full day and there's a week to talk about it first."

A Palace veteran laid out the misunderstanding to me.

"If you are an actress on a TV show in America, you have a number of staff who are literally paid by the hour to work for you." So your business manager, your agent, your stylist, maybe your publicist, et cetera, are there to meet your demands without question. You are therefore never wrong, and it is all exactly what you want. It's just billable hours. But when you move to a situation where you've got full-time members of staff who work for an institution—the Palace—they're employees, not contracted people, they work within a policy framework. There are rules around accepting gifts. There are rules around accepting hospitality. Not rules that we just make up, but because it's a public institution. One assumes that the transition was probably not easy for Meghan, and for someone from the States, not welcome at all. And a big cultural shock about, "Well, here I am, I've become much more famous than I could have ever imagined." . . . And yet, the way she is served, in her mind, has not risen with that.

What the Palace staff saw as her willful blindness to institutional culture was a direct clash with Meghan's worldview. In the ranking system of the entertainment world, star power—wattage—equals leverage. She was not becoming a member of the Royal Family to argue, like the minor actress she was in her past life, about the size of her perk package. Successful screen actors have only one response to attempts to curtail their demands: Call my agent.

"They just couldn't deal with Meghan's level of directness," a Palace source explained to me. In other words, "Why didn't that invite go out?" rather than "I wonder if you could just check if that invitation did in fact go out if you don't mind, Allegra?"

"I suspect Meghan was trying to be herself, and trying to get things done the way she had been brought up in the industry, as well as in the States," one of the **Suits** executives told me.

Either not understanding how to get what she needed done, or thinking she had more seniority. Whatever it was, I'm sure that almost everywhere she turned she was banging into a wall, and simply did not know how to handle it. And after a while, the graciousness just disappears when you constantly make wrong turns.

Harry, who had always chafed at the hierarchy himself, was the last person to want to tell her to slow down. They were both now drunk on a shared fantasy of being the instruments of global transformation who, once married, would operate in the celebrity stratosphere once inhabited by Princess Diana. Meghan couldn't, and wouldn't, bide her time to get there. She was thirty-six. This was her big break. Alas, she seemed oblivious to the one critical factor that would determine the outcome of her plans for the future: primogeniture. Calling her agent just wouldn't help there.

Yet this age-old institutional truth could not have been more clear. The Duchess of Cambridge was pregnant for the third time, causing Meghan's future husband to slip even further down in the line of succession. When Kate became queen, Meghan would have to curtsy to her. In royal terms, Prince Harry, second son of the Prince of Wales, brother to the future king who would soon have three children, was—just as Meghan had been in **Suits**—number six on the call sheet.

CHAPTER
2 2

MAGIC KINGDOM

———

A Wedding Transforms the
House of Windsor

———

MAY 19, 2018. WINDSOR CASTLE.

It was a day of enchantment that suspended any doubt, any sniping, any courtier condescension. The wedding of the newly minted Harry, Duke of Sussex, to his mixed-race American Duchess achieved something remarkable. It turned the gray nine-hundred-year-old redoubt of Windsor Castle into a hotbed of cultural transformation.

Maybe there have been more mythic royal weddings. The swirl of doom around Prince Charles's marriage to the too-young Lady Diana Spencer was foretold in the moment just outside St. Paul's Cathedral when the blushing child-bride's taffeta train unfurled from her pumpkin carriage, as crumpled as her fairy-tale hopes would soon be. And there have certainly been weddings that were more consequential. The nuptials of the translucent twenty-one-year-old Princess Elizabeth to the Greek god Prince Philip at Westminster Abbey was one such, a rare moment when the future Queen chose her heart's desire over fusty Palace counsel. (And as usual, her own judgment was sounder than theirs.)

But Harry and Meghan's wedding was magic in its dictionary definition—a seeming power to influence the course of events by calling upon mysterious, possibly supernatural forces. It conjured up a vision of England as its dreamt-of best: a welcoming place, a place of inclusion, of freedom, of possibility, of love, a place where history and tradition fused effortlessly with uplifting social progress.

I was on network TV duty that day for CBS News, crammed onto a tiny balcony of the Harte and Garter, the ancient inn that overlooks the gates of Windsor Castle. I was sharing anchor duties with the morning show's consummate queen bee and Oprah best friend Gayle King, who got into the swing of things by switching to a different bobbing fascinator during every commercial break. I had forgotten how small Windsor is, with its tight alleys and closely packed pubs and novelty shops. I could hear the sublime soaring of the choir, practicing in St. George's Chapel, as if they were in the next room.

Meghan was going to have to trample on a lot of Harry's dead ancestors under the chapel's marble floors as she advanced up the aisle, including King George III, who was booted out by America.

The Great West Door was wreathed in massive leaf garlands, roses, and white peonies to frame the bride and groom when they emerged into the spring sunshine. The scent of the blooms wafted across the street, adding to the dreamlike quality of the day.

On the afternoon before, a mere hundred feet from my perch, the princely figures of William and Harry—discord put aside—emerged unexpectedly from the castle to plunge in and glad-hand the crowd. The sight was so Shakespearian in its motley Englishness I felt I should be tossing my mobcap over the side and dropping a curtsy. (Was that Falstaff watching and cheering with his tankard below?) As night fell, I looked out from the inn's bedroom window at a violet sky darkening over the castle's Norman battlements.

At 11:25 A.M., we saw the first glimmer of Meghan behind her silk tulle veil in the Rolls-Royce Phantom IV sweeping out of the majestic drive of Cliveden House, the former home of the Astor family, where she had spent her wedding eve dining alone with her mother. Beside her in the car was the awed, loving face of Doria with her tiny nose ring and small, pale green button hat with braids peeking out. An impeccably attired Prince of Wales, almost seventy now, silver-haired and ruddy of face, exuded welcoming charm as he waited to walk the bride up the aisle in place of her absent father. At the end of the service, he gallantly offered his arm to Doria to escort her out, a gesture rapturously received by a British public that saw its least favorite royal fogey magically (yes!) transformed into Chaucer's "verray, parfit gentil knyght."

The rush of indelible moments kept coming. It was impossible not to be touched by the yearning vulnerability of Harry's face when he first saw his bride approach the altar. It was suddenly clear what a desperately unhappy man he had been before. The broken boy who never fully recovered from losing his mother, with all the years of pain and blame in between, had now been made whole by the love of a strong, demonstrative woman, ready to wrap around him. He could fall into her arms, weeping with relief that, at last, he had someone of his own to share the strange solitary state of being royal. "You look amazing," he whispered, as she took her place beside him in her boatneck alabaster silk gown. The light through the chapel windows illuminated the fifty-three flowers of the Commonwealth that had been hand-sewn into her sixteen-foot veil.

Other memorable images: the deep dignity in the ramrod back of the almost ninety-seven-year-old Prince Philip, as he endured an hour on his feet just six weeks after a hip operation. Beside him, unchanged in six decades of attending royal weddings, the Queen's boot-face for the ages, framed by a lime-green boater hat. Oh, how the cameras loved the joyful tumble of tiny bridesmaids and pages, with the graceful figure of Kate dropping down to sweetly hush them.

The unexpected triumph of the hour was the music. Rousing boarding-school hymns—"Guide Me, O Thou Great Redeemer," one of Diana's favorites—were followed by Karen Gibson's gospel choir rocking out "Stand by Me," an inspired touch suggested not by the bride as everyone assumed but by her ever-surprising father-in-law. It was capped only by the WTF look creeping across aristocratic poker faces under feather-laden, flying-saucer head-gear when the African American bishop Michael Curry blasted out his nearly fifteen-minute roof-raising, theologically charged sermon: "Set me as a seal upon your heart, as a seal upon your arm; for love is as strong as death, passion fierce as the grave. Its flashes are flashes of fire." His gusts of raw spiri-tual fervor, probably the ultimate inspired injection of Black joy into British traditionalism, generated forty thousand tweets a minute. Most of the con-gregation, expecting the usual comforting disen-gagement of the waning Church of England's pallid bishopric, were too dumbstruck or baffled to listen to his message: that love (as novelist Tara Isabella Burton noted of the sermon) is "a necessary, chaotic, and political force. Love, for Curry, provides hope in the face of social injustice, even as it provides a blue-print for overturning it."

Open-carriage rides of a royal bride and groom usually have a theme-park flavor. After their Westminster Abbey nuptials, William and Kate also took a victory trot, but London's streets are broad, diluting the crowd's intimacy. Windsor, however, is such a compact English town that the cheering, flag-waving spectators could almost touch Meghan and Harry's carriage as it passed below the balconies. On our own precarious ledge, Gayle King and I saw the bride and groom jingle out of the castle gates right underneath our noses, were able to ogle every detail of the scarlet cavalry uniforms, the sparkling polish of the brass, the prancing white steeds, the whole thrilling rousing riot of red and gold as the breeze lifted Meghan's veil. Harry's military back was as straight as his grandfather's, as the horses clip-clopped through the cobbled streets to cries of royalist goodwill. There was a wonderful moment of genuine emotion when the couple approached the end of the Long Walk, the historic two-and-a-half-mile avenue south of the castle, and Meghan could be seen, with her hand at her slender throat, almost gasping as if to say, "Oh my God, I am blown away."

Nothing, not even Hollywood, had prepared her for this. And nothing had prepared Britain for the loved-up, uninhibited celebration that was so utterly unlike anything hitherto associated with the Windsor family in their castle on the hill. There were multiple references to the presiding presence of Harry's mother in the commentary, from her favorite forget-me-nots in the bride's bouquet to the eerily similar voice of her elder sister Lady Jane Fellowes reading from the Song of Solomon from the pulpit. But perhaps the most powerful Diana echo was from the days after her death when strangers of every race, creed, and color embraced one another in the weeping crowds outside Buckingham Palace. At the end of the day, I was so emotionally spent with ambient goodwill, all I could do was collapse in my hotel room in London and watch the reruns.

II

For the Palace, the kumbaya moment was even more remarkable because of the shit-show that preceded it. After almost two years of getting to know the bride-to-be and witnessing her mesmerizing hold over Harry, the Palace staff was reeling. Compared to the jovial team effort for the wedding of William and Kate, Palace sources report that the preparation for the Sussex union was all drama, all the time. Meghan's MO was seen as revving up Harry when she sensed any obstruction.

The last person anyone at the Palace wants to offend is the woman who sees the monarch four times a day in her pantyhose. Angela Kelly is Her Majesty's dresser. Her large, powder-puff face, silver-blond bouffant, and twinkly cornflower-blue eyes belie a steely wielding of court power. Not only is the sixty-something daughter of a Liverpudlian crane driver the first-ever in-house designer of the Queen's seasonal wardrobe of colorful outfits, she is also the curator of the Queen's priceless jewelry collection.

Endowed with the job title of personal adviser, she coordinates the monarch's medical appointments and personal calendar. Her intimacy is such that she breaks in the Queen's shoes for her (the same stumpy-heeled style in black, cream, or white for the last fifty years) and joins the "recce" team before her public engagements to ensure that her boss's cerise bouclé coatdress ensemble will not clash with the curtains on the podium or that the plumage on Her Maj's

Ascot hat will not obscure the camera's view. She sits alone with the Queen behind the privacy screen in the Robing Room of the House of Lords before the opening of Parliament and gently drapes the ceremonial robe on her sacred shoulders before she enters the chamber to deliver the annual ritual of the Queen's Speech. Kelly's unfettered access is, not surprisingly, resented in some Palace factions, particularly when she was granted permission to write two books about her Palace role, a privilege disallowed to any royal servant since Crawfie broke her omertà in 1950. Around the Palace, she is known, not always affectionately, as AK-47.

After so much time together, an unlikely friendship has bloomed between monarch and servant. The Queen appreciates Kelly's caustic humor, valuing her as a truth teller, and though none of this is a secret at court, Meghan did not—or could not—perceive the difference between the Queen's personal aide and a contract stylist at NBC Universal. A blow-up occurred when Kelly willfully—as Meghan and, therefore, Harry saw it—denied the bride-to-be access to the Queen Mary bandeau tiara, on loan from the Queen, that Meghan would be wearing for the wedding. Meghan wanted to try on the tiara **now** for some styling sessions with her hairdresser, and her fiancé fired off like a missile to make it happen.

The removal of any of the historic pieces from the vault in Buckingham Palace involves a rigmarole of permissions and procedures, including the personal sign-off of the monarch and the presence of the

Crown jeweler, who handles the bling in white gloves. Whether the Queen herself told Kelly to refuse Meghan's request was one of the perennial questions of palace Kabuki, as was the process of lending her jewels in the first place. The Queen is said to enjoy offering a "statement" piece or two to female members of the family for big occasions, but part of the ritual is the recipient understanding that an invitation to pick something out is not really a choice. Kelly was deputed in the presence of the Queen to present to Meghan the five tiaras the Queen had preselected. It was suggested by the monarch which tiara Meghan might find most pleasing, i.e., the refined, slim crescent of the diamond Queen Mary bandeau (estimated value $2.7 million) made for the Queen's grandmother. Perfect, don't you agree, Meghan? (It was.)

In **Finding Freedom**, widely accepted as the sanctioned biography of Meghan and Harry, authors Omid Scobie and Carolyn Durand lay out a scenario in which Harry, after repeated calls for access to the tiara for his fiancée's hairdressing rehearsal, was rudely stonewalled by Kelly. What's missing from this account is how fed up, by this time, many Palace aides were with Meghan's demands and those of her husband. "Meghan would say, 'I'll just do whatever you want me to do,'" a source told me, vehemently, "while meanwhile, she eventually got the chapel she wanted, the preacher she wanted, the choir she wanted, the dress she wanted, the tiara she wanted, the candles she wanted, the location for the after-party, the chef, the entertainment, the guest list. No one said no to anything." It's not unusual for a bride to get everything she wants or become over-wrought before her wedding, less usual for the man to turn into groomzilla. Harry was determined his wife should get everything he considered her due. There was a lot of raging, a Palace source told me. "In-person shouting in front of other members of staff, basically in front of too many people, which is why it all started to come out and become the first-ever negative piece of coverage about the behavior of the couple." Meghan got her tiara, but Angela Kelly had made her point.

With tensions rising, there was an altercation be-tween Kate and Meghan at the bridesmaids' dress fitting. The question—now wreathed in legend—is this: Who made whom burst into tears? It was later reported that Meghan had insisted that the little girls—including Kate's three-year-old daughter, Princess Charlotte—dispense with tights beneath their ivory silk dresses, and that this had pushed royal traditionalist Kate to the brink of a panic at-tack. Another version is that Kate was irritated that the flower girls' dresses didn't fit. And that the ex-hausted Duchess of Cambridge, having only recently given birth to Prince Louis, was sick of standing around in the heat being bossed around by the-not-quite-yet Duchess of Sussex.

Who cares? Mainly Meghan, it would seem. When rumors of the spat leaked six months later, generat-ing a rash of "impossible diva" headlines, Meghan demanded that the Palace denounce or correct the story. She was outraged that they wouldn't immediately deny something that, inconveniently, appeared to them to be true, if incomplete. (Best guess: Both of them had meltdowns that day.)

Either way, the culture of the Palace press department is almost never to comment on personal matters relating to the family. According to another Palace source, Meghan was told, "'We don't comment on private matters. Deal with it.' Then she became obsessed with the fact that the Palace wouldn't knock it down."

What makes this picayune controversy worth noting is its curious afterlife. In her March 2021 Oprah interview, Meghan took the opportunity of addressing a global audience of 49 million to assert that it was she, not Kate, who had been made to cry. Three years after the wedding she was still (at the height of the COVID-19 pandemic) obsessing about the Palace's refusal to correct the dopey bridesmaid story in answer to questions she could have briefly dispensed with. For decades, Camilla has had to read the endlessly recycled lie that she was pelted with bread rolls in her local supermarket by an angry Diana fan, but she has smiled creamily and sailed on. Kate said not a word after the Oprah interview, even if behind the scenes the Cambridge briefing machine worked overtime. Katie Nicholl, royal correspondent at the **Daily Mail,** was told, "Kate is not in a position to respond, and Meghan and Harry know that." The power of a royal silence is the monarchy's ultimate mystique.

So why didn't Harry help navigate Palace culture for his future wife? He didn't want to. Their new complicity required Meghan to fight all the norms he had kicked against for so long. She was now his comrade in arms. An aide described their confrontational stance to me as a mutual "addiction to drama."

Plenty was coming their way and, as happens so often, was partially self-inflicted. It was probably a mistake for Meghan to ghost the rambunctious Piers Morgan as soon as she met Harry. After their first convivial dirty martinis at the Scarsdale Tavern, Morgan never heard from Meghan again. It was a snub for which he later extracted sweet revenge, mocking her relentlessly, as only he knows how, on his morning show and in his **Daily Mail** column, two of the most powerful media platforms in the country. A wedding invitation to the man she had once eagerly DM'd to try to get a meeting would have reaped PR dividends. He said as much in his **Mail** column that appeared at the time of the engagement under the friendly headline "Hearty congratulations, Harry, you picked a real keeper."

"I didn't hear from Meghan again after her royal romance erupted into the public gaze, which is perfectly understandable under the circumstances," he wrote. "All will be forgiven though if I get an invite to the wedding of the year."

It didn't arrive and he didn't forgive.

Serena Williams, David and Victoria Beckham, Priyanka Chopra, Elton John, and the cast and producers of **Suits** all received gold-embossed invitations. ("The American visitors were decked out. The locals were wearing morning coats that hadn't been ironed in twenty years," one of the **Suits** team told me.) The celebrity guests were a portrait not of Meghan's intimate circle but of the friends she most wanted to recruit. Oprah, whom Meghan had scarcely met, if at all, was seated in prime pew real estate opposite the Queen. Her pastel pink Stella McCartney dress had been whipped up overnight to replace the one in beige she suddenly feared would photograph white. Human rights lawyer Amal Clooney, who floated up the steps of the chapel in a stunning liquid yellow dress and wide-brimmed tea-tray hat, was seated with the debonair George opposite Princess Margaret's son, Viscount Linley. Rachel Johnson, sister of Boris, alleged in a column that Princess Diana's former flatmate turned to the star couple alongside her in the pew and asked how they knew Harry or Meghan. " 'We don't,' " she said the Clooneys answered "brightly."

The speed with which Meghan seemed to dispense with people was becoming a meme. Bad karma rained down from her spurned half siblings. Living in Florida and Oregon, respectively, Samantha, fifty-three, and Tom Jr., fifty-one, had always been cash-strapped loose cannons. Samantha had called Meghan "narcissistic and selfish" as early as November 2016, before Meghan and Harry were engaged, but she was stirred up again by Harry's insensitive remark on BBC Radio 4's **Today** show about the royals being "the family, I suppose, that [Meghan's] never had." This seems rich, given what Harry has since told the world about his miseries as a misfit in the royal cage. Scattered, discordant, and mutually resentful, the Markles were never a **Leave It to Beaver** American household. But in a contest of dysfunctional families, the Markles versus the Windsors is probably a toss-up.

Though Americans are more inclined than the British to exclude difficult or embarrassing relatives, wiser heads would have recommended that Meghan grit her teeth and invite Samantha and Tom, with PR clamps firmly in place. "We all have black sheep in our families, don't we?" Lady Glenconner said to me. "But you know you have to somehow round them up and get them on side and bring them all in and stick them somewhere." One can imagine in the same situation with recalcitrant relations Carole Middleton flying the whole feuding clan over first-class, billeting them in the Boring Goring, and entertaining them with VIP sightseeing tours of London until the big day. Meghan opted not to go this route. She was a brand now as much as a bride, and the famous, the beautiful, and the influential would fill the pews of St. George's Chapel.

Reduced to the role of Cinderella's step-siblings, Samantha and Tom Jr. doubled down on the trash talk about Meghan to the receptive tabloid press. Tom Jr., in an interview with the **Daily Mirror**, blabbed that Meghan's refusal to invite them has "torn my entire family apart." Samantha let fly a barrage of negative tweets: "It's time to 'man up' . . . "Shout outs' about humanitarianism don't work when you are allowing Meg to ignore the Markles."

In one of the more grotesque moments of the family smackdown, Tom Jr. wrote an open letter to Prince Harry that appeared in **In Touch**. It was "not to [sic] late," Tom Jr. said, to realize "this is the biggest mistake in Royal Wedding History," and, in prose that sounded like it was written with a bread knife, proclaimed Meghan is a "jaded, shallow, conceited woman that will make a joke of you and the royal family heritage. Not to mention, to top it all off, she doesn't invite her own family and instead invites complete strangers to the wedding. Who does that?"

Reeling, Meghan called her father and begged him to tell her half siblings to call off the dogs. "She was getting mad at me," he told me when he spoke to me from Rosarito. "She kept saying it was up to me to handle it, but I don't know of any parents that can control their fifty-year-old children. I can't defend what my son said or why he said it. I would actually blame most of the things that were printed on a couple of reporters that drove up to Oregon and took him out every night to a bar. And I do mean literally every night. They would feed him things and then they reported it."

Wow, that's evil, I suggested.

"You want to hear evil stories about reporters?" Tom Markle said. "I can keep you here for a long time."

III

Today, the overall public perception of Meghan Markle's father is of a sorry, money-grubbing loser. Not content with embarrassing his daughter by selling fake pictures of himself to the media prepping for the wedding, he then stiffed her before the Royal Family and the world on the biggest day of her life after torturing her about whether or not he would show up.

Markle is, indeed, a difficult man with a stubborn curmudgeon's pride that means when he's in a hole, he keeps digging. After fifty years of blinkered professional life, working overnights on soap operas, now living by himself and finding his pension hasn't stretched as far as he'd hoped, one senses all he wants is to be left the fuck alone.

Yet it rankles him to this day that Harry failed to show him the respect of coming in person to meet him even once before asking for his daughter's hand in marriage on the phone. He prefers not to admit that Meghan was likely too embarrassed by how he came off to introduce him to her royal boyfriend in person. ("Embarrassment is a choice that an individual makes. It's not the fault of the other person," Wendy Riche, Tom's former boss as executive producer of **General Hospital**, opined to me.) It did not help Tom's mood that his ex-wife received a visit at her house in L.A. from two reps from the British consulate bearing the official engagement announcement by the Palace, but that he, her father, was treated like a second-class citizen.

When the world's press showed up in Rosarito banging on his door, looking for dirt, Tom found the experience rattling in the extreme. He thought Harry's exhortations on the phone not to speak to reporters were unrealistic—easy to say for a prince living in a palace, not so easy when they're swarming the sleepy Mexican town where he was grocery shopping and sitting in the launderette.

"On the street I live on, they rented porches on the left and the right of the street," he told me. "Every time I come out of my house, someone would take a picture of me. I couldn't get in and out of my car or in or out of my house. Anytime I drive downtown, they'd follow me. Anytime I get a haircut, they take pictures of me. I took to only going out at midnight, at one A.M. to go to my ATM machines and do some shopping." A humiliating torrent of images of Tom hauling beer cans and shopping for flatulence medication appeared in the tabloids, depicting him as some shambolic hobo rather than how he saw himself, a once-successful former lighting director enjoying his beachfront retirement. "All of us who worked on **General Hospital** were horrified about how Tommy was portrayed," one of the production team told me.

A desire for a less disheveled public image made Tom fall afoul of the dastardly sting perpetrated by Jeff Rayner, the silver-tongued co-founder of a low-life celebrity photo and gossip agency in Los Angeles. Rayner suggested a shoot that purported to follow Tom getting measured for his morning suit, lifting weights to get in shape, and poring over a copy of the book **Images of Great Britain.** His daughter Samantha, with her unerring combination of bad faith and bad judgment, thought it was a great idea, particularly as Rayner offered her a cut on the syndication money. (They ultimately netted around £100,000.) So she urged her dad to do it. In one of the more poignant setups, Tom's bulky back is humped over a computer screen at an internet café as he scrolls through engagement shots of Meghan and Harry, unaware that he looks like the ultimate sad voyeur to his daughter's ascendance out of his league.

The sham fell apart when **The Mail on Sunday** published closed-circuit footage showing that Tom had colluded, with the footage held for maximum impact until the week before the wedding. The supposed tailor—he looks about fourteen—was revealed to be a party-store clerk who was tipped fifteen dollars to "measure" Markle. With the wider camera angle, it's clear that the alleged workout space was a derelict hillside scattered with mattresses and tires.

"I thought I was doing the right thing, which obviously I was not," Markle told me gruffly. "It was a mistake."

It is hard to imagine more mortifying revelations for Meghan, who thought she'd finally crossed the bridge into her fairy-tale future, only to have her banished kin rear up to grab her by the ankles and drag her down into the slimy deep. After a tip-off that the **Mail** was about to expose the truth of the photo shoot, the bride-to-be, in obvious pain, called her father to ask if he was indeed in on the scam before she asked if the Palace could get the story killed. For reasons known only to him—guilt, or mounting panic—he denied it. Reflecting later to a friend about his conduct, Meghan said, "My dad never sought this out. I really believe he was a victim and now I feel sad because I believe he's been fully corrupted." Markle's refusal to call Kensington Palace communications secretary Jason Knauf for assistance—as his daughter had urged him to do—can be ascribed to his defensive refusal to admit how vulnerable he really felt.

Palace officials began, for the first time, to feel sorry for Meghan, while among the senior royals, the anxieties about her joining the Firm entered a whole new realm of alarm. Forget about her imperious demands and worrying hold over Harry; the malign indiscretions and folly of her relatives would likely keep the tabloids in business for years. It was doubly painful for Harry because the Sturm und Drang validated the caution of all the stuffy Meghan naysayers and his censorious brother.

Texts to Tom Markle from Harry in this fevered moment—which later emerged in the Sussexes' court case against **The Mail on Sunday**'s parent company, Associated Newspapers Ltd.—show that he was terrified when Tom wanted to issue a public apology in case he got himself further embroiled. "Tom, Harry again!" he wrote. "Really need to speak to u. U do not need to apologize, we understand the circumstances but 'going public' will only make the situation worse."

Media micro-management by Harry at this late date only made Markle feel further disempowered—perhaps even emasculated. The shock of finding himself the butt of the world's scorn was so shameful to Tom, it doubtless contributed to what happened next—a minor heart attack.

Meghan was now living her own version of Harry's **Truman Show.** Her father was talking to the celebrity website TMZ instead of to her. She had to log on to discover, first, that he was feeling too embarrassed to attend the wedding, and next, that he had changed his mind and was coming after all. There followed a tabloid **opera buffa** that riveted the world about whether or not the bride's father would get on the plane to London and walk his daughter down the aisle at Windsor.

Then, nothing: silence, a second heart attack, and Tom Markle bailed on the wedding for good. With his daughter's frantic texts beeping on his phone, the father of the bride sank beneath the waves like a traveler on the **Titanic.**

He blamed his vanishing act to me on a last berating phone call from Harry—something Meghan has denied—while he was recovering in his hospital bed. "Harry said, 'If you had listened to me, this would not have happened to you.' At that point I said, 'That's the snottiest man I've ever heard in my life.' And I hung up on him. I said, 'That's it, no more.' After that, they never called me again, ever," he told me. Meghan has since claimed she called him over twenty times.

At the bride's request, Prince Charles immediately agreed to step in to perform the role of walking her down the aisle. Whatever the private collective sighs of relief from Windsor Castle, for the weeping Meghan—as she wrote to her father in August 2018—it was a blow that "broke my heart into a million pieces." The turbulent week of family drama had exposed to the world unadmitted humiliations. The ugliness of her relatives' fighting, and the proud lonely figure of her mother without one relative or friend beside her in the pew, suggests Meghan had worked her way up through more meanness and discord than she had let on. In their last mother-daughter evening together at Cliveden, how much crying did she do about the indignities inflicted on her that last week? The discreet Middleton family was a Praetorian guard around Kate before her wedding. Meghan could trust only the sweet composure of her mother, Doria.

The drama was almost as traumatic for Harry as it was for Meghan. Once again, the media had found a way to wreak incalculable damage on someone he loved, this time by ensnaring her father. As the Prince said when the news of their love first broke, "Some people think this is a game. It's not a game. It's her life."

The pre-wedding torture of Tom Markle was press malfeasance at its most unpardonable, driven by a commercial cynicism that had a tragic human outcome. "At the heart of this is the very great harm that a small number of newspapers have done to the Markle family," Paddy Harverson told me. "Basically, the driving of an enormous permanent wedge between Meghan and her father. It's worth remembering that when Harry and Meghan first went out together, the Palace officials officially reached out to all the press on background and said Thomas Markle lives privately alone and doesn't want to speak to media. The press ignored all this. They groomed him; they broke him down to the point where he succumbed. There was no public interest in it. All the stuff that happened stemmed from the ruthless way the media broke into his life."

Ultimately, a ravaged Tom watched the fairy-tale wedding of his daughter on TV, like everybody else, alone in a $30-a-night Airbnb in Tijuana that he rented to get away from the press. "My baby looks beautiful," he said. "I will always regret not being able to be there and not being able to hold my daughter's hand."

CHAPTER 23

UNRAVELING

The Monarchy's Morning After

I SAW THE CAR FLIP AND THOUGHT 'FUCKING HELL.'" On a frosty January morning in 2019, seventy-five-year-old local barrister Roy Warne was startled to see a Land Rover somersault across the A149 motorway at Babingley, in Norfolk, and roll onto its side. An elderly male voice could be heard shouting, "My legs, my legs!" The vehicle had collided with a blue minivan—now giving off plumes of smoke—driven by a woman with a female passenger and a nine-month-old baby in the back seat. Warne got the screaming infant out, then rushed to the Land Rover to help extricate the driver. At which point, the gob-smacked Warne had occasion to think "**fucking hell**" again. Shaken but uninjured, the Duke of Edinburgh was lifted up and staggered out.

For some time, the ninety-seven-year-old Prince Philip had refused to consider the fact that he was too old to be behind the wheel. He was always a demon driver and never wore a seatbelt while careening around his estates. As soon as he totaled this Land Rover he ordered a new one, and the next day was cautioned by the police after being photographed driving unbuckled. When the incident hit the news media, it triggered a national debate about getting geriatric menaces off the road. It doubtless caused Philip some grim amusement that the populist tabloids were now hollering that he should be driven around by a chauffeur.

For once, the Queen was not entertained by her husband's contumacy. If the two women and baby in the minivan had been killed, it would have been the monarchy's Chappaquiddick, raising similar "what if" questions as Camilla's car accident twenty-two years earlier. The Duke, moreover, was stubbornly unwilling to take the blame, insisting that the sun in his eyes caused him not to see the other car coming. The passenger in the minivan told the **Mirror,** "It would mean the world to me if Prince Philip said sorry but I have no idea if he's sorry at all. What would it have taken for him and the Queen to send me a card and a bunch of flowers?" She added that she only received a terse message via a police family liaison officer, which said: "The Queen and the Duke of Edinburgh would like to be remembered to you." It was clear that the aggrieved woman remembered perfectly well, thank you.

Philip was cajoled (or perhaps in this instance commanded) into writing the woman a letter of apology the next day in which he implausibly claimed he'd just been told she had broken her wrist and re-iterated what an excellent driver he usually was. There was a deep sigh of relief at the Palace the next month when he finally yielded to pressure and gave up his driver's license. It was a humiliating blow for a man who had insisted on independence over a lifetime—and guarded it without compromise.

The incident was another sign to the Queen that her beloved consort was losing his grip. Four months earlier, she had blessed his decision to retire from royal duties. It had been more than six decades since the thirty-one-year-old Philip Mountbatten, Duke of Edinburgh had sworn his oath of allegiance as her **liege man of life and limb.**

By the time he stepped down in August 2017, he had accompanied the Queen on all 251 of her overseas tours ("Don't jostle the Queen!" he would sometimes bark if the press got too close) and had completed 22,000 royal engagements on his own. More than 780 organizations could claim him as their patron, president, or honorary member, and he showed up for them again and again, even for such dutiful duds as touring the headquarters of the British Dental Association in Brighton, after which one reporter noted, "The weather could just not have been worse." One patronage he held proudly for nearly sixty-five years, the captain generalcy of the Royal Marines, he relinquished to his grandson Prince Harry. "Don't cock it up," Philip told him, advice that seems, today, to be not in the least bit gratuitous.

In his retirement, Philip took himself off to his man cave at Wood Farm, the cozy and unpretentious royal property on the Sandringham Estate, where he organized his papers, painted watercolors, and read history voraciously. He was often visited by Penny Romsey. She shared the Duke's love of painting, a quiet and unobtrusive passion for both. Still obsessed with technology, Philip often extolled the joys of his Kindle until, disgusted by all the direct marketing of books that he didn't want to read, he threw it in the bathtub.

With typical decisiveness, he'd made it clear that he was not only physically absenting himself when he retired but also getting out of the royal advisory business altogether. Though the Queen was personally happy that Philip was spending his final years as he pleased, the absence of his unfailing good counsel left her with a void. His retirement unwittingly caused the loss of another wise man from her most trusted inner cabinet. A rare undiplomatic move by her private secretary Sir Christopher Geidt created an opportunity for Princes Charles and Andrew to push the Queen's savvy and most senior counselor out the door.

Andrew had never forgiven Geidt for working political back channels to get him removed as the UK's trade envoy in 2011 because of his general awfulness and dodgy financial deals. And Charles was outraged when Geidt summoned a staff meeting of the five hundred members of all three royal households to announce Philip's retirement and called for them to unite in support of the Queen. The thin-skinned Charles's reaction can be parsed as "Bloody outrageous!" This should have been a Prince of Wales moment. Charles was about to turn seventy and was desperate to signify that his mother had begun her glide path down and he was now lifting off.

Charles had always resented Geidt's power. The Queen trusted her formidable private secretary not least because he had a keen antenna for the national mood. A former colleague told me, "Geidt has a finger on the pulse of the country like no one else I know, including politicians." (He was subsequently hired by Prime Minister Boris Johnson as his ethics adviser in 2021.) While Geidt understood that his role was to manage the delicate transition from the reign of a revered long-reigning queen to that of her less popular son, he is said to have believed that the convulsions of Brexit had made the Queen an important unifying symbol of stability.

The optimism of Brexiteers after they won the vote to leave the European Union had turned into a rancorous fear that it wasn't, after all, going to happen. Theresa May's Tory government was at war with itself, and there was a strong belief that the still-balking Remainers would find a way to make it a Brexit in name only. Even though Charles now accompanied Her Majesty to the opening of Parliament and took on more of the Palace investitures, it was Geidt's view that the British people had to be reassured, in the middle of all the political turmoil, that the Queen was not going anywhere—yet. This was the very opposite of what Charles wanted.

Charles went to Mummy and demanded Geidt's head on a platter. In what was surely not her finest hour, the Queen caved to her son's tantrum. The rare fraternal alliance of Andrew and Charles was too rattling for the ninety-one-year-old monarch to resist. She showed her private anguish over Sir Christopher's unfair dismissal after ten years of service by loading him up with honors on the way out and throwing him a farewell party for more than four hundred guests at Buckingham Palace. Every senior royal attended except the backstabbing Charles and Andrew. The bruised Geidt went off and buried himself on a sheep farm in Orkney. Edward Young, the deputy who replaced him, had been the head of communications at Barclays before joining the Palace staff in 2004 and, though he had excelled overseeing the details of HM's Irish tour, possessed nothing like his predecessor's wide-ranging tentacles. There are many who believe that subsequent royal troubles would not have blown up so badly if the Queen could have turned to Geidt.

II

Meanwhile, the insistent Meghan kept asking for Palace meetings about how to "shape her role"—a role that was, to the Palace, blindingly clear. It was to support the monarchy with a considered agenda of

multiple local patronages and appearances, punctu-
ated with overseas tours judicially selected by the
Foreign Office. To show Meghan how it was done,
the Queen invited the family fledgling to accompany
her a month after the wedding to open a six-lane toll
bridge in the town of Chester, near Liverpool. One
should, perhaps, detect Her Majesty's dry sense of
humor in the choice of engagement. The Queen wore
a festive lime-green **Cat in the Hat** trilby, matching
coat, and white gloves, and had rarely been seen having such a good time at a public engagement that
wasn't about horses. It happens to be a fact that the
Queen adores anything to do with bridges and tunnels,
often fishing out invitations from her private secretaries'
"decline" pile. Even so, as a message to a glamorous new
American granddaughter-in-law attempting to understand what service to the monarchy looked like, this
particular excursion to Merseyside was a useful method
of instruction. To rephrase George V's consort Queen
Mary's dictum, "We are the Royal Family and we love
infrastructure."

Hatless (gasp!), with her hair down, Meghan chose
to wear a cream Givenchy pencil dress with a cunning shoulder cape. She was heard to ask the monarch
as they stepped out of the royal train at Cheshire
how she would like to proceed into the waiting
Bentley.

"What is your preference?" asked Meghan.

"You go first," the Queen replied with a twinkle in
her eye as she let the former **Suits** actress take precedence.

Harry and Meghan were then dispatched on an agreeably undemanding tour of Ireland. The Duchess arrived in Dublin in a skin-tight, moss-green Givenchy skirt and top, rang the massive Peace Bell with Harry, attentively watched a game of hurling at Croke Park, and admired the young oak tree planted by the Queen on her own celebrated visit six years before. It was meat-and-potato royal stuff, but executed with an actress's élan. The Paddy Harverson doctrine of "all you have to do is smile and look as if you enjoy doing it" paid off with ecstatic reviews. In 2018, there were eight hundred thousand references to Meghan as a "breath of fresh air."

The Duchess, in fact, came up with two well-considered royal projects of her own. She created a book of recipes from immigrant women displaced by the tragic inferno that killed seventy-two residents of the Grenfell Tower in June 2017. The project was a winner on multiple levels. It was authentic—Meghan is a talented cook herself. It was compassionate, a way to remind the public and the media that the families were still bravely suffering after the cameras had moved on. And it was effective. **Together: Our Community Cookbook** raised over £500,000 for the fire's victims and was an instant bestseller on Amazon.

At a time when 37 percent of the residents of London were born outside the United Kingdom and their very status as residents was being impugned by vocal Little Englanders in the post-Brexit rancor, the sight of the Duchess of Sussex in an apron at the Al-Manaar mosque churning rice in a cauldron alongside head-scarved mothers was a solid public relations success. No one in the Royal Family but Meghan could legitimately utter the words "On a personal level, I feel proud to live in a city that can have so much diversity."

The Grenville Tower tragedy had exposed the existence of shameful racial and economic inequity in London just a stone's throw from one of the city's most expensive neighborhoods, Notting Hill. It became a celebrity cause for the likes of Adele and Lily Allen. By shining her own spotlight on the grassroots London cause du jour and marrying it to her kitchen cred, the new Duchess preserved her brand of "foodie feminist activist royal."

In another well-received move, she helped launch a clothing line for Smart Works, a charity that provides a business wardrobe for needy women going on job interviews. Meghan had first visited the charity secretly two months before her wedding and eagerly returned five times. Smart Works' mission included providing workplace coaching and styling sessions for their clients, some of which Meghan conducted herself. "Not a handout, a hand held," she posted catchily on Instagram. The founder of Smart Works, Juliet Hughes-Hallett, said, "She's a natural coach. She helps our clients feel safe, comfortable and protected. There is a real natural empathy about her. There's something about her which is mighty."

It was a win for the Sussex brand, upholding the

working-woman ethos versus Kate's stay-at-home-mom template, and contributing Meghan's **Tig** sense of style to the usually glum fashion arena of thrift shops. "Why are there so many lilac jackets in here?" she pondered, while surveying the dowdy offerings in the Smart Works racks.

It was all an excellent run-up before the higher stakes of the Sussexes' sixteen-day tour of Australia, New Zealand, and Fiji in October 2018. Meghan's Commonwealth debut was a smashing success. Echoes of Charles and Diana's famous first Australia conquest were irresistible in the number and excitement of the fans who turned out. Meghan was photographed in full Diana mode, hugging toddlers who gave her flowers, dropping to her knees to clasp both hands of an ancient granny in a wheelchair in Sydney, and clapping with delight at a baby koala bear at the Taronga Zoo. She made a solo speech in Fiji, beating the drum for the education of girls.

Harry, too, seemed in his finest form, opening and closing his fourth Invictus Games in the middle of the tour. It helps to be in love with your wife—and to be proud of her rather than jealous. Unlike Charles, who seethed at suddenly playing second fiddle to Diana's charisma, Harry had star power in his own right. But for the first time, he also had a woman he loved to share it with.

The New York Times acclaimed the couple as "young, diverse and exuding cool, the new face of royalty." Powering through seventy-six engagements, Meghan showed the promising stamina of a royal workhorse, particularly encouraging now that she was four months pregnant. The couple announced their joyful news on the eve of the tour, telling the crowds at Sydney Opera House, "We're excited to join the [parent] club!"

So, Meghan must have been thrilled with it all . . . right? No. She apparently hated every second of it. She found the itinerary of engagements "pointless," a former Palace employee told me. "She didn't understand why things were set up in that way. Instead of being excited when thousands of people showed up at the opera house, it was very much like, 'What's the purpose? I don't understand this,'"—the "this" being the representational role of the British monarchy and its traditional agenda, rather than the focus on causes she wanted to spotlight. Such engagements are old school, yes, but create classic royal ties that bind.

The way Meghan read the crowd response was the direct opposite of the way Prince Philip understood it when he accompanied the Queen on their first Commonwealth tour of Australia in 1954. As he told Gyles Brandreth, "More than a million people came out and cheered the Queen, a million! It wasn't about her. They came because she was the Queen. If you start thinking it's about you, you're lost." But it was head-turning for Meghan to experience the full-throttle motorcade-purring, outrider-vrooming, crowd-roaring adulation of a popular young royal on a tour planned to the last teacup by the Palace machine. Megmania, as it was called in the Australian press, was markedly more enthusiastic than the reception for William and Kate on their own Aussie tour in 2014. Meghan seemed to interpret the success as a call for Brand Sussex to be elevated in the Palace hierarchy.

Her aggrieved mood mirrored Harry's. He fulminated over the customary presence of the royal press pack, even though the copy they filed was overwhelmingly complimentary. The **Times** correspondent Valentine Low remembers him being "pretty grumpy." During "a long and incredibly boring welcome ceremony in Fiji . . . Harry was just glowering. He was cross with the media, and he spent the entire welcome ceremony diverting his gaze to one side just to stare daggers at the press pack." When the Palace team encouraged him to go to the back of the plane and chat up the traveling press, Harry un-endearingly told them, "Thanks for coming, not that anyone invited you." Did he forget that it was a taxpayer-funded trip?

Back home, Meghan felt snubbed that there was no particular display of Palace appreciation. A former aide acknowledged to me that it's often a "massive anticlimax when you get back from a royal tour. . . . You're just back into your normal life. The Queen would send the principals a note after a trip but you don't come back to a ticker-tape welcome." Diana experienced the same disappointment after the success of her own Commonwealth tour in 1983. "She couldn't understand why nobody said, 'Well done,'" a Palace veteran recalled to me. "The reason is that they all do their duty, and they wonder what is so unique." Diana sensed that the snooty silence meant that other senior royals were jealous of her appeal overseas. Harry believed the same was true about Meghan. "[My family] was very welcoming until after the Australia tour," he told Oprah darkly. "It was the first time that the family got to see how incredible she is at the job and that brought back memories."

But Diana, aged twenty-one at the time and raised in a family of courtiers and ladies-in-waiting, interpreted the meaning of her first major royal tour in a significantly different way from Harry's thirty-seven-year-old wife. The Princess told Martin Bashir that the grueling six-week trip (fraught with backstage unhappiness about the chill from Prince Charles), "when we flew back from New Zealand, I was a different person. I realized the sense of duty, the level of intensity of interest, and the demanding role I now found myself in." For Diana that was an almost sacred feeling. Meghan appeared to draw a different conclusion from her first tour: that the monarchy likely needed her more than she needed them. She had starred in the equivalent of a blockbuster movie and wanted her leading-lady status to be reflected in lights.

The Queen, determined not to fail Meghan as it was privately recognized Diana had been failed, offered Meghan the ear of her most senior lady-in-waiting, Lady Susan Hussey, a wily court infighter who had been around since 1960, and Samantha Cohen, a brisk Australian Palace veteran who was the monarch's most trusted communications aide, and who agreed at the Queen's personal request to return from the private sector specifically to support the new Duchess's learning curve. In early 2019, HM personally bestowed on Meghan two plum honors. For forty-five years, the Queen had been patron of the National Theatre. She granted the juicy cultural honor to the former actress. And, in an index that she did indeed appreciate the success of the Australia tour, she named Meghan vice president of the Queen's Commonwealth Trust (Harry was its president) with a remit to support young people, especially women and girls. It was a clear signal that the Sussexes would have their own high-profile territory as ambassadors of the organization that is one of the Queen's most treasured expressions of her sovereign power. She had made it a priority in her reign to visit all but two of the fifty-four countries in the Commonwealth's voluntary association of independent and equal countries, most but not all of which are former British colonies.

Meghan was said to be genuinely chuffed with this new platform. For years she had dreamed of UN goodwill ambassadorships. Now she had something even better, the gravitas of the Commonwealth imprimatur. The organization's dusty image was ripe for a rebrand. The world's most appealing royal couple could sprinkle their stardust and bring its mission of collaboration and outreach alive with new purpose. It was soft power with bells on, especially in the post-Brexit era when Britain's trade alliances were being redrawn and its internationalism was in some peril.

But modernizing the imagery of the Commonwealth's mission would take not only care and tact, but time. And time, it seems, was something that Meghan did not have.

The grating problem was money. The royal predicament is all status and no quo. It was becoming clear to Meghan that without financial freedom, every effort to fulfill the Sussexes' global dream was hitting a wall. Sharing office resources with the Cambridges meant they were junior partners in an underfunded operation. Harry was at the mercy of his father's watchful dispensation of funds, his grandmother's largesse for a roof over his head, his elder brother's prior claims on the allocation of budget, and the approval of tour expenses from the Sovereign Grant.

In his army days, Harry hadn't been a big spender. His allowance gave him ample coverage for his bar bills at Boujis, and he was perfectly content with his modest Nott Cott digs. He was used to flying commercial and getting in line for the occasional royal use of the two government private jets. Like every aspect of Palace existence, there was a pecking order for who got to fly on them. The Queen had first dibs, then the prime minister, then Prince Charles and a few generals, followed by Prince William and some top cabinet officials. If the chancellor of the exchequer needed to fly to Scotland, he could bump Prince Harry off the manifest, a somewhat undignified prospect for a bride who aspired to be the House of Windsor's Melinda Gates.

In his pre-Meghan years, Harry had always

indicated to his brother that when he married, he would dig into country life like most of his upper-class friends or disappear off-piste to an African farm. But that all changed when he met Meghan. In their early fever dreams of world conquest, it's unlikely her fairy-tale prince emphasized his financial realities. The returns on the share of his mother's and grandmother's bequests provided the Duke with a more than comfortable living, but a parched liquidity. For Meghan, the unpalatable fact was that, at the age of thirty-seven, after fifteen years of supporting herself, she was financially dependent on a husband who was as reliant as a teenager on the Bank of Dad.

While her **Suits** friends might imagine her swanning around palaces in princessly splendor, the couple was still crammed into the two-bedroom Nott Cott with a baby on the way. They were waiting for the renovation of the Duke and Duchess of Gloucester's former twenty-one-room apartment next door to the Cambridges in Kensington Palace. Meanwhile, for a weekend country retreat, the Queen had offered them York Cottage on the grounds of Sandringham. No thanks to that. "York Cottage is a perfect hell hole," a Norfolk neighbor told me. "So poky and dark. Sandringham is so gloomy anyway, terrible sandy soil. You can't even plant a rhododendron." The Sussexes preferred to rent a farmhouse in the Cotswolds, a stone's throw from Soho House's rustic outpost and David and Victoria Beckham's countryside estate.

It was soon depressingly apparent that their intended London digs in the Kensington Palace apartment would take years to fix up, given its asbestos and other creaking structural problems. They had to ask Granny to flip through her available Crown Estate properties and come up with something else. Her Maj offered Frogmore Cottage, a white stucco eighteenth-century **Wind in the Willows** rabbit warren, twenty-two miles from London on the grounds of Windsor Park. At the time divided into five flats for Windsor estate workers, it had, as realtors like to say, plenty of potential charm; it was already slated for an upgrade, and could be made ready in time for the baby.

Many Americans were baffled by the British media outcry about the £2.4 million spent from the Sovereign Grant (the couple paid for "fixtures and fittings" themselves) on doing up Frogmore. Such a sum wouldn't even buy a two-bedroom teardown in the Montecito neighborhood in California where the couple lives today. A **Daily Mirror** journalist once explained to me that though the tabloids feast on negative scoops, all they really want is a new narrative to milk, whether it's saccharine or sensational. They hadn't had a juicy story of royal real estate extravagance since the 1990s with the Queen's gifts of "South York" to Andrew and Fergie, and the overly grandiose Bagshot Park to Edward and Sophie Wessex. The Frogmore follies became a fun new episode. Inventive hacks churned out "Spendarella" myths about Meghan's overweaning demands for a lavish copper bathtub and a private yoga studio, with an ongoing refrain of "Who does she think she is?"

She was HRH The Duchess of Sussex, and she couldn't even put in a new kitchen without being called Imelda Marcos. It was a morale-sapping drag. Where was the glamour? After years of striving on the celebrity B-list and watching swag-stuffed gift bags being handed out by luxury brands to Oscar presenters, she was now forbidden to keep the designer bling and other freebies that came her way as a royal influencer. Her own staff confiscated it! Ever since the Peat report gave its thundering rebuke to factotums like Fawcett and members of the royal household accepting the spoils of privilege, the Palace and the Royal Family, too, were supposed to operate like politicians under scrutiny for taking favors. There was an ugly (and unsurprising) flap when Meghan wore Chopard diamond chandelier earrings given as a wedding present by Saudi Crown Prince Mohammed Bin Salman three weeks after the regime-backed murder of dissenting journalist Jamal Khashoggi.

Meghan wanted a job, a paying job, she told the Palace team. And so did Harry. There was precedent. William had worked as an air ambulance pilot, but he had donated his salary to charity.

The Palace reviewed the way other European royal families addressed the question of royals with a day job. A bunch of Scandinavian princelings, lurking around the feature pages of **Hello!** magazine, had paid careers in everything from banking to walking the catwalk for Burberry and Dior. But these royals were no longer performing official duties and showed up a couple of times a year for family occasions. One outlier was King Willem-Alexander of the Netherlands, who, for twenty years, including after he became king in 2013, was a part-time pilot for KLM Airlines.

The Sussexes wanted a hybrid model: royal patronages, Commonwealth tours, HRHs—plus a commercial arm. I'm told the couple was talking with Netflix as early as 2018. Elton John's husband, David Furnish, had introduced Meghan to his connections at the entertainment behemoth to discuss an animated series, and the prospects broadened from there. Harry and Meghan saw lucrative opportunities in streaming entertainment. They were told by the Palace they could do all the TV projects and documentaries they wanted (as both princes had done with the 2010 documentary **Prince William's Africa** and the 2016 documentary **Prince Harry in Africa**). They just couldn't get paid for them.

There was history here that made the family squirm. Edward and Sophie Wessex still carried the stigmata of their attempts, as members of the innermost circle, to secure a personal income while remaining senior royals. "You're in or you're out," they had been told firmly by Prince Philip. Conflict of interest issues made it impossible to combine the privileges and responsibilities of the monarchy with commercial opportunity. **Basta.**

III

A sulfurous cloud hung over the House of Sussex. As a young, celebrated couple expecting their first child, they should have been radiating felicity. Instead they had a beleaguered air. Harry had waited so long for this personal happiness, pining for a family of his own while his brother settled into a fulfilling domestic life. But his wife's discontents were contagious, and he blamed the press for destroying her morale. "He just seemed incredibly unhappy, partly because she was unhappy," a Palace source told me. At social gatherings, even at farewell parties for trusted Palace advisers, they stood in a corner and talked only to each other.

Meghan found England itself an exhausting conundrum. George Bernard Shaw's maxim that Britain and America are "two nations separated by a common language" asserted itself every day. Like many Americans, she felt excluded or rebuffed by British reserve, which, among the Royal Family and the Palace, was at the extreme end of the usual upper-class denial of emotion. "I really tried to adopt this British sensibility of a stiff upper lip. I really tried," she later told ITV's Tom Bradby. She found it draining to traverse the chasms between her California effusiveness and British understatement. It was her earnestness versus their irony, her explicitness versus their words unsaid. The **Daily Mail,** depicting the Duchess as a bull in a Palace china shop who didn't have a clue about royal tradition or English mores, dubbed her "Hurricane Meghan."

She was hopelessly at sea with England's drier, more satirical sense of humor that's especially aroused by the smiley-face sensibility in which Americans are adept. In February 2019, she made an unannounced (read "stunt") visit with Harry to a Bristol sex workers charity and wrote—"You are loved! You are brave!"—messages on bananas destined for the sex workers' food parcels. What would probably have been reviewed as a heartwarming celebrity gesture in Hollywood was greeted with snickers and eye rolls in the UK. On the 2019 Africa tour when she declared to the women in a Cape Town township, "I am your sister," it came across to Brits as an embarrassing **de haut en bas** gesture from someone who had not yet earned it. She failed to see why it was not a Princess Diana moment. To assume that sharing equals caring in England is always a risk.

The Queen usually shows empathy with indirection. A former member of her staff told me how at a Palace lunch for worthy citizens, Her Majesty was seated next to a surgeon who had operated on the front lines in Iraq. He began to tear up as he described what it was like, and the Queen said, "I think this is a very good time to feed the dogs, don't you?" She asked for the corgis to be sent in, and she and her guest surreptitiously slipped them morsels under the table until he had regained his composure. It was a gesture that to a British eye suggested exquisite tact, but to an American might read as a kind of rebuff. (Sometimes it was hard to read otherwise. "Thank goodness he hasn't got ears like his father!"

was Her Majesty's comment when she first saw her baby grandson Prince William in the incubator at the hospital.)

More generally, the Queen opts in public to show very little emotion at all. "Because she has spent her entire life being such a closed book, people project onto her whatever they want her to be," one of her former advisers told me. "I remember seeing this in an organ recital in Windsor Chapel. I was watching the Queen, and she was just completely dead tired. There were lots of people who are clearly loving this music and looking at her probably thinking, 'Look at the Queen, she is loving this.' And there were probably lots of people in the room thinking, 'I wish this concert would just be over. Look at the Queen. I bet she's hating every minute of this.' But because she's not showing any emotion at all, she's not dividing that audience. She's not on one side or the other. And that must be exhausting for her." He added that when she comes off duty, she often emotes with vigor. As in . . . "What a simply frightful concert. It went on forever!"

The unceasing drip-drip-drip of a tone-deaf Duchess of Sussex narrative created tensions within the Firm about how to deal with it. The couple was obsessed with punishing the royal press pool by withdrawing access to photo ops when news organizations transgressed. But that affected media relationships cultivated by the other senior royals and their communications teams. As it was summarized to me, "The family was saying, 'Look, we get that it's horrible that you have to do an engagement. And there's that reporter who wrote that horrible thing about you. You just have to deal with that. We're public figures.' Harry and Meghan just wouldn't agree with that, and that got really tough." The Sussexes felt the Palace was too pusillanimous in its approach to the press, at least when it came to its newest family member. "Meghan thought their way of handling the media was old-fashioned," a former Palace insider told me. "Her way of handling it is Hollywood 101—you have a bad story about you, so you put out a good story to counteract it, but at the Palace we never play that game. It's an approach that just sends you into a spiral. Meghan saw that as a lack of imagination, and creativity, and energy."

Meghan turned for succor to the American PR company Sunshine Sachs. An obsequious puff piece soon appeared in **People** magazine in which anonymous "close friends" gushed about Meghan's humble relatability. It backfired in the UK, where the media smelled PR machinations and, worse, prodded the wounded bear Tom Markle to come roaring out of his Rosarito hideaway. One of the article's violin themes was that Meghan had been misrepresented as an uncaring daughter when, **People** related, she had written her father a "heartfelt" letter in an attempt to repair their relationship.

Actually she wrote the letter to appease her in-laws: Tom Markle's continued sporadic interviews with the likes of Piers Morgan were a source of ongoing exasperation to both Charles and the Queen.

For Harry, it was a source not only of exasperation but of family tension. In an email made public in a later legal action, Meghan wrote to their communications secretary Jason Knauf:

> Even after a week with [Harry's] dad, and endlessly explaining the situation, his family seem to forget the context and revert to "can't she just go and see him and make this stop?" They fundamentally don't understand so at least by writing [Harry] will be able to say to his family, "she wrote him a letter and he's still doing it." . . . By taking this form of action I protect my husband from this constant berating and while unlikely, perhaps it will give my father a moment to pause.

There was little chance of that. Meghan crafted the letter with the knowledge that it might well be leaked by her father. "Given that I have only ever called him Daddy," she strategized in a message to Knauf, "it would make sense to open as such despite him being less than paternal. And in the unfortunate event that it leaked, it would pull at the heart strings."

As predicted, **The Mail on Sunday** goaded Tom into giving them nine extracts from the five-page letter handwritten in his daughter's best wedding calligraphy. In one she wrote, "I have only ever loved, protected, and defended you," but then bitterly called him out: "You continue fabricating these stories, manufacturing this fictitious narrative, and entrenching yourself deeper into this web you've spun."

"There was more I didn't release," Tom told me ominously.

It's a good thing he didn't. Every professional publisher knows that the physical letter belongs to the person who received it, but the content of the letter belongs to the person who wrote it. The verbatim publication of Meghan's plea to her father to desist from talking about her to the press went well beyond any reasonable fair use—it was a flagrant breach of the Duchess of Sussex's copyright.

Copyright infringement is one of the few things the Royal Family sues over. Prince Charles won a case against the **Mail**'s parent company, Associated Newspapers Ltd., in 2006 for publishing extracts of a journal he sent to friends during Britain's handover to China of Hong Kong. ("At the end of this awful Soviet-style display, we had to watch the Chinese soldiers goose-step on to the stage and haul down the Union Jack and raise the ultimate flag.")

In the 1980s, **The Sun** had to grovel and make a compensatory charitable donation for publishing a letter written by the Queen and Prince Philip about Prince Edward's decision to leave the Royal Marines. In 1993, the paper settled a breach of copyright case over a leaked copy of the Queen's Christmas speech, the publishing of which broke the long tradition of polite embargo on its less-than-earth-shattering content. Harry and Meghan were determined to sue for both copyright breach and invasion of privacy, a grayer area fraught with legal hazard that conservative Palace lawyers felt was unwise to incur. With a skepticism that was widely shared by media savants, the **Guardian** columnist Roy Greenslade asked, "Is Harry taking a sledgehammer to crack a nut here? I think he may well find that this is counterproductive."

The Sussexes disregarded them all. Harry wanted justice, not the institutional protectiveness of the Palace's mumbling mandarins. **The Mail on Sunday**, the publisher of the letter, was the very same tormentor that had ruined their pre-wedding happiness with the iniquitous Tom Markle photo set-up. Instead of using the royals' go-to law firm of Harbottle and Lewis, Harry hired the flashy celebrity legal shop Schillings, reputation bodyguards of such clients as Lance Armstrong, J. K. Rowling, and the retail shark Philip Green. Two years later, it was clear the Sussexes had made the right choice. The Duchess was victorious in her suit. In February 2021, Schillings won a High Court summary judgment, a bravura vanquishing of the Sussexes' foes, and in December prevailed again in Associated Newspapers' appeal. It was a sweet win, and Meghan didn't hold back in her gleeful victory statement, name-checking not just the paper for having "broken the law" but also its owner, Lord Rothermere.

To be sure, the appeal kicked up some embarrassing revelations for Meghan that showed she had been economical with the truth in repeated coy assertions that she had not collaborated with the authors of **Finding Freedom**. In texts back and forth with Knauf, it was shown that she had been guiding the hagiography with talking points throughout. She had to issue an apology to the court for "not remembering" her involvement. The knight-in-shining-armor posture of Harry also lost some luster. In an email to Knauf, Harry, now on the board of the Aspen Institute's Commission for Information Disorder, told him, "I totally agree that we have to be able to say we didn't have anything to do with it."

But the victor owns the narrative, and Meghan made sure she did, casting it as a triumph for all those "collectively brave enough to reshape a tabloid industry that conditions people to be cruel, and profits from the lies and pain that they create. . . . Tomorrow it could be you. These harmful practices don't happen once in a blue moon—they are a daily fail that divide us, and we all deserve better."

Champagne flowed in Montecito, but whether the Duchess was right about "reshaping the tabloid industry" is another question. The press is both mightily rude and rudely mighty. As the Tory MP Enoch Powell once noted, "For a politician to complain about the press is like a ship's captain complaining about the sea," and the same can be said about members of the Royal Family.

"The media in the UK are going to be more toothless but she has poked a stick in a hornet's nest not just against the UK media but against global media," Mark Stephens, one of London's leading experts in media law, told me when the verdict came down on December 2, 2021, after the Sussexes had left England for Montecito. "Now they are no longer working royals and members of the Royal Family, they only have their reputations to market. If they are traduced in the media, they won't be as valuable to Netflix, or indeed anyone else. . . . Even if she won this round, in the wider context of the war between the media and the Sussexes, I suspect the media wins."

CHAPTER
24

PRIVACY AND PREJUDICE

———

Surviving the Windsor Fishbowl

———

THERE WAS A HISTRIONIC (EVEN HYSTERICAL) quality to the way the Sussexes declared they wanted to be private. A desire for privacy is understood (if not respected) by the media; an obsession with secrecy is not, particularly when combined with high-profile socializing. It's a phenomenon of Hollywood that actors who become suddenly famous go from eagerly trying to get the attention of the press to making scenes in restaurants whenever fans spot them (which, of course, ensures the attention of the press).

If privacy is what you crave, Kensington Palace is the ultimate gated community. The Sussexes' choice to give up prime London digs at KP baffled many at the Palace, even though they had to wait for the apartment renovation. After her divorce from Charles, Princess Diana hung on to her home in Apartments 8 and 9 for dear life, recognizing it as an unbeatable symbol of royal belonging. The Prince of Wales was mystified why the Sussexes—or anyone—would want to live at Frogmore in the flight path of Heathrow airport. The house had one major benefit—it was inside the security perimeter of Windsor Park. Meghan could exercise the dogs and perambulate a new baby in its lush gardens without being spied on, or stroll in the "mulberry walk," where staff used to pick the fruit for Prince Philip's mulberry gin. It's a five-minute jog up the hill for tea with Granny on a Sunday afternoon. But the Duchess had few friends in the Windsor area aside from the Clooneys in nearby Sonning Eye. (George found trying to be a movie star from Berkshire not optimal, and got his way in the COVID lockdown to relocate with Amal to L.A.) And popping out for a little retail therapy in a town as parochial and gift shop–ridden as Windsor seems an unlikely fit with Meghan's **Tig** sense of style, nor would it offer her much anonymity.

Harry's own determination to hide from his pursuers was explicable given past invasions, but his suspicious nature was compounded by Meghan's inflated sense of celebrity and persecution. It was the opposite of the Kate-William dynamic, said a friend of both. When William got riled up, Kate calmed him down. When Kate was rattled by the press, William talked her through it. The Sussexes fueled each other's distrust of everybody else, and Harry's wife was as temperamentally combative as he was.

The mentally fragile Harry had the worry of

seeing his wife now flailing herself. Their secrecy verged on the paranoid. The couple treated the impending birth of their baby like a state secret, denying the press the routine Palace announcements about where he would be born, or which doctor they'd be assisted by. They also tossed overboard the royal custom of releasing the names of the godparents, later easily identified as Harry's cherished nanny Tiggy Pettifer (née Legge-Bourke), his mentor Mark Dyer, and his childhood friend Charlie van Straubenzee. When Meghan attended Wimbledon in 2019 with two college friends to watch Serena Williams play, her protection officers annoyed nearby spectators by asking them not to take her picture—even though the Duchess was in a public place. It didn't help Meghan's prima donna rap that Kate had watched the tennis from the same VIP section just two days earlier, serenely unfazed by the cell phone cameras trained on her from every side.

There is an art form to being private in the Royal Family. Philip used to drive around town to see London friends at the wheel of a black taxi he kept for occasions when he wanted to stay under the radar. The Queen's equine life enabled her to make discreet visits to see her American friends William and Sarah Farish on their horse farm in Kentucky, or play hooky every year on her birthday at the Polhampton Lodge Stud Farm near Sandringham, where she treated herself to a meet and greet with the new foals. Whenever they wanted quiet off-season weekends alone, Philip and Elizabeth stayed in the cottages on their Balmoral or Sandringham estates, where there were few staff in attendance and Her Maj sometimes preferred to do the dishes herself. Charles and Camilla have always had an extensive network of mutual friends who, in the couple's illicit years, were willing to protect their affair. It was clear on the leaked Camillagate tapes, as the lovers ran down a list of possible accommodating hosts, that half the noble names in the shires were in on the adultery.

The key to being private in the Royal Family is to truly—not performatively—want to be so. That means old friends who are loyal, socializing at houses rather than restaurants, cultivating a circle of trust that will never tip off the press. Harry had many such friends from Eton and the army, but he had distanced himself from them by the time he was married. Meghan's own friends were in the United States or recently acquired and famous. Meghan would later tell Oprah that she lost her freedom when she married Harry and depicted a life that sounded more like the House of Saud than the House of Windsor—locked down before the lockdown, her keys and passports "taken."

"I remember so often people within the Firm would say, 'Well, you can't do this because it'll look like that. So, even, 'Can I go and have lunch with my friends?' 'No, no, no, you're oversaturated, you're everywhere, it would be best for you to not go out to lunch with your friends.' I go, 'Well, I haven't... I haven't left the house in months.'"

If going out to lunch with your friends means

flying to Manhattan for a girls' afternoon with Serena Williams, Jessica Mulroney, et al., at one of Manhattan's most expensive hotels, you will indeed be everywhere. Even in London, it's possible to disappear. Isn't that what the private dining rooms at Soho House are for? On one awkward occasion during her pre-engagement sojourn with Harry at Nott Cott, Meghan ran into Kate at Kensington Palace, heading out to go shopping on the same street, though Kate had not invited Meghan to join her. The truth was, though, they didn't really know each other yet and perhaps Kate wanted to avoid the press pandemonium that would ensue at the sight of the two most high-profile women in Britain hitting the aisles together. She is used to slipping in and out undetected.

II

The Duchess of Cambridge has had years of practice. After more than a decade as a royal, she has learned to negotiate the taxing duality of a life close to the Crown. She often drives George and Charlotte to school in her Range Rover—with her protection officer sitting inscrutably beside her. Her Spanish nanny is trained in defensive driving and self-defense in case of kidnapping threats to her charges. For evening engagements, the Duchess's tiara has to be worn at a forty-five-degree angle, her nail polish has to be as sheer as her mandatory hose, and she cannot sign an autograph in case her signature is copied and forged.

"William and Kate have a really good sense of the ridiculous," a friend of theirs told me. "They will laugh a lot together about stuff that is quite stressful. There's a lot of weirdness in their lives." The oddness of being Kate is reflected in the widespread awe expressed when she pulled out of the Tusk Conservation Awards dinner with William in November 2019 because one of the children was feeling unwell and they didn't have a babysitter. What, no butler, housemaid or yeoman of the pantry who could step in and play hide-and-seek? Actually, no—not one who was qualified in martial arts and defensive driving.

Sometimes, to nourish her inner life, Kate steals off on her own to museums and art galleries that open early for her. Although she is surrounded by some of the world's most priceless paintings and artifacts in the royal palaces, they must sometimes feel more like trophies of royal claustrophobia than pleasure to the eye. In 2012, the venerable advocate Jeremy Hutchinson—a professor at the Royal Academy of Arts—was viewing a David Hockney exhibit there at eight A.M. when a young woman sat beside him on a bench to gaze at a picture. He asked her how she managed to get in so early, and she replied, "I just needed to come on my own so I asked for a favor. I miss my History of Art so much and I never get to see paintings. . . . It's what I do to get my fix." As Hutchinson caught sight of a lurking protection officer, the mysterious morning visitor extended her hand. "I'm Catherine," she said.

In their parallel Norfolk world, the Cambridges have managed to construct a particular, ingenious normality. As a child of warring parents, William married a woman who understands his need for insulated domestic stability. The couple can often be sighted making sandcastles with their children on Holkham beach, relishing apple juice and biscuits at the local tea shop, or letting the kids splash paint around at Mable's Paint Pot in the old market town of King's Lynn. "William and Kate have done it brilliantly up here," a member of their Norfolk set told me. "They get their privacy. People really respect them. Everybody leaves them alone. They've chosen a place where they can be pretty anonymous."

A local charity they diligently support is the East Anglia's Children's Hospices, where Kate serves as royal patron. The chatelaine of the nearby stately home Houghton Hall, Lady Rose Cholmondeley, is a patron, too. At a charity dinner supporting the hospices at Houghton in 2016, the room was divided up into small groups to meet the Duke and Duchess of Cambridge, who chatted to each guest with synchronized informal expertise. "I was struck by how absolutely perfect William and Kate are at making people feel at ease," recalled Euan Rellie, a British-born, New York–based investment banker who was present. After dinner, Rellie was privy to a winning offstage William incident.

One of the most generous donors to the hospice charity, an elderly Park Avenue lady who had come over from the United States for the function and was a huge William fan, was stuck in her room feeling unwell, and could not come down to join the other guests. "Someone mentioned to William, 'It's a shame our highest roller donor is too ill to meet you,'" Rellie told me. "William said, 'Is there any chance someone could make a pot of tea and put a couple of biscuits on a plate?' And he went and knocked on the lady's door and said, 'I know that you were too ill to come to dinner and thought I'd bring you a cup of tea and just say thank you very much for supporting the hospices.' She was so over the moon." Hard not to be. It was a gesture that showed the imagination and empathy of his mother. "It was a classic Diana Spencer move," said Rellie, "just a natural, gentle human kindness, and had much more effect than a grand act. We all thought, wow he learned something from his mum."

William and Kate have got the evasion of royal stuffiness down to a fine art. An annual hazard in pre-COVID days was the merry purgatory of Christmas as the Queen's guests at Sandringham. The schedule includes a groaning black-tie blowout on Christmas Eve when gifts are opened. As anyone who saw the movie **Spencer** knows, there's a honk-honk tradition of family members getting weighed like French geese, first on arrival and then on departure, to record precisely how much justice they, and their livers, have done to the artery-clogging feast.

The Cambridges know how to do the essential bits, like church and Christmas Day lunch (blessedly brief because it has to be wrapped up in time for the Queen's pre-recorded speech at three P.M.), then flee back to the twenty-first century at Anmer Hall, where they do what every other English family does: open their stockings and watch telly. Any telly, that is, not starring members of their own family.

Cambridge loyalists will tell you that the couple is so used to being branded as the Duke and Duchess of Dull that they wear it as a proud moniker. But there is an assumption, because Kate is by temperament equable, that she's also impervious to the cruelties of her public position. In March 2019, rumors were seeping into the press that there was a rift between the Duchess and her Houghton charity friend Lady Cholmondeley (pronounced Chumly). The thirty-four-year-old marchioness, a long-limbed former model who looks not unlike Kate, might have been in the running to marry William in his bachelor days, but Rose Hanbury, as she was formerly called, has the kind of who-gives-a-damn aristocratic flair that suggests that she—like Diana before her—would have found life as the consort of the heir to the throne a bourgeois bore.

As the wife of a peer, Rose is herself a pedigreed woman not easy to banish from the Cambridge social circles should Kate, as alleged, have wanted to do so. The Cholmondeleys, who live a stone's throw from Anmer in one of England's most imposing stately homes, are coveted guests at some of the same shoots attended or hosted by the Cambridges. Rose's husband, David, serves as Lord Great Chamberlain, tasked with carrying the Imperial State Crown at the opening of Parliament. Rose's grandmother Lady Elizabeth Longman was a bridesmaid at the Queen's wedding to Prince Philip. The Cholmondeley twin boys were playmates of Prince George.

Social feuds have never been the Duchess of Cambridge's inclination. So what was behind this one? Speculation circulated at Norfolk dinner parties that William was paying Rose too much attention. Gossips suggested that after giving birth to her third child and suddenly outglammed by Meghan, Kate was not at the top of her glossy game, and looked under strain. Tell me any woman who wouldn't feel demoralized opening a newspaper—even if it's **The Sun**—to read a headline such as "Kate Middleton Has Gone from Fab to Drab in the Royal Style Stakes." The phone lines from Anmer to Coach Carole at Bucklebury must have been burning up. According to Vassi Chamberlain in **The Telegraph**, a friend of Kate's tells how, whenever the Duchess gets bad press, her parents tell her, "Remember you chose this life, you had a lot of time to think about joining the family before you got married, you have to be strong and learn to get on with it."

As Norfolk gossips persisted in touting the supposed rivalry as a face-off between a queen bee and a queen-to-be, the Cambridges believed it was all being spread by the older generation in Norfolk, whose own years of sub-rosa activities made them assume most rumors were true. The two couples were so distressed by the talk of a fallout and marital trouble that Richard Kay of the **Daily Mail** leapt in to refute it. The well-sourced royal scribe affirmed to me that he strongly believes there was nothing there, a sentiment echoed in a legal warning reportedly sent to the press by William's lawyers, making clear that the speculation was false. (In January 2020, the Cambridges and the Cholmondeleys were in fact spotted attending the same church service.)

Was the desire to reward Kate's forbearance in the face of the rumor mill a factor in the Queen's decision to honor her in April 2019 on her eighth wedding anniversary with the Grand Cross of the Royal Victorian Order? The inescapable truth is that in the unlikely event that the Cambridge marriage ever becomes troubled, the whole Windsor house of cards could come tumbling down. Kate has become a cherished national icon of flawless motherhood. The breakup of Charles and Diana was traumatic enough, but in the social media age, the monarchy would be unlikely to survive a messy rift in the House of Cambridge.

Kate is aware of her leverage. Very occasionally she exercises it, as she did in 2020 when **Tatler** published what purported to be a flattering cover story titled "Catherine the Great" but snickered about her mother's nouveau taste infiltrating the Cambridges' Norfolk home ("like a gleaming five-star hotel, with cushions plumped and candles lit . . . very Buckinghamshire"), and said that Pippa was "too regal and"—using a common dog-whistle snobbery phrase—"try-hard." Neither Kate nor her mother have ever expressed how much the unrelenting class condescension rankles, but getting these mild gibes scrubbed from the **Tatler** website after a forceful statement by Kensington Palace lawyers about inaccuracies must have been a gratifying expression for Kate of her ascending royal power. It was also a sign that she had become used to press that was uniformly glowing.

Little by little, Kate has exercised almost complete control of her image and of the Cambridge brand. Always a keen amateur photographer, she has appointed herself the chronicler of their nuclear family, with all her pictures under the Cambridge copyright. Permission to reproduce is closely held. The Cambridge Instagram account is populated with her carefully chosen snaps of the family's fresh, adorable domestic life: for Father's Day, a pile of the whole squealing brood on top of Daddy William; for the national Big Butterfly Count, the touching image of six-year-old Princess Charlotte gravely holding a red admiral in her cupped hands; for Louis's third birthday, a shot of their youngest astride his jolly little red two-wheeler. The usually beaming gap-toothed Prince George in his short-trouser phase was so appealing that he's the only child I have ever followed on social media except my own. The Cambridges are "us five," the monarchy's embodiment of family virtue.

William is such a control freak that he refuses to

let his father release pictures of himself with his grandchildren without explicit Cambridge permission. In 2020, Kate managed to conjure up a tender William and Charles Instagram moment, with the younger prince in his tweed flat cap, clasping the ruddy-faced Charles round the shoulder, as if they are two country-bumpkin mates heading off for a pint at the village pub.

When Kate is herself the focus of the cameras in public, her affect is more expressive than the Queen's. But she has studied and mastered the monarch's art of conserving her real thoughts and feelings, allowing people to project on her any emotion they want. A resting stone face like Her Majesty's would not work for a modern royal Duchess. Kate's chosen public expression is one of eternal joy—at climate change conferences, at air force bases, at canine training centers—it's smile, smile, smile. Unless it's Remembrance Day, in which case her side-saddle saucer hat is balanced atop an appropriately solemn countenance.

After more than ten vigilant years embedded in the heart of the Firm, Kate the Relatable has undergone a stealth transformation in the power dynamics of the Palace. While the public obsesses on her wavy new blowout or whether her decision to forgo a clutch bag is a sign of "new confidence," she has become a savvy dynastic strategist who wholeheartedly buys into both the monarchy's mission of duty and its priority of survival.

I learned of a fascinating exchange between Kate

and an intimate member of the royal circle shortly after the Brexit vote in which she meditated on the collapse of trust in institutions that seemed to many to be at the heart of Brexit. Her concern was fixed on how the monarchy might be buffeted by the mercurial national mood. Such theorizing comes not from a passive partner or a walking photo op but, like the Queen Mother, from a marital consigliere to a future king. It was unspoken that the task of rebuilding trust fell in part on Kate's slim shoulders. She could not know then, of course, that members of the Royal Family would once again undermine the Firm more than any exterior forces.

III

William and Harry had always been brothers-in-arms, two refugees from the tumult of their childhood. Many, including William himself, have observed how much Harry depended on William's protective arm, but Harry's unconditional love, too, was an essential solace to William in his hyper-responsible life. Harry's irreverence toward his elder brother was a refreshing antidote to the sycophancy that inevitably surrounds the heir to the throne and the monarch, just as Philip's was for the Queen. Not having Harry at his side is "an emotional weakness for William," says a Palace insider. "William is not a confrontational person. He wants peace in his life." Within months of Harry's involvement with

Meghan, he reportedly told his father that his younger brother's obsession with her was "like something I have never seen . . . it feels like I have lost my best friend," the very sentiment that Harry had expressed when William paired off with Kate.

William was supportive when the Sussexes wanted to split operations from the Cambridges. He lobbied their father for the additional funds. Harry wanted to establish a discrete Sussex office team. Its communications head would be the high-powered political operative Sarah Latham, a former adviser to Bill and Hillary Clinton. An office was allocated to Harry and Meghan at Buckingham Palace, not ideal as far as the Sussexes were concerned, as they were now under the beady eye of the Queen's press operation, run by Donal McCabe. But at least it was their own turf.

William was more than agreeable, too, to divide the foundation. It was inevitable that their philanthropic ventures would need to be separate. They weren't the royal "boys" anymore. They were thirty-seven and thirty-five years old, and their competing interests and the complexity of the activities of their wives were increasingly challenging for aides to adjudicate.

But there were other reasons why the Cambridges were relieved when the Sussexes hived off their operation. William and Kate like to treat their staff as a collegial professional family. Interviewees for jobs with the Cambridges are struck by how much the principals rely on the steering of their communications team for every decision big and small. The royal couple was allegedly shocked by the way Meghan treated their shared employees. A typically uncomfortable incident had taken place during the rollout of the wedding plans when I was told Meghan yelled at a junior employee who held an announcement back because it clashed with something scheduled with the household of another senior royal. An insider privy to the pre-wedding incident told me, "I wouldn't say it was bullying behavior but I've certainly never heard of a member of the Royal Family talking like that to a member of staff." Harry said he would talk to Meghan, who then apologized. But contrition became increasingly rare.

Charges of Meghan's harsh conduct would follow her out of the Palace in the form of three staff complaints leaked on the eve of the Oprah interview and vehemently denied by the Duchess. In November 2021, she dispatched her lawyer Jenny Afia to appear on Amol Rajan's BBC documentary **The Princes and the Press** to rebut the bullying charges as massively inaccurate. "What bullying actually means is improperly using power repeatedly and deliberately to hurt someone physically or emotionally," Afia said, adding that Meghan "wouldn't want to negate anyone's personal experience."

One result of the split in operations was that there were now two ducal power centers with dueling Instagram accounts, a source of joy to those in the press who loved to keep tally. The Sussex fan base was clear in the launch of their now-defunct

@SussexRoyal account in April 2019, which attracted one million followers in five hours and forty-five minutes, faster than any previous Instagram account at the time, earning them a place in Guinness World Records. Always digitally smart, Meghan hired away Burberry's Instagram wizard David Watkins to manage the content. The Cambridges, as if by digital magic, always managed to keep a close, but appropriate, lead over @SussexRoyal. Team Cambridge's effort to maintain their superiority of position was quiet but insistent. "There seems to be a shift at the Palace," a source told **Vanity Fair.** "There's a focus on William being set up as a future king and Kate as his Queen Consort. This order seems to hint at the Cambridges' importance in the royal ranking." The dutiful, diligent Cambridges versus the "charismatic," "progressive" Sussexes. Was there room on the royal stage for both?

The divide was deepened by competition between Palace factotums. One of the most toxic aspects of the senior royals' dynamic is the long-established habit of communicating sensitive issues through their private secretaries rather than face-to-face. "It increases the dysfunction of not seeing each other that often," a Palace source told me. "So, if the Prince of Wales wanted to give William and Harry a difficult message, he wouldn't give it himself. That instantly creates a subset of people who exercise power, and who try to understand the family dynamic and act in line with it. And that magnifies any problem." Harry and William always refused to do that with each other in the past, but when the offices and foundation parted, their open lines of communication became jammed.

If Kate was being yawned at as the drab Duchess, Meghan saw a nastier pile-on coming her own way. While pregnant Kate had been written up as a serene Madonna "tenderly cradling her baby bump," Meghan was blasted with a boldface **Daily Mail** teaser: "Why can't Meghan Markle keep her hands off her bump? Experts tackle the question that has got the nation talking: Is it pride, vanity, acting? Or a new age bonding technique?" It would have been consoling for both women if they had united over the egregiously sexist campaign to pit them against each other. But the vast difference in their life experience was greater than any sisterhood of the royal tiaras.

In theory, Kate was one of a cadre of Windsor wives—and one ex-wife—who could share their own war stories with Meghan and offer her maps of the difficult terrain: Camilla, for instance, who is said to have offered much chummy, plummy advice; Andrew's ex, Sarah Ferguson, whose whole post-divorce life had been an apology tour; Sophie Wessex, who had been trampled underfoot in the Fake Sheikh fiasco of the nineties; even the much-derided "Führer," Princess Michael of Kent. However, except for Kate and the preternaturally tough Camilla, they must have looked to Meghan like the walking wounded. They had all been crushed on the Palace wheel after years of being brutalized by the press.

The glaring but unspoken problem was that none of these experienced Palace hands were women of color. As for the lady-in-waiting the Queen had offered for support, what on earth did the eighty-year-old Lady Susan Hussey have of use for a thirty-eight-year-old biracial American actress trying to navigate the treacherous Palace system? She hailed from the Jurassic period of court etiquette, and had also been proffered for guidance to Diana (who couldn't stand her).

Kate, Camilla, Fergie, Sophie—they were all white, British-born women educated at similar upper-class schools with deep networks of social support. As for Princess Michael, she had had to apologize for wearing a "blackamoor" brooch to a 2017 Buckingham Palace Christmas lunch she knew Meghan was attending.

There is currently only one Black member of the British aristocracy whom Meghan could have turned to, had she known her. Her direct expression, long brown hair, and striding pose jump out among the haughty pale faces in the gallery of her predecessors at Longleat House in Wiltshire, of which she is now the chatelaine. The thirty-six-year-old former model and chef Emma McQuiston, daughter of a Nigerian father and an English mother, became England's first Black marchioness in 2020 when her then-forty-five-year-old husband, Ceawlin Thynn, inherited the title of eighth Marquess of Bath (and, with it, the iconic stately home and safari park of Longleat).

The ravishing Lady Bath has found a way to thrive

in a life that could have been suffocated by her husband's heritage and openly expressed family prejudice. Unlike the Duchess of Sussex, she was raised British, her father is an oil billionaire, and she attended Queen's Gate, the same elite London school as Camilla Parker Bowles. But all that still didn't cut it with her mother-in-law. Lady Bath's husband, a dashing Mr. Darcy type, barred his mother from their wedding after she apparently asked him, "Are you sure about what you're doing to four hundred years of bloodline?"

Now with two sons of her own, Emma prefers not to speak about her monster mother-in-law and has already triumphed as the chatelaine of Longleat and the mother of the heir (especially after the domestic mayhem wrought by Ceawlin's priapic father, who entertained a revolving harem of over seventy "wifelets," as he called them). "There isn't a rule book. There isn't an example. How could there be?" Emma told me. "Our children, their generation are the focus and the reason I feel so motivated about positive change. I see that diversity is the future, here and internationally."

Michelle Obama's experience may have been closer to Meghan's. She too is an American who broke the racial barrier of a powerful institution whose corridors are lined with oil paintings of her all-white predecessors, and was intimately familiar with what she has called "the quiet, cruel nuances of not belonging." After her husband was elected president, she carried the burden of being the first Black

First Lady into every room she entered. Even then, she was called "Barack's baby mama" by Fox News. Her strategy against all of it was, "When they go low, we go high." She later explained, " 'Going high' doesn't mean you don't feel the hurt, or you're not entitled to an emotion. It means that your response has to reflect the solution. . . . I'm not trying to win the argument. I'm trying to figure out how to understand you and how I can help you understand me."

Michelle, who forged a close relationship with Prince Harry during the 2016 Invictus Games, is said to have offered private counsel to Meghan in her struggles about how to hang in and use her royal position for the greater good. In a **Good Housekeeping** interview in 2018 before the Sussex wedding, she was asked what advice she might offer the future Duchess. "My biggest piece of advice would be to take some time and don't be in a hurry to do anything," Mrs. Obama replied. "What I'd say is there's so much opportunity to do good with a platform like that—and I think Meghan can maximize her impact for others, as well as her own happiness, if she's doing something that resonates with her personally."

A major difference from Meghan is that Mrs. Obama is married to a man who for eight years was the most powerful leader in the world and had an exit ramp from the White House with a post-presidential life. Meghan was married to the fifth spare to the heir with the knowledge that royal pressure had no expiration date.

IV

It's worth conjecturing how Meghan might have absorbed her first experiences of England if she had arrived in the multicultural Peak London zenith of 2010–12 or after the racial reckoning following the murder of George Floyd in May 2020. In the immediate post–EU referendum years of 2016–19, England was not a congenial place to be, even for a feted, fabulous royal duchess. It was a time of corrosive negativity in the political climate and social fabric. The discourse, if you can call it that, on social media was increasingly polarized, angry, and misogynistic. It was often anti-Semitic on the far left and racist on the far right. The disgruntled middle-aged white voters who comprised many of the Brexiteers posted vicious attacks against Remainer women MPs. "It became very personal," Nick Lowles, the chief executive of the UK advocacy group Hope Not Hate, told me, and Meghan was soon a target. "She was mixed-race and spoke against Trump and for women's rights. She fitted into that box." When the Duchess of Sussex opened her Twitter feed, it was crawling with vile abuse. In a survey Hope Not Hate conducted on her Twitter feed, 70 percent of the five thousand snarling messages posted between January and February 2019 were revealed to have originated from the same twenty hostile accounts.

Until the crisis of Meghan's unhappiness, the Palace had never had cause to consider the meager level of diversity within its ranks—and the dangers this could pose. A Palace source admitted to me something that both the royals themselves and the combined Palace personnel have yet to forcefully confront in public statements. "We didn't take race seriously enough," the source said. "There were hardly any Black people that worked in the household or almost none in senior positions." That sorry fact alone made them insensitive to negative coverage and comments when viewed through the prism of race. They had contacts enough to ask advice from Black leaders themselves, but they chose not to do so. While the Queen's commitment to her subjects has always been impeccably impartial, and her lifelong dedication to the Commonwealth never open to question, HM did not hire a Black equerry until 2017, when Nana Kofi Twumasi-Ankrah, a Ghanaian-born army officer, joined her personal staff. And it had been sixteen years since Colleen Harris led Prince Charles's Clarence House communications team as the first (and still the only) Black press secretary. "We made a mistake as a household," the Palace source told me, "not a mistake in the family."

Actually, the family was plenty capable of making mistakes, and did. Until he fell in love with Meghan, Harry himself was an unregenerate Hooray Henry in his racial attitudes. "I wasn't aware of [racism] to start with, but my God, it doesn't take very long to be suddenly aware of it," he told Oprah. All he needed to do was conjure up the faces in the Windsor photograph albums.

There is, of course, a world of difference in social

attitude between the younger royals and the ancien régime. The Queen Mother died with her colonial condescension unreconstructed. Prince Philip was capable of brusque disrespect, as when he asked an Australian Aboriginal person in 2002 if he was still "throwing spears." An uncomfortable number of Philip's notorious "gaffes" had a racial component that suggests they were not truly gaffes—that is, clumsy mistakes—but revelations of what he actually thought. Philip had to apologize in 1999 after a walkabout at an Edinburgh electronics factory when he commented that a fuse box bursting with wires looked "as if it was put in by an Indian." Such comments were numerous, but there were always royal sycophants available to rush in and minimize the intent of conduct, that, even then, would have got him fired as a CEO. "Once again Prince Philip misses the target with what he thought was a jovial aside and offends more people than he entertained," said Scottish Tory deputy home affairs spokeswoman Lyndsay McIntosh, offering an excuse that only reinforced the offense. A "jovial aside" that was meant to "entertain" means the only people who are offended are those without a sense of humor, and presumably of the race he has just insulted.

Princess Margaret remained an old-school bigot to the end of her days. Penny Mortimer, the widow of the playwright and barrister Sir John, told me that in 2000 her husband was seated next to Margaret at an All Souls College dinner in Oxford. "I do hope my sister will come and stay with me in Mustique,"

Margaret sighed. "She's so tired after this ghastly Commonwealth prime minister conference. Every day a different blackamoor crying on her shoulder and you know, she's so wonderful. She knows all their names!"

The last fight between Princess Diana and her mother in 1997 was about Frances's explosion over her daughter's "relationships with Muslim men" when she learned Diana was dating Gulu Lalvani. (He is actually a Punjabi Sikh, but still, to Frances, unacceptably brown.) No one will be surprised to learn that the Duke of York remains firmly entrenched in the basket of deplorables. The former Labour foreign secretary Jacqui Smith said on LBC radio in 2019 that at a 2007 state banquet at Buckingham Palace for the Saudi king, she and her husband were left "slack-jawed" by the "awful jokes" Andrew made "involving camels."

"That he thought we might find these amusing was a terrible situation to be in," Smith said, and added: "But he's at the worst end of the royal family, I think."

The generational change in attitudes did not pass William and Harry by, but it's unlikely anyone in the family would have been pulling on their young coattails in private saying this or that casual gesture or comment was racist. It's lucky for William—and all of them—that his twenty-first birthday party, a jungle-themed **Out of Africa** jamboree at Windsor Castle in 2003, occurred in the days before selfies and Twitter. The young heir to the throne's blithe racial assumptions are captured in his remark with a "wide grin" to the UK's Press Association before the party. "Lots of people will be wondering if we're actually going to be eating crocodile, but obviously we won't be doing that."

It was not until Harry was caught on a video leaked in 2009 calling a fellow soldier "my little Paki friend" and another a "raghead" in jocular tones that he was called out for his insouciant racism. Days after that leak, it was revealed that Prince Charles had affectionately called his Punjabi-born polo friend Kolin Dhillon "Sooty." Loyally and probably even sincerely, Dhillon defended Charles as a man of "zero prejudice." Charles, no doubt, would agree, because like most of his class, he is both blind and deaf to the nuances of modern racial literacy that have become newly urgent since the wake-up call of Black Lives Matter.

Class trumps race in the rarefied ether of the British establishment and has a compounding effect. Wyndham Lewis famously said that Englishmen are born branded on the tongue. If you are Black but to the manor born, and if you have the right accent, racism alone is unlikely to defeat you.

The novelist Aatish Taseer—son of a Pakistani father and an Indian mother—dated Princess Michael's daughter Lady Gabriella Windsor for three years in the early 2000s. "British racism," he suggested in **Vanity Fair** in 2018, "is more casual than its American coeval but more insidious, because its animating prejudice is class."

In the Royal Family, Taseer expanded to me, "the conversation is similar to what you read in certain nineteenth-century writers about Indians being sly, or Indians not being very good at anything. Even so, with Indians, there's quite a lot of romance and a kind of respect. . . . The Windsors would certainly have no comparable form of appreciating someone who was African-American. . . . It is really dinosaur territory."

Whatever degree of intimacy the royals might have with people of color could not possibly equal, for example, the experience of even the most benighted American president. Royal circles are dictated by generations of breeding and the same overwhelmingly white elite schools. It's notable that Downing Street has been occupied by two Eton-educated prime ministers in the last ten years, though Eton is now a much more diverse environment than it was in Boris Johnson's and David Cameron's day.

In a 2016 **Daily Mail** column that she now disavows, Boris's sister, Rachel Johnson, wrote that Meghan's "exotic DNA" would "thicken" the Windsors' "watery, thin blue blood," and reprised the "Straight Outta Compton" smear of Doria Ragland as "a dreadlocked African-American lady from the wrong side of the tracks." And it was Boris himself who, in 2002 when he was a member of Parliament, referred in a **Daily Telegraph** column to Commonwealth crowds of "flag-waving piccaninnies" and Africans with "watermelon smiles"—and still got elected as mayor of London.

For Meghan, accustomed to the liberal interpretive filter on race that prevails in the more cosmopolitan cities of America, nothing could have been more alienating than the flippant shared assumptions of the British upper class. No wonder she swept out so many of Harry's old friends. Two Christmases at Sandringham with those barking voices and blasting guns must have felt like Hell Week in the Navy SEALs. In Aatish Taseer's judgment, to any outsider the members of the royal circle are "really forbidding people. . . . The manners. The lifestyle. The world of the shoots and the country houses. The generations of the same friends. The sense of superiority is awe-inspiring." Even Diana, who was herself a member of one of the oldest aristocratic families in England, couldn't stand the stultifying sameness of it all.

And yet, one should not ignore that iconic family photograph, the one that carried so much hope and meaning, taken on May 8, 2019, when the bonny seven-pound, three-ounce Archie Harrison Mountbatten-Windsor was formally presented to the world. The national desire to see the Sussexes' baby son had reached febrile proportions. Archie arrived two weeks late, at 5:26 A.M. on May 6, and was born at London's Portland Hospital. But for an undeclared reason—one that the media read as Sussex peevishness—it was not until eight hours later, after the couple had returned to Windsor, that Harry shared the happy news. Adding to the confusion, just forty-five minutes before Harry's announcement,

Buckingham Palace revealed only that the Duchess had gone into labor that morning.

Because the new parents slipped out of the hospital undetected, the press and the British nation were deprived of the traditional front-page shot of an elated but exhausted young royal couple posing on the hospital steps showing off a crinkle-faced newborn, a unifying media tradition that celebrates not only a joyful new life but a welcome green shoot on the ancient royal family tree. The images of William and Kate with their babies and Diana and Charles with both of theirs outside the Lindo Wing of St. Mary's Hospital Paddington passed into royal iconography. As distinguished British broadcaster Sir Trevor Phillips pointed out, "It became clear that [Meghan and Harry] had not really grasped that in return for the fairy tale you have to give the people outside the castle something, or they just decided they didn't want to play the game. The point at which you decide you're not going to play the game, well don't expect other people to play by the rules." Even so, the press's sour sense of being cheated lifted when the first images of Archie and his parents were finally seen.

Swaddled in an ivory woolen shawl, the Sussexes' first child snuggled in his mother's arms with an ecstatic Harry beside her at Windsor Castle. In the frame, the Queen, wearing the cozy blue cardigan of any British granny, and the beaming ninety-eight-year-old Duke of Edinburgh, gaze dotingly at their eighth great-grandchild. Alongside them is a tenderly over-the-moon Doria Ragland. Immediately, the wedding magic surged again, restoring the fading promise of a diverse England and a Royal Family that had evolved at last from the ultimate bastion of white Protestant values to a closer representation of its own changing people. Patrick Vernon, a prominent Black activist and campaigner, rejoiced: "The presence of the mother is significantly important as it reminds the public and the royal family there is black in the Union Jack." And the **Sunday Times** journalist Grant Tucker spoke for many when he tweeted, "When the Queen ascended to the throne the last remnants of the British Empire were still brutalising many on the African continent. Sixty-five years later that same woman looks down upon her great-grandson, alongside his African-American grandmother."

That's why it was crushing for all who jumped for joy at this historic baby picture to hear from Meghan only twenty-three months later on Oprah's special that there were several "concerned" conversations within the family—not, they hastened to update afterward, with the Queen or Philip—about "how dark Archie's skin might be." And it was baffling to the British people more familiar with royal tradition that Meghan alleged that Archie had been denied his right to be a prince because of his skin color. Her husband knew full well that protocols laid down by George V meant that the Sussex children will not be named prince and princess until Charles ascends the throne.

After a thunderstruck royal silence, the Queen responded with a carefully judged sixty-one-word statement. After repeating that Harry, Meghan, and Archie remain much-loved family members, she dispatched the unforgettable zinger "Some recollections may vary." Never has the passive voice been more artfully ambiguous.

Was Her Majesty's gnomic statement a way of saying, "It depends who you talk to"? Or was it, "You hear what you want to hear—you interpret innocent comments as racist if that is how you were raised"?

And if it's the latter? Well, shouldn't the royals have thought to become at least passingly literate in the language of race and racism, the language that Meghan—raised in the United States with its very different history—"spoke" as her own? Was it really her obligation to give tutorials on modern racial attitudes, just to get on with her in-laws?

And shouldn't Meghan—on her side of the chasm—have recognized that attitudes that had defined (white) privilege in a thousand-year-old monarchy were unlikely to change overnight?

Evidence of how sensitized the royals are becoming since the Black Lives Matter movement is the speed with which William condemned the ugly online abuse of three Black soccer players after the Euro 2020 final, held in July 2021, when they missed penalty kicks in the shoot-out. "I am sickened by the racist abuse aimed at England players after last night's match," he tweeted. "It is totally unacceptable that players have to endure this abhorrent behavior. It must stop now and all those involved should be held accountable. W."

Harry, Duke of Sussex, and the woman he loves have played their own distinctive part in the attitudinal evolution of the House of Windsor. They have achieved something no one can take away from them—Doria Ragland and Queen Elizabeth as grandmothers in the same family, a twin victory over entrenched attitudes toward race and class.

So hold that picture! Two years later, Philip was gone, the Sussexes had fled, the brothers were at war, and the notion of a harmoniously integrated Royal Family is a souvenir gathering dust in our psychic Windsor gift shops.

In November 2019 a Palace old hand, now retired, spoke to the Duke of Cambridge at a charity function in London. William apparently said to him with a worried air, "We may need you to come back for a bit. I'm afraid the wheels are going to fall off with Harry."

CHAPTER
25

SCORCHED EARTH

———

"Annus Horribilis" Redux

———

THE SUSSEXES' DECISION TO GET OUT OF Dodge had much in common with the American exit from Afghanistan: a necessary end executed with maximum chaos. Harry takes vehement issue with the term "Megxit," as the couple's announcement in January 2020 to "step back" from their duties as senior royals came swiftly to be styled. The Duke calls the term "sexist."

"Inaccurate" would be a better word. The decision was Harry's with acceleration from Meghan.

The couple's intent was clear from as early as the fall of 2018. The Commonwealth havens of Canada, where Meghan had roots of her own, and South Africa, where Harry had always dreamed of disappearing, were both canvassed as new Sussex homes. At least one former Palace staffer who cared about Harry supported the idea of his leaving for good. "I thought one of the best things that Meghan could do for Harry was to take him out of royal life because he was just so unhappy for so long," the person told me. "He needed a wife to come in and say, 'Actually, the best thing for you is that I take you out of this.'"

The family saw the split coming only months later, in the summer of 2019. "I think the Queen found herself genuinely very conflicted," said the same Palace source. "They could all see how unhappy Harry and Meghan were. Everybody was supportive of them leaving. But they wanted it done in an orderly way. And they also wanted it done in a way that set the right precedent. William's got three kids. The precedent they set for this generation would affect his children. He's very mindful of that. So they wanted it done properly."

"Done properly" has a very royal ring to it. But what does it mean? Like any divorce, much of the conflict came down to money, and, as usual in this saga, there were hot temperaments and cold misunderstandings.

It was clear to everyone except Meghan and Harry that a blurred part-time arrangement threw up multiple conflicts of interest. If, say, the high-visibility couple tacked a few days of shooting a paid Netflix documentary onto the back of a Foreign Office–funded Commonwealth tour, there would be an uproar—just as Andrew saw when he mixed business sidebars with his trade ambassador trips. Ethics issues of this kind have killed many a promising political career and are red meat for the media. And even if each commercial activity was carefully delineated, it was the Sussexes' royal status that was being packaged and sold. As one Palace veteran put it, Harry "is a deeply caring person who wants to make a positive difference. He doesn't understand that the reason he's getting to do that is because he's a Prince."

The Sussexes wanted to be free to have "a voice" to speak up on causes in which they believed. But what if the cause was controversial? Would they be embracing it as royal personages or in this other status? That issue arose in November 2021, the year after they left, when Republican senators Susan Collins and Shelley Capito received calls on their cell phones from Meghan to lobby for paid family leave, which the GOP opposed. The caller identified herself as the Duchess of Sussex, which Collins said she "found kind of ironic." If Meghan was lobbying in her capacity as a duchess, wouldn't she be in breach of the Royal Family's pledge to be apolitical?

Private security was another headache. Between Harry's entitled casualness and Meghan's blinkered assumptions, the question of who was going to pay for the hefty annual cost of police protection seems to have eluded the Sussexes. Yet Harry knew full well that royal security is not determined or funded by the Crown. Once the Sussexes left the country and were no longer working royals, British taxpayers would not spring for it—and the media would never let them. Was the security detail supposed to hang around while the Sussexes temporarily reverted to private citizenship?

At the core of the difficulties was determining whether the Sussexes were celebrity royals or royal celebrities, two very different states of being. A royal is representing Queen and country. A celebrity is representing himself or herself. The summer of 2019 confirmed to the media that the Sussexes had made the decisive and deadly pivot to the meretricious side of the equation.

After all the tumult of the first six months of that year, Meghan owed herself a long British maternity leave after giving birth to her son. At last ensconced in her new home at Frogmore, it would have been a good moment to take stock of her first year as a royal and reassess the way forward. Sometimes, in the words of the supercomputer Joshua in the science fiction thriller **WarGames,** "the only winning move is not to play." Tabloid sanctification awaited Meghan if she took up the Queen's invitation to bring Archie up to Balmoral with Harry and post the odd snap of their baby son dabbling his tiny pink feet on the edge of Loch Muick. But downtime was not in Meghan's lexicon. Nor were gung-ho picnics on a tartan blanket in the Scottish Highlands.

Instead, she couldn't wait to cram down every cake offered on the celebrity buffet. In the dog days of summer, British newspaper readers were given frequent sightings of the Duke and Duchess of Sussex on luxe jaunts bound to stir up the tabloid hornets' nest. An invitation from Elton John to fly private to his south-of-France villa just two days after a sun break in Ibiza to celebrate Meghan's thirty-eighth birthday? Two big slices please! A hop back to the U.S. Open in New York to watch her pal Serena play Bianca Andreescu in the finals? Yummy, yummy! An offer to guest-edit British **Vogue** for the big, fat door-stopper September issue? Can't resist! As for Harry, he showed up at the annual Google summer camp in Sicily to do a barefoot presentation about climate change to the billionaire bros of Silicon Valley. Between them, Harry and Meghan took four private jets in eleven days.

The media, still resentful of the secrecy over Archie's birth, hit the couple with a sneering backlash over these conspicuous summer travels. It was noted—many times over—that they seemed willing to accept any invitation except the Queen's to show up at Balmoral. It hardly seemed a coincidence when photos suddenly appeared of William, Kate, and their three children boarding a budget flight to Aberdeen, the nearest airport to the Queen's Scottish home.

It was the **Vogue** project, a collaboration with Edward Enninful, one of the UK's most influential taste barons, that was Meghan's unexpected Waterloo. Celebrity guest-editing is usually a risk-free media suck-up. Prince Charles had thrice done it for **Country Life** magazine. Harry received approving reviews when he took over an episode of Radio 4's prestigious **Today** show in 2017, the same year Kate's digital foray at **Huffington Post UK** was lauded for its championing of early-childhood mental health. Meghan's **Vogue** issue about female role models of the moment was titled "Forces for Change," and she had no reason to doubt she would be hailed for her efforts as a millennial moral leader in a tiara. To keep the project under wraps, Enninful, the fashion bible's first male and first Black editor-in-chief, turned Vogue House into the fashion version of Bletchley Park. Unsuspecting staff worked on a decoy issue, and layouts winged back and forth to the code-named duchess with the final pages transported to the printer facedown.

The issue's big reveal united every element of caustic British ridicule and confirmed the Palace's fears about a member of the family wading into political territory. What drew the most fire were the uniformly liberal convictions of the Duchess's anointed change agents—a "right-on roll call" as **The Times** called the list—including climate activist Greta Thunberg, New Zealand prime minister Jacinda Ardern, and trans actress Laverne Cox. Only five of the fifteen icons were British. (Where, the press asked, was Her Majesty Queen Elizabeth II amongst the women Meghan admired?)

The glossy package was seen as snotty piffle by the tabloids, a pious fluff package by upscale columnists, and a mystifying bore by traditional **Vogue** subscribers who would have preferred solutions for more immediate problems like where to find the best camel hair coat with a kimono tie. Harry's Q&A for the issue with the revered primatologist Jane Goodall included his comic Malthusian pronouncement that he and Meghan were limiting their reproductive urges to two children to help save the planet. That went over in the media like a flatulent blast of methane, given that the Duke had just loaded up his carbon footprint flying private to the Google camp.

Meghan's chagrin over the issue's critical reception went to the very core of her aspirations. Once again she had been defeated by the renegade British sensibility, and the national inclination to laugh at earnest intent. The controversy that howled around the issue was God's gift to **Vogue**'s buzz and its newsstand sales (higher than any in its 103-year history), but Meghan wanted a halo, not just ratings. Like many global influencers, she still hankered for the gravitas of old media's validation. Feelings of rejection, cultural and social loneliness, and what sounds like a wave of postpartum depression engulfed her. She found herself considering suicide. "I was really ashamed to say it at the time and ashamed to have to admit it to Harry, especially, because I know how much loss he's suffered," she told Oprah. "But I knew that if I didn't say it, that I would do it. And I just didn't want to be alive anymore."

"The scariest thing for her was her clarity of thought," Harry has recalled. "She hadn't 'lost it.' She wasn't crazy. She wasn't self-medicating, be it through pills or through alcohol. . . . She was absolutely sober. She was completely sane. Yet in the quiet of night, these thoughts woke her up."

And what did her princely husband do about it? "I went to a very dark place as well," he told Oprah. "But I wanted to be there for her and . . . I was terrified. . . . I guess I was ashamed of admitting it to [my family]. . . . I didn't have anyone to turn to."

It was a statement that was not only unsatisfactory but also, surely, disingenuous. Perhaps it was an index of Harry's panic that, after seven years of therapy himself, he seemed paralyzed about turning to the same Palace advisers who had supported him in the past. What about the crack MI6 advisers who could find experts at purging the demons of patients striving to reconcile assumed roles with private lives? Harry had campaigned with courage to ease the stigma surrounding mental health problems, even co-founding Heads Together, whose mission statement is to ensure that "people feel able to support their friends and families through difficult times and that stigma no longer prevents people getting the help they need." If he was now too afraid of the pile-on that would follow an admission of Meghan's ordeals, should he not own the fact that it was he—rather than the Palace or members of his family—who had failed to get his wife help in her hour of need?

In October 2019, the couple chose a different route for talk therapy—Tom Bradby, the royal brothers' longtime media crony at ITV News. Network producers had fully expected Bradby's documentary, **Harry and Meghan: An African Journey**, filmed during their highly successful ten-day tour, to be an uneventful royal tag-along. There were great visual moments to capture on camera—face time with Nelson Mandela's widow, Graça Machel; Archie's adorable nestle with Archbishop Desmond Tutu;

and Meghan's "I am your sister" proclamation to the women of Cape Town's Nyanga township. There was also the expectation of a little newlywed charm thrown in. But, to the astonishment of the Sussexes' communications team and the show's producers, Harry and Meghan hijacked their own humanitarian message during their end-of-tour interview with Bradby by talking about how bummed out they were in their private lives.

For Harry, it was another jeremiad about their persecution by the media. This, after ten days of glowing coverage, including a **Telegraph** front-page Indiana Jones shot touting his earnest op-ed inside the paper about South African conservation, a contribution unlikely to have made it into print—or been given splashy front-page treatment—without a royal byline. Would William be envious of such prime media real estate was the question that crossed my mind when I saw it, presciently as it turned out, because Harry's comment to Bradby—"We are certainly on different paths at the moment"—detonated headlines about an open breach between the brothers.

Meghan took the opportunity to spill forth about her new-mum vulnerability, her bruising struggles to cope with the British stiff upper lip (and life), and her exhortations to Harry about the need to "thrive" rather than simply "survive." Asked by Bradby how she was coping, her response—which convulsed the internet—was, "Thanks for asking because not many people have asked if I'm okay." Not many people ask the women in the Nyanga township if they are okay either, was the media consensus. "I never thought that this would be easy, but I thought [press coverage] would be fair," she told Bradby, unleashing yet more backlash about one of the world's most privileged women complaining about her own press coverage after ten days of witnessing the intense poverty and challenges of parts of South Africa.

On the eve of their departure from Johannesburg, Harry planted a news bomb on the official Sussex website, announcing their lawsuit against **The Mail on Sunday** for publishing Meghan's letter to Tom Markle. Rather than relying on the power of restrained legal language to speak for itself, the Duke announced the lawsuit with a Spencerian tirade:

There comes a point when the only thing to do is to stand up to this behaviour, because it destroys people and destroys lives. Put simply, it is bullying, which scares and silences people. We all know this isn't acceptable, at any level. We won't and can't believe in a world where there is no accountability for this.

Though this action may not be the safe one, it is the right one. Because my deepest fear is history repeating itself. I've seen what happens when someone I love is commoditised to the point that they are no longer treated or seen as a real person. I lost my mother and now I watch my wife falling victim to the same powerful forces.

His evocation of Diana was a window into Harry's free fall. As William had feared, Harry's wounds from the loss of their mother remained too raw for him to cope with the triggering burden of protecting his high-profile wife from the furies of the media. At the Google camp, he told another guest that he was tormented by the conflict of how to shield Meghan and still serve as a senior member of the Royal Family.

Harry's Johannesburg announcement hit the mark with seventy-two cross-party female MPs who, after three years of post-Brexit misogyny, signed an open letter in support of Meghan against "the often distasteful and misleading nature of the stories . . . concerning you, your character and your family. . . . We share an understanding of the abuse and intimidation which is now so often used as a means of disparaging women in public office from getting on with our important work." It's the kind of statement Meghan had longed for from the Palace as an institution. What if the wives of Windsor—the Duchesses of Cornwall and Cambridge, and the Countess of Wessex—had made a similar declaration of collective female outrage? A thrilling, but as yet inconceivable, notion.

In mid-November, the exhausted Harry and Meghan announced they were taking a six-week sabbatical with Archie in Canada. "I couldn't help but notice how incredibly tired, even burned out he [Harry] looked," Tom Bradby later reflected.

Christmas was coming and there was no way the Sussexes would be caught dead at the annual weigh-in at Sandringham.

II

The Windsors' latest round of troubles was just beginning. While the Duke and Duchess of Sussex went off to implode in a rented $13 million waterfront mansion on Vancouver Island, Prince Andrew, in November 2019, decided to strap on a suicide vest and sit down for an ask-me-anything hour-long interview with Emily Maitlis, one of the BBC's most probing broadcasters. No doubt it was inadvertent that he chose the moment when Charles had just set off on a six-day tour of New Zealand with Camilla. Shortly after the Prince of Wales arrived in Auckland to sparse crowds, his phone lit up with news that had nothing to do with his impending meetings about sustainability with concerned Kiwi leaders. Andrew's **Newsnight** performance was a catastrophe. "I expected a train wreck," was a sample tweet from Charlie Proctor, editor of Royal Central website. "That was a plane crashing into an oil tanker, causing a tsunami, triggering a nuclear explosion-level bad." Another tweet, from Dickie Arbiter, the Queen's former press secretary, "If Prince Andrew thought he'd drawn a line in the sand over the Epstein saga, he was in cuckoo land."

Why Andrew imagined he could emerge unscathed from a fifty-minute, free-ranging interview about the sexual allegations against him on a hard-hitting news show was a classic example of Dunning-Kruger delusion. Despite vehement opposition to the interview by Jason Stein, a respected PR adviser who had been newly installed on Andrew's team with the mission of steering the soiled prince back toward respectability, Andrew was confident that he could hold his own with the implacably prepared Emily Maitlis. She had been pursuing him for an interview even before Jeffrey Epstein was arrested on July 6, 2019.

Epstein had been taken into custody after he flew into New York from Paris on his so-called Lolita Express, and was charged with one count of sex trafficking of a minor and one count of conspiracy to commit sex trafficking. Four weeks later, the same day Andrew arrived for his annual Scottish sojourn with his parents at Balmoral, his onetime financial mentor and frequent host was found hanged by a bed sheet tied to the top bunk in his cell at Manhattan's Metropolitan Correctional Center. The question of whether Epstein's death was suicide, or murder carried out to protect the powerful friends he might have implicated, renewed focus on all those who had consorted with him, including Andrew. Virginia Roberts Giuffre's sexual accusations against the Duke of York erupted again and, to make it more darkly tantalizing for the media, his old friend Ghislaine Maxwell was now on the lam. He needed to clear his name!

Palace veterans blame the absence of Sir Christopher Geidt for the fact that the fatal interview took place at all, let alone that it was conducted in the Blue Drawing Room of Buckingham Palace. Andrew clearly hoped the intimidating trappings of royalty would boost his own threadbare gravitas. A Palace source told me that

Andrew went directly to Mummy to get permission
to film there—after already telling the BBC they were
cleared to do so. He positioned the broadcast to the
Queen as a discussion about his official duties and his
success with Pitch@Palace, his entrepreneurial initiative. Expecting just that, Her Majesty, I am told by a
source close to her, watched the broadcast alone in her
private sitting room at Windsor after enjoying a light
dinner on a tray. One only hopes she did not upend
her favored champagne nightcap.

The interview was an exercise in self-immolation as
epic as Windsor Castle going up in flames. Headline:
"Astonished Nation Watches Prince Squirm" (**The
Mail on Sunday**). Andrew, whose demeanor was that
of a cordial blowhard at a gentlemen's club, told
Maitlis that he had no recollection of ever meeting
Giuffre (then all of seventeen years old), much less
having sex with her. He said that he could not have
been with her at Maxwell's home that evening because
he took his daughter Beatrice to a birthday party at a
Pizza Express in Surrey, an occasion he remembered
vividly because, well, he didn't go to Pizza Express that
often. Headline: "I Did Not Have Sex. I Have a Pizza
Alibi." (**The Sunday Times**). As for sweating profusely
on a nightclub dance floor as Giuffre claimed, that
wasn't possible, he said, because he had a medical condition at the time, since remedied, which meant he
could not sweat, an affliction that he said derived from
an overdose of adrenaline from when he was serving
in the Falklands War. Headline: "His Royal Dryness"
(**New York Post**). He expressed not a word of

sympathy for the underage girls who had been trafficked by Epstein and zero remorse for consorting with the sordid man who had done so. Headline: "No Sweat and No Regret" (**Sunday Mirror**).

Asked why he visited Epstein at his home to end their association—rather than just call or email him—Andrew attempted the faux-manly excuse that it was the "chicken's way" not to tell him in person.

As it happened, Prince Philip agreed with the in-person method. The Queen's ninety-eight-year-old consort may have retired from his enforcer role, but this was one last family intervention he was keen to execute himself. Andrew was summoned to Wood Farm at Sandringham for a father-son meeting to explain himself. "There was no screaming or shouting," a royal insider told **The Telegraph**. "Philip told him in no uncertain terms that he had to step down for the sake of the monarchy. Philip doesn't like trial by the media but he's realistic enough to realize that Andrew's actions were a danger to the very fabric of the royal family." The disgusted disciplinarian told his fifty-nine-year-old son to "take his punishment." A statement thundered out from the Palace that the Duke of York was "step[ping] back from public duties for the foreseeable future." Headline: "Outcast" (**Daily Mail**). Left unaddressed was how long Andrew's limbo would be. Much to the military's chagrin, he managed, for the moment, to retain eight of his honorary titles, including the prestigious rank of Colonel of the Grenadier Guards, who, among other duties, are the stoic guardians of Buckingham Palace, beloved by every tourist for their towering bearskin hats and scarlet tunics.

Racing back from media eclipse in New Zealand, Charles found a way to make lemonade out of lemons. This was the moment for the Prince of Wales to go straight to Sandringham to see his father and reinforce his own position as the head of the family. Andrew was once again summoned to make the 140-mile drive from Windsor to Norfolk to give Charles the opportunity of firing him again. At last, there was a conclusive reason to boot his embarrassing younger brother from the ballooning "slimmed-down" monarchy. The Andrew crisis was not unwelcome either for the Sussexes, who got to see the shit rain down on another senior royal for a change. Andrew's ex-wife, Sarah Ferguson, galloped to the rescue with an Instagram post that caused yet more ridicule, calling him a "giant of a principled man that dares to put his shoulder to the wind and stands firm with his sense of honor and truth."

The Duke of York's disgraces came thick and fast. His name was wiped from Pitch@Palace. (He tried to cling on even as its blue-chip sponsors fled.) He was told to step down as patron of more than 230 organizations, including the Outward Bound Trust, London Metropolitan University, the English National Ballet, and the Royal Philharmonic Orchestra. At the family's annual Christmas gathering at Sandringham, Andrew was missing from photographs at the St. Mary Magdalene Church service the rest of the family attended. The Queen canned the glittering sixtieth birthday she had planned to host for him in February 2020 and, for the first time in Andrew's life, he didn't wake up that day to flags flying on government buildings in his honor. Since he left the navy, the one role in which he could truly claim to be a success was as a father. To his chagrin, it was deemed prudent to exclude him from the wedding photos released when Beatrice, who twice postponed the occasion to evade the stench of her father's scandal, married real estate developer Edoardo Mapelli Mozzi the following summer at the Royal Chapel of All Saints at Royal Lodge.

Overnight, the overbearing, rank-pulling, unperspiring Duke of York became a ghost royal. Born with a destiny of descending in importance, he had now disappeared altogether into a pit of shame. The only person who was willing to be seen with him was his mother. Two days after the announcement that he was a dead parrot, the Queen was spotted riding with Andrew on the Windsor Castle estate. While Charles and William were both of the opinion that Andrew was toast, mother and son held on to the belief that, after the passage of time, Andrew could be returned to the fold with a reduced role rather than full banishment.

For her starring role in Andrew's downfall, the BBC's Emily Maitlis was named 2020 network presenter of the year, ironically by the Royal Television Society. "A lot of people ask how it feels to be interviewing a royal, a senior royal, in the middle of Buckingham Palace, and I guess the thing I would say is it wasn't actually about the royal," she said on receipt of the award. "It was an interview for women watching around the world who were waiting to see if we asked the right questions, at the right moment, to things that we needed answering."

It's worth noting that Andrew was punished not for consorting with a known pedophile or accusations of having sex with a trafficked teenage girl, but for talking about it to the skillful Ms. Maitlis.

III

Meanwhile, the Sussex sabbatical on Vancouver Island soon became a working vacation. In between walks in the woods with Archie, Harry and Meghan furiously refined their exit plan. Meghan reactivated her former publicist Keleigh Thomas Morgan at Sunshine Sachs to map out the new Sussex Royal foundation, and tapped the former designer of her **Tig** website to secretly create the digital expression of their future modus operandi as part-time royals. The snag was that no one at the Palace had yet agreed. The shiny new trademark of "Sussex Royal" needed the Queen's permission, which Her Majesty had not given, and the pronouncement that they were going to forgo their share of the Sovereign Grant and work toward "becoming financially independent" was still based on the dubious proposition of being adjunct royals with lucrative side hustles.

Tant pis. If the Sussexes had any residual misgivings about whether they wanted out, those doubts vanished when they viewed the Queen's 2019 televised Christmas message. With their own eyes, they saw that they had been kicked to the margins of the monarchy. Her Majesty eloquently made the point in her speech by saying nothing. The subtext was all in the flotilla of carefully arranged family photographs positioned on her writing desk, a grouping that, in case anyone thinks is accidental, has been artfully changed every year since the monarch's first televised seasonal message in 1957.

The previous Christmas, a family portrait of Charles, Camilla, the five Cambridges, and Harry and Meghan was exhibited at Her Majesty's elbow. But in December 2019, the Sussexes had evaporated, their image excised as skillfully as Stalin would have done to an apparatchik out of favor. According to author Christopher Andersen, the Queen told the director of the broadcast that all the displayed photographs were fine to remain in the shot except for one. Her Majesty pointed at a winsome portrait of Harry, Meghan, and baby Archie. "That one," said the Queen. "I suppose we don't need that one."

And a happy Christmas to you too, Granny! William was said to have been appalled when he saw the Sussexes had been edited out. He knew his brother well enough to predict a Category 5 tantrum brewing.

It was time for the Sussexes to pull the trigger. Harry says that far from blindsiding his family, he spoke from Canada about his exit plans with his grandmother three times and his father twice. The conversations went deep enough that Charles, Harry claims, told him to itemize their "step back" concept in writing, not an unreasonable request given the serious ramifications to the monarchy of funding, taxation, official duties, titles, and public positioning—all of which had become even more sensitive after the Andrew debacle. But trust was at such a low ebb between father and son that Harry was convinced Charles was stalling. Hot words were exchanged, culminating in Charles, Harry says, refusing to take his calls. That's when the Red Prince decided, as he put it opaquely to Oprah, to "take matters into his own hands."

Ominous mood music. The Sussexes sans Archie flew back to London on January 6, 2020. Harry's last-ditch strategy was to bypass his father and the Palace gatekeepers and talk directly to the Queen, whose affection for him he believed was strong enough to trump his father's disfavor. Her Majesty promisingly invited her grandson for tea or dinner at Sandringham on arrival. But as soon as the Vancouver flight touched down in London, Edward Young canceled the meeting. The monarch, her private secretary said, was otherwise engaged for the rest of the week. Some deft ostriching had occurred since the Queen offered the friendly invitation.

"There is something in my diary that I didn't know that I had," his grandmother demurred when Harry then called her from Frogmore. "What about the rest of the week?" he appealed. Uh, "That's busy now as well," the monarch weaseled.

Today, Harry prefers to blame Her Majesty's decision not to meet with him on "bad advice," but he knew this drill very well. As one veteran of the Palace staff explained to me, "One thing the Queen is very good at is she has a distinction between being the sovereign and being the grandmother. And the family always knows whether they were going to see her in one or the other capacity." In this way, Elizabeth II is no different from any other dynastic head, whether it's King Lear or Logan Roy.

It sometimes falls to the Queen's private secretaries to alert her to family members trying to blur the lines to secure inappropriate outcomes. In corporate terms, it's called CEO deniability. In this case, Harry's goal to make an end run past the Queen's advisers was very clear. "Such conversations [as the Sussexes' plans] would have to be done in the spirit of Elizabeth II as sovereign so there would've been agendas. Talking points would've been agreed on beforehand between private secretaries. . . . What the Sussexes tried to do was circumnavigate that and go and see her because, on her own, she famously says yes. She caves," said a Palace source privy to the events. Had she done so, could she have talked sense into Harry to slow this momentous decision down? She clearly thought that it was more likely her charming grandson would talk her into agreeing to something that was not in the Crown's interest.

Who leaked the ready-to-go Sussex Royal website to **The Sun**—just before Meghan skipped off back to Canada to rejoin Archie—is still a matter of furious contention. There have been suggestions emanating from the Sussex camp that loose lips passed it to the Palace, who leaked it to **The Sun** to make the couple look bad. Plunging the Royal Family into PR chaos in order to score a point sounds like an unlikely strategy and, instead, was seen unilaterally in the Palace as a Sussex ploy to force their hand. "What Harry and Meghan did was a terrible blow," Dickie Arbiter said. "The Queen is feeling very let down—more disappointed than she felt after Andrew's terrible BBC interview."

Whatever conversations Harry insists had taken place, the Sussexes' fully baked proclamation of intent on their website was an insult just by its very existence. "It was total madness," was the verdict of an intimate Palace source. For once, the monarch and the Prince of Wales were united in feelings of offense. Laying out rules of the new "working model" was a bit like making public your terms of employment as a **fait accompli** before any job had actually been offered. Hollywood public relations–speak was naïvely apparent in the manifesto's language. After the redefinition of their roles, it declared, the Sussexes would continue to "collaborate" with Her Majesty the Queen, as if the monarch were the co–executive producer of a TV series.

But the Queen does not collaborate. She commands—as her impetuous grandson was about to find out.

The tense conclave that came to be known as the Sandringham Summit took place at two P.M. on January 13, 2020, in the house's Long Library. It was attended by the Queen, William, Harry, Charles, and all their private secretaries, serving as human shields. In times past, the library was the secluded cozy room where the young William and Harry had gathered with their York cousins for high tea at Christmas. Now it was the scene of a bitter royal divorce. "Harry and Meghan overplayed their hand," opined one who was privy to the discussions. "They thought if they leaked [the website], it would force the Royal Family to respond by saying . . . "Okay, Harry and Meghan, what do you want? We're going to give you what you want.' . . . They thought this was their nuclear weapon. And so they deployed it. But the Royal Family went, 'Okay, off you go.' "

It's always an unwise idea to give an ultimatum to Queen Elizabeth II. I am told that, far from yielding the floor to her advisers, this was a process in which her sovereign self, not her granny persona, was very much in control. Nothing about the Sussexes' headstrong behavior to date suggested any "part-time" arrangement could have worked then or now. There would be no stepping "back" for them. There was only stepping down.

Megxit was not so much a deal as an edict. Harry and Meghan could keep their HRH titles but couldn't use them. They could not, they later learned, brand their enterprises Sussex Royal. They could no longer represent the Queen with all their royal patronages, including their Commonwealth roles. They had to repay the £2.4 million cost of renovating Frogmore. Though they could keep the house as their UK base, they would have to pay commercial-rate rent. Prince Charles ended up funding them just until the summer of 2020. Most devastating to Harry was that, though he could keep his private Invictus Games and Sentebale charities, he had to relinquish all his military titles, including his much-prized captain generalcy of the Royal Marines. That was particularly galling, and many would argue un-fair, given that the toxic Prince Andrew had been allowed to keep his military titles, to the outrage of many in the forces. "Make no mistake," wrote Camilla Tominey of **The Telegraph**, "[this was] the hardest Megxit possible for the Duke and Duchess of Sussex. While insisting Harry, Meghan and Archie 'will always be much loved members of my family,' the 93-year-old monarch could not be clearer on their ongoing role in the Firm. It's over."

"Harry and Meghan were really stunned," said a former adviser. "They did not expect that to hap-pen." After the two-hour meeting, the participants pulled out of the Sandringham drive to go their sep-arate ways. There was shell shock in each person present that the family alliance could have shattered in this way.

For William and Kate, Megxit had more direct implications than anyone other than the Sussexes. The Cambridges, with three young children, would have to not only absorb the Sussex workload but also fill the charisma vacancy left by Harry and Meghan. That was made abundantly clear in a now-iconic spontaneous snap of the Sussexes taken in March 2020 on a last royal engagement in London. Sharing an umbrella against the shimmer of raindrops, the now-liberated couple shone with a star power as sizzling and romantic as the ardent way they gazed at each other. The familiar, conservative brand of royalty that William and Kate represent is, without doubt, better suited to occupy the throne in the future. But holding the public's attention is altogether more difficult.

For Charles, who saw himself as a modernizer, it was crushing to lose the two members of the family who had proven they could resonate with a younger and diverse British public. The missed opportunity to create a space for a beloved, fallible prince—"dear old Harry" as Charles affectionately called him— and the monarchy's only woman of color was another failure that would be laid at his door. This was intensely painful for the man who had so gallantly stepped in and walked Meghan down the aisle at St. George's Chapel on that glorious May morning in 2018.

And for the Queen, who reverted to a grandmother as soon as the Sandringham Summit was over, one can only surmise the sorrow of being obliged, just as she had with Princess Margaret, to dash the happiness of someone she deeply loves. From her perspective, Harry and Meghan could have chosen a path of duty and service that would not have made them wealthy in global terms, but offered the longevity of influence and reach that had enabled Philip to make his mark, even if it posed some irksome constraints on their freedom. The Princess of Wales gave her royal role seventeen years. Meghan gave it twenty months. Even in her darkest moments, Diana understood—as she extended her hand to a patient in an AIDS ward—that the most powerful way to be a change agent was from within.

At a private dinner for Sentebale six days after the Sandringham Summit, an emotional Harry told the assembled crowd, "It gives me great sadness that it has come to this. Our hope was to continue serving the Queen, the Commonwealth and my military associations but without public funding. Unfortunately that wasn't possible. I have accepted this, knowing it doesn't change who I am and how committed I am. But I hope it helps you understand what it had to come to that I would step my family back from all I have ever known to take a step forward into what I hope will be a more peaceful life."

But peace was not, and perhaps never will be, in Harry's future. The cheerless day he departed England to return to Meghan and Archie in Canada was January 21, St. Agnes Day. The ancient English myth the date memorializes was conjured up by John Keats in his great, chilly narrative poem **The Eve of St. Agnes,** about a young star-crossed couple who flee the granite walls of a castle after being driven out by a hostile court. I have always found the lines in its concluding stanzas haunting:

The chains lie silent on the footworn stones;
The key turns, and the door upon its hinges
    groans.

And they are gone: ay, ages long ago
These lovers fled away into the storm.

EPILOGUE

EMBERS

———

AND THEN FROM OUT OF NOWHERE CAME A great plague, and the world stopped.

The blanket of sorrow and suffering that descended on the British nation with COVID-19 called on the Queen to fulfill her role as consoler of her people, just as her parents had offered up their balm to a traumatized people in the Blitz. As hospitals filled, governments flailed, and fear of sickness drove us behind the walls of our own barricaded castles, Elizabeth II, who had never had freedom of movement herself, calmed the nation from hers.

On April 5, 2020, the Queen made a televised address, recalling the moment when she and Margaret spoke from Windsor in 1940 to the children who had been evacuated from Nazi bombing and faced painful separation from their families, just as loved ones were now kept apart by the pandemic. "I want to reassure you that if we remain united and resolute, then we will overcome it," she said. "While we have faced challenges before, this one is different. This time we join with all nations across the globe in a common endeavor, using the great advances of science and our instinctive compassion to heal." She closed with the words "We will meet again" from Vera Lynn's defining song of World War II. The broadcast was watched by twenty-four million people, as many as three times more than the audience for her Christmas message.

For most of us, Zoom reduces the closeness of human intimacy, but as a new method of royal outreach, it had the opposite effect. Technology brought the royals into every home in ways that were idiosyncratic and informal. A video of Princess Anne teaching her mother how to log in connected with similar scenes in every British household. Charles, speaking from Balmoral in front of shelves overflowing with books, family photographs, and, inevitably, a teddy bear, described the lockdown as a "strange, frustrating and often distressing experience."

"Would Prince Charles have talked so candidly about lockdown separation and really wanting 'to give people a hug' if he was face-to-face with an interviewer rather than doing it remotely via a laptop? Maybe. Maybe not," noted the BBC. Engagement on Clarence House's digital platforms reportedly increased tenfold.

As the banging of pots and pans to celebrate the valiant National Health Service workers could be heard every Thursday night in doorways across Britain, the Royal Family were in their doorways too. At Anmer Hall, the Cambridges, their three children never more adorable, clapped with the nation. As did Charles and Camilla—cozy and accessible in her blue jeans—outside the rustic front door of Birkhall. Sophie Wessex was snapped volunteering at a London vaccination center.

The Duchess of Cambridge was a luminous and perennial Zoom presence, chatting about the challenges of helping with homeschooling (she graded her math skills at negative 5) and cutting her children's hair. She released **Hold Still,** a book of portraits submitted by the public that captures the British people in lockdown. Princess Charlotte delivered packages of homemade pasta to isolated pensioners in Norfolk. There was something endearingly old-school about William's decision not to make public the fact that he had gone through a very bad case of COVID himself, quarantining at Anmer "because he didn't want to worry anyone." In a video call as patron of the National Emergencies Trust, he praised the public's response to the crisis, insisting, "Britain is at its best, weirdly, when we're in a crisis: we all pull together." Community spirit, he said, had come rushing back. Even forgoing the traditional forty-one-gun salute for the Queen's ninety-fourth birthday was a unifying act. Her people weren't celebrating, and nor was Her Majesty.

But the Queen did receive one unexpected blessing. The pandemic meant she was able to spend a year locked down at Windsor and Balmoral with the love of her life. Philip helicoptered back from his Wood Farm haven on March 19, 2020, and the royal couple bubbled together with a reduced team that included Angela Kelly, Paul Whybrew, and Prince Philip's private secretary Brigadier Archie Miller-Bakewell. The ninety-three-year-old monarch rode every day in Windsor Home Park with her head groom and plowed through her red boxes, while Philip, now increasingly ailing, fended off efforts to engage him in conversations about his one hundredth birthday celebrations in June 2021. He was on record as saying he had no desire to reach his centenary. "I can't imagine anything worse. Bits of me are falling off already," he said.

It was the longest time the Queen and Prince Philip had ever spent together alone as a couple in their seventy-three-year marriage. Theirs was a bond that didn't need a constantly reinforced presence. Though they permitted themselves no displays of affection in public, in private they had a "wonderful teasing intimacy," their friend Alastair Bruce told me. "They played off each other the way two people who love each other do, in a way that makes their inner sanctum very trusting."

The wartime flavor of their last year together evoked their early courtship in the 1940s. For Philip, it was reminiscent of being back at sea. In a memo to the "HMS Bubble" staff, the Queen's master of the household and a former Royal Navy officer Tony Johnstone-Burt wrote: "The challenges that we are facing, whether self-isolating alone at home or with our close household and families, have parallels with being at sea, away from home for many months, and having to deal with a sense of dislocation, anxiety, and uncertainty."

From the moment the COVID pandemic gripped the world by the throat, the Sussexes were starkly cut off from the surge of patriotic feeling in the country they had left behind. Ensconced in one of Hollywood's more preposterous mega-mansions, loaned to them by the entertainment superstar Tyler Perry, they confronted something they had never expected: irrelevance in Britain. With one stroke, their goal of global platform-building was at emphatic odds with the zeitgeist. Sounding off about generic humanitarian virtue was suddenly out of style when something as brutal and specific as COVID tore through the world. The couple managed to get in only one lucrative headline performance at a J.P. Morgan Alternative Investment Summit in Miami Beach before everything closed down into eerie seclusion. In England, the media pilloried them as California sybarites who had dissed the Queen and got what was coming to them—a life of luxury, yes, but also public opprobrium.

In the United States, their bid for freedom wasn't scoffed at. It was applauded, and better understood. The Sussexes rode a dealmaking wave that would make them financially independent at last. They landed a rumored $100 million score from Netflix for movies and documentaries, a $25 million podcast deal with Spotify, a multiyear deal with P&G, an approximately $700,000 children's book deal for Meghan, and a fancy corporate title for Harry as chief impact officer of BetterUp, a digital start-up that offers mental health coaching. The banned trademark Sussex Royal was torn up and relaunched as Archewell. In June 2020, the couple bought a $14.7 million Mediterranean-style estate in Montecito, the Santa Barbara enclave for tech billionaires and celebrities between the Santa Ynez Mountains and the Pacific Ocean.

The deal that kicked them into the stratosphere was their interview with Oprah. It was the shrewdest move after a year of floundering to refocus the spotlight. For Meghan, it was irrefutable validation that she was a world-class celebrity. For Harry, it was a firebomb thrown into the heart of a family with whom he could find no other way to communicate. It sank into the Sussexes that the British government was not going to cough up the over seven-figure annual cost of their police protection and, now that Harry and Meghan were Netflix moneybags, nor was the Royal Family. Harry's explosive chagrin can be attributed to the fact that entitlement was literally in his DNA. "I never thought that I would have my security removed, because I was born into this position," he told Oprah. "I inherited the risk, so that was a shock to me. That was what completely changed the whole plan."

One new Sussex income stream produced a collective shudder in the three royal households—

a reported $20 million, four-book deal with Penguin Random House that included a memoir from Harry that would "share, for the very first time, the definitive account of the experiences, adventures, losses, and life lessons that have helped shape him."

Mercifully, some would say, Prince Philip was one member of the family who didn't hear that announcement. In January 2021, he had gone into his last decline due to a combination of heart issues and an infection. Hollow-eyed and gaunt, he walked into London's King Edward VII Hospital with no assistance. Because of COVID rules, the Queen could not visit him there, and she would not seek special privileges. As the weeks ticked by, the country knew his prolonged stay was a death watch. Philip had vowed not to die in the hospital, and on March 15 the public had its last glance of the Queen's staunch consort sitting bolt upright in the back of a car as he was driven back to Windsor Castle to spend his last weeks with Lilibet.

On the morning of April 9, 2021, the Queen's frail liege man found heavenly release from his life of service. Gently, and with love, she let him go.

II

Prince Harry was asleep when the call came from Britain that his grandfather had died. At the request of the British embassy, an officer from the Santa Barbara County Sheriff's Office was dispatched to bang on his door in Montecito at three A.M. so that he would not read it first in the media.

Harry has said that whenever he flies into London, he finds it "a trigger." Nothing could have been more triggering than his return to quarantine at Frogmore, his brief marital home with Meghan now frozen like Pompeii in the ashes of their own Vesuvius, before attending his grandfather's funeral at St. George's Chapel, Windsor. Only six weeks after going nuclear on Oprah, Harry had to face his grieving family at a Church of England service for Philip that COVID rules had reduced to a sacred minimum. Which was, as it happened, just what Philip would have chosen. There were only thirty guests, and the ceremony lasted less than an hour. Among the few mourners outside the family were the Duke's private secretary and Countess Mountbatten, Penny Romsey.

With his customary obsession with detail, Philip had designed a modified Land Rover repainted dark bronze green with a custom-made rear section to carry his coffin, on which was set his gold-braided naval cap and the sword presented to him by his father-in-law, King George VI. Only one of the expected protocols—that the family men wear military dress—was not honored. It was piercing for Harry, now stripped of his military titles, that he was not entitled to wear a uniform. In a characteristic tantrum, Andrew demanded to wear an admiral's regalia even though he had never been promoted to that rank and was holding on to his existing military titles by a thread. The Queen, ever the grown-up in the room, deftly defused the etiquette bomb by decreeing that all the Windsor men wear morning dress.

Walking behind Philip's coffin with his siblings was a shattered Prince Charles, whose relationship with his father had been full of complicated mutual disappointment. Now he had inherited the patriarch's role at a time of seemingly unquenchable family conflagration. Beside him, Princess Anne, in a long black coat adorned with military medals, was the most martial figure in the lineup, not least because more than any of her three male siblings, her brusque temperament resembles her father's.

In the third row, William and Harry, who had once walked with Philip behind their mother's coffin, now walked behind his. **If I walk, will you walk with me?** That tender question to his grandsons is now seen as the monarchy's cruel prerogative of duty. But Philip's breed of self-sacrifice belonged to a different era—and a different ethos.

The media was riveted by the suspense of a possible fraternal reconciliation. Palace planners denied photographers a brothers-at-war close-up by positioning their burly cousin Peter Phillips to walk between them. Trained to always be cordial in front of cameras and determined to cheat the press of any narrative drama, the once inseparable royal boys did not betray the depth of their alienation. Despite a promising moment when Kate dropped back to let them speak to each other, there was no bro-hugging adjournment to the castle's private apartments.

Instead, the image that was soldered on the heart of the nation was of the Queen, small and bereft in her black mask and simple black hat and coatdress, grieving alone in the corner of the cavernous carved oak pew of the chapel. In normal times, she would have been surrounded by consoling family and the world's dignitaries, but, like everyone else who had lost a loved one in pandemic England, she was mourning in isolation.

III

Living their best lives in Montecito, now with a baby girl called Lilibet Diana, the Sussexes found that being non-working royals takes a lot of work. Deals have to be serviced. Unaffiliated celebrity needs to be buffed and maintained. Exile from the monarchy does not offer a confirmed place in the world order, or even, sometimes, at the biggest red-carpet events. Three days after Meghan was snapped doing earnest rounds of UN dignitaries with Harry, clutching an Archewell Foundation brochure and wearing an I-am-serious heavy camel coat, Kate showed up at the London premiere of the latest James Bond film **No Time to Die** in an eyeball-popping, shimmering golden gown with a deep V-neck and high heels. WTF?

Without the Palace platform, a constant hustle is required to insert yourself in the global conversation or get in on the issue of the day. For Meghan's fortieth birthday, the Archewell website featured a video of the Duchess sitting at what looked like an oversized spa desk and inviting forty high-profile women friends to donate forty minutes to mentor a woman rejoining the workforce. As comic relief, the Queen's grandson could be glimpsed juggling outside the window.

When every leader of note assembled in Glasgow in November 2021 for the UN Climate Change Conference, and Prince Charles and Camilla and Prince William and Kate played host, you could almost feel the gusts of FOMO from Montecito in the letter the Sussexes sent to attendees asking them to take action in this "window of opportunity." William had just launched the Earthshot Prize, his signature environmental initiative in partnership with the most beloved man in Britain, the naturalist and broadcaster Sir David Attenborough. The Sussexes reportedly offered a video message to the conference but were bumped when the Queen recorded hers. Her Majesty spoke of "the great pride to me that the leading role my husband played in encouraging people to protect our fragile planet, lives on through the work of our eldest son Charles and his eldest son William." Not a mention of Harry's conservation work. The next day, he and Meghan released a statement pledging to make their Archewell Foundation carbon neutral by 2030 and noting their "long-standing commitment to the planet."

But the Sussexes were undisputed world superstars to the roaring throng of sixty thousand attendees of the Global Citizen Live concert in New York's Central Park during UN week 2021, when the topic **du jour** was vaccine equity. Harry bestrode the stage holding hands with Meghan, who wore a Valentino minidress, under a screen declaring "Defend the Planet/Defeat Poverty!" Harry said: "My wife and I believe that the way you are born should not dictate your ability to survive." It was ephemeral star power versus the institutional gravitas of monarchy.

That gravitas took a severe hit when Prince Andrew's decade-long attempt to stonewall Virginia Giuffre's allegations ran out of road. In August 2021, Giuffre filed a civil lawsuit against him, repeating her accusations that he sexually abused her when she was underage. Turning up the heat even further, Ghislaine Maxwell was convicted four months later in a Manhattan courtroom of five federal sex-trafficking charges after spending her sixtieth birthday behind bars. The potential for reverberations of a trial of Andrew and the collateral damage for the Queen and the entire Royal Family during the 2022 Platinum Jubilee year was a full-blown nightmare. When a federal judge in the US refused to dismiss the case, the panicked Duke was left with a choice between two dire outcomes: enduring the eviscerating circus of a trial or ponying up a prodigious sum he could ill afford. In January 2022, Andrew filed court papers denying all of Giuffre's allegations and demanding a jury trial.

Andrew's moment of truth, like Harry's, was a potent reminder that Elizabeth's affection for her family and the Sovereign's need to protect the Crown had become mutually exclusive. If the Queen had any residual hopes that Andrew could stage a comeback, an open letter from more than 150 veterans pleading with her to strip the Duke of York of his honorary military roles was decisive. "Officers of the British armed forces must adhere to the very highest standards of probity, honesty and honourable conduct. These are standards which Prince Andrew has fallen well short of," they wrote. "We understand that he is your son, but we write to you in your capacity as head of state and as Commander-in-Chief of the Army, Navy and Air Force."

On January 13, just hours after receiving this blistering petition, HM summoned Andrew to Windsor Castle and confiscated the last vestiges of his royal status—his titles and all his military patronages. Like Harry, the Duke of York would no longer be known as His Royal Highness in any official capacity. The triumvirate of the Queen and her direct heirs, Charles and William, abandoned him to fight his lawsuit in America as a "private citizen." By so publicly humiliating him in an effort to inoculate the monarchy, they all but acknowledged Andrew's guilt. In the Palace statement, there was no reference as there twice was with Harry to the Duke of York remaining a "much-loved member of [the] family." Canceling her own son was perhaps the Queen's most bitter sacrifice to the commands of duty. But four weeks later, she threw him one last lifeline, topping up the funds he needed to settle with Giuffre. His reputation was shredded regardless.

THE QUESTION OF HOW the buffeted institution can maintain its mystical stature after the Queen dies has begun to creep through the British nation like a low-grade fever. How much tarnishing can the Crown endure? Take Elizabeth II out of the frame at the splendor of state dinners for visiting presidents, the solemn obsequies for fallen war heroes, and the glorious theater of the opening of Parliament, when the mere glimpse of her scarlet velvet ermine robe makes even the unruliest of MPs sit up straight, how will anyone know how to be British anymore? In an age when everyone has opinions, she has maintained the discipline of never revealing hers. Her epic stoicism has come to signify the endurance of the nation.

As the close of the second Elizabethan age approaches, the words the first Elizabeth used to rally her troops at Tilbury against the Spanish Armada could just as well have been uttered by her modest but stalwart namesake:

I have always so behaved myself that, under God, I have placed my chiefest strength and safeguard in the loyal hearts and good-will of my subjects; and therefore I am come amongst you, as you see, at this time, not for my recreation and disport, but being resolved, in the midst and heat of the battle, to live and die amongst you all; to lay down for my God, and for my kingdom, and my people, my honor and my blood, even in the dust.

There is a sense of foreboding about the impending national identity crisis. In his biography of Queen Victoria, Lytton Strachey wrote of the astonished grief that swept over the country when she died, "as if some monstrous reversal of the course of nature was about to take place. The vast majority of her subjects had never known a time when she was not reigning over them." If that was true of Victoria, who reigned for almost sixty-four years, how much more true will it be of the present Queen? Elizabeth II has beaten the world historical record, except for Louis XIV, who doesn't count, because he ascended to the throne when he was ten.

After a series of maladies in the fall of 2021 and her first hospitalization in years, the Queen had to cancel a season of official engagements. No more Dubonnets in the evening. No more long walks with her corgis in Windsor Park. Hardly surprising at her time of life, but the British people are anything but reconciled—in the way one might expect—to the gradual fade-out of a nonagenarian monarch. The news in February 2022 that the Queen had tested positive for COVID-19 was another cold gust of advancing inevitability.

When the dreaded moment comes, every broadcaster and media outlet knows the drill. The Queen's private secretary will contact the prime minister and utter the fateful code words, "London Bridge is down." The prime minister will contact the foreign secretary, who will notify the leaders of the fourteen countries of which she is head of state and the thirty-six other Commonwealth countries. A news alert will go out to the world's media. A black-edged notice of death will appear on the Buckingham Palace website and then . . . what?

The edifice of British self-image will creak and sway, but the old, tribal, and atavistic beliefs in the monarchy, both mortal and majestic, will trundle on.

Amidst the deluge, the tsunami, the engulfing torrent of world mourning, the man who has spent seven decades in the waiting room of his destiny will finally walk through its door. In the Middle Ages, they would have dubbed him Charles the Green. For years, it looked as if the Prince of Wales would be but a husk of history by the time he became king. But in a miraculous accident of timing, he will ascend the throne at a moment that uniquely calls on his lifelong passion to save the planet. However muddied by scandal the crown he inherits may be, the power to convene is an undimmed royal prerogative, and Charles will use it, even as he will have to muzzle his well-known opinions.

At exit ceremonies for Britain's ever-shrinking global dominions, Charles offers more than the Queen's perennial benedictions to inevitable forces of change. In November 2021 in Barbados, he used the island's republic celebration, where he had the odd experience of being guest of honor as his mother was deposed as head of state, to speak about the "appalling atrocity of slavery" that "forever stains our history"—words the Queen—incredibly—is constitutionally prohibited from saying by her oath to be non-political but that Charles said while he still could.

His reign will be too short to acquire his mother's ingrained rings of collective national memory, but a monarch whose Aston Martin runs on a bioethanol blend of cheese and English white wine by-products will find a different way to be loved. Pinker by the minute, like a Thomas Rowlandson cartoon of a gouty squire, he's growing into his role of grandfather of the nation. Like his ancestor Edward VII, who waited fifty-nine years to follow the endless imperial reign of his mother, Victoria, Charles will need a shock-and-awe coronation to blow the door off for his arrival. After which, he will execute long-held plans to reduce the pomp and circumstance of the monarchy. He's expected to live in a private apartment atop Buckingham Palace and will allocate more of the space (there are 52 Royal and guest bedrooms and 188 staff bedrooms) to year-round public tours. Balmoral Castle may well become a museum of his mother's reign while his beloved Highgrove and Birkhall remain the Kingly retreats.

And what of Camilla, who has proven herself to be such a staunch second wife to Charles? At the end of 2021 she moved one step closer to that goal when the Queen appointed her to Britain's oldest and most senior order of chivalry as a Royal Lady of the Most Noble Order of the Garter, the triple crown of honors before the big one that came next. On the eve of her Platinum Jubilee in February 2022, the Monarch, in a move that was both magnanimous and strategic, announced that she wishes the Duchess of Cornwall to become Queen Consort when Charles ascends the throne, protecting her heir from any wounding controversy had he announced the decision himself. It was not only a dynastic gift to Charles but it acknowledged something new and even seismic: that duty and loyalty to the Crown—as we have also seen with Kate Middleton—are more defining of royalty than bloodlines. Once again, the glacier of monarchy has moved. For Charles, his mother's validation of his devotion to Camilla was the last exorcism of Diana's ghost.

It is ironic that, after so much talk of duty, perhaps the most powerful survival element of the monarchy has turned out to be marital love. Without the caring resolve of the Queen Mother, George VI would have been a stammering introvert who could never have led the country in its hour of need. Without Philip's bracing loyalty, the Queen could have been a lonely conformist, run by her courtiers. Without finally being allowed to marry Camilla, Charles would have suffered a slow death of the soul instead of his late flowering into an unapologetically happy man. And without Kate's serene empathy,

William might have collapsed under the pain of his childhood and the weight of his future. Diana's two boys have each found the sustaining love that eluded her, even though in Harry's case he chose to leave rather than allow his wife to be crushed by the media and the Palace machine.

The fascination of monarchy is that its themes repeat themselves because its protagonists are earthly. When George V rebranded the monarchy as the House of Windsor and turned it into the emblem not just of the British family but of a sacralized exemplary version of the British family, there was one central flaw: their humanity. There will always be the rebels, the problem children, and the miscreants, because the Crown rests on a family as fallible as any other. The Queen has given her entire life over to the path set forth by her grandfather and her father, a concept frozen in time, to which only her unique properties of character could hold fast. But her unbreakable rectitude has come at a price. Will historians of the future consider the length of her reign a fatal impediment to dynastic evolution? A pileup of heirs and unresolved problems of minor royals who became casualties and roadkill?

In November 2021, I attended the Salute to Freedom Gala in Manhattan aboard the warship **Intrepid,** at which Prince Harry presented awards to veterans living with the invisible wounds of war. I was struck by how small and vulnerable Meghan looked in her bravura scarlet ball gown clutching Harry's hand, and also by how, up close, the Prince's complexion is as flushed and transparent as Diana's. It was impossible not to be touched by the Prince's natural sweetness, his earnest desire to do good—and to feel, with a pang, that the wounds of war of which he spoke so eloquently were also his own.

The days of implacable royal silence are over. It was not only William's Earthshot Prize that made a powerful statement about the concerns of a future king. It was also his podcast, **Time to Walk**, that let the public in to hear him ruminate as a man and a father of three about his experiences of pain, and the joy of his family life. He has found a way to accept both his destiny and his own emotional complexity. In doing so, King William, with his consort Queen Catherine, may find a way to reinvent the monarchy in ways that none of us can anticipate.

While we celebrate the mightiness of Elizabeth II's allegiance to a life of service, we should also acknowledge that an antiquated version of monarchy must now pass into history. The jubilee to mark her seventy years on the throne stands as a widespread valediction—not just to the Queen while she's still alive, but to what the monarchy has been on her watch.

"I cannot lead you into battle," she told the nation in her first televised Christmas message in 1957. "I do not give you laws or administer justice but I can do something else, I can give you my heart and my devotion to these old islands and to all the peoples of our brotherhood of nations."

Never again.

ACKNOWLEDGMENTS

THE PALACE PAPERS SPANS A PERIOD OF twenty years of the British monarchy—and what felt like twenty years to me in its writing.

As for so many of us in the traumatic era of a worldwide pandemic, pretty much everything about my life changed from that jaunty summer day in 2019 when my brilliant WME agent, Eric Simonoff, called to tell me that Gillian Blake, the accomplished new publisher and editor-in-chief of Crown, was enthusiastic about my book proposal and would like to be its publisher.

Gillian and I had worked together at Henry Holt on my last book, **The Vanity Fair Diaries**. I knew her sharp clarity of editorial direction and copy judgment would be an invaluable asset on this book, and I was not disappointed. It was an added gift to receive the keen insights throughout from a British perspective offered by my UK publisher Ben Brusey, publishing director of the Cornerstone imprint Century and their excellent respective teams I name below.

The support of my editor and publishers had never been so important because during the writing of this book I lost the most brilliant editor of all, my husband, Sir Harry Evans, who died on September 23, 2020, of congestive heart failure, leaving me in an abyss of grief and disorientation. To say I miss Harry's wonderful moral energy, his soaring intellect, his generous open heart, and his unwavering optimism that goodness would and could prevail is of course a heartbreaking understatement. During our magical forty years together, he would read my pages every night at warp speed then disappear into his study saying, "I just have a few tweaks," which turned out to be a seamless reorganization of the whole chapter with a new lead, a point of view, and a mysteriously brilliant thematic paragraph in the middle that somehow bound it all together.

Unable to face a winter writing alone at the house in Quogue on Long Island where we shared so much happy industry, I decamped to a rented house in Santa Monica, California, with my two adult children. There, with a laptop in a garden scattered with lemons and limes from the overhanging trees and the sun on my back, I spent a healing four months in a locked-down cocoon. I was consoled in between labored efforts to write by Saturday-morning walks with my wonderful friends from **Vanity Fair, New**

Yorker, and **Daily Beast** days: Caroline Graham, Gabé Doppelt, Angela Janklow, Arianna Huffington; and WME partner and my agent for dramatic rights, Nancy Josephson. There was also the comforting fire-pit company of some new friends: the British painter Damian Elwes and his wife, Lewanne, and their vibrant family, and our next-door neighbors Sally Hibbard and Mike Moody, who one evening left a tray of margaritas on our doorstep as a thank-you for a basket of limes, a stunningly genial gesture to anyone used to brief, preoccupied eye contact with neighbors in elevators, as we are as apartment dwellers in New York City.

My shipwrecked family was the greatest, most joyful compensation—my valiant thirty-six-year-old son, Georgie, who missed his father every aching minute, and my equally devastated documentary-producer daughter, Izzy, thirty-one, who proved she has inherited Harry's eagle eye for a sloppy sentence and was a tireless reader and re-reader of my recalcitrant prose. Perhaps her greatest gift to me and her brother was the adoption on Christmas Eve of an English bulldog puppy. We became convinced that Gimli, as Izzy called her after the wise dwarf in **Lord of the Rings,** was sent by Harry to console us, as she shares so many of his characteristics: dogged (literally) tenacity, fearlessness when wrestling with dogs three times her size, and being never more content than when chomping through a manuscript.

By the time spring 2021 came around, I returned to NYC for freezing convivial dinners outside with all the wonderful East Coast friends I had started to sorely miss. The brainy, always opinionated Amanda Foreman, Gillian Tett, Holly Peterson, Edward Jay Epstein, Marie Brenner, Susan Mercandetti, James Wolcott, Vicky Ward, and Stephen Schiff were wonderfully willing to chat about new angles.

The Palace Papers would have foundered on the rocks of personal and logistical setbacks if I had not been borne up by a remarkable cohort of researchers and contributors:

Jacqueline Williams, my unwearying London-based researcher, who brought such diligent expertise to my previous book about the Royals, **The Diana Chronicles,** and did so again with this equally intense enterprise. Brigid Graff, my chief of staff at Tina Brown Live Media, who moved to Cambridge to join her academic husband, Thomas, at the height of the pandemic and cleverly produced a beautiful baby daughter in April 2021. She worked every second a newborn allows to manage research and ensure the accuracy of a multitude of details. She smartly recruited Thomas to ably annotate the sources for every chapter, giving me a brilliant editorial duo. Cindy Quillinan, my husband's treasured former executive assistant, who joined the team and became the keeper and tracker of every change in the manuscript—reconciling drafts, locating paragraphs lost in the ether, and devoting ungodly hours to make the deadline. Kara Simonetti, former VP of programming at Tina Brown Live Media, and Olivia Messer, a meticulous former **Daily Beast** reporter who resolved queries in complex chapters, and the able help of Susanna Jennens.

Throughout the summer and fall, the pandemic was still spinning the world into uncharted territory and so was the story I was trying to tell. Meghan and Harry's interview with Oprah in March 2021 had blasted a new hole in the Royal narrative, requiring fresh reporting and research, as did the explosions around Prince Andrew, the feuding of William and Harry, and the death of Prince Philip. For additional firepower to push **The Palace Papers** to the finish line in time, I turned to the multi-talented Karen Compton, Emmy Award–winning TV writer and producer whose keen news sense and intellectual rigor had been such a source of strength at Women in the World—the live journalism platform I ran from 2009 to 2020—for which she had been one of our most valued senior producers. In marathon phone sessions and side-by-side deadline crunching, we cracked the last half of the book in a joyful collaboration that crescendoed in the last two days of the year, storming through every legal query as the Omicron variant inflicted fresh paralysis on our lives. To Karen and to all the **Palace Papers** team, I cannot thank you enough for your care and commitment.

There are many reasons to value the sophisticated intelligence of my friend, writer, and editor Tunku Varadarajan, but I do so even more now since he agreed to be a first reader of all I wrote and apply his critical eye (and pencil) before it landed on my publisher's desk. His multiple improvements appear on every page. I thank also Hendrik Hertzberg, former editorial director at **The New Yorker,** who remains my esteemed emergency-sentence doctor when I brood over how to fix a clunky paragraph.

Thanks to the spot-on recommendation of **Tatler's** editor-in-chief, the always-generous Richard Dennen, it was an enormous pleasure to do what every ex–magazine editor loves best, work with a top-flight picture editor—in this case Vivien Hamley—to find the best, most surprising images for the book. It's to Vivien's rare curatorial gifts that I owe the picture of the nineteen-year-old Prince William in real time gazing up at fellow St. Andrew's student Kate Middleton as she sizzled her way down the runway at a charity fashion gala dressed in a see-through dress—an Henri Cartier-Bresson "decisive moment" with bells on. My magazine-editing nostalgia was further increased by persuading the deft writer and editor Louis Glucksmann-Cheslaw to crank out the captions. Creating the beautiful inserts and endpapers with Crown designer Barbara Bachman was a piquant flashback to all those days in the art departments of glossies.

Writing a book about the royals is a fraught process at the best of times. There are so many who helped make this narrative more accurate, more fair, and more honest but whom, because of ongoing or intimate past relationships with the Palace, I cannot name or thank. No author likes to use unattributed quotes, but in this particular realm, the alternative is a version so sanitized that the truth is compromised and the perspective is skewed. I am enormously grateful for all those who took the time in person, and on Zoom, sometimes multiple times, to answer my questions and offer unique insights about the events consuming the House of Windsor in the last twenty years. Profound thanks to all of you.

The landscape of this book is broad and required a historical perspective. Fortunately, my passion for stories of the past has brought some brilliant historians into my happy orbit. To brainstorm with dear friend Sir Simon Schama is the ultimate intellectual luxury. His throwaway thoughts are the stuff of other people's Pulitzer prizes. To Zoom with David Starkey about the monarchy is as invigorating as a hike in the Balmoral hills and far more entertaining; to chat with Sir David Cannadine about the inspired dullness of George V is a treat I would pay good money for (and did, reading his wonderful short biography over Christmas). To download the expertise of distinguished Commonwealth scholar Professor David Dilks is to understand the meaning of that hitherto opaque institution for the first time. No author of a royal book can get by without the perceptions of Hugo Vickers, the strikingly well-informed chronicler of the aristocracy and the monarchy. On the question of how to view the House of Windsor's attitudes about race, it was critical to hear the insights of my old friend from **New Yorker** days Professor Henry Louis Gates Jr., Alphonse Fletcher University Professor and Director of the Hutchins Center for African & African American Research at

Harvard University, and creator of the hit TV show **Finding Your Roots.** Juliet Nicolson, author of sparklingly readable books about the social atmosphere of England in the early twentieth century, was always gracious about helping access information. Thanks, too, to Andrew Marr, a crackling brain with a rich store of quotable information, and to an old and trusted friend, Robert Lacey, not only one of the best regarded of royal biographers but now the historical consultant to the hit Netflix series **The Crown.** I had a riveting discourse, too, with legendary broadcaster and author Jonathan Dimbleby from the book-lined study of his country home, about his seismic 1994 biography of Prince Charles.

Listing Lady Anne Glenconner as an admired author is a particular pleasure. For the many years I have known her, her penetrating insights, glorious sense of humor, and remarkable stoicism in the face of so much tragedy was a joy to be savored only by her friends. It was clear she had the unmistakable voice of a writer but less clear she would ever commit it to the page. When she finally did with her memoir, published at the age of eighty-seven, the rest of the world recognized it, too, and made **Lady in Waiting** a barnstorming 500,000-copy bestseller. I have turned to it often in my portrait of her former boss Princess Margaret as I did to the always entertaining Craig Brown, author of **Ninety-Nine Glimpses of Princess Margaret.**

I thank so many other friends for their help at critical moments: Nicholas Coleridge, the former president of Condé Nast International whom I depended on to set me right on forgotten matters of English tone and mood; **The New Yorker**'s jewel, critic Anthony Lane, and the celebrated British poet (and beloved old friend) Craig Raine were always willing to offer their brilliance in my search, at knotty moments, for the **mot juste.** Former Condé Nast editorial director James Truman was generous with observations of the social and culinary atmosphere of Peak London, as was **The Guardian**'s Andy Beckett, who christened the era with that name. A trio of distinguished Irish public servants—former presidents Mary Robinson and Mary McAleese, and former taoiseach Enda Kelly, helped bring alive to me the Queen's historic state visit to the Republic of Ireland. Former Chancellor of the Exchequer George Osborne was invaluable for his political and financial acumen. A Zoom with the witty and original Stephen Fry yielded infinite subtle insights. A drink at Dean Street Townhouse with the versatile Gyles Brandreth yielded golden nuggets about Prince Philip and so much more. Musing about the respective heroines of Charles Dickens versus Anthony Trollope as the best template for Kate Middleton, I turned to the fertile brain of **New Yorker** critic Adam Gopnik to hear his always provocative take. Friend and editor Courtney Hodell constantly challenged me to elevate my thinking. Most helpful, too, was the unvarnished perspective of gifted novelist and journalist Aatish Taseer, and the perceptions offered by **British Vogue** editor-in-chief Edward Enninful, who connected me to the stylish, high-energy Emma Thynn, Marchioness of Bath, and her welcome insights.

For the intersection of royalty, politics, and media, I am grateful to the shrewd analysis of the communications guru David McDonough, who also initiated me into the gourmet appeal of the celebrated Mayfair restaurant Wiltons, where he regularly holds court with his fabled and fabulous partner, Lady Mary-Gaye Curzon. Always helpful, too, was David Muir, former director of political strategy for Prime Minister Gordon Brown, who is deeply knowledgeable about the ebb and flow of complex political currents.

A book on the monarchy is inevitably also a book about the Royal Family's co-dependent warfare with the press. The urbane communications strategist Mark Bolland and his partner, Lord Black of Brentwood, offered invaluable guidance, as did the BBC's Amol Rajan, creator and presenter of the controversial yet fascinating two-part documentary **The Princes and the Press.** I am warmly grateful, too, to the forensic media insights of two friends with stellar legal minds who are also friends with each other, Geoffrey Robertson, and media lawyer Mark Stephens.

The more I studied Prince Harry's tormented experience with tabloid invasion, the more it became clear that I needed a deep source in the world of journalism's darkest arts—hacking, blagging, and stalking. At the suggestion of Peter Jukes, executive editor of **Byline Times,** whose fearless coverage of the Murdoch newspapers' phone-hacking case I had often published at **The Daily Beast,** I invited the investigative journalist Graham Johnson, who briefly had personal involvement with the hacking culture, to be my guide through this world and conduct some critical interviews for the chapter titled Snoopers.

Another world explored in **The Palace Papers** is the cable TV entertainment culture Meghan Markle experienced in the filming of her hit show **Suits** on USA Network. I am indebted to the creative team of **Suits** executive producer David Bartis, writer and creator Aaron Korsh, director Kevin Bray, and casting director Bonnie Zane. I'm a longtime fan of the show, and it was wonderful to hear about the painstaking process that made the show such a success and gave Meghan the break that changed her life.

Covering the Royal Family is a hazardous and often thankless business involving tedious deniability from sources. I am indebted to all the biographers and reporters who have beaten the path before me. Fortunately, there are many who are superbly accomplished at penetrating the spin. Anthony Holden, first official biographer of Prince Charles and a beloved friend who was always willing to help my efforts; Clive Irving, author of the excellent recent book **The Last Queen;** news-making journalist and author Anna Pasternak; and the irrepressible bomb-thrower Piers Morgan. His **The Insider: The Private Diaries of a Scandalous Decade** remains a raw classic about tabloid life in the "Belly of the

Beast." Today his TV presence and unmissable **Daily Mail** columns land with as much of a punch on both sides of the Atlantic.

One of the best royal memoirists of the Diana era is her former private secretary Patrick Jephson, who was ever willing to share his acute observations and historical perspective, as was the documentarian Nick Kent, whose outstanding films **Diana, Our Mother: Her Life and Legacy** and **Prince Philip: The Royal Family** show sensitive understanding to the unique loneliness of the royal predicament. A biographer always worth reading is Tom Bower, whose **Rebel Prince: The Power, Passion and Defiance of Prince Charles** is groaning with hitherto unreported, and often comic details of both the upstairs and downstairs of Windsor World (as were his two peerless Maxwell books). I am indebted to him especially in the chapter titled Servant Problems.

Others I would be remiss not to mention: I am a longtime fan of the **Daily Mail**'s Richard Kay, whose depth of knowledge after he owned the Diana story twenty years ago has continued to accrue and deliver new insights in the unfolding royal saga. **The Telegraph**'s Graham Turner is invaluable for his superb reporting on the earlier years of the Queen's reign and her relationship with the Queen Mother. Current scoops from the House of Cambridge and Sussex rain down from **The Telegraph**'s sharpshooter Camilla Tominey, who first broke the news about the arrival of a certain, stunning TV actress in Harry's life; there is no royal commentator better wired than Robert Jobson of the **Evening Standard** for his insights into the monarchy's evolution. **The Telegraph**'s Robert Hardman is superb on the Queen as a global figure, and there is none more readable than Penny Junor, whose biographies I turned to so often for the freshness of her observations and reporting. Angela Levin, Duncan Larcombe, Ingrid Seward, Christopher Wilson, Katie Nicholl, Tom Quinn, Lady Colin Campbell, Nigel Cawthorne, Omid Scobie, and Carolyn Durand are essential for insights into the royal story. Caroline Graham (no relation to the above) of **The Mail on Sunday** was helpful with access to Tom Markle. No book that covers the House of Windsor in the last twenty years is free of the debt to Andrew Morton, whose **Diana: Her True Story** broke the biggest royal scoop of the late twentieth century and keeps on yielding its secrets to this day. Sarah Bradford and Sally Bedell Smith are authors of excellent, indispensable books about the royals that are both distinguished and reliable.

There are so many others to whom I offer my grateful thanks, either behind the scenes or on the page, on tape, or on my speed dial. Gillian Blake's Crown team of the punctilious associate editor Amy Li and the indefatigable duo of managing editor Sally Franklin and production editor Mark Birkey made the entire publishing process a joy, as did publicity, marketing, and production dynamos Penny Simon, Julie Cepler, and Linnea Knollmueller. The laser-sharp copyediting of Michelle Daniel is also to be commended, as is Ben Brusey's Century team in the UK, ably buoyed by associate editor Jessica Ballance, and Penguin Random House managing editor Joanna Taylor and production manager Anna Cowling. I also extend special thanks to Amy Musgrave, who created a stunningly clever cover design, and the UK's publicity, serial, and marketing gurus Etty Eastwood, Penny Liechti, and Claire Bush. I am more than grateful for the rigorous, and patient, attention of Penguin Random House legal experts Matthew Martin and Amelia Zalcman in the United States and Tim Bainbridge in the UK. I further thank Martin Soames for his judicious appraisal.

Special thanks are due to many remarkably kind people who helped me with different aspects of **The Palace Papers** along the way:

John Arlidge, Cherie Blair, David Boies, Graham Boynton, Peter Brown, Chris Bryant, Gerry Byrne, Alastair Campbell, Basil Charles, Martin Childs, Jacqueline de Chollet, Joanna Coles, Chris and Ryan Cuddihy, Stephen Daldry, Danny Danziger, James Danziger, Baron Darroch of Kew, Nick Davies, Charles Delevingne, The Rt. Hon. Lord Donoughue, Marty Edel, Ed Felsenthal, Niall Ferguson, Amy Finnerty, Debbie Frank, Stephen Frears, James Fox, Anthony Geffen, Geordie Greig, David Griffin, Lloyd Grove, Barbara Guggenheim, John Guy, Tony Hall, Baron Hall of Birkenhead, William Hague, Baron Hague of Richmond, James Harding, Nicky Haslam, Marie Helvin, Reinaldo Herrera, Lady Pamela Hicks, Lynn Hirschberg, Lyndall Hobbs, Steven Hoffenberg, Mark Hollingsworth, Major General Francis "Buster" Howes, Mort Janklow, Sir Simon Jenkins, David Jones, Stuart Karle, Alan Kilkenny, Cynthia Knights, Jesse Kornbluth, Brian Lang, Gulu Lalvani, Jolene Lescio, Magnus Linklater, Shelley Curtis Litvack, Natalie Livingstone, Nick Lowles, Lainey Lui, Thomas Markle, Catie Marron, Sir Donald McCullin, Dame Helen Mirren, Penny Mortimer, Andrew Neil, Vanessa Neumann, Fay Nurse, Bruce Oldfield, Catherine Ostler, Antony Phillipson, Erin Pizzey, John Preston, Jennifer Pryor, Euan Rellie, Wendy Riche, Andrew Roberts, Antonia Romeo, Conchita Sarnoff, Mark Saunders, Ivan Schwarz, Clarissa Sebag-Montefiore, Jonathan Shalit, Lisa Shields, Alexandra Shulman, Dan Snow, Sir Nicholas Soames, Roderick "Rory" Stewart, Skip Stein, George Stroumboulopoulos, Nona Summers, Ken Sunshine, Ben Tai, Colin Tebbutt, Taki Theodoracopulos, Mark Thompson, Malcolm Turnbull, Simon Walker, Krista Webster, Sir Peter Westmacott, Anthony "Burghie" Fane, 16th Earl of Westmorland, Ken Wharfe, Ed Williams, Michelle Williams, Dr. Rowan Williams, Lynn Wyatt, Peter York.

Writing a book is a lonely business, and all the above have helped me fill those intimidating white pages. I thank you again, each and every one.

NOTES

PROLOGUE. KRYPTONITE

xi   **"Were you silent"**   Duke and Duchess of Sussex, interview by Oprah Winfrey, **Oprah with Meghan and Harry**, CBS, March 7, 2021.

xii   **Meghan Markle is the first**   Jennifer Meierhans, "Buckingham Palace Reveals 8.5% Ethnic Minority Staff," BBC News, June 24, 2021.

xiii   **"What does it mean"**   Duke and Duchess of Sussex, **Oprah with Meghan and Harry.**

xiv   **"You are a member"**   Sondra Gotlieb, "Queen Mary Superstar," **The New York Times**, June 29, 1986.

xvi   **"I didn't do any research"**   Duke and Duchess of Sussex, **Oprah with Meghan and Harry.**

CHAPTER I. NEVER AGAIN: THE ROYALS CONFRONT A POST-DIANA WORLD

9   **"morning glory"**   David Dilks, **Churchill and Company: Allies and Rivals in War and Peace** (London: I. B. Tauris, 2012), chap. 1.

10 "A different monarch" Elizabeth Longford, **Elizabeth R: A Biography** (London: Weidenfeld and Nicolson, 1983).

10 "Where's Philip?" Marion Crawford, **The Little Princesses: The Story of the Queen's Childhood by Her Nanny, Marion Crawford** (New York: St. Martin's Griffin, 1950), chap. 10.

11 "Our late" Craig Brown, **Ninety-Nine Glimpses of Princess Margaret** (New York: Farrar, Straus and Giroux, 2018), chap. 84.

13 "Did his Royal Highness" Gyles Brandreth, interview, February 26, 2020.

15 in a cottage Robert Lacey, **Monarch: The Life and Reign of Elizabeth II** (New York: Free Press, 2003), chap. 15.

17 "I'd like to be" Princess of Wales, "An Interview with HRH The Princess of Wales," interview by Martin Bashir, **Panorama**, BBC, November 20, 1995.

17 "she was pleased" Gulu Lalvani, interview, January 11, 2021.

19 "One of your jobs" Mark Bolland, interview, May 13, 2005.

21 the Queen replied, "Why?" Graham Turner, "The Real Elizabeth II," **The Telegraph**, January 8, 2002.

21 "just wanted to lead" Peter Mandelson, **The Third Man: Life at the Heart of New Labour** (London: HarperPress, 2010), chap. 6.

21 "people had gained" Ibid.

22 "At least for me" Ibid.

23 "She grasped" Tony Blair, **A Journey: My Political Life** (New York: Vintage Books, 2010), chap. 5.

24 "One of the hardest" **Diana, 7 Days**, directed by Henry Singer, BBC, aired August 27, 2017.

24 "The shock" Duke of Cambridge, **Mind Over Marathon**, directed by Peter Coventry, episode 2, BBC One, aired April 20, 2017.

24 "**The trauma**" Alastair Campbell, "Alastair Campbell Interviews Prince William About Diana: 'She Smothered Harry and Me in Love,'" **International Business Times**, updated August 30, 2017.

25 "**consumed by a total**" Alastair Campbell, "Thursday, September 4, 1997," in **The Alastair Campbell Diaries**, vol. 2, **Power and the People, 1997–1999** (London: Hutchinson, 2011).

26 "**the somberness**" Geordie Greig, interview, November 16, 2005.

26 "**we will not allow**" Earl Spencer, "Full Text of Earl Spencer's Funeral Oration," BBC News, September 6, 1997.

27 "**[She] proved**" Ibid.

27 **Diana's astrologer** Debbie Frank, interview, March 14, 2006.

27 "**vengeful and spiteful**" Robert Crampton, "Just Marry Camilla Now, Charles," **The Times**, June 1, 2004.

27 "**Very bold**" Hugo Vickers DL, interview, July 28, 2005.

27 "**I hope you feel**" Glenda Cooper, "Diana's Calming Waters," **The Washington Post**, July 7, 2004.

28 "**It's good to see you**" Penny Junor, "Getting On with the Day," in **Prince William: The Man Who Will Be King** (New York: Pegasus Books, 2012).

29 "**duly materialized**" Anthony Holden, **Based on a True Story** (London: Simon and Schuster, 2021), chap. 15.

29 "**a truly healthy sign**" Stephen Fry, interview, April 7, 2021.

30 "**fresh air**" Andrew Alderson, **The Sunday Times**, January 28, 1996.

32 **When William turned to** Robert Lacey, **Battle of Brothers: William and Harry; The Inside Story of a Family in Tumult** (London: HarperPress, 2020), chap. 23.

33 The **Daily Mail**'s **Richard Kay** Richard Kay, interview, November 21, 2019.

CHAPTER 2. SEX AND SENSIBILITY: WHY CHARLES LOVES CAMILLA

36 **At the time Alice** Tom Quinn, **Mrs. Keppel: Mistress to the King** (London: Biteback Publishing, 2016), chap. 8.

36 **"brilliant, goddess-like"** Diana Souhami, **Mrs. Keppel and Her Daughter: A Biography** (New York: St. Martin's Press, 1996), chap. 1.

36 **"She invariably knew"** Ibid.

37 **"resplendent"** Ibid.

38 **"a right dirty bird"** Quinn, **Mrs. Keppel**, chap. 10.

38 **"I don't mind"** Anthony Holden, "Diana's Revenge," **Vanity Fair**, February 1993.

39 **"He did not seem"** Christopher Wilson, **The Windsor Knot: Charles, Camilla, and the Legacy of Diana** (Los Angeles: Graymalkin Media, 2008), chap. 7.

40 **"a pleasant young man"** Roy Strong, "2 March 1971," in **Splendours and Miseries: The Roy Strong Diaries, 1967–1987** (London: Weidenfeld and Nicolson, 2019).

41 **"was coming for a drink"** Catherine Mayer, **Born to Be King: Prince Charles on Planet Windsor** (New York: Henry Holt, 2015), chap. 2.

41 **"enormous sympathy"** Penny Junor, **The Duchess: Camilla Parker Bowles and the Love Affair That Rocked the Crown** (New York: Harper, 2018), chap. 2.

41 **"Now, you two"** Ibid.

41 **"My great-grandmother"** Gyles Brandreth, **Charles and Camilla: Portrait of a Love Affair** (London: Arrow Books, 2006), chap. 2.

42 **"One of his"** James Fox, email correspondence, March 26, 2021.

43 **"quite fierce"** Geordie Greig, "EXCLUSIVE: Ca-

milla Up Close! Duchess of Cornwall Opens Up as Never Before, Saying: 'If You Can't Laugh at Yourself, You May as Well Give Up,'" **Mail Online**, updated May 28, 2017.

44 "a serpent" Camilla Long, "One Long Party," The Times, April 27, 2014.

44 "a real-life" "Mark Shand—Obituary," **The Telegraph**, April 24, 2014.

44 "When I heard" Greig, "EXCLUSIVE: Camilla."

46 "Poor Charles" Robert Hardman, **Queen of the World** (New York: Pegasus Books, 2019), chap. 12.

47 "I was to be treated" Jonathan Dimbleby, **The Prince of Wales: A Biography** (New York: William Morrow, 1994), part 2.

47 "stern rebuke" Anthony Holden, **Charles at Fifty** (New York: Random House, 1998), chap. 6.

48 "shit-scared" Brandreth, **Charles and Camilla**, chap. 5.

49 "You knelt a boy" Sir John Betjeman, "A Ballad of the Investiture 1969," Royal Collection Trust, rct.uk.

50 "I can even see" Wilson, **Windsor Knot**, chap. 11.

50 "Pretend I am" Kitty Kelley, **The Royals** (New York: Grand Central Publishing, 2009), chap. 11.

51 "Camilla used to come" Marie Helvin, interview, February 27, 2020.

52 "We used to complain" Greig, "EXCLUSIVE: Camilla."

53 "where the girls" Brandreth, **Charles and Camilla**, chap. 4.

53 "We had to stop them" Theo Aronson, **Princess Margaret: A Biography** (London: Michael O'Mara, 1997), chap. 1.

55 For ten minutes Tony Allen-Mills, "Party Animal Camilla Fired for Being Late," **The Sunday Times**, October 30, 2016.

55 "It sounds" Greig, "EXCLUSIVE: Camilla."

56 **"If good girls"** "Camilla the MAN EATER: She Was Fired from Her Posh Job for Too Much Partying and Revelled in the Fact That Her Great-Grandmother Was Edward VII's Mistress—Her Biographer Reveals How She REALLY Spent the Swinging Sixties," **Daily Mail**, updated November 5, 2016.

58 **"After such a blissful"** Dimbleby, **Prince of Wales**, part 2.

58 **"in pieces"** Christopher Wilson, "The FIRST Her Royal Hotness: New Film Reveals the Startlingly Racy Love Life of the Young Princess Anne," **Daily Mail**, January 18, 2016.

59 **"His power"** Nigel Dempster and Peter Evans, **Behind Palace Doors** (London: Orion, 1993), chap. 7.

60 **"When I was with Andrew"** Ibid.

60 **"tight"** Marie Helvin, interview, September 18, 2006.

61 **"You often hear"** James Whitaker and Christopher Wilson, **Diana vs. Charles: Royal Blood Feud** (Los Angeles: Graymalkin Media, 2017), chap. 1.

61 **"I said, 'Better luck'"** Taki Theodoracopulos, interview, June 7, 2020.

61 **Andrew and Paravicini invented** Junor, **Duchess**, chap. 8.

61 **"They fucked him"** Patrick Anson, Earl of Lichfield, interview, May 11, 2005.

62 **"secondly a seven-foot"** Clare Conway, "Andrew Parker Bowles on Being Painted by Lucian Freud," **Tatler**, October 11, 2019.

64 **"I'm so proud"** Lynn Barber, "Quite Grand, and She Doesn't Tip," **The Telegraph**, October 21, 2003.

65 **"very randy"** Tina Brown, "The Wilts Alternative," **Tatler**, July/August 1980.

65 **"Her face"** Turner, "Real Elizabeth II."

67 **"extremely posh"** Lyndall Hobbs, interview, May 12, 2020.

69 **"The pain"** Alexis Parr, "'Mummy Was Called Mad.

She Committed the Cardinal Sin of Talking About Prince Charles': Lady Kanga Tryon's Daughter on Her Mother's Obsession," **Mail Online,** March 7, 2011.

70   "**The hauling down**" Wilson, **Windsor Knot,** chap. 5.

70   "**Christopher Soames unwisely**" Michael Shea, interview, September 9, 2006.

70   "**And pray God**" Wilson, **Windsor Knot,** chap. 5.

72   "**Don't ever, ever**" Dempster and Evans, **Behind Palace Doors,** chap. 9.

73   "**On and on**" Wilson, **Windsor Knot,** chap. 5.

73   "**HRH is very fond**" Ibid.

74   "**exquisitely pretty**" Dempster and Evans, **Behind Palace Doors,** chap. 3.

74   "**to keep myself**" Andrew Morton, "In Her Own Words," in **Diana, Her True Story—In Her Own Words** (New York: Simon and Schuster, 2009).

74   "**She's never stuck**" Lady Colin Campbell, **The Real Diana** (New York: St. Martin's Press, 1998), chap. 6.

74   "**We're extremely relieved**" Kate Nicholson, "Royal Prediction: How Princess Margaret Knew 'Camilla Will Never Give Charles Up,'" **Express,** February 11, 2020.

75   "**The Spencers are difficult**" Sarah Bradford, **Elizabeth: A Biography of Her Majesty the Queen** (London: Penguin, 2012), chap. 16.

76   "**My baby**" Mary Corbett, "Frances Shand Kydd: The Last Interview with Princess Diana's Enigmatic Mother," **Hello!,** June 15, 2004.

76   "**extensive malformation**" Max Riddington and Gavan Naden, **Frances: The Remarkable Story of Princess Diana's Mother** (London: Michael O'Mara, 2003), chap. 1.

76   "**Her mother's testimony**" Barbara Gilmour, interview, September 27, 2005.

77   "**The house was so huge**" Corbett, "Frances Shand Kydd."

78 **"That's from all"** Jack Royston, "Diana: Her True Voice; We Publish the Full Transcript of the Bombshell Diana Tapes as Her Former Private Secretary Backs Channel 4 Documentary," **The Sun**, updated August 2, 2017.

78 **"[It] gave me"** "Diana Revealed: Never-Before-Seen Videotapes of Princess Diana," **Dateline**, NBC News, November 29, 2004.

CHAPTER 3. THE WILDERNESS YEARS: HOW CAMILLA HUNG IN

80 **"It was like"** Morton, **Diana: Her True Story**, foreword.

81 **"It was entirely normal"** Tom Parker Bowles, interview by Tracy Grimshaw, **A Current Affair**, Nine Network, July 27, 2015.

81 **"I'm certainly not"** Sally Bedell Smith, **Prince Charles: The Passions and Paradoxes of an Improbable Life** (New York: Random House, 2017), chap. 18.

81 **"Ernest Simpson"** Dempster and Evans, **Behind Palace Doors**, chap. 23.

82 **"Why don't you"** Katie Nicholl, **William and Harry: Behind the Palace Walls** (New York: Hachette, 2010), chap. 6.

82 **"It's fiction"** Wilson, **Windsor Knot**, chap. 7.

83 **"The Queen and Prince Philip felt the same"** Shea, interview.

83 **"Something happened"** Campbell, **Real Diana**, chap. 10.

83 **"Oh God, it's a boy"** Morton, "In Her Own Words," in **Diana, Her True Story**.

83 **"One day, he'd had"** Howard Hodgson, "It Wasn't Always Bad (1981–86)," in **Charles: The Man Who Will Be King** (London: John Blake, 2007).

84 "Diana saw Charles" Dempster and Evans, **Behind Palace Doors**, chap. 15.

85 "bad blood" Sarah Bradford, **Diana** (New York: Viking, 2007), chap. 17.

85 "The Queen, or anybody else" Andrew Morton, **Diana: In Pursuit of Love** (London: Michael O'Mara, 2004), chap. 4.

85 "Camilla has been" Bob Colacello, "Charles and Camilla, Together at Last," **Vanity Fair,** December 2005.

86 "Game, set" Ken Wharfe with Robert Jobson, **Diana: Closely Guarded Secret** (London: John Blake, 2015), chap. 16.

87 "I couldn't really" Greig, "EXCLUSIVE: Camilla."

88 "I am genuinely" Wilson, **Windsor Knot**, chap. 8.

88 "She has no desire" Mary Riddell, "Prince Charles Has Missed His Chance to Marry Camilla," **The Times,** May 28, 2004.

88 "I remember" Greig, "EXCLUSIVE: Camilla."

89 "rather nervously" Woodrow Wyatt, **The Journals of Woodrow Wyatt,** ed. Sarah Curtis, vol. 2 (London: Pan Macmillan, 2000).

89 "Have you no shame?" "Charles Is Heckled Over Tapes," **Herald Sun,** January 30, 1993.

90 "not King material" Holden, **Charles at Fifty.**

90 "is not beautiful" James Lees-Milne, "Saturday, 4th September 1993," in **Diaries, 1984–1997,** ed. Michael Bloch (London: John Murray, 2008).

91 "Wouldn't the media" Dempster and Evans, **Behind Palace Doors**, chap. 24.

91 "the paradise of exiles" Ibid.

92 "The Queen reportedly" Brandreth, **Charles and Camilla,** chap. 9.

93 "to be faithful" **Charles: The Private Man, the Public Role,** directed by Christopher Martin, Dimbleby Martin Productions, aired June 29, 1994.

93 "I only saw" Lees-Milne, "Tuesday, 28th June 1994," Diaries, 1984–1997.

94 "The programme" Morton, **Diana: In Pursuit of Love**, chap. 5.

94 "It was terrible" Kate Ng, "Teach Young People About Osteoporosis, Says Camilla Duchess of Cornwall," The Independent, October 24, 2021.

94 "pain and ignominy" Henry Bokin, "Duchess Recalls 'Agonising' Deaths of Mother and Grandmother to Bone Disease," The Telegraph, October 17, 2017.

96 "William would blame" Chris Byfield, "'Terrible Fights' Prince William 'Would Blame' Camilla for 'Hurt She Caused,'" Sunday Express, November 14, 2021.

96 "I didn't help" Bowles, interview.

100 "While the Prince" Smith, **Prince Charles**, chap. 22.

100 "appeared like a missile" "Parker Bowles to Escape Prosecution Over Car Crash," The Independent, July 11, 1997.

101 "I think in shock" "Prince Charles' Lady Leaves Bruised Feelings in Auto Crash," AP News, June 12, 1997.

101 "I don't want" "Parker Bowles to Escape Prosecution."

102 "entirely wrong" Christopher Wilson, "Camilla Loses Her Rock," Mail Online, June 12, 2006.

CHAPTER 4. MOTHER OF THE NATION: THE QUEEN'S TWENTY-FIRST-CENTURY HEADACHES

109 "Please don't tell me" Blair, **Journey**, chap. 9.

109 "a damp squib" Alastair Campbell, "Friday, December 31, 1999," in The Alastair Campbell Diaries, vol. 3, **Power and Responsibility, 1999–2001** (London: Hutchinson, 2011).

110 "TB [Blair] worked away" Ibid.

111 "My Golden Jubilee" Lacey, **Monarch**, chap. 32.

112 **"Dearest Lilibet"** Victoria Mather, interview, May 22, 2006.

112 **"No, no, not for the sake"** Gyles Brandreth, **Philip and Elizabeth: Portrait of a Marriage** (London: Century, 2004), chap. 10.

114 **"will have spanned"** Her Majesty the Queen, "A Speech by the Queen at the Sydney Opera House," March 20, 2010.

115 **declared himself an "Elizabethan"** Tory Shepherd, "Republican Malcolm Turnbull on Meeting Queen Elizabeth II, Says He Is an 'Elizabethan,' " News Corp Australia, July 12, 2017.

115 **"one of the prime instruments"** Tom Bower, **Rebel Prince: The Power, Passion and Defiance of Prince Charles** (London: William Collins, 2018), chap. 4.

116 **"The Golden Jubilee was the culmination"** Robert Hardman, **Her Majesty: Queen Elizabeth II and Her Court** (New York: Pegasus Books, 2012), chap. 1.

117 **"Today marks the 37th Anniversary"** Ozzy Osbourne, Twitter, January 20, 2019, 4:04 P.M.

117 **"a whale of a time"** Sally Bedell Smith, **Elizabeth the Queen: The Life of a Modern Monarch** (New York: Random House, 2012), chap. 18.

118 **"It makes her look"** "U.K. Reaction: Queen's Portrait Pleaseth Not," **The Washington Post,** December 22, 2001.

118 **"Very interesting"** Conway, "Andrew Parker Bowles."

118 **"Haven't you been painted"** Brandreth, **Philip and Elizabeth,** appendices.

118 **The invitation to Charles's fiftieth** Graham Turner, **Elizabeth: The Woman and the Queen** (London: Macmillan, 2002), chap. 8.

120 **"No secret"** Rebecca Adams, "Charles and Camilla Pictured Together for the First Time Was a Sight to Behold," **The Huffington Post,** updated December 7, 2017.

121 "lying in its vastness" Anthony Holden, **Charles: A Biography** (London: Bantam Press, 1998).

122 "If she'd spent" Turner, "Real Elizabeth II."

123 "He's coming out of" Ibid.

124 "Well, when the weather" Lady Pamela Hicks, interview, November 22, 2019.

125 "a marshmallow" Selina Hastings, "Fluffy and Steely," **The Telegraph**, November 20, 2005.

125 "unaware or unconcerned" Hugo Vickers, **Elizabeth: The Queen Mother** (London: Arrow Books, 2006), chap. 28.

125 "Oh, your Majesty" "The Truth Is, He Still Needs Her Terribly," **The Age**, April 14, 2002.

127 "He has to have" Turner, "Real Elizabeth II."

128 "Charles is absolutely desperate" Ibid.

131 "I've never seen" Ryan Parry and Hugo Daniel, "EXCLUSIVE: Jeffrey Epstein and Ghislaine Maxwell's Place of Honor as Prince Andrew's Special Guests at 2000 Royal 'Dance of the Decades' Ball in Windsor Castle Is Revealed in Souvenir Program," **Daily Mail**, December 23, 2020.

133 "ghastly British brush-off" Bower, **Rebel Prince**, chap. 20.

133 "I once said" Peter Brown, interview, July 17, 2019.

134 "had been bullied" Ingrid Seward, "Why a Footman Gave Andrew a Black Eye and It Was the Queen Who Was Livid with Edward for Quitting the Marines: More Intimate Details from the Royals' 70 Years of Marriage," **Daily Mail**, updated November 10, 2020.

134 "You wouldn't pick" Julie Carpenter, "Sophie Wessex: The Queen's Favourite," **Express**, December 19, 2007.

136 "incandescent" Ian Katz, "It Was Me What Spun It," **The Guardian**, October 27, 2003.

136 "fucking idiot" Piers Morgan, "Thursday, 27 September 2001," in **The Insider: The Private Diaries of a Scandalous Decade** (London: Ebury Press, 2005).

137 **"We call him"** Gaby Hinsliff and Burhan Wazir, "Word by Word, Sophie Digs Herself Deeper into Trouble," **The Guardian,** April 8, 2001.

138 **"close the door"** Hardman, **Her Majesty,** chap. 1.

139 **"Who cares about the boys"** Morgan, "Thursday, 12 February 1998," **Insider.**

142 **"It is not an easy option"** "The Royal Statements," **The Guardian,** April 9, 2001.

142 **"It is quite obvious"** "Queen Pays Edward £1/4m to Quit TV," **The Guardian,** March 2, 2002.

CHAPTER 5. A QUESTION OF INDEPENDENCE: HOW ELIZABETH AND PHILIP MADE IT WORK

144 **"I, Philip, Duke of Edinburgh"** Tina Brown, "Prince Philip, the Man Who Walked Two Paces Behind the Queen," **The New York Times,** April 9, 2001.

145 **"What do you mean"** Brandreth, interview.

146 **"Part of that love"** Brown, "Prince Philip."

147 **"I am the only man"** Philip Eade, **Prince Philip: The Turbulent Early Life of the Man Who Married Queen Elizabeth II** (New York: Henry Holt, 2011), chap. 20.

148 **"close to tears"** Ibid., chap. 16.

148 **"Queen only wishes"** Smith, **Elizabeth the Queen,** chap. 6.

148 **"German junker"** Lacey, **Monarch,** chap. 14.

149 **"He might as well"** Stephanie Linning, "The Bond Between a Grandmother and Grandson: Touching Personal Letters from the Queen Mother Reveal How She Championed a Young Charles as He Struggled with His 'Distant' Mother," **Mail Online,** March 29, 2017.

150 **"I used to enjoy"** **Prince Philip: The Royal Family Remembers,** directed by Faye Hamilton and Matthew Hill, BBC One, aired September 22, 2021.

150 **"Your country"** Helena Horton, "48 of Prince

Philip's Greatest Quotes and Funny Moments," **The Telegraph,** April 17, 2021.

151 **"How do you keep"**   "Prince Philip's Gaffes from Decades on Royal Duty," BBC News, May 4, 2017.

153 **"Flirtatiousness at his age"**   Richard Kay and Geoffrey Levy, "One's Still Got It! As He Flirts Outrageously at 93, Friends Say Philip's Bond with a Blonde Aristocrat Keeps Him Young. But What DOES the Queen Think?," **Mail Online,** May 18, 2015.

154 **"She shrugs her shoulders"**   Ibid.

154 **"the wonderful moment"**   Selina Hastings, interview, March 14, 2006.

154 **"Good God woman"**   "Philip: I Could Never Get Away with Affair," **Sunday Mirror,** January 14, 1996.

157 **"First was when"**   Bernard Donoughue, **Westminster Diary,** vol. 2, **Farewell to Office** (London: I. B. Tauris, 2017).

157 **"Her Majesty is my lifelong best friend"**   The Rt. Hon. Lord Donoughue, interview, July 31, 2020.

159 **She once urged her dresser**   Angela Kelly, **The Other Side of the Coin: The Queen, the Dresser, and the Wardrobe** (London: HarperCollins, 2019), chap. 1.

160 **"I consider we got to know"**   Smith, **Elizabeth the Queen,** chap. 18.

160 **"with her nose"**   Ibid.

161 **"A dog isn't important"**   Ibid.

164 **"so wise and so true"**   Hardman, **Queen of the World,** chap. 6.

164 **"These are dark"**   "Text of the Queen's Message to New York," **The Guardian,** September 21, 2001.

CHAPTER 6. SWAN SONGS: MARGARET AND THE QUEEN MOTHER LEAVE THE PARTY

165 **"Yes, someday"**   Smith, **Elizabeth the Queen,** chap. 1.

166 **"The Queen was always able"**   Richard Kay and

Geoffrey Levy, "Mystery of Royal Love Burnt by the Queen's Sister: Princess Margaret Had Chauffeur Destroy Thousands of Romantic Royal Correspondence—Including Those from Diana," **Daily Mail**, March 14, 2016.

166 **"Oh look"** Major Colin Burgess, "Don't Mention Diana! Charles Was the Queen Mum's Most Cherished Grandchild—Which Is Why, When His Marriage Ended, She Never Allowed Diana's Name to Be Uttered in Her Presence Again . . . as Revealed by Her Own Loyal Equerry," **Daily Mail**, April 24, 2017.

166 **"Oh, it's so much easier"** Sarah Bradford, "The Woman Who Wasn't Quite Queen," **The Telegraph**, February 10, 2002.

167 **"In all the years"** Kay and Levy, "Mystery of Royal Love."

167 **"like a big sister"** Anne Glenconner, **Lady in Waiting: My Extraordinary Life in the Shadow of the Crown** (New York: Hachette, 2020), chap. 10.

168 **"She was thrilled"** Ibid., chap. 17.

168 **"Your leaving us"** William Shawcross, **The Queen Mother: The Official Biography** (New York: Vintage Books, 2010), chap. 16.

171 **"utterly oyster"** Vanessa Thorpe, "Queen Mother Was 'Ruthless' to Royal Nanny," **The Guardian**, June 25, 2000.

171 **"What, no mustard!"** Tina Brown, "What Colin Tennant Does for Princess Margaret," **Tatler**, June 1980.

172 **"What do you think"** Penelope Mortimer, interview, January 8, 2021.

173 **"This is a terribly sad day"** The Prince of Wales, "Charles: My Darling Aunt," BBC News, February 9, 2002.

173 **"probably been a merciful release"** Shawcross, **Queen Mother**, chap. 24.

173 "slightly strained"   Glenconner, **Lady in Waiting,** chap. 13.

174 **"Mummy and Margaret"**   Bradford, "Woman Who Wasn't Queen."

174 **"Of course I looked sad"**   Glenconner, **Lady in Waiting,** chap. 4.

175 **"Carry on with your house party"**   Andrew Morton, "Princess Margaret Accused the Royals of Ignoring Her Mental Anguish—Years Before Diana and Meghan: ANDREW MORTON Reveals How She Took Pills and Whisky, Sobbed on Chauffeur's Shoulder and Threatened to Throw Herself from Window," **The Mail on Sunday,** updated March 21, 2021.

175 **"For God's sake"**   Brown, **Ninety-Nine Glimpses of Prince Margaret,** chap. 90.

176 **"Every time I try"**   Glenconner, **Lady in Waiting,** chap. 17.

176 **She rebuked Princess Diana**   David Griffin, interview, August 30, 2006.

176 **"Princess Margaret was kind"**   Ibid.

177 **"didn't have one"**   Glenconner, **Lady in Waiting,** chap. 10.

177 **"I may not have achieved"**   Ingrid Seward, "A Brilliant Mother Despite Everything," **Mail Online,** February 11, 2002.

179 **"life, above all"**   Charles Nevin, "Princess Margaret," **The Guardian,** February 9, 2002.

180 **"It was the saddest"**   Smith, **Elizabeth the Queen,** chap. 18.

182 **"Africa's quite gone"**   Lacey, **Monarch,** chap. 21.

183 **"The Queen's picture"**   Ben Pimlott, The Queen: Elizabeth II and the Monarchy (London: HarperPress, 2012), chap. 11.

183 **"dangerously progressive"**   Private Lives of the Windsors, directed by Ben Reid, Renegade Pictures, 2019.

184 "I had a short opportunity" Brandreth, **Philip and Elizabeth**, chap. 10.

184 "Apart from insisting" Ibid.

184 "Here comes the problem" Turner, **Elizabeth**, chap. 5.

185 "like a dumping-ground" Ibid.

185 "a horrid little house" Ibid.

185 "Perhaps they would" Shawcross, **Queen Mother**, chap. 17.

186 "It's Mummy that matters" Douglas Keay, interview, February 15, 2007.

186 "there was an awkwardness" Brandreth, **Philip and Elizabeth**, chap. 10.

187 "Everything at Glamis" Geordie Greig, **The King Maker: The Man Who Saved George VI** (New York: Open Road Integrated Media, 2014), chap. 11.

187 "He needed to marry" Michael Thornton, "Revealed for the First Time—the Other Woman in the Queen Mother's Marriage," **Mail Online**, August 14, 2009.

188 "engulfed by great black clouds" Shawcross, **Queen Mother**, chap. 17.

188 "If only Mummy" Richard Kay and Geoffrey Levy, "The Queen's Power Struggles with the Mother She Adored: They Shared a Mutual Love of Horse Racing, but Her Majesty and Her Mother Were Far from Alike," **Daily Mail**, March 16, 2016.

189 "great delicacy" Shawcross, **Queen Mother**, chap. 17.

189 "he must have said" Vickers, **Elizabeth**, chap. 24.

189 "I realized suddenly" Shawcross, **Queen Mother**, chap. 17.

190 "She was shouting" Kay and Levy, "The Queen's Power Struggles."

191 "a little 'Mmmm'" Ann Morrow, **Without Equal: H. M. Queen Elizabeth, the Queen Mother** (Thirsk, North Yorkshire: House of Stratus, 2012), chap. 25.

191 "affectionately suggest" Turner, **Elizabeth**, chap. 5.

191 "Really" Lacey, **Monarch**, chap. 18.

193 "there had been no sign" John Arlidge, "The End of an Aristocratic Era of Style, Opulence . . . and Overdrafts," **The Guardian**, March 31, 2002.

193 "Was this yours?" Shawcross, **Queen Mother**, chap. 19.

193 "You now have" Ibid.

194 "Darling, lunch" Andrew Alderson, "The Day Great Granny Did Her Ali G Rap at the Dinner Table," **The Telegraph**, April 7, 2002.

195 "a very serious look" Tom Quinn, **Backstairs Billy: The Life of William Tallon, the Queen Mother's Most Devoted Servant** (London: Robson Press, 2016), chap. 11.

195 "We really are" Ibid.

196 "She was later shown" Elizabeth Longford, **The Queen: The Life of Elizabeth II** (New York: Alfred A. Knopf, 1983), chap. 19.

197 "outlived her usefulness" Matt Wells, "BBC Defends 'Respectful' Coverage," **The Guardian**, April 1, 2002.

197 "an embarrassing spectacle" Bower, **Rebel Prince**, chap. 13.

198 "My 37th birthday" Morgan, "Saturday, 30 March 2002," **Insider**.

199 "panache, style" Prince of Wales, "A Tribute by HRH The Prince of Wales Following the Death of Her Late Majesty Queen Elizabeth, The Queen Mother on Saturday, 30th March, 2002, London," princeofwales.gov.uk, April 4, 2002.

200 "Paper that got it" Torin Douglas, "Public Mood Takes Media by Surprise," BBC News, April 9, 2002.

200 "It was a huge mix" Roy Strong, "8 April 2002," in **Scenes and Apparitions: The Roy Strong Diaries, 1988–2003** (London: Weidenfeld and Nicolson, 2016).

200 "a friend of the Queen Mother" Bower, **Rebel Prince**, chap. 13.

201 "slightly upbeat tone" Matt Seaton, "The Accidental Laureate," **The Guardian**, September 16, 2002.

201 "reflected her thoughts" "'Mysterious Origin' of Funeral Poem," BBC News, April 11, 2002.

203 addressed simply to "England" Strong, "8 April 2002," **Scenes and Apparitions**.

CHAPTER 7. JUBILEE GIRL:
THE QUEEN'S ENCORE

207 "We need to face" "A Spectacular Jubilee," **The Guardian**, June 4, 2002.

208 "The Golden Jubilee" Strong, "4 June 2002," **Scenes and Apparitions**.

CHAPTER 8. SERVANT PROBLEMS:
WHAT THE BUTLER SAW

212 "If I say it" Diary entry, March 2006.

212 "lump[ing] her" Griffin, interview, 2006.

212 "They didn't give" David Griffin, interview, October 7, 2020.

214 "You must be quite mad" Bower, **Rebel Prince**, chap. 24.

214 "I had three" Smith, **Prince Charles**, chap. 32.

214 "He never, ever" Rebecca English, "'Charles Is the Most Difficult Person in the World to Buy a Present For': Camilla Pays Tribute to 'Workaholic' Husband as He Celebrates His 65th Birthday," **Daily Mail**, November 14, 2013.

215 "I would never" Major Colin Burgess, **Behind Palace Doors: My Service as the Queen Mother's Equerry** (London: John Blake, 2007), chap. 12.

216 "I can manage"   "Michael Fawcett: Trusted Aide," BBC News, November 7, 2003.

216 "I could never quite work"   Burgess and Carter, **Behind Palace Doors**, chap. 12.

218 "Do you have"   Bower, **Rebel Prince**, chap. 9.

218 "My darling"   "Butler 'Stole Diana's Belongings,'" BBC News, October 14, 2002.

218 "Her Royal Highness"   Bower, **Rebel Prince**, chap. 9.

219 "It's full of boxes"   Ibid.

219 "I want white lilies"   Ibid., chap. 11.

219 potentially explosive   Ibid.

219 "This man is a monster"   Ibid., chap. 9.

221 "the Prince of Wales is distraught"   Ibid.

221 "Burrell has chronic"   Riddington and Naden, **Frances**, chap. 17.

221 "my rock"   Griffin, interview, 2020.

221 Diana's loyal chauffeur   Colin Tebbutt MVO, interview, October 7, 2020.

222 "Barrack-Room Bertha"   Bower, **Rebel Prince**, chap. 11.

222 "I can't take anything"   Ibid., chap. 9.

223 "what's in [Burrell's] head"   Morgan, "Wednesday, 17 January 2001," **Insider**.

223 "A cornered Burrell"   Ibid.

223 "I wish to emphasize"   Warren Hoge, "London Journal; Diana's Faithful Butler: In the End, Was He False?," The New York Times, October 18, 2002.

224 "You know what it's called"   Paul Vallely, "Sir Michael Peat: Once Holder of the Purse, Now Keeper of the Royal Honour," **The Independent**, November 8, 2003.

224 it was Peat   Griffin, interview, 2020.

224 "Michael was charm"   "Profile: Sir Michael Peat," The Sunday Times, March 9, 2003.

226 Those summoned   Tebbutt, interview.

226 "Her Majesty has had a recollection"   Bower, **Rebel Prince**, chap. 15.

227 "star non-witness"   Stephen Bates, "Queen's Flash of

Memory Saved Burrell. But What Took Her So Long?," *The Guardian*, November 2, 2002.

228 **"being hit"** Bower, **Rebel Prince**, chap. 11.

228 **"Because the Queen's personal property"** Bates, "Queen's Flash of Memory."

229 **"Only a golden bullet"** Bower, **Rebel Prince**, chap. 15.

229 **"The Queen came through"** Stephen Bates, "What the Butler Said: 'The Queen Came Through for Me,'" *The Guardian*, November 2, 2002.

230 **"air stewardess"** Bower, **Rebel Prince**, chap. 15.

230 **"I, for one"** "Royal Butler Attacks Spencer Family," BBC News, November 7, 2002.

231 **"a complete fuck-up"** Ian Katz, "Prince Is Very, Very Weak, Says His Former Top Aide," **The Guardian**, October 25, 2003.

232 **"None came forward"** Susan Clarke, "Tiggy Attacks Fawcett: The £250,000 Fixer for Charles," **The Mail on Sunday**, September 4, 2005.

233 **"Sir Michael Peat"** Warren Hoge, "Prince Charles's Top Aide Quits After Inquiry," **The New York Times**, March 14, 2003.

233 **"Michael Peat did his best"** Clarke, "Tiggy Attacks Fawcett."

233 **"Quite frankly"** Ann Pukas, "The Fugitive Butler—Burrell Faces 10 Years in Jail," **Express**, March 5, 2008.

234 **"She will be merciless"** Dipesh Gadher, Roya Nikkhah, and Gabriel Pogrund, "Camilla Wants Prince's 'Damaging' Aide Pushed Out Over Charity Scandal," **The Sunday Times**, October 31, 2021.

CHAPTER 9. CAMILLA'S LINE IN THE SAND: A NEW DUCHESS IN THE WINNERS' ENCLOSURE

237 **"I remember"** Mark Bolland, interview, September 27, 2005.

237 "I'm not the block"　Ibid.

237 "Nobody knows"　Bower, **Rebel Prince**, chap. 21.

238 "Is that true?"　Ibid.

238 "in every respect"　"The Queen Gives a Toast at the Prince of Wales' 70th Birthday Party," royal.uk, November 14, 2008.

239 "Toy Town"　Tom Bawden, "Prince Charles Discovers 10 Ways to Antagonise Architects with List of 'Geometric Principles,'" **The Independent**, December 21, 2014.

239 "very proud"　"Prince Charles—Poundbury," YouTube, 1:50, November 24, 2009.

239 "I only hope"　Stephen Bates and Robert Booth, "You'll Miss Me When I'm Gone, Says Charles as He Flies Off to Schmooze US," **The Guardian**, October 29, 2005.

240 "Countryside in 1970"　Duke of Edinburgh, "A Speech by HRH The Prince of Wales at the Countryside in 1970 Conference, Steering Committee for Wales, Cardiff," princeofwales.gov.uk, February 19, 1970.

241 "He was a curious mixture"　Blair, **Journey**, chap. 5.

242 "the shanty town"　Smith, **Prince Charles**, chap. 29.

242 "The trouble"　Ken Wharfe MVO, interview, March 15, 2006.

243 "What is wrong"　Stephen Bates, "Tribunal Exposes Prince's 'Edwardian' Attitudes," **The Guardian**, November 18, 2004.

244 "a monstrous carbuncle"　Duke of Edinburgh, "A Speech by HRH The Prince of Wales at the Royal Institute of British Architects (RIBA), Royal Gala Evening at Hampton Court Palace," princeofwales.gov.uk, May 30, 1984.

245 "degree to which"　Rob Evans and Robert Booth, "Prince Charles Faces Fresh Meddling Claim Over Letters to Ministers," **The Guardian**, December 19, 2009.

245 **"poor performance"** Duke of Edinburgh to Elliot Morley, October 21, 2004.

245 **"If we, as a group"** Caroline Davies and Charles Clover, "'Black Spider' Letters Catch Charles in Web of Controversy," **The Telegraph,** September 26, 2002.

245 **"the risk of being"** Duke of Edinburgh to Elliot Morley, October 21, 2004.

246 **"environmentally friendly"** Ben Webster, "How Prince Charles Lobbied Tony Blair Over Ban on 'Romantic' Fox Hunts," **The Times,** October 9, 2017.

247 **"The men were"** Tina Brown, "Wednesday, November 9, 1983," in **The Vanity Fair Diaries: Power, Wealth, Celebrity, and Dreams; My Years at the Magazine That Defined a Decade** (New York: Henry Holt, 2017).

248 **"one of the domestic"** Blair, **Journey,** chap. 10.

248 **"seen as a direct"** "Camilla Banned from March," The Times, August 27, 2002.

249 **"It's too small"** Bower, **Rebel Prince,** chap. 10.

250 **"Haven't you read"** Ibid., chap. 20.

250 **"Camilla is nervy"** Mark Bolland, "Windsor Wedding," **The Sunday Times,** April 10, 2005.

251 **"His instructions"** Junor, **Duchess,** chap. 28.

252 **"being frozen out"** "People with Andrew Pierce," The Times, May 12, 2004.

252 **"The Prince will become"** Andrew Pierce and Alan Hamilton, "After 30 Years, Charles Put His Affair in Order," The Times, February 11, 2005.

253 **"Prince William could"** Strong, "2 June 2003," **Scenes and Apparitions.**

254 **"I thought she"** Junor, **Duchess,** chap. 28.

254 **"It was most noticeable"** Ibid.

254 **"I think there was"** Andrew Pierce, "Prince 'Lost Chance' to Wed Camilla," **The Times,** May 28, 2004.

255 **"He is the heir"** Crampton, "Just Marry Camilla Now, Charles."

256 "The trouble is Charles" "War of the Wedding," **Mail Online**, updated November 4, 2004.

258 "Although he loved" Junor, **Duchess**, chap. 28.

259 "It's nonsense" Brandreth, **Charles and Camilla,** prologue.

259 "regulariz[ing]" Ibid.

261 a "substantial" trust Robert Jobson, "Prince Sets Up Trust Funds for Camilla's Son and Daugther," **Evening Standard,** April 13, 2012.

261 "taken to the cleaners" Andrew Alderson, "Charles Ignores Lawyers and Insists There'll Be No Pre-nup with Camilla," **The Telegraph,** March 27, 2005.

263 "just coming down" Caroline Davies, "Charles to Marry Camilla," **The Telegraph,** February 11, 2005.

263 "approved premises" Marriage Act 1994, chap. 34.

265 "Do I put" Stephen Bates, "Through Gritted Teeth," **The Guardian,** April 1, 2005.

265 "Bloody people" "I Hate Facing Media, Says Charles," BBC News, March 31, 2005.

265 sitting on a Bates, "Through Gritted Teeth."

266 willingness to sanction Stephen Bates, "Royal Couple 'Must Apologise for Adultery Before Receiving Blessing,'" **The Guardian,** March 28, 2005.

266 "It might have been" **The Spectator,** February 26, 2005.

267 "Will the nastiness" Brandreth, **Charles and Camilla,** prologue.

267 "really good" Ibid.

269 "crown jewels" Andrew Pierce, "Wedding Overcomes New Hurdle as BBC Puts Back the National," **The Times,** April 6, 2005.

269 "She was really ill" Junor, **Duchess**, chap. 29.

269 "She literally couldn't" Ibid.

271 "There is very little" Bower, **Rebel Prince**, chap. 22.

272 "We acknowledge" **The Book of Common Prayer,** 1549.

273 "I have two important announcements" Bower, **Rebel Prince**, chap. 22.

273 "There was a moment" Fry, interview.

274 "Oh, look" Bower, **Rebel Prince**, chap. 22.

274 "It was transparent" Junor, **Duchess**, chap. 29.

CHAPTER 10. THE PRINCES NEXT DOOR: WILLIAM'S AND HARRY'S COMPETING REALITIES

277 "You couldn't help" Junor, "Partners in Crime," **Prince William**.

278 "He's really interested" "Playful Prince William, Latest Royal Public Speaker," **The Times**, June 13, 1984.

279 "Poppa says" Wharfe, interview.

279 "out of control" Robert Lacey, **Battle of Brothers: William and Harry; The Inside Story of a Family in Tumult** (London: HarperPress, 2020), chap. 8.

279 "a holy terror" Christopher Andersen, **William and Kate: And Baby George; Royal Baby Edition** (New York: Gallery Books, 2011), chap. 2.

279 "Basher Wills" Junor, "His Royal Naughtiness," **Prince William**.

280 "Harry is quieter" Lacey, **Battle of Brothers**, chap. 9.

280 "You take care" Lady Colin Campbell, **Meghan and Harry: The Real Story** (New York: Pegasus Books, 2020), chap. 2.

280 "There were bedrooms" Patrick Jephson, **Shadows of a Princess** (London: William Collins, 2017), chap. 8.

281 "an extraordinarily natural" Smith, **Prince Charles**, chap. 19.

281 "It glows sometimes" "Prince William Lends Support for Children's Cancer Centre in Exclusive Interview for CBBC's **Newsround**, BBC, March 18, 2009.

282 "You'll be king" Lacey, **Battle of Brothers**, chap. 9.

282 **"Tower Records, Over"** Chris Hutchins, "Diana, 'Uncle James' Hewitt and the Emotional Wounds That Haunt Harry: Fascinating Psychological Insight into the Forces That Shaped the Playboy Prince," **Mail Online,** updated April 9, 2013.

283 **"One of her mottos"** **Diana, Our Mother: Her Life and Legacy,** directed by Ashley Gething, ITV, 2017.

283 **"Some hours later"** Junor, "Partners in Crime," **Prince William.**

284 **"I am not telling"** Angela Levin, **Harry: Conversations with the Prince** (London: John Blake, 2019), chap. 2.

285 **"If he doesn't"** Ingrid Seward, **William and Harry** (New York: Arcade Publishing, 2011), chap. 15.

285 **"Colditz with Kilts"** Christopher Wilson, "Punched as He Slept, Friends Tortured with Pliers: As It's Revealed the Queen Mother Tried to Stop Charles Going to Gordonstoun, No Wonder He Called It Colditz with Kilts," **Mail Online,** February 1, 2013.

287 **"My boy's got"** Caroline Frost, "Prince William: Reticent Royal Icon," BBC News, June 19, 2003.

287 **"The grown-ups"** Juliet Nicolson interview, February 19, 2021.

288 **"He really doesn't"** Wharfe and Jobson, **Diana,** chap. 3.

289 **"The Princess believed"** Ibid., chap. 17.

290 **"everyone is not rich"** Frost, "Prince William."

290 **"I want them"** Princess of Wales, "An Interview with HRH The Princess of Wales," **Panorama.**

290 **"Sleeping rough"** "Prince William: 'Seeing People Overcome Such Adversity Is Incredibly Moving,'" **The Big Issue,** December 14, 2015.

291 **"forget me not"** Robert Hardman, **Queen of the World** (New York: Pegasus Books, 2019), chap. 13.

291 **"I always wanted"** Duke of Sussex, **The Me You**

Can't See, executive produced by Oprah Winfrey and Prince Harry, Apple TV+, May 21, 2021.

292 "Ooh, look, boys" Holden, **Based on a True Story,** chap. 14.

293 "my little wise" Simone Simmons, **Diana: The Last Word** (London: Orion Books, 2006), chap. 6.

294 **"Mummy, [Bashir] is"** Richard Kay, "Hasnat Khan Wields the Knife: He Was Princess Diana's Lover as She Filmed Her Secret **Panorama** Interview. Now, Inflamed by the Unfolding Scandal, the Heart Surgeon Gives His First Interview in 12 Years—and It Is Devastating," **Daily Mail,** January 8, 2021.

294 **"literally anything"** Morgan, "Thursday, 16 May 1996," **Insider.**

295 **"This has happened"** "A Class Act in the Saga of Splitsville," **The Herald,** September 7, 1995.

295 "She's milking it" Morgan, "Thursday, 16 May 1996," **Insider.**

297 **"I hate you"** Andrew Morton, "William of Wales: The Path of the Prince," in **William and Catherine: Their Lives, Their Wedding** (London: Michael O'Mara, 2011).

297 **"Harry loves animals"** Levin, **Harry: Conversations,** chap. 2.

298 **"It gives you"** Princess of Wales, "An Interview with HRH The Princess of Wales," **Panorama.**

298 **"I remember going"** Diana, **Our Mother.**

301 **"better"** if she departed Lacey, **Battle of Brothers,** 90.

301 **"smoking and guzzling"** Morgan, "Wednesday, 28 May 1997," **Insider.**

301 **"had a go at [her]"** Ibid.

302 **"I am not"** Junor, "Outside the Gilded Cage," **Prince William.**

302 **"One of the great"** Patrick Jephson, interview, February 4, 2021.

CHAPTER 11. THE LOST BOYS: HOW THE PRINCES SURVIVED THEIR CHILDHOOD

303 "I'm not very good" **Charles: The Private Man, the Public Role.**

304 "I hope" Junor, "A Very Public War," **Prince William.**

304 "Your lenses are very daunting" Mark Saunders and Glenn Harvey, "Mark, April 1994," in **Dicing with Di: The Amazing Adventures of Britain's Royal Chasers** (London: Blake Publishing, 1996).

305 "It was Diana" Saunders and Harvey, "Glenn, November 1993," **Dicing with Di.**

305 "One of the feelings" Duke of Sussex, **The Me You Can't See.**

306 "Is it true" Morton, "William of Wales: The Path of the Prince," **William and Catherine.**

306 "May I say" Wharfe and Jobson, **Closely Guarded Secret,** chap. 3.

308 "Is that really" Simmons, **Diana,** chap. 6.

309 "After a few" Saunders and Harvey, "Mark, November 1995," **Dicing with Di.**

309 "Mummy, I think" Princess of Wales, "An Interview with HRH The Princess of Wales," **Panorama.**

309 "slumped on the sofa" Lacey, **Battle of Brothers,** chap. 12.

310 "What have I done" Simmons, **Diana,** chap. 6.

311 "It's very tragic" Mark Saunders, interview, August 19, 2021.

311 **William was so angry** Junor, "Uneasy Relationship," in **Prince William.**

312 "It was very, very" **Diana, Our Mother.**

312 "comforted enormously" "UK Princes Say Let Diana Rest," BBC News, September 2, 1998.

313 "We cannot believe" Ian Katz and Stephen Bates, "Princes Vent Fury at Butler," **The Guardian,** October 25, 2003.

313 **"These photographs"** "These Photographs Are Redolent with the Tragedy of Diana's Death," **The Guardian,** June 5, 2007.

314 **" 'Nicholas, can I' "** Nicholas Coleridge, **The Glossy Years: Magazines, Museums and Selective Memoirs** (London: Penguin, 2020), chap. 15.

316 **"Whether Harry's Bar"** Lalvani, interview.

316 **"He's sold me out!"** Simmons, **Diana,** chap. 4.

316 **"I saw his Adam's apple"** Mark Stephens CBE, interview, November 21, 2019.

317 **"He told me that Diana"** "For the First Time, **Princess in Love** Author Anna Pasternak Tells the Full Story Behind Her 1994 Book About Diana and James Hewitt," **Daily Mail**, June 30, 2019.

318 **"It is my view"** David Brown et al., "Prince William's Statement on Bashir's Diana Interview: 'BBC Lies Fuelled My Mother's Paranoia," **The Times,** May 20, 2021.

320 **"I'm glad I did it"** Lalvani, interview.

320 **"She was walking"** Saunders, interview.

321 **"She indicated left"** Saunders and Harvey, "Mark, November 1995," **Dicing with Di.**

CHAPTER 12. ENTER KATE: WILLIAM MEETS AN EXTRAORDINARY, ORDINARY GIRL

326 **"Her hair was dark brown"** Anthony Trollope, **The Duke's Children** (London: Penguin, 1995), chap. 28.

327 **"go back as far"** Jane Fryer, "Hardly Buck House, Was It Kate? Inside Kate (and Pippa) Middleton's Very Modest Childhood Home," **Daily Mail**, May 20, 2011.

329 **"wanted to be"** Claudia Joseph, **Kate: The Making of a Princess** (Edinburgh: Mainstream Publishing, 2010), chap. 5.

329 **"I'm a Thatcher child"** Camilla Tominey, "Is Gary Goldsmith Really the Black Sheep of the Middleton Family?," **Express**, March 24, 2013.

330 "Butter wouldn't melt"   Lacey, **Battle of Brothers,** chap. 6.

330 "the amazing white"   Fryer, "Hardly Buck House, Was It Kate?"

332 "Girls can be"   Giles Hattersley and Francesca Angelini, "Beauty and the Bullies," **The Sunday Times,** April 10, 2011.

333 "You pick up"   "Kate Middleton 'Quit Her First Public School Because She Was Bullied,'" **Daily India,** April 3, 2011.

333 "She was regarded"   Hattersley and Angelini, "Beauty and the Bullies."

333 "were encouraged"   Jo Macfarlane and Simon Trump, "No Hockey, No Boys and a Hotbed of Oestrogen: Why 'Bullied' Kate Quit Her First Public School," **Daily Mail,** updated April 8, 2011.

334 could not return   Matthew Ball, "Just the Ticket," The Spectator, August 6, 2005.

335 "was quite an old-fashioned"   Rebecca English, "The Remaking of Kate," **Daily Mail,** August 27, 2005.

335 "her V-plates"   Ball, "Just the Ticket."

336 "My focus is on winning"   Pippa Middleton, "Pippa Middleton: My Schoolgirl Sports Confessions," **The Spectator,** September 7, 2013.

336 "Kate was always"   "The Other Middleton Girl," **The Scotsman,** November 3, 2008.

337 "It's easy for them"   Andrew Neil FRSA, email correspondence, February 24, 2021.

337 "poshos"   Ibid.

339 "Look at my"   Katie Nicholl, **Kate: The Future Queen** (New York: Weinstein Books, 2013), chap. 4.

339 "one of the fitter"   "Revealed . . . How Kate Followed William on His Chile Mission," **Evening Standard,** April 21, 2011.

341 "With deepest sympathy"   Sam Greenhill, "The Student Prince," **The Telegraph,** September 23, 2001.

341 **"Any good parties"** Ben Summerskill, "No Disre-spec' as Princes Recall a Lifetime of Laughter," **The Guardian,** April 7, 2002.

341 **"Hmmn, this will"** Brian Lang, interview, March 27, 2021.

342 **"Andrew [Neil] said that"** Lord Black of Brentwood FRSA, interview, November 4, 2019.

343 **"But people who try"** "Student Prince Starts Col-lege," BBC News, September 22, 2001.

344 **"William the bashful"** Robert Jobson, **William and Kate: The Love Story; A Celebration of the Wedding of the Century** (London: John Blake, 2010), chap. 7.

344 **"Usually I was"** Vanessa Thorpe, "William: I Can't Have a Serious Girlfriend," **The Guardian,** June 22, 2013.

346 **"grit, determination"** "The Queen's Speech," BBC News, July 1, 1999.

346 **"Do you have any idea"** Andrew Neil FRSA, inter-view, December 10, 2021.

348 **"He actually told"** Katie Nicholl, "Wills and the Real Girl," **Vanity Fair,** December 2010.

349 **"You looked so"** Brown, **Diana Chronicles,** 140.

353 **"doors to manual"** Esther Addley, "The Middletons—Finding Common Ground with the Royal Family," **The Guardian,** April 30, 2011.

353 **"Pardon?"** Vicky Ward, "Will's Cup of Tea," **Vanity Fair,** November 2008.

353 **"At first"** "Kate Middleton's Parents to Contribute Six-Figure Sum to Cost of Wedding," **Vanity Fair,** March 14, 2011.

353 **"But the voice"** Lisa Armstrong, "Exclusive: Carole Middleton's First Interview: 'Life Is Really Normal—Most of the Time,'" **The Telegraph,** November 30, 2018.

354 **"could be flip"** Morton, "William and Kate: A Street Called Hope," **William and Catherine.**

CHAPTER 13. QUEEN IN WAITING:
KATE CLOSES THE DEAL

358 "Bitch!"   Junor, "Gaining a Sister," Prince Harry.

359 "Only if she"   "Kate's Not Precious. She Mucked in at Jigsaw," Evening Standard, July 12, 2008.

359 "I don't want"   Patrick Harverson LVO, interview, November 19, 2019.

359 "Listen, do you"   "Kate's Not Precious."

360 "When we first"   Oliver Marre, "Girl, Interrupted," The Guardian, March 18, 2007.

360 get a "real job"   Susie Kellie, "Kate Middleton's 'Invidious Position' as Queen Demanded She 'Get a Job,'" Express, June 3, 2021.

361 "Army boys"   Marre, "Girl, Interrupted."

361 "was acutely aware"   Nicholl, Kate: The Future Queen.

361 "genuinely wanted"   Megan C. Hills, "Kate Middleton Asked for a Part-Time Job Due to Her 'Relationship with This Very High Profile Man' According to Royal Expert," Evening Standard, June 12, 2020.

363 "You must be"   Oliver Burkeman, "William Passes Muster with Grandma (and Kate)," The Guardian, December 16, 2006.

364 "more than anything"   Sam Knight and David Byers, "Paparazzi on Prowl as William's Girlfriend Turns 25," The Sunday Times, January 9, 2007.

365 "concern about"   Nicholl, Kate: The Future Queen, chap. 6.

365 "She openly admitted"   Charlie Bradley, "Kate Middleton's Anger at Prince William over His Lifestyle: 'Making Me Look Bad,'" Express, December 5, 2021.

365 "too young to settle"   Rebecca English, "William and His Two Other Women," Daily Mail, updated April 16, 2007.

366 "far as Kate"   "Prince William and Kate Middleton Split," **The Sunday Times,** April 14, 2007.

367 **She had to excuse herself**   Lacey, **Battle of Brothers,** chap. 18.

367 **"Recuperate on holiday"** Stephanie Marsh, "Did You See?," **The Sunday Times,** June 26, 2007.

368 **"the big sister"** Angela Levin, "Exclusive: Prince Harry on Chaos After Diana's Death and Why the World Needs 'the Magic' of the Royal Family," **Newsweek,** June 21, 2017.

368 **"lost puppy"** Nicholl, **Kate: The Future Queen,** chap. 8.

369 **"clear and persistent harassment"** "Self-Regulation of the Press," House of Commons, Culture, Media and Sport Committee, July 3, 2007.

370 **"Remember, this"** Morton, "William—and Catherine: 'A Total Shock,'" **William and Catherine.**

370 **"There is no doubt"** Julie Carpenter, "Is This Proof That Kate Has Won Back Her Prince?," **Express,** August 8, 2007.

371 **"my way"** "In Full: William and Kate's 2010 Engagement Interview, ITV News," YouTube, 1:48, November 16, 2010.

372 **"She married William"** Kate Nicholson, "Kate Middleton 'Wanted Loads of Kids and No Royal Obligations,'" **Express,** January 4, 2021.

373 **"I hear that you've"** Tamara Davison, "Queen's Cheeky Joke to Royal Cake Maker Before Prince William and Kate's Wedding," **Mirror,** April 7, 2021.

374 **"I sometimes still"** Carolyn Durand and Gabriel O'Rorke, "An Insider's View on the Royal Family," ABC News, May 19, 2018.

375 **"You don't always"** Robert Hardman, **Our Queen** (London: Arrow Books, 2012), chap. 2.

375 **William would "recognize" her** Morton, "William

and Catherine: The Wedding Day," **William and Catherine.**

377 "**There will be massive expectations**"   Marre, "Girl, Interrupted."

378 "**They knew what**"   Dr. Rowan Williams, interview, April 29, 2021.

379 "**equal part**"   Gordon Rayner, "Royal Wedding: Prince William Insists on Role for Kate Middleton's Family," **The Telegraph,** November 25, 2010.

379 "**The minute**"   Camilla Tominey, "Is Gary Goldsmith Really the Black Sheep of the Middleton Family?," **Express,** March 24, 2013.

381 "**That was really**"   Martina Bet, "Queen's Heartbreaking Words to Prince Philip on Kate and William's Wedding Day," **Express,** April 9, 2021.

CHAPTER 14. THE GREAT ESCAPE:
HARRY THE HERO FINDS HIS WAY

384 "**Lieutenant Wales**"   Carmen Nobel, "Prince Harry in Afghanistan: Miguel Head Shares the Story of a Historic Media Blackout," **The Journalist's Resource,** April 18, 2019.

384 "**£46 million flying**"   Duncan Larcombe, **Prince Harry: The Inside Story** (London: HarperCollins, 2017), chap. 7.

384 "**to remove Saddam**"   "Tony Blair's Address," BBC Radio 4, March 20, 2003.

385 "**bullet magnet**"   "Prince Harry Dismissed 'Bullet Magnet' Fears," **The Telegraph,** February 28, 2008.

385 "**I hope**"   Stephen Bates, "Harry at 21 on Camilla, the Media and AIDS Children in Africa," **The Guardian,** September 15, 2005.

385 "**knees brown**"   Jamie Lowther-Pinkerton LVO, MBE, DL, interview, March 11, 2021.

386 "**We'd have had**"   Junor, "Thwarted," **Prince Harry.**

386 "We used to say" Levin, **Harry: Conversations,** chap. 6.

387 "hoped to piss" Charles Spencer, **The Spencer Family** (London: Penguin, 2000), chap. 8.

387 "Family members have said" Caroline Davies, "Meghan, Diana, Drugs and Therapy: What Harry Said in Apple TV Series," **The Guardian,** May 21, 2021.

388 "burst out of the car" "Harry in Paparazzi Brawl," **Evening Standard,** October 20, 2004.

389 "Maybe it's just part" "£45,000 Damages for Teacher Who Accused Prince Harry of Cheating," **The Guardian,** February 14, 2006.

389 "the best escape" Levin, "Exclusive: Prince Harry."

389 "I do enjoy running" Bates, "Harry at 21."

390 "Prince Harry will" Rebecca English, "About Time, You 'Orrible Little Prince!," **Daily Mail,** May 9, 2005.

390 "This is what" Audrey Gillan, " 'I Think This Is as Normal as I'm Ever Going to Get,' " **The Guardian,** February 29, 2008.

390 "He's got extraordinary" Major General Francis "Buster" Howes CB, OBE, interview, March 4, 2021.

391 "You 'orrible little prince!" Andersen, **William and Kate,** chap. 5.

391 "I feel it is important" Larcombe, **Prince Harry,** chap. 6.

392 "The first time" "Prince Harry—I'm better Than Prince William 2009.mpg," YouTube, 3:18, May 23, 2011.

392 "He is a seriously" Junor, "By Hook or by Crook," **Prince William.**

393 "know the fear" Hardman, **Our Queen,** chap. 9.

396 "We want to know" Larcombe, **Prince Harry,** chap. 6.

397 "The competitive nature" Nobel, "Prince Harry in Afghanistan."

398 "Get out of the way" Caroline Davies, "Charles and

His Cantankerous Canter," **The Guardian**, December 30, 2007.

400 **"They're calling him"** Matt Drudge, "Prince Harry Fights on Frontlines in Afghanistan; 3 Month Tour," **Drudge Report**, February 28, 2008.

400 **"He was very upset"** Nobel, "Prince Harry in Afghanistan."

401 **"It was the first time"** Ibid.

402 **"It's a shame"** Michael Smith, "'I'm No Hero,' Says Prince Harry," **The Sunday Times**, March 2, 2008.

402 **"It was simply"** Nobel, "Prince Harry in Afghanistan."

CHAPTER 15. SNOOPERS: HOW THE PRESS STALKED THE ROYALS

405 **"there were monkeys"** Helen Rumbelow, "Chelsy Davy: 'It Was Full-On—Crazy and Scary and Uncomfortable,'" **The Times**, June 27, 2016.

406 **"I wish I could spend"** Klara Glowczewska, "Prince Harry Joins a Pioneering Conservation Outfit in the Fight to Save Africa's Wild Animals," **Town & Country**, September 28, 2021.

409 **"I've got a young man"** Junor, "Gap Year," **Prince William**.

409 **"Harry is a thoroughly"** Chris Tryhorn, "Clarence House Attacks 'Ill-Informed' **Express**," **The Guardian**, February 20, 2004.

411 **"If you go out"** Rumbelow, "Chelsy Davy."

411 **"It was so full-on"** Ibid.

412 **"In the evening"** Graham Johnson, "**Daily Mail** Dragged into Murdoch's Prince Harry Hacking Scandal," **Byline Investigates**, May 27, 2020.

413 **"Jamie said he had been"** Patrick Harverson LVO, interview, November 4, 2019.

413 **"The story—a stupid"** Tom Bradby, "The Phone

Call to Prince William That Changed All Our Lives," **Express,** July 16, 2012.

414 **"We started to twig"**   Harverson, interview, November 4, 2019.

414 **"There was a clear"**   Ibid.

415 **"a mix"**   "Prince Harry," **Armchair Expert with Dax Shepard,** podcast, 33:30, May 13, 2021.

417 **"I called the number"**   Graham Johnson, "Prince Harry Hacking Exclusive: Top **Mirror** Private Investigator Targeted Diana, Princess of Wales," **Byline Investigates,** October 29, 2019.

420 **"the average Fleet Street"**   Alan Rusbridger, **Breaking News: The Remaking of Journalism and Why It Matters Now** (New York: Picador, 2019), chap. 16.

421 **"She can turn"**   Roy Greenslade, "Empress of the Sun," **The Guardian,** January 14, 2003.

424 **"Mazher got nothing"**   Graham Johnson, "Murdoch CEO Brooks Illegally Spied for a Year on Teenage Prince Harry," **Byline Investigates,** April 7, 2020.

424 he felt **"embarrassed"**   Ian Katz, "It Was Me What Spun It," **The Guardian,** October 27, 2003.

424 **"It was all about"**   Gavin Burrows, personal conversation with Graham Johnson.

427 **"It wasn't long"**   Ibid.

428 **"nearly got shot"**   Lisa O'Carroll, "Prince William's Messages for Kate Middleton Were Hacked, Court Told," **The Guardian,** December 19, 2013.

429 **"The readers wanted youthful"**   Greg Miskiw, personal conversation with Graham Johnson.

429 **steady stream of "shorts"**   Ibid.

430 **"The problem was this"**   Glenn Mulcaire, personal conversation with Graham Johnson.

433 **"the office cat"**   Peter Walker, "Ex-**NoW** Journalist Dan Evans Gets Suspended Sentence Over Hacking," **The Guardian,** July 24, 2014.

434 **"the most humble"**   "Rupert Murdoch: 'The Most Humble Day of My Life,'" BBC News, July 19, 2011.

434 **"next to nothing"**   Andy Davies, "Revealed: The Rupert Murdoch Tape," **Channel 4 News**, July 3, 2013.

435 **"part of the culture"**   Josh Halliday, "Scotland Yard Seeks Rupert Murdoch Secret Tape," **The Guardian**, July 5, 2013.

435 showed **"wilful ignorance"**   "News International and Phone-Hacking," House of Commons, Culture, Media and Sport Committee, Eleventh Report of Session 2010–12, vol. 1, April 30, 2012.

437 **"sensational stories"**   Lisa O'Carroll, "Levenson Report: Key Points," **The Guardian**, November 29, 2012.

437 **"people will not assume"**   "Leveson: Where Does It Leave the Internet?," BBC News, November 30, 2012.

438 **"I was basically"**   Gavin Burrows, "The Princes and the Press," interview by Amol Rajan, BBC Two, November 22, 2021.

CHAPTER 16. GLORIANA:
THE WINDSORS' WINNING STREAK

440 **"our despised"**   "The Queen's Jubilee: Diamond Is Not Forever," **The Guardian**, June 1, 2012.

440 **"Suave and charming"**   Robert Booth and Julian Borger, "Christopher Geidt: The Suave, Shrewd and Mysterious Royal Insider," **The Guardian**, May 31, 2013.

442 **"The boat was there"**   William Borders, "Lord Mountbatten Is Killed as His Fishing Boat Explodes; I.R.A. Faction Says It Set Bomb," **The New York Times**, August 28, 1979.

442 **"unjustified and unjustifiable"**   "Bloody Sunday Killings 'Unjustified and Unjustifiable,'" BBC News, June 15, 2010.

444 "For a lot of people" Andrew Marr, interview, May 12, 2021.

445 "was brave" Bernard Donoughue, email correspondence, May 7, 2021.

445 "This is named" Mary McAleese, interview, May 25, 2021.

445 The Queen told Enda Kenny, interview, May 13, 2021.

446 It was McAleese McAleese, interview.

446 "So much of" "Full Text of Speech by Queen Elizabeth II," The Irish Times, May 18, 2011.

446 "It was incredibly moving" David Cameron, For the Record (New York: William Collins, 2019), chap. 23.

447 "Bejaysus" Ibid.

447 "It was the biggest" Marr, interview.

447 "prepared to go" Ibid.

447 "the influence of" Kenny, interview.

448 "All I did" Cameron, For the Record, 459.

449 "Prince Harry was" "Prince Harry 'Such a Gentleman' Says Bash Kazi, Who Was Helped by British Royal After Polo Accident," The Washington Post, March 18, 2012.

450 "I had a dream" "Cheryl Cole: 'I Dreamt I Married Prince Harry,'" Marie Claire, April 3, 2012.

450 "oiled and manacled" Stephen Bates, "Thames Flotilla to Mark Queen's Diamond Jubilee," The Guardian, April 5, 2011.

451 "the kind of weather" Simon Schama, email correspondence, May 20, 2021.

451 "she had thought" Cameron, For the Record, chap. 27.

453 "As a member" Anne: The Princess Royal at 70, directed by Ian Denyer, ITV, 2020.

454 "given a Faroe Isle cardigan" Stuart Jeffries, "How

the Royals Became Cool," **The Guardian,** April 11, 2012.

455 **"A rich old toad"**   Hugo Vickers, interview, May 12, 2021.

458 **"Bottles and bins"**   Ross Lydall, "Camilla Hit by Rioter Through Car Window as Protesters Attack Royals," **Evening Standard,** April 12, 2012.

459 **"So where am I"**   Seb Coe, **Running My Life: The Autobiography** (London: Hodder and Stoughton, 2012), chap. 24.

460 **"Princess Anne has all"**   Ibid.

460 **"I think this person"**   **Anne: The Princess Royal at 70,** 13:12.

461 **"I wanted to wring"**   Cameron, **For the Record,** chap. 27.

461 **"the Geiger counter"**   "Factbox: Memorable Quotes from the 2012 London Olympics," Reuters, July 30, 2012.

464 **"I remember there was"**   Andy Beckett, interview, May 17, 2021.

465 **"They were thinking"**   Marr, interview.

466 **"Now we can"**   Beckett, interview.

467 **"Prince Charles also phoned"**   Matt Dathan, "London Riots: Prince Charles Cares More Than Cameron, Miliband and Clegg Says Senior MP," **The Independent,** March 18, 2015.

469 **Her only real concern**   Stephen Daldry CBE, interview, May 19, 2021.

470 **"Of course"**   Kelly, **Other Side of the Coin,** chap. 3.

470 **"It was messy"**   Amy Raphael and Danny Boyle, "The Opening Ceremony of the 2012 London Olympics," in **Creating Wonder: In Conversation with Amy Raphael** (London: Faber and Faber, 2013).

470 **"If we had judged"**   Coe, **Running My Life,** chap. 27.

471 **"None of them"**   Ibid.

472 **"What was so"**   Daldry, interview.

CHAPTER 17. THE DUKE OF HAZARD:
ANDREW'S MONEY PIT

475 **"have a word"** Sasha Swire, "2011," in **Diary of an MP's Wife: Inside and Outside Power** (London: Little, Brown, 2020).

478 **"Golly, I could"** "A Life in Quotes: The Queen Mother on . . . ," **The Guardian**, March 31, 2002.

479 **"disastrously diddled"** Andrew Roberts, "The Bitter Row That Blighted the Queen Mother's Fortune," **The Telegraph**, May 12, 2002.

480 **"Bloody Osborne"** Peter Brookes, **The Times**, 2012.

481 **"old newspapers"** "The Queen Net Worth—**Sunday Times** Rich List 2021," **The Sunday Times**, May 21, 2021.

481 **"The Queen was just"** "Eleanor Steafel, "My Life Up Close with the Queen—the Most Famous Woman in the World," **The Telegraph**, June 12, 2021.

483 **"we're talking relatively discreetly"** Jonathan Calvert, George Arbuthnott, and Tom Calver, "Prince Michael of Kent 'Selling Access' to Putanistas," **The Sunday Times**, May 8, 2021.

484 **"little tiny spot"** Stephen Castle, "From Prince Andrew, Critical Words for U.S. on Iraq," **The New York Times**, February 4, 2008.

485 **"Materi was"** Stephen Day CMG, "It's Now Getting Really Bad . . . ," **Royal Musings**, March 10, 2011.

485 **"[I] am deploying"** Laura Roberts, "Duke of York Pleads for Government Support Over Dinner with Tunisian Dictator's Relation," **The Telegraph**, March 5, 2011.

487 **"The sale of Sunninghill Park"** Guy Adams, "The Truth About Andrew's £15m House Sale," **Daily Mail**, updated May 23, 2016.

487 **"Kazakh oligarchs"** Tom Sykes, "Just What Is Prince

Andrew's Relationship to a Kazakh Oligarch?," The Daily Beast, updated April 13, 2017.

487 "absolute twaddle" Emily Fairbairn, "His Royal Rudeness: Prince Andrew's Decades of Unpleasantness Revealed—from His Huge Ego to the Diva-Like Meltdowns," The Sun, November 21, 2019.

488 "I'm the last person" Darren Johnson, Twitter, August 30, 2019, 10:49 A.M.

488 "Isn't it increasingly" "Prince Andrew: Envoy Career Plagued with Controversy," BBC News, July 21, 2011.

489 "There appears" Nicholas Watt, "Prince Andrew Special Trade Role to Be Downgraded," The Guardian, March 6, 2011.

489 "Nobody called him" Philip Williams, "Invincible and Prince Andrew Home from War," UPI, September 17, 1982.

490 "Prince Andrew is" Nigel Cawthorne, Prince Andrew: Epstein, Maxwell and the Palace (London: Gibson Square Books, 2020), chap. 3.

491 "Whenever she hears" Edward Klein, "The Trouble with Andrew," Vanity Fair, August 2011.

492 "natural boss" Cawthorne, Prince Andrew, chap. 2.

494 "six feet of sex appeal" Ibid.

494 "We want Andy!" Ibid.

495 "the world's quietest" Elton John, Me (New York: St. Martin's Griffin, 2019), chap. 14.

495 "He walked" Sarah Oliver, "Koo Stark Reveals the Truth About Prince Andrew: After 32 Years' Silence, Prince's Ex-Lover Gives Account of Affair to Defend Him from 'Sex-Slave' Claims," The Mail on Sunday, updated February 15, 2015.

495 "Oh I do wish" Phil Dampier, "Publishing Koo," The Royal Observer, June 3, 2021.

495 "Overnight" Annabel Sampson, "Prince Andrew's Ex Koo Stark Loses Annual Payment," Tatler, February 17, 2021.

496 **"I was desperately fond"** Dempster and Evans, **Behind Palace Doors,** chap. 19.

496 **"assassinations of character"** Dominic Kennedy, "Koo Stark Defends Duke Against Sex Allegations," **The Times,** February 16, 2015.

497 **"a breath of fresh air"** Hilary Rose, "My Mills and Boon Life—the Duchess of York's Story," **The Sunday Times,** January 14, 2021.

497 **"Diana may take"** Karen DeYoung, "Fergie: Bedlam Over the Bride," **The Washington Post,** July 22, 1986.

498 **"Fergie lightens"** Brown, **Diana Chronicles,** chap. 13.

498 **"Her mother leaving"** Kate Waddington, interview, September 14, 2006.

499 **"Oh good"** Sarah, The Duchess of York, with Jeff Coplon, **My Story** (London: Simon and Schuster, 1996), chap. 2.

499 **"damask curtains"** Ibid., chap. 9.

499 **fifty stuffed teddy bears** Emily Kirkpatrick, "Prince Andrew's Former Maid Reportedly Had to Be Trained on How to Arrange His Teddy Bear Collection," **Vanity Fair,** January 24, 2022.

500 **"My solution"** Sarah, The Duchess of York, with Jeff Coplon, **My Story,** chap. 9.

501 **"The ridiculous thing"** Waddington, interview.

502 **"Although [Fergie] did not live there"** Paul Sims, "Prince Andrew Kept Fergie's Wedding Dress in His Wardrobe After They Divorced," **The Sun,** January 20, 2022.

502 **"Prince Andrew, poor fellow"** Wyatt, "1993," **Journals of Woodrow Wyatt,** vol. 3.

502 **"I joined Fergie's staff"** Waddington, interview.

502 **"The redhead"** Richard Kay, "The Night Diana Told Me 'The Redhead's in Trouble' as I Confronted Fergie's Toe Sucking Lover: As We Begin a Spectacular Series on Palace Scandals, Legendary Royal Writer

RICHARD KAY Looks Back," **Daily Mail,** November 1, 2014.

503 **"The jungle"**   Sarah, The Duchess of York, interview by Oprah Winfrey, **Finding Sarah Ferguson,** OWN: The Oprah Winfrey Network, 2011.

503 **"I remember one"**   Camilla Tominey, "The Duchess of York: 'I Am Proud of My Failings," **The Telegraph,** July 23, 2021.

503 **"When I met"**   Christine Lennon, "Duchess of York: Diana, the Queen and I," **Harper's Bazaar,** February 28, 2007.

505 **"That opens up"**   Stephen Bates, "Sarah Ferguson Offered Access to Prince Andrew for Cash, Says Tabloid," **The Guardian,** May 23, 2010.

506 **"I stand by him"**   Frances Hardy, " 'I'm Not Divorced from Andrew—I'm Divorced TO Him': In Her First Full Interview for 20 Years, Sarah Ferguson Discusses Her Weight Issues, Complex Personal Life, Eugenie's Wedding . . . and THAT Remarriage Gossip," **Daily Mail,** updated November 10, 2018.

508 **"I abhor pedophilia"**   "Duchess of York Apologises for 'Gigantic Error of Judgment' Over Debt," **Evening Standard,** April 12, 2012.

CHAPTER 18. AN INCONVENIENT FRIEND: THE LURE OF JEFFREY EPSTEIN

511 **Epstein was part of**   Malia Zimmerman, "Billionaire Sex Offender Epstein Once Claimed He Co-founded Clinton Foundation," Fox News, July 6, 2016.

513 **"hair-raising"**   Hannah Gold and Marie Lodi, "The Décor in Jeffrey Epstein's NYC Townhouse Is the Stuff of Nightmares," **The Cut,** updated August 15, 2019.

513 **" 'You know, you Americans' "**   Conchita Sarnoff, interview, June 8, 2021.

514 "The younger the better" Philip Weiss, "The Fantasist," **New York,** December 7, 2007.

515 "house arrest" Sarnoff, interview.

520 "entered into" Steve Hoffenberg, interview, July 25, 2021.

521 "This is what Daddy" Eleanor Berry, **My Unique Relationship with Robert Maxwell: The Truth at Last** (Market Harborough, Leicestershire: Book Guild, 2019).

522 "One minute" "The Strange and Lonely Life of Britain's Would-Be Playboy Prince," **The Times,** March 12, 2011.

522 Epstein's former handyman Klein, "Trouble with Andrew."

522 "full of pictures" Guy Adams, "Ten Questions Buckingham Palace MUST Answer Over Prince Andrew's 'Under-Age Sex Slave' Scandal," **Daily Mail,** January 6, 2015.

524 showed her off as his "girlfriend" Bradley J. Edwards, **Relentless Pursuit: Our Battle with Jeffrey Epstein** (New York: Gallery Books, 2020), chap. 28.

525 The depraved complicity Ibid.

525 "until he finished" Ibid.

525 "Their whole entire lives" Benjamin Weiser, " 'Massage' Was Code for 'Sex': New Epstein Abuse Revelations," **The New York Times,** August 9, 2019.

526 "she said, 'they're nothing' " Vanessa Grigoriadis, " 'They're Nothing, These Girls': Unraveling the Mystery of Ghislane Maxwell, Epstein's Enabler," **Vanity Fair,** August 12, 2019.

526 "whiff of chicanery" John Preston, interview, June 22, 2021.

528 "The Duke assured his mother" Klein, "Trouble with Andrew."

530 "I am an ideas factory!" John Arlidge, "The Maga-

zine Interview: Prince Andrew on Being the Palace's 'Entrepreneur-in-Residence,'" **The Sunday Times,** December 3, 2017.

CHAPTER 19. NUMBER SIX ON THE CALL SHEET: MEGHAN MARKLE'S WORLD

533 **"Meghan turned to me"**   Chris Bradford, "Meghan Markle's Estranged Dad Thomas Reveals She Told Him 'Daddy I Want to Be Famous' When She Was on Red Carpet Aged 12," **The Sun,** June 23, 2021.

534 **"people are fighting"**   Collette Reitz, "Meghan Markle Stood Up for Women as a Young Girl & Is Our New Feminist Icon," **Elite Daily,** December 1, 2017.

534 **"He said, 'She's so bright'"**   Wendy Riche, interview, December 16, 2019.

534 **"It's six hundred dollars"**   "Home Video Shows a Day in the Life of Meghan Markle circa 1999," You-Tube, 5:11, December 8, 2017.

535 **"Her first year"**   Thomas Markle, interview, August 27, 2021.

535 **"closet filled with fashionable"**   Meghan Markle, "I'm More Than an 'Other,'" **Elle,** December 22, 2016.

536 **"'She's black!'"**   Samantha Markle, **The Diary of Princess Pushy's Sister: A Memoir, Part 1** (New York: Central Park South Publishing, 2021), chap. 9.

536 **"black girls and white girls"**   Duchess of Sussex, "Birthday Suit," **The Tig Archives,** September 2014.

537 **her mother's eyes fill with tears**   Markle, "I'm More Than an 'Other.'"

538 **"I would end up"**   Matt Goulet, "Meghan Markle Grew Up Around TV Decades Before She Starred on **Suits,**" **Esquire,** February 14, 2018.

538 **"I've had to freeze"**   Emma Duncan and Valentine Low, "Can Meghan Markle Modernise the Monarchy?," **The Economist,** May 23, 2018.

540 "**brutal**"   Duchess of Sussex, "Birthday Suit."

541 "**She was just an actor**"   Bonnie Zane, interview, January 9, 2020.

541 "**a spa resort**"   James Walcott, "Suits Me," **Vanity Fair,** May 2018.

541 "**They wanted someone**"   Kevin Bray, interview, January 29, 2020.

542 "**I loved her**"   Zane, interview.

542 "**We need**"   Bray, interview.

542 "**They always think**"   David Bartis, interview, January 29, 2020.

542 "**I wanted it**"   Duchess of Sussex, "A Suitable Beginning," The Tig Archives, January 2015.

543 "**think hair pulled back**"   Ibid.

544 "**Even [an established player]**"   Aaron Korsh, interview, December 16, 2019.

544 "**coloreds**"   Erica Gonzales, "Meghan Markle Opens Up About Her Family's Experience with Racism," **Harper's Bazaar,** January 18, 2017.

545 "**carefully tossing**"   Duchess of Sussex, "A Love Letter," The Tig Archives, May 2014.

546 "**pear on stilts**"   Markle, **Diary of Princess Pushy's Sister,** chap. 8.

547 "**I always felt safe**"   Riche, interview.

547 "**It was a weird life**"   Shelley Curtis Litvack, interview, August 12, 2021.

548 "**beautiful bean**"   Markle, **Diary of Princess Pushy's Sister,** chap. 12.

548 **He underwrote**   Thomas Markle, interview.

550 "**an organic fluidity**"   Bray, interview.

551 "**I had no idea**"   Duchess of Sussex, "Suitable Beginning."

552 "**She was 'marrying up'**"   Lady Colin Campbell, **Meghan and Harry: The Real Story** (New York: Pegasus Books, 2020), chap. 3.

556 "**Going for a trail run**"   Julianne Carell, "Actress

Meghan Markle's Favorite Toronto Beauty Spots," **Glamour,** August 21, 2014.

557 **"sister-wives"**   Sarah Madaus, "Meghan Markle's Former Co-Star Gina Torres Says Motherhood Is a 'Dream Come True' for the Duchess," **Town & Country,** July 28, 2019.

559 **"show's moral conscience"** Salamishah Tillet, "Meghan Markle Left 'Suits.' Here's What She Took with Her," **The New York Times,** April 25, 2018.

559 **fit within**   Delap, "**Suits** Star Meghan Markle."

562 **"You didn't hear"**   Bray, interview.

564 **"all the energy"**   Cath Clarke, "Anti-Social," **Time Out,** April 27, 2015.

565 **"Celebrity MasterChef"**   Jonathan Shalit, interview, August 9, 2021.

566 **"an old PR ruse"**   Katie Hind, "The Night Meghan Markle Begged Me to Get Her IN the Tabloids: The Duchess of Sussex Spoke Movingly About the Pressures of the Media Spotlight, but as KATIE HIND Reveals, She Wasn't Always So Reticent," **The Mail on Sunday,** updated October 27, 2019.

566 **"scholarships, financial aid"**   Amy Mackelden, "Meghan Markle's First Royal Tour Speech Was an Emotional Call for Female Empowerment," **Harper's Bazaar,** October 24, 2018.

567 **"I work long hours"**   Andrew Morton, **Meghan: A Hollywood Princess** (London: Michael O'Mara, 2018), chap. 8.

568 **"larger than life"**   "How These Visionary Women Are Carving the Path for Gender Equality," YouTube, 14:09, October 17, 2014.

568 **"While most"**   Duchess of Sussex, "Meghan Markle for **Elle:** 'With Fame Comes Opportunity, but Also a Responsibility,'" **Elle,** November 8, 2016.

570 **"Women need a seat"**   "Meghan Markle UN Women," YouTube, 8:23, March 13, 2015.

571 **"Were it not"** Duchess of Sussex, "Meghan Markle for **Elle.**"

573 **"We were talking"** "Meghan Markle Was on the Hunt for 'Famous British Men' Before Meeting Prince Harry," **The News International**, September 21, 2021.

573 **"I'm in London"** Piers Morgan, "Hearty Congratulations, Harry, You Picked a Real Keeper (Even If Your Romance Did Destroy My Beautiful Friendship with the Amazing Meghan Markle)," **Mail Online,** November 27, 2017.

575 **"There's no way"** Kate Mansey, "It's Meghan and Haz! Royal Bride-to-Be Gave Harry His New Nickname Weeks After Their First Meeting—and It WASN'T a Blind Date, Says Her Friend and Advisor," **The Mail on Sunday,** updated April 8, 2019.

CHAPTER 20. FLASHMAN'S FLAMEOUT: HARRY CONFRONTS HIS DEMONS

577 **"Oh really?"** The Duke and Duchess of Cambridge, Twitter, April 29, 2016, 3:55 P.M.

577 **"a classic example"** "Prince Harry 'Let Down Family' Over Vegas Photos," BBC News, January 21, 2013.

583 **"Having been a soldier"** Lowther-Pinkerton, interview.

583 **"he looked at me"** Howes, interview.

585 **"I would love"** Tom Sykes, "Why on Earth Is Prince Harry Single?," **The Daily Beast,** April 13, 2017.

585 **"Cringe de la cringe!"** "Everything You Ever Needed to Know About Cressida Bonas," **Tatler,** September 9, 2013.

587 **"I can feel"** **Diana, Our Mother.**

590 **"on the verge"** Hannah Furness, "Prince Harry: I Sought Counselling After 20 Years of Not Thinking About the Death of My Mother, Diana, and Two Years

of Total Chaos in My Life," **The Telegraph,** April 19, 2017.

591 **"You need to feel it"** Ibid.

591 **"only two years"** Ibid.

591 **"Every time I put a suit on"** Duke of Sussex, **The Me You Can't See.**

592 **"My brother, you know"** Duke of Sussex, "Prince Harry," Bryony Gordon's **Mad World,** April 16, 2017.

593 **"was as if something had changed"** Duke of Cambridge, **Time to Walk,** Apple Fitness+, 2021.

594 **"It was in many ways"** "Battle of the Somme Centenary Commemorations," royal.uk, July 1, 2016.

595 **"I thought, 'Okay' "** "FULL Interview: Prince Harry and Meghan Markle," YouTube, 3:51, November 27, 2017.

CHAPTER 21. SMITTEN: THE STARS ALIGN FOR HARRY AND MEGHAN

597 **"dirty dancing"** Morton, **Meghan: A Hollywood Princess,** chap. 9.

598 **"It was as if Harry"** Omid Scobie and Carolyn Durand, **Finding Freedom: Harry and Meghan** (New York: Dey Street Books, 2020), chap. 3.

598 **"Do I sound crazy"** Ibid.

599 **"I was looking forward"** Ibid.

601 **beaded blue bracelets** Ibid., chap. 4.

601 **"so incredibly quickly"** Ibid., chap. 8.

601 **"totally happy"** "Prince Harry and Girlfriend Buy Christmas Tree in London," ITV, December 14, 2016.

602 **"Mail Order Bride"** "Mail Order Bride? How the Middletons Made Their Millions," **The Times,** November 26, 2010.

603 "shop-window" Hilary Mantel, "Royal Bodies," **London Review of Books,** February 21, 2013.

603 "your devoted" Lauren Collins, "Prince Harry, Meghan Markle, and Royal Romance," **The New Yorker,** May 14, 2018.

603 "I wouldn't want" Camilla Tominey, "50 Years On: How the Duchess of Cornwall Finally Won Over the Nation," **The Telegraph,** August 20, 2021.

604 **"Vagina Monologues"** Lauren Collins, "Mail Supremacy," **The New Yorker,** March 26, 2012.

605 **"Plagued by crime"** Ruth Styles, "Exclusive: Harry's Girl Is (Almost) Straight Outta Compton: Gang-Scarred Home of Her Mother Revealed—So Will He Be Dropping By for Tea?," **Daily Mail,** updated January 10, 2020.

606 **"Meghan felt sick"** Scobie and Durand, **Finding Freedom,** chap. 5.

608 **"the smear on the front page"** Gordon Rayner, "The Duke of Cambridge Approved Prince Harry's Plea to Trolls to Leave Meghan Markle Alone," **The Telegraph,** November 26, 2016.

609 **"As I read it"** Charlie Brinkhurst-Cuff, "Prince Harry's Woke Statement Doesn't Mean We Should Start Dreaming of Being Princess," **The New Statesman,** November 15, 2016.

610 **"We're a couple"** "Meghan Markle, Wild About Harry!," **Vanity Fair,** September 6, 2017.

613 **"I've just been"** Carolyn Durand and Katie Kindelan, "Meghan Markle Speaks Out About #MeToo Movement, Calls for Women to Be 'Empowered' to Use Their Voice," **Good Morning America,** February 28, 2018.

614 **"Women don't need"** "Meghan Markle Wants to 'Hit Ground Running' with Royal Charity Work," BBC News, February 28, 2018.

CHAPTER 22. MAGIC KINGDOM: A WEDDING TRANSFORMS THE HOUSE OF WINDSOR

622 **"You look amazing"** Scobie and Durand, **Finding Freedom,** chap. 14.

623 **"Set me as a seal"** " 'The Power of Love': Address by U.S. Bishop at Harry and Meghan's Wedding," Reuters, May 19, 2018.

623 **"a necessary"** Tara Isabella Burton, "Bishop Michael Curry Just Stole the Show with His Sermon at the Royal Wedding," **Vox,** May 19, 2018.

629 **"Kate is not"** Chloe Morgan, "Kate Middleton Is 'Mortified' by Claims That She Made Meghan Markle Cry During Row over Bridesmaids Dresses Because She's 'Very Careful' with How She Treats Others' so as Not to Spark Feud Rumours, Royal Expert Claims," **Mail Online,** updated March 16, 2021.

630 **"I didn't hear from Meghan"** Morgan, "Hearty Congratulations, Harry."

631 **" 'We don't' "** Rachel Johnson, "Sussex Fatigue: Meghan and Harry Are Making the British Yearn for the Queen Mum," **Air Mail,** October 24, 2020.

632 **"the family, I suppose"** " 'It Was Fantastic': Prince Harry Tells **Today** on BBC Radio 4 About Christmas with Meghan Markle and Says Royals Are 'the Family I Suppose She's Never Had,' " **The Sun.**

632 **"We all have"** Lady Anne Glenconner, personal conversation.

632 **"torn my entire family apart"** Christopher Bucktin, " 'Maybe We Embarrass Her': Meghan Markle's Brother Thomas Says Their Family Is Torn Apart over Royal Wedding Snub," **Mirror,** updated April 19, 2018.

633 **"It's time"** Joseph Curtis, " 'It's Time to Man Up, Harry!' Meghan Markle's Sister Blasts the Prince for 'Allowing Meg to Ignore' Her Family in Extraordinary

Twitter Tirade Right in Middle of Meghan's First Official State Appearance," **Mail Online,** April 18, 2018.

633 **It was "not to [sic] late"** "Meghan Markle's Estranged Brother Writes a Letter to Prince Harry (Exclusive)," **In Touch,** updated May 19, 2018.

634 **"Embarrassment is a choice"** Riche, interview.

635 **"On the street"** Thomas Markle, interview.

636 **"I thought I was doing"** Ibid.

637 **"My dad never"** Scobie and Durand, **Finding Freedom,** chap. 12.

638 **"Harry said"** Thomas Markle, interview.

639 **"Some people"** "A Statement by the Communications Secretary to Prince Harry," royal.uk, November 8, 2016.

640 **"At the heart"** Harverson, interview, November 4, 2019.

640 **"My baby looks beautiful"** James Beal, "Dad's £23 Hideout: Meghan Markle's Shamed Dad Thomas Watched Royal Wedding from a £23-a-Night Airbnb in Mexico," **The Sun,** May 22, 2018.

CHAPTER 23. UNRAVELING: THE MONARCHY'S MORNING AFTER

641 **"I saw the car"** Emily Andrews, "Iron Duke: Prince Philip, 97, Yelled 'My Legs, My Legs' After Car Crash 'Caused by Dazzling Sun,'"**The Sun,** January 18, 2019.

642 **"It would mean"** Haroon Siddique, "Prince Philip Has Not Said Sorry for Car Crash, Injured Woman Claims," **The Guardian,** January 20, 2019.

643 **"The weather"** Johnny Dymond, "The Royal Visit—Prince Philip Accepts His Certificate," **British Dental Journal** 230 (May 2021): 546–66; extracts originally published in vol. 104 (March 1958).

643 **"Don't cock it up"** "Harry and Meghan Not Return-

ing as Working Members of Royal Family," BBC News, February 19, 2021.

646 **"shape her role"**   Polly Dunbar, "Getting Up at 5am, Bombarding Aides with Texts and Her Eyebrow-Raising Fashion: Meghan Is Shaking Up the Royals Six Months After the Wedding," **The Mail on Sunday,** updated November 19, 2018.

647 **"You go first"**   Simon Perry, "How the Queen Avoided an Awkward Car Moment with Meghan Markle: 'You Go First,'" **People,** June 14, 2018.

649 **"On a personal"**   Rebecca Mead, "Meghan Markle's Ever-So-Slightly Radical Cookbook," **The New Yorker,** September 25, 2018.

649 **"Not a handout"**   Emily Nash, "Not a Handout, a Hand Held," Instagram post, September 12, 2019.

649 **"She's a natural"**   Simon Perry, "Meghan Markle Steps Out in Her First Maternity Dress as She Visits One of Her New Patronages," **People,** January 10, 2019.

650 **"young, diverse"**   Isabella Kwai, "Harry and Meghan Charm Sometimes Skeptical Subjects in Australia," The New York Times, October 16, 2018.

651 **"More than a million"**   Brandreth, interview.

652 **"pretty grumpy"**   **The Princes and the Press,** presented by Amol Rajan, directed by Grace Hughes-Hallett, BBC Two, 2021.

652 **"She couldn't understand"**   Brown, **Diana Chronicles,** chap. 10.

653 **"[My family] was very welcoming"**   Duke of Sussex, **Oprah with Meghan and Harry.**

653 **"when we flew"**   Princess of Wales, "An Interview with HRH The Princess of Wales," **Panorama.**

657 **"fixtures and fittings"**   Valentine Low, "£2.4m Bill for Renovation of Meghan and Harry's House, Frogmore Cottage," **The Times,** June 25, 2019.

660 **"I really tried"**   **Harry and Meghan: An African**

Journey, directed by Nathaniel Lippiett, ITN Productions, 2019.

661 **"Thank goodness"** Morton, "Diana, Princess of Wales in Her Own Words," **Diana: Her True Story.**

663 **"close friends"** Michelle Tauber, "Meghan Markle's Best Friends Break Their Silence: 'We Want to Speak the Truth,'" **People,** February 6, 2019.

664 **"Even after a week"** Caroline Davies, "Meghan Chose to Write Letter to Father to Protect Prince Harry, Texts Reveal," **The Guardian,** November 12, 2021.

664 **"Given that"** Sean Coughlan, "Duchess of Sussex Weighed Up Calling Father 'Daddy,'" BBC News, November 10, 2021.

665 **"There was more"** Thomas Markle, interview.

665 **"At the end"** "Charles' Diary Lays Thoughts Bare," BBC News, February 22, 2006.

666 **"Is Harry taking"** "Meghan Sues **Mail on Sunday** Over Private Letter," BBC News, October 2, 2019.

666 **"broken the law"** Gareth Davies, "Meghan's Statement in Full: Duchess Says She Is 'Reshaping' Tabloid Media Industry as She Takes Swing at 'Daily Fail,'" **The Telegraph,** December 2, 2021.

667 **"I totally agree"** Nicholas Witchell, "Meghan Apologises to Court for Forgetting Biography Briefing Notes," BBC News, November 11, 2021.

667 **"collectively brave enough"** Caroline Davies, "Meghan Calls for Tabloid Industry Overhaul as **Mail on Sunday** Loses Appeal," **The Guardian,** December 2, 2014.

667 **"The media in the UK"** Mark Stephens, interview, December 2, 2021.

CHAPTER 24. PRIVACY AND PREJUDICE:
SURVIVING THE WINDSOR FISHBOWL

672 **"I remember so often"** Duchess of Sussex, **Oprah with Meghan and Harry.**

674 **"I just needed"** Nicolson, interview.

675 **"I was struck by how"** Euan Rellie, interview, July 23, 2021.

678 **"remember you chose"** Vassi Chamberlain, "What the Duchess of Cambridge Is Really Like Behind Closed Doors," **The Telegraph,** January 8, 2022.

679 **"like a gleaming"** " 'Very Buckinghamshire': How 'Society Bible' **Tatler** Fell Out of Royal Favour," **The Guardian,** June 1, 2020.

683 **"like something"** Christopher Andersen, **Brothers and Wives** (New York: Gallery Books, 2021), chap. 5.

684 **"What bullying actually means"** The Princes and the Press.

685 **"There seems"** Katie Nicholl, "The Real Meaning of Kate Middleton's Very Personal Honor from the Queen," **Vanity Fair,** April 30, 2019.

686 **"tenderly cradling"** "Why Can't Meghan Markle Keep Her Hands Off Her Bump? Experts Tackle the Question That Has Got the Nation Talking: Is It Pride, Vanity, Acting—or a New Age Bonding Technique?," **The Mail on Sunday,** updated January 28, 2019.

687 **"blackamoor"** Patrick Greenfield, "Princess Michael of Kent Apologises for 'Racist Jewellery' Worn at Lunch with Meghan Markle," **The Guardian,** December 23, 2017.

688 **"Are you sure"** Stephen Bates, "The Marquess of Bath Obituary," **The Guardian,** April 5, 2020.

688 **"There isn't a rule book"** Emma Thynn, Marchioness of Bath, interview, October 29, 2021.

688 **"the quiet, cruel"** Michelle Obama, **Becoming** (New York: Crown, 2018), chap. 6.

689 **"Barack's baby mama"** "Fox Refers to Michelle Obama as 'Baby Mama,' " **Today,** June 13, 2008.

689 **" 'Going high' doesn't mean"** Raisa Bruner, "Michelle Obama Explains What 'Going High' Really Means," **Time,** November 20, 2018.

689 "**My biggest piece**"   Megan Sutton, "Michelle Obama Reveals the Advice She'd Give to the Duchess of Sussex," **Good Housekeeping**, March 12, 2018.

690 "**It became very personal**"   Nick Lowles, interview, October 21, 2021.

691 "**I wasn't aware**"   Duke of Sussex, **Oprah with Meghan and Harry.**

692 "**throwing spears**"   "Prince Philip's Gaffes from Decades on Royal Duty," BBC News, May 4, 2017.

692 "**Once again**"   Gerard Seenan, "Prince Apologises as Latest Gaffe Offends Indians," **The Guardian**, August 11, 1999.

692 "**I do hope**"   Penny Mortimer, interview, January 8, 2021.

693 "**slack-jawed**"   Talia Shadwell, "Prince Andrew Made 'Unbelievable' Racist Comments About Arabs, Ex–Home Secretary Says," **Mirror**, November 19, 2019.

694 "**Lots of people**"   "African Theme Shows Wild Side of Wills," **Wales Online**, updated April 1, 2013.

694 "**zero prejudice**"   Owen Bowcott, "Polo Friend of Charles Addressed as 'Sooty,'" **The Guardian**, January 14, 2009.

694 "**British racism**"   Aatish Taseer, "Race and the Royals: An Outsider's View Inside Kensington Palace," **Vanity Fair**, May 2018.

695 "**the conversation is similar**"   Aatish Taseer, interview, March 15, 2021.

695 "**exotic DNA**"   Johnson, "RACHEL JOHNSON: Sorry, Harry."

695 "**flag-waving**"   "PM's Past Comments About Black People 'Deeply Offensive,'" BBC News, June 12, 2020.

696 "**really forbidding people**"   Taseer, interview.

697 "**It became clear**"   **The Princes and the Press.**

698 "**The presence**"   Nadine White, "Meghan's Mother Doria Ragland's Appearance in Royal Baby Photo Cel-

ebrated as Watershed for 'Multicultural Britain,'" The
Huffington Post, updated May 9, 2019.
698 "When the Queen"   Grant Tucker, Twitter, May 8,
2019, 5:23 P.M.
699 "Some recollections may vary"   David Hughes,
"Buckingham Palace Statement in Full: Read the Royal
Family's Succinct Response to Harry and Meghan Interview," I News, March 10, 2021.

CHAPTER 25. SCORCHED EARTH:
"ANNUS HORRIBILIS" REDUX

701 "sexist"   Hannah Furness, "Prince Harry: I Warned
Twitter Boss About a Coup Before the Capitol Riots,"
The Telegraph, November 10, 2021.
703 "found kind of ironic"   "A Major Celebrity Is Pitch-
ing Senators from Both Parties on Paid Family and
Medical Leave: Meghan Markle," Politico, November 3, 2021.
706 "right-on roll call"   Melanie Phillips, "Meghan's
'Woke' Vogue Is Shallow and Divisive," The Times,
July 29, 2019.
707 "I was really ashamed"   Duchess of Sussex, Oprah
with Meghan and Harry.
707 "The scariest thing"   Duke of Sussex, The Me You
Can't See.
707 "I went to a very dark place"   Duke of Sussex, Oprah
with Meghan and Harry.
708 "people feel able"   "About," Heads Together, headsto-
gether.org.uk.
709 "We are certainly"   Harry and Meghan: An African
Journey.
709 "Thanks for asking"   Ibid.
710 "There comes a point"   "Statement by His Royal
Highness Prince Harry, Duke of Sussex," sussexofficial
.uk, October 1, 2019.

711 "the often distasteful"   Brownen Weatherby, "Female MPs Pen Open Letter to Meghan Markle in Support of Her Stand Against 'Distasteful and Misleading' Articles," **Evening Standard,** October 29, 2019.

711 "I couldn't help"   Tom Bradby, "Prince Harry and Meghan: ITV African Journey Documentary Shows They Can Only Take So Much," **The Times,** October 20, 2019.

712 "I expected a train wreck"   Bonnie Christian, "Prince Andrew Faces Barrage of Criticism Over 'Plane Crash' Jeffrey Epstein Scandal Interview," **Evening Standard,** November 17, 2019.

712 "If Prince Andrew"   Dickie Arbiter LVO, Twitter, November 16, 2019, 10:26 P.M.

715 "There was no"   Camilla Tominey, "Prince Philip Told Prince Andrew to 'Take His Punishment' After Summoning His Son to Sandringham," **The Telegraph,** December 5, 2019.

715 "step[ping] back"   Duke of York, Twitter, November 20, 2019, 6:02 P.M.

716 "giant of a principled man"   Sarah Ferguson, Instagram, November 15, 2019.

717 "A lot of people"   Freddy Mayhew, "Prince Andrew Interview Wins Top Prizes for Cuts-Hit BBC **Newsnight** at Royal Television Society Awards," **Press Gazette,** February 27, 2020.

719 "That one"   Andersen, **Brothers and Wives,** chap. 5.

720 "take matters into his own hands"   Duke of Sussex, **Oprah with Meghan and Harry.**

720 "There is something"   Ibid.

722 "What Harry and Meghan did"   Andersen, **Brothers and Wives,** chap. 1.

724 "Make no mistake"   Camilla Tominey, "Queen Delivers Hardest Possible 'Megxit' as Cost of Harry and Meghan's Decision Becomes Clear," **The Telegraph,** January 18, 2020.

726 **"It gives me great sadness"** Bonnie Christian, "Harry Breaks Silences on Royal Crisis Saying He and Meghan Markle Had 'No Other Option' but to Stand Down," **Evening Standard,** January 20, 2020.

EPILOGUE. EMBERS

728 **"I want to reassure you"** "The Queen's Coronavirus Address: 'We Will Meet Again,'" BBC News, April 5, 2020.

729 **"strange, frustrating"** "Coronavirus: Charles Speaks Following Virus Diagnosis," BBC News, April 1, 2020.

729 **"Would Prince Charles"** Sarah Campbell, "Coronavirus: How the Royal Family Is Changing in Lockdown," BBC News, July 1, 2020.

730 **"because he didn't"** "Covid-19: Prince William 'Tested Positive in April,'" BBC News, November 2, 2020.

730 **"Britain is at its best"** "Coronavirus: 'Britain Is at Its Best, Weirdly, When We're in a Crisis,' Says Prince William," ITV, April 12, 2020.

731 **"I can't imagine"** Abbie Llewelyn, "Prince Philip Said He 'Couldn't Imagine Anything Worse' Than Living to 100 Before Death," **Express,** June 10, 2021.

731 **"wonderful teasing"** Brown, "Prince Philip."

731 **"The challenges"** Katie Nicholl, "Inside the Queen's Lockdown 'Bubble,'" **Vanity Fair,** June 1, 2020.

733 **"I never thought"** Duke of Sussex, **Oprah with Meghan and Harry.**

734 **"share, for the very first"** "Prince Harry to Author Book Reflecting on Lessons Learned Throughout His Life," Archewell, July 19, 2021.

734 **sitting bolt upright** Richard Kay, "The Sun on His Face and a Rug on His Lap," **Daily Mail,** April 9, 2021.

735 **"a trigger"** Duke of Sussex, **The Me You Can't See.**

738 **but were bumped**   Kara Kennedy, "Meghan Markle and Prince Harry Dropped for COP26 Video Speech After Queen's Message," **Express,** November 8, 2021.

738 **"the great pride"**   Alex Kleiderman, "COP26: Act Now for Our Children, Queen Urges Climate Summit," BBC News, November 1, 2021.

738 **"long-standing"**   Jack Royston, "Prince Harry's Carbon Pledge Pressures Royals Day After Queen Omits Him from Speech," **Newsweek,** November 3, 2021.

739 **"My wife and I"**   Jaclyn Roth, "Meghan Markle & Prince Harry Look So in Love at 'Global Citizen Live' Event—Details!," **The Royal Observer,** September 25, 2021.

740 **"Officers of the British armed forces"**   Former members of Britain's armed forces to Queen Elizabeth, "Prince Andrew's position in the armed forces," 20–22 Wenlock Road, London, January 13, 2022.

740 **she threw him one last lifeline**   Victoria Ward and Josie Ensor, "Queen to Help Pay for £12m Prince Andrew Settlement," **The Telegraph,** February 15, 2022.

741 **"I have always"**   "Elizabeth's Tilbury Speech, July 1588," Timelines: Sources from History, British Library, bl.uk.

744 **"appalling atrocity"**   Caroline Davies, "Praise for Prince Charles After 'Historic' Slavery Condemnation," **The Guardian,** November 30, 2021.

747 **"I cannot lead you into battle"**   Her Majesty the Queen, "Christmas Broadcast 1957," December 25, 1957, royal.uk.

PHOTOGRAPH CREDITS

PAGE 5

Top: PA Images/Alamy Stock Photo
Bottom left: Shutterstock
Bottom right: Private Collection © The Lucian Freud
    Archive. All Rights Reserved 2021/Bridgeman Images

PAGE 6

Top left: Tim Rooke/Shutterstock
Top right: John Swannell/Camera Press
Second row left: PA Images/Alamy Stock Photo
Second row right: Terry Fincher/Princess Diana Archive/
    Getty Images
Third row center: Toby Melville/PA Images/Alamy
Bottom left: PA Images/Alamy Stock Photo
Bottom right: Chris Jackson/Getty Images

PAGE 7

Top: Gareth Cattermole/Getty Images
Second row left: Tim Rooke/Shutterstock
Second row center: Max Nash/AFP via Getty Images
Second row right: Sang Tan/AP/Shutterstock
Bottom left: Shutterstock
Bottom right: Joanne Davidson/Shutterstock

PAGE 8

Top: Reuters/Alamy Stock Photo
Center: Ian Jones
Bottom: Reuters/Russell Cheyne/Alamy

INSERT 2

PAGE I

Top left: Malcolm Clarke/ANL/Shutterstock
Top right: Malcolm Clarke/Daily Mail/Shutterstock

Bottom left: PA Images/Alamy Stock Photo

PAGE 2

Top: Reuters/Dominic Lipinski/Pool/Alamy
Bottom: Shutterstock

PAGE 3

Top: Samir Hussein/WireImage/Getty Images
Bottom: Richard Gillard/Camera Press

PAGE 4

Top: Shutterstock
Second row left: James Breedon/The Sun/News Licensing
Second row center top: Canadian Press/Shutterstock
Second row center bottom: Shutterstock
Second row right: Owen Humphreys/Pool via Reuters/
    Alamy

PAGE 5

Samir Hussein/Wireimage/Getty Images

PAGE 6

Top left back: Mirrorpix
Top left front: News Licensing and Shutterstock
Top right: Max Mumby/Indigo/Getty Images
Center: Shutterstock
Bottom left: Shutterstock
Bottom right: Alamy and Camera Press/Rota

PAGE 7

Top: Jonathan Brady/WPA Pool/Shutterstock
Center: Chris Jackson/WPA Pool/Getty Images
Center right: David Hartley/Pool/Shutterstock
Bottom left: Danny Lawson/WPA Pool/Shutterstock
Bottom right: Ian Vogler/WPA Pool/Shutterstock

PAGE 8

Top: Max Mumby/Indigo/Getty Images
Top right: Christopher Furlong—WPA Pool/Getty Images
Center right: Panorama/BBC
Bottom: Max Mumby/Indigo/Getty Images

ENDPAPERS

PAGE 1

Top left: Jeff J Mitchell/AP/Shutterstock
Top right: Pictorial Press/Alamy Stock Photo
Second row left: Reginald Davis/Shutterstock
Second row center: Max Mumby/Indigo/Getty Images
Second row right: PA Images/Alamy Stock Photo
Third row left: Karwai Tang/WireImage/Getty Images
Third row right: David Hartley/Shutterstock
Bottom left: Andrew McCaren/LNP/Shutterstock
Bottom center: Yousuf Karsh/Camera Press
Bottom right: Tim Rooke/Shutterstock

PAGE 2

Top left: Nils Jorgensen/Shutterstock
Top center: Shutterstock
Top right: Dominic Lipinski/PA Archive/PA Images
Second row left: AP/Shutterstock
Second row center: PA Images/Alamy Stock Photo
Third row left: Guy Corbishley/Alamy Stock Photo
Third row right: Max Mumby/Indigo/Getty Images
Bottom left: David Hartley/Shutterstock
Bottom center: BBC
Bottom right: Hannah McKay/Reuters

INDEX

ABOUT THE AUTHOR

TINA BROWN is an award-winning writer, the former editor in chief of **Tatler, Vanity Fair,** and **The New Yorker,** and the founder of **The Daily Beast** and of the live event platform Women in the World. She is the author of the #1 **New York Times** bestseller **The Diana Chronicles,** and in 2017 she published **The Vanity Fair Diaries,** chosen as one of the best books of the year by **Time, People, The Guardian, The Economist, Entertainment Weekly,** and **Vogue.** In 2000 she was awarded the CBE (Commander of the British Empire) by Queen Elizabeth II for her services to journalism. She lives in New York City.